# Ancient Rome

## A History

D. Brendan Nagle
*University of Southern California*

2010
SLOAN PUBLISHING
Cornwall-on-Hudson, NY 12520

Library of Congress Cataloging-in-Publication Data

Nagle, D. Brendan
Ancient Rome: a history / D. Brendan Nagle
p. cm.
ISBN 978-1-59738-021-8
1. Rome--History. I.Title.
DG209.N253 2009
937--dc22

2008052516

Cover photograph: Hadrian's Pantheon in Rome. Photo: D. Brendan Nagle
Cover designer: Amy Rosen


Sloan Publishing, LLC
220 Maple Road
Cornwall-on-Hudson, NY 12520



Printed in the United States of America
10 9 8 7 6 5 4 3 2 1

ISBN-10 1-59738-021-0
ISBN-13 978-1-59738-021-8

# Ancient Rome

A History

# Contents

# List of Maps

# Preface

History has many cunning passages, contrived corridors
And issues, deceives with whispering ambitions,
Guides us by vanities

T. S. Eliot, *Gerontion* 34.

The justification for a new book on Roman history would seem to involve a great deal of cunning, even more ambition if not hybris, and not a little vanity. Surely enough books have already been written on the subject? Can anything new be said about ancient Rome?

If it is true that every generation writes its own history, then perhaps it is time for a book on Rome that reflects the experiences of a generation that enjoyed a vacation from history in the last decade of the twentieth century only to see the sudden, violent revival of history in the early twenty-first century. Globalization has united our world in ways that are at times reminiscent of the world of Rome's day when glass and linen from Egypt, silks from China, spices from India and the East Indies were in demand by elites all over the Mediterranean and Europe. Our generation has witnessed the rise of an economic, cultural, political and military colossus—the United States—and we are all too well aware of the dependencies, resentments, and fears it has generated world-wide. Inevitably comparisons arise with Rome's apparent domination of a unipolar world and the challenges it faced from the unpredictable churning of pre-political, pre-state peoples in Eurasia and elsewhere, and a powerful, resurgent Iran.

Rome's footprint on the world, like that of the modern West, was large. Its ghostly presence continues to influence our contemporary world. Languages based on Latin are spoken by millions of people who today live far beyond the confines of the original Roman Empire. English, heavily affected by Latin and Greek, is also spoken by millions. It is the second language of more millions and has become the de facto lingua franca of the world. To speak a modern European language is to be influenced, none too subtly, by Roman culture and through it by Greek culture. The great monotheistic religions of the modern world, Judaism, Christianity and Islam, were deeply affected, though in very different ways and in different degrees, by their Roman and Greek heritages. The fact that Christianity originated within the Roman Empire and its Scriptures were written in Greek, the second language of the Empire after Latin, has something to do with an enduring focus on Rome because to understand Christianity one needs to understand Rome. In its Hellenized and Romanized form, that religion has spread over much of the world, bringing with it embedded patterns of Greek thought and Roman law and organization. The continuing ability of Rome to impact popular culture should not be ignored. That capacity was magnified by nineteenth and twentieth century fiction writers and by Hollywood's instant recognition of the ability of gladiators, Roman feasts and festivals and the races of the Circus Maximus to attract and hold the interest of masses of people.

This book is organized around a number of perennially important questions in Roman history: How did Rome succeed in creating an empire based on the city-state or *polis* when every other city-state—Athens, Sparta, and Carthage, for example—that attempted to do so failed? Why, after such stunning military success did the government of the Republic under which most of the Mediterranean and a good portion of temperate Europe were conquered, collapse? Even more astonishingly, how did the Republic, phoenix-like, revive and recreate itself? Then, finally, in the fourth century A.D. under pressure from the powerful Empire of Persia in the East and numerous warrior bands and migrating peoples in the West, we see that Rome nearly collapsed again only—miraculously—to pick itself up once more and this time fundamentally transform itself socially and culturally.

This approach undoubtedly oversimplifies or over-generalizes the long and complex history of Rome from its legendary founding in 753 B.C. to A.D. 732 when the Frankish successors of Rome turned back the conquering Arabs at the Battle of Poitiers in France. However, as an approach it has the advantage of making Rome's history comprehensible by dividing it up into seven, relatively digestible segments. Rather than a continuous narrative where one event follows another chronologically, events and chronologies are subordinated to a master narrative—the questions posed at the beginning of each of the seven sections. These "master narrative questions" are traditional topics that are discussed in all Roman history courses and are by no means novel in themselves. All the usual subjects of Roman history will be found in this book, but they are not examined individually. For instance, art, architecture and religion are treated as parts of Roman political and institutional history rather than as topics in their own right. Similarly the household and other social-cultural topics are folded into the broader narrative of Roman history. Underlying this approach is the assumption that the society of the Mediterranean city-state and Rome's version of it was very different from the kind of society and culture we know in the modern world. Perhaps in seeking justification for treating Rome once again we should settle for Eliot's own explanation of how history works:

> She (history) gives, gives with such subtle confusions
> That the giving famishes the craving.

In writing this book I had the advantage of calling on the patience, kindness and talent of a number of friends and colleagues who read either the whole or parts of the manuscript and provided me with invaluable comments. That the book still contains many flaws and shortcomings is due in no way to them. I wish to thank in particular Stanley M. Burstein, Arthur M. Eckstein, Richard I. Frank, Brigette Russell, Richard Saller, Mehmet F. Yavuz, Walter Scheidel, Jane Laurent, and Steven Tuck. Stefan Chrissanthos supplied information on mutinies in the Roman army from his on-going research. William L. MacDonald provided me with images from his matchless collection of photos of Roman imperial architecture, and Sandra Potter kindly gave permission to use photos taken by her and her late husband Tim Potter. Deborah Stewart and the staff of Dumbarton Oaks Library in Washington D.C. gave invaluable supporting help. My thanks also goes to Bill Webber of Sloan Publishing who first suggested the idea of a Roman history text and from the beginning proved to be an outstanding source of sound advice on every aspect of the book's writing and production. To my wife Pat and daughter Eliza I owe a particular debt of gratitude and affection for their patient and loving support.

*In memory of*
*Gerald and Elizabeth Connolly*

# Part One

# The Rise of Rome

## 1. INTRODUCTION AND OVERVIEW

### Is Roman History European History?

It is tempting to think of Roman history as a part of, or perhaps just an episode in, "European" history. This tendency should be resisted, however, because it projects into Roman history perspectives that only became dominant thousands of years later when there was, finally, such a thing as "European" history. It is better to see Rome as part of a much older story rather than as being history's highpoint. Despite its 1,000 year length Roman history was an episode in the even longer history of the Mediterranean and Middle East, and a phase in the slow process of introducing Mediterranean practices into Europe. Chronologically Rome comes before Europe, but the Mediterranean comes before Rome.

WHAT ROME INHERITED Romans inherited from the near and distant past of the Mediterranean a whole assemblage of technologies (e.g., the alphabet, coinage); political institutions and ideas (the city-state, the rule of law); military organizations and techniques (the hoplite phalanx); an economy based on inherited plants and specific agricultural practices; a pre-existing network of Mediterranean-wide contacts; and much more. Rome was not an isolated island in the middle of an ocean, but rather, at least initially, just one community among many that shared a common Mediterranean material, social, and political culture. This Mediterranean world provided Rome with the ingredients out of which the Romans were enabled to create over time their own particular version of Mediterranean culture.

That is what it was and remained: a variation on an already well-established theme. Once this is understood, the genius and originality of Rome in fashioning its own individual inheritance can be better appreciated.

## 2. THE ROMAN EXPERIMENT

### Other Challengers: The World in 350 B.C.

This global, Mediterranean approach to Roman history gets us only so far. Rome in 350 B.C. had been recently sacked by the Celts, and its future was uncertain. At that same date other states had been making their mark on a much larger historical canvas and had been doing so for centuries. The great Persian Empire dominated all of western Asia from Afghanistan to the Aegean. For many years it had posed an imminent threat to the Greeks living around the Aegean, and the Greeks, or at least some of them, had fought epic wars in defense of their freedom. Hundreds of Greek city-states in the Black Sea and Mediterranean possessed a kind of cultural—and at times military—hegemony, over large portions of those regions. Carthage, just across the Tyrrhenian Sea from Rome, was a flourishing city-state. It exercised an extensive hegemony over the western Mediterranean. By 350 B.C. the transformation of Macedonia to the north of Greece into a super-state was underway. Under Philip and then his son Alexander, Macedonia was to destroy the Persian Empire and establish Macedonian sovereignty over much of western Asia and the eastern Mediterranean.

### So Why Rome?

None of these states was to establish as long-lasting a dominion over the Mediterranean and parts of the Middle East and Europe as Rome did. The most powerful of the Greek city-states, Athens and Sparta, had each established short-lived hegemonies in Greece, but in the end they failed to find a way around the shortcomings of their political structures. City-states worked well as long as they remained small but faltered when they had to expand and become large territorial states. The Persian Empire was swept away by the Macedonians, but the Macedonians, in turn, were unable to replace the unitary, stable empire of the Persians with a single empire of their own and fell to quarreling among themselves. In the end they carved up the old Persian Empire into three feuding, territorial states ruled by kings.

The question of what enabled Rome to rise to power first in Italy, then in the western and finally the eastern Mediterranean, was a challenge to historians, politicians, and political thinkers from the time its growing presence in Italy was first detected by Greeks in the fourth century B.C. The discussion goes on into the present day. It is the main theme of Part I of this book.

THE GREEK EXPLANATION The Romans themselves ascribed their success to their traditions and the favor of the gods, which was a fairly standard, but not particularly helpful, way of explaining the rise of successful states in antiquity. Greeks, however, alone among the peoples of the Mediterranean, had a long tradition of secular inquiry into the rise and fall of states. While acknowledging the roles of morals and the gods, they looked for more practically useful explanations of why some constitutions (in Greek, *politeiai*) were more successful in undergirding the strength of one state rather than another. Sparta, for example, was seen as a model of stability and power, while other states seemed to be forever in a state of *stasis*, or civil unrest. Direct democracy and tyranny were regarded as the most unstable of all constitutions.

Plato and Aristotle, to name just two of the best-known thinkers, put political science on a firm basis in their writings on politics and ethics. Plato is usually thought to have had a more theoretical approach to political analysis, while Aristotle was more empirical and pragmatic. Aristotle and the students of his school collected, for example, the constitutions of 158 states, Greek and non-Greek, to analyze what made them work or not work. Hence when Rome burst on the scene, Greek thinkers were ready with explanations for what made its constitution so spectacularly successful. Down to modern times historians have, in one modified form or another, followed the Greek mode of analysis in attempting to discover what made Rome great.

WHAT MADE ROME SUPERIOR According to this explanation, Romans were first and foremost great politicians and statesmen, and only secondarily great fighters. They were excellent people-managers who came up with a wholly original form of citizenship that, unlike citizenship elsewhere, transcended race, ethnicity, language, and culture. The Ro-

**Chronology of the Development of Complex Societies**

*The gap between the time when urban life and states were established permanently in the Middle East and in Europe is noticeable.*

| | |
|---|---|
| ca. 3100 B.C. | The Urban and State Revolution: True cities and/or states are *permanently* established in Mesopotamia, Egypt, Syria, Palestine, and Anatolia (modern Turkey). |
| ca. 2000 B.C. | Palace Culture, quasi-urban society, develops in Crete and Mainland Greece. |
| ca. 1200 B.C. | Collapse of Palace System throughout Aegean. Failure of first indigenous European effort at urbanization and state formation. |
| ca. 800 B.C. | Revival of complex societies in Greece, the Aegean, and parts of the western Mediterranean including Italy and north Africa. The *polis* or city-state makes its appearance. |
| 753 B.C. | Traditional founding date of Rome. |
| A.D. 500 | Decline of cities and states in much of western and central Europe ("Fall of western Roman Empire"). Second failure of the city and state to take permanent root in the West. |
| ca. A.D. 1000 | Final *permanent* establishment of cities and states in western and central Europe. |

man war machine was formidable, but the Roman legion was not intrinsically better than the Macedonian phalanx, nor was Rome's navy—when it finally created one—better than Carthage's.

It was neither technology nor bloody-mindedness that ultimately led to Roman suzerainty of the Mediterranean, but rather flexibility—in political, social, and military matters—combined with a deep seriousness. Ultimately, what made Rome's military superior to the formidable war machines all around the Mediterranean was Rome's first class, unmatched political culture. It was this culture that enabled it to sustain as many as 90 severe defeats on the battlefield in the period of the Republic. As late as 105 B.C., long aafter Rome had become the acknowledged suzerain of the Mediterranean, it suffered a staggering defeat at the hands of migrating Celts and Germans losing, it is said, 80,000 men in a single day. It was this same culture that enabled Rome to reinvent itself again and again throughout its extraordinarily long history.

## 3 ORGANIZATION AND ARGUMENT

Part I of this book is devoted to explaining how Rome rose to power. Chapter 1 traces the deepest roots of Roman strength to its generic Mediterranean heritage. Its aim is to provide a very general background sketch of the environment—natural and human—out of which Rome emerged. What kind of advantages did Italy and the Mediterranean offer that enabled the Romans—one small group among many competing groups—to succeed as spectacularly as they did? Conversely, what kind of obstacles in their environment did Romans have to overcome in order to succeed? Chapter 2 gives a brief survey of where our information on Roman history comes from, such as archaeology, literary sources, inscriptions, and coins. Chapter 3 sketches the complex geography and ethnography of Italy, which provided the background for Rome's earliest years. Chapter 4 tells the story of Rome's struggle—first for survival in Italy, and then for control of the peninsula. Chapter 5 offers an explanation of how Rome managed its rise. The remaining chapters of Part I (Chapters 6 and 7) recount the history of Rome's Mediterranean wars with the Carthaginians, Macedonians, and Greeks. The section ends with Rome, having defeated all of its enemies, standing supreme in the Mediterranean, but ready to collapse internally as a result of its conquests.

# 1

# Themes and Perspectives: Rome and its Mediterranean Environment

## 1. THE CONNECTING SEA: THE MEDITERRANEAN CONTEXT OF ROMAN HISTORY

### The Mediterranean: Frontier or Highway?

Unlike the Atlantic or the Pacific, the Mediterranean was never an obstacle to communication. It was not a frontier the way the Atlantic and Pacific were before the fifteenth and sixteenth centuries A.D., but rather a major highway. Throughout much of history (with some notable, centuries-long interruptions), Syrians, Egyptians, Greeks, Tunisians, Italians, and Spaniards were connected, if not united, by the Mediterranean.

Reflecting the meaning of its name, "The Middle-Earth Sea" or "The Mid-Land Sea," the Mediterranean should be thought of as more like a large land-locked lake or groups of lakes than a sea. Certainly it is not an ocean, and although it appears from the map to be a single "lake," the Mediterranean is really a series of connected smaller "lakes," such as the Aegean and Adriatic Seas, and what eventually became Rome's own lake, the western Mediterranean. Yet another connected "lake," the Black Sea, serves as a link to the great plains of Eurasia and the Caucasus.

Among the reasons for the connective capacities of the Mediterranean is its relatively small size. Much of it can be traversed without ever, except for fog and recently smog, losing sight of land. Currents and perennial winds contribute to the connectedness of Mediterranean lands by aiding navigation. High evaporation draws water into the Mediterraneanp

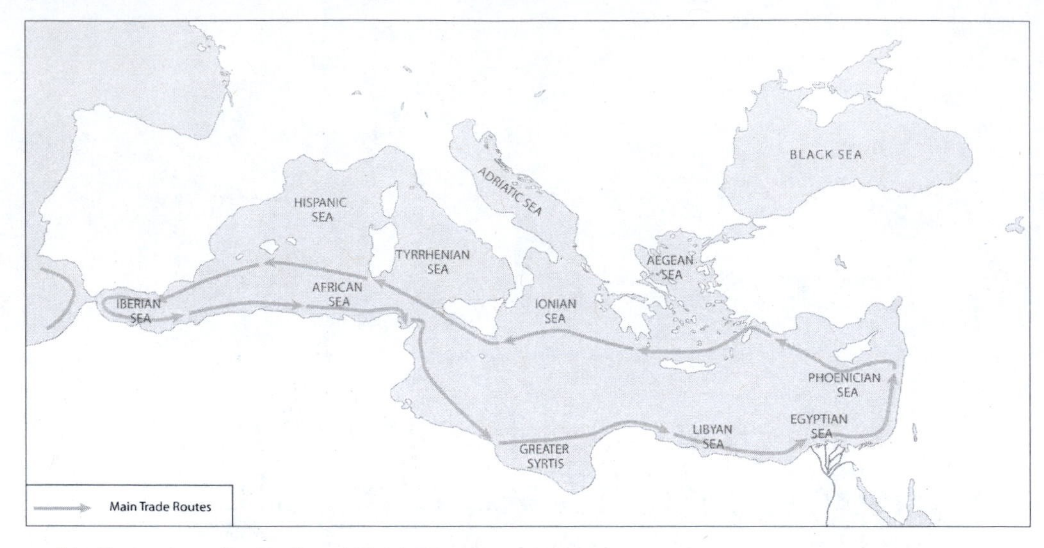


Mediterranean "Lakes" and Trade Routes

from the Atlantic through the Straits of Gibraltar. This influx creates currents that circulate around the coasts of the southern rim of the Mediterranean in a counter-clockwise direction, while the prevailing winds tend to blow perennially from north to northeasterly directions. Innumerable islands, headlands, coves, and harbors provide safe havens and useful stopping points for travelers—not that the Mediterranean is a particularly safe sea to navigate as the thousands of shipwrecks, ancient and not so ancient, indicate. However, as a navigable body of water it is a lot safer than the great oceans of the planet.

## Quicker, Cheaper, Easier: The Advantages of Water Over Land Transportation

It is a truism that in pre-modern times transportation by water was cheaper, more efficient, and often safer than transportation by land. It is estimated by one scholar that in Roman times a given item could be transported for 5 miles overland, 25 miles by river and, 115 miles by sea for the same price.[1] Before the coming of the railroad and the super highway, canals were the preferred means of states aiming to solidify their control over territory and advance commerce. For almost all of human history the fastest bulk goods could be moved on land was the pace of a horse, mule, or ox pulling a wagon or barge.

Travel by sea had, and continues to have, its own hazards—of pirates, storms, reefs, and currents (in the Mediterranean tides were not much of a problem)—but nothing compared to the hazards of land transportation. Throughout history river crossings, mountain passes, and forest paths have been places where robbers and governments have coerced tolls from travelers and thereby restricted trade. There were always the natural challenges of bad

[1]Duncan-Jones, R. P. *The Economy of the Roman Empire* (Cambridge, 1982), 368.

weather, floods, deserts, high mountains, swamps, forests, etc. The size and nature of the "Middle Earth Sea" made it possible for travelers and traders to make an end-run around most of the obstacles to land travel and make it one of the most connected, if not unified, regions of the world. If Egypt was, as the Greek historian Herodotus said, the "gift of the Nile," the prosperity of the lands around the Mediterranean was the gift of the Mediterranean. The analogy, however, is not exact. The Nile contributed to Egypt's homogeneity, while the Mediterranean had the opposite effect: it contributed to the diversity of the cultures around it. Why this was so may be explained as follows.

## Diversity and Dominance

Mediterranean connectedness had an important consequence: It was difficult for any single power to dominate it, partly because the Mediterranean Sea places extreme limitations on the degree of control that can be exercised over it. As we will see later, Rome, a wild exception, was the one empire able to successfully dominate the Mediterranean.

With the exception of Egypt the Mediterranean region was—and to an extent still is—an enormously complex bundle of micro-ecologies and micro-regions requiring for their proper cultivation and maintenance (not to say profitable exploitation) a high degree of agricultural and land-management skill. Compared to the agricultural surpluses that states such as Mesopotamia and Egypt generated, those of the Mediterranean were relatively meager and hugely scattered. In imperial as in all ruling affairs, whoever controls the surplus of an economy has, at least potentially, the means to command obedience. In the case of the Mediterranean, a ruling power had to take into account the variety of economies in the region and to beware of squeezing any one region too much for fear of destroying its productivity and thereby its surplus. It took a calculating and cool mind to recognize that only so much could be drawn out of any given place or people before resistance or agricultural decline would end the source of income completely. Equally, it took high political skills to persuade elites in these scattered regions that it was to their advantage to share their meager surplus. Rome was successful in both these endeavors. Since Roman times, no state has had the right combination of skills or the will to achieve the goals of uniting the Mediterranean in a single state, let alone, as Rome also did, unite the Mediterranean with the equally diverse cultures of continental and Atlantic Europe.

## The Roman Paradox: An Empire Without a Heartland

Paradoxically, to be a major power-wielder in the Mediterranean did not require the possession of a large landmass and a large population *if* the power in question could draw on the resources of rich—and willing—overseas satellites. In time Rome discovered this secret. Its main food and mineral supplying regions were, when its empire was consolidated, not primarily in Italy (much of which was hard to reach from Rome), but the grain fields and mines of southern Spain, Egypt, Tunisia, Sicily, and Sardinia. Even recruitment for the army was eventually outsourced. By the Early Empire the main recruiting grounds for soldiers and cavalry were, except for officers, in the provinces—anywhere but Italy. Native elites in these satellite provinces were gradually integrated into the ruling elite of the Roman Empire itself, just as Rome had earlier integrated the elites of Italy in the rule of Italy. In the second century A.D., for example, one of Rome's most distinguished emperors was a north African from Leptis Magna in Libya (Septimius Severus), and by the third century emperors were being drawn from Syria (Elegabalus), Arabia (Philip), north Africa (Aemilianus), and the Balkans (Aurelian, Diocletian, Constantius, Constantine)—again, any place but Italy. There was a downside to all of this. A network of overseas elites was fragile and difficult to maintain, and it worked only as long as the interests of the elites coincided with Rome's. The lack of a spacious, well-developed, populous, accessible, homogeneous heartland was a weakness for which Rome was always forced to compensate. When the overseas network collapsed in the fifth century A.D. there was no substitute for it in fragmented, mountainous Italy.

## 2. CLIMATE, FOOD, AND THE ECONOMY

### Climate(s) and the "Mediterranean Triad"

Geography books often refer to portions of the earth such as Chile, southern California, and the southern peninsulas of Australia as having a "Mediterranean climate"—meaning a climate that has mild, wet winters and hot, dry summers. While this is generally a true description of climate in the Mediterranean, it is also the case that there are many subtypes to be found within the region. One reference work, for instance, speaks of 64 climatic sub-types without even listing the inland sea's more numerous micro-climates. It is possible, for instance, to drive a few hours from Rome and find oneself among the snow-capped peaks and the alpine forests of the Abruzzo National Park in the Apennines. In one of his odes, the Roman poet Horace speaks of the "deep and dazzling snows" on Mt. Soracte just north of Rome (*Odes* 1.9). Travelers along the Saronic Gulf in Greece may be surprised in winter to see high ranges of snowy mountains suddenly pop up in front of them as they drive toward Corinth from Athens.

THE MEDITERRANEAN TRIAD Land and climate lend themselves to the production of a healthy, essentially vegetarian diet known as the "Mediterranean Triad" consisting of cereals, wine, and olive oil. The commonest cereal in antiquity was wheat, but barley, oats, and millet were also cultivated. Millet was considered a "famine" food to which people turned in times of crop failures in other cereals. Dried figs were another such famine food. The fact

| **Chronology of Roman History** | |
|---|---|
| Traditional Founding Date of Rome | 753 B.C. |
| The Roman Republic | 509 B.C.–30 B.C. |
| The Early Empire (The Principate) | 30 B.C.–A.D. 284 . |
| The Late Empire (The Dominate) | A.D. 284–A.D. 476 |
| Eastern Roman or Byzantine Empire | A.D. 476–A.D. 1453 |

that cereals could be produced in abundance in such places as Sicily, Sardinia, Tunisia, and Egypt and transported in bulk cheaply by sea gave Rome the advantage of an assured food supply independent of the capacities of its own homeland. Naturally, this dependence on overseas suppliers created its own problems, requiring the control of these distant lands and the connecting sea lanes, but the diversity of these sources tended to guarantee that food could be obtained from at least one or more of them on a dependable basis.

To cereals of the triad should be added high protein legumes or pulses—peas, beans, and lentils, the "poor man's meat." A stock joke of Greek and Roman comedy, which suggests how commonly pulses were eaten, was the emphasis given on stage to the anti-social consequences of bean consumption. Shortage of water and forage makes cattle-raising in the Mediterranean a limited affair, at least compared with northern Europe where large quantities of beef were, and are, regularly consumed. By necessity most Mediterranean peoples were vegetarians. Oxen were traction animals and were too valuable to be used as a source of meat. Poultry, pigs, goats, and sheep, however, were common and a valuable source of protein. In antiquity meat was always a prestige food and the only time ordinary people had an opportunity to eat it was at religious festivals. Fortunately these were frequent, and an added bonus was that the well-to-do were expected to foot the bill for the sacrifices, which provided the meat. The availability of free meat might help explain why religious festivals were so popular everywhere throughout antiquity. One scholar has calculated that the typical Athenian had an opportunity to receive a share of meat from sacrifices every eight to nine days. Athens, however, may have been exceptional in this regard. Another exception to the general rule was Rome, whose inhabitants were the beneficiaries of 20,000 pounds of pork distributed daily by the state during the third century A.D. Fish was not, as might be expected, a common item of diet, in part because most ancient peoples were farmers and unless salted, fish had a short shelf life. One way of preserving fish was to turn it into a paste or a sauce. The recipe for one of these, a pungent sauce know to the Romans as *garum*, is still available.

## Food, Civilization, and Barbarism

Olives and olive oil were considered one of the gods' greatest gifts. Olive oil was used principally for cooking and as a condiment, but it also served many other—sometimes unexpected—purposes: as a contraceptive; as a soap; for lighting (only poor qualities were used for this purpose); for controlling fleas; as a medicine; as a perfume base; as a food preservative. Its health properties are well known today but were also appreciated in antiquity. Olive trees were often designated as sacred and the oil produced from them was given as a prize in athletic contests. High quality oil was valued the same way vintage wines were. They were transported all over the Mediterranean. So highly did the peoples of the Mediterranean think of the olive and its products (and, of course, the grape and its products), that they identified civilization with its cultivation. Northern and central Europeans who ate large amounts of meat, milk, and milk products, especially butter, were identified as barbarians by their diet alone (and supposedly their distinctive smells). Barbarians such as the Celts, who under Roman influence exchanged their trousers for the toga and began to cultivate the vine and olive where that was possible, were thought to be on their way to being civilized. Eastwards beyond the Rhine, where neither olive nor vine could grow, was the true heart of barbarian Europe.

## The Backbone of the Economy: The Farmers

Prior to industrialization, 90 percent or more of all peoples world-wide were involved in agriculture. By contrast today the sign of a developed economy is the small proportion of the population engaged full time in agriculture. The figures given today for the U.S. vary but they range from a high of 3 percent to what is considered statistically negligible amounts (agriculture in India and China still involves 50 percent to 60 percent of their populations). Wealth, therefore, was derived largely from land ownership or the control of the surplus generated by agriculture. This is not to say that other forms of economic activity—commerce, mining, and the production of goods of all kinds—did not also generate significant amounts of wealth. Such cities as Tyre, Sidon, and Carthage were famed and alternately praised or envied for the material wealth they generated. The ancient economy, however, was by and large equivalent to the economy of an undeveloped modern country. Exceptionally, when the Mediterranean was at peace, much higher levels of productivity and trade were achieved, but never for extended periods. In ancient times the principal growth period was between 200 B.C. and A.D. 200, when Rome was at its height, as the figure showing shipwrecks demonstrates.

SURVIVAL: CULTIVATE A LITTLE OF EVERYTHING The key to the successful exploitation of the complex environment of the Mediterranean by farmers was diversity. Because so many regions possessed a diverse landscape of plain, hill, and marsh, it made sense to cultivate a variety of crops each suited to a particular area, soil, and micro-climate. Olives resisted drought but did not fare well in areas subject to frost. They required relatively little cultivation and were extraordinarily long-lived. Grape vines grew well on a number of soils, ranging from gravelly ground to marshy conditions. Their cultivation required, however, constant attention and a high level of skill. "The cultivation of the vine," said the Roman agricultural writer Columella (first century A.D.), "is more complicated than that of any other tree, and the olive, the queen of trees, requires the least expense of all" *(On Agriculture* 5.7). Cereal crops could be grown in between rows of fruit trees. Flocks of goats and sheep did well on hillsides where nothing else could be grown successfully. Herds of pigs foraged in oak, beach and chestnut forests. The key was to cultivate a little of everything; then if one crop failed there was something else to fall back on. Exchange networks through local markets were also keys to survival in the risky environment of the Mediterranean. The best way to provide against risk was to produce the maximum that was possible. If there was a surplus it could be stored in the form of olive oil, vinegar, wine, dried fruits, preserved vegetables, grains, and cheeses. Animals constituted a form of stored food.

Mediterranean farmers were not technologically backward. They were canny exploiters of every environmental opportunity that presented itself. As a result, a typical farm consisted of a series of patches of land, small gardens, orchards, and grain fields scattered throughout the landscape. Children looked after their family's flocks and herds in other

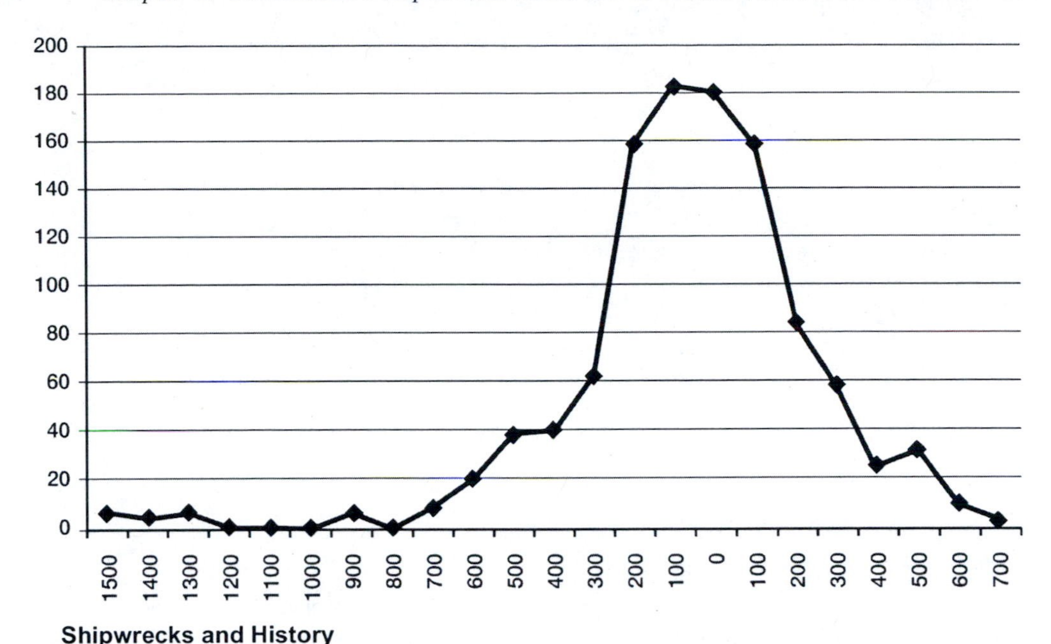


**Shipwrecks and History**

*Shipwrecks in the Mediterranean from ca. 1500 B.C. to ca. A.D. 700. The figure shows graphically the great increase in commercial activity that occurred between the rise of the Greek city-states around 700 B.C. to the collapse of trade following the fall of the Roman Empire and the Muslim invasions of the seventh century A.D.*

parts of the neighborhood. Mostly people lived in villages, but many also constructed huts on distant plots where they could live at harvest time.

SLAVES Compulsory labor in some form was endemic to the Mediterranean and a constant throughout world history. The nature of agricultural work—and indeed all forms of heavy manual labor—made it attractive to engage as many hands in it as possible. The Roman agricultural writer Varro writing in the first century B.C. describes the labor component of farming this way:

> All agriculture is carried on by men who may be either slaves, or freeborn men or a combination of both. In the case of freemen farming is conducted when they cultivate the soil by themselves as many poor people do, with the help of their children or with hired hands when the heavy farm operations such as the vintage and haymaking take place. Then there is farming carried on by debtors, large numbers of whom are still to be found in Asia (*modern Turkey*), Egypt and Illyricum (*modern Balkans*) (*On Agriculture* 1.17).

There are thus in Varro's classification two basic classes of agricultural labor: freemen and forced laborers. The latter category is broken down into true slaves—chattels that could be bought and sold—and freemen who, usually because of debt, could be forced to repay their creditors through the labor. From the third century B.C. onward, however, the use of chattel slaves and not just unfortunate debtors down on their luck, became common in parts of Greece, Italy, and north Africa and grew in importance, reaching a high point in

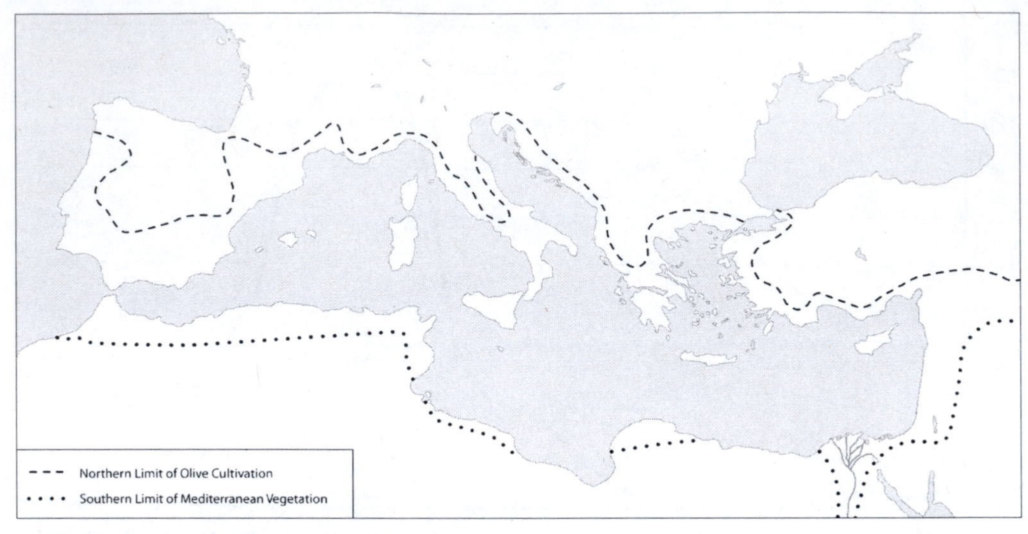


Mediterranean Vegetational Limits

Greeks and Romans popularly associated the cultivation of the olive and the vine with the limits of civilization. By that definition "civilization" did not penetrate very far beyond the shores of the Mediteranean.

the late Roman Republic and early Empire (ca. 200 B.C.–A.D. 200). The development of chattel slavery coincided with the rise of cash-crop farming and monoculture throughout the Mediterranean and was aided and abetted by Rome's wars of conquest from the Second Punic War (218–202 B.C.) onward.

## Risky Behavior: Monoculture and Famine

Monoculture—the dedication of an entire landscape to a single crop—was invariably the result of the intervention of some outside power, whether an overseas imperial power like Rome or a local elite who forced the neighboring farmers to produce a single crop for sale in the market. Needless to say such single crops were highly risky, being subject to the vagaries of weather, plant disease, and insect infestation. Their destruction could easily result in famine for the cultivators. Naturally, in such situations the elite only suffered loss of income. Throughout much of Mediterranean history there was chronic tension between the demands of elites for a larger share in the agricultural surplus and the limitations of the farming environment. It was commonplace to say that "Famines are blue-blooded," meaning they were generated by the bad agricultural polices of ruling elites. This is, of course, the commonly accepted view of what causes famine today: famines are not caused by actual shortages of food, but by the maldistribution of existing food supplies due to wars or poor governmental policies.

INSURANCE THROUGH NETWORKS One of the principal resources of all Mediterranean farmers was their kin and friendship networks. The cultivation of good relations with relatives and neighbors was an essential key to survival. In a society without lending institutions and government social safety nets, the only alternative in bad times was to turn to one's social contacts. One "banked" favors with ones' neighbors—lending tools or work animals or one's own labor—in the expectation that the favor would be reciprocated. Unfortunately for these resourceful people this effort to control risk could be frustrated by the intervention of outsiders whose considerations were other than the good of the farmers. Like other Mediterranean peoples, Romans too placed heavy emphasis on networks of friendship. These networks extended throughout their social, political, and economic system and to a considerable extent sustained it.

## 3. POPULATION AND DEMOGRAPHY

What held population down before modern times was not so much epidemics of diseases, lack of food, or low levels of technological development, but rather unsettled political conditions, marriage practices, inheritance laws, and more generally, low levels of health. Contaminated water supplies, bad human waste disposal habits, and lack of personal cleanliness were sources of such killers as typhoid, which were still life-threatening even in nineteenth and early twentieth century Europe and America. Throughout the pre-modern world, life expectancy at birth was low. Approximately half of all children died before reaching their fifth birthday. Those who survived the barrage of early childhood diseases had a good chance of living into their thirties or longer. It took the health and sanitary revolutions of the nineteenth and twentieth centuries to break this cycle and produce the population surges that are still underway in some parts of the globe.

### Family Planning

The most effective and commonly practiced form of family limitation in ancient times was infanticide. The practical reasons for having few children are stated with clarity by the eighth-century B.C. Greek poet Hesiod. He argued that, ideally, a family should have only one son because "An only son preserves his father's name and keeps wealth within a single household, whereas if you have two sons you will need more wealth and live a longer life" (*Works and Days*, 376). Hesiod goes on to say, however, that with the help of Zeus wealth can be found to support a larger family and concludes: "More children mean more help and greater wealth." Both strategies were risky. There was the possibility that, given the hazards of life in the ancient world, having only one or two children might leave a couple without any children at all, in which case old age would be truly bleak. The Greek statesman and historian Polybius, writing in Rome in the second century B.C., commented on this as a threat not just to individual households but to the state itself: "In situations where there are only one or two children and one is carried off by war and the other by sickness, it is clear that houses will be left unoccupied. As in the case of swarms of bees cities end up without resources and are enfeebled by slow degrees" (36.17). One well-known Roman, Cornelia, mother of the famous Gracchi brothers, had 12 children, but only three of them survived into adulthood. Too many children, on the other hand, led to family disputes and the probable impoverishment of the whole family unit. Traditionally, one of the advantages of having an empire was the possibility that surplus children—at least males—could find jobs in imperial service overseas.

### An Alternative to Malthus

There was, fortunately, an alternative to this grim scenario. The axiom of Malthus that in the long term, increasing populations outstrip food resources did not always happen even in pre-modern times. Rising population could and often did lead to more intense exploitation of existing farmland and the bringing into production of new land. This was frequently the case in Greece, Italy, and North Africa, as archaeology demonstrates. In Greece this happened between 600 B.C. and 300 B.C. and in North Africa in Roman times. Italy was a rich land—far more so than ancient Greece—and could, with good government, support a thriving population. The archaeological and documentary picture of Italy shows a significant population increase beginning in about the third century B.C. at the same time that new agricultural land in the Po valley and the Pomptine Marsh area of Latium in central Italy was being exploited. Elsewhere in Italy there was more intense agricultural exploitation of existing land, especially near large cities, which provided markets and stimulated production. Specialized farms came into existence to supply cities with vegetables, fruits, flowers, and animal products. More distant markets supplied grain, wine, and oil. A huge, 118-foot high artificial mound in Rome called Monte Testaccio near the Aventine, consisting entirely of broken pieces of amphora (ceramic food containers), testifies to the approximately 6 billion liters of olive oil estimated to have been imported by Rome over a few centuries during the Early Empire, initially from Italy and then later from southern Spain and north Africa.

## 4. POLITICAL AND CULTURAL THEMES

### The Power of the *Polis*: The Technology of Political Organization

From a cultural viewpoint the most important inheritance of Rome from the eastern Mediterranean was politics. It may seem perverse to make a claim like this for the much-derided realm of politics, yet good politics is at the heart of all successful states. If a people cannot get their politics (i.e., their governments) and their political culture (i.e., citizen understanding of, and participation in, politics) right, in the long run they can get nothing right. Good governments guarantee personal security and property rights, restrain internal violence, administer justice, and protect people from outside aggression. Yet, how good governments are created—and maintained—is one of the most elusive of all human undertakings. In a sense, the maintenance of justice—which is what government is all about—is the ultimate "technological" achievement. It is the breakthrough that provides the foundation for all further human progress.

In human history there have been relatively few major political or governmental breakthroughs. The most important of these in ancient times was the invention of the city-state and an idea of citizenship in Sumer, Mesopotamia around 3,000 B.C. from where it spread to the Mediterranean coastlands of the Levant (Syria/Palestine). Beginning around 750 B.C., Greeks in the Aegean area developed a very different version of the city-state and citizenship. In Greek the word for such an entity is *polis*, from which comes such English terms as "politics," "police," "polity," and "polite." Some scholars feel that "city-state" is not a good translation for the Greek term *polis* and suggest "citizen-state" instead. The Latin equivalent for *polis* is *res publica*—constitutional state or commonwealth—from which we get "republic." Instead of the Greek term *polites* for citizen, we use the Latinized "citizen" (from *cives* for citizen and *civitas* for state).

THE SUPERIORITY OF THE *POLIS* Greeks regarded the *polis* as a form of government and a way of life superior to any other because, among other things, it guaranteed legitimate rule under law; personal and communal freedom; an effective military; and the participation in public life of a higher proportion of people than under another form of government. Greeks felt that more people could develop and exercise their talents to the fullest in a *polis* rather than in any other type of human community. That Greek citizenship did not extend to all *polis* inhabitants is beside the point. The fact that a small number of people achieved high levels of political awareness and personal freedom was miraculous enough in a world where almost everyone, male and female alike, were unfree. How this was possible and under what circumstances will be explored later in the book. However, one fundamental assumption will be touched on here.

From the Greek and later the Roman viewpoint active participation in government was considered to be the highest form of human activity, since it involved the exercise of the most important virtues—moderation, courage, practical judgment, and justice—at levels not possible in the private sphere of life. Neither family nor work offered an adequate venue for full human growth. Primarily, of course, this ideology was true of males, but it was also indirectly true of females whose roles as shapers of citizens and sustainers of citizen households was regarded as vital to the survival of the *polis.* Women had a higher status in a *polis* than in any other political environment. At its best, the *polis* was a community of confident, well-informed, highly motivated, self-governing people.

MILITARY PARTICIPATION RATIOS One of the most important features of the *polis* was the military advantage it conferred on its citizens; its military power was disproportionate to its numbers. The reason for this was that the *polis* had an extraordinarily high military participation ratio (i.e., a higher proportion of the citizens of a *polis* were available for military service, and were better trained, than under any other form of government). Proportionately speaking the *polis* had, as a result, a distinct military advantage over any other form of political organization with which it came into conflict other than another *polis*. It also had the advantage of rapid decision-making. Assuming the *polis* was functioning as it was supposed to, consensus could be hammered out on important issues such as war and peace in private and public debates quickly and decisively. That is not to say that consensus always led to wise policies, but it did mean that it was possible, for example, to wage war with a higher level of popular support than is the case in modern free societies. Athens' endless Peloponnesian War (431–404 B.C.) and Rome's wars with Carthage, the Punic Wars

(264–241 B.C. and 218–202 B.C.) could not have been sustained without a high level of popular support, which was in turn based on political and social cohesion.

DRAWBACKS OF THE *POLIS* Despites these advantages the *polis* had significant weaknesses. Greeks felt that if a city grew too large citizens would lose control and the city would cease to be a *polis* and become something like Babylon. Aristotle said that Babylon was so large that when it was captured "a considerable part of it was not aware that had been captured until three days later" (*Politics* 3.1276a28). The result was that in the Greek *polis* (of which there were some 1,500 scattered around the Mediterranean and Black Sea), citizenship was severely restricted. *Poleis* (plural of *polis*) remained small, with perhaps an average of 700–1,000 households per city and a phalanx of just a few hundred. The largest number of hoplites (heavy infantry) the Greeks ever managed to field was 39,000 at the Battle of Plataea in 479 B.C. against the Persians. Aristotle was right when he said that if the Greeks had been able to unite they would have ruled the world (i.e., the Mediterranean). This was, however, a feat they could never accomplish (or, for that matter, never attempted).

The *polis* was for Greeks a kind of political and military cul-de-sac. They were unable to solve the problem of combining the ideals of *polis* life—freedom and the rule of law—with territorial expansion. It took the Romans to figure out a solution to this enigma and take the *polis* to the next level by inventing a more flexible and extensive form of citizenship detached from language, ethnicity, race, and culture. It is to this model that the modern constitutional state is heir. It was Rome's genius to be able to find a formula that enabled it to preserve many of the most desirable forms of the small city-state—its freedom, its emphasis on the rule of law, its high level of citizen participation in self-rule, and citizen responsibilities of military service—with territorial and demographic expansion. In its early years, the *polis* constitution allowed Rome, with its relatively small population, first to defend itself against its neighbors, then defeat and incorporate them in its state, and eventually to dominate Italy and then the Mediterranean.

# 2

# The Sources of Roman History

## 1. SOURCES: WHAT DO WE KNOW ABOUT ROMAN HISTORY, AND HOW DO WE KNOW IT?

### The Written Sources: Historiography

It has been said that the study of antiquity is like trying to reconstruct the contents of the rooms of the Palace of Versailles by looking through keyholes. Some rooms are in complete darkness, and nothing is visible. Others are full of light, but only a few of the objects in the room can be made out. Yet others are poorly illuminated so that we can only guess at each room's contents. Whole floors are completely unavailable for examination, even if only through keyholes.

The construction of Roman history presents similar challenges. The elite of Roman society and its interests are over-represented in the historical record, while ordinary people are woefully under-represented. Even among elites only a tiny percentage are known to any extent at all. The representation of women's viewpoints—by women—is virtually non-existent. Elite women feature prominently in the Roman historical narrative, but all the narratives were written by men, so that when these women "speak" in the sources, their speeches are the compositions of male authors. Except in the case of inscriptions, no woman's voice is heard unmediated and direct. Even when they do speak to us from inscriptions, their messages are for the most part formulaic, that is, they repeat standard phrases that were used by males and females alike, often chosen from sample books provided them by the producers of the inscriptions.

The written sources, which constitute the bulk of the evidence for Roman history, have their own built-in biases. Inscriptions, as noted in the previous paragraph, tend to be formulaic and repetitive. As for literature, it is estimated that only about five percent of all the compositions of ancient writers actually survives. Why this particular five percent survived was not purely a matter of accident, but rather the product of a complicated process of selection. Some choices were made in antiquity. An ancient critic by the name of Dionysius of Halicarnassus said of the historian Polybius (much of whose history has perished) that he was "an author whom no one could bear to read to the end" (*de comparatione verborum*, 4). Most, however, were chosen for their educational value in a curriculum that gave priority to studying the classics of fifth and fourth century B.C. Athens. Still other choices were made by medieval intermediaries who were ultimately responsible for passing on this potpourri of antiquity to later generations. The evidence for Roman (and Greek) history ranges, as a consequence, from the highly polished literary works of *some* historians, *some* poets, *some* playwrights, and so on, to scraps of papyrus containing lists of purchases and sales and the crude and misspelled graffiti found on lavatory walls and elsewhere. On occasion we know more about days or weeks of some periods than we do about years or whole centuries of other periods.

BUT ARE THEY REAL SOURCES? Then again ancient sources are not sources in the modern sense. Ancient historians draw mainly on literature, not archives. The kinds of sources social historians use for later periods of history such as wills, marriage contracts, title deeds, letters, commercial contracts, property registries, and the like have mostly vanished. There is no equivalent for ancient historians to the archives of courthouses, churches, presidential libraries, or the Library of Congress. Although military affairs predominate in Roman and Greek historical narratives, there are no minutes of the meetings of generals and their staffs before battles such as we have for modern times.

## Inscriptions

Other important sources for Roman history are inscriptions and coins. Hundreds of thousands of inscriptions in Latin and Greek, most inscribed on stone but some on metal, provide a great deal of information about the public and private life of individuals and cities throughout the Mediterranean and parts of Europe. Rome's earliest extant public document, for instance, is a religious inscription in archaic Latin in the shape of an obelisk known as the "Black Stone"(the *lapis niger*). It was found buried in the Roman Forum and dates from around 500 B.C. The most distinctive inscriptions are those recording the laws of cities, the decisions of town senates, the regulations of cults, letters from emperors and governors, votes of honor, and the careers of notables.

The habit of erecting inscriptions ("the epigraphic habit" as it has been called) was not limited to institutional practice and the highest levels of society. For example, our only substantial body of information about the all-important centurions of the Roman army comes from inscriptions. Innumerable inscriptions commemorate the lives and deaths of individuals of every class including freedmen (indeed, especially freedmen), and slaves. A gravestone put up by a slave at Rome reads simply *Zena, cocus*— "Zena, cook," suggesting that though she was a slave she was proud of her occupation and well enough off to afford to have the inscription cut in stone and erected. Thousands of grave inscriptions help us understand the duties and affectionate relationships that Romans thought went into making a happy family. It comes perhaps as no surprise that most funerary monuments were put up by members of the nuclear family—husband and wives, parents and children, and siblings—to each other, while only 5 percent were put up to other kin—grandparents, aunts, and uncles—outside the immediate nuclear family. Again, not surprisingly, the most common terms used to describe family members in these inscriptions were: *benemerens* (well deserved), *dulcissimus/a* (sweetest), *carissimus/a* (dearest). Another common term, *pius* (devoted), was used of parents, children, and siblings reciprocally, meaning that all members of the family were expected to be affectionately devoted—to have *pietas*—to each other. As a source of information, however, inscriptions have their limitations. They represent urban rather than rural life, for the most part the well-off rather than the poor, and some periods rather than others. Certain social groups, such as ex-slaves, tend to be over-represented, while the poor free citizen population is under-represented. Despite the existence of huge numbers of tomb inscriptions, which provide the deceased's age at death, such inscriptions provide little of worth about life expectancy in the Greco-Roman world.

LITERACY Inscriptions tell us something about levels of literacy in the Roman world, but exactly what is hard to say. Probably a majority of scholars think literacy was most highly developed among members of the Roman elite (including women) and in the Roman Empire period (first century A.D. onwards) among army officers and bureaucrats. Urban dwellers, who were surrounded by inscriptions, were likely to have been more literate than rural dwellers. At a minimum the former must have known enough to figure out basic abbreviations and formulas such as the omnipresent SPQR—"The Senate and the Roman People"—and some inscriptions such as epitaphs were so standardized that most everyone must have known what they meant. Longer, more complex inscriptions that contained laws, poems, official letters, philosophic doctrines, and the like would have presented greater challenges.

**Image of SPQR from the Arch of Titus**

*The short formula "SPQR"—The Senate and the Roman People—summed up the ideology that underpinned the Roman state. Though often more Senate than People, it expressed a basic truth about Rome so that even after the state came under the rule of emperors, the formula was still used widely.*

## Coins

Another important, but very different, source of information about Roman history is coinage. Coins survive in huge numbers and varieties. They offer some advantages over other ancient sources in that they were produced officially and thus convey the issuer's message directly. They also tell us how the issuers hoped to influence their target audience. Thus, for example, when the Italians revolted against Rome they struck coins in 90 B.C. depicting a bull (which stood for Italy) trampling a wolf (standing for Rome). After the revolt was put down, Rome issued coins proclaiming the reconciliation of Rome and Italy represented by two women holding hands. It was reconciliation, however, with a reminder of who won: One of the women has her foot on a globe of the earth. In his war with Mark Antony, Octavian—Julius Caesar's adopted son and heir—issued coins with the legend: "champion of the freedom of the Roman people" (*libertatis populi Romani vindex*). This had the double purpose of portraying Octavian as a traditional Roman (he was anything but) and making Antony seem like a foreign enemy. The fact that Antony was allied with Cleopatra and was headquartered in Egypt helped give substance to this clever piece of propaganda.

## Archaeology

Archaeology provides much of the information we have for early Rome and a good deal regarding the material culture of Rome in later periods. There are, however, problems of interpretation and built-in biases in archaeology just as complex as those found in other sources. Cemeteries are often the most important (or only) source of information for ancient peoples. Modern cities or towns are at times located on ancient sites and make the archaeology of urban settlement spotty. Excavations for telephone cables, sewers, and subways bring to light artifacts of earlier occupation haphazardly and accidentally—that is, if the excavators do not rush to cover them up to prevent the archaeological authorities from intervening to stop or slow down the work.

The earliest archaeological excavations of the eighteenth and nineteenth centuries were often no more than plundering expeditions in search of valuable pieces of art for museums or wealthy private collectors. Hence temples, palaces, or villas were systematically looted or later excavated, while the artifacts of ordinary people were ignored and cast aside. To this day, while thousands of elite sites have been explored throughout the Mediterranean, the number of small farm sites excavated can be counted on a single hand. Careers are not made by excavating cottages or stables. There is also a bias in terms of what is being looked for. In an excavation more recent levels (i.e., levels closer to the present), were frequently just shunted aside in favor of what was assumed to be the more "important" periods of the past or, for that matter, just the particular period in which the archaeologist in charge (or his or her sponsors) was interested. There was also a tendency to look for the supposed ancestors of a particular ethnic group or to burnish the past of the nation conducting the excavations.

To the extent that they can, modern archaeologists have labored to correct these tendencies. Many excavations are models of careful, scientific enterprises. Attention is paid to a much wider spectrum of finds than in the past. Where funds are available sites are studied for all aspects of the lives of the inhabitants. Pollen, seeds, bones, and animal and human

**Italy and Rome; Caesar/Aeneas**

**A.** Italia *and* Roma *clasp hands, but note that* Roma *has her foot on the globe indicating her preeminence.* **B.** *A coin issued by Julius Caesar around 47 or 46 B.C. showing Aeneas escaping from Troy, carrying his father and a statue of Athena (the Palladium). Caesar was here establishing his claim that his family, the* gens Julia, *as legend had it, was descended from Aeneas and the goddess Venus.*

excreta are collected for analysis, along with the usual pottery, coins, mosaic tesserae, etc. Locally made coarseware pottery, which in the past was passed over in favor of imported, high-status ceramics, is given increasing attention. Field or landscape archaeology, which surveys large tracts of the countryside for all signs of human habitation, has helped fill out the picture of the role of the "silent majority" of rural dwellers in history.

Making connections between a collection of material remains and a particular ethnic group is now a much more cautious affair than in the past, to the point where in some instances archaeology has virtually severed itself from the evidence of the written record. In some extreme cases, history and archaeology have become two disconnected fields of study of the past. Some problems, however, cannot be overcome even by the most conscientious excavators; for example, uneven geographical representation and the amount of time and resources a particular society is willing to put into archaeology. Some countries in western Europe have been combed by archaeologists for centuries while others, especially in the lesser developed countries of the Mediterranean, have little by way of an established archaeological record. This should be kept in mind when we consider the past before the existence of written records, and in the case of the vast majority of non-elite peoples who remained mute even after the upper classes acquired the techniques of record keeping. The record is often haphazard and full of pitfalls of cultural misrepresentation.

Despite the shortcomings of our sources they constitute in their totality an amazing assemblage of materials. Pulling them together required the labor of thousands of highly competent scholars from dozens of countries over many centuries. Simply establishing the texts of the surviving written documents occupied generations of scholars since the Renaissance (not to mention the work done by ancient scholars prior to that time). Epigraphists have labored to gather inscriptions from all over the Mediterranean and Black Sea areas,

**The Battle of the Teutoburg Forest: A Victory for Freedom or a Defeat for Civilization?**

An interesting example of the kinds of issues archaeology can raise for modern people is the discovery of the presumed site of the slaughter of three Roman legions by German tribesmen under their leader Arminius (later dubbed "Hermann the German"—his actual German name is unknown) in A.D. 9. An amateur archaeologist looking for coins stumbled on the site in 1987 and today a popular museum and park have been established on the spot. However, long before the discovery of the site of the great battle, Arminius had become a symbol for German nationalists. In 1808 a German playwright wrote a play, *Die Hermannsschlacht*—"Hermann's Battle"—to stir up anti-Napoleonic sentiment and to urge Germans to unite for their freedom as their ancestors had against the oppressive, imperialist Romans. A memorial statue to Arminius at Detmold, the presumed site of the battle in the nineteenth century, became a symbol of pan-German nationalism after the defeat of France in the Franco-Prussian War of 1870–1871. Needless to say, the French and others who suffered at the hands of German militarism interpreted the Roman loss not as a victory for freedom but as a triumph of barbarism and a catastrophic setback for civilization. What, the thinking went, would European history have been like if Germany had been successfully brought within the Roman Empire and "civilized"? A similar monument to that at Detmold is to be found in New Ulm, Minnesota. The museum at Kalkriese, the presumed site of the battle, has a web site: http://kalkriese-varusschlacht.de.

publish them, and where possible, preserve them in specialized museums and institutions. Numismatists perform similar functions for coins. Papyrologists sift through hundreds of thousands of fragments of early forms of paper (mostly papyrus, hence the name) found mainly in Egypt to reconstruct valuable literary, economic, and social texts. Despite the shortcomings of archaeology, the problem for scholars today is how to absorb and properly use the mountains of evidence that generations of fieldwork have produced.

# 3

# The Rise of Rome I: The Founding of the City

At the time of Rome's emergence in the fifth century B.C. states such as Carthage, Syracuse, Athens and Persia—the great power of the eastern Mediterranean—seemed better positioned to achieve hegemony in the Mediterranean than Rome. During the fifth century Rome was mired in purely local conflicts with its immediate neighbors. In 390 B.C. it was humiliatingly sacked by a band of Celts, and for much of the remainder of the century it was in contention with other Italian powers for control over the peninsula. It took another century to decide whether Rome or Carthage would be dominant in the western Mediterranean. Yet of all the potential candidates for Mediterranean supremacy, only Rome was able successfully to exploit its opportunities while simultaneously overcoming its myriad external and internal handicaps. Here we begin the analysis of Rome's rise to power by looking first at the advantages and disadvantages of Rome's geographical position in Italy, and then at Rome in its wider Mediterranean context.

## 1. THE ENVIRONMENT OF ROME'S EARLY HISTORY

### Italy: A Geographically Fragmented Land

Italy is not a naturally unified land. Geographically it is a mosaic of separate regions and sub-regions that have had difficulty connecting with each other at all times in history. It does not have a large natural "center" the way, for instance, France and England have geographically coherent central homelands or as Egypt or Mesopotamia had in antiquity. Symbolic of the way the ancients thought about Italy was the fact that for a good portion of their history, Romans did not think of the Po valley, today Italy's most productive region, as part of Italy—and with good reason. The Po constituted what amounted to a separate country, being generally more in contact with continental Europe through the Brenner Pass than with peninsular Italy to the south where the Apennines impeded communication. The Romans called the Po valley *Gallia Cisalpina*—that is, "Gaul-on-this-side-of-the-Alps." (Gaul proper or modern France was *Gallia Transalpina*—"Gaul-on-the-other side-of-the-Alps"). It was an alien land inhabited by barbarian Gauls (Gaels—or, as we know them more commonly, Celts). Vestiges of this sense of regional diversity persist to the present. An active political movement currently seeks to detach northern Italy from the rest of the country, arguing that as the most developed and wealthiest part of Italy the north should not be forced to subsidize backward parts of southern Italy and Sicily. Other parts of Italy besides the Po valley are even at the present difficult to reach from each other. Without the modern magnificent tunnel under the central Apennine massif, the "Gran Sasso d'Italia"—a long and terrifying drive—central and eastern Italy would be hard to access from the Roman or western side of the mountains. Before the building of the modern autostrada, the drive from Naples to Reggio (which connects travelers by ferry to Sicily) was a nightmare of winding roads and hair-pin bends.

THE MOUNTAINS OF ITALY Peninsular Italy (i.e., Italy south of the Po) is about 100,000 square miles (slightly larger than Oregon), 680 miles in length and 150 miles wide at its widest point. Only seven percent is plain; the rest of it is mountainous or hilly. In World War II the Allies made a costly mistake in thinking they could easily march up the Italian peninsula from the south and drive into central Europe through the Po valley. Time and again they were stopped by the Germans who made skillful use of the mountainous terrain to block their advance. It is no surprise that some of Rome's most hard-fought wars were conducted in these very same mountains against the hills peoples of Italy and that one of its greatest defeats, the battle of Caudine Forks, came at the hands of Samnite highlanders who dominated the central and southern backbone of Italy. The Samnites remained unruly and at times rebellious down to the first century B.C., long after Rome had conquered most of the Mediterranean. Even granted the excellence of Roman roads, Italy remained a fragmented land. More than in most countries, geography had a profound effect on the course of Rome's history.

THE PLAINS OF ITALY The zigzagging of the Apennines back and forth across Italy creates three great natural lowland regions. The first two, the Po valley in the north and Apulia in the south, open onto the Adriatic. In early times the valley of the Po, although immensely fertile, was covered with forest and marsh. The process of reclaiming it for agriculture was launched but not completed in the Roman period. Apulia in the south was also something of an independent mini-country, forming a natural sub-region with the lands facing it across the Adriatic. Its most natural lines of communication were with Illyria (modern Serbia, Croatia, and Albania) across the Adriatic.

The most important part of Italy in ancient times was the third region, made up of the districts of Etruria (Tuscany), Latium (Lazio), and Campania. It opens directly onto the Mediterranean proper and faces towards Sicily, Sardinia, and Corsica, and beyond them

Physical Features of Italy

to Algeria and Tunisia. Between Apulia and Campania the mountains flatten out to form a large plateau, known to the Romans as Samnium, which dominates the plains on either side. The richest agricultural land and almost all the mineral wealth of Italy were to be found in these southwestern lowlands. Peninsular Italy's main rivers, the Arno, Tiber, and Volturno drained the region and made access to the sea from the landward side relatively easy.

POOR HARBORS Italy has about 2,000 miles of coastline but relatively few good, natural harbors. Those in the south, Naples and Taranto, were seized early on by colonizing Greeks. Rome's harbor at Ostia was a poor one, clogged with mud banks and sand bars.

This, and the strength of the Tiber's current, made access to Rome upriver from Ostia a challenge so that for many centuries ports north and south of Rome at Civitavecchia and Puteoli had to be used. It took the resources of the empire in the time of the emperor Claudius, supplemented later by the work of Trajan, to make Ostia into a practical alternative. Even then, maintaining Ostia was an expensive proposition.

ALL ROADS LEAD TO ROME The natural lines of land communication for all Italy, as is still true today, passed through these lowlands rather than through the difficult central highlands or the narrow Adriatic coastal plain. Long before there were any roads leading to Rome all the lines of communication naturally converged on the site where a number of low hills overlooked a ford on the lower reaches of the Tiber. Rome, with its central location astride these natural communication routes, had internal lines of communication and a hugely important strategic location in Italy. It could—at least in theory—control all movement north or south or from the Mediterranean into the interior. Conversely, however, Rome's geographical position could be a liability if the city was weak, since it could be approached by hostile forces from two, three, or four different sides. It was sacked by Celts, Germans (three times), and Arabs in ancient and early medieval times.

## Italy: A Culturally Fragmented Land

Italy was not only a land divided by geography but also by culture. It is natural to assume that because today Italy is thought to possess a "Latin" culture—meaning its people speak a language based on Latin—it must always have been so. But in early Roman history Latin was very much a minority language confined to the small area of the peninsula known as Latium. Rome itself was but one of a number of Latin speaking communities. Forty languages or dialects are known to have been spoken in Italy ca. 400 B.C. at about the time Rome's expansion began.

More important than the linguistic divisions of Italy were its cultural divisions. The cultural world of the peninsula was starkly divided between those peoples who chose the *polis* or city-state way of life and those who adhered to looser forms of society such as the tribe and the chiefdom. The mountain dwellers followed more traditional ways of life while the peoples of the plains tended to be urbanized, regardless of their ethnic or linguistic origins.

THE OSCO-UMBRIANS The most widespread group of Indo-European languages in Italy in early times was Osco-Umbrian (also known as Sabellian), a group of related languages and dialects spoken by the inhabitants of central Italy reaching from Umbria in the north to Lucania in the south. Messapian in Apulia in the southeastern corner of Italy may have been related to Illyrian, the language spoken across the Adriatic in the ancient Balkans.

The speakers of Osco-Umbrian were the most widely dispersed peoples in Italy and possibly the most populous also. They were not, however, a unified people. Their lands were principally the Apennine highlands where they practiced some settled agriculture but primarily a form of pastoralism known as transhumance. Most of the mountains are not suited to arable cultivation, but the raising of animals can be practiced with great success. Transhumance, which survived down to the nineteenth century in some parts of Italy, in-

The Principal Languages of Italy around 400 B.C.

volved moving flocks into the mountains in the spring once the snows had melted and the alpine meadows had begun to produce fresh grass, and then reversing the process at the end of summer when the dry season in the valleys was ending. This terrain did not lend itself to the kind of settled agriculture that was practiced on the coastal plains of Italy.

When the agricultural villages of central Italy began coalescing into cities in the seventh century B.C., the internal regions of Italy where the Osco-Umbrians lived remained faithful to the old ways. There was to some extent a movement towards the production of field crops in the valleys of central Italy, but in terms of political development the highlanders preferred to maintain their independence and refused to make the kinds of sacrifices of personal freedom required by urbanization. In times of threat the Osco-Umbrians could coalesce as a confederation, especially the four Samnite tribes: the Hirpini, Pentri, Caraceni, and Caudini, who possessed a common religious sanctuary and meeting place in the highlands of central Italy.

There thus existed a kind of economic, social, and political fault line through the middle of Italy from north to south that inevitably led to prolonged warfare in which eventually the urbanized plains-dwellers, championed by Rome were victorious. It was in this competitive and risky environment that Rome's warlike character developed.

GREEKS From ca. 750 B.C. a flood of Greek migrants began moving across the northern rim of the western Mediterranean, paralleling the path of the Phoenician traders who were moving primarily along the coast of Africa toward the Atlantic. Greek colonies were founded along the Spanish coast and also the French Riviera where Massilia (modern Marseilles) was the principal foundation. In Italy so many Greek colonies were founded along the Ionian Sea in the south that the region became known as "Greater Greece," Magna Graecia. Of the many Greek colonies in Sicily Syracuse was the most important, while nearer to Rome was Naples. Both Phoenicians and Greeks colonized Sicily, but the interior remained in the hands of the original inhabitants, called Sicels by the Greeks, who were supposed to have come originally from mainland Italy.

PRESTATE CELTS AND GERMANS By contrast with the urbanized littoral of the Mediterranean, all the interior regions of Africa and Europe remained resolutely pre-urban, pre-state, and tribal. From at least the sixth century B.C. the area north of the Mediterranean, stretching from Spain through France, southern Germany, and Austria, was occupied by warlike Celtic-speaking peoples. Much longer than the Greeks and Romans, they resisted the Mediterranean impulse to form states or build cities and generally remained content with less complex forms of society. In response to Greek and Roman presence some of the Celtic tribes began to form proto-states, but aggressive Roman intrusion into France and the Balkans terminated these tentative efforts. Celtic peoples left to their own devices in fringe areas of Europe such as Scotland and Ireland, resisted state formation down to the eve of modern times. The same was true of the interior regions of Spain and north Africa where warlike peoples lived in fragmented societies that constantly warred with each other and with their sedentary neighbors.

From the fifth century B.C. Celts from Gaul infiltrated the Po valley and spread down the Adriatic coast. Celtic has close linguistic affinities with Latin, although the speakers of the two languages parted company centuries earlier, with one group, the Latins ending up in Italy while Celtic languages spread throughout much of continental Europe from Ireland to Romania and as far south as central Spain. The fate of the two languages could not, however, be more different. Today speakers of Latin-based languages (Italian, French, Spanish, Portuguese, and Romanian) number in the hundreds of millions whereas Celtic is spoken by less than a million (mostly in Wales) in the isolated "Celtic Fringe" of Europe. The consequences of successful imperialism are not insignificant.

THE ETRUSCANS The Etruscans inhabited the agricultural and mineral rich area north of Rome known today as Tuscany. Apart from the Greeks of the south the Etruscans were the most technologically and politically advanced people of Italy.

Linguistically, Etruscan is not related to any known language. Perhaps like Basque, another stand-alone language, it was a survivor of an earlier more widespread language that, under pressure of invasions or immigration, ended up being spoken in just one region while dying out elsewhere. About 11,000 very brief inscriptions in Etruscan survive, mostly the names of people, gods, and spirits.

One of the great unresolved mysteries of ancient history is the origin of the Etruscans. In antiquity, Dionysius of Halicarnassus, an historian of early Rome, believed that the Etruscans were native to Italy, whereas Herodotus maintained that they were transplanted Lydians from Asia Minor. There are undeniable similarities between Etruscan arts and practices and those of the east. Tholoi—beehive shaped—tombs similar to those found at Mycenae in Greece and on Crete have been found in Etruria, and their practice of divination by means of the entrails of animals has parallels in Mesopotamia. Many artistic motifs are also found in both areas. There is even an inscription in what appears to be Etruscan on the Aegean island of Lemnos, which could, logically, have been the site of one of the stages of Etruscan western migration. On the other hand the archaeological record shows no break in the development of Etruscan cities from the previous indigenous, Villanovan culture. Every known Etruscan city is preceded by a Villanovan settlement, a fact that has led to the debate about whether the Etruscans were transformed Villanovans or whether the new culture should be explained by the arrival of immigrants from somewhere else, usually the east. We will never, it seems, know the answer to this particular riddle.

**Villanovan Ceremonial Vessel**

*Bronze Villanovan* situla *dating from the 8th–7th centuries* B.C. *The ceremonial bucket was used in religious rituals and sacrifices.*

THE LATINS If the Osco-Umbrians were the most widely dispersed of the native peoples of Italy and the Etruscans the most advanced, among the least dispersed and least numerous were the Latins, among whom the Romans constituted simply one group.

Latin speakers inhabited the small coastal area of Italy known as Latium (modern Lazio). Its boundaries were the Tiber river to the north, the Apennines to the east, the Monti Lepini to the south and the Mediterranean Sea to the west—approximately a square with sides of 30 miles—for a total of just over 900 square miles. This represents about 1 percent of peninsular Italy. For comparison's sake, the city of Los Angeles is 464 square miles; Greater London is 650 square miles—and we are talking not just of Rome and its territory, but of all of Latium.

The Latins had, however, the great advantage of location, and as real estate agents always remind buyers, location is everything. To their south along the coast the Greeks had established a flourishing urban civilization as early as the late eighth century. To their north, the Etruscan-speaking peoples of Tuscany were equally well located, and like their Latin neighbors were the recipients of powerful technological, economic, and cultural influences that were spreading westwards from the heartland of the then-developed world, namely, the Middle East. Although a dangerous environment, Latium was well situated to benefit from a confluence of influences not just from overseas but also from Italy and its own, indigenous, diverse cultures. Nevertheless, location alone does not explain Rome's success in defending its homeland and eventually extending its sway over first Italy and then the whole Mediterranean.

## Rome and its Mediterranean Neighbors

Rome was not just an Italian power. It was also part of the larger Mediterranean world and in particular what was to become its own lake, the western Mediterranean. Although less obviously a "lake" than the smaller Adriatic and Aegean Seas, the western Mediterranean has clearly defined, lake-like boundaries with only narrow exits in the west to the Atlantic through the Gulf of Gibraltar and to the east by way of the strategically placed island of Malta.

ROME'S LAKE The shores of this "lake" were the coastal parts (the littoral) of modern north Africa, Spain, France, Italy and Sicily. The interiors of these lands are cut off from their coastal areas by high mountain ranges which prevent easy communication with the land behind them. Coastal Algeria and Tunisia are naturally oriented northward toward Italy, France and Spain, while the principal agricultural regions of Italy—Tuscany, Lazio, and Campania—look toward Africa. In the south of France the Cévennes and the Alps direct the inhabitants of that region away from continental Europe and toward the Mediterranean. The great rivers of the western Mediterranean have the same effect. The Ebro in Spain, the Rhône in France, and the Arno and Tiber in Italy all flow into the Mediterranean. In the process they draw the peoples of the uplands toward the coasts, which is where all the great cities, in ancient as in modern times, are located. Islands such as the Balearics, Sardinia, Corsica, Sicily, and Malta aid communication. In antiquity they served as handy stopping-off places for its coast-hugging maritime traffic. Understandably the inhabitants of the shores of the western Mediterranean often found it easier to trade and interact with each other than they did with their fellow countrymen of the interior, though it would be a mistake to think of any of these Mediterranean lands in antiquity as being made up of "fellow countrymen" rather than diverse and competing populations which often had nothing, not even a language, in common with each other. There was not then, and not for a long time afterwards, a "France" or a "Spain" or an "Italy" or an "Algeria" or a "Tunisia."

PHOENICIANS, BERBERS, IBERIANS The western Mediterranean was as diverse a mixing bowl of peoples and cultures as was Italy. From the ninth century B.C. Semitic speaking Phoenician traders from the area of Syria and Lebanon began to establish trading bases along the coast of north Africa. Some of these developed into cities, the greatest of which was Carthage in modern Tunisia. It looked directly across the Tyrrhenian Sea at Rome.

The Phoenicians were the first to stumble across the mineral wealth of Spain, and in time it became the Mediterranean world's principal source of silver, copper, and tin. Stimulated by contact with the Phoenicians, the native peoples of Tartessus in southern Spain, the Iberians, began to urbanize; by Roman times a flourishing city culture existed there. Central Spain remained less developed and from around 500 B.C. was subject to invasion and infiltration by groups of Celtic-speaking peoples from across the Pyrenees. They settled in central Spain and Portugal and their decentralized, warlike, tribal forms of society slowed the incorporation of Iberia into the urbanized culture that predominated elsewhere in the Mediterranean basin.

Most of North Africa—modern Morocco, Algeria, Tunisia, and Libya—was inhabited by Berber-speaking, pre-Arabic inhabitants. Berber is a non-Semitic, Afro-Asiatic lan-

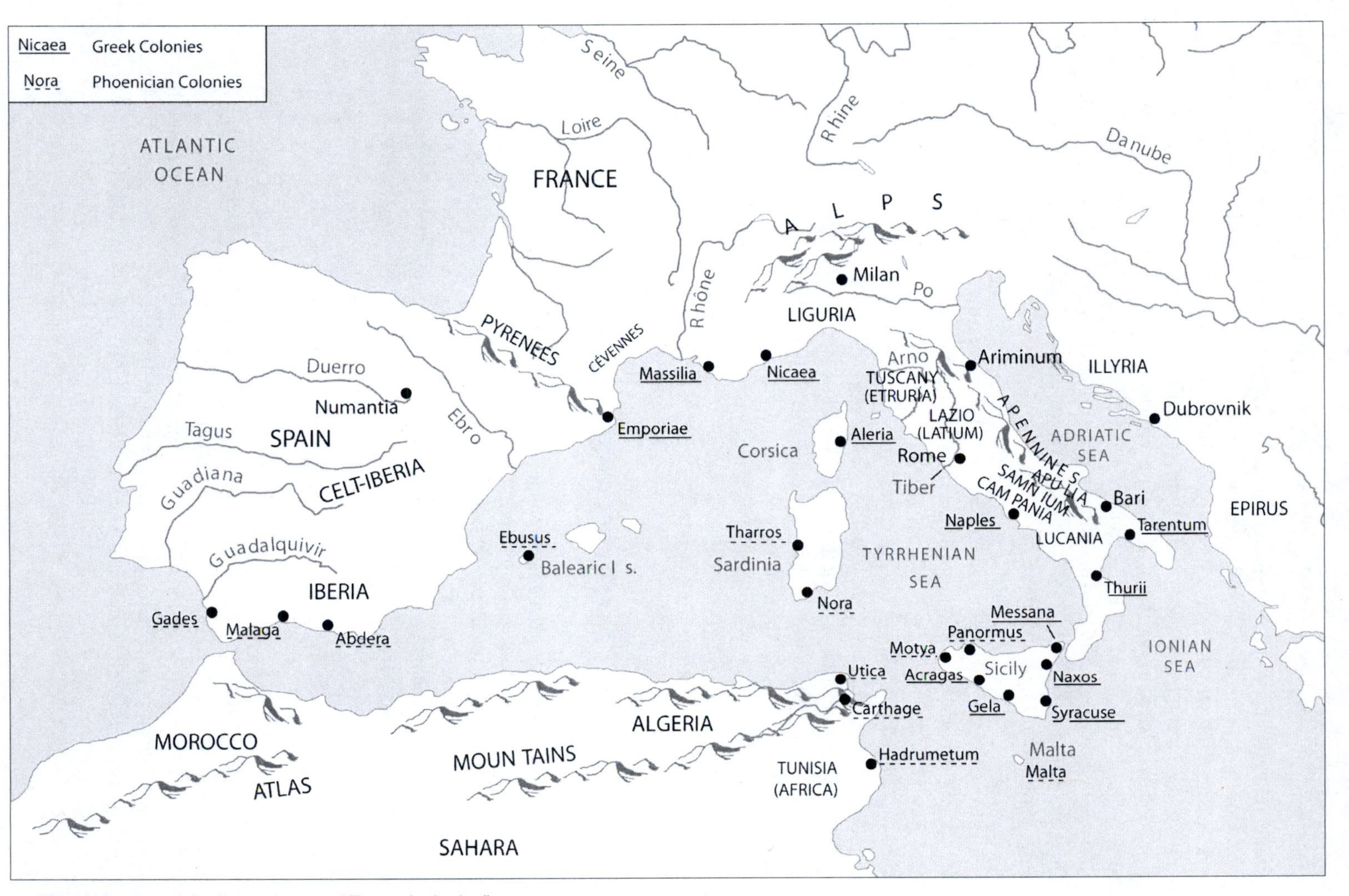


The Western Mediterranean: "Rome's Lake"

guage, related to the languages spoken all across north Africa as far as and including Egypt. It was not until after the seventh century A.D. that that region was incorporated into the Arabic-speaking world. Even today large numbers of north Africans, particularly in Morocco and Algeria, continue to speak Berber. Like the inhabitants of central Spain the indigenous peoples of Libya, Tunisia, Algeria, and Morocco maintained a pre-urban form of society until stimulated by the arrival of the Phoenicians, who established themselves along the coast. Even after the Roman conquest of north Africa the Berber inhabitants of the Atlas Mountains tended to remain independent and were a recurrent threat to the urbanized, plains-dwelling people.

DISTANCE AND DANGER Distances are short in this maritime world of the western Mediterranean. In one of the more dramatic scenes from the Roman Republic, Cato the Elder (second century B.C.), who was arguing in the Senate for the destruction of Carthage in Tunisia, opened the folds of his toga and let fall a bunch of ripe figs that had been picked outside Carthage just three days before, lending emphasis to his point that a vigorous neighbor such as Carthage, even though in Africa, was much too close for comfort. What Plato said of the Greek cities of the Aegean— "We sit like frogs around a pond" —could be repeated of this western, though somewhat larger, pond. Although the Romans were not a sea-faring people the way the Greeks were, they benefited from their proximity to the sea while being far enough away from it to avoid what they regarded as the physical and moral hazards that came with nearness to the sea.

## 2. PHASE ONE OF ROME'S RISE TO POWER

The first phase of Rome's rise to power was hidden in a much larger development: The rise of cities and organized states in the western Mediterranean. By the first millennium B.C. when urbanization got underway in the west, the state was already thousands of years old in the eastern Mediterranean. Growth of the state and the city in the west was a slow and fitful process that did not achieve permanence in northern and Atlantic Europe for nearly another millennium and a half.

### The Rise of Cities

The period 900–700 B.C., which coincides with the beginning of the Iron Age, sees the development of what is known as Villanovan culture, so called after a small village near Bologna, in north-central Italy. This culture represented a distinct break with the past. Old Bronze Age sites were abandoned and new large nucleated settlements were established on them or sometimes on previously unoccupied sites. In Etruria residents left their hut villages for large, defensible plateaus. The significance of Villanovan culture is that all of the known city-states of Etruria—the first indigenous cities of Italy—evolved out of Villanovan sites. This period, therefore, is regarded as the proto-urban stage of the development of the city and the state in Italy.

The next stage, 700–500 B.C. sees the emergence of true cities, again, first in Etruria and then slightly later in Latium. Villages coalesced into genuine urban centers, some laid out architecturally on grid patterns with identifiable public buildings such as temples, large paved open meeting places, and fortifications. This is evidence that a ruling class was able to gain control of whatever surplus the economy managed to produce and devote needed funds to public works and not just the enrichment of individual clans or kin groups. Toward the end of the period the development of "princely tombs," richly furnished burials in Etruria and Latium, confirms the presence of an energetic, warlike aristocracy. If the previous proto-Villanovan period had been characterized by tribal organizations led by individual chieftains, the new urban society suggests a much higher level of social and political complexity. The beliefs that kings presided was an historical memory, but these rulers should not be confused with the kind of dynastic, hereditary kings who ruled in the ancient Middle East or in Europe before the twentieth century. At least in Rome, and probably elsewhere, such kings were not hereditary; kin or clan groups (*gentes* in Latin) retained significant amounts of power. To come to power rulers needed, in some measure, the approval of the citizenry.

WHY THE EARLY URBANIZATION OF ETRURIA AND LATIUM? The facts are clear enough, but the question remains: Why did indigenous Italian states and cities first make their appearance in Etruria and then Latium and not elsewhere? The influence of Greek cities being constructed in southern Italy and Sicily is often cited as an explanation, but their presence is more a condition than a cause. Plenty of peoples with whom Greeks were in contact in Italy (and elsewhere in the Mediterranean) did not choose the path of urbanization and statehood. The ultimate answer is unattainable at this point. We lack the kinds of documentation that are available for state and urban formation in modern times—how, for instance, France or Germany or Japan—evolved into modern nation states. We are left with written sources that are difficult to interpret and analogies with the evolution of other ancient cities and states elsewhere. We know a good deal more about the process as it occurred a short time earlier in Greece and much earlier in the more distant ancient Middle East. In the Americas, where documentation is also largely absent, scholars have used archaeology and the techniques of social anthropology to create plausible scenarios for the evolution of states and urban centers in Meso- and South America.

In Greece many cities (*poleis*) emerged by a process called synoecism, literally "the coming together of households," or households grouped in villages, to form cities. In most instances villages were abandoned in favor of a central location, which was usually fortified and equipped with a water supply, public buildings, meeting places, temples, and residences. A somewhat similar process seems to have occurred in Etruria and Latium. Throughout coastal central Italy villages were abandoned and individually advantageous sites evolved into true cities. Saying this, however, does not get us very far. We are still left wondering what initiated the process of synoecism in the first place. In the case of Etruria and Latium the following is a possible scenario of what might have occurred.

NATURAL RESOURCES Etruria, and to a lesser extent Latium, had a number of significant natural resources that were suddenly in high demand when the technology of iron extraction began to become widespread sometime after 900 B.C. The essential ingredients for

**Chronology: Pre-Historic Italy**

| *Dates* | *Archaeological Definition* | *Historical Definition* |
|---|---|---|
| 1000–900 B.C. | ProtoVillanovan/ Final Bronze Age | Pre-urban |
| 900–700 B.C. | Villanovan/Early Iron Age | Proto-urban |
| 700–500 B.C. | Orientalizing | Urban |

this process were: iron ore, preferably good quality; limestone; and plenty of timber for conversion into charcoal. Etruria had all of these in abundance and in convenient locations. They were not buried in the high Apennines but rather right on the coast, or nearby, as was the case with the iron-rich island of Elba. Populonia on the mainland opposite Elba was also well supplied with iron ore. So much slag was produced there in antiquity that it has proved profitable in recent times to reprocess it using modern techniques. Etruria and Latium were both rich in forests and good agricultural land in addition to the metals. They had excellent local communications, and were accessible by land as well as by water. The climate was mild and rainfall was sufficient so that agriculture could be conducted without the expense or immense labor of irrigation.

If ever there was an area ripe for colonization and exploitation by outside powers, this was it. The ships of land-hungry Greeks and energetic merchants of Phoenicia prowled the Mediterranean looking for just such opportunities. Greeks had earlier settled key portions of southern Italy helping themselves to good agricultural land and key harbor sites, pushing the original inhabitants into the interior. In Sicily Greeks and Phoenicians together carved up the island, seizing its best sites and likewise driving the original inhabitants into the interior. A similar process began on the western coast of Italy. Greeks picked the island of Ischia off the bay of Naples in Campania as an initial base, and as their fortunes improved they settled first at Cumae on the mainland, and then built a new city nearby, *nea polis* in Greek or—as we know it, Naples. This site gave Greeks access to the agricultural riches of Campania, but that was as far north as they got. What was significant about Etruria and Latium was that no Greeks or Phoenicians, outside strictly regulated trading enclaves, were able to carve out colonies exclusively for themselves in either region. There was no repetition there of the land grabs that occurred in southern Italy, Sicily, Africa, Spain, and southern France. Why not?

URBANIZATION Apparently Etruscans and Latins were sufficiently far along in economic, social, and political development that they were able to resist the aggressive colonization of the Greeks and Phoenicians while benefiting from the trading contacts these foreigners offered. Perhaps initial contacts with Greeks and Phoenicians and knowledge of what happened to others clued Etruscans and Latins into what might happen if they did not do something to resist the aggressive outsiders. But what where they to do? The only solution was for them to become like Greeks and Phoenicians (i.e., by urbanizing and forming states that would give them the resources and armies to defend their mineral and agricultural resources). When Japan was challenged by outsiders in the nineteenth century it made a somewhat similar decision and was able to fend off colonizing western powers by becoming like them (though only up to a point). The Japanese had the self-assurance to take what they needed from outside sources, but not any more than they needed.

A similar pattern of self-confident borrowing seems to have characterized the peoples of western, central Italy. The process of evolution was not geographically or chronologically even. Initially southern Etruria made rapid strides in the development of a flourishing city-state system. Northern and central Etruria lagged behind as did Latium, but eventually both areas caught up, and by around 500 B.C., a string of fully developed, powerful political centers were in existence between the rivers Arno and Liris.

To push the question farther and ask where the self-assurance for this self-transformation came from is to go beyond our evidence. Probably stimulation from the outside word coincided with internal developments in central Italy to allow Etruscans and Latins to launch themselves on an independent path of political and social evolution. It is true there were many borrowings from Greeks and Phoenicians; indeed in the early stages of their growth there were so many that the period is referred to as "orientalizing," meaning that many goods and cultural influences from the east appeared in the societies of Etruscans and Latins. The alphabet, for example, was an "oriental" import in the sense that it was invented by Canaanites (ancient inhabitants of Lebanon, Syria, and Palestine) about 1200 B.C., perfected by Greeks (who added vowel signs) and sometime in the ninth century (or perhaps later), imported into Etruria. It was then finally borrowed by the Latins from the Etruscans. The alphabet—a superb information storage and retrieval technology—contributed to the development of both peoples and aided their rapid evolution from low to high levels of social and political complexity. But it was not a wholly one-way process. The massive technology transfer met with a willingness on the part of the Italian natives to transform themselves and invent for themselves new identities based as much on their own indigenous traditions as on the extraneous techniques they took from Greeks and Phoenicians. In the case of the Romans this process of adaptation was to produce a wholly new type of state that outstripped its models in many respects.

## 3. THE ROMAN VERSION OF WHAT HAPPENED

Understandably Romans would not have appreciated this modern explanation in which archaeology, economic theory, sociological speculation, and abstract political models dominate. Their belief was that history was made by individual human beings, usually (but not always) elite males, practicing warfare and statecraft or some combination of the two, and enjoying divine favor. They shared this view with the Greeks and indeed with most peoples until modern times, when historians began to expand the definition of history beyond elites, warfare, and institutions to the rest of society and to deeper "forces" of various kinds, especially economic forces.

Although they were literate from the sixth century B.C., it took expansion into the western Mediterranean in the third century B.C. (300–200 B.C.) to jolt the Romans into awareness that they needed to pay attention to the public opinion of the Mediterranean at large and not let others tell their story for them. In political campaigns candidates are strongly advised to define themselves before their enemies do it for them, and in the campaign for public opinion the Romans initially lagged behind. Greeks such as Timaeus of Tauromenium (modern Taormina) writing in Sicily around 260 B.C. had already begun to sketch out a version of Roman history. Greek intellectuals in the company of Rome's great enemy Hannibal composed histories of the great war with Rome (218–202 B.C.) from the Carthaginian viewpoint. Romans had thus to come up with an explanation of who they were, where they came from, and most importantly, what justified and enabled them to conquer successfully large swathes of the Mediterranean. They needed to establish that their wars were just and that they were a force for good or, preferably, a force destined by Fortuna or Providence to rule.

## Early Roman History Writing

The fifty years from 200 to 150 B.C. saw the appearance of the first histories of Rome. The early historians, known as annalists (because they wrote chronological accounts of Roman history on a year-by-year basis), initially wrote in Greek. They were not professional writers, let alone historians, but rather Roman senators who, in addition to putting a good spin on Rome's activities, also had personal axes to grind. The first of these writers, Fabius Pictor, for example, stressed the importance of his own *gens*, the Fabii, at the same time that he set out the greatness of Rome. Later writers emphasized the role of other great families such as the Valerii, Claudii, Cornelii, and others. Most of their work has vanished, however, and survives only in fragments or incorporated in the history of later writers whose work has survived.

The result is that the early history of Rome is, even to the present, a quagmire of scholarly dispute. What little there was by way of public records of early times was destroyed when an invading band of Celts sacked Rome in 390 B.C. The chroniclers of the principle surviving sources of early Roman history—Polybius, M. Tullius Cicero, Titus Livius (Livy), Dionysius of Halicarnassus and Plutarch—lived between 600 and 800 years after the events they claim to describe.[1] What follows summarizes and synthesizes their accounts. Since no actual hard data existed in their time for Roman origins, all these writers constructed their own versions of early Rome from differing ideological viewpoints. Their sources were those early annalists whose versions of Roman history were skewed by the tendencies and viewpoints sketched above. For centuries historians have sifted the sources to separate the various layers of history writing, the legendary from the factual and, as archaeological evidence became available, to connect both in coherent narratives. Despite progress in all these endeavors, much of the writing about early Rome still reflects individual historians' premises and has a distinctly personal character.

## The Foundations of Rome

The version made canonical by Fabius Pictor around 200 B.C. has Alba Longa being established by the descendants of Aeneas some time around 1150 B.C. (The most popular date for

[1] Polybius: ca. 200 B.C.–ca. 118 B.C.; Cicero: 106 B.C.–43 B.C.; Livy: 59 B.C.–A.D. 17; Dionysius: ca. 55 B.C.–ca. 10 B.C.; Plutarch: ca. A.D. 50–ca. A.D. 120.

**Capitoline Wolf**

*The statue of the wolf foster-mother of the founders of Rome, Romulus and Remus, dates probably from the sixth century B.C. The twins were added at the time of the Renaissance. The wolf was an ancient, totemic symbol of Rome. She appears in Rome's earliest coins first issued in 269 B.C. In 91 B.C. when the Italians rose up against Rome they produced coins picturing Italy as a bull goring the Roman wolf. A similar tale of the intervention of a savior animal is told of many heroes including Cyrus the Great, the founder of the Persian Empire.*

the fall of Troy was 1184 B.C.).[2] Romulus and Remus, natives of Alba, then founded Rome some 400 years later. Six additional kings were given schematic reigns to fill the gap between Romulus and the traditional date of the next major event, the founding of the Republic in 509 B.C. These kings were: Numa Pompilius, Tullus Hostilius, Ancus Marcius, Tarquinius Priscus, Servius Tullius, and Tarquinius Superbus.

The historical reality behind these kings is impossible to recover at this point. All we can say is that they probably represent early leaders of the developing community, of whom some were Sabine (Numa and Ancus), some Latin (Romulus and Tullus Hostilius), and some Etruscan (the two Tarquins and possibly Servius Tullius, despite his Latin-sounding name).

ROME'S HETEROGENEOUS ORIGINS The Romans used these stories of origins to their own propaganda advantage. Unlike many Greek peoples (such as the Athenians) who claimed to have been sprung from the earth (called autochthony, the most noble form of origin), the Romans chose to emphasize the simplicity and heterogeneity of their beginnings and the fact they had many founders, not just one. They pointed out that from the start they were an amalgam of peoples and customs.

ROME'S BALANCED OR MIXED CONSTITUTION In the schematic account of Rome's early history presented by the sources, Servius Tullius played a key role in the evolution of the Roman constitution. According to tradition he was responsible for the creation of the Centuriate Assembly (i.e., a voting assembly of Roman citizens made up of units called "centuries"), which took over some of the responsibilities of the old clan or Curiate Assembly. According to Cicero this act of Servius Tullius in establishing the Centuriate Assembly rounded out the process of constitution building because now Rome possessed the three elements of the best or mixed constitution: monarchy (the king); aristocracy (the Senate); and democracy (the Centuriate Assembly).

In Cicero's scheme (which he borrowed from Greek political theorizing), the natural cycle was now complete and the balanced constitution began to decay. Servius was murdered by the son of the first Tarquin—also called Tarquin—who, to distinguish him from his father, was given the name "Superbus"—the "Arrogant." The usurper lived up to his name. Unlike

[2]The importance of the connection between Troy and Rome is discussed at length in chapter 8, section 2.

**The Roman Melting Pot**

*The historian Livy (59 B.C.–A.D. 17) incorporated the melting-pot view of Rome's origin in his description of the thoughts that ran through the mind of Tanaquil, the ambitious wife of Tarquinius Priscus, who became Rome's fifth king. She argued with herself that her husband was getting nowhere in their native Tarquinii in Etruria, where the people despised him because his father had been a foreigner, a Greek. If he would only go to Rome, she believed, things would be different:*

> Rome was a most attractive place. Here was a new people among whom things happened quickly and where individuals rose because of merit. Surely there would be opportunities there for a courageous and energetic person. After all, Tatius, a Sabine who ruled jointly with Romulus for a short time, had been king in Rome; Numa had been summoned from foreign parts, from Cures, to rule there; King Ancus had a Sabine mother, and only Numa was of noble ancestry in his lineage (Livy, 1.34).

the previous six kings who had governed justly and according to the law, Tarquin acted tyrannically. He oppressed the Senate and forced the people to work on huge building projects such as the completion of the Capitoline temple to Jupiter and the great sewer that drained the Forum area (the *Cloaca Maxima*) whose exit point into the Tiber can still be seen. In foreign affairs he extended Roman hegemony over Latium. As the cycle of constitutional decay continued, an uprising by the nobility occurred, led by L. Junius Brutus "The Liberator." This uprising led to Tarquin's expulsion and the establishment of a new constitution that was based on the old but guaranteed *libertas*, "freedom," to the people. This was the Republic, established supposedly in 509 B.C.

## And the Truth?

For centuries scholars have wrestled with the innumerable problems raised by this schematic account of the regal period of Roman history. How much truth, if any, is to be found in the (often conflicting) stories of the kings? The answers range from extreme skepticism to guarded hope that the outline of the story contains at least some kernels of truth. There is no general consensus, but on some points there is agreement. For example, no one believes that there were just seven kings; there had to have been more to fill the gap between 753 B.C. and 509 B.C. Much of what we read in the stories are clearly simple projections by later historians into the ancient past of practices that became common centuries later. The following points may be noted as having some grounding in historical events.

1. All of the kings, with the exception of Servius Tullius, were confirmed in their power to rule—*imperium* in Latin—by the passage of a confirming law called a *lex curiata* passed by the Curiate Assembly, the clan assembly of the people. The next step in the appointment of the king was the endorsement given by the Senate (*patrum auctoritas*) to the whole process. This method of selecting kings seems suspect in that it conforms to Greek theories of what constituted legitimate rule and also looks like the procedures that were used during the period of the Republic in the selection of magistrates. On the other hand it may reflect a genuine tradition that insisted that Rome's early kings were not tyrants, but rather leaders selected by a political process in which the clan heads still had a good deal of influence. When elected they ruled according to established traditions.

**Brutus and Liberty (*Libertas*)**

*On this coin issued about 54 B.C., Junius Brutus (rev) proclaims his supposed family connection with the Brutus who liberated Rome from the tyranny of the kings and launched the Republic some 400 years earlier. The coin was issued just ten years before Brutus felt himself called upon to eliminate another tyrant, Julius Caesar. Liberty is portrayed as a woman (obv).*

2. The presence of two Sabines in the list of kings, Numa Pompilus and Ancus Marcius, suggests there is some truth to the tradition that Rome was founded as a joint venture of a variety of ethnic and linguistic groups of which Latin and Sabine speakers were the foremost. One scholar suggests that the original synoecism of Rome was the coming together of the communities of the Palatine, which was inhabited by a group of Latins, and of the Quirinal, which was the abode of Sabines.

   The presence of peoples of different ethnic backgrounds, especially at the elite level, in the newly evolving cities of Italy is well established. At the time of initial urban development in Italy a much more fluid relationship between citizenship and ethnicity existed. Greek cities in the south included many indigenous peoples in their populations and the presence of Greeks and Phoenicians in some Etruscan cities is also well known. From inscriptions we know that there were also high status Latins in Etruscan cities. In a rich burial at Tarquinii an inscription in Etruscan to "Rutile Hipukrates" (Rutilius Hippokrates in its Latin form) was found. The name is a composite of Latin and Greek elements. At Caere there were Ate Peticina (Latin, Attus Peticius), Tita Vendia, and Kalatur Phapena (Kalator Fabius) in the seventh century and Ati Cventinas (Attius son of Quintus) in the sixth. At Veii there is a tomb to Tite Latine (Titus Latinus). A Roman literary tradition recalls the migration of a group of Sabines led by Attus Clausus (Appius Claudius) to Rome. In these circumstances the presence of non-Romans, non-Latins, in Rome during its early history is plausible. How strong a presence this was is difficult to estimate, but it was at least sufficient to leave its mark in the historical tradition and provide sanction for Rome's willingness to find a place for non-native Romans in their state in later times. This practice, as will be seen, became a central feature of Roman expansion and a key mechanism of its eventual integration of Italy.

3. Servius' reforms may represent the moment when the army came to vote on political issues. The Centuriate Assembly was the civilian version of the army (i.e., the army assembling outside the boundary of the city (the *pomerium*) without arms). Originally the army probably consisted of only those men who could afford hoplite equipment. An ancient source refers to a distinction between the *classis* "the class," and the *infra classem*, that is those below the class, probably those who could not afford the requisite weaponry for service in the phalanx but nevertheless could serve as light-armed skirmishers and consequently deserved a role, if only a minor role, in the political deliberations of the state. The *infra classem* had representation, but it was unequal representation. Some citizens had by definition more influence or more votes than others.

   The Centuriate Assembly had a long and complicated historical evolution lasting many centuries, and it is extremely difficult to disentangle the early phases of its development from later development. The reconstruction of the Servian reforms presented here is speculative and is based to a considerable extent on analogies with the better-known role of the army in the evolution of Greek cities.

THE ROME OF THE KINGS The Rome that developed under the leadership of the kings was a dynamic, expanding state. By 500 B.C., it had expanded from an area of perhaps 75 square miles to 300 square miles, and its population may have been as much as 35,000. Rome, however, suffered from internal problems of governance whose nature are difficult to grasp. Aristotle's explanation of why it was that monarchies came to an end in the city-states of Greece may suggest a way of understanding them. He says that in early times in Greece "it was unusual to find outstanding men, especially as in those days people lived in small cities," hence kings were common. As time went on, however, and the city-states expanded and "many men were found who were alike in respect of excellence and they would no longer submit to monarchy" but sought a different form of government, namely a commonwealth, which would more fairly—from their viewpoint—reflect the new social reality (*Politics* 3.1286b). This comment of Aristotle suggests that the kings became the victims of their own success. As the *polis* expanded so did the size, wealth, and sophistication of the governing class. Given the competitive nature of aristocracy, it became intolerable that one single individual—the monarch—should have all the honor, glory, and power in his hands alone.

## 4. THE END OF THE MONARCHY

### The Historiographic Problem

For the historians of the late Republic (133–30 B.C.) it was conventional to portray the last king of Rome, Tarquin the Proud (Tarquinius Superbus), as a corrupt and brutal tyrant. He and his sister-in-law (who eventually became his wife) conspired first to kill their respective spouses and then the ruling king. Begun with such savagery, the reign progressed from one outrage to another until finally a Roman nobleman by the name of Lucius Junius Brutus had the courage to organize a coup and drive out the Tarquins. In this version of things, after

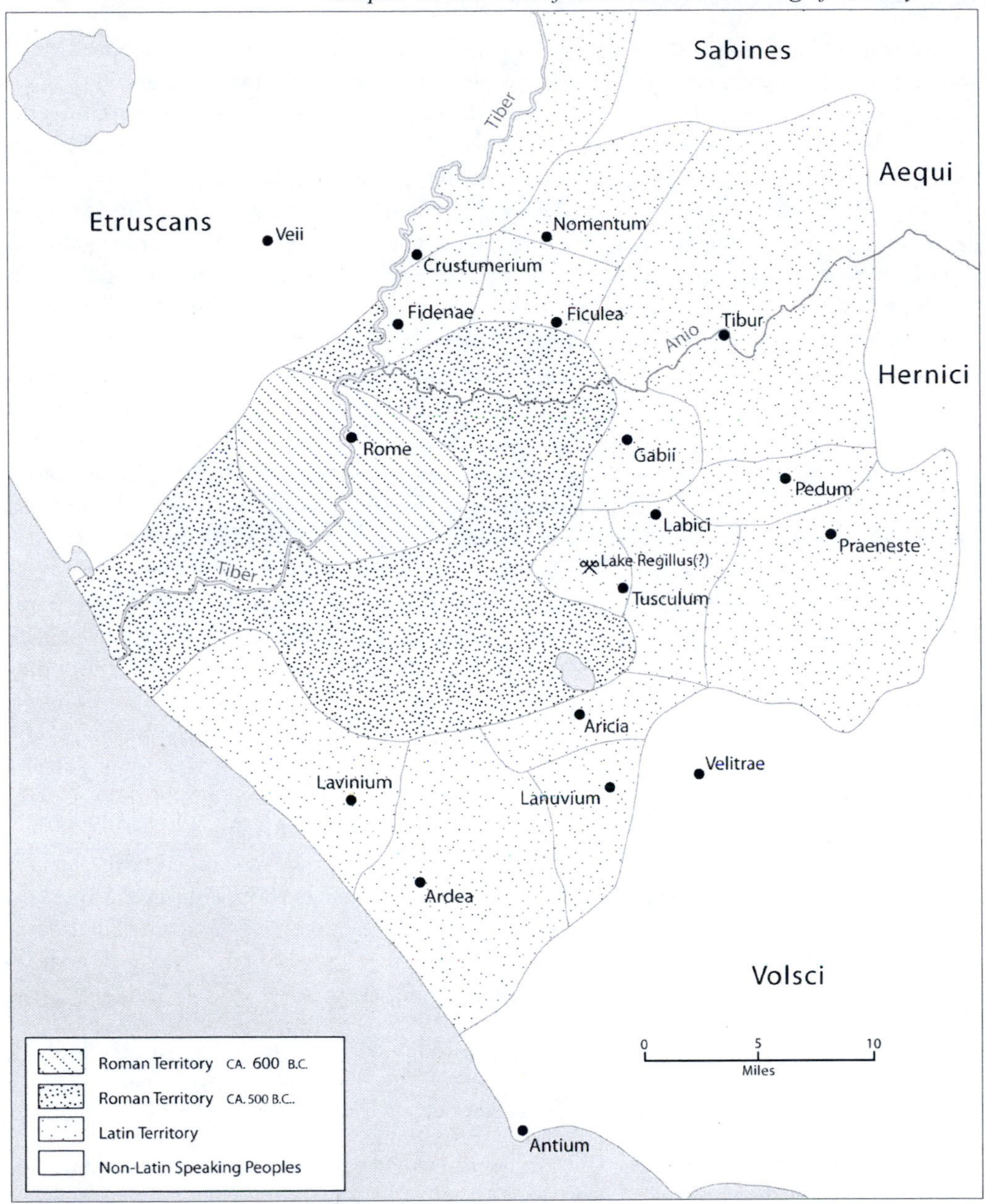


Rome and Latium 600–500 B.C.

Although the largest, Rome was still one of a number of Latin states and Latium itself was surrounded by non-Latin speaking peoples.

the successful expulsion of the tyrant two consuls were chosen to replace the deposed king, and so without civil war or bloodshed or much fuss of any kind Roman freedom was won. An alternate, much less emphasized tradition has the king of the Etruscan city Clusium, Lars Porsenna, capture Rome and expel the tyrant (Tacitus *Hist.* 3.72; Pliny *n.h.* 34.139). In this scenario it is possible that the outsider Porsenna ended the monarchy.

It is understandable how the story of the expulsion of the Tarquins and the liberation of the Roman people by the aristocracy could have achieved the level of an heroic national saga, and equally understandable that modern historians would be skeptical of the tale. Much of the narrative looks as though it was borrowed from stock, moralising Greek accounts of tyrants of whom the Greeks knew plenty. Other parts of it have the appearance of an historical romance. There may also have been apologetic implications behind the tale. The lurid account of the excesses of the Tarquins and the emphasis on the smooth transition from the kings to the Republic may have been aimed at defusing the revolutionary implications of the dethronement of a legitimate king by force. Later Romans looking back at early Rome might have worried that such a coup might have encouraged would-be "liberators" to proclaim freedom for themselves against alleged oppressors. The first century B.C. was, in fact, to produce quite a few such "liberators" using precisely this argument.

The trouble is that there is little in the historical record to put in the place of these two traditions. They each raise an equal number of objections and counter theories. Perhaps we may have to be satisfied with an application of Aristotle's generalizing version of the evolution of the early Greek polis. According to this theory Rome had reached the stage where a monarchy was no longer politically viable and it came to an end either by internal coup, bloody or otherwise, or by outside intervention or by some combination of the two. The one thing that does seem certain is that around 500 B.C. the rule of the kings ended and a new republican constitution was introduced to replace the old monarchical one.

Reflecting his own troubled times when the need of a firm hand seemed necessary for Rome, Livy took a positive view of the kings, or at least those before Tarquinius Superbus. He claimed that without the discipline of the kings the anarchic character of the early Romans might have led them to look for democracy, but fortunately the "tranquil moderation" of the kings, as he calls it, forestalled that eventuality:

> For what would have been the consequence if that rabble of shepherds and vagrants, fugitives from their own countries, having under the protection of an inviolable asylum (Romulus established Rome as an asylum to attract migrants to the new city) found liberty, or at least impunity, uncontrolled by the fear of royal authority? In such circumstances they would no doubt have been distracted by the demagoguery of tribunes and would have engaged in contests with the patrician rulers. This would have happened before the influence of wives and children, and the love of the soil, all of which take time to develop, had united their affections. The nation, not yet matured, would have been destroyed by discord. Luckily, the tranquil moderation of the government of the kings before Tarquin allowed the people, their strength being now developed, to produce wholesome fruits of liberty (Livy, *Preface to Book 2*).

# 4

# The Rise of Rome II: The External Challenges

## 1. LIFE IN A DANGEROUS ENVIRONMENT

"All states are by nature fighting an undeclared war with all other states." (Plato)

INTERNATIONAL ANARCHY Romans lived in a dangerous neighborhood. The whole of Italy was an anarchic world of contending tribes, independent cities, leagues of cities, and federations of tribes. The Mediterranean world beyond Italy was not much different. During the period of Rome's emergence (ca. 500–300 B.C.) the Persian Empire had first consolidated its hold on the Middle East and the eastern Mediterranean, and then lost it to Alexander the Great and the Macedonians. The Macedonian successor states of Alexander's empire fought each other to a standstill. They put down internal revolts and battled invaders.

Greeks fought with and against the Persians for two centuries. Individual Greek city-states waged incessant wars with each other as did alliances of Greek states. Wars lasted for generations. The great Peloponnesian War raged in two phases from 460 to 446 B.C. and from 431 to 404 B.C. During Rome's early years the Phoenician colony of Carthage in Africa emerged as a belligerent, imperialistic power in the western Mediterranean, driving the Greeks first out of most of that area and then fighting centuries-long campaigns against them in Sicily. They waged similarly aggressive wars against the Berbers of north Africa. Continental Europe, although we know little about its history in detail in comparison with the Mediterranean world, was probably even less settled and certainly as warlike to judge from the hoards of weapons, armor, and chariots that have been excavated by archaeologists and can be found in huge quantities in northern European museums. Historically we know of the impact of raiding warrior bands of Celts from Ireland to what is today Turkey. Fear of the Celts, *metus Gallicus*, was lodged deeply in Roman cultural perceptions and, as we will see, with good reason.

A corollary of Plato's assertion that all states were in reality always at war with each other was that they were always prepared for war. Perhaps a truer statement of the international situation might be that "*some* states are by nature fighting declared *and* undeclared wars with *some*, *possibly many* other states." The irony was (and is) that the absence of organized states leads to anarchy, but so does the existence of organized states. The harsh world of interstate anarchy of the Mediterranean and European worlds fostered a culture of belligerence, militarism, and aggressive diplomacy among all parties. International law was minimal and in any case unenforceable. War "is a harsh instructor" said the Greek historian Thucydides who witnessed the Peloponnesian War at first hand (3.82). If the Romans were good at war it was, in part, because they had so many and such good teachers.

## The Regal Period

Under the kings there were no serious external threats either from within or outside of Italy. Roman power expanded so that by the end of the fifth century the city was probably the most powerful of the Latin states. But the historical situation changed quickly. First Rome was challenged soon after 500 B.C. by its Latin neighbors. Then there occurred one of those demographic shifts to which Italy was periodically subject: the movement of the highlanders to the plains. Unfortunately for the Romans these population movements coincided with the infiltration of an even more aggressive, warrior people from outside Italy, the Celts. Coping with these threats took over two centuries and in the case of the Celts, even longer. As late as 225 B.C. a Celtic horde was able to reach within 50 miles of Rome before being defeated, and during the make or break war with Hannibal (218–202 B.C.) the Celts were among his staunchest supporters.

## Rome and the Latins

First the Latins, aiming to trim Rome's power, attempted to reinstall the recently expelled king of Rome, Tarquinius Superbus, but were defeated by the Romans at the Battle of Lake Regillus in 496 B.C. This was a crucial victory—even if historically obscure—in that it confirmed the recently won independence of the Republic. Later generations of Romans who passed through the Roman Forum were reminded of this battle by the large temple to Castor and Pollux which was vowed to the two gods by the commander Postumius during the battle and subsequently built in a prominent position. It occupies that position to the present day. Three of the fine columns that date from a rebuilding of the temple in 117 B.C. can still be seen.

Following their victory over the Latins, the Romans in 496 B.C. entered into a pact with them; the Cassian Treaty (*Foedus Cassianum*) regulated relations among them for the next century and a half. Its terms are not precisely known, and whether it was a treaty among equals or unequals is disputed.

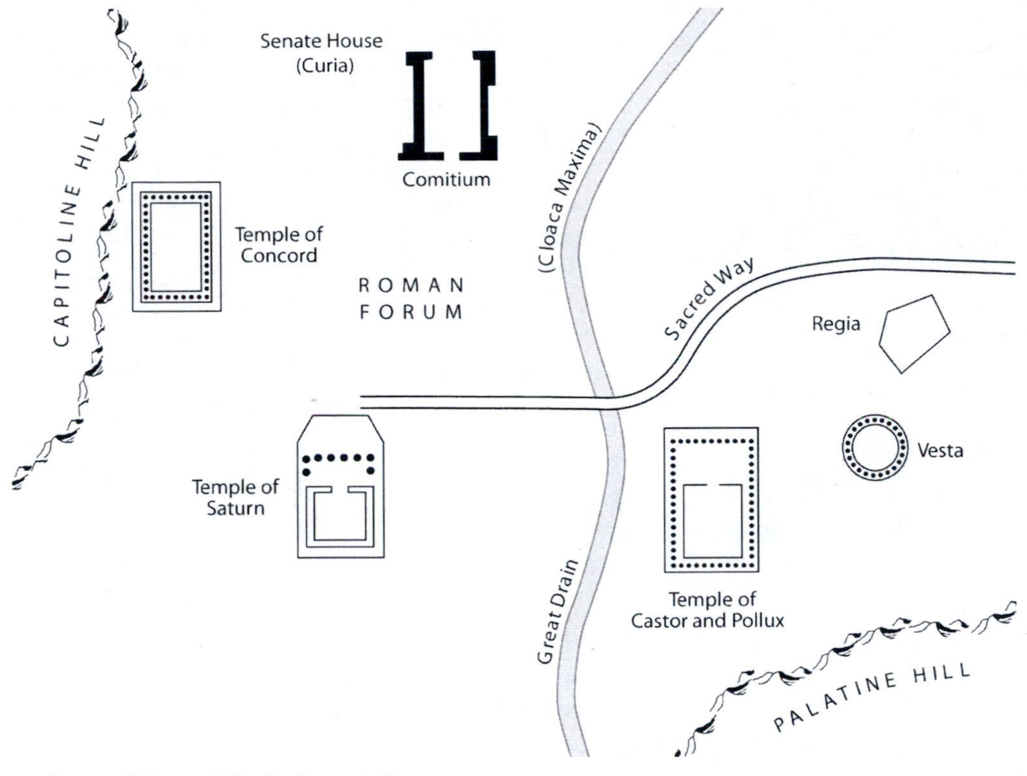


**Ground Plan of Early Roman Forum**

*Before the area known as the Roman Forum could be put to use it had to be drained. The "Great Drain"* (Cloaca Maxima), *which was built for that purpose in the sixth century* B.C., *still functions although it is now integrated with the main sewer system of modern Rome. Its mouth, framed by three concentric arches, is a conspicuous landmark on the Tiber embankment. The drain was much admired in antiquity for its engineering qualities that enabled it to support the great buildings constructed over it and to resist the backwash of frequent floods. The Sacred Way* (Sacra Via), *Rome's oldest street, was lined with porticoes and shops. As the main route to the Capitol it was used by triumphal processions.*

The task of the alliance was to defend Latium against attack and, where possible, expand its boundaries. The league started with a number of advantages. Latium was a geographical unit with no major mountain ranges to disrupt communications and isolate Latin cities from each other. By 500 B.C. the Latins were already an urbanized people who shared a common ethnicity. Their cities were little self-governing republics, in many respects like Greek *poleis*, but with the advantage that, in addition to speaking the same language, they shared a number of key legal rights and had a long tradition of religious association. Festivals were celebrated jointly among them at sanctuaries such as that of Diana on the Aventine in Rome, Venus at Lavinium, and— most important—every spring in the Alban Hills there was the great Latin festival in honor of Jupiter Latiaris— "Jupiter Guardian of the Latins." Common sanctuaries existed elsewhere in Latium such as those at Gabii and

**Temple of the Twins Castor and Pollux**

*The sorry remains of a once-great temple that dominated one end of the Roman Forum from the earliest days of the Republic.*

Satricum. Latins could intermarry among themselves (the right known as *conubium*), own property, and enter into contracts that were recognized in each others' cities (*commercium*). They also possessed the right of migration (*ius migrandi*) from one Latin state to another. This right included the automatic grant of full citizenship in the new domicile. Collectively these rights were known as the Latin Right (*ius Latii*), and the Romans designated the Latins as Allies of the Latin Name (*socii nominis Latini*).

These shared rights and cultural similarities, important though they were, did not bring about political unity. The Latin states did not evolve or, for that matter, aim to evolve, into a federal union. Nevertheless, from the viewpoint of potential military cooperation and greater political unity, the Latins had a major advantage over the other inhabitants of Italy such as the Greeks, Etruscans, and Oscans. These peoples, too, had similar cultural and ethnic backgrounds among themselves but had even less political unity than did the Latins. For example, when the Etruscan city of Veii was besieged by the Romans, it received no help from the members of the longstanding Etruscan league to which it belonged. As in the Greek cities, they were notorious for their endless squabbles and their inability to get along with each other.

## The Oscan Threat

It was good that the Cassian Treaty came into existence when it did because both Latins and Romans almost immediately found themselves under severe pressure from migrants and invaders from the mountainous interior of Italy. For the next century Latins and Romans together struggled to maintain themselves against these intruders.

Peninsular Italy was, from the viewpoint of demographics and economics, an inherently unstable region. The plains' peoples were committed to settled agriculture and a form of the state based on the city. The interior mountainous regions offered only limited opportunity for this kind of agriculture. The olive, for instance, is sensitive to cold and does not do well above a certain altitude. The mountains, however, were ideal for extensive herding, and in consequence settlements there were much less permanent. Whereas urbanized centers were the core of the Italian states in the plains regions, the Oscan and Umbrian states in the interior, to the extent they can be called states, took the form of loose tribal confederations. Their populations lived in scattered settlements or hamlets. At least in the case of the

Samnites, however, their lack of urbanization did not affect their ability to cooperate among themselves for military purposes.

**Chronology: Wars of the Republic 1**

|  |  |
|---|---|
| Wars with the Oscans | ca 500–400 B.C. |
| Capture of Veii | 396 B.C. |
| Sack of Rome by the Celts | 390 B.C. |
| Latin Revolt | 340–338 B.C. |
| Samnite Wars | 326–304; 298–290 B.C. |
| Battle of Sentinum | 295 B.C. |
| War with Pyrrhus | 280–275 B.C. |
| First Punic War | 264–241 B.C. |
| Second Punic War | 218–202 B.C. |

THE SACRED SPRING A challenge the Oscans had to face on a regular basis was that of overpopulation. Their solution to this recurring problem was the institution of the "Sacred Spring" (*ver sacrum*). This was a religious ritual in which all of the creatures born in a particular year—human as well as animal—were declared "sacred" (Lat. *sacer*, i.e., dedicated to the gods). At the end of the year all the animals so designated were sacrificed to the gods and so passed into their possession, while the humans were allowed to live but with the understanding that upon reaching adulthood they would emigrate to make a livelihood for themselves elsewhere in Italy. Needless to say such an arrangement made for unstable and unfriendly relations with neighbors. The settled, less aggressive agricultural inhabitants of the lowlands were the most likely victims of the *ver sacrum*. Without warning a group of warlike and desperate young people might appear out of the mountainous interior and fall on an agricultural settlement or city intending to take over or perish in the attempt.

The institution of the *ver sacrum* was highly successful, at least from the highlanders' viewpoint. During the fourth century Oscans infiltrated Campania and took over the flourishing Etruscan city of Capua and the Greek city of Cumae. The same fate befell many other Greek cities on the Tyrrhenian Sea coast. In Apulia in the south, massive walls had to be built to defend the towns of that region, and by 350 B.C. Lucania and Calabria were overrun by the Oscans.

AEQUI, VOLSCI, AND SABINES While Romans and Latins were squabbling among themselves around 500 B.C., the nearby hill peoples, identified in the sources as Aequi and Volsci (probably Umbrian-speaking), seized their opportunity to expand their possessions and moved down into the plains of Latium and Campania. They overwhelmed the strong Latin towns of Tibur and Praeneste and occupied the Alban Hills and their important sacred sites. Further south they occupied the Monti Lepini and reached the Mediterranean coast where they established themselves at Antium and Terracina. The nearby Etruscan city of Veii took the opportunity of Roman and Latin weakness to seize control of the mouth of the Tiber and the valuable salt route, the Via Salaria, by which salt was carried into the interior of Italy. The Sabines, a hill people with a long history of involvement with Rome—peaceful as well as warlike—now posed an additional threat directly to Rome from the northeast. A significant economic downturn in Rome is detectable in the archaeological record at this time, and the long temple-building program, which had been begun under the kings, came to an abrupt end in 484 B.C. It seems that at this time many Latins took the opportunity to migrate to safety at Rome. A dangerous consequence of the success of the Oscans in fighting their way through Latium to the coast was that the urbanized people of the nearby

**The Fate of a Greek City at the Hands of the Oscans**

*The story is told by the historian Aristoxenus of Tarentum who lived about the time of the conquest of Poseidonia (modern Paestum, south of Naples) by Oscan highlanders.*

> We act like the peoples of Poseidonia who live on the Tyrrhenian Sea. Although they were originally Greeks, it happened that they were completely barbarized, and became Oscans. Nevertheless they still celebrate one festival that is Greek to the present. For this event they gather together and recall those ancient words and institutions which were once theirs and after lamenting them and weeping over them in each other's presence, they return home (Athenaeus 14.632a).

Trerus River valley, the Hernici, were cut off from their natural cultural allies, the Latins.

A DESPERATE SITUATION? It is hard to estimate how desperate the situation was at this time for the Latins, Romans, and Hernici. In the absence of any genuinely useful information, the historians of later periods inflated what little information they had and give the impression that the armies of the contenders were locked in constant warfare. That there was constant warfare is undoubtedly accurate, but armies (at least not large armies) are unlikely to have been involved. The experience of the Romans and Latins was not at all like the epic collision that occurred at about the same time between the Greeks and the Persian Empire where genuinely large armies and fleets were involved. More often than not the clashes of the Latins with their foes were in the forms of skirmishes, raids, and counter-raids, as Livy notes.

Some perspective is provided when we consider the size of the region in dispute. Most of the action of the century and a half of war took place within a radius of 12 to 25 miles of Rome. Veii, the nearby threatening Etruscan city, was just 10 miles from Rome. Another major Etruscan city, Caere, was 24 miles away; the important Latin city of Tibur was 18 miles and Tusculum about 12. Neverthless, we should not overly discount the reports of the sources. The fact that warfare kept up for over a century suggests that despite the resources of the Latins, a significant struggle, whatever the size of the forces involved, took place. Romans and Latins and their institutions were tested severely. Fortunately for them they proved, in the end, capable of outlasting their more simply organized, if more aggressive, opponents. It is worth spending time on this early period because it was precisely in this only vaguely known segment of Roman history that its character and institutions were developed. When better sources become available (say, after 300 B.C.), Rome's childhood and a good part of its adolescence, so to speak, were already over. By then it was already a highly successful, functioning state.

COUNTER-MEASURES What looked like small steps to counter the invaders had important results. Like American frontier forts, Latin fortresses were established at the strategic locations of Cora, Signia, Norba, and Setia with the aim of containing the Volsci in the Alban Hills and the Monti Lepini. Their powerful defensive walls are still impressive.

These fortresses put the invading Oscans on the defensive, though as late as 350 B.C. the Volsci were still in possession of Velitrae in the Alban Hills and Privernum in the Monti Lepini. An alliance was made with the Hernici and a little later with the Samnites. The cli-

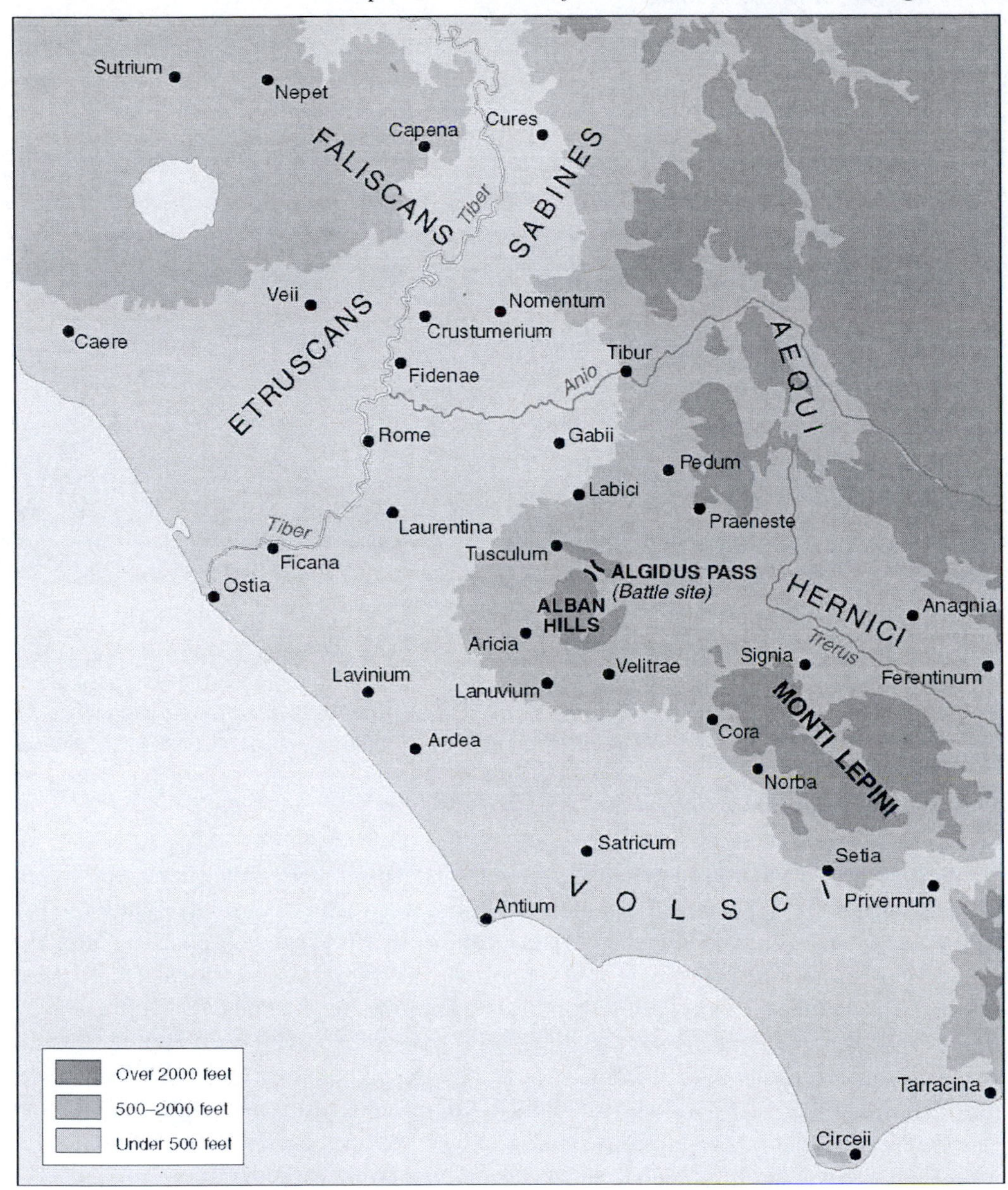


Early Rome and her Neighbors

mactic battle of the war took place in 431 B.C. at the Algidus Pass, just 18 miles from Rome. Vague recollections of these events were stored in the memories and archives, such as they were, of great Roman families such as the Quinctii (to which clan Cincinnatus belonged), the Valerii, Claudii, Cornelli, Julii, Postumii, Manlii, Fabii, and others. These tales were heavily embroidered by later historians, who liberally borrowed from Greek sources and later periods of Roman history.

**The Walls of Norba**

*The massive east gate of Norba. Norba was one of a string of colony-fortresses established on impregnable positions in the foothills of the Monti Lepini to contain the raids of the Aequi and protect the great north-south highway, the Via Appia. Norba, along with her sister fortresses, served Rome and the Latins well in all their wars in Italy.*

## The Fall of Veii

By dint of constant fighting the Sabines, Aequi, and Volsci were either defeated, driven back into the hills, or contained. By 400 B.C. Rome was ready to turn its attention to the nearby Etruscan city of Veii, which given its location just 10 miles away, posed an immediate threat to Rome. After an epic siege of supposedly 10 years (suspiciously like the 10 year siege of Troy by the Greeks), Veii fell and Rome appropriated its gods, its people, and its territory. By the ritual of *evocatio* ("calling-forth"), the gods of Veii were invited to abandon the fallen city and move to Rome, where they would continue to be worshiped. The most famous of the Veian gods who migrated to Rome in this fashion was the goddess Juno (the Greek equivalent was Hera), who ended up with her own temple on the Aventine Hill where she was worshiped as Juno Regina, Queen Juno. By this process Rome not only propitiated the angry gods of Veii but also eliminated the political claims of Veii by delegitimizing its right to divine protection. *Evocatio* was to become a feature of Roman statecraft and imperialism during the Republic. A particularly prominent example of the use of *evocatio* in later time was the calling forth of the gods of Carthage, Rome's mortal enemy, which in 146 B.C. was eliminated as completely as was Veii.

THE SPOILS OF VICTORY Apart from removing a dangerous strategic rival, the conquest of Veii immensely expanded Rome's economic and military resources. It is estimated that Rome's territory was increased by about 60%. Veii's land was divided up into parcels of seven iugera or about four and one-half acres and distributed, according to Livy, to every member of the plebeians (5.30). An important side effect of individual (*viritim*) land grants of this type to poor citizens was that by being bumped up in the census they became eligible to serve in the phalanx of the army, and not merely as skirmishers or light infantry as they had been in the past. For the same reason they moved up within the political system to higher levels of participation and influence. In Rome's political culture, higher levels of civic responsibility in both military and political domains followed upon elevation in economic status. In the class-census (*classis*) system privileges were nicely balanced with responsibilities (more on this in the next chapter). This technique of individual land grants, which was used throughout much of Rome's history, had the multiplying effect of reducing poverty while at the same time increasing the state's citizen manpower reserves, its citizens' political participation, and overall economic strength.

## Conquest and Colonies

The conquest of Veii represented Rome's most significant independent (i.e., independent of the help of the Latin League) acquisition of territory to date. Paradoxically, however, as Rome expanded its borders it became proportionately exposed to new threats—the problem of all expanding states, imperial or otherwise. As old buffer zones were eliminated, Rome found itself with new—often hostile—neighbors and new borders to defend. Expansionism of this type had to balance the gains of new territory with new defensive responsibilities. Given a sufficient level of paranoia—or aggressiveness—this process could go on forever.

To address this challenge Rome relied on an old technique used in the past in conjunction with the Latins: the construction of a jointly sponsored fortress in recently conquered territory. The Latin term for these frontier posts is "colony" (*colonia*), but that term has become so loaded with modern meanings that we need to keep in mind that for Romans and Latins the term originally had a specific, defensive connotation.

THE PROBLEM OF ANNEXATION Few ancient states, and certainly not Rome or any other Latin state in this period, had the capacity to annex and bureaucratically administer new territory. *Polis*-type states de facto had minimal governments and no standing bureaucracies whatsoever. The "administration" of such states was made up of a handful of annually elected magistrates, a council made up of ex-magistrates, and at certain regular times, citizen assemblies. Occasionally committees of these assemblies served in administrative capacities, but only for very carefully defined periods of time, usually no more than a year. No administrative position had a salary attached to it. Compensation for those who served in these capacities was psychic and political. The individual gained in honor and enhanced powers of patronage; his family gained in glory and authority. There were no paid professional politicians or administrators in ancient *poleis*, and Rome was no exception. At most the state covered the expenses of magistrates and administrators, but there was nothing like, for example, the bureaucracies the British built up to administer India or the Ottomans the Middle East. In the absence of such complex governmental bodies Romans and Latins had to find other means to protect their territory. Hence the invention of the "colony."

THE LATIN COLONY The Latin colony was a sovereign state, an autonomous, self-governing entity with its own citizen assemblies, elected magistrates, and Senates (councils made up of ex-magistrates) but with loyalties to the larger Latin community. It drew its membership from throughout the Latin League, allowing citizens of different Latin cities (including Rome) to leave their home states and start a new life for themselves among a whole new set of faces. Just this opportunity alone must have appealed to a certain number of people. There was also a very significant material incentive: a decent size grant of land elevated the founding members of a colony to a new and higher socio-economic status. For a second or third son who had little chance of making it in the home state, the availability of new land represented an escape from a possibly poverty-stricken existence.

There was, however, a price of sorts to be paid: the loss of citizenship in one's native state. Thus a citizen joining a new Latin colony ceased to be a Roman citizen or a citizen of his native state and acquired the Latin citizenship of the new colony. Settlement among hostile indigenous peoples far from home and among strangers from other states, although fellow citizens, must have created difficulties of all sorts. Nevertheless, the fact that so many Latin colonies were successfully established over so many centuries (eventually there were 34 of them) and under such difficult conditions says a great deal about the capacity of the Latins to cooperate among themselves in new ventures.

About a dozen Latin colonies (sometimes called *priscae Latinae Coloniae*—earliest, "old time" Latin colonies) were established before the Latin League came to an end in 338 B.C. Fidenae, Sutrium, and Nepet guarded the northern approaches to Rome and Latium. Velitrae, Signia, Norba, Cora, and Setia protected the Latin plain from the Volsci and Aequi who had taken possession of the Alban Hills and the Monti Lepini. Satricum and Ardea covered the southern approach to Rome and backed up Cora and Norba farther north. Antium and Circeii were fortresses on the coast. All these fortresses were situated in naturally strong positions, some on hilltops, some on the sides of steep ravines or on rivers or streams. They guarded roads, rivers, and mountain passes and were impossible to conquer except as a result of extended sieges, which could not be conducted without inviting an attack from other colonies, from Rome itself, or its allies. Together they formed a deep defensive network protecting the Latin heartland. In the course of centuries fortresses of this type were established at strategic points throughout Italy. They were to become Rome's most faithful allies—its primary shield—and over time the most effective dispensers of Latin culture from the Alps to Magna Graecia in the south.(for a map of the colonies, see pages 49 and 60).

## The Warlike Celts (Gauls, Gaels)

Despite success in containing the Etruscans, Sabines, Aequi, and Volsci, as well as having expanded north of the Tiber by incorporating Veii, neither Rome nor Latium was secure. Warlike Celtic tribes from across the Alps had been settling in the Po valley for a number of generations and had already dislodged the Etruscans from that region. They were now threatening Etruria itself. These events occurred toward the end of the fifth century B.C., but the bulk of the migration seems to have taken place primarily during the fourth century. In due course the Po valley itself came to be know to the Romans as *Gallia Cisalpina*—Cisalpine Gaul ("Gaul This Side of the Alps"). News of these settlements and awareness that the Celts could launch attacks through various passes in the Apennines was available to Romans and Latins alike. Livy notes that one of the reasons the Etruscan cities did not come to the aid of Veii when it was under Roman siege was that preoccupation with "new settlers of strange nationality with whom their relations were ambivalent and far from comfortable" in parts of Etruria (Livy 5.18).

THE SACK OF ROME Of the Latin cities, Rome, being the farthest north, was the most exposed. Still, while not unexpected, the appearance of a Celtic horde just north of Rome, the quick and overwhelming defeat of the Roman army at the battle of the Allia (390 B.C.), and the subsequent capture of Rome itself, must have been an overwhelming shock to the Romans. It undoubtedly contributed to the defensive paranoia that fueled much of Rome's expansion in later years. For ever after, July 18, the *dies Alliensis*, "The Day of the Allia," was observed officially as an "inauspicious day" in the Roman calendar. Fear of the northerners, *metus Gallicus*, became embedded in the Roman psyche more deeply than any other fear, and was reflected even in its law. A special state of emergency known as the *tumultus Gallicus* could be called by the magistrates. It suspended all exemptions from military service and gave the authorities a free hand to call up whatever reserves they thought were necessary to meet the threat. The state had made a decision that the sack of Rome would not be repeated.

THE FAILURE OF THE LATIN LEAGUE At this critical juncture it was clear that the Latin League, and the concentric lines of defense built up in the previous century, had failed spectacularly. This revelation of the city's vulnerability deeply influenced its future strategic thinking and led to a fundamental re-evaluation of the usefulness of the Latin alliance. The success of the first invasion, it was felt, would surely encourage the Gauls to raid again and indeed for the next two centuries this was the case, particularly worrying because it occurred unpredictably. A powerful force appeared in 358 B.C. at Pedum, just 14 miles from Rome. Less than 10 years later they were again in Latium, this time in alliance with a Greek fleet from southern Italy. To meet this particular threat took one of the largest call-up of troops in Roman history.

## Roman Recovery

The opportunity to reorganize Rome's defenses came soon enough. The Celts moved on in search of new opportunities for glory and plunder, and the Romans set about building proper defenses for the city. Stone walls about six miles long, made of rock from the quarries of Veii, were constructed around the core of the built-up area. (So strong were these walls that a good stretch of them, the so-called "Servian Walls" can still be seen just outside the main train station in Rome). Their construction is an indication of both Rome's fear of future attacks and its resourcefulness. Colonies were established to the north at Sutrium and Nepet, and at Setia and Satricum to the south. Nearby Tusculum was fully incorporated into the Roman state in 381 B.C. Its citizens were given the full Roman franchise while be-

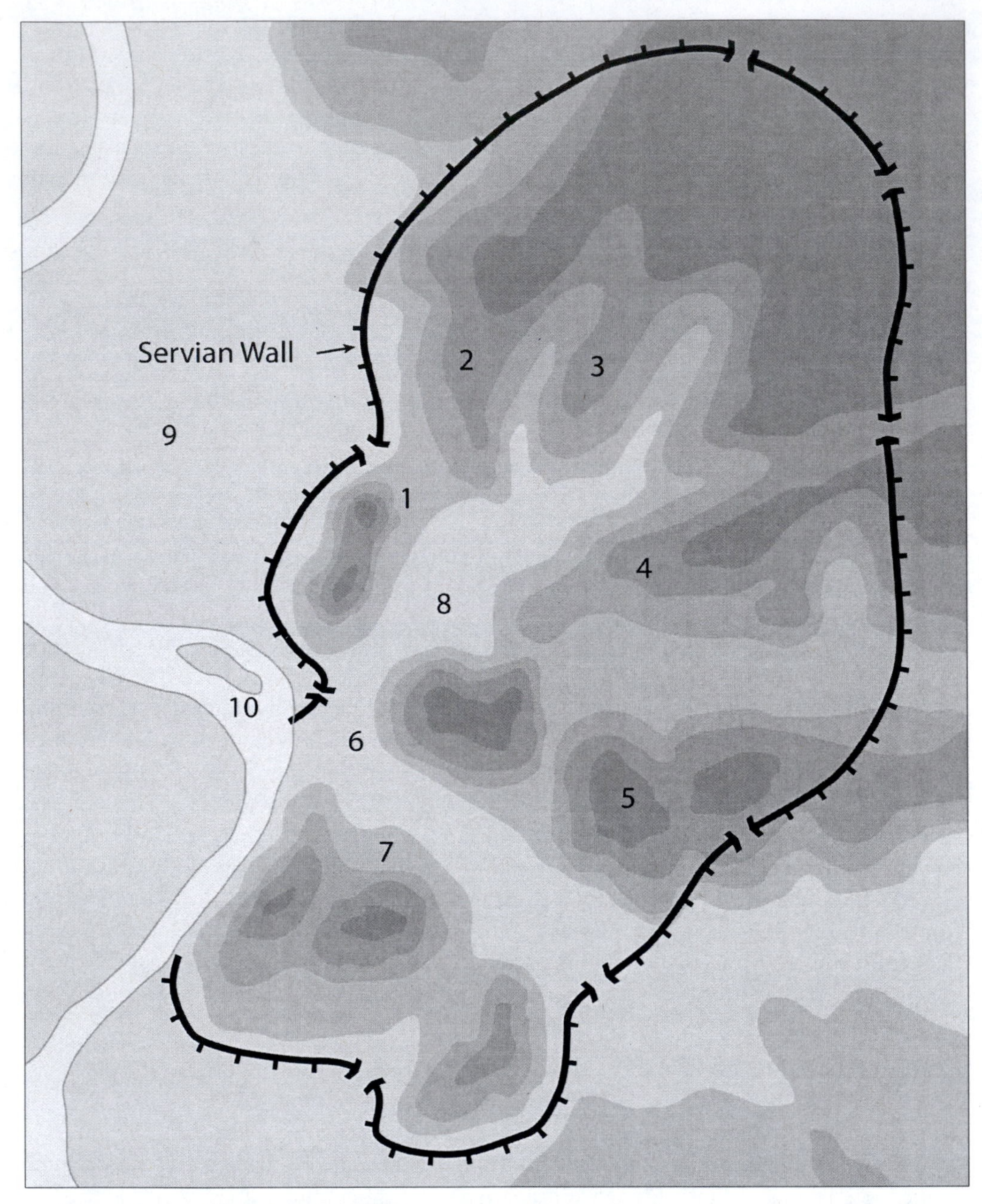


**Rome, Seven Hills, Servian Walls**

*The Seven Hills of Rome and the so-called "Servian Wall," actually built in the fourth century after the Celtic sack of the city. The Romans disagreed as to which of the hills should be counted among the "Seven Hills" of Rome. The most likely are the following:* **1.** *Capitoline;* **2.** *Quirinal;* **3.** *Viminal;* **4.***Esquiline;* **5.** *Caelian*; **6.** *Palatine;* **7.** *Aventine. Also included are* **8.** *The Forum, and* **9.** *The* Campus Martius *or "Field of Mars" located outside the* pomerium, *and* **10.** *The Tiber Island where the Tiber was most easily crossed. The Servian Walls are indicated by the dark perimeter line.*

ing allowed to administer their own internal affairs as they had in the past. A city of this type, having local autonomy but with Roman citizenship, came to be known as a *municipium*— viz., a city that shared the burdens (*munera*) of the Roman state, mainly the responsibility of military service. The nearby city of Caere was given a limited form of cititzenship called *hospitium*, a kind of honorary citizenship, in recognition of services rendered to Rome during the Celtic occupation.

LATIN UNHAPPINESS The Latins also began to re-evaluate their relationship with Rome. Secure for the time being against outside aggression, they took a critical look at Rome's growth and came to the conclusion that the conquest of Veii and the settlement of its territory by Roman homesteaders had created a huge imbalance in their relationship. Then in 354 B.C. the Romans made an alliance with the Samnite federation, which was a significant power to the east of the Latins. This was followed in 348 B.C. by an alliance with Carthage, which essentially recognized Rome's preeminence in the central plains region of Italy.

The main trigger, however, for the dissolution of Rome's relationship with the Latins came as a result of a request for help from the Campanian city of Capua, which found itself threatened by Samnite encroachment. This action, taken independently of the Latin League, gave Rome a toehold on the southern side of Latium. From the Latin viewpoint this amounted to a form of envelopment.

A TURNING POINT IN HISTORY The decision of Rome to abandon its recent alliance with the Samnites and aid the Campanians was both logical and strategic—and opportunistic. Capua was the head of a rich, well-established federation in Campania, and in terms of political culture closer to Rome than the Samnites. In choosing to take up the cause of a *polis*-type state, the Romans began the long process of defending urbanized peoples throughout the Italian peninsula—and eventually outside Italy—against the tribal Celts and Oscans. This decision by the Romans, despite its apparent unimportance, was actually a turning point in their history and possibly, not to overly exaggerate, in world history. Romans of later generations recognized this, and the belief found its reflection in the work of Livy, the great historian of the late Republic. Livy noted that the alliance with Capua led inevitably to war with the Samnites. Victory over the Samnites in turn had the effect of projecting Roman power deep into southern Italy. This then provoked the enmity of the powerful Greek city of Tarentum, which turned for help to Pyrrhus, a Hellenistic king from Epirus, just across the Adriatic from Tarentum. Roman victory over Pyrrhus and Tarentum led them, finally, into war with the Carthaginians (Livy 7.29).

The conflict with the Samnites ended soon after it began (the First Samnite War 343–341 B.C.). An agreement was worked out by which the Samnites recognized coastal central Italy, including Campania, as part of the Roman sphere of interest while the Romans recognized Samnite suzerainty of the inland areas of central Italy and the left bank of the Liris River in Campania. Probably thinking that at this point their situation, wedged between Rome and Roman-dominated Campania was critical, the Latins rose in revolt (340–338 B.C.). They rightly recognized that their autonomy was at stake. The war was hard fought, but its details are unknown. With help from their erstwhile enemies the Samnites, the Romans defeated the Latins decisively by 338 B.C., and a whole new era of Roman history began.

# 2. A NEW BEGINNING: ROME AFTER THE LATIN WAR

The settlement worked out with the Latins after the war was crucial to Rome's future development. Despite the obscurity of the period, which comes as a result of poor documentary evidence, we know enough to conclude that a major historical milestone was passed. Principally it was this; The old rule for *polis*-type societies was that once a certain size had been reached in terms of population and territory, further development was impossible without loss of the fundamental constitution and way of life of the *polis*. Most Greek *poleis* were in the realm of 700 to 1,000 families and a territory of perhaps 25 to 100 square kilometers. Even Athens, which had a much larger population and territory than most *poleis*, had built-in limitations to its growth. Rome, after the defeat of the Latins, found a way out of this cul-de-sac that allowed for growth, while at the same time retaining the characteristics of its *polis* or Republican constitution.

## The End of the Latin League: Terms of the Settlement

The momentous solution worked out by Rome for its defeated adversaries did not spring out of nothingness. Latins and Romans, as previously noted, had much in common both culturally and politically. They had such mutually interchangeable rights as marriage, trade, and migration. The establishment of the institution of the colony showed how expansion could be achieved without loss of autonomy. Basing its solution on this past experience the Romans settled on the following:

1. While some land was confiscated from the conquered Latins, Volsci and Campanians, and assigned to individual Roman settlers, the bulk was left in the possession of its original inhabitants. The conquered were neither enslaved nor reduced to the level of serfs but rather given new legal, social, and political relationships with Rome.
2. The Latin League was abolished as an institution. A small number of Latins were incorporated in the Roman state and given full citizenship rights while being allowed to continue to administer their own internal affairs. Citizens of such states became Roman citizens in the fullest sense (*cives optimo iure*), and their states became known as *municipia optimo iure.*[1] They could vote in Roman assemblies and run for Roman political offices. At the same time they had control of their own internal affairs. What they lost was the ability to conduct foreign affairs as independent states.

   On the whole the number of citizens inducted into the Roman citizenship body at this time was small. Nevertheless, cautious as it was, an important precedent was established, namely, that non-citizens could be given all the rights of Roman citizens *while* retaining citizenship of their own, native communities. The connection between citizenship and place was severed. In the past a person could be only a citizen of the place of his native birth and present domicile. After 338 B.C. it was in principle possible for a community anywhere in Italy (or elsewhere for that mat-

[1] The English dictionary equivalent of *municipium*, municipality, does not much help our understanding of the Roman term. In this instance it seemed better to keep the Latin term.

ter) to have full Roman citizenship while retaining its own local autonomy and citizenship.

3. The large Latin states of Tibur and Praeneste, which were too large to be absorbed at least at this time, remained as Latin states but with individual treaties with Rome and no capacity to act independently in the matter of foreign relations. In this regard all diplomatic arrangements, declarations of war, treaties with foreigners, and so forth, were a matter for Rome to decide. Cora also received this status as a reward for service on the Roman side during the recent war. These were *civitates foederatae*, allied states with separate treaties with Rome.

4. Seven old Latin colonies founded before 338 B.C. remained as Latin colonies, but their relationship was now exclusively and individually with Rome, not with each other as autonomous members of the Latin League. These were Sutrium, Nepet, Ardea, Circeii, Signia, Setia, and Sutrium. They were forbidden to consult with each other as they had in the past and their mutual rights of *commercium* and *conubium* were abrogated. The territories of Antium and Velitrae were annexed.

5. The truly major problem that needed a solution was what to do about peoples such as the Volsci and the Campanians who differed from Romans in language and culture. The traditional solutions—enslavement or enserfment—were not considered. Instead the Romans came up with a new legal status for them: second-class citizenship and partial incorporation into the Roman state. Such states were designated as *civitates sine suffragio* or *municipia sine suffragio*—states without the vote but having to bear the burdens (*munera*) of military service in the Roman army.

   It was an unpopular status as Rome found out quickly, but it had its uses, and it was certainly a lot better than some of the usual alternatives that defeated states suffered in ancient (or more recent times). Citizens of such states could migrate to Roman territory and achieve full citizenship. They were in a better position to familiarize themselves with Roman law, political practice, and culture than would otherwise have been possible and could thus move towards full incorporation in the Roman state. Their elites were able to establish important personal relationships with their opposite members at Rome. De facto, the status of citizenship without the vote became a preparatory phase for full citizenship. From the Roman viewpoint to have whole groups of cities and peoples in the *sine suffragio* status served to create a buffer zone between Roman territory and more distant allies who had less constricting relations with Rome. The Hernici, old-time allies of Rome but enemies during the Latin war, opted to remain as allies rather than accept the status of *sine suffragio*.

6. There was an important religious and cultural component of the settlement of 338 B.C. Ancient myths that told of Rome's founding by the venerable Latin state of Alba Longa and of the shared Trojan origin of Latins and Romans, were emphasized. Although the Latin League as an association of independent republics was over, its religious traditions were maintained. As in the past, joint religious festivals were held at the traditional Latin shrines throughout Latium. Thus practice cemented the idea of ethnic unity, although the new state engineered in 338 B.C. was not based on ethnicity.

In fact, the genius of the Roman invention of 338 B.C. was that any ethnic group anywhere in Italy (and eventually anywhere in the Mediterranean) could be incorporated in some fashion into the Roman state; neither ethnicity nor language nor culture were obstacles to Roman growth—provided, of course, the incorporated peoples were willing to agree to the rules of the new state. The Republic had begun to evolve from a *polis*-type state into a proto-territorial state, without losing the advantages of a *polis*-state or acquiring the administrative disadvantages that normally went with the acquisition of large amounts of conquered territory and resentful subject populations.

## Consequences of the Settlement of 338 B.C.

WHAT ROME AVOIDED First, a permanent class of serfs or slaves was not created. As a result, Roman garrisons were not needed to police the newly conquered territories. Second, no oppressive administrative bureaucracies were imposed by Rome. Roman appointees did not run the dozens of cities that now came under Roman overlordship. Except for the states without the vote (*civitates sine suffragio*) the conquered states paid no tribute to Rome. No Roman judges, tax collectors, or police intruded in the lives of the conquered peoples. What Rome demanded was soldiers in time of war, not taxes. The conquered ran their own internal affairs much as they had in the past. The new Roman state was in fact just a loose confederation of self-administering cities and communities dependent to a considerable extent on mutual tolerance and trust. This goes a long way to explaining why Roman civic ideology and political propaganda stressed *fides*—trust, good faith, dependability—so much. It underpinned domestic culture and social relations in Rome itself and therefore it was logical to promote it also in foreign relations. The worship of Fides personified as a goddess was, in fact, very old. Livy claims that Rome's second king, Numa, instituted her cult, and her symbol—a pair of joined hands—often appeared on coins in later centuries. Her temple was located on the Capitoline Hill in a prominent position overlooking the Forum. The Senate met there occasionally.

WHAT ROME GAINED From economic and military viewpoints, the settlement of the Latin war produced huge gains for Rome. Direct annexation of population and territory was small, but the transformation of its former allies as described above resulted in an overall 37 percent increase of territory and a 42 percent increase of population. The core area of central coastal Italy came under Roman direct control. In emergencies it could call up large bodies of troops and, assuming success in war, could reward all inhabitants of this area with booty and land grants. To order and stability, Rome added tangible material benefits.

## The Roman Footprint in Italy

Although Romans were not present in large numbers anywhere outside their central homeland, their fortress-colonies and the roads that connected them with Rome were visible manifestations of their presence or near presence. The existence of allies and colonies in distant places gave emphasis to the need for good communications at all times of the year and in all weather.

Some of these places were genuinely hard to reach and Rome launched a road-building program to link them with each other and with Rome itself. It took centuries to complete.

*Coin with* Fides *legend*

CENTURIATION The division of land confiscated from enemies also left a powerful visible imprint on the landscape of Italy. Whether it was a matter of founding a colony or individual allotments, an elaborate process known as centuriation (*centuriatio*) was used to guarantee an orderly transfer of land to the settlers and their descendants. Roman surveyors divided up the land to be assigned into squares, rectangles, and irregular areas marked by stone boundary markers, a number of which survive. Registers were kept of the allotments to keep control of the land-distribution process and avoid future disputes.

The work of centuriation is most visible from the air where the marks of the original grids can still be seen in the ground throughout Italy but most especially in the Po valley and in Apulia in southern Italy.[2] The unit of measurement was the *actus* and the normal size of a century was 20 x 20 *actus*, or about 125 acres. The actual lines (*limites*) of the grid were marked by walls, roads, and ditches and it is these that have left their mark in the countryside to the present. *Limites* that ran east and west were known as *decumani*; north-south lines were *kardines*.

Centuriation, the presence of Latin-speaking peoples in powerfully fortified colonies, and roads linking the colonies to each other and to Rome were constant reminders to the native peoples that although they may have been a majority in terms of population, real power

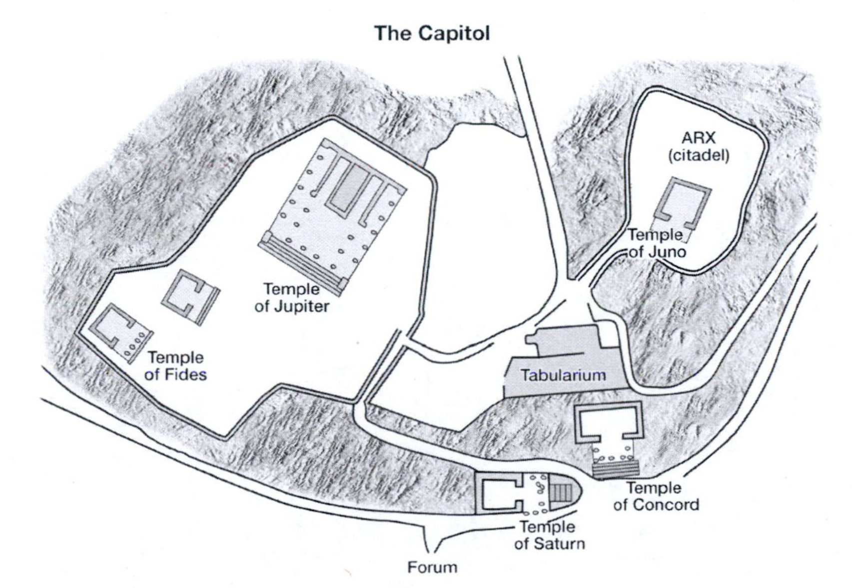


**Plan of Capitoline Hill**

*The Romans gave visual emphasis to their ideology. The Temple of Fides was located in a prominent position on the Capitol overlooking the Forum as a perpetual reminder to Romans and visitors to Rome of the stock Romans claimed to put in trustworthiness and dependability. The clasped hands on the coin proclaim the dependability of the armies (first century A.D.).*

[2]Centuriation is still visible over large areas of Tunisia, France, Germany, the Danube Valley, and parts of the Middle East.

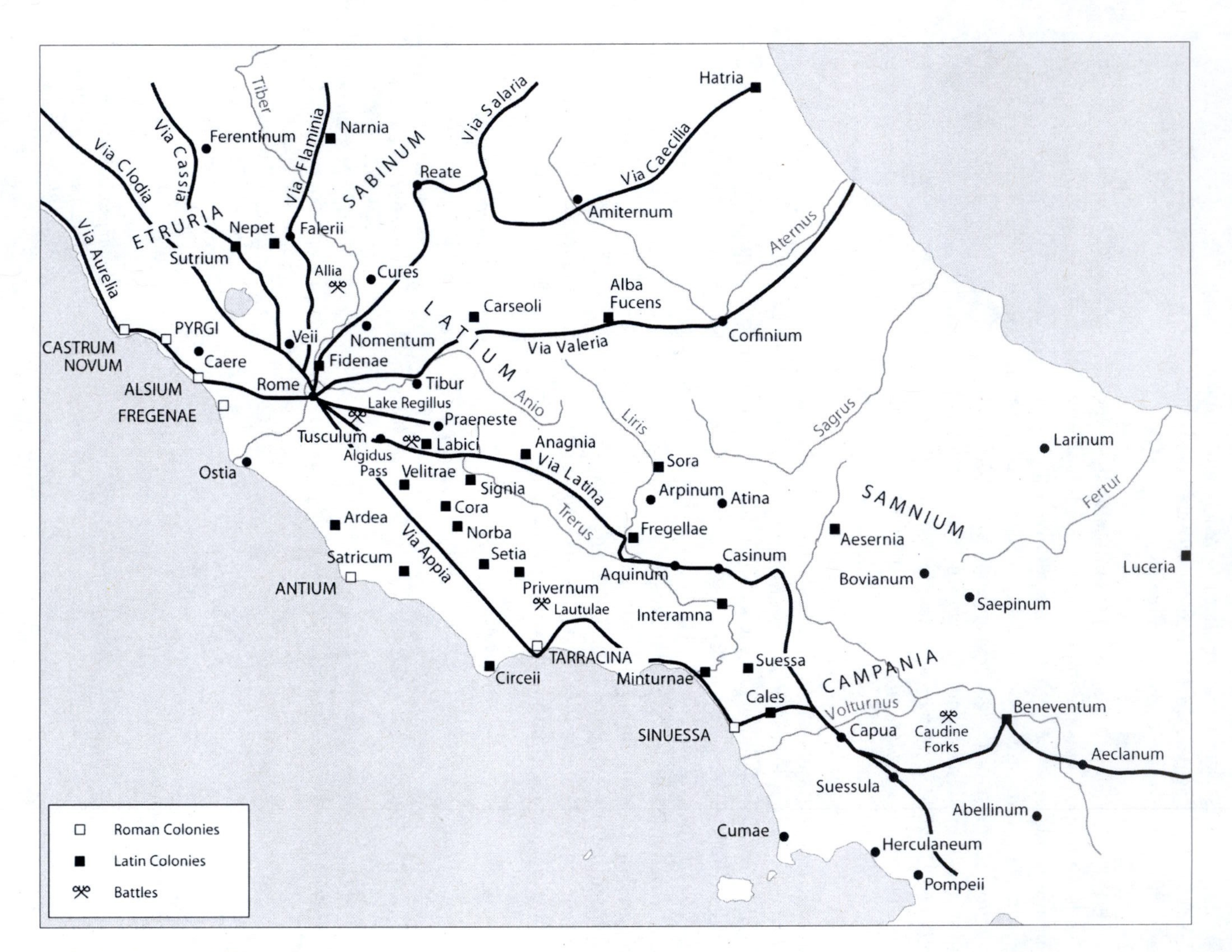

Colonies and Roads

no longer lay with them. For native elites there was little choice but to cooperate with the new authorities. Thus began the slow, uneven process of "Romanization." Long before the term "divide and conquer" was invented, Rome was following the procedure throughout Italy as a matter of self-interested statecraft. Eventually it would do so throughout the Mediterranean and a good portion of Atlantic and continental Europe.

### The Roman Military

The Roman army had originally been modeled on the close-order fighting unit of the phalanx used by Greek armies. The Roman phalanx, perhaps 4,000 men strong, was made up of heavily armed infantrymen or hoplites who were equipped with cuirass, greaves, helmet, and round shields. Packed closely together in files eight deep the purpose of the phalanx was to drive enemy forces from the field and hold the ground captured.

For the siege of Veii the legion was expanded from 4,000 to 6,000 men, probably by expanding the single class system to five classes. Pay may have been introduced at this time for the purpose of covering the individual soldier's living costs while away from home. The cavalry unit of the army went from 6 to 18 centuries. By mid-fourth century the single legionary army was split into two legions, and by the end of the century there were four legions. By that time also the phalanx legion had been transformed into the more flexible manipular legion made up of 30 subunits called "maniples" (*manipuli*— "handfuls"), and each maniple was in turn divided into two "centuries" (of 60 to 80 men) commanded by centurions. It took most of the century for the Romans to complete the restructuring of their army, but in the end it was an extraordinarily efficient fighting force.[3]

AUXILIARIES AND THE ALLIES What we think of when we hear the term "Roman army" is, reasonably enough, an armed body of men made up of Romans. In reality, however, a Roman army was rarely made up of just "Romans." Brigaded alongside the Roman legions was an equal number of soldiers drawn from its Latin and non-Latin allies. Thus a consular army of two legions would be accompanied on campaign by two legion-equivalents of allies. Under treaty arrangements with Rome the allies at the beginning of each year were told how many troops they needed to provide and when and where they were to appear. Allied units were made up of 500 men in *turmae* or cohorts, 10 of which made a wing (*ala*)—the term for the legion-equivalent. Their equipment, so far as we can tell, was the same as that of the Romans themselves. The individual allied cohorts were commanded by their own officers called *praefecti*. Somewhat confusingly the whole allied *ala* was commanded also by prefects, but these were Roman officers appointed by the consuls.

## 3 . THE SAMNITE WARS: THE CAMPAIGN FOR ITALY

Down to the settlement of 338 B.C. Rome had been buffered against direct contact with the Samnite federation by the presence of its Hernican and Latin allies. The settlement of 338

[3]The next chapter has an extended discussion of the military changes that took place in the fourth century. See Chapter 5, Section 5, page 90.

B.C., however, put Rome, through its Campanian involvement with Capua, in direct confrontation with the Samnites.

As the Romans were expanding their hegemony, so were the Samnites. Strategically located on a saddle of mountain land overlooking two of the major plains of Italy, Campania and Apulia, Samnium was in a position to dominate all of central and southern Italy. By the mid–fourth century B.C. it was well on the way to doing so. Previous Oscan incursions from the highlands had, as we have seen, swept the Greeks and Etruscans out of Campania (with the exception of Naples), but when Rome incorporated the Campanians into its commonwealth in 338 B.C., it came into direct competition with the Samnites for control of that area. The Samnites in turn were confronted for the first time not just by individual cities as they had been in the past, but by an organized block of peoples reaching from south of Naples to Etruria. The confrontation between the two powers came in the Liris valley. It is unlikely that at this time either side thought they were about to enter into a multi-phased, decades-long war for supremacy in Italy. But that is what occurred.

Rome strengthened its position in the Liris valley by founding Latin colonies at Cales in 334 B.C. and Fregellae in 328 B.C., as well as a Roman colony at Tarracina on the coast in 329 B.C.[4] The founding of Fregellae, which was on the left bank of the Liris, may have been seen as a particularly provocative act because the Samnites had for some time been moving to control that area. In addition Rome had interests in Apulia, into which the Samnites were infiltrating, where the cities of Arpi and Luceria had requested Roman help. The great conflict was thus a struggle throughout most of central and southern Italy between the urbanized, agricultural populations of the plains and the pastoral highland peoples. For almost a generation the wars dragged on—bloody, confused, unending. They occurred in two phases: the Second Samnite War between 326 B.C. and 304 B.C., and the Third Samnite War between 298 B.C. and 290 B.C.

## The Strategic Issues of the Samnite Wars

Each side had strategic advantages and disadvantages. Geographically the Samnites had a major advantage over Rome throughout their protracted contests. "No position in war is stronger," says the military analyst Correlli Barnett, "than a strategic offensive coupled with a tactical defensive."[5] Translated for the war between Rome and Samnium, this means that Italian topography made it easy for the Samnites to attack Roman territory but difficult for the Romans to attack the Samnite homeland. The most natural approach to Samnium for Roman armies was through Campania, but rugged mountains on Samnium's Campanian side made any assault from that direction difficult. The Romans always had to attack uphill, as it were, into the mountain fastnesses of the Samnites.

Samnium had a weakness, however: Its rear was vulnerable to an attack from the plains of Apulia. The only problem with an Apulian strategy for Rome was how it was to get its ar-

[4]Distances from Rome were not great. Fregellae was just 60 miles away, directly on the line of the *Via Latina*, about halfway between Rome and Campania. Warfare, in other words, was still being conducted within a day or so's walking distance of Rome.

[5]Correlli Barnett, *The Swordbears*, Indiana University Press: Bloomington, 1975, p. 96.

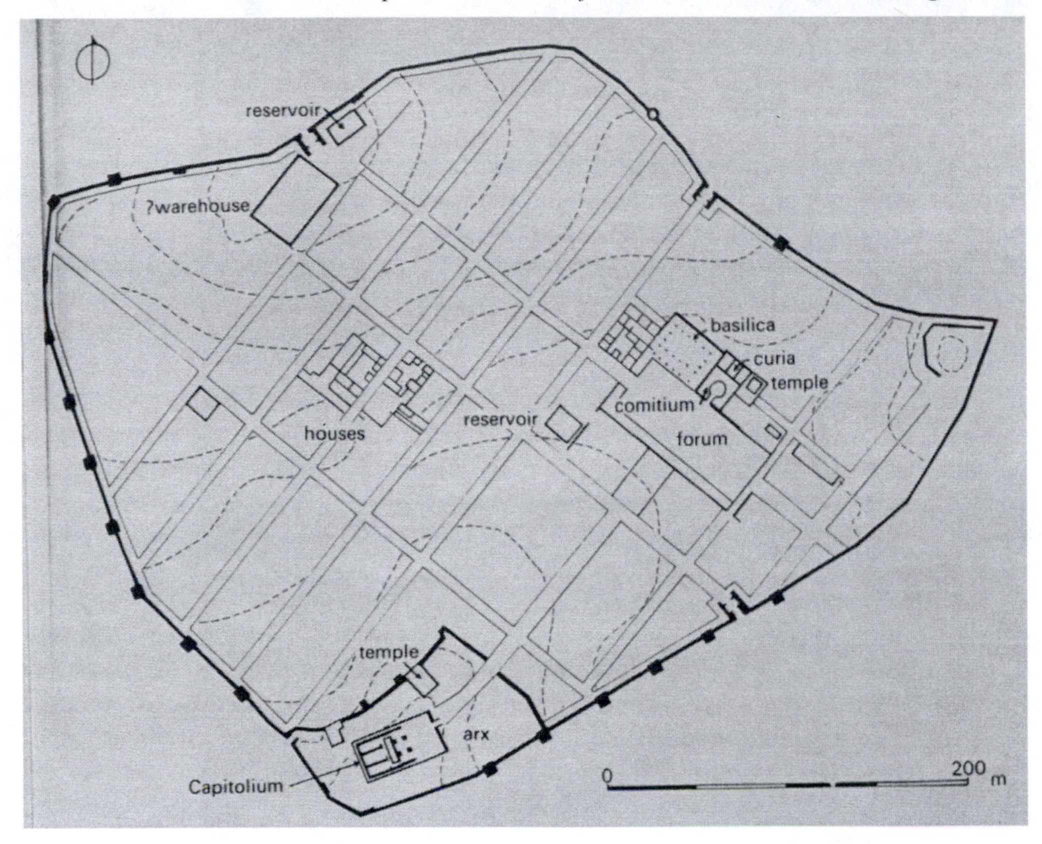


**Ground Plan of Cosa**

*Cosa was founded in 273 B.C. as a frontier outpost on the coast north of Rome. The colony had to cope with pirates and the nearby hostile Etruscan city of Vulci. It was surrounded by walls. Eighteen towers facing the sea strengthened the defenses. Its* capitolium *or tripartite temple to Jupiter, Juno, and Minerva was located on the hill above the colony in the* arx *or citadel. It was built in imitation of its counterpart in Rome. Such "Capitols" were a standard feature of all Roman colonies.*

mies into Apulia. Not by sea—Rome lacked a fleet, and even if it had one the dangers of shipping men and equipment all around southern Italy into the Adriatic would have made that approach too risky. That left a two-step assault, first a move across central Italy to the Adriatic, followed by a march down the coast into Apulia, as the only alternative. This strategy, too, had its problems. Central Italy's mountains were full of belligerent tribes, and the terrain was horrendous for campaigning.

Rome's choices were all bad choices, but of these the frontal assault on Campania seemed at first the only practicable one. The Romans tried this and, predictably, they failed badly. The battle of Caudine Forks in 321 B.C., which resulted in a whole Roman army being forced to surrender, was, in the opinion of the Romans, their worst defeat in history. Rome was compelled to give up its recently established fortresses at Fregellae and perhaps Cales, and its links with Campania, the Via Latina and the Via Appia, were cut. An uneasy five-year truce followed. With the failures of the first round of the war in mind, Rome was forced to rethink its options. It decided on a combined Adriatic-Apulian strategy.

## A New Strategy: Isolating North and South

Ever since its first encounter with the Samnites in the 350s B.C., Romans had been conscious of the danger of having to fight a two-front war with the Samnites on one side and an alliance of Etruscans, Celts, and Oscans on the other. Its worst-case scenario was for these two groups of enemies to unite. To avoid this possibility Rome had to exploit its central place location, its main strategic asset.

In the diagram below, hypothetical country B has central place location relative to countries A and C. At first glance, B's position looks dangerous because it could be attacked simultaneously by A and C. However, B has the natural advantage of internal lines of communication which allow the rapid movement of armies from one frontier to another. The attacking nations have no such advantage. If they are to succeed they have to coordinate their attacks exactly, a difficult task under any circumstances. However, there is a caveat: To exploit the advantages of internal lines of communication requires high levels of national self-discipline and a willingness to engage in long-term planning.

Romans were conscious of the advantages and disadvantages of their position in central Italy from early times. Their discipline and attention to organization were the product of a society militarized by necessity. They knew what they had to do to survive in a dangerous environment. Their strategy, based on central place location, even if not always followed, was reflexive. Nevertheless the sheer doggedness and intelligence with which the Romans pursued their strategy in the period following Caudine Forks is one of the more visionary feats of statecraft and military planning in history. Less well known than some of Rome's other achievements, it deserves to be looked at in some detail.

BUILDING A BARRIER IN CENTRAL ITALY Rome's initial approach to its two-front problem was necessarily diplomatic. It could not conduct wars in the north with much hope of success while simultaneously contending with the Samnites in the south. From the 350s B.C. on, Rome sought to neutralize the northern threat by seeking long-term truces with key Etruscan and Umbrian cities. A major achievement was a 30-year truce negotiated in around 330 B.C. with the Senonian Celts (Gauls) who had settled on the Adriatic side of It-

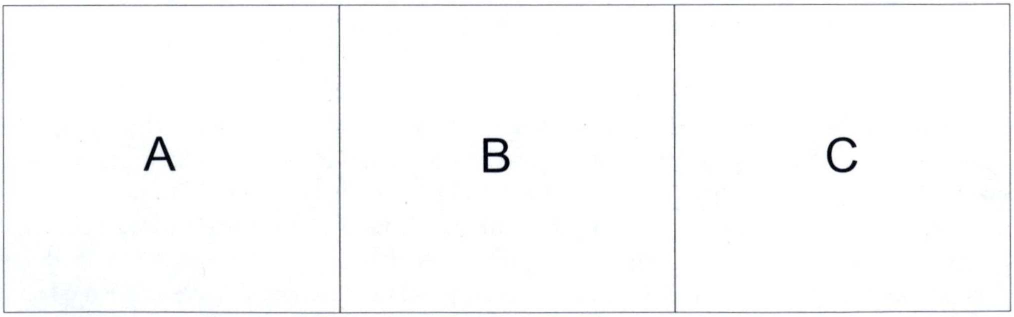

| A | B | C |
|---|---|---|

aly. These were the most threatening (and closest) of all the Celts, and it was vital to keep them quiet while wars with Samnium were in progress. Almost to the end Rome was successful in isolating north and south, although there was trouble in Etruria between 311 B.C. and 308 B.C. When the Celts and Etruscans finally did join in the fighting (culminating in the Battle of Sentinum in 295 B.C.), it was too late to make a difference. Nevertheless, Sentinum was a near thing.

If Latium was Rome's original central place location, it now planned to develop this advantageous position by building a political and military barrier all the way across the Italian peninsula from the Tyrrhenian to the Adriatic Sea. The work on this project began immediately after the humiliation of Caudine Forks but was not complete until 266 B.C. By expanding to the Adriatic, Rome could accomplish the dual task of making a two-front war unlikely—or at least manageable if it occurred—and secondly of defeating Samnium through the Apulian strategy.

THE ADRIATIC-APULIAN STRATEGY The plan was marvelously conceived but difficult to execute. When Germany and the U.S. built their internal lines of communication—networks of roads and railroads—they were doing so in peacetime, with huge resources, and in territories that were under their direct control. The Romans, on the other hand, had to accomplish their task over generations, while engaging simultaneously in war and diplomacy with the Samnite Federation, bands of Celts, Etruscan cities, and literally dozens of tribal peoples in the mountainous interior of Italy. Unfortunately we lack the kinds of records that would allow us to bring these events to life in any detail. We can only imagine the kind of discussions that must have taken place in the Senate, in the homes of commons and elite, among Romans, Latins, and their allies. Every technique of cajolement and intimidation must have been used. Some potential enemies were no doubt bought off, while others were browbeaten. The amount of detailed knowledge of Italy's geography, languages, peoples and cultures acquired by Roman senators and ordinary people during this process must have been huge. Fortunately for Rome there were none of the rapid changes in the makeup of the Senate that occur in modern governments, where it is difficult to pursue consistent strategies from year to year let alone from generation to generation, and where institutional knowledge and memory is shallow.

EXECUTION OF THE STRATEGY Except for occasional notices in the sources we can only follow the general course of Rome's Adriatic strategy. From the start it was successful. We know, for instance, that in 319 B.C. the Frentani made an alliance with Rome, and there followed other alliances with states in Apulia, which were looking for help against infiltrating Samnites. By 315 B.C. Roman armies were operating in Apulia and a major success was achieved that year when the key strategic site of Luceria, a Samnite stronghold, was captured. It was immediately converted into a large Latin colony. By this move Rome established an important fortress from which attacks could be launched on the vulnerable rear of Samnium. In case of disaster, Roman armies could retreat to the defenses of the colony.

But even while Roman armies were having success in Apulia they were in difficulties in their home territories. They suffered a crushing defeat at Lautulae, a few miles from Terracina, and the victorious Samnite army marched to within 25 miles of Rome, as far as

Battlefield Italy

By extending its power across the peninsula, Rome separated its northern and southern enemies. It then held onto its newly conquered territories by planting colonies at strategic locations.

the colony of Ardea, which blocked its progress into Latium. The following year, 314 B.C., saw yet another reversal of fortunes. This time the Samnite army was heavily defeated near Terracina, and Rome was able to re-establish its colonies at Cales and Fregellae and create four new colonies at Saticula, Suessa, Interamna, and on the island of Pontiae off the coast of Campania. The aim of this latter colony was to provide sea access to Campania in case the land routes were severed again. One scholar has rightly called Luceria and these new colonies the fetters of Samnium. The Second War with Samnium came to an end in 304 B.C.

THE FINAL ROUND: THE THIRD SAMNITE WAR Rome now set out to consolidate its hold on the three routes across central Italy to the Adriatic. Large Latin colonies were established at Narnia in Umbria to secure the Via Flaminia route (299 B.C.), and at Carseoli and Alba Fucens to secure the Via Valeria (303 and 302 B.C.). Sora was sent out to protect the all-important connecting route to Campania, the Via Latina, from incursions from the north (303 B.C.).

It was good that Rome took such actions to secure its grip on central Italy. In 298 B.C. the most dangerous round of the three wars with Samnium broke out and Rome's nightmare scenario of Samnites teaming with Celts, Umbrians, and Etruscans in the north came to pass. Rome had to fight a two-front war after all. In 296 B.C. the Samnite general Gellius Egnatius managed to march an army north through Rome's central Italian barrier and join up with the northern alliance at Sentinum near the Via Flaminia route to the Adriatic. Unfortunately for Egnatius, his army did not receive all the support he expected as he marched north. Rome's new colonies and alliances managed to hold down local populations who might otherwise have joined him. Roman armies were then able to concentrate their forces at Sentinum and crush the Samnites and their allies in one of the most crucial battles in Rome's history (295 B.C.). Two years later the Roman armies defeated the Samnites at Aquilonia in their own homeland. Nevertheless, in the closing years of the war Rome was still heavily engaged in the northwest with central Italian peoples who had risen to join the Samnites. This remained the case until 290 B.C. when one of Rome's legendary heroes, M'. Curius Dentatus, put down the remnants of the revolt and added large areas of Sabine and Praetuttian lands to the *ager Romanus*, Roman territory.

CONSOLIDATION The war with the Samnites ended in 290 B.C., but the Celts were still in the field and a Roman army was badly beaten at Arretium in northern Etruria in 284 B.C.. The Celtic forces managed to reach Lake Vadimon, just 50 miles from Rome before being finally defeated.

Once again Rome set about consolidating its gains by planting colonies at strategic locations. Along the Adriatic coast Hadria, Castrum Novum, Sena Gallica, Ariminum, and Firmum were established as colonies between 289 B.C. and 264 B.C. Large numbers of individual Romans were settled on land confiscated by Dentatus in Sabine and Praetuttian territory. A large Latin colony was established in Apulia at Venusia in 291 B.C. With these fortresses in place the Romans had made good on their strategy of severing Italy in half—or so they hoped. Their planning was quickly put to a test by the invasion in 280 B.C. of southern Italy by a Hellenistic king, Pyrrhus of Epirus, at the head of a powerful professional Macedo-

**The Importance of Colonies: Fortresses of Empire**

Is every place of such a kind that it does not matter to Rome whether a colony is founded there or not, or are there some places which demand a colony, some which clearly do not? In this affair as in other matters of our state it is worth remembering the care of our ancestors who located colonies in such suitable places to ward off danger that they seemed not just towns in Italy, but fortresses of an empire (Cicero, *de lege agraria* 2.73).

nian-style army, and towards the end of the century by the great Carthaginian general Hannibal.

UNANTICIPATED CONSEQUENCES It is a commonplace to say that victories in war often generate unanticipated and unwanted consequences for the victors. After a generation or more of almost continuous warfare the Rome that emerged in 290 B.C. was a different one from the Rome that found itself involved with Samnium in 350 B.C. Early in the wars with Samnium, Rome had difficulty holding onto its fortress colony at Fregellae in the Liris valley, a mere 60 miles from Rome. Much of the early campaigning took place within a few days' march from Rome. The decisive battle of the Second Samnite War was at Terracina in 314 B.C., also only 60 miles from Rome and directly on the *Via Appia*. Yet, by the end of the Third Samnite War in 290 B.C. Roman armies were regularly deployed far from Rome, and Roman fortresses—principally its Latin colonies in Apulia, Samnium, and on the Adriatic coast—were hundreds of miles from Rome. The presence of these centers of Roman power far from the metropolis, often in the heart of hostile territory and difficult to reach, was a new development. The dispersion of Romans, their separation from their homeland and their oversight was to be at the heart of the constitutional crisis that was to confront Rome over the next couple of generations. By this early date, however, it was evident to at least some perceptive Romans that the city had already outgrown its traditional city-state or *polis* constitution, and resistance was building to the further expansion of Roman territory.

## The War with Pyrrhus

There was another consequence of Roman expansion in Italy that became apparent much more quickly than the brewing constitutional crisis. Involvement with Campania led to the wars with Samnium, but once Rome was victorious in that conflict it found itself involved with new neighbors and new sets of problems.

Rome's founding of two major colonies in Apulia put it into competition with the Greeks of Tarentum and the protectorate they attempted to maintain over the other Greek cities of the south. Given the usual feuding both within Greek cities between upper and lower classes and among Greek cities themselves it was inevitable that some internal party would supply the impetus or at least the pretext for Rome to intervene directly and displace Tarentum's protectorate with its own.

The occasion was supplied when the Greek city of Thurii found itself under pressure from the Oscans of Lucania and appealed for help not to Tarentum but to Rome. The Romans obliged and provided Thurii with a garrison of Roman troops. About the same time three other Greek cities, Locri, Rhegium and Croton, also were garrisoned by Rome.

**Annoying Greeks: "Incompetent to manage their own affairs but thinking themselves competent to dictate war and peace to others."**

*The event recorded here occurred in 320 B.C. when the Romans were campaigning in Apulia to the north of Tarentum. The spin, on the event, however, is purely Roman. The time for Greek fecklessness was over. The Greeks had had their shot at hegemony; now it was Rome's.*

Just at that moment, as both sides were getting ready for battle, ambassadors from Tarentum arrived and ordered both Samnites and Romans to stop fighting. They threatened that whichever army was responsible for preventing an end of hostilities they would take on themselves on behalf of the other. The consul Papirius listened to the envoys as if he were persuaded by what they had to say and replied that he would have to confer with his colleague. He sent for Publilius [*the second consul commanding the other Roman force*], but went about getting ready during the interval. Then, after he had discussed the situation with Publilius, he gave the signal for battle.

The two consuls were involved in the usual matters that occurred before battle, both religious and practical, when the Tarentine envoys appeared again, hoping for an answer. "Men of Tarentum," Papirius said, "the keeper of our chickens [*the augur*] tells us that the auspices are favorable and that the omens from the sacrifice are also good. So, you see, the gods are with us as we go into action." With that he gave the order for the standards to advance and led out his troops, commenting on the folly of a people which was incompetent to manage their own affairs because of internal strife and discord, but thought themselves qualified to dictate limits of peace and war for others (Livy 9.14)

In retaliation Tarentum sank part of a Roman flotilla that had supposedly entered its territorial waters, expelled the Roman garrison at Thurii and installed a democracy in place of the oligarchy Rome had been supporting. When the Romans protested, their ambassadors were grossly insulted publicly in the theater by the people of Tarentum. After Rome declared war, the Tarentines appealed for help to one of the great military adventurers of the post-Alexander the Great world, Pyrrhus of Epirus.

Pyrrhus imagined he could duplicate in the west the victories over Persia of his relative Alexander the Great. In 280 B.C. he arrived with a force of 25,000 men and 20 elephants. To justify his war he claimed that as a descendant of Achilles he was waging a second Trojan War on behalf of the Greeks against the (Trojan) Romans. At Heraclea he won a battle against the Romans but not before suffering heavy casualties. He offered peace but the Senate rejected his proposal saying Rome would not treat with an enemy as long as he was on Italian soil. Pyrrhus marched on Rome and reached Anagnia, just 35 miles from Rome, before turning around and returning to southern Italy. None of Rome's allies abandoned their alliance. He won a second battle at Ausculum in 279 B.C. but again suffered heavy casualties. After this defeat he was supposed to have replied when someone congratulated him on his victory: "Another win like this and I'm finished" (Plut. *Pyrrh*. 21.9). Hence the proverbial term "Pyrrhic Victory." A proposal to create a federation in southern Italy with Tarentum at its head was rejected by the Romans who were backed by their Carthaginian allies. Never known for his ability to devote himself for long to any one task, in 278 B.C. Pyrrhus left Italy to help the Sicilian Greeks clear their island of Carthaginians. When this expedition failed, he returned to Italy, where in his third battle with the Romans, near Malventum in 275 B.C., he was held to a draw. That was enough, and Pyrrhus withdrew from Italy. To celebrate their win, the Romans changed the name of the city from the evil sounding Malventum to Beneventum. Three years later Pyrrhus removed his garrison from Tarentum, and the city fell to the Romans.

Pyrrhus' invasion encouraged a revolt by the Samnites and Lucanians that lasted for 10 years. When finally put down, the Romans acted decisively to break up the Samnite Confedration by founding powerful colonies at key sites in their midst, at Beneventum in 268 B.C. and at Aesernia five years later. With the fall of Tarentum and the establishment of these new colonies Rome's conquest of the peninsula, except for the Celtic north, was complete. No power remained to challenge Rome. Its defense of the urban, settled populations of the peninsula against their traditional enemies—the Oscans and the Gauls—won Rome credit in the eyes of Greeks throughout the world. Pyrrhus was one of the most colorful characters of the period, and was respected for his military abilities. Roman success against him was evaluated accordingly. The Macedonian king of Egypt, Ptolemy II Philadelphus, sent a delegation bearing gifts to Rome in 273 B.C. Greek historians, ever on the look out for something to write about, took note of the new power rising in the west. Timaeus, a Sicilian Greek historian, identified Rome as a defender of Greek liberties against Carthage, another traditional enemy of the Greeks. To lend dramatic emphasis to his point he made a synchronism between Rome's and Carthage's founding dates.

This chapter has briefly set out the story of the rise of Rome to dominance in Italy, but it has not addressed the question of how it happened from an internal Roman viewpoint. The formal techniques by which Rome made its conquests such as the incorporation of conquered peoples into its commonwealth, the building of roads and the establishment of colonies, have been discussed. We have now to deal with the specific mechanisms Rome used to achieve its hegemony. This will be the subject of the next chapter.

# 5

# The Rise of Rome III: Internal Reorganization

This chapter attempts to account for the remarkable growth of Rome discussed in the previous chapter. There we saw how all through the fifth and early fourth centuries (ca. 400–380) B.C., Rome had difficulty coping with its immediate neighbors and invaders from the nearby hill country. In 390 B.C. it suffered a humiliating defeat at the hands of the Celts during which Rome itself was captured and burned. Yet by 290 B.C. it had achieved sovereignty over the whole peninsula of Italy, vanquishing in the process its old Celtic enemies as well as the powerful Samnite confederation. A few years later it was able to take on and drive from Italy a professional Hellenistic army led by Pyrrhus, the capable king of Epirus (modern Albania). How did it manage to achieve this spectacular turnaround?

## 1. THE MOST FUNDAMENTAL EXPLANATION: THE NATURE OF THE *POLIS*

At its most fundamental level Rome's success depended on its *polis* constitution. It was argued in chapter 1 that the Greek *polis* was a revolutionary breakthrough in human social and political engineering that produced a new type of state. Relative to its population more people were involved in its civic and military affairs than in any previous form of society. As a consequence more talent was tapped and more human energies and loyalties were released than was possible, for example, in much larger but less free states such as the older empires of the Middle East.

When functioning properly, *polis*-type societies were extraordinarily efficient institutions. Major policy matters such as decisions for war could be made quickly and had the advantage that those who were going to execute them—pay the bills or fight the wars—were directly involved in the decision-making processes themselves. They therefore had only themselves to blame if things went wrong later. *Polis* armies were made up of well-trained and motivated citizen militias, not unwilling draftees who had no share in the government of their states. In proportion to their populations a very high number of citizens were directly involved in the military. The high military participation ratios of *poleis* allowed them to achieve an unusual degree of military success and sustain their political independence despite the presence of powerful neighbors. This combination of being able to establish political consensus and high levels of citizen participation in the military gave *poleis* a potency out of proportion to their population. Small colonies of Greeks were able to carve out territories for themselves in hostile lands from Georgia in the Black Sea to the western end of the Mediterranean. A handful of them were able to fend off the might of the Persian Empire during two invasions of the Greek homeland.

THE CONSTITUTION Polybius was thinking along these lines when he said, while analyzing Rome's rise to hegemony, "the most powerful agent for success or failure of any state is its constitution" (6.1). By constitution (or *politeia*, the Greek term) he meant something much more than our limited idea of a constitution as a written document setting out a government blueprint. A *politeia* included the whole way of life of a state—its combined religious, social, cultural, military, and political traditions—even its music, its art, and architecture. Every *polis* had its own characteristic *politeia* that defined its identity over against other *poleis* and non-*poleis*. This chapter will attempt to describe Rome's *politeia* in approximately these terms.

## Roman Exceptionality?

While the constitutional approach is a useful place to begin, we come up immediately against the challenge: So what? What was special about Rome? After all, Rome was only one of many *poleis* in the Mediterranean, so making the claim that Rome's success was due wholly to its generic *polis* character will not get us far. There were many successful *polis*-states in Italy itself such as Tarentum and Naples in the south and the many in Etruria to the north. Not far away across the Tyrrhenian Sea was the prosperous city of Carthage. Yet none of these *poleis* ever achieved anything near Rome's power, though Tarentum and Carthage certainly tried, nor, for that matter, did any of the *polis*-states of Greece or Phoenicia. Again, it was not for want of trying. Athens and Sparta each had large ambitions of hegemony over other Greek states. Their rule, however, was short-lived and unpopular. Rome, as Polybius (among others) recognized, had or developed something these other states did not possess or could not develop.

THE ROMAN DIFFERENCE What that "something" was will be discussed in detail in this chapter. In brief, however, the argument is that the "something" that made Rome different was its success in transforming its basic, generic *polis*-format, its *politeia*, into a hybrid form of the *polis* that preserved the best features of the traditional city-state while overcoming most of its inherent disadvantages. Specifically Rome created two states, one of which served the interests of the elite, thus binding the elite to the state, and the other which served the rest of society and assured it that its interests were also satisfied. In this way Rome managed to solve the problem that plagued many—if not most—*poleis*, namely, the tendency of factions within a state, at moments of internal crisis, to seek outside help to settle their differences.[1] These factions, whether oligarchic, aristocratic, or democratic, were, in effect, willing to betray their states to their enemies for their own narrow purposes. Rome solved this problem and created a powerfully unified, although complex, state. The process by which its social and political consensus was achieved took more than a century to complete. Unfortunately, the development is poorly documented, which may explain why it has not received the attention that later periods have been given. Furthermore, historians disagree over many factual matters as well as interpretations.

## 2. THE MAKING OF ROME'S HYBRID *POLIS* STAGE I: HOW ROME ATTACHED THE ELITE TO THE STATE

### The Aristocratic State

The group that benefited from the expulsion of the kings at the end of sixth century B.C.—however that actually happened—was an aristocratic elite made up of two groups of wealthy, land-owning families. The first were the patricians, who claimed descent from clans who joined Romulus at the time of the founding of Rome as well as select others who joined the patriciate later. An example of this latter group was the Iulii (the *gens Iulia*) who were supposed to have come to Rome after the defeat of their hometown, the nearby city of Alba Longa. This was the *gens* or clan lineage to which the famous Julius Caesar belonged. The heads of these clans were the *patres*—the Fathers or Elders—of Rome—hence the term "patrician."

Whatever their origins, patricians possessed important religious prerogatives, and their political power rested on this basis. They had an exclusive hold on all the main religious offices and claimed to have provided the membership of the advisory council of the kings, the Senate. The auspices, the right to consult the gods, was said "to return to the Fathers" during an interregnum, after a king died. Only a patrician could be an *interrex*—the officeholder who presided over the process of selecting the new king. When confirmed, the king then received the power to take the auspices. These powers passed over into the new state and were jealously guarded by the patricians. Thus, ultimately, political power in the new Republic had religious roots.

The second group among the elite was made up of wealthy landowners who could not claim patrician privileges or origins and were designated historically as "plebeian"—belonging to the masses. This segment of the elite, despite its non-patrician origins, was indis-

[1]For the historian Polybius treason in Greek states was such a big issue that he devoted an entire essay to the subject, 18.13–15. Rome by contrast, he noted, avoided this problem.

tinguishable economically and culturally from the patricians. Although the term plebeian was derogatory it did not have the implications of a lower cultural class or caste. The term in its broad sense applied to all those—rich, poor, or in between—who belonged to the *populus Romanus*, the Roman people, but who did not have patrician status. Initially in the Republic it seems both plebeians and patricians shared high office, but during the fifth century (when is uncertain), patricians managed to establish exclusive control over the magistracies, the most important priesthoods, and the Senate.

THE PROBLEM OF ARISTOCRATIC RULE The problem faced by the patricians was characteristic of all aristocratic or even oligarchic city-states.[2] This was the problem of deciding who was in fact the best and thus entitled to rule among a competing mob of touchy, arrogant aristocrats. It might have been possible once in a great while for aristocrats to have agreed among themselves that some one of them was an outstanding individual, but aristocracies generally solved the problem by arranging for political power and honors to circulate among their membership. The method involved the creation of a system of magistracies and honors that were open to all qualified aristocrats, thus enabling the highest prizes to be won—and then exchanged—in a fair manner. The rules of the game were generally straightforward. Qualifications for entry included good birth, wealth, excellence in battle and civic affairs in general, and an ability to speak convincingly in public and offer wise council. A physically imposing presence and good looks could also be important.

## How to Succeed in the Roman Aristocracy: The Ideology of Virtue

The performance of great deeds for the state—civilian as well as military—which in turn led to personal glory and fame for the individual, was the essence of Roman virtue (*virtus*) and the basis of political power. The private cultivation of personal virtue apart from public service was not regarded as a fit activity for an aristocrat, whose main function was to provide leadership for the state as commander, orator, senatorial councilor, and legal defender of his friends and clients. Wealth was necessary for the aristocratic lifestyle, but it was not its object.

VIRTUS *Virtus* is a difficult term to translate and has little in common with the English term virtue. Perhaps "manly excellence" would be a translation that comes nearest the Roman understanding of the term. *Virtus*, however, was a broad, umbrella term that contained under it all the other Roman markers of quality that were expected to be found in males of the elite class. These included *fortitudo* (bravery, steadfastness, especially in battle, but also in civic affairs, which often required the much less common quality of moral courage); *gravitas* (weightiness, seriousness—as opposed to *levitas*—lightness, inconstancy, undependability); *severitas* (sternness, strictness—Roman fathers were supposed to maintain strict discipline in their households and their military units); *comitas* (affability) and *amicitia* (friendship), which balanced *severitas* and led to the making of many friends essential to an active, political life. Individuals who remembered their friends and repaid favors (*beneficia*), were said to possess *gratia* (esteem, personal influence, grace). Other qualities included *industria* (activ-

[2] "Aristocracy" was the rule of the alleged best, meaning best in terms of noble lineage, wealth, and theoretically talent. "Oligarchy" was the rule of a small number of wealthy, not necessarily aristocratic, individuals.

ity, devotion to work in the public realm as opposed to *inertia*, avoidance of public responsibilities); *fides* (faith in English, but for Romans it mean something more like trust, dependability, solidity; its opposite would have been untrustworthiness, undependability, flakiness if the Romans had had such a word; *levitas* would have come close); *prudentia* (a weak English translation is prudence; in Latin it meant sound practical judgment, the ability to sort out the important from the unimportant in complex situations); *pietas* (reverence for the gods, one's parents, ancestry, and one's country). Success in battle led to glory (*gloria*) and an increase in the individual's reputation (*fama*), which in turn led to higher levels of earned *honos* (honor as in English, but also a burden, an office, a public responsibility), *dignitas* (dignity), and *auctoritas* (authority, influence).

In concrete terms these qualities were made visible to the Roman community at large by the successful holding of public office, the command of armies, the defense of friends and clients in court, and the possession of a large following of friends and clients. *Virtus* was displayed by the recirculation of booty won in war in the form of gifts to the gods (temples, sacrifices, statues, shrines, and altars), entertainment for the people, and gifts to friends, relatives, and clients.

THE TRIUMPH To conduct a triumph was the ultimate public manifestation of *virtus*. The triumph was a ritual of thanks to Jupiter and the other gods of Rome for success in war. It was a stunning piece of theater, a ritual of community affirmation that assured the people of Rome that the gods favored them over their enemies, that their leaders were brave, and that the Senate directing Rome's wars and diplomatic activities was worthy of their trust. The triumphing general's name was added to the *fasti triumphales*, the very select list of those who, over the centuries, had been granted this signal honor. The names on the *fasti triumphales* were carved into the marble of the Regia, the house of the *pontifex maximus* on the *Via Sacra* in the Forum, where they could be read by all who passed by. Later the *fasti* were inscribed on an arch in the Forum, whence they have come down to us. A triumph required a special vote of the people to allow the general to retain his military *imperium* within the city and could only be awarded to one who had achieved a victory in which at least 5,000 of the enemy had been slain.

The triumphal procession began outside the *pomerium* in the Campus Martius and made its way by a circuitous route to the Capitol. The procession was led by the triumphing general's attendants or lictors. He rode in a four-horse chariot dressed as Jupiter with his faced painted red, as was Jupiter's statue. A slave at his shoulder whispered, "Remember, you are but a man." In attendance were the magistrates of the year and the entire Senate. The rest of the procession was made up of important prisoners of war, captured booty piled in carts, musicians, the general's army singing bawdy songs, and animals to be sacrificed and eaten. The route was lined by cheering spectators. Large open spaces such as the Circus Maximus provided ample space for the crowds to gather. Temples and streets were decorated with banners and paintings of battles and sieges.

THE HOUSES OF THE ELITE There was nothing subtle about Roman elite display. In a particularly concretely form *virtus* was made manifest for all to see in the great houses of the elite. Remains of four such houses of the early Republic have been discovered over-

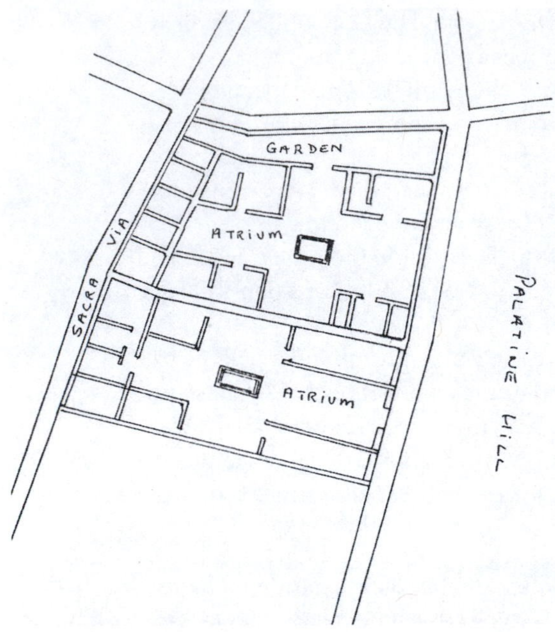


**Ground Plan of Roman Houses on Palatine**

*The Old Roman house reflected the hierarchical structure of the Roman family itself. The blank exterior walls were a protective cocoon around a rigorously ordered interior world where the authority of the father was absolute. The essential features of the house were a broad entrance passage and a sky-lighted hall or atrium with rooms ranked around it in terms of importance. The spatial clarity of the house articulated the clarity of the social structures of the family. It "expressed and guided duty, discipline, and decorum" (Frank E. Brown,* Roman Architecture *(New York, 1961, 14).*

looking the Forum on the northern slope of the Palatine Hill in Rome. These huge houses, built of stone, some of them two stories high, had enough space in their reception halls (*atria*) for as many as 500 people to meet comfortably at a time. The houses were continuously occupied from the late sixth to the second century B.C.

The size and prominence of the houses of the elite are such to challenge the distinction between public and private, since in many respects the houses competed with and overshadowed ostensibly public buildings. They are suggestive, however, of the kind of power the elite in Rome possessed and what a huge investment that elite had in the city from early times onward.[3] Although technically private, elite mansions were both public symbols of their owners' status and practical, well-located bases for the individual owner's exercise of power. Here, it is true, he lived with his family, but here he also conducted his public life. His house was a combined private residence, sacred dwelling, political office, rallying place, theater, and permanent advertisement of his family's place in society and the state. When he died his body was laid out in the atrium for up to a week and heralds were sent throughout the city to invite the citizenry to visit the house and pay their respects to the dead man.

A *domus frequentata*, a house full of people, was an easily understood visible proof of social and political power. Every morning crowds of friends and clients gathered to greet a distinguished man at his house in a ritual known as the *salutatio*, the greeting. At the *salutatio* gifts were presented, favors begged, information exchanged, and contacts made. These grand houses were key exchange nodes in the information and social networks of Rome. When the owner went out to the nearby Forum his friends, clients, family members, and slaves accompanied him in a great swarm, a marvelously staged work of public relations. The larger the group and the more prominent the individuals who made it up, the higher the status and power of the individual.

When a great family died out and a new owner bought the house, he was not allowed to remove the memorabilia of the old occupants. The house was a sacred place, possessed its

[3]These houses were not exceptional. In the late Republic the prominent aristocrat M. Aemilius Scaurus had a house whose atrium has been estimated could hold 2000 people.

**Roman Noble Holding Busts of Ancestors**

*A nobleman holds the wax busts of his ancestors. The Roman nobility exploited every opportunity to promote the status of their family and simultaneously their own careers. Funerals offered a particularly rich opportunity for self-promotion. Actors wearing realistic looking wax masks and appropriate garb impersonated ancestors who held political office. The dead man himself, represented by an actor, walked immediately in front of the bier. When the "ancestors" reached the Forum they sat on the ivory chairs of offices they had used during their time as magistrates. The eulogy praised not only the dead man but also the great deeds of his ancestors. In the late Republic women, too, were honored in this way.*

own spirit (the *genius loci*), and was where the family, in the words of a later Roman writer, "eternally celebrated their triumphs even after their owners had changed."[4] When such a house was razed by public decree because of the outrageous behavior of its owner it was regarded as the symbolic annihilation of the family, its lineage, prestige, and influence in the state. One writer, describing the destruction of the house of the accused revolutionary Spurius Cassius, commented that the "Senate and the people of Rome, not content to execute Sp. Cassius, also destroyed his house so that he would also be punished by the trashing of his household gods" (Valerius Maximus 6.3.1). Located in key sectors of Rome, not just concentrated in particularly favored areas, these great mansions were both the visible manifestation of the elite character of the early Republic and also an affirmation that the elite was an integral part of the state, not above, beyond, or apart from the state.

## Roman Honors: The Magistracies

While their great houses provided the elite with the basis for the physical display of their lineage and power, it was the offices of the state conferred by vote of the Roman people that constituted their true prestige and sustained their place in society.

The offices that conferred the highest level of honor and dignity were the consulate and censorship. The ultimate mark of recognition was to be declared the *princeps senatus*, First Man of the Senate, by the censors who every five years drew up the list of eligible senators.

THE EXECUTIVE The state set up in 509 B.C. to replace the monarchy was rigged to suit the needs of a highly competitive aristocracy. The kings were gone, but executive power had to be wielded by someone or some group of people. As we have seen, there was no effective method of choosing a single "best" man to rule. Thus, the Romans opted for two general principles to ensure that no single individual ever achieved super eminence over

[4]Pliny the Elder, *Natural History* 35.7.

**Roman Honor**

*The grave inscriptions put up in the third and second centuries* B.C. *to honor the Scipio family are an important source of information on what motivated the politically active segment of the Roman elite. The following is the epitaph of Gnaeus Cornelius Scipio Hispanus, active around 150* B.C. *Although Hispanus did not make it to the highest honor, the consulship, he was still capable of boasting of his other achievements in the race course of honors, the* cursus honorum.

Cn. Cornelius Scipio Hispanus, son of Gnaeus, praetor, curule aedile, quaestor, twice military tribune, member of the Board of Ten for Judging Lawsuits; member of the Board of Ten for Offering Sacrifices. By observing our ancestral customs I increased the distinction of my family. I raised children. I imitated the deeds of my father. I upheld the honor of my ancestors, so much so that they are glad I was born of their line. The magistracies I held ennobled my family (H. Dessau, *Inscriptiones Latinae Selectae*, Berlin, 1892, 6)

his fellow aristocrats, but nevertheless could effectively wield executive power. These principles were collegiality and annuality. Collegiality meant the sharing of power with one or more equal colleagues, and annuality simply meant that after a year in office the office holder was automatically out of power.

The first officers of the new state seem to have been a group of magistrates called praetors, ruling in collegial fashion and presided over by a *praetor maximus*. Later two of the group were given preeminence as *praetores majores*, who exercised power jointly. During the later fifth century and early fourth century B.C., officers called military tribunes with consular power were chosen, first in groups of three or four and eventually groups of six. These magistrates had the power to take the auspices to determine the will of the gods, raise and command armies, call assemblies of the people for electoral and legislative purposes, and convene the Senate. By exercising these powers, what was later known as the "Consulate" was gradually elaborated. The term "consul" did not come into general use until after 367 B.C. It is unlikely that the Romans, as was once thought, invented the consulship in 509 B.C. as it existed in later times: a collegial body of two magistrates, elected annually, with equal powers. Instead, the stress of events, particularly the demands of warfare, probably dictated the selection of two individuals from among the magistrates to provide leadership. During the following half-century the constitutional aspects of the complicated working of two individuals, each holding supreme power but working closely together, were worked out. To carry on the religious duties of the kings, the Romans created the King of Sacrifices (*rex sacrorum*), who, like the kings, was solemnly inaugurated for life. Unlike them, however, he had no political, military, or judicial roles.

As need dictated other magistracies were created in the course the following century. Together with the consulate, these offices constituted a kind of "race course of honors" (*cursus honorum*) that spelled out the career track for the politically ambitious among the elite. From early times the tradition developed that in this career ladder certain offices were prerequisites for election to the following positions. Romans, however, were flexible in this regard and as circumstances dictated on occasion violated this tradition by reaching for younger, more capable candidates from the lower ranks.

## Elections, Legislation, Decision-Making: The *Comitia Centuriata* or Centuriate Assembly

In the confusing days after the departure of the Tarquins, the only force in Rome that could be depended on for stability was the army, controlled by the aristocracy. More and more it became the ruling body of the city. Set up as a deliberative assembly, it carried on the legislative, judicial, and elective responsibilities of government. From the centuries, or units, of which it was composed, the assembly came to be known as the Centuriate Assembly (*comitia centuriata*). Eventually there were 193 of these units.

GEOMETRIC NOT ARITHMETIC The centuries were not distributed arithmetically (i.e., in proportion to the population and the principle of one person one vote), but geometrically (i.e., in proportion to the estimated worth of the individual citizen and what he was capable of offering to society). According to this principle those who could offer more in terms of public service—the well born and well-off—got more votes. But they also had to deliver more in terms of state service. In addition, half of the centuries were assigned to the cohort of older men (45 to 60 years of age) who had restricted military duties, and half to the younger men (17 to 45 years of age) who were conscripted for full military service. This meant that in the actual voting of the Centuriate Assembly the votes of the older men, the *seniores*, who composed fewer than 30% of the total electorate, counted for more than twice that of the younger, the *iuniores*. The Centuriate Assembly could only meet when called by a consul, the magistrate who had the authority to summon it. This was true for all other Roman assemblies as they came into being. There was no free discussion from the floor of the assembly, which was essentially called only for the purpose of voting up or down a measure proposed to it by the presiding officer. Thus once a bill had been presented it could not be amended or otherwise modified; the voters could only say yes or no.[5]

## The Senate

The Senate was originally a council of the most important clan heads. It advised the kings, probably on an ad hoc basis (i.e., the king called it when he thought he wanted advice or needed to drum up support among the people). Although it had no formal or constitutional power it had a great deal of informal influence. When the ruling king died, the all-important auspices were said to return to the Senate, which meant that it had the job of finding someone acceptable—to both the gods and the Senate—to replace him. Another ancient source of authority, summed up in the phrase the "authority of the fathers" (*auctoritas patrum*) was the Senate's claim to have the power to ratify resolutions of the Centuriate Assembly before they were enacted. Under the Republic, the Senate, consisting of about 300 ex-magistrates, continued its advisory role, and its influence increased as the power and complexity of the state expanded. By the third century B.C., in practice if not by law, consuls and other magistrates were obliged to seek the Senate's advice on all major internal and

[5]See page 84 for chart of assemblies and their competences.

external policies, but how this came about is part of the evolving history of Rome. Just getting into the Senate was a mark of honor but membership in the Senate was not hereditary. From an institutional viewpoint the presence of ex-magistrates, especially former consuls, in the Senate guaranteed that there was always a well-informed, talented leadership pool present at Rome. Institutional memory was also strong in the Senate as there was no rapid change-over of membership after elections. Romans would have been appalled at Jefferson's idea of intermittent revolutions to purge the body politic or other less violent modern versions of "tossing out the rascals."

### A Winning Formula for the Elite

From the perspective of Rome's aristocratic elite families (mostly, but not exclusively, made up of families belonging to the ancient patrician order), the founding of the Republic was a success. Under the kings the most ambitious members of the leadership class were denied the exercise of supreme power; as senators they were mere advisors to the kings. All glory, honor, authority, and dignity belonged to the monarchs, but with the institution of the Republic the truly able, ambitious, and well-connected could make it to the pinnacle of the state at least for short periods of time. They too could achieve *virtus*, and their success in this endeavor would in turn cast luster on their families, friends, and clients. In addition to honor and glory there were the spoils of victory in warfare: land, movable goods, and slaves.

If the constitution of the early Republic was a winning formula for the elite and embedded it firmly in the state, what of the rest of society? What did the less well-off but still prosperous land-owning classes get out of the expulsion of the kings? Were the poor and the truly destitute any better off because the kings were gone? Did they care as much about the welfare of Rome as did the elite?

It is rare in history that a ruling class willingly gives up power and advantage to help the less well-off in society. Generally advantages for others have to be pried from elites by various means, some brutal, some less so. In the case of Rome after the initial success of the founding of the Republic, what followed was nearly two centuries of mostly non-violent give-and-take among elites and between elites and non-elites, the result of which was the completion, by 287 B.C., of the classical constitution of the Roman state in which a satisfactory balance of power between all involved parties was achieved.

## 3. THE MAKING OF ROME'S HYBRID *POLIS* STAGE II: THE PLEBEIAN STATE

### The Crisis of the Fifth Century

As we saw in the last chapter the fifth century was a period of extreme crisis for Rome. Highland tribes moved into the plains of Latium and the Monti Lepini, and there was extended warfare of a local nature for most of the century. Patricians and plebeians alike lost property and land to the invaders, but generally it seems that the major losers were those who were less able to defend their land, namely the plebeians, especially the poorer members of this group. One result was that the patricians were able to strengthen their hold on the state, and rich plebeians who had previously had access to high political office were excluded from power. Some, perhaps many, small landowners lost their farmsteads and became indebted to the major land holders. Debt bondage, *nexum*, became a desperate alternative for many free Romans. By means of *nexum* a property owner obtained a loan in which the collateral was the debtor himself. In the event of failure to repay the loan the debtor was obliged to pay off the debt by self-enslavement to the creditor. The overall result of the fifth century B.C. crisis was to create an unstable mix of powerful, rich patricians and unhappy, frustrated but well-off plebeians, now excluded from high office, and a much larger number of poor plebeians, forever in debt to their richer neighbors. Inevitably, the power of the state declined, and there was an intrinsic military reason for this decline in power.

THE MILITARY CRISIS Rome, like other *polis*-type societies, depended for its defense on heavily armed infantrymen fighting in a closely packed unit, the phalanx. These infantrymen (hoplites) were expected to supply their own arms, armor, and whatever food was necessary to sustain them on campaign. The patricians and other members of the elite provided the officers, commanders, and the cavalry. The economic foundation of the hoplite infantryman was, however, land; without it he was unable to sustain his membership in the phalanx. Hence the problem for the patricians. As they gained in power and wealth at the expense of the smaller property owners, there were fewer plebeian families who could produce or sustain hoplites for the phalanx. In conditions of peace the narrow patrician oligarchy could probably have sustained itself indefinitely without making concessions, but in the dangerous circumstances of the fifth century, when war was almost constant, this was impossible. In many *poleis* the crisis might have led to a popular uprising in which either the aristocrats were driven out or, less often, slaughtered; or the plebeians were put down and their leaders driven out or, quite often, slaughtered. That this did not happen is a measure of the political maturity of Rome even at this early date. The patricians were not as stupidly obstinate as they might have been and the plebeians were not driven by desperation to extreme measures. In addition, the plebeians had important leverage and good leadership, which they used to good advantage. In the end a compromise was worked out, but it took more than a century of agitation for it to be completed.

## Rome's Response to the Crisis

SOURCE PROBLEMS The Struggle of the Orders is the term given by most historians to the two hundred years of constitutional development in Rome between approximately 509 B.C. and 287 B.C. Unfortunately, as for most of Rome's early history, the sources are meager and difficult to interpret and there are almost as many interpretations as there are scholars writing on the subject. Most agree that the social problems of the later Republic (from about 150 B.C. to 30 B.C.) have been projected backwards into accounts of fifth and fourth centuries B.C. Rome, thus contaminating the accounts of the earlier struggles. Scholars rightly protest that the social and economic difficulties of the late Republic may have been quite irrelevant to those of earlier periods and that it is wrong to assume that the problems of

450 B.C., for instance, were necessarily the same as those of a hundred years later. It is reasonable to assume, however, that because of the overwhelmingly agrarian character of the Roman economy throughout its history, the themes of debt, loss of land and land hunger were likely to be present to some degree in all periods as were, naturally, ambition, greed, hunger for power, and venality.

PLEBEIAN DIVERSITY The plebeians of the fifth century B.C. were a heterogeneous collection of prosperous, ambitious landowners, small holders, and an indeterminate number of landless peasants, many of whom had previously been landowners. Many were debt slaves to the wealthy. Understandably, not all plebeians had the same goals. As a category all plebeians would have benefited from some kind of legal protection from the arbitrary actions of the powerful patrician magistrates who had the authority to flog and execute those they deemed wrongdoers. Perhaps for some this form of protection, along with economic security, would have been sufficient. But at least one group, the well-off plebeians, resented their exclusion from the exercise of political power and chafed at patrician arrogance. Altogether this was a volatile mix of competing and often antagonistic goals, so it says something about the leadership of the plebeians that it was adroit enough to give a focus to these demands while at the same time finding effective tactics to compel the patricians to pay attention and eventually make concessions. We know little of these leaders although some of their names are preserved in the titles of the laws that were passed during the Struggle of the Orders.

THE TWELVE TABLES: ROME'S FIRST LAW CODE After years of agitation the plebeians were finally able, by mid–fifth century, to pressure the patricians into making public the ancient traditions by which Rome was governed. In 451 B.C. the work of codifying these laws was given to a body of ten men (the *decemviri* or decemvirs). Tradition regarding who they were and what precisely their responsibilities were is murky. The sources say that for two years the decemvirs worked to produce the laws as demanded but at the end of the period refused to step down. This prompted a secession (see below, page 83) of the plebs and eventually the decemvirs gave up. The consuls of 449 B.C., L. Valerius Potitus and M. Horatius Barbatus, managed to work out a general settlement that included the publication of the decemvirs' law code (the Twelve Tables) and possibly modifications to the law of appeal (the *lex de provocatione*).

THE RULE OF LAW The Twelve Tables was considered by the Romans of subsequent generations to be the source of all law, private and public, governing such matters as the rights and duties of families, forms of marriage, inheritance, the definition of some crimes and their punishments, and the right of appeal. It was learned by heart by children and played a role analogous to the Magna Carta or the Bill of Rights. The laws themselves were not favorable to the plebeians, and for a long time the administration of the law itself remained under the control of the patricians. Nevertheless, the fact that some aspects of the law had been made public was an achievement, and the general principle of establishing a single code that applied to all members of society by a uniform, universally known process was a step of major importance. It represented a continuation of the conscious molding of institutions to serve the needs of the people rather than the tacit assumption that the law was divine and outside human control, requiring a sacred priesthood to administer it, or in this instance a tiny select group of political figures.

In other respects the Twelve Tables show attempts to bridge the gap between the conflicting elements of the state. For example, the ostentatious display of luxury at funerals, a practice the patricians shared with the Etruscan nobles, was restricted. Various crimes were mentioned and assigned specific penalties—another step toward curbing the arbitrary actions of aristocratic judges.

APPEAL: *PROVOCATIO* Perhaps as a way of relieving plebeian frustration the consuls of 449 B.C. passed legislation restraining the power of the magistrates. According to this law, Roman citizens were granted or acknowledged to have *provocatio*, or the right of appeal to the people (i.e., to demand a trial before an assembly of the people), if they were threatened with flogging or execution by a magistrate. Magistrates henceforth could not summarily flog or execute Roman citizens within the *pomerium*, the sacred boundary of Rome, though outside it they had unrestrained power over citizens. It is hard to estimate how much practical use this law was to ordinary citizens since the majority of them lived outside the *pomerium*. Perhaps it benefited well-to-do plebeians who, like their patrician counterparts, had town-houses as well as country villas and could at least benefit from *provocatio* while they were in the city. From a political viewpoint, however, *provocatio* represented an important step in the protection of individuals against the use of magisterial powers for political purposes. It helped deter magistrates tempted to use their powers as ways of weakening or destroying their political enemies.

SECESSION AND TRIBUNES The method used by the plebeians to extract concessions from the patrician elite was a cultural device traditional among Italian peoples: the formation of a Sacred Band. In times of crisis armies were raised and the soldiers would take an oath, to follow their leaders to death. Anyone who broke the oath was declared accursed or dedicated to the gods (*sacer*), together with his family and property. On a number of occasions the plebeians organized themselves as a Sacred Band, took an oath to their leaders, and withdrew to a hill outside Rome known as the Sacred Mount. Three secessions are recorded: 494 B.C., 450 B.C. and 287 B.C., but more were threatened. The historicity of these events is much discussed among historians and only a general picture of the process and its outcome can be given.

By invoking the protection of the gods and acting as a religious community, the plebeians legitimated their activity, and by timing their secessions to coincide with moments of crisis when the defense of the city depended on the phalanx, they were able to bring maximum leverage to bear on the patricians. The plebeians as a Sacred Band were able to assume the authority to hold their own meetings and choose their own leaders. These officers were known as tribunes of the plebs. To oppose the two patrician consuls the tribunes were initially two in number, but the numbers grew to become a college of ten by the middle of the fifth century. Protected only by the oath of the Sacred Band tribunes could step in between victim and persecutor and interpose their veto in judicial or legislative affairs (*intercessio*) or, more generally, offer protection (*auxilium*). The historian Livy tells of patrician magistrates being brought to trial before plebeian assemblies and even being condemned to death. It is hard to know what was the reality behind this memory. One possibility is that it referred to the lynching of patricians who had violated the sacred character of the tribunes.

**Roman Assemblies in the Republic**

| | *Comitia Curiata* | *Comitia Centuriata* | *Comitia Tributa* | *Concilum Plebis* also called *Comitia Tributa* |
|---|---|---|---|---|
| Number of Voting Units | 30 *curiae,* 10 each from the ancient Tities, Ramnes, and Luceres clan tribes | 193 centuries: 18 *equites*, 170 *pedites* divided into 2 age groups and 5 property classes, plus 5 unarmed centuries | 35 tribes, classified into 4 urban and 31 rural tribes | 35 tribes, classified into 4 urban and 31 rural tribes |
| Presiding Officer | Consul, praetor, or *pontifex maximus* for religious matters | Consul, praetor, dictator. If no consuls an *interrex* for consular elections | Consul, praetor, or curule aedile for judicial matters | Tribune or plebeian aedile |
| Membership | People not present. In late Republic one lictor represented each *curia* | All citizens | All citizens | Plebs only, no patricians |
| Elections | | Consuls, praetors, censors | Curule aediles, quaestors, lesser magistracies, special commissions | Tribunes, plebeian aediles, special commissions |
| Legislation | The *lex curiata* confirmed the *imperium* of magistrates; adoptions | Declarations of war, treaties of peace, confirmation of legislation | Legislation | Legislation. After 287 B.C. *plebiscita* had the force of laws. |
| Judicial | | Capital charges | Crimes against the state punishable by fines. | |
| Place of Meeting | *Comitium* in the Forum or on the Capitol. | Usually the Campus Martius outside the *pomerium.* | For elections: Campus Martius. For legislation: the *comitium* or the Capitol | |

As part of the secession movement the plebeians established their own temple to the goddess Ceres on the Aventine as a counter balance to the Temple of Jupiter on the Capitoline Hill, the religious center of the patrician state. Custodians called aediles (*aedes* is term for what we would call a "temple") were elected to care for it. Both tribunes and aediles were protected by the Sacred Band's *lex sacrata* which endowed them with *sacrosanctitas* (i.e., made them personally "sacrosanct"). Technically, things that were *sacer* belonged to the gods so that anyone who injured either a tribune or an aedile could be held to be "devoted" or "consecrated" meaning that anyone who violated tribunician or aedilican *sacrosanctitas* was by that very act handed over to the gods for vengeance. They could then be killed in a form of extra-judicial homicide without fear of retribution, either divine or human.

THE COUNCIL OF THE PLEBS In the early stages of the struggle between patricians and plebeians the objectives of the plebeians were largely defensive and protective, and their method of procedure was informal. Gradually, however, the plebeians developed a sense of political identity and began to see themselves as constituting a quasi-independent political community within the Roman state. From this consciousness derived the second major assembly of Rome after the Centuriate Assembly, the Council of the Plebs (*concilium plebis*), a parallel and alternative meeting to the patrician-controlled Centuriate Assembly. By tradition it came into existence in 471 B.C. at the instigation of the tribune Publius Valero. Patricians were not allowed to attend.

The organization of the *concilium plebis* was based on tribes into which the Roman population had been divided since the time of the kings. Originally there were three of these, broken down into units called *curiae*. By the time of the Republic the tribes, however, had become territorial units and had nothing to do with kinship, ethnicity or national origin. By 495 B.C. they numbered 21, four urban and 17 rural. After the conquest of Veii four new tribes were created out of the newly conquered territory. Over the next century and a half, ten more tribes were added as new territory in Italy was conquered. By 241 B.C. the number of tribes reached 35 and it remained at that number thereafter.

The convening officer of the *concilium plebis* was a tribune of the people, and the assembly elected tribunes and aediles, passed resolutions (*plebiscita*, plebiscites), and conducted trials. Some years after the formation of the *concilium plebis* the Tribal Assembly or the *comitia populi tributa* was created in imitation of the *concilium plebis*. It too was based on the 35 tribes but could be called into session by consuls (and later praetors), and patricians were allowed to attend. It had electoral, legislative, and judicial functions.

## 4. PROGRESS–AT LAST

The reforms mentioned above had the effect of improving but not solving the embittered social relations of Rome. In external matters Rome's situation improved also. Alliances with the Latins allowed the Romans to fare better militarily against their joint enemies, the Oscans. Gradually land lost to the invaders was recovered and the number of small property owners began to rise, and consequently the manpower pool for the phalanx expanded. Between 445 B.C. and 367 B.C. consular tribunes with consular power, in number ranging from three to six replaced the two consuls, and plebeians were allowed to stand for the office.[6] As was to be expected, few were elected, at least until after 400 B.C., but the principle of plebeians standing for, and on occasion holding, supreme office, was established once again. Pay (*stipendium*) for service in the army to cover food and equipment costs may have been introduced in 406 B.C. at the time Rome began its siege of its most threatening Etruscan neighbor, Veii, when soldiers could expect to be away from their homes for longer than the usual short, summer campaign. Possibly at the same time the single class (*classis*) was divided into five classes each with a different census classification depending on wealth. The point of the reform of the *classis* was to provide a census basis for the imposition of the tax (the *tributum*), which made the *stipendium* possible.

## The Importance of Pay

The effect of the introduction of pay and the division of the *classis* was to expand further the manpower pool of the army because now more citizens became eligible for service as hoplites and light infantry. Pay was an enormously important change since it fundamentally altered the character of the Roman military, shifting it from a restricted, hoplite citizen militia serving strictly at its own expense to a much larger army sustained by the whole community. The overall result was a much more efficient use of available resources. This point will be developed further in Section 5 on the military revolution that occurred around this time.

The slow movement of reform that can be seen in the events listed above suggested that Rome, despite its social problems, was by 400 B.C. sufficiently united to be able to impose a tax on everyone, not an easy task at anytime, especially because the *tributum* fell most heavily on the propertied classes. This surely reflects a willingness of the elite, plebeian and patrician alike, to set aside their quarrels on behalf of the larger needs of the community, not to mention their own long-term interests. As was the admission of plebeians to candidacy for the highest offices of the state, the introduction of pay, even if only on an ad-hoc basis, was an important concession and must have been recognized as such by the plebeian majority. Plebeians knew that with increased participation in the military their influence would grow, a consequence that would naturally have been clear to the patricians too. It was a price the patricians were apparently willing to pay. As noted before, the Roman aristocracy, unlike many in history, was not self-destructive. Throughout its history it opened its ranks periodically to talented newcomers and made concessions when it thought such action was necessary for the preservation of the state and its own political dominance.

## Land Shortage and Debt

Contributing to the improvement of social relations in Rome was the beginning of the solution of the problem of land shortage and debt. The battle against the invading hillsmen had gone on throughout most of the fifth century B.C. and toward the end Rome and the Latins

[6]Military tribunes were legionary officers. Periodically in the early Republic, for reasons unknown, consuls were replaced with colleges of from three to six military tribunes invested with the power of consuls.

**The Five Classes of Centuries**

| *Class* | *Number centuries of seniores* | *Number centuries of iuniores* | *Total* |
|---|---|---|---|
| I | 40 | 40 | 80 |
| II | 10 | 10 | 20 |
| III | 10 | 10 | 20 |
| IV | 10 | 10 | 20 |
| V | 15 | 15 | 30 |
| Cavalry | | | 18 |
| Engineers and Musicians | | | 4 |
| Proletarii | | | 1 |
| Total | | | 193 |

began to gain the upper hand. As they did so they recovered lost land and made new conquests. Colonies were sent out jointly: Circeii (432 B.C.), Labici (418 B.C.), Vitellia (395 B.C.), Conca (385 B.C.), Setia (383 B.C. or earlier), Sutrium and Nepet (ca. 382 B.C.). The conquest of Veii by Rome (the Latins were not involved in this event) in 396 B.C. resulted in a huge expansion of Roman territory, which increased by a gigantic 60 percent. The land won from Veii was distributed in individual allotments (*viritim*) to needy Roman citizens (see Chapter 4, pages 50–51). Colonies and viritane distributions such as that of Veii must have gone a considerable distance toward answering the need for land while at the same time providing more small holders for service in the army.

A PATTERN OF CONQUEST At this point a pattern begins to emerge in Roman social and political relations as a result of conquests. The great landowners found in slaves a substitute for unwilling, unhappy Roman debt-bondsmen. Debt bondsmen escaped their servitude to the rich by migrating to colonies or to individual allotments on newly conquered territory. In this fashion the poor were elevated to hoplite status and those who had lost their land and their status regained both. Elite and non-elite thus discovered a vested interest in conquest. The downward spiral of the fifth century, in which as land was lost small farmers suffered and became reluctant—or ineligible—warriors, was reversed. Another bonus of military success was that as Rome found ways of incorporating the inhabitants of newly conquered lands in its commonwealth, the defeated too began to discover the rewards of joining the victor in further conquests. Yet another consequence of the constant warfare of the fifth century was the creation of an experienced cadre of plebeian leaders who were willing to challenge the political monopoly of the patricians. With their experience came the prestige and qualifications necessary to press home successfully their demands.

LICINIAN SEXTIAN LAWS The Celtic or Gallic invasion and sack of Rome in 390 B.C. if anything accelerated the development of a unitary Roman state. The unreliability of the Latin League was made clear and at least some at Rome must have come to the conclusion that a unitary state rather than a federation of allied, independent city-states offered the best solution to both internal problems and external threats. These external developments added to the pressures for internal reform and reconciliation between the contending interests of patricians and plebeians. In 376 B.C. two tribunes, C. Licinius Stolo and L. Sextius Lateranus proposed that the consulship be restored in place of the consular tribunes and that one of the consuls should be plebeian. Not until 367 B.C. were these measures enacted into law, along with restrictions on the amount of public land (i.e., land won by the state in war) that an individual could own. Plebeian access to public land was guaranteed. The Licinian-Sextian laws addressed the problem of debt by decreeing that interest already paid should be deducted from the principal. The whole amount was then to be paid in full in three years. Subsequently attempts were made to cope with debt and high interest rates, but it was not until the *lex Poetelia* (326 or 313 B.C.) described by Livy as "a new beginning for liberty," that imprisonment for debt was prohibited.

## The New Patrician-Plebeian Nobility

The admission of non-patricians to the consulship in 367 B.C. under the Licinian-Sextian laws did not involve the repeal of a law against their admission because no such law existed—plebeians had in fact been elected to the consulship in the early Republic—but rather the breaking of what had become a fixed custom. Slowly plebeians once again began to make their way into the highest offices, and a new elite, know by historians as the patrician-plebeian nobility, emerged. Some of the old patrician families cooperated with their rising plebeian counterparts. Among these the Aemilii, Fabii, Servilii, and Sulpicii found willing partners in the Licinii, Plautii, and Sextii. The name of these great families appeared regularly in the lists of Republican magistrates for the next three and a half centuries.

Plebeians succeeded in obtaining access to other magistracies. The same year that the Licinian-Sextian laws were passed (367 B.C.), the board of commissioners which regulated some key religious functions was expanded from two to ten, and five of them were to be plebeians. These were the *decemviri sacris faciundis*. In 367 B.C. the patrician curule aedileship, was created to share in the administration of the city with the plebeian aediles. It was soon opened to plebeians, and the important new office of praetor (established in 366 B.C.) was opened to them in 336 B.C. The praetorship was established to relieve the consuls of their civil jurisdiction over the city. The dictatorship (a temporary emergency magistracy) was opened to plebeians in 356 B.C. and the censorship (which conducted the census and examined the membership of the Senate) in 351 B.C. Plebeians did not, however, gain admission to the important priesthoods of the pontiffs and augurs until the passage of the *lex Ogulnia* in 300 B.C.[7] At that time the number of pontiffs was raised from five to nine, and the number of augurs from four to nine. In both cases the additions were all plebeians. In 300 B.C. the right of appeal in capital cases under the *lex Valeria* was established, confirmed or modified. It should not be imagined that the plebeians who sought entry into these magistracies, priesthoods and offices were doing so as representative of the people as though they were motivated by modern liberal, egalitarian sentiments. Quite the contrary. They were merely seeking entry into the *cursus honorum* with the aim of ennobling their fami-

[7]For more on the role of religion in the state see Chapter 5, Section 6.

lies, increasing their prestige and building their wealth. There was only one prevailing ideology in Rome. The amalgamation of patricians and plebeians in a new and wider aristocracy was not a victory for democracy but it was a moment of *concordia* and *consensus*—concord and agreement. The entry of plebeians into high office coincided with the emergence of the Senate as the dominant institution in Rome and the reduction of the assemblies, for the time being, to impotence.

## Appius Claudius Caecus

Appius Claudius Caecus (the Blind) is the first major Roman statesman about whom we know enough to call him a real historical personality rather than the kind of cardboard figures who appear in traditional Roman biographies and histories. He seems to have had a hand in furthering opportunities for plebeians. His censorship in 312 was as spectacular as it was controversial. He distributed the poor among all the tribes thus increasing their influence. This move, however, was reversed by the censors of 304. In drawing up the list of senators he included the sons of freedman while passing over others deemed worthy by the elite. He contracted for Rome's first aqueduct, the aqua Appia, and had a highway from Rome to Capua constructed (the via Appia).

In 304 B.C. the aedile Cn. Flavius, the son of a freedman of Caecus, took further steps toward breaking down the exclusivity of the patricians. He made public a handbook of legal phrases and procedures (*legis actiones*) and the posted a calendar in the Forum that showed days on which public business could be transacted. These measures were significant because the expanded on the reforms introduced by the Twelve Tables. They made public the techniques by which the law could be actually put into practice and how it was manipulated by the elites.

THE LEX HORTENSIA One of the most important and final steps in the creation of the patrician-plebeian state came in 287 B.C. when the plebiscites (*plebiscita*) or decrees of the Plebeian Assembly (*concilium plebis*) acquired the force of law and became binding on the whole state not just on plebeians. From 287 B.C. onwards the decisions of the Plebeian Assembly had the same force as those of the Centuriate Assembly. One practical result of the *lex Hortensia* was that the Tribal Assembly, which had the same organizational structure as the Plebeian Assembly, became the principal legislative body of the state rather than the more difficult to organize Centuriate Assembly. Around about this time the Tribal Assembly also became a court of appeal and acquired the right to ratify treaties with foreign powers.

ESTABLISHING ELITE ALLEGIANCE With the passage of the *lex Hortensia* the blending of the two predominant political and social elements of the state was formally completed. A highly competitive, mostly talented and relatively enlightened elite was guaranteed sole access to the high offices, secular as well as religious, of the state. In return the patrician-plebeian nobility guaranteed the loyalty of the elite to the state. Even in the worst days of the war against Hannibal the elite never weakened. In any state, ancient or modern, the depth of the loyalty of this group is of critical importance to the state's existence, not to mention its morale and its likelihood of flourishing. On the other hand, the non-elite element in the state also had its guarantees. It received or could expect to receive the legal security of their persons and possessions, consultation to some extent on major policy and legislative issues, and a share in the loot of war. This consensus or compact was to hold for over a century before the Republic's success in war undermined it.

## 5. THE MILITARY REVOLUTION OF THE FOURTH CENTURY B.C.: ROME'S HYBRID ARMY

The next item in the interlinked list of causes being marshaled in this chapter to explain Rome's rise to power is the military revolution of the fourth century. It might be thought that, given Rome's reputation as a hyper-militarized state, the development of its lethal military would have been listed first, but it is not, for good reason. Rome's military transformation was a by-product, not the cause, of the great internal social, political, and economic upheavals of the same period. Without them the military revolution could not have taken place.

Military revolutions are not just the result of changes in military technologies, equipment, or formations, although these elements are almost always involved. They are, rather, the product of, and accompany, the transformation of a state's social, political, economic, and military relations. As argued above, by the mid- to late fourth century (ca. 350–325 B.C.) Rome either had already transformed or was well on the way to transforming these. Once it had achieved a stable inner equilibrium it could direct its abundant energies outwards, conduct major military campaigns and, most importantly, sustain catastrophic defeats without losing its internal cohesion. What follows is, briefly, an analysis of the military side of this development.

### The Limitations of the Phalanx

There were a number of built-in limitations to hoplite or heavy infantry style warfare, the dominant form of warfare in fifth and fourth century Italy.

1. A single battle could practically wipe out an entire generation of heavy infantrymen, and a city could be rendered essentially defenseless until the next generation grew up. As a result, hoplite battles between *poleis* were often rather carefully choreographed, inconclusive affairs.
2. Hoplite warfare required that the individual infantryman, sustained by his own economic resources, provide his own weapons, armor, and food while on campaign. Needless to say this convention limited by definition the number of possible candidates for the phalanx to only those landowners who had sufficient resources to finance their role in the phalanx. All things considered, the larger and richer the territory and the more equitably agricultural land was distributed, the larger (and more motivated) the phalanx.
3. A phalanx depended for its success on its cohesion at the moment of collision with the enemy phalanx. Training and experience was the key here. For example, in Greece the

Spartan phalanx was famous for its steadiness in battle, but the price of this was constant, lifelong training. This kind of training was in turn made possible only by the existence of a huge subject population which freed the Spartan hoplite from the usual round of farm work. No ancient state matched the level of training achieved at Sparta, nor, for that matter, was any ancient state willing to do what it took to reach that level of expertise.

4. The distance at which campaigns could be fought was limited. Most phalanxes on the march could carry enough food for only a few days. If the aim was not to devastate an enemy's territory, raiding for food could alienate otherwise friendly local populations. A supply train was both expensive and vulnerable as at each depot troops had to be left behind for its defense. In a campaign using a supply column, the number of soldiers actually available when battle with the enemy was joined inevitably declined.
5. As a tactical unit the phalanx was supreme on level ground but had difficulty when attacking over broken ground or in hilly or mountainous terrain. Its strength lay in its weight rather than its flexibility. It was vulnerable when it lost its cohesiveness.

ROME SOLVES THE PHALANX PROBLEM All of these problems were alleviated or solved by the military revolution of the fourth century. The first problem, shortage of manpower, was resolved by Rome's unconventional method of incorporating conquered peoples in its commonwealth. In 338 B.C. it had access to a total free population of nearly 350,000, and by 264 B.C., on the eve of the great wars with Carthage, that figure was around 900,000. Instead of depleting Rome's resources, conquest increased them. Pay helped here too by defraying the expenses of legionaries and making it possible for even smaller landowners to go on long campaigns. The whole community subsidized the war effort, not just the landowners with the necessary resources.

Training and experience was provided by the constant warfare of the fifth and fourth centuries B.C. Initially this was local, but as time went on campaigns took place farther and farther afield. By the late fourth century Roman armies were campaigning regularly for months on end in Apulia on the Adriatic side of Italy, hundreds of miles from home. Again, manpower resources and a large tax-paying population allowed for proportionately more Roman soldiers to gain the kind of experience that led to superiority in stand-up fights. Pay alleviated the problem of collecting food from an unwilling population. The size of the army's supply column was reduced making it more mobile.

## The New Modular Legion

The Romans were long familiar with the disadvantages of the phalanx as a tactical unit, especially as a result of their experiences campaigning in the difficult terrain of central Italy. At some point in the fourth century the phalanx was abandoned in favor of a new, flexible arrangement that distributed infantrymen in 30 units called maniples ("handfuls," from *manus*, a hand). The maniples fought in three lines of 10 maniples each, in quincunx formation, each maniple separated from its neighboring maniple by a distance equal to its own front. The first line, the *hastati*, was made up of the younger men; the second was the *principes*, made up of the next age group, and the third line, the *triarii*, was made up of the older men. The second and third lines arranged their maniples to cover the gaps in the lines in front of them. Precisely how the manipular legion functioned in combat is uncertain, but there does seem to be an understanding that a system existed that enabled individual maniples to move back and forth through the gaps in the line, reinforcing or relieving units that needed help as the battle progressed. The *hastati* were first fed into the battle. Then, if necessary, the second line could advance to take their place while the first line retired. Finally the last line, the *triarii*, would take part in the battle.

THE *GLADIUS* Each maniple was made up of two centuries of 60–80 men commanded by centurions. Throwing javelins replaced the old thrusting spears. Breast plates and greaves were discarded. Legionaries were equipped with a more open helmet that allowed for better lateral vision. These changes conceal an important shift that accompanied the abandonment of the phalanx. Spears killed at a distance, and their use was relatively easily mastered. The new and more efficient—but more demanding— method of killing involved the introduction of the short (18 inch) stabbing sword, the extremely sharp carbon steel *gladius*. The use of this weapon involved a change in psychology as well as in training tactics. For one, it took longer to master the use of *gladius* than the spear—and it took more courage.

The old phalanx consisted of men packed in ranks who stood literally shoulder to shoulder displaying a wall of shields and spear points to the enemy. Its aim was to seize and hold ground by pushing back the enemy unit—whether another phalanx or something less organized—until it broke and fled. The new system changed all that. Instead of relying on the close order of the phalanx, which limited movement, Roman infantry men were now separated from each other by six or more feet. They became individual combatants whose capacity rested on their initiative, their ability to handle their *gladius*, and their courage in being willing to move to within inches of their opponent in order to engage him. In skilled hands the *gladius* was a deadly weapon. It was not a slashing sword—the kind used by Celts and medieval knights—which tended to wound rather than kill, but rather a thrusting sword, which was aimed at the groin or stomach in an upward movement. Not much penetration was required for lethal results, and it saved energy, an important factor in all combat situations. A line of Roman legionaries, protected by their curved, oblong shields scythed without wasted effort through enemy lines stabbing and thrusting methodically. As they tired they were replaced by fresh soldiers.

All of this took more training. Open order fighting is, by definition, more demanding than combat in massed formations where men on either side, behind and/or in front, provide physical and moral support, and where the key to success is cohesion. By contrast, the new style of fighting demanded initiative on the part of both individuals and their units, the maniples. It was much easier to train soldiers for the phalanx where basic discipline could be reduced to a few commands, the most basic being: "Keep your place" in the file. Much more time was required for the individual legionary to reach the proficiency necessary for the manipular legion. That Rome could afford to field such sophisticated tactical units is indicative of its experience in warfare, its flexibility, its wealth, and the serious thought that went into developing the new fighting unit.

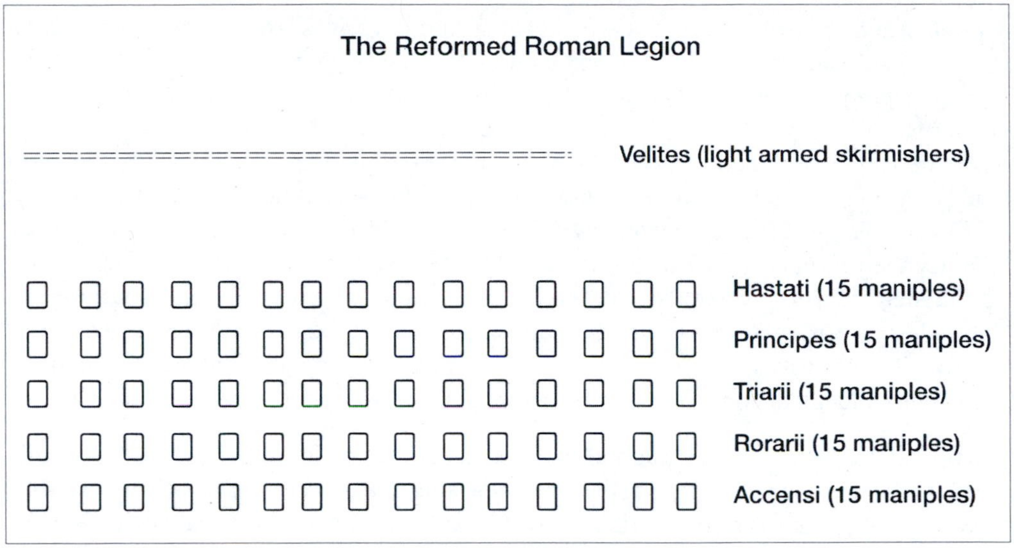

**The Reformed Roman Legion**

Velites (light armed skirmishers)

Hastati (15 maniples)

Principes (15 maniples)

Triarii (15 maniples)

Rorarii (15 maniples)

Accensi (15 maniples)

**The Reformed Roman Legion**

*The* manipular *legion of about 340* B.C. *according to Livy 8.8. The maniples of the* hastati *were made up of young men; those of the* principes *of more mature experienced soldiers; the* triarii *were older veterans. The* rorarii *and* accensi *were less dependable, back-up troops. Each maniple was made up of two centuries of varying size from 60 to 80 men. Each century was commanded by a centurion. Total strength of the legion varied from 4,200 to 5,000 men. There were 300 cavalry.*

## Numbers and Leadership

The key age cohort in all wars involving massed infantry units is the 18- to 25-year-old age group. The larger that age–cohort the larger the recruiting pool for the state. There are many advantages to using young men from the 18 to 25 age cohort rather than older men. Men of this age are frequently unmarried (as was the case at Rome where late marriages for males were common), and so unencumbered by the emotional attachment of wives and children. They bond more easily with the men of their immediate units. They are more impressionable, more susceptible to strict group discipline, more conscious of peer expectations, and perhaps in better physical condition. Because of Rome's huge general population pool it had, relatively, more men in this age cohort than any other ancient *polis*-state.

MOTIVATION Motivation, an essential factor in successful campaigns, was sustained by strong unit cohesion, good leadership, the expectation of victory and booty, and, finally, the improving social and economic situation at Rome. Even an ordinary soldier, the *gregarius*, might come home with a significant amount of loot along with an enhanced local reputation and the bragging rights that came with successful campaigning. Attention was given by the leadership to formalizing the ideology of war and victory. The innovating censor Appius Claudius Caecus gave prominence to the old Roman war goddess Bellona ("The Frenzy of Battle") by building a temple in her honor in the Campus Martius outside the *pomerium* and promoting the public worship of the hero Hercules. The cult of victory (*Victoria*, the Roman equivalent of the Greek goddess Nike) was borrowed from the Hellenistic east and a temple was erected to her in 294 B.C. high on the Palatine Hill where it overlooked the Forum.

There were other factors that contributed to the strength of the new legion. In the traditional *polis* the phalanxes were small and made up of citizens who already knew each other. Motivation was provided principally by the desire not to let down one's neighbors and kinsmen. By the fourth century Rome's army had long passed the point where it could be assumed that citizens were also comrades who knew each other from civilian life. Comradeship was now developed artificially at the level of the maniple, which at a size of 120 to 160 men, was small enough for everyone to know each other, at least by sight. In such units it did not matter where in the territory of Rome the individual soldier originated.

THE CENTURIONS Discipline and professionalism were provided largely by the centurions. These men were drawn from the ranks, not from the elite classes, which provided the higher officers, such as military tribunes, quaestors (financial officers), and consuls. Centurions were thus not officers in the traditional sense of being outsiders from a different class who represented a potentially different set of interests from those of the enlisted men. They were instead rankers promoted on the basis of competence and trust. Unlike the officers who belonged to the legion as a whole, centurions were attached directly to the individual maniples, the tactical units of the legion. They had vast experience and, like modern non-commissioned officers (NCOs), were the backbone of the army. They maintained discipline and engendered confidence in the ranks, but unlike modern NCOs they had greater authority in the legion as a whole and greater access to the commanders.

THE OFFICERS The quality of leadership among the officers was high. Roman commanders and officers had as great if not a greater interest in victory than did the ordinary troopers. Motivated by a highly competitive aristocratic ethic that put the highest premium on *virtus*, *gloria*, and *fama*, Roman generals and officers were aggressive if not always well trained or overly talented.

The political necessity of rotating commands tended to work against competence, although most officers would have had a considerable amount of experience from their many previous campaigns. Yet Romans were not fools. They calculated that in the end a rotating system of command was essential to keeping the elite content and attached to the state, not working against it, and it had the added benefit of weeding out incompetent generals. It was an expensive method, but it generally worked. Besides, there were other ways around the system of rotation. In times of truly great danger to the state successful commanders were often re-elected (*iteratio*) or kept in office (prorogation, *prorogatio*), a legal fiction that preserved both political principle and military competence. In the fourth century, during the wars for control of Italy, a majority of consuls held office more than once. In the 75 years between 366 and 291 B.C., 54 consulships were held by just 14 individuals, and 38 by 8. At the great battle of Sentinum in 295 B.C. the two consuls present could boast 9 consulships between them: Fabius Maximus Rullianus had five and P. Decius Mus had four. After that the number of repetitions declined as new systems evolved to distribute honors more widely and evenly among the competing aristocrats, and the Senate began to exercise controlling power over the individual magistrates and commanders. The dictatorship, an office that lasted a maximum of just 6 months, was another important fall-back in case of military emergency. Between 367 and 300 B.C. dictators held office in two out of every three years, suggesting, as did the iterations of consulships, the level of danger Rome experienced during these years of wars with the Samnites.[8] Later, prorogation took the place of the dictatorship in most instances.

The manipular legion (and its later descendant, the cohort legion) were the final and ultimate development of heavy infantry-style fighting perfected originally by the city-states of Greece. Heavy infantry units of one kind or another were supreme on the battlefields of the Mediterranean and Europe from the seventh century B.C. to the fifth century A.D. The evolution of the legion shows a typical tendency of Romans to imitate and perfect. They did not hesitate to borrow from friends or enemies and had the self-assurance to integrate these borrowings into an overall, more effective political, social, or military entity. The *polis* was not a native Italian institution; it was borrowed. Yet in borrowing the *polis* the Romans were not wedded rigidly to its format. Their innate conservatism made them cling to many of its institutions while at the same time they were willing to make bold innovations to improve it. The military developments of the fourth century, although important, were only part of the larger transformation of Roman society that took place during that little-known century. Rome's openness to outsiders, a characteristic it had from the beginning, its capacity to absorb and adapt them to its own political and military needs, its inner flexibility and ability to find ways for the different classes to interact were the essential foundations for its success in this and succeeding centuries. There were, however, deeper foundations for Rome's cohesion.

# 6. THE SOCIAL UNDERPINNINGS OF THE ROMAN STATE

## The State Religion

That the gods had a lot to do with Rome's success was a widespread belief among Romans. Thirty nine triumphs in the 33 years between 200 B.C. and 167 B.C. was surely proof of the power of Rome's gods, their love for Rome, and Rome's devotion to them.[9] In addition to being successful Roman wars were believed to be always just. Rome had a priestly college, the *fetiales*, devoted to international affairs, one of whose main responsibilities was to establish ritually that wars being contemplated by Rome had the approval of the gods. Aurelius Cotta, one of Cicero's spokesmen in his dialogue on the *Nature of the Gods,* declared: "Romulus, by his founding of the ritual of taking the auspices, and Numa by establishing the state rituals (*sacra*), set the foundations of our state which certainly would never have been able to become so great without having taken such care to obtain the favor of the immortal gods" (3.2.5). Outsiders such

[8] Numbers from T. J. Cornell, *The Beginnings of Rome* (London: Routledge), 1995, 71–72

[9] There were 100 triumphs between 220 B.C. and 70 B.C. For a triumph to be authorized by the Senate there had to be proof that at least 5,000 of the enemy were killed. Sometimes when fewer than this number were slain, an ovation, a lesser form of a triumph, was allowed.

as Polybius, the Greek statesman on whom we depend for so much of our information about Rome of the Republic, agreed. "It is my opinion," he said, "that the arena in which the Roman constitution is conspicuously superior to others is in the nature of the Romans' views of the gods... it is their piety towards the gods that holds the state together" (6.56).

These attitudes were not unique to Romans. Similar views were shared by the citizens of other successful *poleis* in regard to their own states, and of course none of it is subject to verification. Yet the argument of this chapter has been that it was the modification of the basic *polis* constitution that made Rome successful. We should therefore ask ourselves, given the importance of religion to Rome's self-understanding, to what degree was Roman religion affected by the transformation of the *polis* that took place in the fourth and third centuries? What modifications—if any—did the Romans make to the standard forms of *polis*-religion? Can an argument be made that their way of integrating religion with their political and social systems contributed to their civic and military successes?

THE NATURE OF ROME'S *POLIS* RELIGION Religion in Rome, as in all *poleis*, was hugely complex and multiform. There were innumerable gods, goddesses, spirits, and heroes. The city was stuffed with temples of all sizes and shapes, chapels, shrines, altars, statues, sacred spaces, and even sacred trees. Temples and shrines housed holy objects such as the sacred books of the Sibylline oracles and oddities like the shields that were believed to have fallen from heaven and were used in the dances of the Leaping Priests. There were rituals so old that no one quite understood them anymore. For example, the ashes of the blood of the "October Horse" sacrificed to Mars in October were kept by the Vestal Virgins and later sprinkled by them on bonfires at the feast of the Parilia. In May a solemn assembly of pontiffs, Vestal Virgins, magistrates, and priests of Jupiter gathered at the Tiber to toss 30 straw figurines of humans into the river. No one quite understood what these rituals meant but they were still executed faithfully. Some festivals lasted a day, others for weeks on end.

Prophecies and tales of prodigies poured into Rome constantly from all over Italy. Livy offers an example of this in the long list of prodigies that occurred just before the disastrous battle of Trasimene in 217 B.C.:

> In Sicily, some arrows caught fire among the soldiers. In Sardinia the same thing happened to the baton of a cavalryman as he was checking the guards on the walls. The coasts shone with many fires; two shields sweated blood. Soldiers were struck by lightning and the orb of the sun was seen to diminish. At Praeneste burning stones fell from the sky. At Arpi, shields were seen in the sky; the sun was seen fighting the moon [*the list goes on and on*] (22.1).

What were the Romans to make of such prodigies? What was to be done about them? Of course, in this particular instance, it all became clear but too late when, not long after their appearance, the consul Flaminius was killed and his army annihilated by Hannibal on the banks of Lake Trasimene.

INTERPRETING PRODIGIES The preceding examples suggest the kinds of problems religious phenomena posed for the authorities in Rome. Failure to act after a prodigy was reported would be held against them if later something went wrong, but what if incorrect expiatory rituals were performed? They could be blamed for that mistake too. What if the rituals to be offered to a particular god fell on the wrong day because the calendar was off, or the rituals were badly executed, or the festivals started late? The sacrifice of animals was central to almost all worship, but who knew, by inspecting entrails, whether they were acceptable to the gods? What did a good or bad liver look like? Consider, for example, the problems encountered by the consuls of 176 B.C. on the day they were to take up office:

> In the consulship of Gnaeus Cornelius and Quintus Petilius, on the very day they entered office they were both sacrificing the customary ox to Jupiter when no lobe was found in the liver of Petilius' victim [*there followed a problem with Cornelius' sacrifice: the victim's liver was found to have dissolved while it was being boiled in preparation for being offered to the gods. The whole affair was then reported to the Senate*]. The senators were appalled by this prodigy and Petilius (whose victim's liver had lacked its lobe) added to the gloom by reporting he had sacrificed three more oxen and still had not achieved favorable omens [*he never did get the omens he sought and later died in battle with the Ligurians. Cornelius also died in office, though of natural causes*] ( Livy 41.14–15).

Then there was the problem of alien cults that kept creeping into Rome. Although pagan religions have the reputation of being universally tolerant, this is only partially true. Foreign cults were accepted at Rome only if they could be adapted to existing Roman practices. Thus the cult of Dionysus (Bacchus), which spread in the second century B.C. in Rome and Italy, was crushed savagely in large part because it involved secret meetings for the worship of the god. The authorities saw such meetings as an inherent threat to public order and their political control. The Sibylline books, an import in regal times, were not available like Bibles for consultation by anyone. They were under the strict control of a college known as the decemvirs, who alone could consult them and then only at the direction of the Senate and the magistrates.

ROMAN STYLE RELIGIOUS ADMINISTRATION Clearly the administration of religion was a complex and demanding business. Calendars needed to be made and maintained accurately, no easy task. Sacrificers needed to know their business as did those who interpreted omens and prophecies. And there was always a need for money. Sacrifices and festivals were expensive as was the maintenance of the physical infrastructure of religion—the temples, shrines, and so forth—which forever seemed to be either falling down or burning down. The temple of the goddess Vesta, the heart of the Roman religion, which could not be moved without the city's destruction, burned down five times and was threatened by fire on several other occasions.

From a management viewpoint there were really only two solutions to these problems. The first was to create a permanent class of specialist clergy who would be responsible for the religious affairs of the community, or at least be knowledgeable in religious matters, such as the druids among the Celts and the priesthoods of the Middle Eastern states. The other, a much trickier solution, was somehow to integrate religious management with the political administration of the city. The first approach was unacceptable in *polis* communities since it could, and often did, lead to the creation of power centers outside and independent of governmental authority. Hence the second strategy was the one generally adopted in *poleis* and the one followed in Rome.

Comparisons are difficult, but perhaps what made the Roman experiment in religious management different from the experience of other *poleis* was the degree to which Romans were able to blend systematically priestly offices, social standing, and career paths. Much later, long after this blending had been accomplished, Cicero commented: "It is well that the worship of the gods and the interests of the state are in the hands of the same men" (*de domo* 1). In the end Rome created a satisfying balance between the hunger for honor and control on the part of the elite, and the ability to assuage the religious needs and anxieties of all Romans. It was a satisfactory solution that, with various modifications, lasted until the fourth century A.D.

RELIGION, POLITICS, AND POLITICIAN-PRIESTS Romans were careful not to confuse the spheres of religion and politics. The two were separate, autonomous fields with independent sources of authority and validation. Religion was not politics, and Romans were not cynical skeptics manipulating religion for political ends (though, understandably, much of that happened, especially in the late Republic). Romans took their gods seriously, not just in early, dangerous times when even the elite believed, but later on when Romans could relax and it became fashionable to be skeptical of the gods. Thus in the late Republic, when it was discovered that a nobleman's house interfered with the capacity of the augurs to take their sightings of the heavens properly, it had to be torn down.

From the time of the founding of the Republic religious authority in Rome was diffuse. There was never a single, controlling religious figure or body responsible for managing the totality of Rome's complex relations with the gods. It was difficult to distinguish between lines of authority because magistrates and priests each had religious roles by virtue of their offices. In the management of divine relations Romans tended to follow a pattern that was similar to their administration of practical affairs, where committees or colleges of officials were created for different areas of administration such as elections, the judiciary, the market place, and so on.

As a natural reflex the same method seems to have been employed in the organization of religious affairs, though its earliest stages of development are only vaguely known. Typically the committees assigned to the management of religion were given different grades of importance. For example, colleges ranked higher than sodalities, which were assigned lesser tasks or less important deities. There were initially three major colleges, the college of pontiffs, the college of augurs, and the college of decemvirs. In time the number of the decemviral college was increased from10 to 15 and it became known as the quindecemviral college. The college of pontiffs, which was presided over by the chief priest, the *pontifex maximus,* was responsible for the all-important calendar and the general oversight of the state cult including sacrifices and festivals. The college of augurs, which was also highly prestigious, provided advice on the taking of the auspices, which remained in the hands of the magistrates. The main function of the decemvirs was to protect and interpret the Sibylline Oracles—ritual texts, not prophecies—believed to have been collected by King Tarquin the Proud in the late sixth century B.C. They were written in Greek and kept in the temple of Jupiter on the Capitoline Hill. The Oracles were consulted at times of national disaster or in response to unusual prodigies and the decemviral college was expected to come up with appropriate religious remedies based on a study of the Oracles. Among the sodalities were the Leaping Priests (the *Salii*) attached to Mars, and the *Luperci* who, at the feast of the

Lupercalia ran, practically naked, around the Palatine striking bystanders, especially women who wanted to become pregnant, with goat skin thongs.

Over time the ensemble of colleges and sodalities became an integrated part of the framework of political life. As new cults such as that of Cybele (Magna Mater) were introduced to Rome, they came under the supervision of the decemviral college. The influence of the colleges, especially the major ones, was huge. They constituted a kind of shadow magistracy. Augurs, for instance, could dismiss electoral assemblies if they observed unfavorable omens, and the advice of the major colleges formed an essential part of political decision-making. Magistrates were nearly always surrounded by priests. So important did the colleges become that eventually pressure built up to make their method of selection, which was by co-optation (i.e., existing members of a college chose new members), open to some public influence. By the third century B.C. the chief priest, the *pontifex maximus*, was elected rather than co-opted, and at the end of the second century most priests were elected. Typically, however, the election of priests was really only a selection from among nominees made by existing priestly colleges.

ATTRACTIONS OF THE PRIESTHOODS Priesthoods were not magistracies, though priests were often magistrates. There was never a priestly lobby in opposition to the magistrates or the Senate. While some acted as the representatives of their colleges, others were expected to operate independently and individually. Most importantly, unlike magistrates, who had a one-year term of office, priests were appointed for life. Holding a priesthood was thus an attractive and useful adjunct to a political career. It gave access to different sources of authority and different kinds of distinction and prestige. A danger for all politicians is that, over time, the electorate would forget them. Thus, whereas a magistracy lasted only a year, a priesthood was for life, and the priest-politician could be assured of constant public visibility as he conducted his religious duties at sacrifices, dedications, and public affairs of all kinds.

When the Republic collapsed in the last part of the first century B.C. and the emperors took over, one of their first acts was to have themselves appointed members of all of the important colleges and sodalities. They could thus control the religions of Rome from within without giving the appearance of violating tradition. As soon as this happened, however, the autonomy and source of the power of the priests of Rome evaporated. The fact that the emperors felt it was important to hold priestly offices suggests how tightly—and successfully—religion and politics had become interwoven during the Republic.

## Rome as Household

Romans thought of themselves as members of a household, and the city of Rome as their family home, which they cohabited with its gods. For Romans the world was divided between *domi et militiae*, the sacred realm of the city-household where peace reigned and they were safe under the protection of their household gods, and the world outside the city where it was either necessary or at least legitimate to bear arms. Weapons could not be carried in the city any more than they could in a home. What was the point? Either the Roman was at home and therefore safe among kin, or safe in his city-home among fellow citizens. Just as Janus, the two-faced god of the door (*ianua*) protected the entry and exit of a house, the city had a cere-

**Coin of Janus**

*The reverse shows Roma crowning a trophy.*

monial door in its sacred boundary (the *pomerium*) over which Janus presided. This was the temple of Janus, the site of the ceremonial beginnings and endings of war and peace.

By visiting the Forum a stranger to Rome would have easily found evidence for the belief that Romans thought of themselves as a family. There, in a prominent position, a designated state "family" hearth burned in the Temple of Vesta attended by six housekeepers, the Vestal Virgins, who had responsibility for seeing that the flame never went out. The Vestals lived in a large, elegant house attached to the temple. The remains of both house and temple can still be seen. So important to the state was Vesta that she was the only deity in Rome that had a full-time staff of priestesses. Vesta's presence guaranteed Rome's permanence; she could not be moved without the destruction of the state. Livy tells the story that after the sack of Rome by the Gauls the people were so downcast they considered moving to the site of recently captured Veii. The dictator Camillus made a powerful speech arguing against this proposal. His main point was that the gods and the shrines of a city could not be moved without danger of sacrilege:

> Observe the difference between us and our ancestors. They handed down to us certain sacred rites to be performed by us on the Alban Mount and at Lavinium. It was felt to be impious to transfer these rites from enemy towns to Rome—yet you think you can without sin transfer them to Veii, an enemy city! . . . We talk of sacred rituals and temples—but what about priests? Does it not occur to you what a sacrilege you are proposing to commit in respect of them? The Vestals have but one dwelling place which nothing ever caused them to leave except the capture of the city. Shall your Virgins forsake you, O Vesta? (Livy 5.52)

The cult of Vesta was the very heart of the state religion. The temple did not have a statue of the goddess, only the fire, the flame of the fire itself being Vesta. Deep inside the temple, concealed from anyone's view but that of the priestesses, was the Palladium, the statue of Athena believed to have been brought from Troy by Aeneas, as well as other sacred objects such as the Penates, the gods of the household's (in this instance, the city's) food supply.

As authority-laden fathers presided over their households, so did Roman magistrates preside over their citizen-family households. Reflecting this aspect of Roman political culture Cicero noted that "without *imperium* neither a household (*domus*), nor a city, nor a people, can stand" (*de Legibus* 3.1). Yet, although heavily vested with authority, consuls were not lawless tyrants. Like the powerful father of a household (the *paterfamilias*) who consulted his council (*consilium*) of key family members before major decisions, consuls sought advice of key members of their *consilium*, the Senate. Technically neither fathers nor consuls were obliged to consult their councils, but custom required it as did common sense. Each had to pay attention to the community he ruled or suffer damage to his *dignitas*.

**Relief of the Temple of Vesta**

## The Roman Household

The fundamental institution underlying and sustaining the Roman state was the household for which the term *familia* or *domus* was used. Unfortunately the term *familia* is not the equivalent of our term family. Of its several meanings none quite fit the modern idea of a nuclear family of parents and children. *Domus* comes closer, but it is better simply to stick with "household" because that term most accurately depicts the reality of the institution in its ancient Roman context.

For Romans the household was made up of a reproductive unit (the parents) as well as an economic unit (the means by which the reproductive unit was sustained—land, farm equipment, animals, olives, vines, etc., and slaves if it could afford them). It was a community of both the living and dead. Like the city the household was a sacred place in its own right, with its own *genius loci* or the spirit of the place, its family altars, its gods, the images of the ancestors and the memorabilia of the family. Its destruction implied the end of the family and its lineage. As the state priests managed the religion of the state. the *paterfamilias* managed the rituals of the household. He was its priest as well as its head and was responsible for the daily rites honoring the household gods and ancestors of the family. He presided over all family rituals including funerals and marriages; no outside officiants were needed (or available for that matter) to perform these rites.

*PATRIA POTESTAS* Roman families were characterized by a feature that according to ancient authorities had no parallel elsewhere in ancient society. This was the power, *patria potestas*, of the household head, the *paterfamilias*, the oldest living male. This power included the power of life and death over his children. All possessions were his: the household's land, movable goods, and slaves. Even when his children were grown and had become adults, and even if they became significant figures in their own right in public life, they still came under their father's jurisdiction insofar as property was concerned. Adult sons did not own property in their own name. They received an allowance, called a *peculium*, from their fathers. Law and custom thus recognized a divorce between property ownership and public life. Legally the *paterfamilias* could break up not just his own marriage but his children's marriages. These powers of the *paterfamilias* were very ancient. They appear in documentary form for the first time in Twelve Tables (450 B.C.) but clearly reflect long usage before that date. Although modified by usage and custom in later times, *patria potestas* was never abolished.

Most of our information about the working of *patria potestas* comes from the late Republic, by which time it had been considerably softened. How far back this lessening of the severity of the powers of the patriarch go is hard to tell. It is a good guess that severity waned after Rome won its empire and early threats receded. It was probably always the case that before invoking severe sanctions against misbehaving offspring or before important financial decisions were taken, the father consulted his family council. He was also restricted by public opinion, which did not welcome excessive use of his powers as head of his household. It has also been estimated by scholars that in practice relatively few sons actually came under *patria potestas*. From a demographic standpoint not many fathers lived to see their grandchildren. Perhaps as many as two thirds of all sons were fatherless by the time they were 25 so that the tensions that might normally be thought to exist between a father who was still ruling his family and a son waiting to take possession of inheritance was dissipated in practice.

Another restraint on the severe exercise of *patria potestas* came from the existence of the institution of slavery. This may seem an odd connection but slavery's prevalence in ancient society was an important factor in determining social norms and behavior. Insofar as slaves were concerned the father was their master (*dominus*), and he exercised tyrannical power over them. He could punish them severely, sell them, or break up their relationships with other slaves. That, however, was not the way a father wanted to be thought of in regard to the free members of his household. He was not to be a tyrant to either his wife or children. Cato, one of the great political figures of the second century B.C., said that a father should not strike his most sacred possessions, his wife and children, and there was quite a strong opinion in the late Republic and Empire against the physical punishment of children. Slaves could receive corporal punishment, but not children. It would be dishonorable to his family and its reputation for a *paterfamilias* to physically punish the free members of the household. There is no proof that this was the case for the early or middle Republic, the period we have been dealing with here, but it is likely that public opinion always played a powerful role in restraining excessively tyrannical behavior on the part of fathers. It is interesting that of the few cases in which fathers killed their sons, most belong in the legendary past of Rome. Some may not even have been exercises of *patria potestas* in the first place but rather punishment meted out by fathers who also happened to be magistrates, as was the case with the legendary liberator of Rome, Junius Brutus, who as consul executed his sons who tried to bring back the exiled king Tarquin.

FUNCTIONAL ASPECTS OF *PATRIA POTESTAS* The extraordinary power of fathers over their households, even when ameliorated in later centuries by social custom, still put their children under obligation to them into their adult years. It put powerful restraints on misbehaving sons who cared nothing for honor or family traditions but who worried that they might find themselves written out of the will or have their inheritance reduced because they brought dishonor on the household. Daughters also remained under the strict control of their families. Even when married they did not escape their father's *patria potestas*.[10] If divorced for misbehavior or any other reason daughters returned to their fathers' houses. The system of *patria potestas* powerfully focused attention on the transmission of property from one generation to the next, making all involved in the process serious about the dissipation of the family patrimony by bad management. Indeed a Roman father was not identified as a "good" father as today by moral or psychological criteria but rather as a good or bad manager of the family's possessions. In itself *patria potestas* was a powerful educational tool requiring little support from the formal powers of the state.

**The Real Power in the Household: Wifely Power—or Child Power?**

Patria potestas *and* materna auctoritas *have been discussed, but what of the power of wives?*

*The first and second century* A.D. *biographer and essayist Plutarch quotes an aphorism of Cato the Censor (234–149* B.C.*) on the subject of wifely power, noting that it is an adaptation of a Greek aphorism.*

> Speaking on the power of women Cato said, "All other men rule their wives; we rule all mankind, but our wives rule us." However, this saying is borrowed from Themistocles who when he found his son giving him many orders which really originated with his wife, told her, "My dear, the Athenians rule the Greeks, I rule the Athenians, you rule me, and our son rules you. Therefore, he must be sparing in the use of his authority because, child though he is, he is the most powerful of the Greeks (Plutarch, *Life of Cato*, 8).

NO SOCIAL SAFETY NETS Perhaps the lessons to be learned from this section on the social underpinnings of the state are the techniques Romans developed to allow them to exercise high levels of authority in both state and family without at the same time becoming inflexibly authoritarian. Households needed firm guidance. They were large, powerful, complex institutions of which modern households are mere shadows. Households had to look out for themselves; they did not have the option of becoming wards of the state. In ancient society there was no governmental social safety net outside existing ties of kinship, patronage and friendship. At the same time the state and society made heavy demands on households. They were expected to produce, especially among the elite, highly competitive, self-motivated offspring, yet offspring that at the same time knew self-restraint.

*Patria potestas* helped here. It forced fathers to live up to their responsibilities to their households and to the state. Lines of blame were publicly and clearly delineated. Failure of the *paterfamilias* to live up to his duties led to personal dishonor and lowered the prestige and power of his household and lineage. Despite high mortality rates among fathers, the male members of Roman households had severe restraints put upon them during the critical years of adolescence and young adulthood. The role of females, particularly mothers, should not be neglected. Mothers were essential to the functioning of complex Roman households. They were formidable rulers in their own right. While they lacked

[10]An exception was the uncommon form of *manus* marriage, which transferred the bride from her natal household to that of her husband's. In that case she would end up under the *potestas* of her husband or her father-in-law if he was still alive.

the equivalent of the legal *patria potestas* possessed by fathers, they had something that was probably more effective in the long run: *materna auctoritas*, matronal or motherly influence. It is an historical commonplace that while males may make the rules of society it is the females, especially the mothers and grandmothers, the matrons of society, who enforce them.

The state helped households in its own way by giving clear indications of where obligations lay and what consequences followed failure to fulfill them. The state was not some distant bureaucracy but the immediate presence of often interfering magistrates and lower officials. Society was not an anonymous urban mass but other households whose members had a good estimate of the worth of each other's families. Career paths for the elite were limited but clearly marked. For ordinary, non-elite Romans there were plenty of rewards and punishments. The authority of the state was unchallengeable and severe, but there were many incentives to go along with whatever it commanded. Rome was a military society through and through as has been repeatedly noted, and its militarization reached from the heights of consular authority to the *patria potestas* of the heads of even the humblest households.

The Republican socio-political system worked well down to the second century B.C. when fissures began to make their appearance. Then there developed periodic resistance to the draft and reluctance on the part of ordinary soldiers to serve overseas for long periods of time. More importantly, the ability of the elite to control its own membership and maintain its cohesion began to fail. The first century B.C. saw the full loosening of the social and political constraints that had made the state as family and the family as state so successful a basis for world conquest.

# 6

# The Wars with Carthage

With the fall of Tarentum in 272 B.C. (following the war with Pyrrhus), Rome's conquest of the Italian peninsula, except for the Celtic north, was complete. This did not mean, however, that Rome "occupied" Italy in the sense that Roman garrisons and administrators could be found everywhere throughout Italy. Far from it. Romans were generally slow to annex territory, and outside of their still relatively small homeland in central Italy they were few and far between elsewhere in the peninsula. What supremacy did mean was that there was no single power left to challenge Rome in Italy, and Rome had garrisons in key sites throughout the peninsula. Ironically, however, Rome's very success in extending its power into southern Italy brought it into contact with a power that could and did threaten it.

That power was Carthage, a great and ancient city in north Africa, just a few days by sail from Rome. Its vast commercial and maritime empire in the western Mediterranean made it one of the richest and most powerful states in the ancient world. It was also one of the most warlike. Rome's wars with this city were the most critical wars it ever waged, both in terms of Rome's own survival and for its ultimate transformation into a major imperial power. During the second war with Carthage, the Carthaginian commander, Hannibal, came close to destroying Rome's hegemony in Italy. As Livy said, quite accurately, "the eventual victors came nearer to destruction than their adversaries" (21.1). If coming events cast a shadow then it was Pyrrhus who first noticed the approaching danger for both Rome and Carthage: "What a field we are now leaving to the Carthaginians and Romans to fight in," he was supposed to have said as he left Italy following his defeat there. Pyrrhus was not alone in seeing the possibility of a collision between Rome and Carthage. The Sicilian historian Timaeus, although he died before the Punic Wars broke out, picked Rome as the defender of Greek liberties against Carthage, the traditional enemy of the western Greeks. To lend dramatic emphasis to his point he made a synchronism between Rome's and Carthage's founding dates. For the Roman historian Livy there was a kind of inevitability to a collision with Carthage. Once Rome became involved in Campania it inevitably became entangled in the affairs of southern Italy, and once there could not avoid involvement with the larger world of the Mediterranean.

## 1. THE PHOENICIANS, CARTHAGE, AND THE WEST

While the Greeks from the eighth to the sixth centuries B.C. were settling key points along the northern rim of the Mediterranean in successive waves, the Phoenicians were doing something similar along its southern rim. From a political-cultural point of view both Greeks and Phoenicians came from a similar city-state background. Just as there was no "Greek" state but rather many independent micro-states, there was no "Phoenician" state either. Greek and Phoenician settlement patterns overseas, however, had different aims and different relations with their mother cities, their *metropoleis*. The Greeks, in addition to trade, were also interested in finding good agricultural land for their excess population, while the main interest of the Phoenicians was commerce. Phoenician colonies tended to maintain much stronger relations with their originating cities, while Greek settlements quickly became independent of the cities that sent them out.

### Phoenicia

The city-states of Phoenicia were ancient, integral parts of the great civilizations of the Middle East. Geographically, they were to be found from Tarsus in Syria to Gaza in Palestine. Among the best known were Tyre, Sidon, Byblos, Aradus, and Berytus (Beirut). The name given to them by the Greeks, *Phoinikes* (Lat. *Poeni*, hence Punic), is thought to derive from the Greek term for red or purple and may be derived from the Phoenician's production and export of a famous purple dye. What they actually called themselves is unknown. Linguistically they spoke a form of Canaanite, the northwest Semitic language spoken by the inhabitants of ancient Syria and Palestine (including Israelites and eventually also Philistines).

With the abundant timber resources in the mountains of Lebanon, they became seafarers at an early date. In this capacity they played a vital role in the history of the Mediterranean by acting as intermediaries between the then highly developed centers of Mesopotamia and the less developed worlds of the Mediterranean and the Atlantic. So impressive were Phoenician achievements that some scholars in the nineteenth century tended to give priority to the role of the Phoenicians in the development of the Mediterranean, setting a kind of Phoenician "miracle" against the Greek "miracle."[1] Phoenicians traveled as far as Britain and down the Atlantic coast of Africa as far as Sierra Leone in search of tin. A Greek version of one of these African voyages of exploration survives, recording encounters with savages, volcanoes, and "hairy men called gorillas." When Persia conquered Phoenicia, Phoenician ships formed the backbone of its navy and provided the Persians with the mobility necessary to invade Greece. When the Persian empire in turn fell to Alexander the Great, the Phoenician cities were very

[1]A fact that may surprise readers of Edward Said's *Orientalism*.

**Passing Children Through the Fire**

*Phoenician, or to be more exact, Canaanite religion, had a practice that drew the horrified attention of ancient Israelites, Greeks, and finally Romans. This was the custom in times of stress—famine or invasion, for instance—of "passing their children through the fire," that is, sacrificing them to the gods. The special burial places of these children have been found at the sites of a number of Phoenician cities. At Carthage thousands of urns containing the remains of sacrificed infants have been discovered.*

*In 310 B.C. when Carthage was threatened by Agathocles, the Greek tyrant of Syracuse, the angry gods were believed to be responsible and needed to be propitiated. Although Romans too believed that the gods could be propitiated by human sacrifice, their resort to this practice was irregular (three times in the history of the Republic) and was not an integral part of their religious culture.*

The Carthaginians, thinking that the gods had brought about this calamity, devoted themselves to all manner of supplication. ...They concluded that Kronos (*i.e., the Greek version of the Carthaginian god Baal Hammon*) had turned hostile because in previous times they had sacrificed to him the children of their most important citizens. Recently, however, these people had bought slave children and, after raising them, had sent them to be sacrificed in place of their own offspring. After an investigation was made it was discovered that some of those who had been sacrificed were, in fact, slave substitutes. After weighing up this and seeing the enemy camped in front of their city, the Carthaginians were filled with superstitious dread, believing that they had neglected the honors due to the gods of their ancestors. Eager to make amends for this failure, they chose 200 of the noblest children to be sacrificed publicly. Others, being under suspicion, sacrificed of their own accord not less than an additional 300. A bronze statue of Baal stood in the city. The palms of its extended arms faced upwards while sloping towards the ground so that when a child was placed on them it rolled down and fell into a kind of gaping pit filled with fire. (Diodorus Siculus, 20.14).

gradually Hellenized. Their distinctive culture and city-state constitutions, however, lasted long after they were incorporated into the Hellenistic world and later still in the Roman Empire.

## Carthage

The most important Phoenician state founded in the west was Carthage in modern Tunisia. By legend it was founded by Elissa (also known as Dido) who fled her native Tyre as the result of a dispute with her brother King Pygmalion. She brought with her the sacred articles necessary for the worship of Melkart (Herakles to the Greeks, Hercules for the Romans), the guardian deity of Tyre. The story may be legendary but fits well with the history of strong Phoenician women such as Jezebel, the formidable consort of King Ahab of Israel. Jezebel is remembered in the Hebrew bible as the scourge of the prophet Elijah and the force behind Ahab. Her sons ruled Israel after her husband's death, and her daughter ruled Judah, the southern kingdom.

Situated on a peninsula at approximately the midpoint of Mediterranean Africa, Carthage had an excellent geographic location and a superb harbor. Its position gave it ready access to both the eastern and western Mediterranean and to the rich agricultural soil of its hinterland. In the fifth century B.C., access to this region became an important ingredient in Carthage's ongoing prosperity. So successful were the Carthaginians in exploiting their agricultural resources that the Roman Senate ordered a translation of a collection of their technical books dealing with the subject.

CARTHAGINIAN IMPERIALISM Founded sometime in the eighth century B.C., Carthage was not a city of energetic, mostly peaceful merchants who were victimized by an aggressive Rome. In the sixth century B.C. in a series of bitter wars Carthage drove the Greeks out of the western Mediterranean and colonized its coasts with strongholds and naval bases. In the fifth century the Carthaginians began attempts to conquer the portions of Sicily that lay under Greek control. They waged five major campaigns there between 480 B.C. and 278 B.C. In the process the Greek cities of Selinus, Himera, and Acragas (Agrigentum) were captured and destroyed. In the end the effort to conquer the Greeks failed, but it was not from lack of effort. In Africa the Carthaginians were more successful and by around 300 B.C. they had conquered from the native Libyan inhabitants of Africa a larger and richer land empire than Rome's.

Carthaginian generals were elected and held office for as long as was necessary for them to accomplish their missions. Failure on their part was treated with great harshness. Unsuccessful commanders were often crucified. By contrast, Roman commanders were sent out on an annual basis to replace the previous commander in the field unless that general had his command extended. This practice left Roman armies exposed to the dangers of inexperienced generalship, but it also tended to stimulate a general's aggressiveness, because he knew that he would soon be replaced and the glory of victory might fall to his successor. Failure in the field rarely affected a Roman commander's political career.

By the third century B.C. the Carthaginians had established a reputation for brutality that far exceeded Rome's. Its generals were legendary for their cruelty to captured cities where the mass slaughter of citizens was used as a tactic to terrify other cities into submission. Carthage was not popular with its Phoenician allies or with the native Libyans. The harshness with which it ruled both was a weakness in Carthage's otherwise powerful empire.

MERCENARIES Compared to Rome, Carthage always suffered from a shortage of manpower. In compensation it had the wherewithal from its commercial and agricultural activities to hire mercenaries to fight for it, and in the third century, the Mediterranean was awash with soldiers of fortune. Because it was always dangerous to create armies made up of mercenaries who all spoke the same language and so could potentially conspire against their employer, Carthage made sure that its armies were polyglot.

One source of mercenaries for Carthage was the Greek world. For centuries Greeks had warred among themselves and as a consequence, masses of professional soldiers from ordinary infantry men to generals were available for hire. There were well-known places in Greece—Cape Teanum in the southern Peloponnese, for example—where such soldiers could be picked up. But Carthage had access to a much-larger pool of mercenaries locally in north Africa among Libyans and Numidians. The Libyans constituted the bulk of Carthage's infantry units and the Numidians provided the cavalry. In addition warlike, footloose Celts, either from Spain or southern Gaul, were available along with Ligurians from the mountains of northern Italy. By contrast, as we have seen, Roman armies were militia armies, made up of drafted citizen soldiers, brigaded with usually equal numbers of allied contingents.

CARTHAGE AND ROME: EARLY CONTACTS Early contacts between Carthage and Rome were matters of mutual self-interest, with Carthage making the initial overtures. As rulers of a large naval empire, and anxious to preserve that rule, Carthaginians needed to keep on top of developments throughout the western Mediterranean. They were especially concerned about the activities of their principal rivals in the region, the Greeks of Sicily and southern Italy. In warfare with the Greeks in the western Mediterranean the Carthaginians found allies among the Etruscans who shared their concerns about the Greeks. Rome inherited a relationship of some sort with Carthage from the time of the kings, and in the first year of the Republic (509 B.C.) the two cities signed their first treaty. A second treaty came in 348 B.C. when Carthage recognized Rome's suzerainty over Latium. Later Carthage was allied with Rome (in 279 B.C.) against Pyrrhus, their mutual enemy, when that predatory warlord crossed from Italy to Sicily to assist the Greeks, who were under severe pressure from the Carthaginians.

## 2. THE FIRST PUNIC WAR (264–241 B.C.)

### Causes and Occasions of War

As might be expected the occasion for the first collision between Rome and Carthage arose in southern Italy and Sicily where their interests overlapped. Mercenaries from Campania known as "Mamertines," who had been serving Hiero of Syracuse, revolted and seized the strategically important Sicilian city of Messana. Under siege in 264 B.C. by Hiero the mercenaries debated what to do. Different factions among them appealed for help to the Rome and Carthage respectively. The Carthaginians responded first and put a garrison in the citadel.

The request for aid at Rome generated a major debate. Some in the Senate regarded the Carthaginian presence in Messana as an attempt to end the old balance of power between the Greeks and Carthaginians in Sicily in favor of the Carthaginians. Messana was only a few miles from Italy and lay within what was traditionally regarded as Greek Sicily. This, coupled with the fact that the Carthaginians already occupied Corsica and Sardinia and all the other islands of the western Mediterranean, suggested that were they successful in this endeavor the entire Tyrrhenian Sea if not the whole western Mediterranean would become a Carthaginian dominated lake. Inevitably this would have had an impact on Italy itself. As Polybius put it, "The Romans foresaw this future and felt obligated not to abandon Messana nor allow the Carthaginians to build themselves a bridge, as it were, across to Italy" (1.10).

Not all of the senators saw the issue so clearly. Some felt qualms about helping brutal mercenaries who had seized Messana from its original inhabitants. Some felt that Rome had more in common with the Greeks of Sicily than with the Carthaginians, their erstwhile allies. Yet others had a personal interest in the fate of the Campanian mercenaries. Campania had been incorporated in the Roman commonwealth in the previous century, and senators from Campanian such as the Atilii and Ogulnii, were powerful in Rome at this time. Deadlocked, the Senate passed the decision to the Roman people, who voted for war with Carthage.[2]

## War Aims—Were they Absent?

When the war began the Romans had a number of unresolved problems. The most important of these was what constituted realistic war aims. What did they hope to gain by taking on Carthage? A minimal, and probably legitimate achievement, would have been the restoration of the balance of power between Greeks and Carthaginians in Sicily. Whether this was a sustainable solution was an important related issue. Another and more extreme option was to drive the Carthaginians out of Sicily altogether or, as Agathocles of Syracuse had recently tried, attack Carthage directly. None of these issues had been fully debated previously and Rome had no precedents for overseas campaigns from its past history. As a result it was unclear how the war should be waged and events were allowed to dominate the early years of the conflict. For the Carthaginians there was concern that the balance of power in Sicily might tip in favor of the Greeks. Over the centuries they had been able to contain the hegemonic ambitions of Syracuse, but the situation might change with the introduction of Roman influence to the island. Once the Romans decided to build a fleet, the Carthaginian position hardened further. They were not about to tolerate a rival at sea where they had been supreme for the past 250 years.

When the Romans finally decided to help the Mamertines, they sent one of the consuls, Appius Claudius Caudex, to the straits of Sicily with an army. When news of this reached Messana the Mamertines managed to persuade the Carthaginian garrison in the citadel to leave. On his return home the Carthaginian commander was promptly crucified "for having shown folly and cowardice in abandoning the citadel" (Polyb. 1.11). Neither Hiero of Syracuse nor the Carthaginians would back down, and the war was on. Hiero, however, rather quickly reconsidered. Estimating that the Romans had a stronger hand, he switched sides and remained faithful to Rome throughout the long war while at the same time making large sums of money for Syracuse by selling them supplies. It was a mutually beneficial deal because the Romans, lacking a navy, were afraid of being cut off from support from Italy by the Carthaginians.

[2]It should be remembered that the term "people" in this context means the Centuriate Assembly, which was controlled by the ruling oligarchy.

## Strategy: The Problem of Winning Asymmetrical Wars

The problem faced by Romans and Carthaginians alike was how to win an asymmetrical war where one side had a powerful army and the other a powerful navy. Theoretically each was unbeatable, at least while fighting its own kinds of battles on its own ground. What would "victory" in such a war look like? The conflict was in some respects like the not-too-distant asymmetrical Peloponnesian War, which pitted the Athenian fleet against the Spartan army. That war ended when the Spartans, subsidized by the Persians, were able to cobble together a fleet and so defeat the Athenian navy.

For the Carthaginians, a winning strategy would have been to prevent the Romans from conquering their holdings in Sicily and so force a peace on the Romans on the basis of the *status quo ante*. The strategy was straightforward enough: Carthage would remain on the defensive in Sicily while using its fleets to harass Roman possessions in Italy. For most of the generation-long war Carthage was successful in this effort. Their aim was to wear down and embarrass the Romans until they made peace.

For the Romans, if they were to choose to drive the Carthaginians from Sicily rather than just drive them back to their own part of the island, the strategy was more complicated. Waging war with a naval power like Carthage was very different from the land campaigns they were used to conducting in Italy. Even assuming Rome could win all of its land battles, there was the problem of capturing Carthaginian port cities. In the Peloponnesian War, Sparta could not capture Athens as long as Athens could bring in supplies from the sea, and it was only when the Spartans had destroyed the Athenian navy that they could successfully besiege Athens and conduct a proper blockade. The same was true for Carthaginian cities in Sicily. Unless the Romans could cut off support by sea, their sieges would not usually succeed. Finally, there was the issue of whether the Romans were willing to pay the price in citizen soldiers of waging an offensive war against an entrenched enemy.

The naval issue became clear to the Romans (if it was not clear long before) after their capture of the city of Agrigentum in 262 B.C. According to Polybius this victory caused on the one hand many inland Sicilian towns to join the Romans because of their fear of Rome's infantry, but "even more coastal towns broke away from them because they in turn feared the Carthaginian fleet.... They also saw Italy frequently ravaged while Africa remained untouched" (1.20).

COSTLY NAVIES By definition navies—ancient or modern—are inherently expensive to build, man, and maintain. Only the wealthiest states can expect to field fleets. Sparta, in its war with Athens, had limited resources and hence needed Persian subsidies to defeat wealthy Athens. Rome was not particularly wealthy—compared to Carthage, a commercial state—but it had resources Carthage lacked, namely allies who could be called upon to supply ships. These allies of Rome were the Greeks of southern Italy and Sicily, and with their help the Romans brought a fleet into being in 260 B.C. Rome, with its vast manpower reserves, could provide the rowers and marines. To circumvent the superior seamanship of the Carthaginians they planned to turn sea battles into land battles by the invention of a device called the *corvus* (the "crow" or "raven," referring to the birds' bill). This was a gangplank with a spike at the end and was to be dropped on the deck of an enemy ship, transforming it

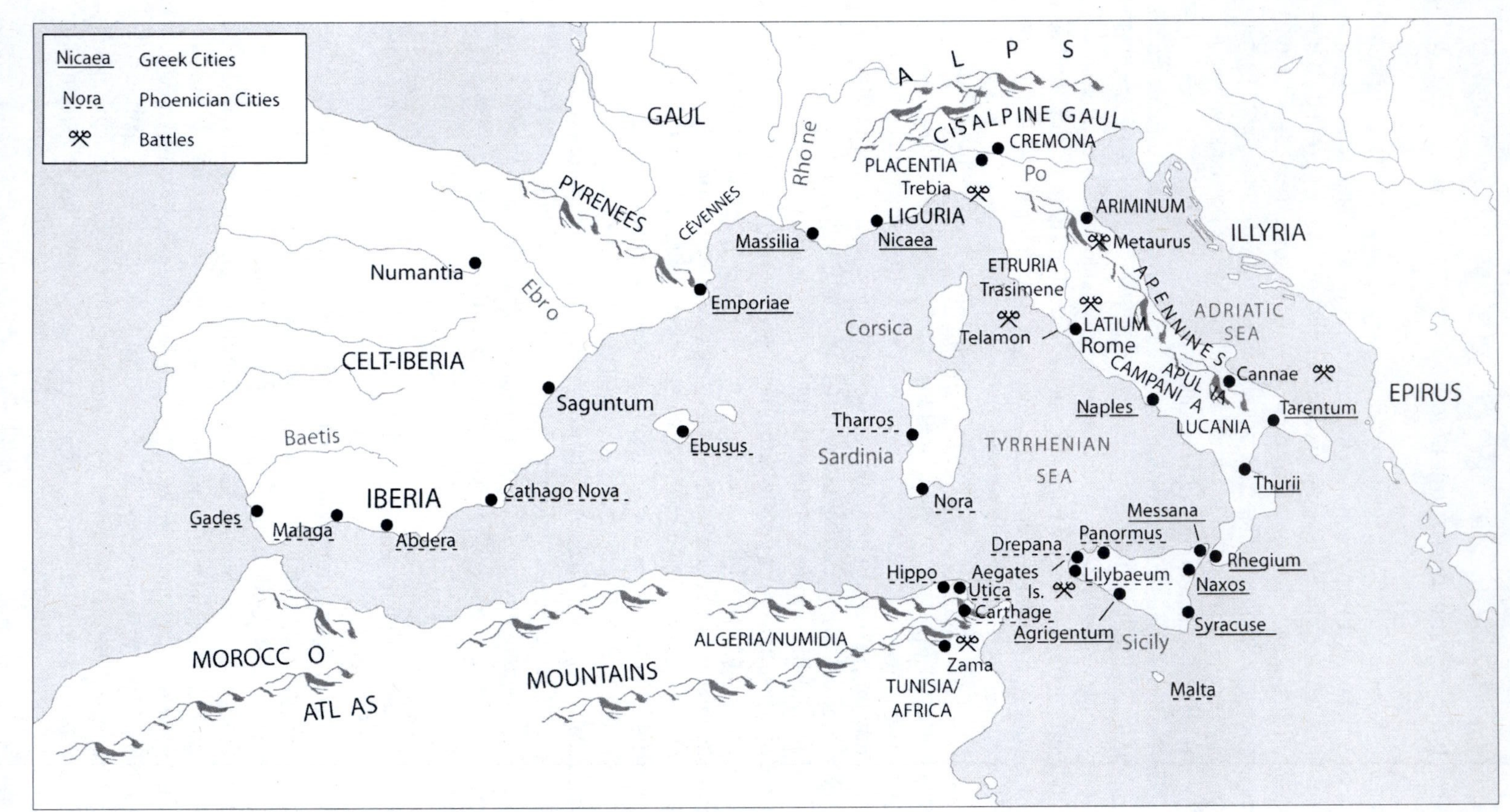


The Western Mediterranean: The Arena of the Punic Wars

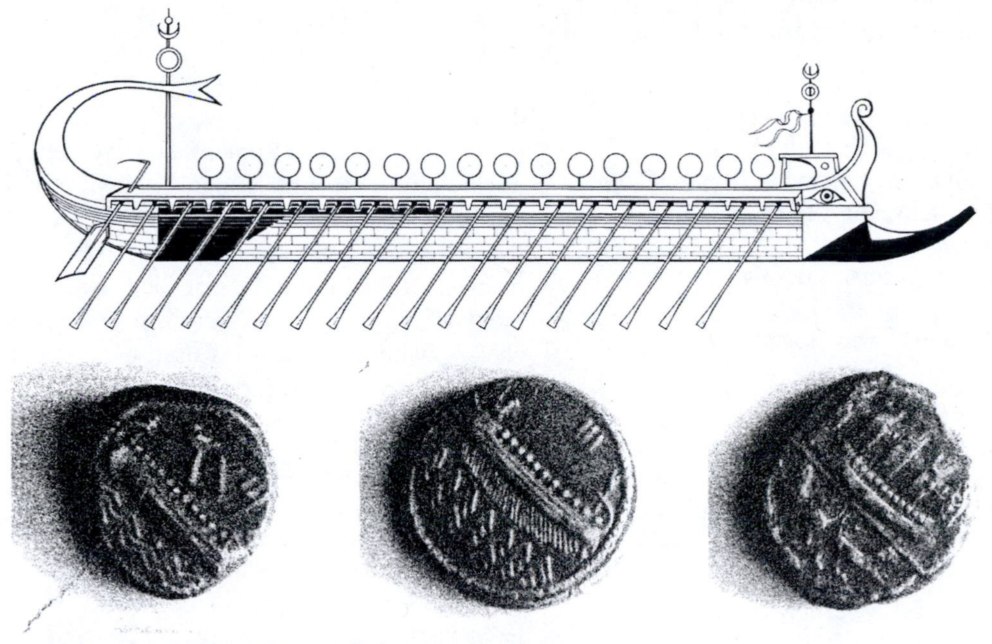

**Carthaginian Warship and Coins**

*A reconstruction of a Carthaginian warship of the time of the First Punic War. The ship was found, along with the wreck of a sister ship, off the coast of Sicily between 1971 and 1973. The hold of the ship illustrated here contained a cache of* cannabis sativa. *The discoverers of the ships speculate that the cannabis was used to help the rowers endure the stress of their long hours at the oars.*

into a grappling iron that locked the two ships together and allowed Roman marines to board the ship and make quick work of their opponents. With the creation of the fleet and the achievement of tactical superiority over the Carthaginians, the slow process of land siege and sea blockade began. Ultimately this approach was to bring victory, but not before the Romans attempted some shortcuts that threatened their whole strategy of naval warfare.

## Short Cuts and War Costs

In 256 B.C. Rome sent an expedition against Carthage in the hope of concluding the war quickly. After some initial successes it failed, and Roman naval power was decimated by storms and mishandling so that by 249 B.C. Rome was back where it started, almost without a fleet. Its manpower losses were staggering. The census for 247 B.C. indicates that the male population of Rome had declined by 17% since the beginning of the war. Apart from the loss of ships, Carthage's losses were minimal because the state depended on mercenaries, of which there was an endless supply as long as Carthage had the money to pay them. Dead mercenaries did not pick up their pay.

For the following eight years the war languished until by one supreme effort the Romans, in 241 B.C., created a new fleet and resumed the Sicilian blockade. In Carthage, meanwhile,

**The Importance of the Auspices**

*In the Roman tradition the defeat of the fleet in 249 B.C. was due to the arrogance and irreligiosity of its commander, Appius Claudius Pulcher. The story is preserved in a small surviving fragment from one of Livy's lost books. There is some suspicion that the tale is a creation of one of Livy's sources, who was known for his hostility to Claudii.*

[Appius Claudius] was anxious to conduct his campaign but was prevented from leaving Rome by a tribune of the people. Thereupon he ordered that the sacred chickens be brought forward. When these refused to eat the grain scattered before them the consul mocked the bad omen and said: "In that case, let them drink," and tossed them into the Tiber. Afterwards, when returning in triumph to Africa he perished at sea along with all his men (Servius, *On the Aeneid* 6.198).

the peace party headed by Hanno persuaded the leadership to concentrate on Africa and undermined the position of Hamilcar Barca (father of the famous Hannibal), who was waging a vigorous war in Sicily. The Romans then won a great naval battle off the Aegates Islands, and Carthage, exhausted and pressed by Hanno's faction, agreed to negotiate (241 B.C.). The settlement resulted in the loss of Sicily, the payment of an indemnity, and various other clauses, which the Romans used as a pretext shortly afterward to seize Sardinia.

### A Balance Sheet of the War

The First Punic War demonstrated the strengths and weaknesses of both sides. The Romans were burdened with the political necessity of having new consuls in office every year and as a consequence often suffered from inept generalship. However, this weakness was compensated for by the unflagging dedication of the elite to the war. Rome's tenacity, its manpower reserves, and its willingness to seek victory served it well when compared to Carthage's half-measures, divisions among its elite, relatively smaller population and, as a result its dependence on mercenaries. Rome had its political divisions too, but was more adept at fixing them. Its leadership class was more broadly based and had greater experience in war and politics than Carthage. It was willing to take risks as well as engage in innovations. An example of its self-confidence was the decision to create a fleet out of nothing. In the perspective of world history it is hard to find an historical parallel to this. The Roman public, in turn, was willing to sustain horrendous casualties whereas Carthage's expenditure of citizen manpower was minimal.[3] Roman luck made a difference too, and its ally, Hiero of Syracuse, more than once helped out in bad times.

## 3. CARTHAGE AND ROME BETWEEN THE WARS

Between the two rounds of wars (264–241 B.C. and 218–202 B.C.) Romans and Carthaginians became deeply involved in their own local affairs. Carthage's most pressing issue was how to replenish its depleted treasure and what to do with the thousands of mercenaries from Libya, Iberia (southern Spain), Gaul, Greece, and Liguria (in northern Italy)

[3] According to Polybius, Rome lost 700 ships during the war compared to Carthage's loss of 400.

who had to be paid off and sent home. Rome had to decide what to do with Sicily, its first overseas possession, how to handle the ongoing Celtic threat from Cisalpine Gaul, and the new issue of piracy in the Adriatic.

## Carthage's War with Its Mercenaries

The process of demobilizing the mercenaries was badly bungled by Hanno and the Carthaginian Senate, who foolishly invited the mercenaries, in view of Carthage's difficult financial situation, to give up part of their pay. Despite the language problem that kept them divided, the mercenaries found a number of charismatic leaders and rebelled. One of the most atrocious wars—Polybius termed it "truceless"—in antiquity ensued, with ghastly atrocities being committed by both sides. Eventually, through the leadership of Hamilcar Barca, the Carthaginians gained the upper hand and the mercenaries were defeated.

## Sardinia, Queen Teuta, Piracy in the Adriatic, and the Celts—Again

While the Carthaginians were involved in putting down the mercenaries, Rome did not intervene and even allowed Carthage to recruit other, more reliable mercenaries in Italy. When the war ended, however, Rome changed its policy and claimed Corsica and Sardinia as part of the peace settlement of 241 B.C. and demanded an additional indemnity. The policy shift seems to have come about as a result of internal politics at Rome where some regarded the treaty of 241 B.C. as too generous. The seizure of the islands seems to have settled the political issue in Rome. In no position to resist after the loss of its fleet in the Punic War and the costs of the Truceless War, Carthage yielded to Rome's shameless demands. Even Polybius, usually sympathetic to Rome, felt this was a clear act of international piracy. The act embittered an already angry and resentful Carthage and laid the foundations for the second round of wars with Rome. To administer the new overseas territories or provinces of Sicily and Sardinia-Corsica, Rome created two new additional praetors in 227 B.C.

In the Adriatic Rome put down the pirates of Illyria who, under their leader Queen Teuta, were terrorizing the Greek coastlands. Shortly afterward, the Celts, who had been quiet all during the war with the Carthaginians, began a major advance on Rome. Terrified, the Romans resorted to human sacrifice and the consultation of the prophetic Sibylline books and finally defeated the Celts at Telamon, just 90 miles from Rome, in 225 B.C. This victory encouraged the Romans to think they had an opportunity to finish off the Gallic threat, and a series of campaigns was launched against the Celts' homeland in the Po valley. Large Latin colonies were established at Cremona and Placentia (Piacenza), but before the full task of subduing the Celts was completed the second war with Carthage broke out. Twenty years elapsed before the Romans renewed their colonial efforts in the north.

## Carthage and Spain

After the loss of Sicily, Corsica, and Sardinia, Carthage found itself confined to Africa, which was not an adequate base for its imperial activities. In casting around for alterna-

### The Truceless War: A Lesson Regarding the Use of Mercenaries

*Polybius prefaces his long story—well worth reading in its own right—of the "Truceless War", with a comment about the danger of the use of non-citizen mercenaries. He emphasizes at length the differences between soldiers-for-hire who were anarchic individualists and citizen soldiers who lived under law in political communities. Unfortunately, the behavior of both groups in the Truceless War makes it hard to see this difference. Polybius remarks at one point that the only term universally understood among the polyglot mercenaries was "stone him"—a method of execution used widely by the mercenaries to quell disagreement in their ranks. Both sides crucified prisoners. On occasion Carthaginians had their prisoners trampled by elephants. The following excerpt from Polybius deals with incidents that occurred toward the end of the war. Hamilcar (the same general who had fought successfully in Sicily) managed to pen 40,000 of the mercenaries and their camp followers, prisoners, and slaves in a canyon.*

Taking them by surprise, Hamilcar encamped opposite them in a position that was favorable for him but not for the mercenaries. Not daring to fight and unable to escape because they were entirely surrounded by a ditch and a palisade, they were driven by famine to eat each other. ...When they had used up their prisoners in this unholy manner and their slaves likewise... the leaders, Autaritus, Zarzas and Spendius, realizing they were themselves in danger owing to the dreadful extremities to which the ordinary soldiers were reduced, decided to give themselves up to the enemy and negotiate with Hamilcar.... [*However, once Hamilcar had the leaders in his hands he proceeded to slaughter the mercenaries. Then, in conjunction with two other commanders, Naravas and Hannibal— not Hamilcar's son—he continued the campaign*]. The Libyans in general gave up and went over to the Carthaginians as a result of their recent victory. After capturing most of the cities, the Carthaginians reached Tunis and began to besiege Mathos (*the last of the important mercenary leaders*). Hannibal encamped on the side of the town next to Carthage and Hamilcar on the opposite side. Their next step was to take Spendius and the other prisoners up to the walls of Tunis and crucify them in the sight of the defenders. Mathos, however, noticed that Hannibal was negligent and overconfident and attacked his camp, killed many of the Carthaginians and took Hannibal himself prisoner. They took him at once to Spendius' cross and tortured him horribly there. Then, taking Spendius down from the cross, they crucified Hannibal alive on it. Around the body the body of Spendius they killed thirty high ranking Carthaginian prisoners. Thus did Fortune, as if it had a plan to compare them, give mercenaries and Carthaginians in turn cause and opportunity for inflicting on each other the cruelest punishments (Polybius *The Histories*, 1.84–86).

tives, Spain to the west came under consideration. For centuries it had been a major source of essential metals for the eastern Mediterranean, with Carthage acting as intermediary. But now Carthage looked to develop southern Spain—ancient Iberia—as a substitute for Sicily and Sardinia. It had for some centuries been urbanized to a degree and had excellent agricultural land, and a Phoenician colony already existed at Gades (modern Cadiz). To the north the tribalized, warlike Celts were both a problem and an opportunity. As perennial raiders they were a danger, but more importantly, they offered a ready source of mercenaries for the Carthaginian army, which was always in need of an adequate manpower pool.

THE BARCIDS IN SPAIN The man entrusted with turning southern Spain into a new Sicily and a base, if necessary, for future war with Rome was the victor in the Truceless War, Hamilcar Barca. Apart from his patriotic duties to Carthage, Hamilcar had a personal grudge to settle against Rome, and the vendetta was passed down to his son. Polybius tells the story of how Hamilcar, while sacrificing to Zeus, invited his nine-year old son Hannibal to join him on the expedition to Spain. When Hannibal responded with delight, "his father took him by the hand and led him to the altar. There he ordered him to put his hand on the victim and swear that he would never be a friend of the Romans" (3.11). How much of this is true and how much the construction of the Roman propaganda machine that dominates the history of Roman and Carthaginian relations, is hard to say. To the Romans the Carthaginians were venal hucksters, an untrustworthy and superstitious people in whom "rapacity and savagery struggled for preeminence," as one of Livy's speakers put it (22.59). Hannibal, who so nearly brought Rome to disaster, was portrayed as the quintessential Carthaginian: unscrupulous, cruel, and calculating, a true prince of darkness.

Hamilcar, his son-in-law Hasdrubal, and his sons Hannibal, Hasdrubal, and Mago established close relations with the Iberian natives. After the death of his wife, Hasdrubal (Senior) married the daughter of a Celtic chieftain. Hannibal, too, married a Celt. Emigrants from Carthage were settled in significant numbers along the southern coastlands and a major city, New Carthage (in Latin *Carthago Nova,* mod. Cartagena), was founded as the capital.

Hamilcar died when on campaign in the winter of 229–228 B.C. and was succeeded by his son-in-law Hasdrubal because his sons were too young to succeed him. However, when Hasdrubal was assassinated eight years later by a Celt seeking revenge for the death of his father, the army chose Hannibal as his successor as it had previously chosen Hasdrubal. The choice was confirmed by the popular assembly in Carthage.

## 4. THE WAR WITH HANNIBAL, OR THE SECOND PUNIC WAR (218–202 B.C.)

As the power of the Barcid dynasty grew in Spain, the attention of the Romans was often drawn to it by Rome's ally Massilia (Marseille) in southern Gaul. Massilia maintained trading posts on the Spanish coasts north of the Ebro and followed the developments in the south with concern. When conflicts with the Celts began to loom in the Po valley the Romans decided to preempt the possibility of a confrontation with the Carthaginians in Spain, and in 226 B.C. they sent a mission to Hasdrubal in Carthago Nova. He agreed not to advance north of

Ebro, but after his death Rome became involved in mediating a dispute in the city of Saguntum south of the Ebro. Although Saguntum was not part of the territory subject to the Carthaginians, and technically Rome did not violate its agreement with Hasdrubal in its mediation efforts, it opened up the possibility for it to make further interventions.

The occasion for the outbreak of the Second Punic War was provided by Hannibal's decision in 220 to expand Carthaginan power northwards towards the Ebro. He won a major victory over the local tribes, and thereafter no one dared to oppose him except Saguntum. Relying on their belief that Rome would come to their aid, the city resisted Hannibal's demands. In due course legates were sent out from Rome to negotiate with Hannibal, but the talks broke down and Hannibal attacked and took Saguntum after an eight-month siege. All its inhabitants were killed. Saguntum received no help from Rome; apparently the Senate did not think the city was worth risking another war with Carthage. Nevertheless, when news of the fall of the city arrived in Rome it provoked a political upheaval in the Senate. A large delegation was sent to Carthage to demand that Hannibal be handed over to them. When this was rejected the delegation then issued an ultimatum which was also rejected. As soon as Hannibal heard the news, he marched his army out of Spain, through France, and toward Italy.

## Strategy: Carthaginian and Roman

The strategies each side used in the Second Punic War were dictated largely by the results of the first war. The Carthaginians, recognizing that Rome could be defeated only on land, conceded control of the sea to Rome; the Romans, for their part, planned to continue where they had left off in 241 B.C., using Sicily as a base to invade Africa while blockading a Carthaginian invasion from Spain. All of these plans, however, were upset by Hannibal's bold plan to attack Rome in Italy: he knew that Carthage could never win merely by staying on the defensive and hoping to wear Rome down.

The problem facing Hannibal, once the decision had been made not to fight this war on the sea, was how to get his army to Italy and then what to do with it when he got there. With Rome's superior naval resources it would have been impossible to ship his army—especially his cavalry and elephants—by sea. A land route had to be found, but this involved a long march from southern Spain, through Gaul, and up the Rhône to a place where the Alps could be crossed. These were, however, essentially tactical issues. From a strategic viewpoint the success of the campaign depended on the fulfillment of a number of reasonable assumptions. The first was that a thoroughly professional general leading professional troops could, on an average, defeat an amateur citizen levy—a militia. This was not an original or unproved idea. Since the mid–fourth century B.C., the time of Philip and Alexander of Macedon (Alexander the Great and his father), professional armies had consistently defeated citizen armies. The second assumption was that as a result of defeats in the field, the Roman confederation, like all other such leagues, would disintegrate. Once deprived of its manpower reserves, Rome itself would revert to being a minor power in Italy.

In the first instance Hannibal proved to be correct, although his own genius was a factor that outweighed the others and made textbook cases out of his battles, confronting the

Romans with a threat they had never before faced. One of the more dangerous aspects of Hannibal's plan was his success in winning over the Celts of northern Italy to his side. It is worth recalling that the Second Punic War was also known to the Romans as the "War Against the Carthaginians and the Gauls." It was on the second presupposition—the collapse of Rome's federation—that Hannibal's grand strategy foundered.

## Hannibal in Italy

Despite the distances involved and the difficulty to be faced in crossing the Alps, Hannibal opted to invade Italy. Having successfully marched out of Spain, he slipped past a Roman army in southern Gaul, marched north up the Rhône, and crossed with difficulty the Alps into Italy. The Romans responded by canceling the planned invasion of Africa and shipping the Roman army in Sicily to Gaul. From 218 B.C. onward, until his return to Africa in 204 B.C., Hannibal remained unbeaten in any set battle. One great Roman defeat followed another, of which Cannae in southern Italy in 216 B.C. was the worst. A classic of double envelopment, the battle is still studied in war colleges.

THE DISASTER OF CANNAE Battle losses in antiquity are notoriously untrustworthy, so we cannot be sure how many Romans (and Roman allies) actually fell at Cannae. Estimates range from 50,000 to 70,000, but even the low figure is suspect.[4] Nevertheless, Roman losses were huge, and adolescents and slaves had to be drafted to fill the newly recruited legions. The annual rites in honor of the goddess Ceres, which could be celebrated only by married women, had to be canceled because too many of them were in mourning and mourners could not participate in the rituals. A delegation was sent to Delphi to inquire what rituals were appropriate for placating the wrath of heaven. Two Vestal Virgins were discovered to have broken their vows of chastity and were executed. The Sibylline Books were consulted and on their authority two Gauls and two Greeks were buried alive in the cattle market—an activity that an embarrassed Livy characterized as "a most un-Roman rite" (Livy 22.57).

Hannibal sent to Carthage a bag containing the gold rings of the knights and senators killed in the battle as proof of his victory. To make the point more dramatic his messenger opened the bag and poured the rings in a heap on the ground in front of the Senate house. As he did after previous victories, Hannibal released the allied prisoners saying to them that he had come to wage war against Rome, not its allies. The key cities of Capua and Tarentum defected, along with Syracuse in Sicily. Some of the Samnite federation and most of the peoples of southern Italy also went over to him. Philip V of Macedonia opportunistically jumped into the fight on the side of Carthage. By the end of the third year of the war Rome had lost 120,000 men—killed or taken prisoner. It seemed that Hannibal's strategy was working. The Romans were put on the defensive. The best tactic they could find was one of avoiding direct confrontation with Hannibal in the field, a tactic that won its proposer, Fabius Maximus, the title of "The Delayer." It worked, but such tactics could not produce victory.

[4]There were 8 legions at Cannae. With their supporting allied troops the total number might have come to something like 80,000 infantry and 6,000 cavalry.

**What was Hannibal Thinking?**

*There is unfortunately no account of the Hannibalic War written from the Carthaginian perspective. Support for the belief that Hannibal knew that to defeat Rome he had to destroy its alliances with Latins and Italians comes from a story in Livy regarding the advice Hannibal was supposed to have later given Antiochus III of Syria. This occurred after the end of the Second Punic War when, for political reasons, Hannibal was forced to leave Carthage and take refuge with Antiochus who was planning war with Rome.*

Hannibal, an exile from his homeland, had fled to Antiochus... and was held in high esteem by the king. Antiochus believed that he could have no better adviser than Hannibal for a war against Rome which he had been considering for some time. Hannibal's view was always the same: The war should be fought in Italy. The reason was that, first, Italy could supply food and soldiers to an invading enemy. Second, if there was no military presence there and Rome was allowed to draw on the manpower and resources of Italy, then neither the king nor any other people for that matter, would be a match for the Romans (Livy 34.60).

## Hannibal's Dilemma

When the Roman federation did not collapse as Hannibal anticipated, he (and Carthage) had no back-up plan. Carthage was too weak or too weak-willed to build up its navy and strongly support him by sea. Indeed Livy tells a story of how Hanno, Hannibal's nemesis and the leader of the peace party in Carthage, joked that surely if Hannibal was as successful as he claimed to be, he did not need reinforcements. Indeed, Hanno went on to say, because Carthage momentarily had the upper hand, now would be the time to negotiate peace with Rome. "We are in a position," he said, "to grant peace terms rather than accept them" (Livy 23.12). Hanno did not have his way, and supplies were sent but only in a half-hearted manner. This was the first, and as it turned out, the only time in the long war that Hannibal was reinforced from Carthage.

THE STRENGTH OF ROME'S DEFENSES Left to his own devices in Italy, the weight of history began to tell against Hannibal. Rome's alliances held; the number of legions continued to grow, not shrink. There were 25 legions in the field by 212 B.C., and the number never fell below 15 until after the end of the war. Then there were the defensive measures Rome had built up to protect the core of its commonwealth in the Samnite Wars. These were the results of the conquests that had deliberately divided Italy into two halves, giving the Romans internal lines of communication, and making it difficult for enemies on either side to unite against Rome. Excellent roads constructed for earlier campaigns allowed the legions to be shifted quickly from front to front and from one colony to another. Strategic colonies—located both to protect Latium and hold down allies if they became restless—protected by massive walls, continued to serve as self-sustaining fortresses and prevented Hannibal from making any serious assault on the Roman heartland. While keeping Hannibal in the south they also made it difficult to impossible for his most important allies, the Gauls of northern Italy, to unite with him or send reinforcements. They proved their worth early in the conflict. After the disaster of Cannae, the remnants of the Roman army were able to retire to the fortress at Venusia. Together with Luceria, the other great fortress in Apulia, Rome was able to maintain a

Battleground Italy: Colonies and Battle Sites

The location of Roman and Latin colonies made it difficult for Hannibal to wage war in Rome's central Italian homeland. Even in the south, where he was confined by Rome's grand straegy, he still had to cope with the colonies of Luceria and Venusia, which he could not capture.

### Why Hannibal Lost

*Why Hannibal's victory at Cannae did not lead to Rome's surrender has been debated since antiquity. According to Livy some of Hannibal's own officers believed he had wasted a golden opportunity to finish the war by not immediately marching on Rome. Maharbal, his cavalry commander, was supposed to have said:* "Hannibal, you know how to win battles, but not how to exploit your victories" (Livy 22.51). *Hannibal, however, was well aware that he could not take Rome by siege. His army was an assault army, not a siege army. Once committed, he had to stick to his strategy of destroying the Roman confederacy. A more sober assessment comes from Polybius. Victory in a long war was as much a political as a military matter.*

> Although the Romans were clearly beaten at this moment and their military reputation had been ruined, yet by the unique character of their constitution and by their sound planning, they not only regained their supremacy in Italy, but in short order became masters of the whole world (Polybius 3.118).

presence in the south throughout the entire war despite Hannibal's superiority in set battles. Hannibal had his liabilities. His ferocious Celts scared many Italians who had long memories of earlier Celtic invasions, and there was always the lurking thought that after Hannibal left, Rome would still be around. This fear was reinforced as Rome methodically re-conquered the rebellious cities of Capua, Syracuse, and Tarentum and treated them with extreme brutality. Hannibal could not prevent their recapture. Finally, with its fleet, Rome could bring in supplies while denying them to Hannibal.

## "He Did Not Lose Faith in the Republic"

STEADINESS OF ELITE AND PEOPLE Still, even with these advantages Rome would not have beaten Carthage had it not been for the steadiness of the Senate and the willingness of the people to endure appalling losses. The state remained united. In the darkest days of the war, the Roman elite never lost its nerve. There was no betrayal or treachery among them as was common in Greek cities under similar circumstances. As Hanno pointed out in his speech to the Carthaginian Senate after the battle of Cannae, no peace overtures came from Rome, despite Hannibal's success in the field. No rogue senators put out peace feelers or made secret visits to Carthage. The Senate and people welcomed back Varro, the surviving consul of the battle of Cannae, despite the view that his bungling contributed or caused the loss of the battle. He was thanked publicly "for not losing faith in the Republic" (Livy 22.61). The Senate refused to ransom the 8,000 soldiers who surrendered after the Battle of Cannae despite great pressure from their families, including many of senatorial rank. Instead of cowering behind its defense network of colonies the Senate took the offensive. It made a strategic decision to take the fight to the Carthaginians in Spain while being content to bottle up Hannibal in southern Italy. The strategy of Fabius Maximus "the Delayer," while prudent for the period after Cannae, was not a strategy that would have won the war. Just enough was done to keep Philip V off balance in Macedonia and Greece. The decision to choose Spain as a battleground reflects the supreme self-confidence of both Senate and people in the face of what most

**The Influence of Roman History on Alfred Mahan**

In 1884 when Captain Alfred Thayer Mahan learned that he had been assigned to the faculty of the U.S. Naval Academy he decided he had to do some fast reading to get his lecture notes in order. One of the books he read was a history of Rome by the great German and later Nobel Prize-winning historian, Theodore Mommsen. In his autobiography Mahan tells us, "It suddenly struck me how different things might have been should Hannibal have invaded Italy by sea." (*From Sail to Steam,* New York, 1907, 277). This thought led to the more general idea that "control of the sea was an historical factor which had never been systematically appreciated and expanded." Mahan developed this insight in his classic work of geostrategic history, *The Influence of Sea Power Upon History* (1890). What Clausewitz's famous *On War* (1832) did for land-warfare, Mahan's *Influence of Sea Power* did for naval power. The book was quickly translated into other languages and was read by naval officers around the world. It was claimed half jokingly by the well-known diplomatic historian Charles Webster that Mahan's book was one of the causes of World War I because of its influence on the Kaiser and the development of German naval power. There is no doubt, however, that its arguments were used by Japanese naval officers in their competition with the army to build up a powerful navy in the run-up to World War II and Pearl Harbor.

states would have regarded as a lost cause. Luck also began to turn in Rome's favor with the discovery—in the person of one of the survivors of the battle of Cannae—of a general of genius. This was the young P. Cornelius Scipio, later known as "Africanus"—or the victor over Africa.[5]

## A Final Scare

HASDRUBAL MARCHES ON ITALY There had been a Roman presence in Spain since the start of the war. Under the command of two Scipios, Publius and Gnaeus, father and uncle respectively of the future Africanus, the Romans had been generally successful. But Carthage undertook to reinforce its army in Spain, and under the leadership of Hannibal's brother Mago, the Roman army was slaughtered and the two commanders, Publius and Gnaeus were killed. This was in 211 B.C. Two years later the young Scipio arrived in Spain at the age of 25 to avenge his father and uncle. His first campaign led to the seizure of Carthago Nova (modern Cartagena), the main base of Carthage in Spain with all its riches and supplies. He next took possession of the gold and silver mines that had been a principal source of Carthaginians' wealth. Having then lost one battle to Scipio,

[5]Africa for the Romans of this period was Tunisia.

Hasdrubal Barca, another of Hannibal's brothers, left Spain and, retracing Hannibal's route, crossed the Alps into Italy.

THE EPIC MARCH OF CLAUDIUS NERO This second invasion of Italy (207 B.C.) might have tipped the balance in favor of Hannibal had the Barcid brothers been able to unite. Roman colonies and control of its central lines of communication, however, now came into play. Gaius Claudius Nero, the consul in command in the south, decided on the dangerous expedient of leaving only a screening force to keep Hannibal occupied at Canusium while he marched 265 miles north to join the other consul, Marcus Livius, at the maritime colony of Sena Gallica near the Metaurus River. Although this was a risky undertaking, it was based on sound reasoning. Hannibal always had to keep an eye on the fortress colony of Venusia, and the screening force had the option of retiring there if threatened. Likewise Nero's march from Canusium to Sena Gallica was through friendly territory anchored either by colonies or allied towns.

Nero in fact managed to slip away without being noticed by Hannibal, and in one of the greatest forced marches in history completed the journey to the Metaurus in seven days. The combined forces of the two consuls was too much for Hasdrubal who was defeated and killed at the battle of the Metaurus River. Nero immediately turned his army around and marched the 265 miles back to Canusium before news of Hasdrubal's defeat could reach Hannibal. Livy tells the story that the announcement of the battle was made by tossing Hasdrubal's head on the ground in front of the Carthaginian outposts, the parading of Carthaginian prisoners in chains, and the sending of two of the prisoners to tell Hannibal what had happened. Hannibal was supposed to have said, under the double blow of personal and public tragedy, "Now, finally I see plainly the destiny of Carthage." Whether true or not such a sentiment summed up the reality of the military situation. Carthage had lost its last chance to defeat Rome.

THE PROBLEM OF SCIPIO Scipio's success in Spain generated opposition in the Senate. In part this was due to his young age and unusual rise to power; he was given consular *imperium* by the people for his command in Spain without ever being elected either praetor or consul. Subsequently he held proconsular command in Spain continuously from 210 to 206 B.C. when he was finally elected consul. His plan to invade Africa was opposed by Fabius Maximus, who could remember the disastrous invasion of Africa in the First Punic War; however, he was finally given permission to do so but not allowed to levy additional troops beyond the two legions made up of survivors from Cannae already in Sicily. Calling for volunteers, Scipio crossed into Sicily and the following year invaded Africa. Lacking Rome's deft capacity to make firm allies, Carthage was never popular in Africa. Many Phoenician cities as well as native peoples switched sides when Scipio and his army landed. Among the most useful allies Scipio gained was a Numidian chieftain of great ability by the name of Masinissa. For once the Romans had decent cavalry on their side. Carthage now recalled Hannibal. In a hard fought battle at Zama in 202 B.C. Scipio defeated him and forced the surrender of Carthage. The terms included the surrender of all of its overseas possessions, all but 10 warships, and a huge indemnity. Carthage was not to wage war in Africa without Rome's consent. Masinissa was recognized as king of Numidia where he set about building a state based on previously quarrelling nomadic tribesmen.

ANALYSIS Rome won for a number of reasons. The first and most important was the solidity of the state itself. This point has been emphasized at length in previous chapters and does not need repeating here. The second reason was Rome's centuries-long investment in building allies in Italy and expanding its own commonwealth to include new peoples and new territories. In the crisis of Hannibal's invasion most of the allies remained loyal to Rome. They also provided an enormous manpower pool, which enabled the Romans to replace destroyed armies and maintain armies in several theaters of war simultaneously. The third reason was the concentric rings of colonial fortresses Rome had built up over the centuries in Italy at strategic locations. Again and again they proved impregnable barriers to Hannibal. They sustained wavering allies and provided safe bases for Roman armies operating in the field.

From a strategic viewpoint, Rome was able to compel Carthage to fight on its terms, even though the genius of Hannibal averted defeat for years. Rome's control of the seas forced Hannibal to march overland to Italy; prevented Philip V of Macedonia, an ally of Hannibal's from 215 B.C. onward, from effectively aiding him; and allowed Rome to make its final assault on Africa from Sicily. The Romans could bring supplies into Italy from all over the Mediterranean while denying the Carthaginians the same facility. In Scipio they finally found a leader who raised their citizen-soldiers to new levels of technical ability, introduced new weapons and sophisticated new tactics, experimented with mobile tactical units (cohorts), and passed on a legacy of brilliant generalship.

There were drawbacks to Rome's success. Victory was achieved in part because Rome was forced to compromise its principle of annual rotation of office to be able to keep its most successful commanders in the field for long periods of time. This violation of precedent, despite opposition, allowed the most successful of these generals, Scipio, to end the war. Although necessary, his extended command, prestige, and charismatic personality constituted an ominous precedent. The war illustrated the difficulty of reconciling a political system that guaranteed freedom through a complex, competitive electoral process with the competing need of the state to maintain its security. The dilemma has confronted all free states to the present day. There were other consequences of the war. New conquests involved new obligations and interactions with new peoples and frontiers even further afield than before. At the same time Rome's manpower resources were depleted, its alliance system was shaken, and much of southern Italy was devastated. The north remained a danger zone.

# 7

# Rome Becomes an Imperial Power

## 1. ROMAN EXPANSION IN ITALY AND SPAIN

After the wars with Carthage, Rome was dominant not just in Italy but in all of the coastal areas of the western Mediterranean. In addition, Rome had interests in the Adriatic. If Italy was its chrysalis then Rome in 200 B.C. was about to emerge from it in all its dangerous splendor.

### The Conquest of Cisalpine Gaul: 200 B.C.–170 B.C.

It was a paradox that while the peoples of the wider Mediterranean world were beginning to look on Rome as an emerging superpower, Rome still had vulnerabilities in its own Italian homeland. In 200 B.C., despite its victory over Carthage and the various peoples of peninsular Italy, the area of northern Italy between the Alps and the Apennines known as Cisalpine Gaul remained a hostile, dangerous region. Not long before the outbreak of the war with Hannibal, Romans were reminded of this when a great army of Celts made its way from Cisalpine Gaul to within 90 miles of Rome before being stopped. In 218 B.C., in an attempt to prevent further raids of this type from happening again, Rome established Placentia and Cremona, two large Latin colonies, at strategic sites on the Po river in central Cisalpine Gaul. Their purpose was to hamper cooperation among the Celtic tribes and provide bases for Roman military activity.

AFTER HANNIBAL Even after the defeat of Hannibal the region was still insecure. In 200 B.C., for example, the Boii (a Celtic tribe) captured and sacked Placentia, a feat that had eluded both Hannibal and his brother Hasdrubal. The Ligurians, a hardy, warlike people who inhabited the Maritime Alps to the west, ravaged the territory of reconstituted Placentia in 194 B.C., and in 177 B.C. overran the recently established colony of Mutina. In 186 B.C. 12,000 Gauls with their families suddenly appeared from across the Alps and attempted to settle in the northeastern sector of Cisalpine Gaul, leading the Romans to establish a colony, Aquileia, to prevent further incursions in that area. Though the conquest of Cisalpine Gaul was complete by about 170 B.C., later in the second century Rome had an unpleasant reminder that beyond the Alps there were threats that could easily flow over into Italy. In 105 B.C. at Arausio (Orange) in southern France, migrating German tribes inflicted the most severe defeat a Roman army had suffered since Cannae. Two consular armies were annihilated with a reported loss, probably exaggerated, of 80,000. Whatever the exact figures, the losses were significant and had important political consequences. Eventually the Germans were defeated, but one tribe made it into the Po valley before being overcome. Even peninsular Italy was not as secure or as well-integrated as it seemed. Fourteen years after the disaster at Arausio much of central Italy rose up in rebellion against Rome in the Social War of 91 to 89 B.C. and nearly brought it down

Rome's wars with the Celts and Ligurians did not reach nearly the magnitude of its struggle with Carthage or even those with the Samnites in earlier times. Nevertheless these conflicts lasted for nearly 30 years and required the building of a dozen good-sized (mostly Latin, but some Roman) colonies connected by a network of roads to secure the region. Even then the tribal peoples of the Alps continued to resist Roman presence in the north to the time of Augustus a century and a half later.

THE RESULTS From the Roman point of view the conquest of Cisalpine Gaul had mixed results. The establishment of colonies and the building of roads meant that after the expenditure of so much blood and treasure, a large and fertile area of Italy was now available for settlement and incorporation into the commonwealth. The effects can be seen to the present day in the form of the centuriation marks in the landscape; superhighways that follow the routes of the old Roman trunk roads, such as the Via Aemelia, which connected Ariminum and Placentia; and great industrial cities that sit on the sites of the original colonial foundations, their streets often reflecting the original colonial grid pattern.

On the other hand, the movement of large numbers of Roman and Latin citizens to places far distant from Rome and Latium revealed a fissure in the old *polis* constitution, which had appeared during the consolidation of Roman power in Italy after the Samnite Wars. The traditional, now quaint, belief was that all citizens should live within walking distance of the metropolis. This, of course, had long since ceased to be the case, but the settlement of the north brought the problem into high relief. The new colonies in the north were an impossible (except for the rich) 200 to 300 miles from Rome. Aquileia was 450 miles away from Rome. The contradiction between ideology and reality was compounded by the fact that the course of conquest being followed by Rome inevitably led to the creation of distant frontiers and then to frontiers even more distant, while political life was still centered in the Forum. The question of how to reconcile these contradictory tendencies was to challenge the statecraft of the Romans of the last generation of the Republic.

**Warfare After Hannibal**

| Warfare After Hannibal | |
|---|---|
| Sporadic wars in the Iberian Peninsula | 197–133 B.C. |
| Second Macedonian War | 200–196 B.C. |
| Battle of Cynoscephalae | 197 B.C. |
| War with Antiochus | 192–188 B.C. |
| Battle of Magnesia | 190 B.C. |
| Third Macedonian War | 172–167 B.C. |
| Battle of Pydna | 168 B.C. |
| Fourth Macedonia War | 150–148 B.C. |
| Achaean War: Sack of Corinth | 146 B.C. |
| Third Punic War: Sack of Carthage | 149–146 B.C. |

## Southern Italy

Many communities in southern Italy had gone over to Hannibal after his victory at Cannae in 216 B.C., and upon Roman re-conquest they lost large amounts of territory. Here the devastation was greater than in northern or central Italy because the south was the principal arena of war among Romans, Carthaginians, and its native inhabitants for over a decade. Much of the confiscated land was distributed as individual allotments to veterans of the war, but large quantities remained undistributed as public land (*ager publicus*) in the great land bank of the state. Unlike Cisalpine Gaul, little actual fighting was required after the departure of Hannibal. For a different reason, however, nearly a dozen colonies, most on the coast, were established during the second century to guard against possible raids by the navies of the Hellenistic powers. As in the north, significant numbers of Roman citizens were settled at great distances from Rome.

## Iberia

The term Iberia refers to the land mass south of the Pyrenees that is today's Spain and Portugal. In ancient times, Phoenicians and Greeks established cities in the Mediterranean coastal areas, and urbanization was undertaken by the native inhabitants of the Baetis (Guadalquivir) River valley. The interior of Iberia was occupied by a mixture of pre-urban Celts and Iberians, and the Atlantic coast was held by the tribal Lusitani. Raiding of the settled areas by these peoples and by the Berbers of Mauretania (modern Morocco) across the sea from Spain was a constant feature of life.

As a result of the War with Hannibal, Rome came to recognize the strategic importance of Spain and determined that it would never allow itself to be attacked from that quarter again. Spain's significant resources had to be denied to a revived Carthage or any other potential rival. Accordingly the peninsula was divided into two provinces, Nearer and Farther Spain and the slow process of bringing Iberia under Roman control was launched. Between 197 and 133 B.C. Rome conducted a series of campaigns resulting in the subjection of much of the peninsula. Challenged, however, by the skillful use of guerilla tactics by their non-state opponents, the Romans resorted to extreme brutality. Not until 133 B.C. when the Celt-Iberian town of Numantia was captured and destroyed by Scipio Aemilianus, the same general who some years earlier had reduced Carthage to rubble, could Rome's hold on Spain be considered secure. Even then campaigins agains the Lusitani in the west of the peninsula were conducted in 112, B.C.,109 B.C. 102 B.C. and 101 B.C. Forty years later Julius Caesar campaigned in the same area, and under the reign of Augustus (died A.D. 14) recalcitrant tribes in the northwestern corner of the peninsula were still resisting the appeal of

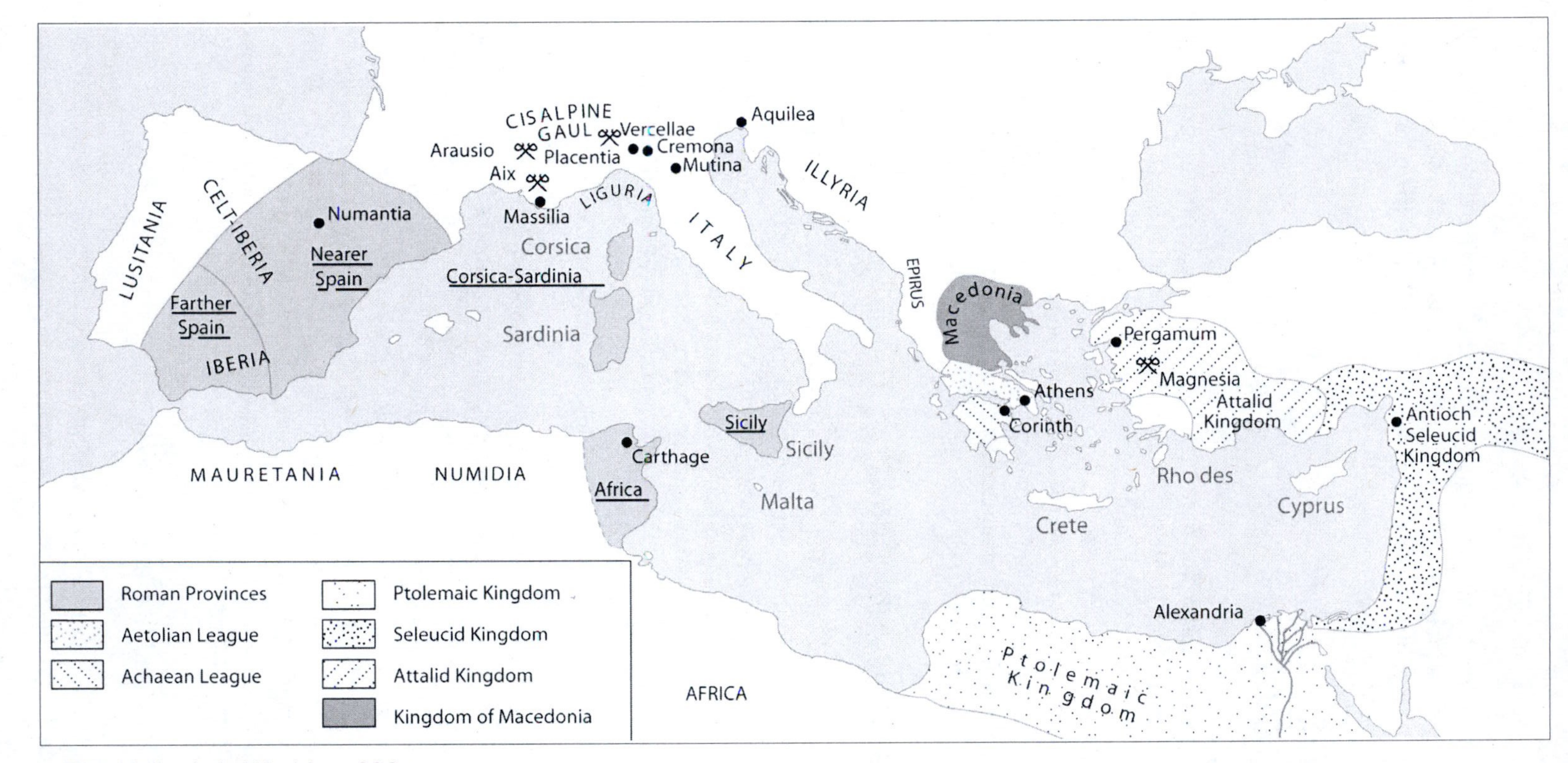

The Hellenistic World ca 200 B.C.

the *pax Romana*. Spain was the grave yard of the reputations of many Roman generals and of Rome's principles of *fides* and just wars. It is not just a coincidence that the decline of the Roman Republic was assigned by some later Roman historians to Rome's poor behavior and disastrous experiences in the Iberian Peninsula.

## 2. MACEDONIA AND THE EAST

Rome's conquest of Tarentum and southern Italy gave it a frontier on the Adriatic and Ionian Seas across which lay Illyria, Epirus, Macedonia, and Greece. Piracy was a time-honored occupation of the Illyrians, and by late third century B.C. had reached epic proportions. Not that Rome was directly affected or that the Senate cared that much about the problem, but numerous Greek cities in Italy were suffering and appealed to Rome for help. In responding to these requests Rome was doing what it did or claimed to have done in Italy, namely, defend the freedom of civilized, urbanized people against unruly mountaineers, bandits, and pirates. As in the past, however, such campaigns tended to have unintended consequences.

### The First Macedonian War

With characteristic efficiency, Rome suppressed the pirates of Illyria in 229 B.C., and with an equally natural instinct for propaganda the Senate sent legations throughout Greece to announce the good news. Envoys went to Athens, the cultural center of Greece, and to Corinth, where the Isthmian Games were being held, thus guaranteeing that Greeks from many parts of the Hellenic world heard of Rome's defense of Greek freedoms. In 219 B.C. Rome was forced, once again, to intervene in Illyria to curtail continuing piracy in that area. Rome, however, had no interest in a permanent presence across the Adriatic and, having taught the Illyrians a lesson, brought its forces back to Italy.

Philip V, Macedonia's young and ambitious king, had plans to expand his influence toward the Adriatic and sought to take advantage of Rome's weakness after the battle of Trasimene in 217 B.C. Hence he felt it astute politically to align himself with Hannibal after the latter's great victory at Cannae in 216 B.C. The Senate, naturally, regarded this opportunistic action as a stab in the back. However, there was not much it could do in response to Philip, given its weak situation in Italy. It was forced to look for an ally to wage war on its behalf against the Macedonians and found the proxy in the Aetolian League, an old Greek enemy of Macedonia. Rome conducted some naval operations against Philip, but its main efforts had to be directed elsewhere. The war petered out in 206 B.C. when the Aetolians made peace with Philip, and a year later the Romans also made peace. Thus ended the so-called First Macedonian War.

### The Second Macedonian War

The causes of the Second Macedonian War are not well understood and are much disputed among historians, ancient as well as modern. Livy simplified the issue, for exam-

**Clouds Looming in the West**

*When the news of the Roman defeat at Trasimene in 217 B.C. at the hands of Hannibal arrived in Greece, the ambitious king of Macedonia, Philip V, was, according to Polybius, inflamed by the possibility of extending his kingdom westwards. The following is Polybius' version of a speech addressed to Philip at a conference. The speaker urged the Greeks to stop the* "wars and the games that we play with one another" *and unite in self-defense against barbarian invaders (meaning Roman barbarians). Polybius adds that Philip agreed with the speaker's sentiments because he had already, for his own reasons, come to a similar conclusion. Whatever the truth of the motives ascribed by Polybius to the king, the speech suggests that concerned Greeks were well aware of what was happening in the west and of the potential consequences for Greece of the struggle between Rome and Carthage.*

"It would be best if the Greeks should no longer make war on one another but rather should regard it as a favor of the gods if they could all speak with one voice and by joining hands like men crossing a river should repel barbarian invaders and protect themselves and their cities. If this kind of unity is impossible to maintain indefinitely I urge you at the present to at least agree on a common plan for safety in view of the size of the armies and the greatness of the war being waged in the west. For it is evident... that whether the Carthaginians beat the Romans or the Romans the Carthaginians, it is not likely that the winners will be satisfied with their possessions in Italy and Sicily, but are certain to come here and extend their ambitions beyond what is right. Therefore I beg you all, and especially you King Philip, to protect yourselves against this danger....If you wait for the clouds that now loom in the west to settle over Greece then I greatly fear that the truces and wars and the games in general that we play with one another will be so rudely interrupted that we will beg the gods for an opportunity to still make war and peace among ourselves, that is, to still have the power to manage our own quarrels ourselves [without the intervention of outsiders]" (Polybius 5.104).

ple, by saying that, as was typically the case, Rome as a good ally came legitimately to the defense of her friends under attack by Philip in the east. Undoubtedly this was an aspect of the situation, but there were other causes at work. Philip was increasing his influence in the Aegean, and the Romans would have preferred to see a weak rather than a strong Macedonia. Then there were internal factors present at Rome. Among the nobles there was a desire to exceed or at least match the great prestige gained by Scipio Africanus in his victory over Hannibal. Campaigns in the east, unlike those in the west, were likely to bring much booty and many clients in addition to glory. Then there were the ever-present lobbyists of Greek cities whose contacts with senatorial households in Rome gave them an ability to affect indirectly the debate in the Roman Senate. The kingdom of Pergamum and the important naval state of Rhodes who were both, along with Athens, at war with Philip, naturally wanted Rome to intervene on their side and raised the specter of an alliance between Philip and the Hellenistic king of Syria, Antiochus III. An important factor driving all of this was weakness or near collapse of the Ptolemaic state of Egypt between 207 and 200 B.C., as a result of native revolts and dynastic instability. Both Philip and Antiochus were tempted to seize the opportunity to enlarge their respective territories, thus altering the balance of power in the whole eastern Mediterranean. Although Rome was still attempting to recover from the long and terrible war with Hannibal, the Senate came to the conclusion that the danger of inaction in the east was far greater than the costs and risks of a decisive intervention there.

FLAMININUS AND CYNOSCEPHALAE Rome challenged Philip to stop attacking the Greek states and, when he refused, launched a war against him. Early commanders had only moderate success, but at Cynoscephalae in 197 B.C. the able general Titus Quinctius Flamininus defeated Philip and forced him to sue for peace. The Senate's object, as in Spain and elsewhere, was not the direct acquisition of territory or the complete destruction of Macedonia as a center of power but only its weakening and curtailment within suitable limits. This was achieved by balancing Macedonia against Aetolia and winning over the Greek states by granting them their freedom. The announcement by Flamininus' heralds that Greece was to be ungarrisoned and tribute-free was made for maximum propaganda effect at the Isthmian games in 196 B.C. and was received with enthusiasm by the Greeks, who thought they could now go back to their—from a Roman perspective—feckless ways. Unfortunately, the Greeks had difficulty in understanding what exactly friendship with Rome meant or how Romans understood the term freedom. It was to take more wars and the breaking up of Macedonia for the ambiguities of their relationship to be finally resolved.

## The Syrian War with Antiochus

The first of these wars was provoked by Rome's old ally, the militarily powerful but culturally backward Aetolian League. The Aetolians had hoped to fill the power vacuum left by Rome's defeat of the Macedonians, but Rome had no intention of allowing this to happen. Disappointed, the Aetolians turned for help to the Seleucid King of Syria, Antiochus III with whose possessions in Asia Minor Rome was now in contact.

Rome's evacuation of Greece after the defeat of Philip had won it much good will so that when Antiochus landed in Greece in 192 B.C. to "liberate the Greeks," he received a cool reception and was easily driven out of Greece by the Romans who quickly returned in 190 B.C. He was followed to Asia Minor by a Roman army under the command of Lucius Cornelius Scipio, the brother of the famous Scipio Africanus, who accompanied Lucius as an advisor. With the assistance of their Greek allies, the Romans completely defeated Antiochus at Magnesia in Asia Minor. An enormous indemnity and arms reduction was im-

**Coin of Flamininus**

*Flamininus issued a gold coin commemorating his victory over Philip V and the Macedonians and his freeing of the Greeks. The reverse shows Victory, by this time a well-established Roman symbol originally borrowed from the Greeks. This coin was the earliest coin portrait of a Roman. In Rome, Flamininus' Greek clients erected a bronze statue to him with a Greek inscription. He was the first to develop a policy of making the cities and leagues of the Greek world clients of Rome—and of himself. A typical patrician noble, he combined patriotism and family loyalty with frank self-promotion.*

posed on Antiochus which eventually led to the destruction of Seleucid power in the east. Rome's allies Rhodes and Pergamum were rewarded, and at the Peace of Apamea in 188 B.C. a new balance of power was established in the eastern Mediterrnaean. Having seen its two old rivals Macedonia and Syria go down to defeat Ptolemaic Egypt, and anyway weak at this time, had no intention of challenging Rome

## The Third Macedonian War

Rome handled Greece by a combination of cynical manipulation and reliance on its old client-patron approach to foreign policy. This approach, however, led to continuing misunderstandings and mistakes by both allies and enemies alike. It also had negative consequences for Rome. By engaging in alliances with Greek states Rome inevitably became involved in the tangle of inter-state relations that had frustrated the efforts of Greek peoples, statesmen, generals, and philosophers for the previous five hundred years. Rome found itself constantly besieged by multiple factions and governments trying to manipulate it in their own self-interest against other factions or states. On one occasion there were no less than four sets of envoys in Rome claiming to speak for Sparta. Such a situation put

The Aegean World ca. 200 B.C.

Greek states at the mercy of Rome but it also dragged Rome into the demoralizing world of Greek diplomacy where it quickly learned or perhaps better, perfected its arts of casuistry, equivocation and trouble making. It is not as though the Romans were unable to comprehend the subtlety and sophistication of Greek diplomacy. Flamininus, the victor over Philip V, spoke fluent Greek and was himself a manipulator of the first rank. To impress Greek public opinion he dedicated trophy shields at the shrine of Delphi; he had nothing to learn from Greek diplomatic techniques. Scipio Africanus wrote to Philip in Greek and another general, Tiberius Sempronius Gracchus, while on an embassy to Greece addressed the Rhodians in Greek. Unlike many other imperial peoples, the mastery of foreign languages and cultures was recognized by the Romans as an essential tool of power.

A suspicious move by one of the states under surveillance by Rome or the complaint of an ally jealous of its neighbor led time and again to investigations by Roman comissions. These in turn provoked confrontations. A combination of circumstances of this type led after the death of Philip V to a final conflict between Macedonia under his son Perseus, and the Romans. A marriage alliance between Perseus and Seleucids and the growth of Macedonia's economic and military resources, together with the allegations of Eumenes king of neighboring Pergamum and a trusted ally of Rome, led to war and the final overthrow of the kingdom of Macedonia at the battle of Pydna in 168 B.C.

AFTERMATH In the aftermath of the war, Macedonia was divied into four autonomous but weak republics, and for the first time tribute was imposed on an eastern state. Thus did one of the world's great nations pass into political oblivion. Thinking of the sudden demise of Macedonia and the vagaries of Fortune, Polybius was reminded of the comparison the philosopher Demetrius of Phaleron had drawn at an earlier time between Persia and Macedonia. Fifty years ago, Demetrius mused, who would have thought that mighty Persia would be overwhelmed by unknow Macedonia—and so quickly forgotten. He goes on to say:

> Fortune never makes deals with life and always defeats our calculations by some novel move. She is forever demonstrating to us her power by foiling our expectations. And now it seems to me that in putting Macedonia in possession of the wealth of Persia she proved to all that her investiture of Macdonia with the insignia of empire was equally revocable and contingent upon her will. (Polybius 29.21)

Polybius was moved to reflect that just as Persia had been defeated by upstart Macedonia now Macedonia had been overwhelmed by upstart Rome. Delicately Polybius left it to his readers to make the obvious conclusion about the eventual fate of Rome.

Neighboring Epirus was punished with the mass enslavement of 150,000 of its population. The Greek Boeotian league was dissolved. Its democratic constitution, which Rome identified with instability, found little sympathy at Rome. Rhodes, Rome's former ally was weakened because it had make the mistake of proposing to mediate between Rome and Macedonia when the Romans seemed to have have difficulty bringing Perseus to a decisive confrontation. Attalus of Pergamum, who was also involved in mediation efforts, was likewise punished and suffered eclipse as Rome's foremost ally in Asia Minor.

## The Achaean War and the End of Carthage

This was not the end of Rome's involvement in Greek affairs. Rome pursued the same policies in Greece it had followed in its conquest of the western Mediterranean. Rome was slow to take on responsibility for the direct supervision and administration of conquered territory but preferred to eliminate one center of power after another and slowly taught inculcate the rules under which state affairs were to be conducted in the future. Its allies were at times slower to understand the new rules than were enemies as the recent examples of Aetolia, Rhodes and Pergamum suggested. Now another old ally of Rome, the Achaean League was about to find out just how much freedom it was permitted to settle affairs in its own area of control, the Peloponnese. The story is worth telling in its own right to illustrate the intractability of so many Greco-Roman interatctions.

EXASPERATING THE ROMANS The tale begins in around 157 B.C. when, for unknown reasons, Athens sacked the Boeotian frontier town of Oropus. Oropus promptly sent a delegation to Rome to ask for redress and the Senate referred the issue to the city of Sicyon for arbitration. The resulting verdict was unfavorable to Athens, which was ordered to pay a huge fine. Athens immediately appealed to the Senate and the fine was reduced. In the meanwhile Athens garrisoned Oropus and expelled those citizens who did not go along

**Victory Monument of Aemilius Paullus at Delphi**

*This monument was originally built by Philip V to commemorate his victories over the Greeks. After the defeat of his son and successor Perseus by Aemilius Paullus the conqueror appropriated the plinth, replaced Philip's statue with his own, and added the inscription: "Lucius Aemilius, commander, captured this from Perseus and the Macedonians." Rome appropriated Greek culture and symbols in more senses than one. Fragments of the frieze around the top of the monument showing Roman soldiers defeating Macedonians, survive to the present day.*

with its highhanded actions. Oropus once again appealed to Rome and, getting nowhere, turned to the Achaean League for help.

They were unlucky there too at first, and resorted to bribing a number of key figures in the League's administration. This worked. The League threatened action, and Athens backed off. But this was not the end of the affair. The bribed League officials began to quarrel among themselves and their fight escalated into a dispute with a reluctant League member, Sparta. Once again the issue ended up in Rome. Meanwhile a revolt had broken out in Macedonia led by a pretender by the name of Andriscus who claimed to be the son of the last Macedonian king, Perseus. Distracted by this, Rome took its time about solving the Oropus (now a League) affair, and a small civil war broke out between the League and Sparta. At this the Senate decreed that Sparta should leave the League. The League responded by declaring war on Sparta, and Rome decided to intervene militarily. The city of Corinth, where a Roman delegation had been insulted and abused by the mob in 147 B.C., was made an object lesson to the rest of Greece. In 146 B.C. this ancient and fabled city was thoroughly looted and then destroyed by the Roman general Lucius Mummius. Its art works were carried off to Italy. The Achaean League survived in a weakened condition. Two years earlier, after the revolt of Andriscus in Macedonia had been finally put down, the four republics were dissolved and the country made subject to direct Roman rule as a province. Now those states that had fought against Rome in the Achaean War were made formally subject to the governor of Macedonia. In this way all of Greece came under the general supervision of Rome.

THE END OF CARTHAGE The same year (146 B.C.) that saw the end of Corinth saw the destruction of Carthage, Rome's old rival in the west. The combination of the complaints of allies and Roman suspicions that brought on confrontations in Greece in the past had the same effect in Africa. There the growing economic strength of Carthage, Roman paranoia and a stream of complaints from the Numidian king Masinissa finally brought Rome to a decision to destroy the city. The case for the destruction of Carthage was argued with great force by the venerable censor Cato who was supposed to have closed all his speeches in the Senate with the phrase "and I say Carthage must be destroyed" (*delenda est Carthago!*).

His opponent, Scipio Nasica said that there was no just cause for war and besides the elimination of Carthage would fatally weaken Rome internally by the removing an external threat which kept Rome from overconfidence and hubris. Carthage, he said, should be considered "a counterweight of fear." Eventually Cato won his point, and war was declared and Carthage put under siege. The fall of the city after heroic resistance to P. Cornelius Scipio Aemilianus is described graphically by the historian Polybius, who was present at the siege. According to Polybius Scipio shed tears and quoted a line from Homer: "The day shall come in which our sacred Troy... shall perish" (Appian 8.132). Scipio, of course, had Rome in mind. The ruins of Carthage were cursed, and yet another province, Africa, was added and came under the direct control a Roman governor.

## 3. ROME'S EMPIRE

In 146 B.C. Rome emerged as the dominant power in the whole Mediterranean. Under its direct control were the provinces of Nearer and Further Spain, Sardinia-Corsica, Sicily, Africa and Macedonia. Not long afterwards Asia Minor and southern Gaul were added. Cowed by Rome's power or enmeshed in its system of client-state relations were the Hellenistic Kingdoms of Seleucid Syria and Ptolemaic Egypt and dozens of independent cities, petty states, and tribal peoples. In skeletal form this was to be the eventual shape of what we know as the Roman empire.

The Romans had no preconceived plans for the conquest of Italy, the western Mediterranean, and finally the Greek east. Some conquests came as a result of responses to importuning allies. "By defending our allies," Cicero wrote with some sarcasm, "we have come to dominate the whole world" (*de re publica* 3.23). Early wars in Italy were defensive in nature, ad hoc, and fueled by a mixture of fear, glory seeking, and land hunger. With reason the Romans feared and hated the Samnites, Celts, and Carthaginians. It was a different story when they encountered the powers of the Hellenistic world, but by then Rome had been hardened by its experiences in the western Mediterranean. Nevertheless, fear was a factor in the Second Macedonian War and the war against Antiochus. Rome had become an imperial power. Inevitably its empire became institutionalized. Vested interests arose and ensured that the empire did not decrease. The elite wanted prestige and the people the tangible benefits of empire. Once taxes and booty began rolling in, Romans were naturally reluctant to let go of their conquests.

### Why Nations Rule Other Nations

Writing in the fifth century, the Greek historian Thucydides reports on a debate at Sparta in which an Athenian ambassador attempted to defend Athens' empire. He did so by explaining why, universally, nations acquire empires, why it is difficult for them to let go of them once they have been acquired, and what, if any, justification can be made for imperial rule. The speaker admits that while Athens had acquired its empire "first through fear," soon afterwards "honor and profit" entered the picture, making it impossible for

Athens to give up its rulership. The speaker goes on to claim that in being driven by the universal human emotions of honor, fear, and profit, the three driving forces for empire, Athenians were not acting contrary to human nature. Furthermore, Athens was not the first to act this way. Empires were always acquired in response to these emotional drives. He goes on: By their nature empires are always unpopular. But, so what? The only true choice is "between governing strongly or endangering one's own security." What counts in the end is whether, when a nation has actually acquired an empire, it rules justly: "Men deserve praise," the Athenian speaker says, "when in obedience to human nature they exercise rule over others, and yet show more justice than the extent of their power allows."[1] The Romans would have agreed.

We should be wary of projecting contemporary concerns with national sovereignty, isolationism, and interventionism into the distant past. At the time when Rome was winning its empire it was considered respectable to want to rule. Thucydides' view was unexceptional. Neither isolation nor pacifism was an option in the anarchic world of Europe and the Mediterranean. War was a normal and accepted exercise of sovereignty and was recognized as such by the international community. Plato opined, perhaps with tongue in cheek, that "in reality all states are in a natural state of perpetual, if undeclared, war with every other state" (*Laws* 625d).

## Restraints on Imperial Expansion

The impulse to having more, however, clashed with a variety of internal constraints at Rome that had nothing to do with the justice or injustice of imperial rule. An important conservative element in the Roman elite recognized that continued expansion posed a threat to the balance of power within the governing class and undermined the republican or *polis* character of Rome. There was strong resistance, for instance, to the settlement of individual Roman homesteaders in the distant Sabine lands conquered during the Samnite Wars and in the *ager Gallicus* on the Adriatic coast. Rome was generally reluctant to annex territory and even more reluctant to take direct responsibility for administering and maintaining order in distant provinces. Then, in the second century B.C. the pattern of warfare changed. Roman armies did not march every year to war as they did in the fourth and third centuries. Periods of intense warfare alternated with relatively peaceful interludes. The elite, despite its yen for glory, did not want to see individual members gain too much glory and rise above their peers in the opinion of the people. In the first century, when glory-seeking leaders were willing to ignore their peers' envy and disapproval and identify their own success with that of Rome's, the way was opened to one-man rule.

## The Historiography of Roman Imperialism

The nature of Roman imperialism was much debated in antiquity, and the debate has continued to the present. Contemporary political, social, and cultural currents inevitably affect historical judgments. In the nineteenth century when empires and emperors were common

[1] Thucydides, *The Peloponnesian War* 1.75–76.

in Asia and Europe, many (though not all) scholars argued that Rome's acquisition of empire was mainly defensive. Empire was justified, they claimed, on the principle that unruly people who could not govern themselves and made the lives of their settled neighbors miserable should be ruled by those who could rule themselves. On the other hand, in the twentieth century the collapse of Asian and European empires after World War II, the war in Vietnam, and the optimism generated by the fall of the Soviet Union in 1991 led some western scholars to categorize all empires as inevitably unjust and unnecessary, beneficial neither to conquerors nor to the conquered. To these scholars, Rome was a uniquely belligerent and violent society. It sent out armies year after year in search of booty and slaves to sustain its insatiable social needs of honor, glory, and material prosperity. Each conquest required another. In this view the Romans were hard wired for imperialism.

More recent scholars, however, are less inclined to see Rome as uniquely violent, arguing, for example, that within the "anarchic interstate [world of antiquity] every major state, every medium-sized state, and even many small states were highly militarized societies, habituated to employing violence and threats to achieve their aims."[2] To this list should be added the presence at times of even more dangerous, even more highly militarized non-state peoples such as Celts and Germans and the violent nomadic peoples of the Eurasian steppe such as the Huns. In the context of the world in which they lived, Rome was no more violent than any other militarized state.

This book does not aim to settle the argument over the justice or injustice of empires and imperial rule. That is properly the role of political philosophers and ethicists. By reviewing previous chapters, readers can make up their own minds whether Rome was justified or not in waging war as it did in Italy against the Samnites, Celts, and others or later with the Carthaginians in the west and the powerful Hellenistic monarchies in the east. The argument presented so far in this book is that what made Rome different from the many other militarized, belligerent states of its day was not that it was more or less just or violent than others, but that it was better organized, better led, more adaptable, and had, at the time of its conquests, greater internal cohesion than its opponents. It did not, as a society, fall apart and lose its nerve when confronted with serious challenges. Its elite did not betray it as did the elites of so many Greek cities. The population at large lived up to its responsibilities and did not feud incessantly with the leadership. This formula won for Rome its empire. The question of its justice came later.

JUSTICE AND IMPERIAL RULE The case for justice was argued by the Greek Stoic philosopher, Panaetius of Rhodes, who was a member of the entourage of Scipio Aemilianus, the destroyer of Numantia and Carthage. Combining the Stoic ideal of moral duty and the old Roman concept of good faith (*fides*) and just wars, he argued that the empire was justified only if the Romans used their strength fairly and conscientiously for the good of the people they ruled. It was to this high duty, he suggested, that Rome was called by destiny and for which it was particularly well equipped. Rome had become great through its pious observance of its duties to the gods, who in turn had repaid piety with

[2] Arthur. M. Eckstein in Craige B. Champion, *Roman Imperialism: Readings and Sources*, Malden, MA: 2004, 6.

prosperity. By divine law good government was owed to conquered peoples. Panaetius' theory was a theory in search of practitioners.

As a people Romans recognized that the environment in which they lived was a dangerous one; they entertained few illusions about human nature and human society. This situation, however, changed. As the level of danger from the outside declined, Rome began to lose its internal social and political balance. That the absence of fear leads to social decline is an old explanation. Sallust, a careerist ally of Julius Caesar, in attempting to explain Rome's social upheaval in the first century B.C., argued that in the past "fear of enemies preserved the good morals of the state, but once this fear was removed, the vices of prosperity, licentiousness, and arrogance rose."[3] He was echoing a common theme. Modern historians, as we will see, prefer different explanations.

The formula that won an empire for Rome was poorly suited to maintaining it once it had been won. Between 133 B.C. and 31 B.C. Rome entered into a protracted period of internal disorder and civil war that nearly destroyed it. That it survived this period of chaos and was able to re-invent itself yet again is itself a commentary on the character of Rome's political culture. This reinvention or transformation of Rome in the second and first centuries B.C. will be the subject of the next section.

[3] *Jugurthine War* 41.

# Part Two

# The Fall of the Roman Republic

## 1. INTRODUCTION AND OVERVIEW

The Fall of the Roman Republic (sometimes known as the Roman Revolution or the Transformation of the Roman Republic) is one of the great events of world history, comparable to the more recent American, French, Russian, and Chinese Revolutions. Like them, it is complex and difficult to understand. It is, however, of special interest to citizens of contemporary constitutional states. The media often draws attention to the number of long-established autocracies that have become free states in the last 50 years, suggesting that, optimistically, history is moving in the right direction (i.e., in the direction of freedom). Perhaps; but it is useful to be reminded that the opposite process, the transition of a long-established constitutional state from freedom to military autocracy, as was the fate of the Roman Republic, is also a possibility. In any case, the acquisition of great power by states, whether constitutional or not, does not occur without generating proportionately large amounts of internal stress. The history of the Fall of the Republic is the story of how Romans handled the internal crisis created by their accession to power in the Mediterranean.

## 2. THE HISTORIOGRAPHIC TRADITION: ANCIENT AND MODERN EXPLANATIONS

Among the Romans themselves there were two basic schools of thought regarding the causes of the Fall of the Republic; both were moral. We have already seen one at the end

### The Corruption of Rome by Wealth

*One of the commonest explanations advanced by Romans for the fall of the Republic was the influence of wealth. Livy, an historian of the late Republic, thought that the rot began with the return from Asia in 187 B.C. of the booty-laden army of Manlius Vulso.*

The origins of foreign luxury were brought to Rome by the returning army [of Manlius]. They were the first to introduce into Rome bronze couches, expensive rugs as covers, curtains and other elaborate woven fabrics, and what *then* were thought to be exotic pieces of furniture—tables with a single leg and marble topped sideboards. To banquets were added women lute and harp players and other pleasures of the feast. The banquets themselves began to be prepared with greater care and expenditure. Then the cook, for our ancestors the lowest of slaves in terms of both actual worth and use, began to have real value. What had been regarded as a mere labor now became an art! Yet these things, which at the time were thought to be remarkable, were merely the seeds of the luxury to come (Livy 39.6).

of the previous chapter. This was the argument that the elimination of all serious rivals freed Romans from the fear of external threats. Once fear was removed the door was opened to destructive rivalries among individual aristocrats who cared more for their interests than for the common good, the *res publica*. The other explanation was that the 187 B.C. return of Manlius Vulso's army, laden with spoils, began the process of undermining the values and morals (the *mos maiorum*) that had made Rome great. Greed, luxury, and corruption destroyed the republic. Cicero cites the aphorism of the third/second century B.C. poet Ennius: "the *res publica* of Rome was founded firmly on ancient customs and men of valor" but then goes on to say "what now is left of the 'ancient customs' on which the '*res publica* of Rome was built'? They have been so completely buried in forgetfulness that not alone are they no longer practiced, they are already unknown" (Cicero, *de re publica* 5.1–2).

In the eighteenth century Montesquieu offered still a different explanation: The size of the empire and the growth of the city of Rome overwhelmed the republic. Armies and generals ceased to serve the state but pursued their own private objectives. The republic failed because members of its elite were no longer able to agree on what constituted the common good. Liberated from restraint, ambition triumphed. Rome foundered on its empire.

In the nineteenth century there was a tendency to see the fall in terms of a struggle between two large, ideologically driven, class-based parties, the one aristocratic and traditional (the *optimates,* "The Best"), the other democratic and reform-minded (the *populares*, "The People's Party"). This view of the Fall emerged in the context of the clash in Europe from the French Revolution onwards of what were seen as similarly minded groups. Twentieth-century scholars preferred to regard the clash between *optimates* and *populares* as a choice of tactics in the struggle for power within the ruling class rather the clash of organized political parties. Factions of nobles made ad hoc alliances to achieve particular goals. Class, at least in the modern sense of the term, is rejected as an inappropriate, anachronistic mode of analysis for ancient Rome.

Most recent interpreters see the Fall as a series of systemic failures, economic, social, military, and most of all political. The empire was too large to be maintained in peace by the old system of government, which at best suited the rule of a small city-state. Rome was now a world state and needed an appropriate form of government to manage it—to the extent it could be managed at all. However effective Rome's citizen army had been in winning wars, it was poorly suited to sustaining the needs of an empire.

## 3. THE CRISIS

Rome's crisis had been brewing for some time, but it was not fully apparent until the revolutionary activities of the Gracchi brothers (133 to 121 B.C.). Both brothers attempted to introduce major reform programs aimed at fixing a number of Rome's most outstanding problems, but both efforts ended in disaster. Tiberius, the elder brother, was murdered in 133 B.C., and his younger brother, Gaius, in 121 B.C. They were ever after thought of as either initiators of dangerous revolution or as martyrs to honest, liberal reform.

With the failure of comprehensive reform efforts in the second century B.C., Rome drifted from crisis to crisis. Some crises were generated by outside events, mostly wars, and others by internal conflicts, within Italy or Rome itself. Reforms were addressed piecemeal. Sometimes the solutions attempted created larger problems than the crises they were supposed to resolve. In the end the solution that was decided upon was the abandonment of the collective rule of the aristocracy and its replacement by the rule of a single man, not wholly an autocrat or dictator but someone more like a popular sovereign.

It is perhaps easy to sympathize with the traditionalists in the face of the tidal wave of change Rome faced from 200 B.C. onwards. Unfortunately for the upholders of the old way of doing things the changes were overwhelming. The traditional *polis*-based system on which Rome had been founded was no longer up to the task. Rome had to adjust to the reality of the newly acquired Empire. It could not let go of what it had acquired and retreat into isolationism and rural, cultural provincialism.

ROME'S CAPACITY FOR REINVENTION Perhaps we should be less surprised by the failure of Rome's reform efforts than that Rome and its empire survived at all. There were a number of occasions in the years of revolution between 133 B.C. and 30 B.C. when it seemed more likely that Rome's rickety empire would collapse rather than survive. It is a tribute to their basic political health that Romans eventually were able to cobble together a system that managed to prolong their empire for centuries. Cicero was right about the collapse of the Republic, but wrong about the "ancient customs and men" on which Rome was founded. With the same energy with which they acquired their empire, Romans plunged into the colossal job of transforming their *res publica* so that they could, as they hoped, keep their freedom while enjoying their empire. In the end they accomplished the latter but not the former; possibly they had no alternative. This is a judgment, however, that can only be arrived at by looking at the long story of the transformation of Rome between the Gracchi and the victory of Julius Caesar's adopted son Octavian over Antony and Cleopatra at the battle of Actium in 31 B.C. Chapter 8, the first in this section, deals with some of the most important problems Rome faced as a result of its acquisition of empire. Each of the remaining chapters in this part deals with a phase in the crisis of the Republic. Chapter 9 is devoted to the Gracchan revolution, while Chapter 10 introduces the first of the military strong-men, or dynasts as they are called, Marius and Sulla. The last chapter of the section, Chapter 11, presents the fall of the Republic at the hands of Pompey and Caesar, leaving alone on the stage the last and most successful of the dynasts, Octavian, later and better known as Augustus.

# 8

# The Consequences of Empire

Rome's transition from dominating Italy to dominating the entire Mediterranean inevitably transformed all aspects of Roman society. The shift from city-state to world-state, however, did not come easily. Rome's *polis* constitution—its *politeia*—had been stretched just to enable Rome to maintain its position in Italy. It failed when the rest of the Mediterranean world was thrust upon it. The problem was finding a replacement: Was there anything to put in its place? No one seemed to know of anything better. The legitimacy of Rome's existing *politeia* was never fundamentally challenged. Even the challengers did not advocate a new order, but that is what they got.

Under the impact of wealth from the empire the Roman economy shifted from one based on small property owners to a much more complex, monetized, mostly cash-crop economy. The elite fragmented, and new classes developed. Small property owners declined in numbers. The city of Rome grew in size and became home to a diverse society, dominated in terms of numbers by poor, free-born citizens, freedmen, and slaves. The cultural Hellenization of Rome, which had been in progress for centuries, was accelerated. The military gradually ceased to be a citizen militia made up of draftees from the property-owning class and became, by some point in the first century B.C., a de facto standing army of professional soldiers. The relationship with the allies in Italy (i.e., the large numbers of non-Romans outside the commonwealth), deteriorated to the breaking point.

## 1. THE ECONOMIC TRANSFORMATION

### The Impact of Empire on the Economy of Rome

The wars of the second century brought a gigantic flow of booty to Rome from the ransacked cities and lands of Greece, north Africa, and Spain. Indemnities from Macedonia,

Carthage, and Syria; taxes from Sicily, Asia Minor, and elsewhere; and the products of the fabulous mines of Spain and Macedonia swelled Rome's income to enormous proportions. Although most of this money stayed at the top, some trickled down to the masses in various forms, such as improved services and communications, a share in war booty for soldiers, and most importantly, the elimination in 167 B.C. of the *tributum*, the principal tax to which Romans were subject.

Outside of land and trade the Roman economy offered little or no opportunity for investment. There was no stock or bond market, and no manufacturing sector that could profitably soak up the surplus income of the empire. Banking was rudimentary. If, however, there were few opportunities for the aristocracy to save and invest, they had powerful systemic impulses towards spending. Understandably so, as public display was how an aristocracy sustained itself. There were other impulses towards spending. The needs of a rapidly growing city, the imperial administration, and the army had to be met. These needs in turn created an expansion of employment in non-agricultural sectors of the economy and drew people to Rome from all over Italy and the Mediterranean. The population of Rome expanded greatly during the second century reaching in the neighborhood of one million by the late first century B.C.

A BUILDING BOOM Rome launched a building boom in the second century B.C. that continued on and off for the next 500 years. Little, unfortunately, is visible of the buildings from the Republican period, and the huge monuments of brick, concrete and marble that can be seen in Rome today are the products of the Empire. Older aqueducts such as the Aqua Appia were repaired and two new ones, the Aqua Marcia and the Aqua Tepula, were constructed. As a result Rome's water supply was more than doubled. In 184 B.C. the censors Cato and Flaccus spent large sums on drainage and sewage systems and over the years new bridges (the Mulvian and Aemilian), basilicas (Sempronian, Aemilian, and Opimian),[1] temples, shrines, warehouses, porticoes, granaries, sidewalks, and shopping areas were built. Statues and arches proliferated. The second century B.C. witnessed the construction of Rome's first marble buildings. The Temple of Jupiter on the Capitoline Hill was adorned with a fine gilded ceiling. Throughout Italy building projects funded by the local elites embellished towns with baths, forums, basilicas, and temples. The art objects L. Mummius had looted from ancient Corinth after he sacked it in 146 B.C. were distributed throughout the towns and provinces of Italy as his surviving inscriptions boast. The simple style of construction that had characterized the private town and country houses of the aristocracy in the past disappeared. Now in possession of huge private fortunes the elites set about constructing lavish country villas and town houses that had every available embellishment that imported Hellenistic architects and artists could devise. Aviaries and fish ponds and heated baths warmed by air ducts in walls and floors, became common. Country villas had their grounds laid out in imitation of natural scenery and were adorned with towers, bridges, pavilions, statues, exotic trees, artificial islands and streams.

ROAD CONSTRUCTION Throughout Italy in the second century B.C. a great network of trunk roads was constructed, linking one end of the peninsula with the other and tying Rome's colonies directly to the metropolis. In the north the Po valley was dissected by the

[1] Basilicas were large public buildings designed for court hearings and other judicial and political functions.

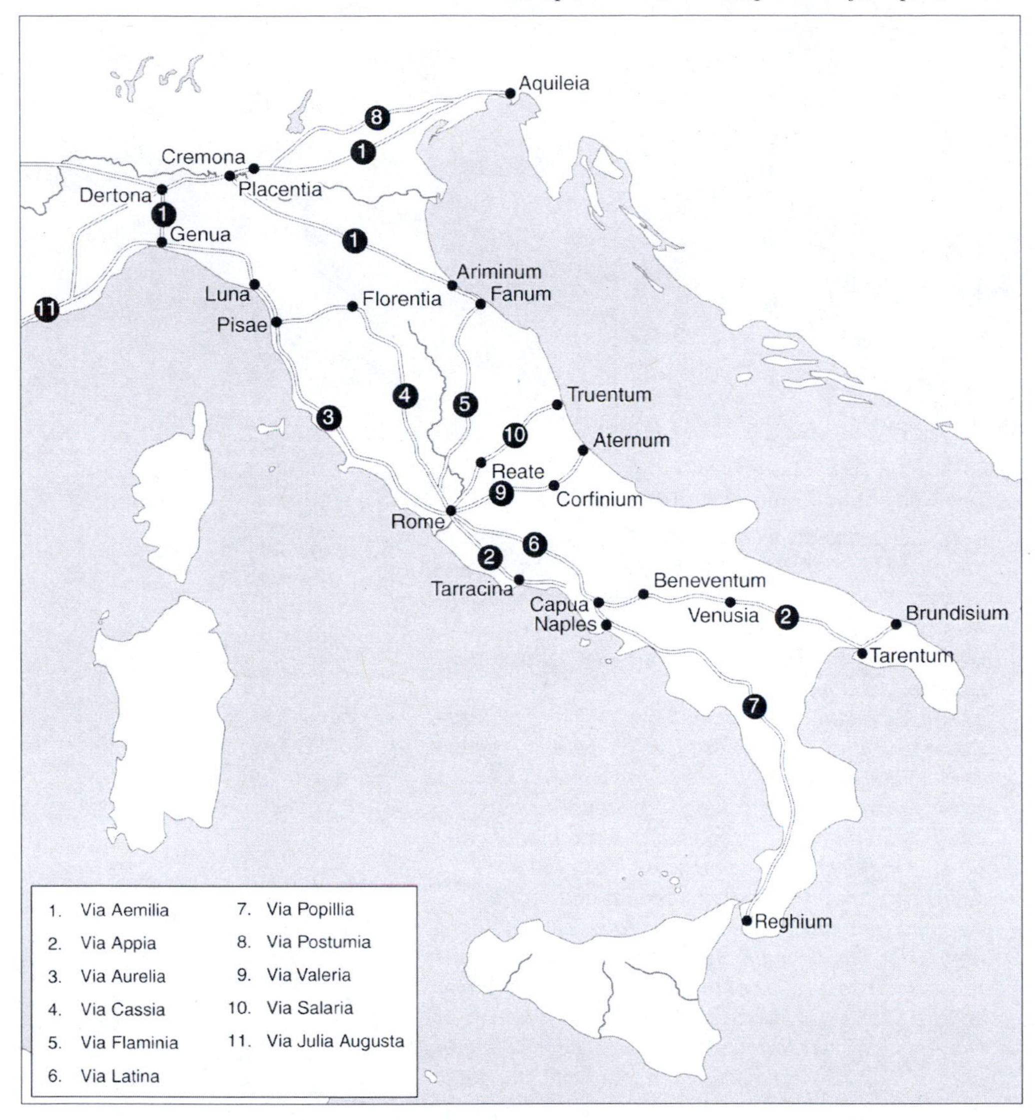


Roads of Italy, Second and First Centuries B.C.

Via Aemilia and the Via Postumia, which linked Genoa on the west to Aquileia and Ariminum on the Adriatic. Another consular road, the Via Aurelia-Aemilia, ran along the coast from Rome to Genoa. Other major roads were built in the mountainous regions of central Italy. The old Via Valeria was reconstructed, and the Via Annia extended the Via Appia all the way from Campania to Rhegium in the toe of Italy. A new route through the Liris valley was established for the Via Latina between Rome and Campania. In addition to these trunk roads, secondary roads sprang up to serve local needs and connect bypassed towns with the main routes. In the provinces, too, roads were constructed, such as the Via Egnatia, which traversed Macedonia, and the Via Herculea in Spain.

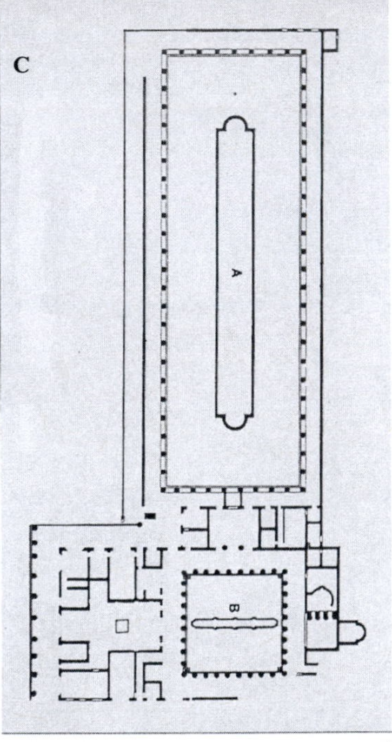


**The Economic Transformation of Italy**

*It is hard to find visual evidence of the huge economic transformation of Rome and Italy that began in the second century B.C. Much of the new construction was either incorporated into or built over in subsequent centuries. There are few surviving buildings datable to the late Republic. The following are a few examples taken from outside Rome. The Villa of the Papyri on which the modern Getty Villa and Museum in Malibu are modeled was frozen in time by its burial in A.D. 79 during the eruption of Mount Vesuvius. It is used as an example of the kind of villas that began to be built in the second century and first century B.C.* **A.** *The still-standing, second century B.C. Porta Augusta gate of Perugia shows the wealth and engineer skills that even an out-of-the way city in Italy possessed as a result of the expansion of the Empire.* **B.** *The second-century B.C. Bridge on the Via Praenestina near Rome still carries traffic.* **C.** *Ground plan of ther Villa of the Papyri, a relatively modest villa at Herculaneum.*

THE AGRICULTURAL REVOLUTION Although road construction was conducted for military purposes and did not have economic objectives in mind, it had the effect of opening up previously inaccessible and unprofitable Roman landholdings to Roman farmers, both large and small. Archaeological surveys show that land use intensified during the second century B.C. in many parts of Italy as the primeval forest was cut down and land came under cultivation for the first time. Northeast of Rome was a large area in which specialized farms produced vegetables, poultry, fish, flowers, and all sorts of luxury items (snails, boars, stags, and thrushes, for example) for the Roman market. Served by three main roads, the Via Flaminia, the Via Cassia, and the Via Clodia, this was a natural area for intensive farming. Similar "truck farming" regions were probably associated with cities throughout the peninsula. Elsewhere in Italy great groves of olive trees and vineyards were planted to supply the needs of an affluent population and to provide exports for growing markets overseas, especially in the west. In the south giant ranches (*latifundia*) were devoted to raising huge herds of cattle and sheep watched over by slave herders.

## Social and Military Consequences

These changes in the economy, coupled with the devastation of southern Italy caused by the war with Hannibal and the continuing demand for manpower for the legions, overflowed into Roman social and political life. The social character of Italian agriculture began to change. The peasant subsistence farmer, the backbone of the army, began to give way to the long-term volunteer, whose loyalty was more likely to be to his commander—or at least to whoever could pay his wages—than to the state.

In Rome, as in all *poleis*, there was an intimate connection between land, political, military, and social life. It was impossible to change the character of one of these without impacting the others. These relationships are so fundamental that they deserve to be reviewed in some detail, for without understanding them it will be difficult to appreciate some of the more explosive aspects of the collapse of the Republic.

REVOLUTIONARY EXPECTATIONS It is hard for modern readers to grasp the importance of land ownership (or at least access to land) to the peoples of pre-modern societies. This was especially true of *polis*-type societies where so much else was related to possession of land. There was nothing that could excite revolutionary feelings among *polis*-peoples than the loss of land or its ancient counterpart, the redistribution of land, (i.e., the process by which large estates owned by the rich were broken up into small parcels for distribution to the poor). Abolition of debt was a closely related revolutionary issue, because debt was the inevitable and natural concomitant of an agricultural economy. To the present, even in advanced economies, farmers every year go into debt for machinery, land, seed, fertilizer, etc., expecting to pay off their debts at harvest time. The market, the weather, insect infestations, and crop diseases—all unpredictable factors—can easily upset these calculations and result in a bad harvest. In modern economies governments try to even out the natural boom and bust cycle of farm life, but in pre-modern societies there were no such state-sponsored programs. In a cash crop economy small and medium-sized landowners went into debt to rich landowners, and in bad years they lost not just their harvests, but their land.

JOBS AND LAND In modern societies upwards of 97 percent of the population is sustained by the 3 percent of the population still engaged in agriculture. In ancient societies these percentages were reversed.[2] The small service and manufacturing segments of *polis* economies were mostly dominated by non-citizens and unfree labor. There was a reason for this. To work on a long-term basis for someone else—to hold a job or be em-

[2]Scholars argue about the percentages. Cities with advanced commercial sectors, particularly maritime cities in the eastern Mediterranean society, had a much lower percentage of their population engaged in agriculture. Athens, for example, was dependent on grain imported from the Ukraine and elsewhere in the Black Sea region for its survival. Athens, however, was an exceptional case.

ployed, as we would say—was not proper for a free citizen. Occasional part-time jobs were acceptable, but full-time employment was incompatible with the free status of citizens and their responsibilities to the state. Technically, therefore, there were no "jobs" in the modern sense of the word in a *polis* economy. Thus for the majority of the inhabitants of any given *polis*—including Rome—there was no alternative to a life engaged in food production. In such societies parents did not discuss what children were going to be when they grew up: they were all, male and female alike, going to be involved in one aspect of farming or another. The only matter of any importance was to how much land they might have access. In the Mediterranean world at least five hectares (12.5 acres), as well as access to common land for grazing, firewood collecting etc., was necessary for subsistence.[3] In the second century B.C., as the value of land increased small farmsteaders found themselves in competition with wealthy Roman and Italian landowners for access to common land. As they were cut off from access to this traditional subsidy their chances for economic survival were proportionately diminished.

HOUSEHOLD FORMATION From birth to death all any people talked about or dreamed about in *polis* society was land, crops, and weather. Everyone knew to the last square yard the quality of each field he owned, what it might or might not be useful for—as well as the quality of the neighbor's land. Everyone knew that no land meant no marriages, no families, no children. No children meant a miserable old age because the bargain between the generations was that parents looked after their children while they were young; and children, after inheriting their parents' property, looked after them when they could no longer work. The threat of loss of land, or its opposite, the possibility of acquiring more land, excited passions that have few parallels in modern society, where people move without much fuss from job to job, and from one residence to another. In the ancient world a family's very existence was tied to access to land.

There were a number of possible escapes from the Malthusian economies of the ancient *polis*. All involved suffering for somebody. For the Greeks, emigration to already established overseas colonies or mercenary service were possibilities. For Romans the principal outlet for surplus population was emigration to newly conquered lands, which as we have seen, tended to be farther and farther from the homeland. Naturally for the dispossessed of newly conquered lands life was bleak indeed, but these were the realities of the ancient agricultural economy.

LAND AND THE POLIS If access to land in all pre-modern societies was a matter of economic and social survival, in *polis* societies much more was involved: There were political dimensions to the possession of land. In a *polis* individuals were not mere peasants, the passive subjects of nobles and kings, but citizens with access to a wholly different kind of life, the life of civic freedom in autonomous states. By contrast, in non-*polis* agricultural society there were no politics, no access to power. There was nothing beyond the household and the village. Such peasants were confined to what Marx called "the idiocy of rural existence."

[3]Common land was a) land won by Rome in war, owned by the state as public land, *ager publicus*; and b) land outside private ownership such as forests, marshes, and hills.

WHAT LAND OWNERSHIP MEANT Here is where land was of overriding importance. In a *polis* ownership of land or property was the foundation of a citizen's rights and duties. It was his portal, his and his household's source of access to the full life of the city. Without land he was effectively marginalized and impoverished in more than an economic sense. The landless man and his household in a *polis* had weak legal rights and either no (or only very reduced) political influence. He could not serve in the main military units (phalanx or legion) of the *polis*, had little access to booty, and often ended up as the dependent of some better-off citizen. At Rome people of this status were known as *proletarii*, meaning they were people whose only possessions were their children (their *proles*) or, to put it another way, their children were the only contribution they could make to the state. At the other end of the spectrum were, of course, the great landowners who dominated the magistracies, the assemblies, and the Senate and provided the officers for the army. Their possessions gave them the leisure time to devote to politics, religion, and military affairs. In between was the great bulk of the Roman population, and on the security of their property depended, in the end, the stability of the state.

THE THREAT It was this great bulk of traditional Roman society that was threatened by the economic changes brought about in Italy as a result of the empire. We should not imagine that the tradition of small landownership was wiped out overnight in Italy, and that masses of landless people migrated to the cities of Italy, primarily to Rome itself. There was some of this, though its magnitude is hard to estimate. The picture is more complex.

In the confiscated lands of southern Italy large tracts of land were devoted to ranching, but around the old established colonies traditional farming went on as in the past. In central Italy, in the highlands, subsistence farming and transhumance continued. In areas where truck farming (i.e., farms that supplied perishable foods to local markets) was possible, subsistence farming disappeared and was replaced by cash-crop production. In the far north, in the Po valley, both subsistence and cash-crop farming coexisted around the urban centers that were evolving out of the old colonial settlements there.

In one way or another, the traditional economy of Italy was turned upside down. There was a strong tradition in Roman historiography that the small farmer, the source of manpower for the legions, was severely impacted, though precisely how this came about is unclear (see box "Social and Military Consequences of the New Economy"). According to this tradition, the land of the small farmers and of absentee soldiers was gobbled up by the rich who had an insatiable hunger for land. They also had the cash with which to exploit it. Maintaining an aristocratic lifestyle had always been an expensive business, and the ownership of large amounts of land was its basis. In the second and first centuries an aristocratic way of life became more expensive and more competitive. An affluent public presence was an essential attribute of aristocratic status, and loss of visibility meant loss of influence. Running for office for those in the elite who chose to pursue a political career was an also an increasingly expensive business. Each side justified its economic claims by reference to ideologies of land ownership (in the case of the poor) or aristocratic privilege (in the case of the rich).

Needless to say there was a price to be paid for the expansion of the land holdings of the wealthy. We have already seen that something like this—but for other reasons—had occurred in the fifth century (Chapter 5, Section 3). If the manpower pool of the army, namely the small farmers, declined, so would the size of the army. Yet the need for a constant supply of soldiers for the army was overwhelming, because the Mediterranean world was an inherently unstable region, and because by the second century B.C. Rome had made itself, perhaps inadvertently, its policeman. A further danger lay in the makeup of the dispossessed, the *proletarii*, although this was not immediately evident. The Roman *proletarii* were not apolitical, apathetic peasants down on their luck, but rather former citizen-landowners and, more to the point, former soldiers. They understood the political system, and they knew how to fight. All they needed to make their influence felt was someone to organize them, help them figure out what their interests were, and then lead them in the fight. That was not, of course, the Roman way, but as time passed there seemed to be no other alternative.

## The Impact of the Empire on the Elite

The expansion of Roman hegemony catapulted some, but not all members of the Roman aristocracy into an international arena that was full of cultural, social and economic temptations. Here we deal with the economic impact of the empire on the elite and some of its political implications.

Roman generals overseas were sometimes treated, and often acted, like gods. Statues were erected in their honor and cult was offered to them. They acquired friends among the conquered elites and became the patrons of whole cities and provinces. Vast fortunes came to them, sometimes under shady circumstances. The booty that had fallen into the hands of Roman generals in the past had been comparatively modest. Sacking some backward Samnite or Lucanian hamlet did not begin to produce the kind of riches that wars in the developed east did. In that part of the world undreamed-of opportunities for self-enrichment were thrown in the way of Roman generals and their armies. After losing the battle of Magnesia in 190 B.C. Antiochus, the Seleucid king of Syria, was forced to pay 18,000,000 denarii for the upkeep of the Roman army, yet Scipio Africanus never provided a satisfactory account of what happened to this great windfall.[4] In 177 B.C. 80,000 Sardinians are said to have been killed or sold into slavery. Ten years later Aemilius Paullus enslaved 150,000 unfortunate inhabitants of Epirus after concluding the war with Macedon. Even less rich provinces could still provide substantial rewards to enterprising generals and governors.

ROMAN-STYLE LOBBYING While much of the loot of empire circulated in the form of rewards to soldiers, gifts to friends, and the building of temples and public monuments, the general result was to create a gap within the elite between those who had access to these riches and those who did not. Further rifts were created in the ruling class when generals who had become patrons of foreign communities exercised their patronage. It was understandable that the elite of conquered areas would turn to their Roman patrons in case of trouble in their homelands or in the hope of influencing official Roman behavior towards

[4]At that time the ordinary Roman soldier made around 100 denarii a year.

**Social and Military Consequences of the New Economy**

*The biographer Plutarch, relying on earlier sources, gives the following account of the impact of the new economy on Italy. Unfortunately for small farmers there was no turning back the clock. Once Rome acquired an empire and Italy was flooded with money and urban populations expanded, it was inevitable that subsistence farming would be challenged and in some places replaced by cash crop farming or, as we know it, "agribusiness." The process is common in the modern world and no less tragic than it was two millennia ago. In Rome's case the elimination of the economic base of the citizen-militia was, however, fatal for the republican constitution. The land referred to was state-owned public land, which was leased out to long-term tenant farmers.*

> [For a time the rapacity of the rich was checked by law] and the poor remained on the land which they had originally been granted... but later on neighboring rich men used the names of fictitious tenants to obtain control of their leases and finally openly took possession of the greater part of the land under their own names. When the poor found themselves forced off their land they became unwilling to serve in the army or even to raise families. Soon a shortage of free men was apparent all over Italy. The places of the small proprietors were taken by gangs of slaves brought in from abroad. It was with these that the rich cultivated the estates from which they had driven off the free citizens (Plutarch, *Life of Tiberius Gracchus*, 8).

them or their communities. Naturally these clients came bearing gifts, and there was a real danger that their patrons would be seen as, or actually became, their lobbyists in Rome. The point was made by the reform-minded Scipio Aemilianus who warned a young African prince by the name of Jugurtha:

> to cultivate the friendship of the Roman people publicly rather than privately and not to make a habit of making presents to individuals. It was dangerous, he said, to buy from a few what belonged to the many. (Sallust, *Jugurthine War* 8.2)

Roman-style lobbying and gift taking was not quite as obvious an evil as it may appear. Laws regulating conflicts of interest are a modern development, whereas gift-giving and the exchange of favors of all kinds were a normal aspect of Roman social relations, especially between social unequals as, for example, between patrons and clients. The complication introduced by the acquisition of an empire was that the patronage of rich, overseas cities and states was of a different order of magnitude than traditional patronal relations in Rome and Italy. There was a fine line between the rights and duties of patrons and the needs of the state. Naturally, the great houses that lacked such overseas connections felt diminished and, when opportunity presented itself, created their own overseas connections. The very existence of the empire and Rome's way of running it thus escalated competition among the members of the ruling class. In the battle for clients and wealth the common good of Rome was not always the beneficiary.

## 2. THE CULTURAL TRANSFORMATION: THE EXAMPLE OF HISTORY WRITING

Following the flood of money to Rome came a flood of talent from the east as Rome began its appropriation of the rich cultural capital of the Greek world. Philosophers, artists, litterateurs, architects, doctors, professors, sculptors, skilled masons, jewelers, mosaicists—whole professional classes—came to fill the needs of the newly affluent, well-to-do classes of Roman society. Rome lacked the accumulated literature, art, and philosophy that centuries of precocious cultural development had produced in the Greek world, but it did not lack self-confidence. Its generals and ambassadors had already demonstrated this to the Hellenic world in previous centuries. Rome had its own ancient traditions of musical performance that were part of its public religious festivals and of the drinking feasts of the aristocracy, as well as an important heritage of art and architecture from the Etruscans. All these arts were transformed as we shall see, but the Hellenization of Rome was far from a one-way process as the following example of the development of Roman history writing shows.

### The Battle for Public Opinion

The Romans had a pressing need to tell their story, or to be more exact, to sell their version of their history to the Greeks. From long experience of contact with the Greek world Romans knew the importance of public opinion, and they recognized it was essential for them to respond to questions being raised throughout the Mediterranean about the origins of Rome, its ability to conquer Pyrrhus, the Gauls, and the Carthaginians (the last two ancient enemies of the Greeks), and what justification, if any, it had for possessing an empire. If the Romans could get their version to stick they would gain a major cultural advantage by capturing the moral high ground from the Greeks. This was no easy task. The battle for public opinion was not a matter of defeating armies, capturing cities, and forming political federations at which Rome excelled, but of winning minds, or at least putting a counter-narrative into circulation. This was a technique the Romans had to learn from the experts. It is worth spending time on this subject as it provides an illustration of how effectively the Romans culturally, and not just militarily, interacted with their conquered subjects.

### The Greek Advantage

The initial problem the Romans faced in their public-relations battle with the Greeks was that they were at a disadvantage when it came to telling the story of their origins. In reality, they knew next to nothing about them other than a few legends. They had a well-grounded suspicion that it must have been impressive—even spectacular—to judge by how well their enterprise turned out in the long run. The Greeks, however, had been in the business of history writing for centuries before the Romans got around to it and had perfected the way in which historical stories, especially those accounting for the distant, legendary past, were to be told. The Romans had little choice but to accept and adapt existing Greek models of how this past should be constructed, though they made sure these models were adjusted to their own quite different needs.

THE IMPORTANCE OF HAVING HOMER There were several reasons Greeks had such an early start on story telling. One was that as a maritime people they traveled a lot in search of trade goods and land to settle and so came into contact with many of the diverse peoples of the Mediterranean and Black Sea regions. When they began to think about their origins they were forced to think in comparative ways. Another was that from early times they had a rich poetic tradition that gave them a strong sense of the past and their connection with it. Their good luck in regard to their poetic tradition was enhanced when, at an early date (usually set at around 725 B.C.), the great poet Homer produced two masterpieces, the *Iliad* and the *Odyssey*, which immortalized the heroes of the Trojan War and made the war itself the central event of early Greek history. Homer's two tales told of things that occurred before, during, and after the siege of Troy. The poet Hesiod, writing about a generation after Homer, came up with a grand scheme that accounted for the origin of the gods and humans. Other poets working in the same tradition expanded and extended these stories. Genealogies, such as the *Catalogue of Women*, explained who was who among the heroes and helped highlight contacts between Greeks from many different areas of the Greek world. Gradually a kind of proto-history of early times developed.

HOW THE GREEKS TOOK CONTROL OF PRE-HISTORY With the Trojan War in place Greeks had a chronological template for the organization of all of early Greek history. This generic framework allowed Greeks everywhere to fit a lot of loose information they had (or invented) about the founders of their own individual cities into the established traditions about the generations who lived prior to and after the Trojan War. Association with the Trojan War gave luster to any city that could make the connection by claiming, for instance, to have sent a contingent to fight there. Wherever Greeks traveled in the Mediterranean and Black Seas they took the poems, genealogies, and stories of Homer, Hesiod, and the other poets with them. In this way a coherent pre-history, a kind of cultural anthropology, of the Greek people was built up. Among Mediterranean peoples only Jews were able to offer a similarly comprehensive account of early times, but the dissemination of the biblical version of human origins did not come until much later in Mediterranean history. That Greek and Jewish accounts of their prehistories are not historical in our sense of the word is beside the point. Both were well integrated, carefully developed stories to which it was hard to find exception because no alternative narratives of such scope existed outside these traditions. Both Greeks and Jews regarded their stories as historical, and this belief was an essential and formative aspect of their cultures.

FOREIGNERS IN THE GREEK NARRATIVE Greek pre-history was not limited to the activities of Greeks though they were, naturally, the prime actors. While working on their own past they established synchronous chronologies for the pre-histories of most of the peoples with whom they had come into contact during their centuries of travels throughout the Mediterranean and Black Seas, linking them with their own pre-history by means of such helpful but vague wanderers as Heracles (Hercules to the Romans), Jason, Odysseus, Diomedes, Evander, and others. Another technique was to deduce the ancestor of a people by analysis of the people's name. Thus, for instance, they could make the late-arriving Persians part of the overall picture by claiming that the Persians were the descendants of the well-known Greek hero Perseus. Even peoples who appeared out of nowhere such as the Galatians, a Celtic horde that terrified mainland Greece and Asia Minor in the third century B.C., were soon found a place in Greek pre-history: They were discovered to have been the descendants of the famous—at least to Greeks—nymph Galataea and the Cyclops Polyphemus (the one-eyed giant who featured in the *Odyssey*).

Romans and Italians were not excluded from this universal interest. For example, Hesiod makes Circe and Odysseus parents of Latinus, the eponymous ancestor of the Latins (a parenthood extended by later writers to all of the people of Italy):

> And Circe, daughter of Helios, the son
> Of Hyperion, loved Odysseus, patient souled,
> And bore great good Latinus and Agrius.
> They, in the midst of holy islands, ruled
> The famous Tyrrhenians so far away.[5]

That Hesiod, in the generation after Homer, had heard of "Latinus" is indicative of the development that was occurring in Italy at this time.

There were many Greek versions of Roman origins. One of them was that Hercules in his wandering ended up in Latium and married the daughter of Evander, an exile from Arcadia in Greece, who had arrived there earlier. They had a daughter named Pallantia, after whom the Palatine hill in Rome was (supposedly) named. Hercules thus becomes an ancestor of the Romans. A later tradition claimed that Evander brought the alphabet with him from Greece. Aristotle has Achaean Greeks settle in "Latinium." Another version says Lavinia, the daughter of Latinus, married the Trojan refugee Aeneas; Romulus was their grandson.

THE POWER OF CULTURAL COLONIALISM This fascination with pre-history was not the childish game it may seem to be from the brief examples cited above. The mastery of the past is closely connected with the pursuit of cultural and political supremacy. The process is as old as the iconography of the great states of the Middle East where the dominant powers—Assyria, for example, or Egypt—displayed their supremacy by depicting their kings seated on thrones while subject kings groveled before them. The Behistun inscription of the great Persian king Darius lists the provinces he ruled—including Greek Ionia—and portrayed the nine kings he conquered with their arms tied behind their back and their necks connected to each other by ropes. Whoever gains control of the dominant narrative of a people—whether by iconography, poetry, song, or written accounts—has the ability to influence how a people think about themselves and how outsiders think about them.

The comprehensive account of pre-history evolved by Greeks from the seventh century onwards was an extraordinarily powerful cultural weapon in their hands. First, it gave to them a strong sense of who they were, where they came from, and what they had accomplished. This was of vital importance since there was no "Greece" in a national, territorial sense, but rather hundreds of Greek settlements scattered from the Atlantic to Georgia in

[5]Hesiod, *Theogony*. 1011–1061 tr. (modified), Wender. The Tyrrhenians were the Etruscans (who lived by the Tyrrhenian Sea).

the Black Sea. Second, Greeks were able to put in their places, so to speak, peoples who had less knowledge of their past than the Greeks claimed to possess. Many foreigners became dependent on, and thus subordinated to, the Greek master narrative of past events, in which, naturally, Greeks figured as the main actors with everyone else playing supporting roles.[6] Needless to say, lots of individual peoples out-of-hand rejected the Greeks and their version of history as ridiculous, but because they themselves had no better explanations to offer, the Greek version tended to predominate.

## Cultural War with the Greeks

Third and second century Romans contended with the Greeks for cultural hegemony over Mediterranean history by selecting from the Greek account the kinds of stories that suited their needs and that could be blended with their own native traditions. Understandably Romans were not eager to acknowledge a Greek founder, though there was some advantage to doing so: Greek culture was the dominant culture throughout the Mediterranean. Any people who could claim Greek origin could therefore claim to be civilized. Fortunately there were alternatives in the huge portfolio of Greek legends. The Trojan hero Aeneas became the connecting link.

AENEAS The *Iliad* itself said that the descendants of the surviving Trojan hero Aeneas would rule over the Trojans. But where? Troy was destroyed, so it could not be there. Besides, Aeneas was known to have escaped overseas as Troy was being sacked by the Greeks. Some places in the Aegean claimed that Aeneas and his band of Trojans had settled there, but most of the stories of their wanderings came from the western Mediterranean, especially Sicily. Aeneas was even a popular figure as far north as Etruria. More than 70 surviving vases, for example, depict Aeneas in one or more of his adventures. This brings the Trojan hero close to Latium. Suggestions were made quite early on, for example by the Greek poet Stesichorus (ca. 600 to 550 B.C.), that the prediction of Aeneas' ruling over Trojans might have been fulfilled in Italy. The great librarian of the museum in Alexandria, Eratosthenes (ca. 285 to 194 B.C.), speculated that Romulus, eponymous ancestor of Rome, was the grandson of Aeneas. The most acceptable version of the Aeneas connection was worked out by Diocles of Peparethos (ca. 250 B.C.) who claimed that the descendants of Aeneas settled at Alba Longa, an important religious center in Latium near Rome, and from there eventually settled Rome. Fabius Pictor, Rome's "Father of History," writing around 200 B.C., accepted this version of the tale, thus melding a Greek legend with local legends of Romulus.

WHY TROJANS? This choice, however, had its own difficulties. Why choose losers? The Trojans had lost their ten-year war against the Greeks, and Troy had been destroyed. The Romans, nevertheless, saw a number of advantages in the choice. First, it guaranteed the antiquity of Rome. Romans could trace their origins back to a famous city that was as

[6]A somewhat similar complaint has been lodged in modern times by non-Western peoples against the West's version of world history and its domination of world media.

old as any Greek city. Second, they could insert themselves into current events with a ready-made justification for their involvement in Greek affairs: They were redressing the injuries suffered by their remote ancestors at the hands of the Greeks. This was not specious propaganda. In the early third century when Pyrrhus invaded Italy in support of the Greek city of Tarentum, which was at war with Rome, his justification for doing so was not the usual claim of supporting Greeks against barbarians, but rather a much larger one. As a descendant of Achilles Pyrrhus claimed that he was continuing the Trojan War against Troy's later descendants, namely, the Romans (this time the Trojans—the Romans—won).

EARLY ROMAN HISTORY WRITING The fifty years from 200 to 150 B.C. saw the appearance of the first true histories of Rome. The early historians, known as annalists (because they wrote chronological accounts of Roman history on a year-by-year basis), initially wrote in Greek. They were not professional writers, let alone historians, but rather Roman senators who, in addition to putting a good spin on Rome's activities, also had personal axes to grind. For example, the first of these writers, Fabius Pictor, stressed the importance of his own *gens*, the Fabii, at the same time that he set out to establish the greatness of Rome. Later writers emphasized the role of other great families such as the Valerii, Claudii, Cornelii, and others. Most of their work has vanished, however, and survives only in fragments or incorporated in the history of later writers whose work has survived.

CATO'S LATIN HISTORY With Cato the Elder, in the first half of the second century B.C., Latin history writing first came into existence, representing a new level of self-confidence on the part of the Romans, who now rose to the challenge of Greek letters by composing a literature in their own language. This was an achievement matched by no other people with whom the Greeks came into contact. For Cato, in fact, the Greeks no longer counted; the Romans and the Italians had nothing of which to be ashamed. On the contrary, they had incorporated the best of the Greek world into the best of their own rich heritage—a pardonable exaggeration with which some Greeks in the second century B.C. might have agreed. From this time on, numerous accounts in Latin by members of the senatorial class provided the growing reading public of Rome and Italy with suitably patriotic, moralizing histories, often laced with polemical tracts from the internal political battles of the century. There were few qualms about adapting history to the political needs of the Roman upper classes, and history was seen as a means of glorifying one's own achievements and the achievements of one's family, as well as propagandizing for further advancement.

THE REAL POINT OF ROMAN PROPAGANDA The deeper message of Rome's maneuvering for media control was that while Greece may have had a glorious past and was still culturally significant, it no longer counted for much politically or militarily. History was now being made by the lone superpower, Rome, which was not just militarily, but also morally, superior. Fabius Pictor portrayed Romans as adhering to a strict moral code that ruled public and private life. Romans, he claimed, won wars because of their immense resources in manpower and materiel, but also because of their bravery, moderation, and good faith. Greek anti-Roman cultural chauvinism only underlined the impotence of Greece. History, so the message went, had moved onwards and westwards.

The Romans were not just good politicians and soldiers, but also superb propagandists. Propaganda, in the sense of individuals or parties or nations getting their message out, is an essential aspect of good politics. To the extent there was a free media in the ancient world, the Romans, being themselves a free people, knew how to use it to get their message across to all Mediterranean peoples, Greeks and non-Greeks alike.

## The Outrage of Latin Plays

Rome's appropriation of Greece's cultural capital was not limited to history writing. Over time it extended to other areas of art, including architecture, sculpture, literature, and the theater.

In the middle of the third century B.C. Rome made the bold move to make Greek-style theatrical productions part of its own festivals. Only the most self-assured of states could have taken on such a formidable task. The theater was one of the proudest and oldest possessions in Greece's cultural repertoire. Professional companies of actors, producers, and writers traveled all over the Greek world putting on plays. Sophisticated theater fans traveled from city to city to hear their favorite plays or see their favorite actors. The staging of plays in some cities such as Syracuse and Athens was legendary. The result was a cosmopolitan, Mediterranean-wide, Greek theatrical culture. One of the key identifying features of any Greek *polis* worthy of the name was its theater, the grander and the larger the better. Non-Greeks might build theaters and invite Greek professionals to put on Greek plays in them, but no barbarian people dreamed of putting on plays written in their own language. That is, except the Romans. Roman statesmen, however, were less interested in the finer points of Greek tragedy than in making a popular success of the city's national religious festivals and expanding its limited offerings of mime and farce. In this context Romans knew they could outdo the Greeks, and in time they did.

PLAYS IN LATIN? The first move towards incorporating plays in the festivals came at an important juncture in Roman history. In 240 B.C. the Senate set the precedent by commissioning Livius Andronicus, a naturalized Greek from Tarentum and a freedmen of the prominent *gens* Livia, to write a play for the Roman Games, the Ludi Romani. These games were a central part of Rome's celebration of its victory over Carthage in the first Punic War, which had just ended the previous year. Thereafter dramatic performances gradually became a standard feature of the state festivals such as the Ludi Plebeii, the Ludi Apollinares, the Ludi Megalenses, and the Ludi Cereales.

The decision by the Senate in 240 B.C. pointed to Rome's conscious decision to become a contestant in the highly popular and competitive cultural world of the Greek theater—a direct challenge to the Greek domination of this well-developed genre. It is indicative of the success of the games that the year following the performance of Livius' play, Hiero, the ruler of the powerful city of Syracuse, came to Rome to attend the games. We know the names of three comedies and 10 tragedies composed by Andronicus, but only a few words from them have survived.

Besides writing (and performing in) plays Livius also translated Homer's *Odyssey* into Latin in a form adapted to Roman taste. It is significant that he chose to translate the *Odyssey*, which had western Mediterranean and Roman connections, rather than the *Iliad*, which was Greece's national epic. In his old age Livius was called upon to compose a hymn for a procession of virgins that was part of a large ritual enacted to beg the gods for help at a moment of great crisis in the war against Hannibal. This was in 207 B.C. when Hasdrubal was poised to cross the Alps and link up with his brother Hannibal in the south. The battle of the Metaurus ended these plans, and Livius was honored for his role in winning the gods' favors with the establishment of a guild (a *collegium*) of writers and actors with its base in the temple of Minerva on the Aventine hill. This was a significant reward for Livius. It showed Rome's appreciation for Livius' part in blending theatrical performances with the festivals, and the city's overall satisfaction with the role of the theater in its religious life. The creation of the guild established an official connection between the professionals who were responsible for the plays and Rome's state religion. There was, however, a difference. In the Hellenic cultural world these professionals performed under the auspices of the god Dionysus; at Rome they came under the patronage of Minerva, one of the three presiding deities of the state.[7] Minerva, the dignified goddess of wisdom, the protectress of cities and their rulers, was a much less permissive deity than Dionysus the "Liberator," the god of wine, excitement, intoxication, and wild animal impulse.

Another non-Roman, Gnaeus Naevius, a close contemporary of Livius, composed patriotic plays and a verse epic based on the Punic Wars. The names of 32 of his comic plays based on Greek models are known, but his main originality lay in introducing Roman historical themes to the theater in the form of two plays, one dealing with Romulus and the other the defeat of the Gauls at Clastidium in 222 B.C. In the next generation Ennius, from Apulia in southern Italy, was the first of the great Latin poets. He too composed plays for the public festivals as well as a narrative epic in 15 books on the history of the Roman people from the fall of Troy to his own time. It emphasized the reversal of fortune the Greek states had suffered after the sack of Troy and the expansion of the Roman Empire under the patronage of the Olympian gods. Ennius' aphorisms, which reflected the nobles' vision of Rome, became commonplaces quoted throughout subsequent Roman history.[8] His epitaph, reported by Cicero, reads: "Gaze, O citizens, at the sculptural portrait of the aged Ennius. He recorded the great deeds of your ancestors" (*Pro Arch.* 22).

The first half of the second century B.C. saw the full flowering of Latin in the plays of Plautus and Terence. Both freely adapted Hellenistic plays to Roman tastes. Comedies, especially those of Plautus, were always popular, although the settings and the stock figures were Greek, for fear of offending conservative Roman tastes. There was no place in Rome for the raw, explicitly political humor of Old Comedy such as that of the Athenian playwright Aristophanes. The Roman aristocracy took its role as a governing class seriously and unquestioningly. Mime and farce, which were native to Italy, were the popular fare of the lower classes and eventually displaced the plays of Roman comedy altogether.

FEAR OF THE NEW Nevertheless there was a genuine fear among traditionalist Romans of the new culture and its clever, mocking ways. Even Scipio Aemilianus, the Roman pa-

---

[7]Minerva was one of the Capitoline "triad" at the head of the Roman pantheon. The other two were Jupiter and Juno. Minerva is usually identified with the Greek goddess Athena.

[8]See above, p. 142, Introduction for Cicero's citation of perhaps Ennius' best known aphorism: "moribus antiquis res stat Romana virisque."

tron and friend of the Greek historian Polybius, attacked the corrupting influence of Greek ideas and the disastrous effect of wealth on the Roman ruling class. Scipio Nasica prevented the building of a permanent theater in Rome in 154 B.C. because he feared it would lead to the speedy corruption of the citizens, and such a theater was not built for a century. A permanent amphitheater for games, which were becoming increasingly popular, was not built in Rome until the end of the first century B.C. In both cases the true reasons were political. Crowds in theaters easily got excited and were difficult to control. Permanent theaters were used throughout Greece as meeting places for the people, but Rome was not democratically minded Greece. One of the best ways of controlling an audience, so it was thought in Rome, was to keep them from becoming too comfortable. The audience, therefore, should be made to stand.

## Culture: A Force for Disruption

ELITE FRAGMENTATION An insidious result of the Hellenization of segments of the Roman elite was the divisions it introduced among the elite. It is understandable that lengthy encounters with the highly developed Greek east might lead most Roman aristocrats to acquire a taste for good living and some of them to develop genuine interests in art, literature, and even philosophy. The danger of acquiring friends among foreign elites and at least the patina of Greek culture was that not all members of the Roman elite had the same opportunity or even approved of this form of cultural competition. Even today, among peer-group competitors, if some become richer and display their riches in the form of cultural superiority, the result is a loss of face—real as well as perceived—for others. For many elites throughout history the introduction of new cultural norms is a zero-sum game.

The practical aspects of Hellenization also had the capacity to create political divisions. The technical command of oratory, expanded knowledge of history, geography, and international affairs could give an individual a political edge over his opponents. The presence of cultivated foreign friends and wealth displayed in the form of art and new knowledge added to existing high levels of competition within the elite. The cult of individuality, which was well-developed in Roman political culture, was given a boost in different directions by all these developments.

NEW OPPORTUNITIES Roman aristocratic expectations in the past were that leisure was for public service, primarily civic and military service. Contact with the Greek world introduced other possibilities, and a new world opened up to wealthy young Romans. Instead of the law courts or the army camp, they had other options. They could put to one side the state with its competitive and often destructive rivalries and devote themselves to the cultivation of the private realm. More often than not this took the form of hedonistic self-indulgence and materialistic excess, and it was on these more crass features of the new culture that the traditionalists focused. Nevertheless, an important minority of Romans seriously cultivated the arts, literature, and intellectual pursuits. They were to produce or patronize the creation of a remarkable body of literature, rhetoric, art, and architecture amid the chaos of the last century of the Republic.

**Theater Building Was Not Welcome at Rome**

*While the Romans were quick to adopt Greek plays they were a good deal slower to warm to Greek theater buildings. No permanent theater was allowed in Rome until the first century* B.C. *on the plausible grounds that theaters were useful not just for plays but for gatherings—lawful and otherwise—of the people. In Greece, they were comfortable for audiences and easily accessible either in cities themselves or close by. Some theaters opened directly on the* agora, *the Greek equivalent to the* forum *or central gathering place of the city. Such permanent theaters were attractive places for loiterers, troublemakers, and especially demagogues, and Greek cities had a long history of political turbulence in which the theater featured as a handy focal point for disaffected mobs. From the Roman viewpoint all of this violated a basic principle of politics that meetings of the people could only be summoned by magistrates and then only under certain carefully choreographed conditions dictated by long-established customs. Meetings were not intended for entertainment or for long discussions of issues. Debate and analysis took place mainly in the Senate where discussion could be safely controlled because only the most senior members spoke, and they spoke in order of their importance. In general, public meetings were functional and business-like. They did not aim to make people comfortable. Everyone stood. If a meeting was called it was to hear descriptions of laws or policies (the* contio*) or to vote (a* comitium*). There was no room for debate. The anarchy of public meetings in the late Republic when the magistrates began to lose control of their meetings was a sure sign of the collapse of the old order. It is interesting that the first permanent theater was built in Rome in 55* B.C. *by the dynast or strong-man, Pompey, one of those who brought down the Republic, at the height of the chaos of that period. Even then Pompey thought it prudent to claim that his theater was only a monumental staircase leading to the temple of Venus Victrix at the top. It was here, in the adjacent Porticus of Pompey, that Julius Caesar was murdered on March 15, 44* B.C.

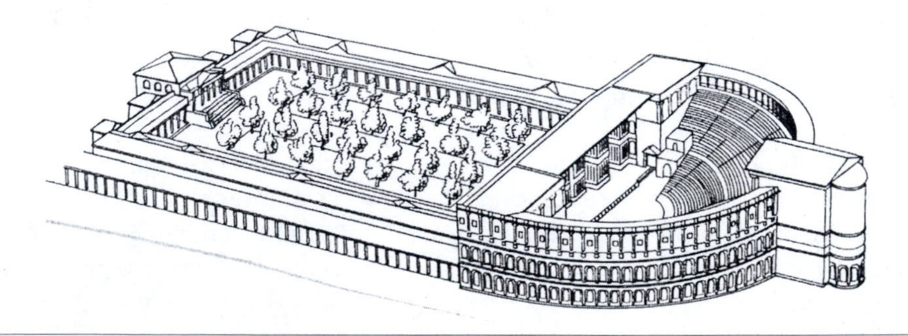

Reconstruction of Pompey's Theater

THE IMPACT OF GREEK PHILOSOPHERS Romans had ambiguous attitudes towards the talented Greeks who came to Rome in the second century B.C. Greek grammarians were expelled from the city in 161 B.C. Some years later three famous philosophers—Carneades, the head of the Platonic Academy; the Stoic Diogenes; and Critolaus the Peripatetic—came to Rome to plead a case on behalf of Athens They electrified the young men of the city with the lectures they gave while waiting for the Senate to decide their case. On one occasion Carneades spoke one day on justice and its application to the problem of empire and on the following day refuted all the theories he had put up on the previous day. Traditionalists were angered by this kind of blatant cynicism and Cato, representing their viewpoint, urged that the philosophers be given a quick answer to their plea so that they "could return to their schools in Athens as soon as possible, while the youth of Rome could listen, as in the past, to their laws and magistrates." Nonetheless it was significant that the young men who so impressed by the philosophers were sufficiently in command of spoken Greek to understand their lectures. By the next century even among the most hardened, self-seeking leaders of Rome there was hardly one who did not have a Greek intellectual or two in his entourage. Pompey, who thought of himself as a second Alexander the Great, was a friend of the Stoic Posidonius whom he regarded as his Aristotle (Aristotle had been the tutor of the young Alexander). Another Greek, Theophanes of Mitylene wrote a highly favorable account of Pompey's deeds in the eastern Mediterranean. Both Julius Caesar and his successor Augustus patronized the Alexandrian philosopher Arius Didymus. Arius first acted as the young Octavian's (as Augustus was then known as) tutor and later lived with the imperial family.

There were practical reasons for having court philosophers. Apart from writing complementary biographies as Theophanes did for Pompey or schooling the young of the elite, they could write speeches and compose panegyrics in honor of their patrons. When their patron's children died they wrote consolationes as did the philosopher Athenodorus for the grieving Octavia, Augustus' sister, on the death of her son Marcellus. Philosophers were useful in helping to manage Greek public opinion. They could be used to convey messages that would otherwise be difficult to transmit. Thus, for example, when Octavian, after defeating Antony and Cleopatra in battle wanted to reassure the Alexandrians that he was not about to loot the city, he made use of the well-known Arius:

> Octavian entered into Alexandria with Arius the philosopher at his side. He gave him his right hand and kept up a conversation with him in order to increase Arius' importance in the eyes of the Alexandrians . . . . When Octavian entered the gymnasium and mounted a platform that had been erected there, the people were beside themselves with fear and fell on their faces before him. Octavian, however, told them to arise and assured them he had no intention of holding their city to blame [*for being on the wrong side of the civil war between Octavian and Antony and Cleopatra*]. This, he said, was for several reasons. First, it was because the city had been founded by Alexander. Secondly, it was because he himself admired its beauty and spaciousness, and finally because of his regard for Arius (Plutarch, *Life of Antony* 80).

Word soon seeped out that Octavian had granted a number of pardons of well-placed people at the request of Arius.

Philosophers might even lend an aura of intellectuality and seriousness to their patrons in the eyes of ever-watchful Greeks. Not all of the interchanges were based on purely pragmatic principles of mutual self-help. Philosophers hoped to influence and ameliorate the behavior of their patrons and their patrons' children. There was always the possibility, remote though it might be, of turning their patrons into philosopher-rulers as Plato had attempted to do with Dionysius, the tyrant of Syracuse. The system worked both ways, and the philosophers might bear the blame for how their patrons turned out. The responsibility for the tempestuous tribunate of Tiberius Gracchus was placed by some members of the elite on two of his intellectual advisers, Blossius of Cumae and Diophanes of Mitylene. Diophanes paid the price for his poor advice with his life but Blossius was exonerated, although though he chose to leave Rome for good.

## 3. THE IMPACT OF EMPIRE ON ROMAN SOCIETY

The acquisition of empire had two principal socio-economic effects. The first was the impact on Roman society of the importation of masses of slaves and the creation of a large freedman class. The second was the creation of a new financial class among the elite, the publicans (*publicani*).

### Slaves and Freedmen

Booty in war came in two forms: movable and immovable wealth. The latter consisted of land and buildings; movable wealth, obviously, embraced everything else, much of it in the form of human beings, namely, slaves. In one brief campaign in Epirus in 167 B.C. (cited previously), the consul Aemilius Paullus enslaved 150,000 people, and in the remainder of the century huge numbers of slaves continued to be brought into Italy. Not all slaves, however, resulted from Rome's military activities. Independent of war the slave trade was big business in the Mediterranean, and had been for centuries. Piracy was always an important source of slaves, and at the free port of Delos in the Aegean slave-traders, it is claimed, could process up to 10,000 slaves per day, no questions asked.

Slaves went where the money was, and in the second and first centuries B.C. that was Italy. One estimate puts the figure of the total number of slaves in Italy by the end of the first century B.C. at around 2,000,000. The use of slave labor became an integral part of the agricultural economy of Italy, contributing to the shift from subsistence to cash-crop farming. Independent of agriculture the public building projects undertaken in Rome and Italy (Section 1 above) supported the labor of masses of free and unfree laborers and enriched the entrepreneurs who contracted to provide them.

FREEDMEN Romans had a tradition of liberating slaves. For example, Sulla, a first-century B.C. general, freed 10,000 slaves on one occasion. Upon being freed former slaves became citizens, though with some legal restrictions. With large numbers of slaves being manumitted, a significant libertine or freedman population grew up in Rome and in the cities of Italy. Freedmen came to dominate the commercial life of Rome, and some became extremely wealthy. At his death one ex-slave, for instance, owned more than 4,000 slaves. An estimate, which may be high, claims that over half the population of Rome in the late Republic was made up of slaves or freedmen and freedwomen.

In the case of freedmen the political problem for the Romans was where to locate them in the political system. Were they to be distributed among all 35 tribes of the Tribal Assembly or bottled up in the four urban tribes? If they were distributed throughout all the tribes they could be much more influential, because freedmen were concentrated in the city and were always available to vote. The concentration in the city of so many freedmen and slaves was also a cause of concern for public safety, especially as order began to break down in Rome in the first century. Without a police force Rome depended entirely on the good behavior of its inhabitants for orderliness. Freedmen and slaves could be organized into gangs or claques or infiltrated into assemblies if a political leader or demagogue had an interest in doing so. It took Roman politicians only a little while before they figured out how to exploit these opportunities to the fullest extent. The involvement of slaves and freedmen in street fighting, and on the periphery of the political process, added to the mayhem of the last years of the Republic.

## The Publicans

THE MONETIZATION OF THE ECONOMY The increasing complexity of its administrative and military needs forced Rome to adopt the coinage practices of the Hellenistic world. Large armies could not be supplied or paid without currency, and during the Hannibalic War Rome began minting a silver coin known as the *denarius*. It is estimated that in a little over 40 years Rome put into circulation some 250,000,000 denarii. This gigantic amount of currency, minted out of the income of mines, indemnities, and taxes, created the basis for the money that circulated in the second and first centuries B.C. In time the denarius-based coinage system became the dominant currency throughout the Mediterranean.

THE BUREAUCRATIC CHALLENGE By the second century Rome was faced with the responsibility of maintaining order and administering huge territories throughout the Mediterranean. Armies needed to be paid and supplied, and roads, aqueducts, and temples built. Rome itself was expanding. Shipping and transportation had to be organized, public buildings maintained, mines exploited, coins minted, provincial taxes collected, and state properties managed. Yet Rome, a libertarian's paradise, had no bureaucratic tradition and no desire to create a bureaucracy to provide these services.

For Romans as for other *poleis*-citizens bureaucracies were dangerous, incompetent, unresponsive power centers operating outside the political system and therefore extremely difficult to control. Rome's solution was to privatize the services it needed by contracting with groups of individual entrepreneurs. Understandably these entrepreneurs had to have large amounts of capital on hand to be able to bid on state contracts, which were not small undertakings. Taxes for entire provinces, for instance, were put up for bid, and the winning contractors were expected to pay the contractual price up front with only the hope of reimbursement later when the actual task of collecting the taxes was complete.

**Roman Coinage**

| *Denomination* | *Asses* | *Sesterii* | *Metal* |
|---|---|---|---|
| Aureus | 400 | 100 | Gold |
| Denarius | 16 | 4 | Silver |
| Sestertius | 4 | 1 | Brass |
| Dupondius | 2 | 1/2 | Copper |
| As | 1 | 1/4 | Copper |
| Qadrans | ¼ | 1/16 | Copper |

In the second century B.C. a denarius was a day's wages for a free man. Slaves were hired out at two sesterces (HS) per day. Soldiers were paid 108 denarii per year. On a wage of 300 denarii a year approximately 90 denarii would be spent on grain and 90 more on other kinds of food according to T. Frank, *An Economic Survey of Ancient Rome* (Baltimore, 1933, 1.189). This calculation would apply to an urban-dwelling Roman.

The only place in Roman society where such well-to-do individuals could be found was, needless to say, among the propertied classes. Senators were forbidden by law to engage directly in commerce over a certain, small fixed amount that enabled them to look after their landholdings. That left the burden, or better, the opportunity, for contracting with the state to the segment of the propertied, equestrian class that was willing to get into this business. These equestrians, who knew one another since they all belonged to the same class, formed companies of publicans (*societates publicanorum*).[10] To be a senator one had first to be an equestrian. The ramifications are a bit confusing. A person could be a member of the senatorial *ordo* or order without being actively involved in politics if one's forebears had been senators. In terms of social standing and culture, however, there was less to distinguish members of the equestrian order from those of the senatorial order. They all belonged to the same elite of Rome. In the late Republic they may together be thought of as a plutocracy sharing in both landed and business interests. The partners of the companies put up the necessary capital and elected managing partners (*magistri*), who in turn supervised the work to be done under the given contract. In the provinces the company was represented by a *pro magistro*, a manager who acted on behalf of the partners. There was often a large staff mostly made up of freemen and slaves.

DIVISION IN THE ELITE One consequence of the rise of the publicans was that a portion of the elite, which might otherwise have given itself in traditional fashion to military and civic service through a senatorial career, instead devoted itself to the financial and service side of the imperial economy. Thus, over time, the Roman elite evolved from being a relatively unified social and cultural body into one with many, often-conflicting interests. Adding complexity to the situation was the fact that senators learned to profit from the system despite the law barring them from doing so. They did this by becoming silent partners in the companies of the publicans through the holding of unregistered shares (*partes*).

[10]In the late Republic the equestrian class was, broadly speaking, made up of the wealthy, propertied people of Rome who had a minimum property qualification of 400,000 sesterces. The inner core of the equestrian class was the senatorial class (i.e., those individuals and their families who were actively engaged in the political life of Rome).

The system as it evolved lent itself to nepotism and corruption. Conflicting political and financial interests were, however, a more serious problem for Rome. The Senate was responsible for managing and maintaining order in the empire, yet it inevitably came into conflict in the provinces with the publicans of the equestrian class, their otherwise social and cultural peers. Governors trying to rule their provinces justly found themselves undermined by the companies of publicans attempting to recoup their investments at any cost. Trying to draw the two groups together into a "concord of the orders" (*concordia ordinum*) was one of Cicero's main, though unfulfilled, goals throughout much of his distinguished political career.

### The Family

The Roman family could not escape the influences of the times, both for good and ill. As Roman society loosened and shook off the discipline of early times, so did the Roman family. The powers of the *paterfamilias* remained technically in effect and could always be called upon when necessary, but there was an overall tendency towards softening the full force of paternal authority. The Roman patriarchy, like the state itself, suffered a devolution of its powers. Women became more independent, aristocratic women notoriously so. Children learned to become more individualistic, less susceptible to parental discipline or respect for the ways of the ancestors. Among the elite it became chic to have one's offspring educated in Greek culture by imported Greek tutors. For polish sons were sent overseas for a year or so, sometimes achieving less than the desired results. It was understandable that the elite would try to keep up with the times and give their children the best possible education they could provide. Greek was the language of learning, culture, literature, the theater, and most importantly of diplomacy. The young had to be prepared to enter this world. And of course families had to keep up with each other. Some like Cato questioned whether Romans would assimilate or choke on this rich social and cultural diet.

## 4. THE DISINTEGRATION OF ROME'S COMPACT WITH ITALY

There is an anomaly in the fact that while Rome by the middle of the second century B.C. was the undisputed ruler of the Mediterranean, its control of Italy was in the process of being undermined. It is true that large numbers of Romans and Latins lived in scattered settlements throughout Italy from the far north to the far south, but the majority of Romans and Latins still lived within the boundaries of their old, central Italian heartland. The bulk of the non-Roman, non-Latin population of Italy, its numerous tribes, cities, and federations were related to Rome by means of hundreds of treaties negotiated over past centuries. These were Rome's allies (*socii*, sing. *socius*) and in every war they constituted a large percentage of Rome's armies. There was a saying among the warlike Marsi of the central Italian highlands that Rome "never triumphed over them—or without them."

ALLIED UNHAPPINESS After the war with Hannibal, however, the allies began to constitute a larger and larger percentage of Rome's armies as Rome's manpower pool

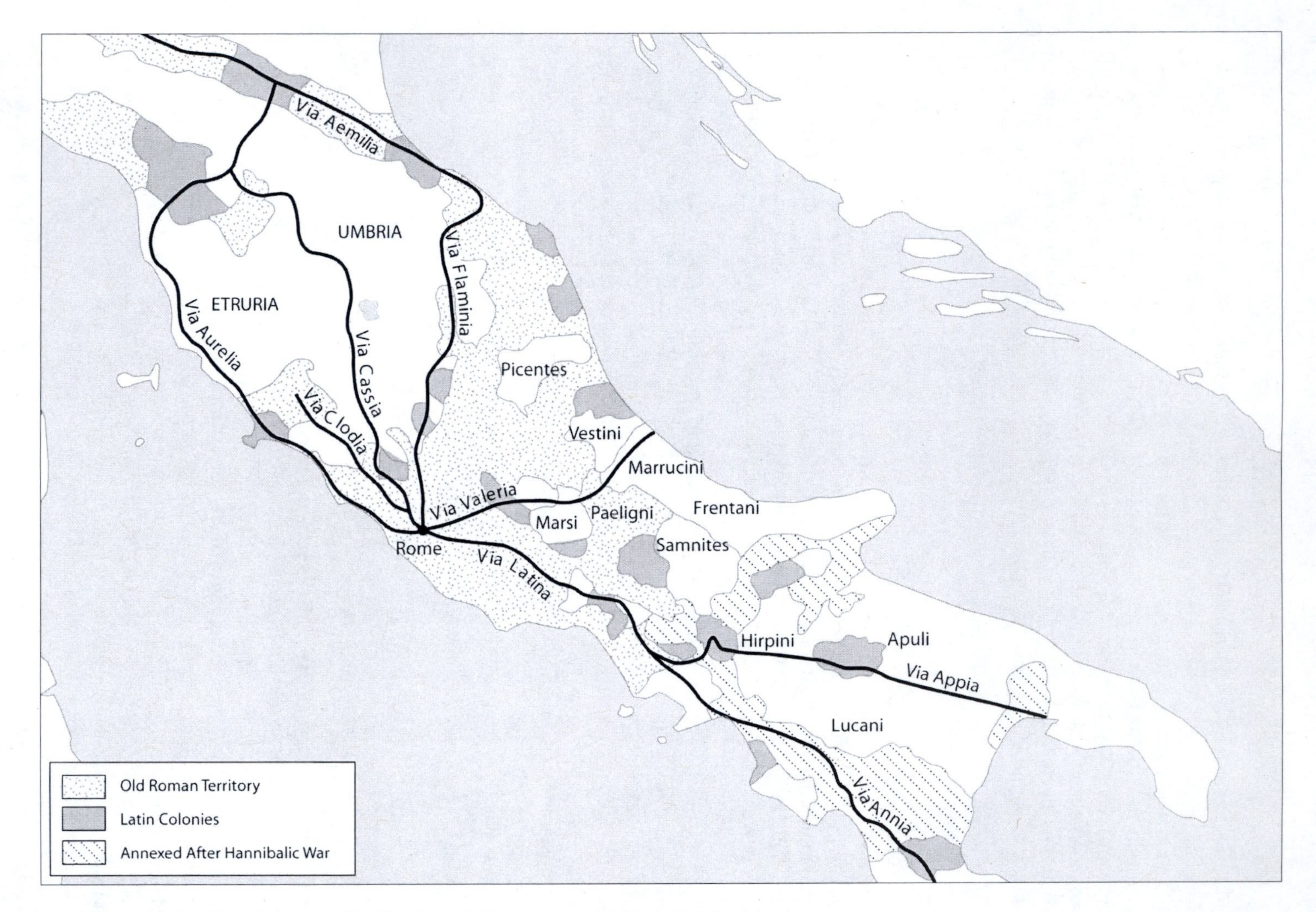


Map of Italy showing the Distribution of Roman and Allied Territory

### Collapse of the Consensus with the Allies

*By the end of the second century* B.C. *the Italian* socii *were fed up with the arrangement that left them perpetual second-class citizens. The Italian view is put by the soldier and historian Velleius Paterculus (born 20* B.C.*) who was of Samnite-Campanian ancestry.*

> [*The Italians were enraged because*] in every year and in every war they served with twice as many infantry and cavalry as the Romans and yet were not given the right of citizenship in the very state which through their efforts had reached such a high position that it could look down on men of the same race and blood as if they were outsiders and foreigners (2.15.2).

shrank and as punishment was inflicted on those allies who had gone over to Hannibal. By mid-second century the number of the allies serving in Roman armies had risen to about the same as the number of Romans, and by the end of the century the percentage was even higher. Although joint Roman-Italian armies conquered the Mediterranean, the allies received less booty and had little choice but to fight the wars Rome chose to fight. Latin and Roman colonies located in their midst, often on the best available land, certainly at the most strategic spots, reminded them who was in control of Italy. Public land, technically Rome's through conquest, but often still occupied by the original possessors, grew to become an issue of major importance towards the middle of the second century B.C. when the Romans began to think of dividing it up and giving it to their own poor. Individual members of the Roman elite behaved as arrogantly among the Italian allies as they did overseas. At the same time the competence of the military leadership of Rome's aristocracy was called into question by a number of spectacular defeats in Africa and Europe beyond the Alps at the end of the second century, in which large numbers of the allies were slaughtered. Slowly the consensus that had sustained Roman power in all previous centuries began to collapse.

From the Roman viewpoint, however, there were no easy solutions to the Italian problem. The Roman elite recognized that if the aristocrats of Italy were fully enfranchised the Italian aristocrats would compete with them for the already-too-few magistracies. The rest of the population felt threatened in analogous ways. The profits of the empire would be diluted if the vast bulk of the Italian population were admitted to a full share in it. Then there were important status considerations. Roman citizenship meant a great deal legally, socially, and culturally. Those who possessed it were members of a privileged class even if they were not individually especially rich or well placed. The presence (or potential loss) of this feeling of superiority was an important factor in the increasing tension between the now closely related peoples.

The four subjects discussed in this chapter are not meant to be an exhaustive list of the problems Rome had to face as a result of its acquisition of an empire. They merely aim to suggest the magnitude of what Rome was up against. Any one of these problems might have been enough to defeat Rome's best efforts at a solution, let alone all of them together. How Rome addressed these challenges, or more often failed to address them, is the subject of the next several chapters.

# 9

# The Crisis of the Roman Republic: The Gracchi

## 1. THE SOCIAL AND POLITICAL CONTEXT

Romans did not ignore the many problems posed by their acquisition of an empire. They were conscious of the challenges they faced and made many efforts toward solving them. Unfortunately, their political system, which had served them so well in the past, failed them at this juncture.

### The Manpower Problem

The manpower crisis for the army, which had been looming since the Hannibalic War, did not emerge fully until well into the second century B.C. For a period of time Rome was able to find ways of postponing this danger.

TECHNIQUES FOR COPING When there was a shortage of draftees during the Hannibalic War, property qualifications for service in the legions were dropped from 11,000 asses to 4,000 (for Roman coinage, see figure on page 166). For the time being this automatically augmented the manpower pool. The colonial foundations and individual allotments made in the second century also helped for a while to maintain the manpower resources. This was because as the poor received individual land grants or were recruited into colonies, they automatically went on the draft registers for the legions. Then, this was still a time when social norms were enforceable. The burden of military service fell principally on the younger males of the family; the unchallengeable authority of the fathers, along with peer pressure and the opportunity for booty, guaranteed that young men would present themselves for the draft. There was also a pool of long-term volunteers who were much sought after by the consuls when they were drafting their armies. We know, for example, of one such volunteer by the name of Spurius Ligustinus. He served in the First Macedonian War against Philip during which he was promoted to centurion. He then fought in the Syrian War against Antiochus in Asia Minor and Greece. He was twice on campaign in Spain. In total, this well-traveled soldier spent 22 years in the legions. He was decorated many times and ended his career as chief centurion.

However, with Italy secure by the 170s B.C. there was no longer a need for new colonies, and most of the land that was available for distribution in individual lots had already been parcelled out by this time. Thus the safety-valve of land distribution, which had maintained the draft rolls, was shut off. Social cohesion declined, and new economic alternatives to subsistence farming became available. At the same time overseas wars continued to create a demand for new recruits who had to be prepared for years of unbroken service overseas.

DISCONTENT IN THE RANKS Recruitment for wars in both Greece and Spain was a constant cause of discontent. There was a mutiny in the army in Greece in 198 B.C. and insubordination there eight years later. In 189 B.C. the consul Manlius Vulso was forced to relax discipline and to bribe his troops to get them to fight. Aemilius Paullus, the victor over Philip V and the Macedonians at Pydna in 167 B.C., had great difficulty initially with his undisciplined troops, and they later complained loudly of the small amount of loot they received and even attempted to prevent his triumph. The Spanish war particularly caused major outbursts. Recruitment was difficult from the beginning, and discontent was chronic. Draft riots broke out in 151 and 138 B.C. Prospective recruits appealed to the tribunes for help, and the tribunes thereupon imprisoned the consuls who were conducting the enlistment. Raw recruits were often sent out when veterans refused to serve.

## Response to the Crisis: General Reform Efforts

Attempts were made to cope with these and other indications of dissatisfaction. An upper limit of 500 *jugera* (625 acres) was put on the occupation of public land (*ager publicus*) in an attempt to control the efforts of the wealthy to create giant estates in the south and elsewhere by acquiring large tracts of public land, it apparently went unenforced. Furthermore, it did not limit the acreage that could be rented, and once begun, rental contracts tended to be renewed automatically. The Porcian laws (*leges Porciae*) so improved conditions of military service and guaranteed the personal rights of Roman citizens so well (*provocatio*) that by 150 B.C. the death penalty for citizens had fallen into general disuse. Secret ballots were introduced after mid-century for elections, trials, and legislation, indicating concessions to popular demands. These ballot laws had the effect of weakening the patronal power of the elite and helped to bring into existence more independent-minded voters. About the same time a tribune, Gaius Licinius, introduced legislation that would have had the effect of breaking the hold of the aristocracy on the priesthoods. It proposed that vacancies in the priestly colleges be filled by popular election rather than by the traditional process of co-option, which allowed the elite to control these important offices closely. It failed but was revived and passed in 104 B.C.

**The Secret Ballot at Rome. Coin of Nerva.**

*The coin shows a voter bending down to receive a ballot from an attendant standing on the ground. The voter has already climbed onto the voting pons or bridge by means of a ladder (not shown). Another voter precedes him and is shown in the act of depositing his ballot in the voting basket. The voting bridge, the ballot, and the basket were all efforts to make the voting process transparent. Nonetheless corruption did occur.*

THE RISING ROLE OF TRIBUNES These efforts at reform, many spearheaded by tribunes, suggest that the latent power of the tribunate was being slowly awakened or reawakened, and in an increasing number of instances tribunes were willing to use their awesome power on behalf of groups or individuals who felt that the state had become unresponsive to their needs. Conversely, some nobles were not above appealing directly to the people and using tribunes for their own self-interest. Scipio Aemilianus, the destroyer of Carthage, was twice elected consul and assigned provinces with the assistance of the people in flagrant defiance of custom and law. This was a model for political action that would reappear later in the century with a much more negative impact. Laws against corrupt electioneering practices (*leges de ambitu*) were enacted in 181 and 159 B.C., and by the end of the century there was a standing court responsible for the examination of such cases.

There was also a reaction against the developing powers of the tribunes. The *leges Aelia et Fufia* limited the number of days that tribunes could call meetings of the Popular Assembly (*concilium plebis*) and generally made it more complicated for them to push through popular measures. These laws also regulated the process by which a magistrate, by announcing that he was going "to look for signs from the gods" (*obnuntiatio*), could shut down an assembly because it could always be assumed that he would find the signs he was looking for. According to Cicero "these laws often weakened and restrained the outrages of the tribunes" (*Against Vatinius* 18). The ruling elite sensed trouble brewing and thought they could avoid taking serious reform action by inventing legal technicalities to hold back assertive tribunes. It was not an unreasonable reaction, but in the absence of constructive counterproposals on their part amounted to mere obstructionism.

A good example occurred in 140 B.C. when Gaius Laelius as consul attempted to do something about land reform. His proposal was that all public land above the law's limit of 500 *jugera* (ca. 625 acres) should be set aside for distribution to veterans of the Spanish wars. There was fierce opposition from the occupiers among the senatorial elite, who argued they had been in possession of this land sometimes for generations and to be told now that they had to give it up now was unjust. They claimed, with some truth but more exaggeration, that they had built homes on this land and their ancestors were buried there. Laelius was forced to withdraw his bill and earned the ambiguous title *Sapiens*, "The Wise" (or perhaps more likely "The Calculator"). Thus by mid-century it seems clear that the Senate itself could neither undertake effective reform nor permit it to develop outside its immediate control.

POLITICAL BREAKDOWN All this points to the gradual breakdown of the old, predictable social and political bonds that had united the elite in a common front and bound the masses to the upper classes by ties of mutual respect, friendship, and patronage. With Rome's lower classes expanding—as dispossessed small farmers and veterans, both citizen and allied, migrated to the city and mixed with increasingly large heterogeneous classes of slaves and freedmen—the social relations of previous times based on kinship and personal connections gave way to new relationships based on common economic or political interests. Votes, which in the past had belonged to a patron by ancient custom, began to be thought of as free and could be sought by anyone caring to solicit or buy them. Laws against corrupt electioneering did not work, and sponsoring expensive spectacles or attaining significant military achievements became alternative ways to gain visibility and high office, although it was not until the next century that the most flagrant abuses were found in this area. Thus the cost of running for office rose dramatically, and the politically active members of the elite needed to find larger and larger sources of income to advance their careers. This in turn drove their search for lucrative overseas commands.

Others among the senatorial and equestrian classes gave up their rigorous ideals of public service and found substitutes in the increasingly attractive private realm, which offered the comforts of luxurious villas, expensive clothes and foods, and the satisfaction of their intellectual, aesthetic, and more often sensual appetites. In the past these were neither affordable nor socially acceptable. Attempts to control conspicuous consumption failed. Taxes introduced by Cato on slaves with special skills or talents, as well as on ornaments, women's clothes, and other items were resisted, and similar taxes on statues and other *objets d'art* had no success. The railings of Cato and other moralists against erecting public statues (including statues to women) and their general allegations of moral corruption point to a major reordering of values in the second century B.C. The values that had made Rome great in war and adversity led in peace to monstrous examples of egomania and self-indulgence. There was a fine dividing line between the acquisition of honor and glory in the service of the state and outright self-inflation. The empire brought vast riches to a small elite and enabled its members to vie for more and more personal power. The maldistribution of wealth was an essential factor in undermining the delicate equilibrium among the competing factions of aristocrats. The unity of the elite, which had to this point been one of Rome's great strengths, began to unravel.

## 2. THE GRACCHAN REVOLUTION

### Tiberius Gracchus and the Emergence of Popular Politics

The enormous social, cultural, and economic changes of the second century B.C. were funneled into a constitutional framework designed for a city and territory that were a fraction of the size of the empire that Rome now possessed. The political machinery of the Republic

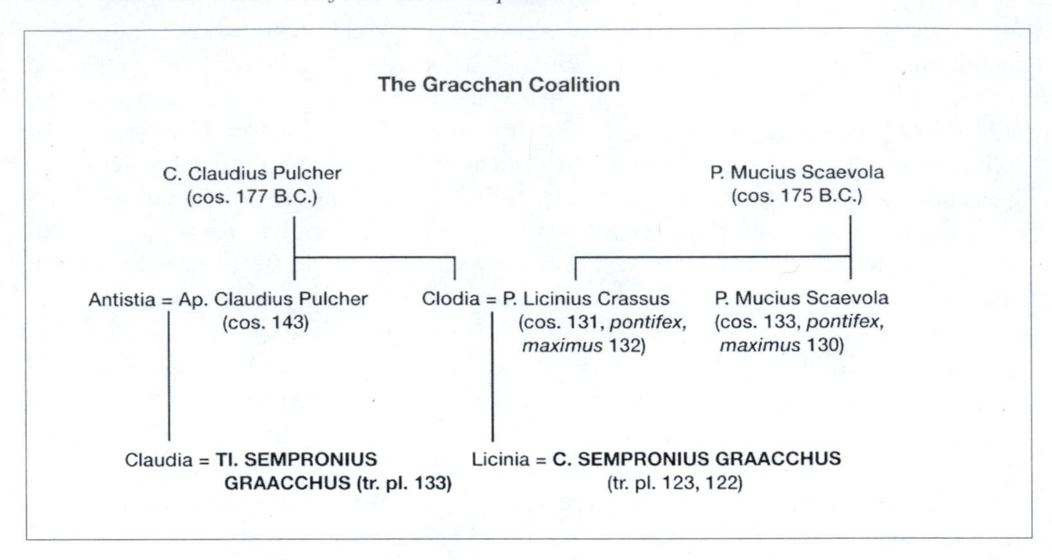


was called upon to perform tasks for which it had not been designed. In 133 B.C., when it was presented with truly major reform legislation that attempted to fix problems that had been developing for half a century or more, it failed catastrophically. The result was a division in the ruling class following roughly the lines of the divisions that had already begun to appear in Roman society at large.

THE REVOLUTIONARY FAMILY The instigators of this revolutionary change were not the product of the new forces at work in Roman society. They were, rather, true insiders, members of Rome's most prominent aristocratic families. The brothers Tiberius and Gaius Sempronius Gracchus were descended from branches of the ancient Cornelian and Sempronian *gentes* or clans. On the Cornelian side—their mother's side of the family—Tiberius and Gaius were related to the great Scipio Africanus, the victor over Hannibal. By marriage they were connected with other distinguished families in Rome. Their brother-in-law was Scipio Aemilianus who sacked Carthage in 146 B.C. and was currently (133 B.C.) in command of Roman forces besieging Numantia in Spain. Tiberius's wife was the daughter of Appius Claudius who had been both consul and censor and was now *princeps senatus*, the foremost man in the Senate. As *princeps* his opinion carried great weight; he was the first to be consulted in any senatorial debate. Gaius's father-in-law, Licinius Crassus, was soon to be *pontifex maximus* (chief priest) and consul. The brother of this same Crassus, Mucius Scaevola, a well known legal expert, was—conveniently—consul in 133 B.C. This was the very year that the elder Gracchan brother, Tiberius, entered into the office of tribune of the plebs with an ambitious reform plan that had multiple political, economic and social aims.

WHAT WAS WRONG WITH ROME In the view of Gracchus and his supporters Rome in the second century suffered from a number of interrelated maladies. The steady disappearance of peasant farmers who were being pushed off their land by the rich had a number of negative social, economic, political and military consequences. The use of slaves on large estates was increasing. Dispossessed farmers and their families had no place go and in many instances ended up in Rome where they had come in hope of finding employment in one of the many building projects being undertaken there. One result of this kind of immigration to the capital was the creation of a potentially dangerous permanent underclass of *proletarii*.

With the reduction in the number of land-owning peasant citizens the manpower pool for the army shrank. The disappearance of the sturdy, independent farmer was regarded as a disaster for Rome for, as Cato said "it is from the farming class that the bravest men and the best soldiers come" (*On Agriculture* 1.1). This loss, it was thought, made it difficult for the state to obtain adequate numbers of the right kind of recruits for the legions. Though largely correct, this analysis failed to do justice to the exceedingly complex developments of the second century B.C., or even to the reasons for the inadequate number of troops. There was surely a decline in the number of peasant farmers on the legionary rolls by mid-century, but there was also a growing reluctance on the part of many to serve in the army. New kinds of wars were now being fought, not just in defense of Rome but for the protection or acquisition of an overseas empire. Many of these wars involved years of service in inhospitable environments at great distances from Italy. As Rome's military needs changed in the second century B.C. so did the aims of the warfare it waged.

There were other factors at work that made recruiting for the legions difficult. New economic opportunities in Italy made soldiering a less attractive alternative. At least some small property owners were able to convert from subsistence to cash-crop farming and sell their produce to the growing urban population of Italy. The growth of Rome and the job opportunities presented by the huge building programs undertaken in many parts of Italy in the second century attracted many rural dwellers to the city.

THE GRACCHAN PROGRAM To address these problems the Gracchans proposed a radical reform program built around the distribution of public land to landless citizens. Their plan was well thought-through and attempted to take into account the failure of Gaius Laelius' similar plan of seven years earlier. Their aim was to draw on the huge land bank of public land (*ager publicus*) over which the state had sovereignty to make grants of inalienable plots of land to individual farmers. Since the assigned plots of land could not be sold two problems would be solved. Their owners would be able to resist the pressures of the rich to sell and they and their descendants would be forever liable to legionary service. From the viewpoint of the state there was an added benefit: these newly settled farmers would have much less opportunity to escape the draft. A bonus for Tiberius' coalition would be the fact that the new assignees would constitute a grateful political constituency for the members of the faction. Thus at a stroke it was hoped that a dependable supply of recruits for the legions would be guaranteed or at least augmented. It was estimated, presumably, that the bait of land ownership would outweigh the growing reluctance of the peasantry to serve in the legions at all. The poor would be moved up from the ranks of the landless *proletarii* to the respectable status of *assidui*, landowning, self-sustaining citizens and cease to be a burden and a danger to the state. The old moral and economic foundation of the state—the peasant household—would be restored.

To offset the opposition of longtime occupiers of public land the law offered clear title to the generous amount of land permitted by law, 500 jugera, plus and an additional 250 jugera for each of two sons. This was a total of over 1200 acres in a world where a 40 acre farm was considered large. Needless to say, none of this legislation applied to land already owned privately; it dealt only with public domain land of the Roman state. The Gracchan land proposal was a popular law but it was not a piece of demagoguery in which the rights of ownership were to be trampled in a grab for political power. Nonetheless, because it involved land, the proposal set off a fire storm, exciting, for different reasons, the landless, the landed elite, and everyone in between. A zero-sum game had been launched. Someone had to lose.

PROBLEMS OF THE LAW There were a number of difficulties built into the program. The public land under discussion had been parceled out over the centuries to renters, and the titles of possession were inextricably confused. There were legal renters and leaseholders who had come to consider themselves de facto owners because of the long time they had been in possession of their properties. They made their point noisily by claiming that if were they forced off this land they would have to abandon the graves of their ancestors. Then there were illegal squatters, both Roman and non-Roman, as well as the original Italian possessors who leased their land back from Rome or who had in some instances simply never vacated their confiscated land. Tiberius and his supporters had first to clear these people off the land and somehow equitably settle a large number of complicated suits before initiating their own settlement program. Because many of the leaseholders as well as the squatters with doubtful title were well-to-do, this proposal was calculated to stir up a storm of protest, which in fact it did and continued to do long after Tiberius' death.

A second problem was unanticipated at least in terms of its size. This was the large number of rural dwellers who suddenly discovered that they could either acquire ownership of land or firm title to land on which they were already squatting. There were naturally many more of these than of the well-to-do possessors. When the law came up for a vote Rome witnessed the extraordinary sight of masses of country people pouring into the city to vote. In a good economic climate for the sale of farm produce the ownership of land or the extension of one's possessions was an irresistible attraction. In this instance the usual obstacles of time and distance that normally kept rural voters from traveling to Rome, were not deterrents.

UNANTICIPATED CONSEQUENCES The Gracchans now found themselves at the head of an unplanned democratic movement, which led to a constitutional confrontation of powers unfolding as follows.

Apparently a decision had been made at the start by the Gracchan faction not to present the land bill to the Senate for pre-approval as was customary, but rather to go ahead and deal with the people directly in the People's Assembly (the *concilium plebis*). This was not unprecedented, and anyway the provisions of the *lex Hortensia* guaranteed that tribunes could call the popular assembly into session and pass legislation binding on all classes. The Senate, however, had the means, also constitutional, of stymieing such legislation. As a member of a college of ten members, Tiberius' actions were subject to veto by any of the other nine tribunes, some of whom were friendly to the senatorial opposition. If that occurred the law would be automatically rescinded, and normally that would be the end of the affair until at least such time as the opposing tribune(s) agreed to withdraw his veto. In due course a tribune, Marcus Octavius, interposed his veto.

At this point most of Tiberius' backers peeled away and accepted the defeat of the law. Tiberius however had other ideas. He proposed to the people that the offending tribune who was—after all—obstructing their will, should be removed. This was an unprecedented action but was not illegal. The problem was that this maneuver pitted a number of key Roman political principles against each other. Such a conflict of principles had always been a possibility, but in the past outside threats and the cohesion of the elite had usually deterred individuals and factions within the elite from pushing their cases to extremes.

THE CONSTITUTIONAL ISSUES First there was a collision between the tribune's sacrosanctity and the will of the people. The removal of Octavius would involve some kind of violation of this ancient principle. There was, however, a more fundamental issue. Rome had a traditional, not a written constitution. Political results were to be achieved by means of consensus worked out among the contending parties without any one of them making full use of his legal powers. Collegiality was supposed to nudge magistrates towards consensus of some kind. However, the removal of a tribune from office by popular vote pitted the powerful principle of popular sovereignty against the equally or even more powerful principle of magisterial collegiality and authority. If it was possible to remove a magistrate from office by the vote of the Popular Assembly, the Senate would lose control of the magistracies. Magistrates would then become subject to the people and power would shift to the assemblies. The people's will would then be supreme. Thus the original bargain between the patricians and the plebeians would be abrogated in favor the latter. Although any issue having to do with land was potentially explosive all by itself, the political tactics being pursued by Tiberius went a step in the direction of subverting the constitution. In the minds of his fiercest opponents his next step had to be *regnum*—one-man rule—in which the Senate would be dispensed with and a single individual would rule Rome in conjunction with the Popular Assembly.

Here indeed was a radical solution to Rome's political problems but not one the ruling class, undoubtedly even including Tiberius himself, was ready for. Nevertheless Tiberius was de facto a pioneer of the popular approach (*popularis ratio*) to politics, which led to the use of the term *populares* ("supporters of the people") for those who subsequently advocated it. Their opponents chose to call themselves *optimates*, "the best," in a moral and social sense, but also best qualified in their eyes to run the state.

TIBERIUS' MOTIVATION Why did Tiberius head off in this direction? The sources offer a number of possibilities, none of them fully convincing. One was that Tiberius had been infected by Greek ideas of popular sovereignty. Among his inner circle of friends and advisors were a number of Greeks, including Diophanes, an orator from Mitylene, and Blossius, a philosopher who was a close friend of the distinguished Antipater of Tarsus, head of the Stoic School in Athens.

Most scholars think it unlikely that Tiberius was ideologically motivated in this way. Members of the Roman elite were fully aware, as were of course the Greeks themselves, of the problems of direct, majoritarian rule. Democracies constantly changed their minds; people had short memories and invariably focused on the short term. It was impossible to run an empire on such principles. As it was, direct democracies lacked the sophistication, patience, and will power necessary for running large territorial states. They also had the unwelcome tendency (from an elite viewpoint) to take money and land from the rich to help the poor. An empire presented even more challenges.

Another theory was that Tiberius had to win this battle or his dignity would have suffered a fatal blow. Already he had been dishonored by having had the bad luck in his early military career of being an officer in a Roman army that was forced to surrender in Spain. The army only escaped after it made a shameful treaty with the enemy. Upon its return the Senate repudiated the treaty and handed the army's commander over to the Spaniards. The same fate would have befallen Tiberius himself if he had not been rescued by his influential brother-in-law, Scipio Aemilianus. This theory assumes that Tiberius was willing to put his career above everything else. Perhaps he was; we simply do not have enough information to pass such a psychological judgment.

A third possibility is that because the city was full of rural voters rather than the usual urban crowd there was a real danger of things getting out of control. Plutarch claims that it was the people themselves who had the greatest influence on Tiberius. The people, he reports "inscribed slogans and appeals on porticoes, monuments, and the walls of houses, calling on him to recover the public land for the poor."[1] Perhaps it was better to go forward and hope for the best than to give up and see street violence and who knows what kind of mayhem. In any case, whatever his final motivation, Tiberius went ahead with his plans and had Octavius voted out of office. The land law was then enacted and a commission for its administration appointed.

THE FUNDING CRISIS Then a new crisis connected with the law arose. The Senate refused to fund the bill (i.e., supply the commission with the necessary resources to complete the land distribution and settle the new owners). At that point Attalus III, king of Pergamum, died and left his kingdom to Rome. Tiberius immediately claimed the inheritance for the Roman people and had legislation passed to that effect. The money was to be used to complete the enactment of the law. This action, however, constituted a clear encroachment on the Senate's prerogatives, which traditionally included both national financial administration and foreign affairs. Tiberius was now explicitly accused by his opponents of seeking one-man rule (*regnum*). In the next century Cicero was to comment that Gracchus created a situation "where there was in one state two Senates and almost two peoples" (*de re publica* 1.31), and even Sallust, who was highly critical of the elite, said that the "Gracchi were so eager for victory they did not show sufficient moderation" (*Jugurthine War* 42.2).

THE MURDER OF TIBERIUS With the passage of the law and the election of a commission (consisting of Tiberius, his brother, and his father-in-law) to administer it, the rural crowd withdrew from Rome, and political life began to return to normal. However, there arose the inevitable threat of prosecution of Tiberius for illegality when his term of office was up on December 9, 133 B.C. To forestall this, Tiberius attempted to have himself re-elected to the tribunate, an unprecedented act. Tiberius' enemies in the Senate called for the presiding consul, the Gracchan supporter Mucius Scaevola, to intervene. When Scaevola refused, a key figure in the opposition and the then *pontifex maximus* Scipio Nasica led a mob of senators

[1] *Life of Tiberius Gracchus*, 8.

and their supporters in an attack on the assembly that was to re-elect Gracchus. In the melee that followed Tiberius and some 300 of his supporters were murdered.

### A Revolution is Launched

*Many Romans of later generations looked at the murder of Tiberius Gracchus as the moment when the Roman revolution began.*

> This was the beginning of civil bloodshed and of the free reign of the sword in the city of Rome. From then on right was overwhelmed by might and the strongest was preeminent. Disputes between citizens that in an earlier age had been settled through consensus were now settled by the sword. Wars were not started for just causes but for what profit could be made out of them. This state of affairs was not surprising: Precedents do not stop where they begin. However narrow their first path, they create for themselves a broad highway where they may wander at will. Once the path of justice has been abandoned, men rush headlong into wrongdoing. No one considers a way too evil for himself which has brought rewards to others (Velleius Paterculus, *A History of Rome*, 2.3).

## Gaius Gracchus

Ten years after Tiberius' death his brother Gaius, who in the intervening years had performed his required military service and acted as commissioner for the discharge of his brother's agrarian law, entered the same office of tribune of the plebeians as Tiberius had held in 133 B.C. but with a new strategy and a new plan of action. He took his mother's advice to avoid direct action against his enemies to avenge himself for the murder of his brother.

Much had been learned from the experience of Tiberius Gracchus. This time an appeal was made immediately to several of the newly emerging power groups in the state, though not in particular to the rural crowds who had proved so difficult to handle in 133 B.C.

Among these emerging groups were the publicans and the equestrian class. The Roman aristocracy had always resisted the creation of anything like a bureaucracy since such an institution would interfere with the way they ran the state. Because someone had to collect the revenue necessary to run the state, contracts for the collection of taxes were leased out to private companies—societies of publicans (*societates publicanorum*)—as they were called. Similarly, contracts were let out for public works, military supplies, the exploitation of mines, the building of roads, and other services. These companies of publicans bid among themselves for these contracts. In the case of tax contracts they were required to put the proceeds upfront, before the taxes were actually collected. Hence, only the well-off, primarily members of the equestrian class, the second rank of the aristocracy after the senatorial class, could participate in this lucrative business. Because senators after 129 B.C. were excluded from the equestrian centuries they could not directly participate in publican enterprises, though they did so indirectly through representatives. The dominant figures among the publicans were the equestrians, and it was to these the Gracchans appealed.

In 123 Gaius Gracchus sponsored a law providing that the revenue for the province of Asia, which had been willed to Rome by its ruler ten years earlier, be sold in Rome by the censors every 5 years. In comparison to previous contracts, the sums involved for the Asian

**A Mother's Advice to her Son**

*Cornelia, daughter of Scipio Africanus and the mother of the Gracchi advised her only surviving son Gaius (she had 12 children but only 3 reached adulthood) not to let his desire for revenge overwhelm his larger goals.*

You will say that it is glorious to take revenge on one's enemies. That seems neither truer nor more glorious to anyone than it does to me—but only if it can be done without injury to the Republic. Since that, however, cannot be, it is better that our enemies not be destroyed and remain as they are rather than that the Republic should be ruined and perish. (Cornelius Nepos, fragment 1)

taxes were spectacular, and the profits proportionately large. The power of the equestrian class expanded enormously. In addition Gracchus sponsored laws promoting contracts for constructing roads, granaries, and public buildings in different parts of Italy. The power of the equestrian class was expanded further when it was given control of the extortion court (*quaestio de repetundis*), which tried cases of senatorial misconduct in provincial administration. Until then the court had been in the hands of the senators themselves.This new arrangement ensured the publicans a high degree of political freedom from senatorial interference as they collected the taxes of Asia. It also served to highlight the emergence of the equestrian order as an order distinct from the senatorial order. Promises of large amounts of land in Africa, grain at a fixed price for the urban crowds, some laws governing military service and personal rights, Roman citizenship for the Latins, and Latin citizenship for the Italian allies were the baits offered to the final elements of the Gracchan coalition.

Many of these proposals addressed pressing problems. Rome had a population at this time of about 250,000 and had outgrown local food resources. Grain had to be imported, but it was dangerous to leave the price of grain to the unpredictable fluctuations of the market. Hence the proposal to guarantee grain, at a subsidized price, for the inhabitants of the city. It was also recognized that the single year that a tribune had to execute his program did not provide enough time so that from the start Gaius planned to run for re-election. Time had been one of the factors in the undoing of his brother in 133 B.C. Therefore, a law was passed making it legal for a tribune to seek re-election.

THE FAILURE OF GAIUS' PROGRAM This extraordinary combination of interests enabled Gaius to wield power for two consecutive years and enact most of the promised legislation, but in time the inevitable negative forces with which the Roman constitution abounded, in particular tribunician opposition, gradually dissolved the alliance. Gaius Fannius, one of the consuls of 122 B.C. who had been elected as a Gracchan supporter, switched sides. He and the tribune Livius Drusus reminded the people that any extension of citizenship would be to their disadvantage, and as a counter to Gaius' colonial law, he proposed a much larger program under more favorable circumstances. In 121 B.C. Gaius Gracchus found himself out of office and without power. During an attempt by his opponents to abrogate one of his laws, the situation became so riotous that the Senate passed an emergency decree that ordered the consul to restore order in the city (*senatus consultum ultimum*). In the ensuing conflict Gaius was killed along with 3,000 of his supporters, including the ex-consul Fulvius Flaccus. Their bodies, along with those of the other slain, were thrown into the Tiber. Their property was confiscated and the proceeds placed in the public treasury.

Once again the *optimates* forces had triumphed. The consul who had executed the *senatus consultum ultimum* hubristically refurbished the temple to the goddess Concord in honor of his "victory." Someone at night carved this graffito on it: "An act of insane discord produces a temple to Concord."[2] The people responded by consecrating the places where the Gracchi were slain, put up statues to them, and brought offerings there on a regular basis "as though they were honoring statues of the gods."[3]

## The Consequences of the Gracchan Reform Movement

The end of Gaius offered a clear illustration of the Senate's inability to rule and of the power of the new forces within the Republic. Tiberius and Gaius together made obvious the paralysis of the old senatorial elite and the ineffectiveness of its ruling techniques. It was not at all clear, however, what were the alternatives to senatorial rule short of one-man rule. Gaius' coalition of equestrians, the well-to-do, and the urban crowds enabled him to control the Popular Assembly for a time, but his reliance on the office of tribune did not constitute a permanent or an alternate basis for government. Even though in the end the Gracchan coalition disintegrated and the old system reasserted itself, it would be only a matter of time before new leaders would experiment, perhaps more successfully, with the emerging forces. One of the immediate consequences of Gaius Gracchus' legislation was to set up the publicans as a new exploiting class unrestrained by the traditions of public service and otherwise unaccountable to the law.

As the Gracchans highlighted the power of the rural voters, the equestrian class, and the urban crowds, and drew attention to the discontent of the Italian allies, they stimulated the political consciousness of these interest groups and whetted their appetite for change. It was to these groups that politicians and generals were to turn more and more. A new approach in political technique, the *popularis ratio*, was at hand for them to use. The Gracchi were both models and martyrs.

In a crisis the elite could generally depend on the loyalty of their personal retainers, clients, and like-minded friends to crush movements like those of the Gracchi. In the first century B.C., however, the new popular leaders (*populares*) learned how to counteract this crude power with mobs of their own. When this happened the possibility of political solutions was even further undermined. There was no alternative but to bring in the army, thus violating the most basic constitutional principle that armed soldiers should not cross the *pomerium*, the sacred boundary of the city. The old distinction between *domi et militiae*—the peaceful, civil atmosphere of the city, where problems were solved by political consensus versus the dangerous world outside the city, where war was the method of resolving problems—disappeared. The public space, where contentious matters could be hammered out peacefully, was gone.

[2]Plutarch, *Life of Gaius Gracchus*, 16.

[3]Plutarch, *Life of Gaius Gracchus*, 17.

# 10

# After the Gracchi

## 1. AFTER THE GRACCHI: FURTHER UNRAVELING OF THE CONSTITUTION

### An Overview

WINDING DOWN THE GRACCHAN PROGRAM After the murder of Gaius Gracchus the internal battles among the elites moved to the courts. Attempts were made there to take revenge on some of the major anti-Gracchan figures such as Opimius, but they were mostly unsuccessful. Some of Gaius Gracchus' laws remained in effect such as his grain subsidies for Rome, his reforms of the court, and his tax farming arrangements for Asia. The land program established by Tiberius Gracchus was not challenged head on but was rather gradually modified. It eventually ground to a halt. Its key inalienability clause, i.e. the prohibition against the sale of land parceled out under the law, was eliminated and Gracchan settlers were allowed to treat their allotments as though they were private land. The land commission was abolished in 119 B.C., and a final law passed in 111 B.C. wound up the agrarian reform program. There was now no peaceful way by which the manpower problem and poverty in the city could be alleviated. The termination of land reform efforts prepared the way for the development of private or client armies by the dynasts in the next century.

PROBLEMS SOLVED AND UNSOLVED For a century after the Gracchi Rome struggled with the great issues their attempted reforms raised. Manpower shortages for the legions were addressed by the consul Marius in 107 B.C. when he ignored property qualifications and enlisted the *proletarii*. Because property qualifications had had been falling since the time of the Hannibalic War Marius' actions were not especially revolutionary, but they did suggest to other generals how to go about filling up vacancies in their legions when the draft produced too few recruits. The truly dangerous issue of what should be done with demobilized, long serving veterans remained to be settled. There were no provisions for pensioning off these troops. The Senate recognized that if it moved to provide them with land or cash they would generate the same kind of problems that the Gracchans faced and failed to solve. It would take large sums of money to acquire land for returning veterans and no one had any idea where that money would come from. In the bloody Social War (91–89 B.C.) the Italian allies fought for and won Roman citizenship, but the full integration of the Italians in the political and social structure of the Roman state was to take several more generations. The military dynast Sulla recognized that the Senate was too small for its role in administering the empire and expanded it to twice its original size. Most of the new members were drawn from the equestrian order. Some problems were unresolvable. The maintenance of public order in Rome without a police force of some kind, especially in times of political crisis, was not solved until Augustus introduced a permanent militarized police force in the form of the Praetorian Guard and the Urban Cohorts. This was only a partial solution and came with its own sets of problems. There were well established reasons why a police force was incompatible with the kind of freedom enjoyed by *polis*-type citizens.

WHO WAS TO RULE ROME? The most intractable of all the problems facing Rome after the Gracchi was the question of who was to rule and by what means. This was mainly a political problem, but it had social and economic ramifications. The old understanding of how a *polis* state should be run had been undermined but there was no clear consensus regarding what should take its place. At issue was the question of the composition of the ruling class and how it conducted itself. In the past, it was accepted that the chief offices of the state were exchanged among a handful of elite families. It was also understood that only be disciplining its own membership could the Senate retain control of the political power of the state. However, by the end of the second century B.C. it was clear that the Senate's control its own members had been considerably weakened and that the consensus among the elite that that had held the ruling class together for centuries was disintegrating. Although it was still possible for the old inner coterie of the elite to put its candidates in highest offices, it was unable to dominate proceedings as it had in the past. By the time of the emergence of a new ruling class almost a century later, most of the old elite families of the Republic were gone. Their replacements came from a much wider social and geographic background than in the past. The ruling elite expanded numerically adding to the difficulty of the Senate's ability to control it. In terms of their economic resources and social viewpoints the newcomers did not essentially differ from their predecessors. What did change was the locus of political power which shifted first to the commanders of provincial armies and then to a single, new political head of state, the emperor.

## 2. MARIUS

### Wars and the Opportunities They Generated

The foreign affairs of the late second century were largely the legacies of the wars conducted earlier in the century. To maintain contact with its provinces in Spain Rome had to

| Chronology | |
|---|---|
| Jugurthine War: Marius in Africa | 111–104 B.C. |
| War with the Cimbri and Teutons | 105–101 B.C. |
| Social War | 90–88 B.C. |
| Revolt of Mithridates VI | 88 B.C. |
| Dictatorship of Sulla | 82–79 B.C. |

secure its lines of communication through southern Gaul. This led to the creation of a new province there in 121 B.C., and the founding of a colony at Narbo in 118 B.C. as its capital. The Balearic Islands were annexed and two Roman settlements sent to Majorca. There was more road building. The *via Fulvia* was constructed in the Po valley and the *via Domitia* in the new province in southern Gaul connected Spain, with Italy.

Rome's external enemies in the generation after the Gracchi were not major powers on the order of Carthage or the Hellenistic states of earlier ages. Many were pre-political, pre-state peoples whose lack of an identifiable apparatus of state made them difficult to control. Wars against them tended to follow the pattern of the guerrilla campaigns that Rome had fought in Spain. They were long, protracted, and unconventional, and often revealed the ineptness and weakness of the senatorial system of command. A Celtic tribe, the Scordisci, was a perennial threat to Thrace, Macedonia and even Greece. They inflicted a serious defeat on a Roman army in 114 B.C. and promptly raided Greece as far south as Delphi. In the following year another Roman army was crushed by a wandering German tribe in what is now Austria. There was a protracted guerrilla war in Africa and a slave revolt in Sicily (103-101 B.C.).

THE WAR IN AFRICA Rome's client kingdom of Numidia in north Africa had been a problem for Rome on and off since the second century. The ruling king Micipsa had, on the recommendation of Scipio Aemilianus adopted Jugurtha who had served with Scipio at the siege of Numantia. Jugurtha was a grandson of the founder of the kingdom Masinissa, but who was not in line for succession. To solve the dispute a Roman commission divided Numidia between Jugurtha and one of the legitimate heirs, but Jugurtha soon disposed of his co-ruler but in the process provoked the ire of the Senate. In 112 B.C. the consul L. Opimius invaded Numidia but quickly made peace, perhaps deterred by the possibility of a long drawn out guerrilla war. When summoned to Rome on safe conduct in 111 B.C. to give testimony in a bribery case, Jugurtha took the opportunity to have a potential rival who happened to be living in Rome, assassinated. Although clearly guilty the well-connected king was allowed to leave Rome in safety. On departing he was supposed to have looked back at it and have said: "There is a city up for sale. Its days are numbered if it can find a buyer."[1]

For a number of years the war dragged on dismally, and Roman commanders did poorly against their wily opponent. The difficulty of waging a guerrilla war and military incompetence were not just the issue; corruption was also suspected. There were accusations of bribery against the consul Calpurnius Bestia who made a peace on favorable terms with Jugurtha. The treaty was rejected by the Senate and war began again but the Roman army sent against Jugurtha was forced to surrender, and was humiliated by being sent under the yoke and then expelled from Numidia. With the appointment of Caecilius Metellus as com-

[1]Sallust, *Jugurthine War*, 35.

mander in 109 B.C. good progress was made, but although competent and incorruptible, two years went by and the war still dragged on.

MARIUS Exasperated by repeated failure, corruption and the slow pace of the war, the people turned to Gaius Marius, a "New Man" (*novus homo*) who promised them a quick end.[2] He was elected to the consulship for 107 B.C. The problem Marius faced in the African war was a basic one of all guerrilla wars: He had to outnumber the enemy by as much as 7:1, but with another war in progress in the north against wandering German and Celtic tribes and permanent manpower shortages, it seemed unlikely that he would be any more successful than most of his predecessors. However, by the simple but bold expedient of enrolling the propertyless (the *proletarii*), Marius resolved his manpower problem. In 105 B.C. Marius brought the war to a successful conclusion, just in time to allow him to return to Italy for another war.

THE GERMAN THREAT Sometime towards the end of the second century B.C. a large German tribe, the Cimbri, were driven from its homeland in Denmark by the flooding of the sea, and began a slow march southward. It was joined by two other German tribes, the Teutones and Ambrones. Like the Celts they planned to pillage their way toward the promised lands of the Mediterranean shore. They made their first contact with the Romans at Noreia (in modern Austria) in 113 B.C. where they routed the army of Gnaeus Carbo. Fortunately for Rome the tribes did not immediately aim for Italy but headed west toward Gaul. They were joined on their march by the Tigurini and other Celtic tribes. With their new province in southern Gaul under threat, the Romans sent out another army under Junius Silanus, consul of 109 B.C. to defend it. It too was defeated and two years later yet another Roman army was defeated and its consular commander killed.

In 105 B.C. the consul Gnaeus Mallius, a "new man," was sent out to take care of the situation. The remaining army in southern Gaul under the proconsul Servilius Carbo was supposed to cooperate with Mallius, but because Mallius was a *novus* the haughty aristocrat Carbo disdained to cooperate. The result, the battle of Arausio (Orange) in 105 B.C., was the Romans' worst defeat since Cannae. There was now the real possibility of an invasion of Italy, but the Romans were fortunate yet again as the German horde chose to head west to plunder Gaul and Spain. The Romans were given one more chance to prepare themselves for invasion. Luckily Marius had just brought the war against Jugurtha in Africa to a successful conclusion. For the next five years Marius was elected consul, flatly disregarding the law that prohibited such successive tenures of office. Immediately Marius set about a thoroughgoing reorganization and retraining of the army. On occasion in the past Roman commanders had grouped the 30 maniples of the legions into 10 larger units called cohorts to give the legion greater coherence in the face of the kind of massed infantry attacks favored by Celts and Germans. Each cohort had about 500 men in it and was further subdi-

---

[2]The term "new man" was an invention of the late Republic for the first man in a family to reach the senate or for such a man to reach the consulship. These men almost never found full social acceptance among the already established senatorial families. Their background was usually the municipal aristocracy of Italy, the *domi nobiles*, men who were nobles in their own home cities. Marius and later Cicero belonged to this class. They were from the mountain town of Arpinum, about 70 miles southeast of Rome, in old Hernican territory. The ancestral language of this region was Oscan, but its people had long been Latinized.

**The Cohort Legion**

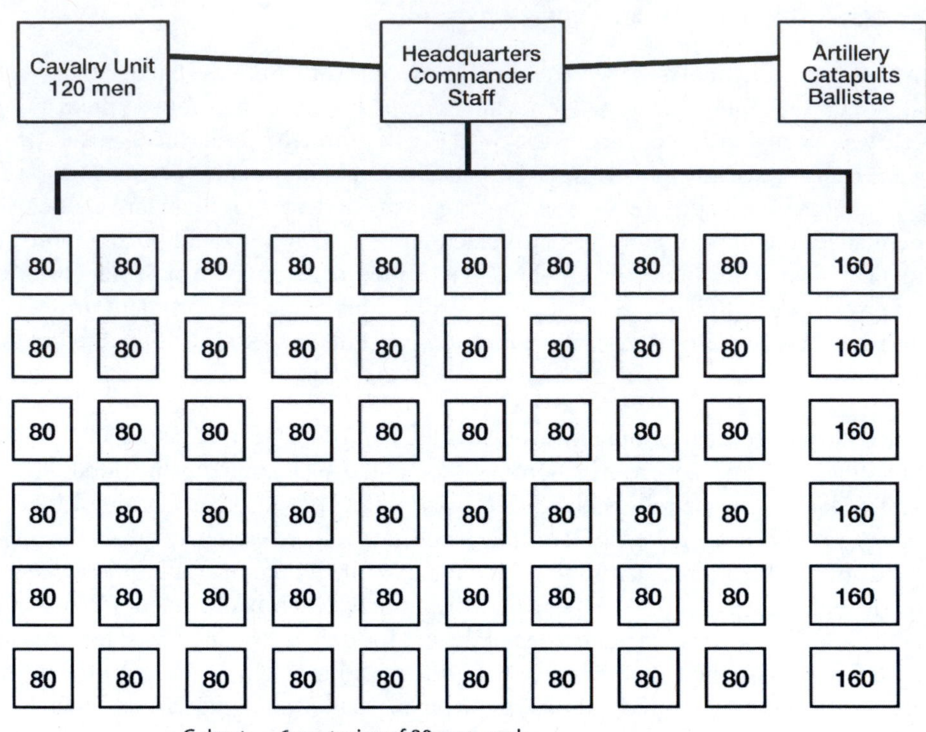


Cohort: 6 centuries of 80 men each.
Legion: 9 standard cohorts plus first cohort of double centuries.
Century: 80 men

vided into six centuries of 80 men, commanded by a centurion. The corporate identity and continuity of the legions were fostered by giving each one its own silver "eagle," or standard. The legionaries were given professional training in arms-use based on the techniques employed in the gladiatorial schools. The mobility of the army was increased by Marius' insistence that every soldier carry his own equipment. Henceforth the infantry were popularly known as "Marius' mules." The reforms either initiated or adopted by Marius had the combined effect of further undermining the traditional ideal of the citizen-soldier and moving the civilian militia in the direction of a mobile, well-trained, full-time army. However, it would take another generation and a half before the transition was complete.

In 102 B.C. the Cimbri and Teutones and their allies returned from their plundering expeditions in Gaul and Spain and finally headed for Italy. Given their large numbers it made sense to divide their forces and converge on Italy from different directions, thus forcing the Romans to divide their forces also. The Cimbri and Tigurini went by way of the Alps into the Po Valley while the Teutones and Ambrones traveled by the coastal route. At Aquae Sextiae (modern Aix-en-Provence) Marius was able to destroy the Teutones and Ambrones, and then return to northern Italy in time to join the other consul, Lutatius Catulus, to confront the Cimbri and their allies. These were defeated in 101 B.C. near Vercellae.

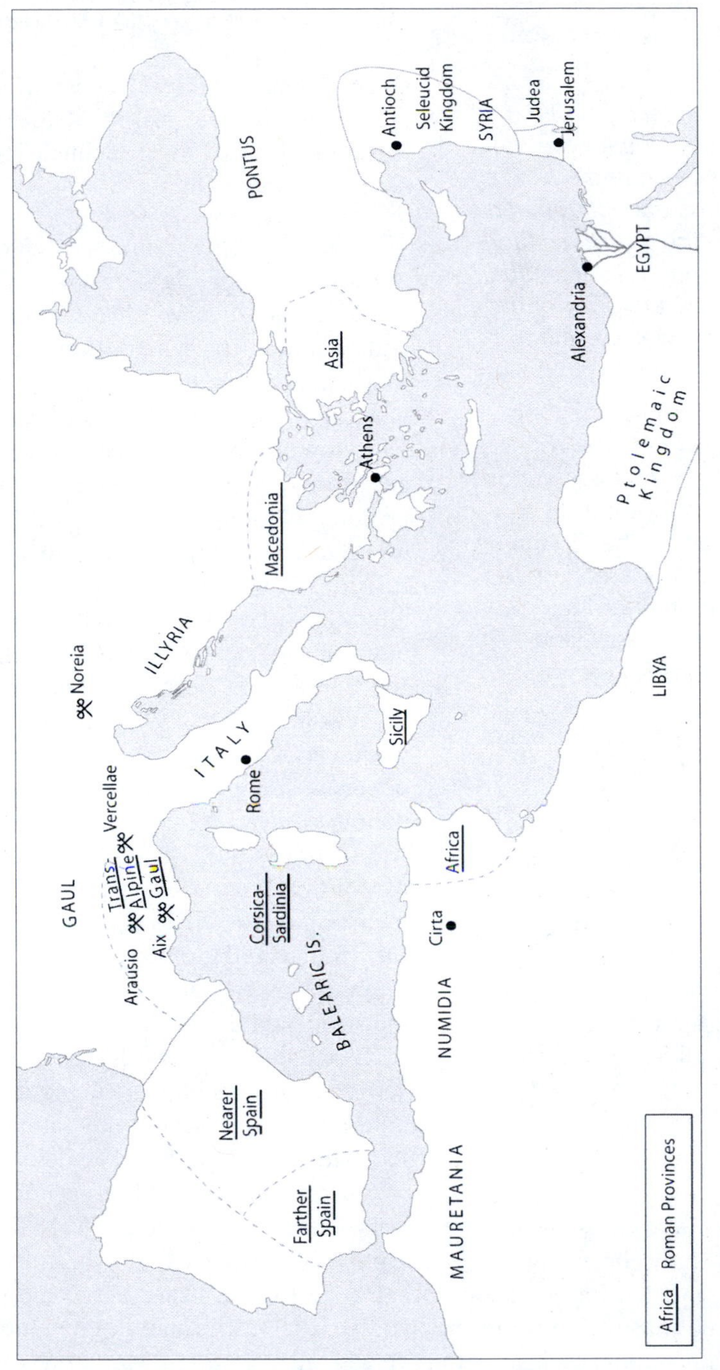


The Mediterranean ca. 100 B.C.

### The End of the Battle of Vercellae

*Plutarch, the author of the following lurid piece, had some good sources for the battle of Vercellae including the accounts, now all lost, of the consuls Marius and Catulus and one of Catulus' officers, the future military dynast Sulla. As can be deduced from the tone of the story the fear and horror of barbarous northerners was a well-developed constant throughout most of Roman history.*

The greater part of the enemy and their best fighters were cut to pieces.... Those who fled were driven back on their wagon lager by the Romans who were then confronted with a terrible sight. The German women, all dressed in black, stood on the wagons and killed the fugitives—their own husbands, brothers, and fathers—and then strangled their small children with their own hands, throwing them down under the wheels of the wagons or the feet of the oxen. Finally, they cut their own throats. It is said that one woman hanged herself from the end of a wagon pole with a child suspended from each ankle. The men, for want of trees, tied themselves to the horns or feet of the oxen and drove the animals forward with goads so that they were either dragged or trampled to death. In spite of all these suicides, more than 60,000 prisoners were taken while twice as many were said to have been killed (Plutarch, *The Life of Marius*, 27).

## Marius, Saturninus, and Veterans

Once the German threat had been dispelled, the old system of senatorial rule began to reassert itself and Marius' power declined. He was a soldier, not a politician.

LAND FOR THE VETERANS Under Rome's old system of fighting wars it was assumed that discharged soldiers would return to their farms and resume life where they had left off. Marius, however, had broken with the system when he filled vacancies in the legionary ranks with propertyless volunteers. They were now an acknowledged part of the army. What was to be done with them on demobilization? Somehow they had to be cared for, and the easiest solution seemed to be to give them land allotments. The Senate, fatally, was unable or unwilling to take on the job. The responsibility for finding the necessary land defaulted to their commanders. They in turn looked to whatever support they could muster among opportunistic politicians at Rome and used their own demobilized veterans in whatever ways were useful. This became a new method of political action among *popularis*-minded members of the elite. Generals who successfully found land for their veterans acquired additional power; the settled soldiers became their dependable clients

To satisfy his veterans Marius aligned himself with the ambitious tribune L. Appuleius Saturninus. An alliance with Saturninus in 103 B.C. had already produced land for his veterans of the African war and Marius hoped to repeat this success for the veterans of the German wars. Passage did not come easily, however, and in the impasse Marius brought his veterans into the legislative assembly and secured passage by force, thus writing yet another chapter in Roman history (100 B.C.). Although Tiberius Gracchus had used a combination of the rural voters and the city mob to pass his measures, and his brother Gaius tried to forge an alliance of the equestrians and the city people, it was not until Marius that the final step of uniting tribunes, military commanders, veterans and *plebs urbana* was taken. It was too effective a combination to be ignored by generals and politicians in the future. Apart from providing a model for political action, the granting of land to Marius' veterans provided an important precedent for ambitious generals who enrolled *proletarii* in their armies. However, when Saturninus resorted to violence in furthering his own ambitions, Marius abandoned him proving he was, at heart, no revolutionary. Saturninus was killed in a riot. The tribune's laws were rescinded by the Senate though it seems likely his law regarding the granting of land to Marius' veterans of the German war remained in effect. Once again the optimates had stopped at the brink and seized control from the *populares*, but the elimination by force of their enemies from the Gracchi to Saturninus did not amount to a constructive reform program. Besides, the *optimate* tools of control by violence were also weakening. There was no guarantee they would work in the future.

## 3. THE SOCIAL WAR

The matter of citizenship for the Italian allies, so pressing at the time of Gaius Gracchus, seems to have disappeared. In 91 B.C., however, it resurfaced violently. In general the Italian allies felt that they were getting less than their share of the spoils of conquest. They served in the army and fought Rome's wars but were losing out in the changed conditions of the second and first centuries B.C. They had lost heavily in the German wars through the

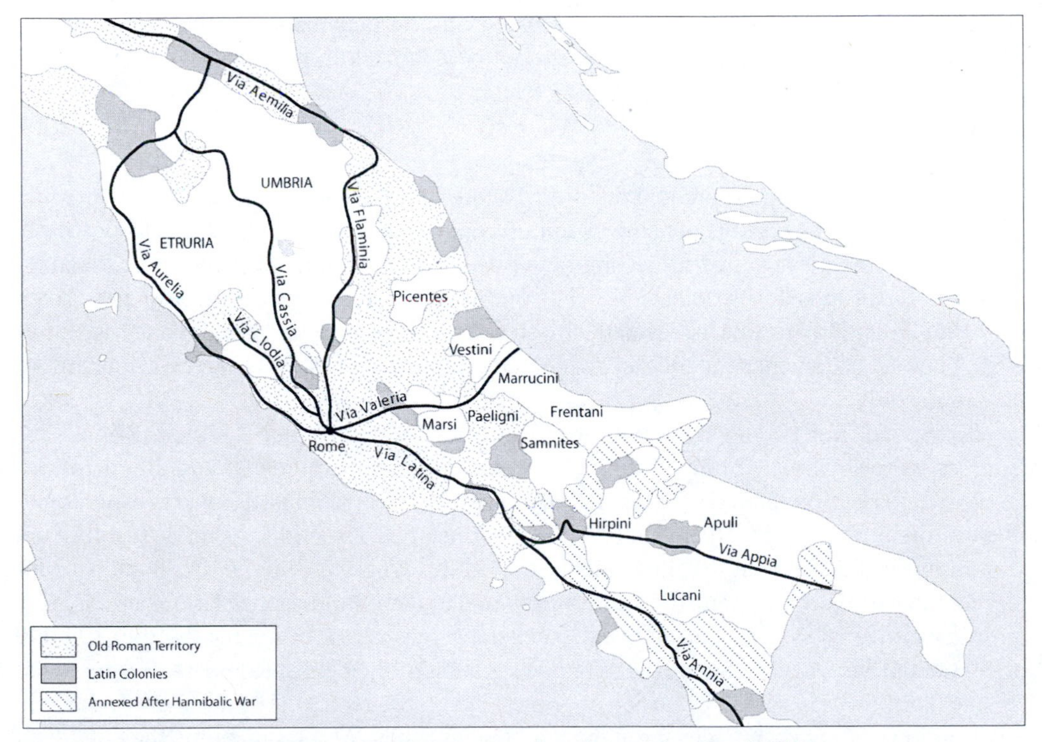


Map of Roman and Allied Territories on the Eve of the Social War

**Social War Propaganda of the Allies**

*The Italian confederates issued coins with* Italia *depicted as a woman. Favorite reverse sides were a bull goring a wolf or a soldier with a bull beside him representing Italy, and a foot on a Roman standard.*

bungling of incompetent Roman generals. Since Gaius Gracchus raised the citizenship issue there had been no letup in the exploitation by Romans of public land all over Italy.

## The Outbreak of the War

In 95 B.C. in an attempt to prevent the illegal acquisition of citizenship by allies who had moved to Rome, the consuls of that year humiliatingly ordered their expulsion from Rome. The issue of the bestowal of citizenship was raised by the tribune M. Livius Drusus in 91 B.C., but the proposal was defeated by the combined shortsightedness of ordinary citizen and elite alike. Drusus was assassinated by an unknown person, and the Italians rose in revolt. They set up an independent state, which they called Italia, with its capital at Corfinium in central Italy.

The Social War (Rome's war with its allies, its *socii*) was bitterly fought. Rome's resources were severely strained militarily in the early stages of the war and allied contingents had to be brought in from outside Italy. By 90 B.C. the main issues were resolved but the war did not come to a full end until 80 B.C. Grants of citizenship were made to cities and communities that had not revolted, and to individuals who gave up the revolt and surrendered. Finally all of Italy south of the Po was united under a single constitution, and a single political and legal system. The numbers listed in the census rose dramatically from 394,000 to 963,000. Even then, however, the optimate segment of the elite at Rome tried to avoid the political implications of the extension of citizenship by preventing for a number of years the distribution of the new citizens throughout all the 35 tribes. At the same time the elite itself was further fragmented as political enemies tried to settle grievances against each other in the courts.

## 4. THE MILITARY DYNAST SULLA

Able and ambitious Romans among the elite still found that war offered the best opportunities for self-advancement. The predominant figures of the next fifty years—Sulla, Pompey, Crassus, and Caesar to mention only the best known—all rose to prominence through their generalship and their ability to convert success on the battlefield into political power in Rome.

L. Cornelius Sulla was a quaestor of Marius in the war against Jugurtha. He served under Catulus in the German war and distinguished himself again in the Social War. He was elected consul for 88 B.C. Almost immediately a new war provided him with an opportunity to further his career. In eastern Anatolia the kingdom of Pontus had been gradually expanded by energetic rulers and found itself in collision with Roman client-kingdoms in the area. A major conflict developed when Mithridates VI, the reigning king of Pontus, invaded the Roman province of Asia in 88 B.C. where he was hailed by many as a liberator. To encourage hatred of Rome and solidify his own position he arranged for the massacre, it is said, of 80,000 resident Romans and Italians. Apart from the affront to Roman prestige, the loss of Asia represented a huge hit to the Roman treasury because Asia was Rome's richest province, and an immediate debt crisis resulted.

### Sulla's March on Rome

As consul for 88 B.C. Sulla inherited the war against Mithridates but his command of it was challenged by Marius, who, in collusion with the tribune P. Sulpicius Rufus, had himself designated commander. Just as Marius had used his veterans to force the passage of a land law, Sulla now went a step further by asking his army to help him "liberate" Rome from its oppressors. Only one of his officers, his relative L. Licinus Lucullus, followed him, but Sulla had no difficulty in convincing the rest of the army that its interest lay with him, not with Marius, who might recruit a new army. As the soldiers knew well, a war in Greece and Asia Minor was bound to be lucrative. This was not to be a war against poor but dangerous barbarians in the west. Rather it was to be against civilized, urbanized, and not very dangerous easterners.

Sulla's six legions followed him to Rome. Marius was driven out, the offending tribune Sulpicius, though still in office, was killed and his laws invalidated. After disposing of some more enemies, and enacting new laws, Sulla and his army left for the east. Not long after his departure Marius, who had fled to Africa, returned and made common cause with one of the consuls of the year, the anti-Sullan, Cornelius Cinna. They raised armies, marched on Rome, captured it and as Sulla did, took vengeance on their enemies. Sulla was outlawed and exiled in absentia, his property confiscated, and his house torn down.[3] Sulla's war against Mithridates was thus, technically, from now on being conducted without a legal mandate. Sulla, however, continued to claim he was the representative of the true Republic. Among the more constructive acts of the new rulers of Rome was an attempt to

[3] On the significance of destroying a citizen's house at Rome—the symbolic annihilation of the family—see above, page 77.

solve the debt crisis and the distribution, finally, of the Italians among all 35 of the tribes. Thus at length the long process of the unification of Italy was brought to an end, though the cultural unification was to go on for many more centuries. Marius, after a record seventh consulship, died in 86 B.C.

**Sulla's March on Rome: The Liberty Argument**

*Liberating Rome from its oppressors was a well established theme in Roman political ideology. At the beginning of the Republic Brutus had freed Rome from the tyrant Tarquinius Superbus. Periodically, in the intervening centuries the claim to be vindicating liberty had been used to quell potential threats to the Establishment. Both* optimates *and* populares *used the liberty argument depending on whether the rights of the elite or of the people were being defended. Here Sulla asserts his version of the argument. Later dynasts such as Caesar and Octavian also made claims to be vindicating liberty.*

Delegates met Sulla on the way to Rome [*at the head of his army*] and demanded why he was marching on his own country under arms. Sulla replied: "In order to free the state from those who were ruling it as tyrants" (Appian, *The Civil Wars,* 1.57).

## Sulla and Mithridates

Having defeated the Romans in Asia Mithridates' forces now crossed into Greece. Athens foolishly allowed itself to be persuaded to join Mithridates, and as soon as Sulla arrived he put it under siege and after its capture allowed his soldiers to slaughter its inhabitants at will and pillage it. Shortly afterwards he won two decisive battles in nearby Boeotia against Mithridates' forces and forced them to evacuate Greece. In the meantime Sulla's enemies in Rome had sent out yet another army of two legions to fight against Mithridates under the command of Valerius Flaccus, but also to challenge the renegade Sulla. A mutiny in Flaccus' army led to the death of Flaccus and his subordinate Fimbria took over. By 85 B.C. Mithridates was ready to negotiate. Terms were worked out by Sulla whereby Mithridates agreed to vacate the province of Asia and pay an indemnity. When finally the two Roman armies made contact Fimbria's troops defected to Sulla and Fimbria committed suicide. His army was incorporated in Sulla's.

SULLA RETURNS TO ITALY In 83 B.C. Sulla returned to Italy, ready to reestablish his political power. With his veteran army and the assistance of a number of young nobles who rallied to him, including M. Licinius Crassus and Gnaeus Pompeius (Pompey), Sulla routed his opponents and most of Italy submitted to him. Only the Samnites and Lucanians held out. In a final effort to attain freedom from Rome they marched on Rome and a desperate battle was fought just outside the city. Sulla prevailed and slaughtered the survivors of the battle arguing "that he knew from experience that no Roman would be able to live as long as the Samnites existed" (Strabo 5.4.11). Strabo, born about 20 years after these events, goes on to remark that what were once cities in Samnium had by his time become mere villages, and some had completely disappeared. The Samnite menace to Rome was finally liquidated.

In 82 B.C. Sulla had himself appointed dictator with special powers for reestablishing the state (*dictator rei publicae constituendae*). The ancient office of dictator had been used in the past in cases of emergency when the threat to the state was from the outside, but now the threat to Rome was from the inside the state itself. He used his position ruthlessly in a vain attempt to reinstate the traditional rule of the Senate and restore the old status quo.

THE PROSCRIPTIONS In his use of violence to achieve that end, however, Sulla showed himself not a traditionalist, but an apt pupil of the violent politicians who had preceded him. To raise money to pay his troops and eliminate his political opponents, he hit upon a novel method of legalized murder and confiscation. This was the proscription list. On the list, which was posted publicly, were the names of his enemies together with the prices he was willing to pay for their deaths. About 200 senators and over 1,600 equestrians perished in these proscriptions, and from the proceeds of their estates, Sulla was able to pay his troops and then settle down without fear of opposition to the task of reforming the constitution. In later years some of those involved in hunting down the proscribed claimed they had done so out of fear. This is not improbable. The proscriptions aimed not only at eliminating Sulla's enemies and finding cash for his troops but also involving or—perhaps better, incriminating—members of the elite in his political reordering of the state. Sharing responsibility for murder or the confiscation of property is a technique dictators have used from time immemorial.

## Sulla's Reforms

Acting as dictator from 82 B.C. to 79 B.C., Sulla enacted a number of major reforms aimed at restoring order to the chaos of recent political life at Rome. The main threat to senatorial control seemed to originate with the tribunate. Hence Sulla curtailed its powers by limiting the tribune's veto power and removing the tribune's legislative and prosecutorial capacities. Holders of the tribunate were barred from holding further public office. It thus became a political dead-end and in theory it would be shunned by the kind of ambitious opportunists who had used it, especially in the recent past, to promote their careers. In view of the demands of imperial administration he increased the number of quaestors to twenty and of praetors to eight, and established a rigid schedule according to which the different magistracies were to be held. The power of provincial governors, like that of the tribunes in Rome, had grown substantially and was increasingly attractive to ambitious individuals. To address this problem Sulla ruled that governors should not start wars on their own or march their troops across the boundaries of their provinces. He restored the courts to the Senate. However the problem of what to do with private, client armies, such as his own, and of what to do with such armies when they were to be demobilized, was not solved.

Probably his most important and lasting change was his reform of the Senate. Its numbers had been halved in the civil wars and by his own massacres. To the approximately surviving 150 or so members he added about 450, mostly from the equestrian order. From this time onwards, the make-up of the Senate was radically altered. The senatorial order was considerably broadened, and if the famous old families still continued to dominate the high offices, it was not in the way they had in the past. The moral authority of the Senate was weakened further by the elimination of those who had been most loyal to the Republic and by the introduction of many who had joined Sulla simply out of opportunism. "New men" began to make their appearance in the lower magistracies. It is against the background of this much enlarged and increasingly incoherent Senate that the events from Sulla to Caesar must be viewed.

## 5. THE NATURE OF THE BREAKDOWN

### Institutional Failure

Unfortunately the Senate could not be easily reformed. It had functioned in the past within a mutually shared culture of restrained competition and tolerance. This culture was deeply inculcated in its members. In the old Senate there were boundaries which individual senators would not transgress. Self-restraint was one of these, and perhaps the most important. If self-restraint was not enough the Senate had sufficient institutional authority to shame or quash its most egocentric, impulsive, corrupt or simply irresponsible members.

By Sulla's time, and in part as a result of the recent civil war with the *populares*, the membership of the senate had been decimated and merely adding new members did not solve the problem of its malfunctioning culture. Shame no longer worked. Honor had been ego-centrically redefined. Institutionally the Senate was broken. The irresponsible, the self-involved and the impulsive could no longer be held back in large measure because these men disdained the restrictions of an authority which, they could argue with some justice, had failed Rome spectacularly for decades. The legitimacy of senatorial rule had been undermined. An assertion of individual noble's *dignitas* became sufficient justification for launching a rebellion.

### The Menace Beneath the Surface

There were other less obvious consequences of the recent wars, civil and foreign. The events of elite history are relatively well known, but below the surface there was a less visible, but nonetheless fundamental transformation taking place among ordinary, non-elite Romans, especially among those who were serving in the armies. The cohort of uprooted, hardened men who found a home for themselves in the legions had increased in size since the Social War. These were professional soldiers in all but name. Being homeless and propertyless, they had little interest in replicating the old fashioned life-style of the traditional legionary. The psychic rewards of patriotism meant little to these men. Many came from rural, recently enfranchised districts of Italy, and had little knowledge of and less interest in obeying the commands of a weakened Senate and its often corrupt, incompetent magistrates. What they wanted were leaders who would win battles and reward them suitably afterward.

The first and most obvious manifestation of the development of an independent minded soldiery was the willingness with which the ordinary legionaries followed Sulla in his march on Rome in 88 B.C. Similarly motivated recruits followed Marius and Cinna in their assault on the capital a few years later. The high number of mutinies in Roman armies in the

80s B.C. point in the same direction. In 89 B.C. the legate Postumius Albinus was stoned to death by his soldiers while besieging Pompeii. Also in 89 B.C., the consul L. Porcius Cato was faced with a mutiny by soldiers, although he managed to escape death. When one of the consuls of 88 B.C., Q. Pompeius Rufus, went to take over the command of his army, he was lynched on his arrival by the soldiers with the apparent connivance of its previous commander, Gn. Pompeius Strabo, the father of the soon-to-be prominent military dynast Pompeius Magnus (Pompey the Great). The list goes on and on. Between 89 and 80 B.C. there were an extraordinary 11 mutinies compared to five in the previous hundred years. In few of the mutinies were either the ringleaders or their followers punished. This was a signal departure from the past when mutinies were savagely put down. The disciplinary power to punish had been lost. The pattern was to continue to the end of the Republic. When the hardened soldiers of the late Republic were matched, finally, in sufficient numbers with equally hardened and ruthless leaders of the elite, they were to combine together to bring down the Republic.

# 11

# The Fall of the Republic: From Sulla to Octavian

## 1. THE POLITICAL TRANSFORMATION

### After Sulla: The Quiet Before the Storm

The shock and horror of the activities of Marius, Cinna and Sulla in the first civil war had the effect of quieting Rome's appetite for a full-scale repetition for about a generation. Sulla's reform —to address the failures of the political system—were comprehensive, but even Sulla, talented as he was, lacked the character and the vision to make Rome a functioning state again. His main reforms focused on the Senate as the traditional ruling body of Rome, and in theory he provided it with all of the legal tools it needed to ensure its success in the future. The reality was that the senators whom Sulla had brought to the forefront of the state were united only in their determination to hold onto power and to resist change. These senators are often referred to as the "Sullan oligarchy," and an oligarchy was indeed what Rome's government had become. Sulla's own example beckoned others to follow. They were not long in doing so.

### The 70s B.C.: Spain, Slaves, and Special Commands

Sulla retired from active political life in 79 B.C. and died the following year. The consul of 78 B.C., M. Aemilius Lepidus, initiated an armed revolt when frustrated in his efforts to undo the Sullan constitution. He sent his legate, M. Junius Brutus, father of the soon-to-be assassin of Caesar, to occupy Cisalpine Gaul and raise troops. From this power base Lepidus intended to launch a new march on Rome. Unintentionally Lepidus set a precedent that Caesar was to exploit some 20 years later. The Senate turned to the young Sullan supporter and supreme opportunist, Gnaeus Pompeius (Pompey), to defend Rome. Although he was not a member of the Senate and had not held any previous magistracies he was given a special command: pro-praetorian *imperium* (i.e., the power to act as a praetor) with two mandates. The first was to put down Lepidus, which he did successfully. The second, which was to attend to a revolt in Spain, was more difficult. In Spain the cause of Marius was still being championed by the governor, a talented general by the name of Sertorius whose charisma made him attractive to Spain's native inhabitants, the Lusitanians and Celt-Iberians. Sertorius proved to be a more determined and capable leader than Lepidus, and the last resistance in Spain did not end until 71 B.C. On his return march to Rome Pompey stopped in northern Italy and mopped up the remnants of the slave revolt of Spartacus who had fled there.

| Chronology | |
|---|---|
| Slave revolt of Spartacus | 73–71 B.C. |
| Pompey's campaign against the pirates | 67 B.C. |
| Pompey's conquest of the east | 66–62 B.C. |
| Conspiracy of Catiline | 63 B.C. |
| Conquest of Gaul by Caesar | 58–52 B.C. |
| Civil wars | |
| Battle of Pharsalus | 48 B.C |
| Assassination of Caesar | 44 B.C. |
| Battle of Philippi | 42 B.C. |
| Battle of Actium | 31 B.C. |

SPARTACUS The revolt of Spartacus broke out in 73 B.C. in the gladiatorial schools in Campania. Spartacus, a former Roman auxiliary soldier from Thrace, led the uprising and was joined, in addition to agricultural slaves, by some of the victims of the civil war who had lost their lands in the expropriations of Sulla ten years earlier. Two of his generals, Crixus and Oenomaus, were Celts. For the first two years he triumphed over Roman armies and led his troops into Cisalpine Gaul from where, according to one source, he hoped his followers would disperse to their homes. Perhaps preferring a life of plunder, they did not. Spartacus turned south again. Once more the Senate resorted to a special command, this time selecting another supporter of Sulla, the praetor M. Licinius Crassus. Crassus collected a large army and finally cornered the slave army in southern Italy and Spartacus was killed in action. His body was never found. Of the captured slaves 6,000 are said to have been crucified along the Via Appia. Together with Pompey Crassus was able to procure his election to the consulship for 70 B.C.

Promptly both men saw to the restoration of the tribunate and set about removing what was left of Sulla's reforms. The Senate had already reduced the Sullan constitution to a shambles by its reliance on special commands. In addition to commands given to Pompey (who was not even a member of the Senate) and Crassus, L. Licinius Lucullus was entrusted in 74 B.C. with the command of the revived war against Mithridates. His province was Cilicia, but gradually he expanded it to include Asia, Bithynia, and Pontus. The same year yet another special command was given to Marcus Antonius (father of Mark Antony and husband of Caesar's sister Julia), against the pirates. The price of these special commands was a progressive loss of control by the Senate of its own foreign policy. As long as things went well it could entertain the illusion that it was in control, but as soon as there was a set-back or a conflict among the wielders of special commands, then the Senate was without a means to remedy the situation.

THE PIRATES In 67 B.C. a law was proposed to give Pompey a special command with unlimited power *(imperium infinitum)* against the pirates, whose depredations had grown ever since Rome had curtailed the independent maritime power of Rhodes. Piracy was an endemic problem throughout the Mediterranean, but it had become particularly dangerous in the first century because of Rome's dependence on imported grain. This was a political and security issue because, since the time of Gaius Gracchus, the urban plebs had been guaranteed either subsidized or free grain. It was too dangerous to let the price of grain fluctuate as the market might dictate. Once again the Senate was forced to act.

The proposed command was so large and so unusual that it provoked a storm of protest in the Senate, where only Julius Caesar, who had been elected to the quaestorship just two years earlier, spoke on its behalf. One prominent senator correctly pointed out that while Pompey was "undoubtedly a great man he was becoming too great for a free republic, and that all power should not be placed in the hands of one man" (Velleius Paterculus, 2.32). This was precisely the problem faced by the Senate. The pattern was common. A challenge of some kind—foreign or domestic—would arise, and when traditional means of handling it proved inadequate, as was the case of the a Mediterranean-wide problem of the pirates, a special command had to be created. If successfully executed the individual commander would then be in possession of such prestige and enlarged financial resources that he would completely outstrip his supposedly equal colleagues. Having generated much envy, he was then faced with the difficult task of maintaining his standing while his rivals would chip away at his overly large *dignitas* and *auctoritas* by any means they could, but especially by means of similar special commands. After its restoration the tribunate became the favorite tool of the ambitious for arranging such commands, further undermining the authority of the Senate.

The bill giving Pompey his command (*lex Gabinia*) was finally passed in scenes of great disorder by the popular assembly, and Pompey entered his command. By means of excellent organization of his resources he largely cleared up the pirate menace in a matter of months and was soon peacefully settling the remnants of their forces on vacant land in Cilicia. However, the pirates remained a problem to some extent, and we still hear of difficulties with the grain supply during the 50s.

MITHRIDATES AGAIN In 66 B.C. another opportunity presented itself to Pompey. The war with Mithridates had started up again, but after initial successes under L. Licinius Lucullus, it was not going well. It was now proposed that Pompey finish it off. Under the terms of the Manilian law, supported again by Caesar and by the "new man" Cicero, Pompey was given command of the provinces of Cilicia, Bithynia, and Pontus and of the war against Mithridates. Between 66 and 62 B.C. Pompey swept through the east, first defeating Mithridates and driving him to flight, then continuing into Armenia and from there back to Syria and into Palestine, where he settled a dispute over the throne of Judaea. Single-handedly, he redrew the map of the eastern Mediterranean, founding cities and making provinces and treaties with client-kings. In the process, he increased Rome's annual income by 70 percent.

The Conquests of Pompey

## Meanwhile: Debt and Discontent in Rome

THE DISPOSSESSED In addition to disturbances overseas the Senate faced destabilizing forces within Italy and in the city of Rome itself. In any society the murder of a good portion of its elite and the expropriation of its possessions is not a policy likely to have a peaceful outcome. Reconciliation after a revolution of this kind is never easy to come by. Sulla's legacy was one of poisonous hatred. The sons and families of those executed in his proscriptions, along with those in the communities of Italy who ended up on the wrong side in the civil war and penalized by him, were a source of disaffection for a generation, ready to join any political or armed group that might help them regain their rights and their properties.

| Provinces Made During the Republic | | |
|---|---|---|
| 1 | Sicily | 241 B.C. |
| 2 | Sardinia-Corsica | 238 B.C. |
| 3,4 | Nearer and Farther Spain | 197 B.C. |
| 5,6 | Africa and Macedonia | 146 B.C. |
| 7 | Asia | 133 B.C. |
| 8 | Transalpine Gaul | 121 B.C. |
| 9 | Cisalpine Gaul | 89 B.C. |
| 10 | Cilicia | ca. 80 B.C. |
| 10 | Cyrene | 74 B.C. |
| 11,12 | Bithynia, Syria | 62 B.C. |

THE URBAN PLEBS Another source of unrest was the urban population of Rome itself, increasingly made up of uprooted rural dwellers, freedmen, slaves, and immigrants from all over Italy and the Mediterranean. By the late Republic the city had reached a population of perhaps a million. Many lived in desperate poverty. The freeborn population was no longer governed by the old rules. These had traditionally imposed a discipline based on regular military service, the responsibilities of farm ownership, and the acknowledgment of the authority (*auctoritas*) of the magistrates and the upper classes in general. Now recruitment for the legions took place largely in rural areas; farms had been lost and the ties of clientage were weakened. The elite seemed to have gone back on its social contract. Many among them appeared, as Cicero complained, more interested in their fishponds than in their customary leadership roles:

> Our leading men think they have transcended the summit of human ambition when the bearded mullets in their fishponds eat out of their hands while they let everything else go to hell (*To Atticus*, 1.2).

Other forms of association, primitive trade unions, fraternal associations, and burial societies (*collegia*) began to assume more and more significance for the urban population. The *collegia*, which had ancient roots in Roman society, taught the ordinary people of Rome the usefulness of informal, low-level organizational techniques. These associations dovetailed with the long-established local neighborhood associations of the city, the *vici*. The existence of a dependable subsidized grain supply from the time of Gaius Gracchus contributed to the growing independence of the *plebs urbana*, the urban people, or the *plebs sordida*, as the upper classes called them. The proletariat (*proletarii*, the lowest census category) should not be confused with the *plebs urbana* of which it was a part; the *plebs urbana* contained a much wider spectrum of people. At least initially none of these groups constituted a focused opposition to the leadership of the Senate, but potentially they were a dangerous element in the already volatile mix of Roman politics. It would take special talent to turn the *collegia*, *operae* (gangs), *tabernarii* (shopkeepers), and *opifices* (artisans) of Rome into an effective political force.

CATALINE'S CHALLENGE A source of difficulty for many members of the ruling elite in the 70s and 60s B.C. was indebtedness or, perhaps more accurately, difficulty with cash flow. Maintaining visibility was an essential but expensive aspect of the political culture of first century B.C. Rome. As time went on it became more and more competitive and more and more costly to stand for office. Candidates needed large sums of money for bribery,

**Making It at Rome: Fishponds**

*Fishponds were an important and all-but-indispensable architectural feature of luxury Roman villas. The Villa of the Papyri at Herculaneum had two, one located in the peristyle in front of the villa* **(A)**, *and the other in the atrium of the villa itself* **(B)**. *Dozens of such villas are known, many with far-grander fishponds. The images here are of the ponds of the Getty Villa, a modern reconstruction of the Villa of the Papyri.*

which had become commonplace, and for games and spectacles to win support among the plebs. Much of the elite's wealth, however, lay in land, and they were forced to borrow heavily against it. In the 70s and 60s a liquidity crisis in Rome drove up the cost of borrowing and with it the cost of maintaining an aristocratic life-style. A failed campaign for an office, especially for one of the higher ones, could lead to serious problems for even the most well-off among the elite. Caesar was supposed to have told his mother on the morning of the balloting for the office of *pontifex maximus* that he would return either "as Chief Priest or not at all" (Suetonius, *Caesar*, 13).

Catiline was a fairly typical representative of the ambitious competitors for office in the late Republic. He made the praetorship in 68 B.C. but failed repeatedly thereafter to win the consulship. In 63 B.C. Cicero was elected consul, in part because he was seen as an alternative to Catiline. Catiline then turned to two genuinely revolutionary measures: A program of land distribution, and the cancellation of debts. In order to put these in place he planned the violent overthrow of the government, but his plans were betrayed, and Cicero had Catiline's co-conspirators arrested in Rome. Catiline escaped and joined a private army, which one of his associates had assembled in Etruria. He was declared a public enemy by the Senate and died in battle when cornered by the forces sent out to suppress his insurrection. There was a problem then of what to do with his allies in Rome. They had not been declared public enemies as Catiline had been, nor were they armed when arrested. Nevertheless, contrary to long tradition they were executed without trial, and Cicero as consul was saddled with the responsibility for their deaths. What he regarded as his great triumph in 63 B.C. was to hound him for the rest of his career.

**The Threat of the "People"**

*The potential for using the people as a political force independent of the Senate was noted by Cicero citing a comment of the maverick aristocrat Catiline.*

> Catiline declared openly at a meeting of the full Senate that there were two bodies politic in the Republic. One was weak and had a poor head on its shoulders [viz. the Senate]. The other was strong but it had no head at all. As long as he was alive, he declared, he would be its head (Cicero, *pro Murena*, 51).

*Another acknowledgement of the potential of the uprooted comes in the form of a letter by an unknown author who pretends to be Sallust writing to Caesar.*

> When men were increasingly driven from their farms, deprived of their work and their livelihood and forced into homelessness, they began to envy the riches of others. Thus they came to sell their services along with their loyalty. Gradually, a people which had been an imperial people and ruled the world, fell from its position and instead of ruling jointly sold itself individually into slavery ([Sallust], *Letter to Caesar*, 2.5.4).

THE RETURN OF POMPEY The return of Pompey with his victorious army from the east raised fears among the optimate oligarchs that he might use his veterans to sustain his unusually high, and in their eyes, unjustified, position in the state. However, Pompey was no Sulla, and he had no intention of starting another civil war. He was content, he told the Senate in a report, to work with it for the ratification of his provisions in the east and for the pensioning off of his veterans by means of land grants. This was promptly seized on by the oligarchs as a sign of weakness. This belief was strengthened when, on his return to Italy in 62 B.C., Pompey demobilized his army.

In anticipation of Pompey's return Crassus had continued to build up his political strength and sponsored the promising career of Julius Caesar. Others also claimed Crassus' support, among them the young patrician Publius Claudius Pulcher. It was Claudius' special genius to see the possibility of building a power base on Rome's *plebs urbana*, but to do so he had to had to make himself eligible for the tribunate, the office par excellence, of the people. Accordingly he had himself adopted into a plebeian family and henceforth called himself Clodius which sounded somewhat more plebeian than Claudius. After his year in office as tribune in 58 B.C. Clodius went on to organize into a powerful political force the artisans, shopkeepers, neighborhood associations, burial societies, and thugs that constituted the urban plebs. What his long-term goals may have been is unclear. His immediate aim, however, was his desire for revenge against Cicero, with whom he had a vendetta. In 58 B.C., he succeeded in having Cicero exiled. Beyond that, perhaps he just enjoyed the exercise of power at the expense of the elites. His gangs were capable of bringing public business to a standstill. He could, at will, shut down assemblies and courts and intimidate powerful magistrates. Even the great military dynasts had to learn to take Clodius into account. Appropriately, his end came some years later when he was killed in a brawl with a rival gang that had been organized by his political opponents.

## The Alliance of Pompey, Crassus, and Caesar

The return of Pompey gave new impetus to Caesar's advance. The oligarchs in the Senate could see more clearly than ever the danger preeminent individuals presented to their collective rule. To date Pompey was undoubtedly the most powerful of these overlarge individuals, and the oligarchy hoped to cut him down to size and so preserve their precarious control of the state. With the demobilization of his troops they thought they could succeed. The ratification of his treaties and of the provinces he had established in the east were held up by procedural maneuvers. He was denied land for his veterans.

**Catiline Stands on His Dignity**

*The Roman historian Sallust preserves a letter from Catiline. Even if forged it gives a good idea of what the members of the elite thought justified going to extremes.*

> Lucius Catilina to Quintus Catulus. ...I have made a resolution not to defend formally my undertakings, but I will offer some explanation, though not out of a feeling of guilt for wrong doing. I am confident you will be able to see its justice. Infuriated by wrongs and insults, robbed of the fruit of my industry and unable to achieve a position of dignity, I openly undertook the cause of the oppressed as I had often done in the past. It was not that I could not have settled my debts by selling some of my estates ...Rather, it was because I saw unworthy men promoted to honorable positions and felt I was reduced to an outcast because of unwarranted suspicions. For this reason, in order to preserve what was left of my dignitas, I have adopted measures which are wholly honorable considering my situation (Sallust, *Catiline*, 35).

THE FRIENDSHIP OF POMPEY AND CAESAR Rebuffed by the Senate, Pompey turned first to a tribune for help and, failing there, to Caesar, one of the consular candidates for 59 B.C. Caesar was able to reconcile Crassus and Pompey who had been at odds with each other, and with the combined support of Crassus and Pompey Caesar was elected consul. Cato, a leading member of the optimate oligarchy, was afterwards to say repeatedly that the downfall of the Republic started not with the enmity between Caesar and Pompey, but with their friendship in 60 B.C. Others agreed with him. Writing some years later under the regime of Augustus, the soldier and historian Asinius Pollio began his account of the civil wars between Caesar and Pompey with the year 60.[1] The poet Horace, a friend and beneficiary of Pollio, saw this year as a year of "deadly friendships," which led to the shedding of "unexpiated blood... and all the earth subdued except the fierce heart of Cato" (*Odes,* 2.1).

This informal alliance of Pompey, Crassus, and Caesar is sometimes, though inaccurately, called the "First Triumvirate." The arrangement was actually a personal agreement among the three not to work against each other and, when possible, to push forward each others' plans. Unlike Pompey, Caesar was free of scruples regarding the use of force

[1]The great modern historian of Rome, Ronald Syme also began his history of the fall with 60 B.C.

and cared little whether his actions were formally legal or not. When his colleague Bibulus announced he was going to watch the skies for unfavorable omens, Caesar went ahead with his legislation anyway, knowing full well that Bibulus' divination might invalidate his laws. Not a member of the Sullan oligarchy, Caesar did not share its interest in limiting the pursuit of fame and honor on the part of the elite. For Caesar, being first trumped all other considerations. Plutarch tells us a story of how on one occasion when he was crossing the Alps, Caesar came across a miserable town and joked that no doubt even here, too, men struggled to get ahead and that there were jealous rivalries among its leaders. "For my part," he then said, speaking seriously, "I would rather be first man here than second man in Rome" (Plutarch, *Caesar,* 11). In Spain when he was quaestor there in 67 B.C. he became upset when he came across a statue of Alexander the Great, remarking that at the same age Alexander had conquered the world. He, on the other hand, had still accomplished nothing (Suetonius, *Caesar,* 7). Caesar was not unusual in his ambitions; they were common among the hyper-competitive nobility of the late Republic. The difference between him and others of his class was that his ambition was matched by outstanding military and political abilities.

CAESAR'S CONSULSHIP On entering his consulship in 59 B.C. Caesar immediately saw to the passage of the measures desired by his allies. After failing in an attempt to work with the Senate he forced through his legislation by violence, ignoring the vetoes and auguries of his fellow consul. Pompey's veterans got their land, and his arrangements in the east were ratified. The contract for the collection of taxes in Asia, in which Crassus had an interest, was revised. Caesar, too, got what he wanted, namely, the province of Cisalpine Gaul with three legions for five years. Later Transalpine Gaul with another legion was added to his command. The strategic significance of this had been evident since the abortive revolt of Lepidus some twenty years earlier. The possession of Cisalpine Gaul provided one of the three cooperating dynasts with a source of military power within a few days march of Rome. It also provided Caesar with the important military option of conquering Gaul should the opportunity present itself. To solidify his relationship with Pompey, Caesar married his own daughter Julia to him.

CAESAR IN GAUL Once in his province, Caesar had no difficulty in finding excuses for a full-scale conquest of Gaul. This was not a challenge, given the traditional raiding practices of the Celts, their internal feuds, their tendency to migrate, and their exposure to threats from what Caesar was to argue were even more barbarous peoples living to their east across the Rhine, the Germans.

The geography and ethnography of Gaul were not well known at this time, and Caesar was to make adroit use of this lack of knowledge to shape popular views of the region. His regular reports (*commentarii*) from his province were artful means of promoting his own achievements as well as justifying his savage wars of conquests. Among his many talents Caesar was a masterful propagandist. Public opinion at Rome always needed to be massaged, and Caesar knew well how to do this. The Senate in general and the small inner core of oligarchs in particular were justifiably suspicious of the activities of overly energetic generals, but there was a way of overcoming this suspicion: success. The extension of

Rome's imperial boundaries, an increase in the state's income, and protection from dangerous enemies triumphed in most Romans' eyes over mere legalities. This view can be found in one of Cicero's speeches:

> Let men think whatever they wish. I for one cannot be other than a friend to someone who has served the Republic well . . . . Under the command of C. Caesar war has been waged against the Gauls whereas in the past the Gauls were merely fended off. The great C. Marius ... drove back vast hordes of Gauls who were pouring into Italy. ... But it is clear that the approach of C. Caesar is different. He does not suppose that it was merely his duty to wage war against those whom he saw actually to have taken up arms against the Roman people, but also that the whole of Gaul was to be brought under our sway. (*On Provincial Govenorships,* 24, 32)

Celts, with whom the Romans were all too familiar, were known to occupy Gaul, but Gaul's eastern frontiers were unclear. Beyond the Rhine were other more barbarous peoples, the Germans. How distinct culturally these people were from the Celts of Gaul is uncertain, but it suited Caesar's propaganda that Rome had already encountered the Cimbri and Teutones who had come from that part of the world. Caesar was able to make good use of Rome's bad memories of the depredations of these peoples and the numerous defeats they had inflicted on Rome's armies a generation earlier.

Caesar's motivation and justification for his conquests were complex. In a battle with the Tigurini he could allege personal reasons: the grandfather of Piso, his father-in-law, had been killed by these people in battle, so that in punishing them Caesar was able to claim he was "avenging a private injury as well as one done to his country" (*The Gallic War,* 1.12). The most salient reasons, however, were the same as those of previous provincial commanders, and most recently that of Pompey: glory, honor, resources—meaning money and clients—and, ultimately, power. Pompey's clients and the main source of his power, were to be found all over the eastern Mediterranean. Caesar needed a similar power base and client network in the west. He had also learned from Pompey's mistakes in dealing with the optimate oligarchy.

CAESAR AND HIS ARMY These motives were well understood at Rome, and the oligarchs rightly feared a successful campaign by Caesar in Gaul. An army's loyalty was to its victorious general and only vaguely to Rome. Rome was distant and to many soldiers irrelevant. Recruits came from all over Italy, and having spent years in the field with a particular commander, it was natural that they would look to him for their pay, their equipment, and the promise of future pensions in the form of land grants. The state was still paying them a ridiculous 108 denarii a year; troops did not serve for such miserable rewards. They also knew that at every opportunity the Senate attempted to block their land grants, and that in the past the only way veterans got what had been promised them by their commanders was through intimidation or outright violence. They had learned not to expect the gratitude of the Senate or the Roman people. What they did expect were generals who would fight for them at home as they fought for him in the field. Charisma, of which Caesar had plenty, counted for a lot, but security and cash were the ultimate motivation of the soldiers in the late Republic. Even Caesar's legions, much as they loved him, were prepared to mutiny if their needs were not met.

THE CONQUEST OF GAUL Between 58 and 50 B.C. Caesar conducted what was essentially a gigantic plundering expedition. Huge numbers of Celts were sold as slaves, their temples and towns ransacked. "In Gaul," noted the biographer Suetonius, "Caesar plundered the shrines and temples of the gods filled with offerings, and more often sacked towns simply because they were rich rather than because they were guilty of doing anything hostile against him" (*Caesar,* 54.2). When two German tribes, the Usipites and Tencteri, crossed the Rhine into Gaul to settle there, Caesar confronted them, aiming to send a message to other German tribes not to cross into Gaul. When their leaders met with him to negotiate, he held them prisoner while launching a surprise attack on their now leaderless tribes. What follows is Caesar's own sparse account of what happened:

> He formed the legionaries into three columns ready to wheel into line of battle and made a rapid march of 8 miles, reaching the enemy's camp before they realized what was happening. The speed of his advance and the absence of their leaders combined to throw the tribesmen into a sudden panic. ... The Roman soldiers could tell they were afraid by their shouting and running aimlessly back and forth ...and broke into their camp. There some Germans were quick enough to seize their weapons and resisted our men for a time, fighting under cover of their wagons and baggage. There was also, however, a large crowd of women and children in the camp, for the Germans had brought their families and all their possessions with them when they left home and crossed the Rhine. These began to flee in all directions, and were hunted down by the cavalry which Caesar sent out for that purpose ...[*The Germans continued to flee until they came to*] the confluence of the Rhine and Moselle rivers where they realized they could flee no more. A large number were killed, and the rest flung themselves into the rivers and drowned, overcome by their fear, exhaustion and the force of the current. Although a major struggle had been anticipated against an enemy that was 430,000 strong, the Romans returned to their camp without suffering a single fatality (*The Gallic War,* 4.13–15).

When the Senate voted holidays and sacrifices in honor of this victory Cato objected, saying that instead Caesar should be handed over to the Germans to free Rome of the guilt of breaking a truce. He does not seem to have been much concerned about the slaughter of the tribes. In any case his motion was overruled. Caesar followed up the massacre of the Usipetes and Tencteri by building a bridge across the Rhine and raiding into Germany with the aim of demonstrating Rome's military capacity and intimidating any more Germans from crossing the river. Two years later he repeated the exercise. For similar reasons he raided across the channel into Britain in 55 and 54 B.C.

By 50 B.C. Caesar had annexed for the empire and his own benefit a gigantic new stretch of territory, reaching from the Pyrenees and the Atlantic coast to the Rhine—double the size of Italy.[2] The resources of this territory, both in manpower and in money, constituted the foundation of what amounted to an independent kingdom. From a larger historical viewpoint, the addition of Gaul and parts of what is today Germany represented a fundamental move away from a Mediterranean axis towards an Atlantic and central European axis. For the first time a strong centralized Mediterranean-style state was directly introduced into continental Europe and eventually also to Britain, breaking the ancient tradition of loosely organized tribal-based polities. The cost for the Celts was high. Caesar, followed by his successors in Gaul and Britain, essentially decapitated Celtic society. Rome snuffed out Celtic cultural independ-

[2]240,000 sq. miles vs. 116,000 sq. miles.

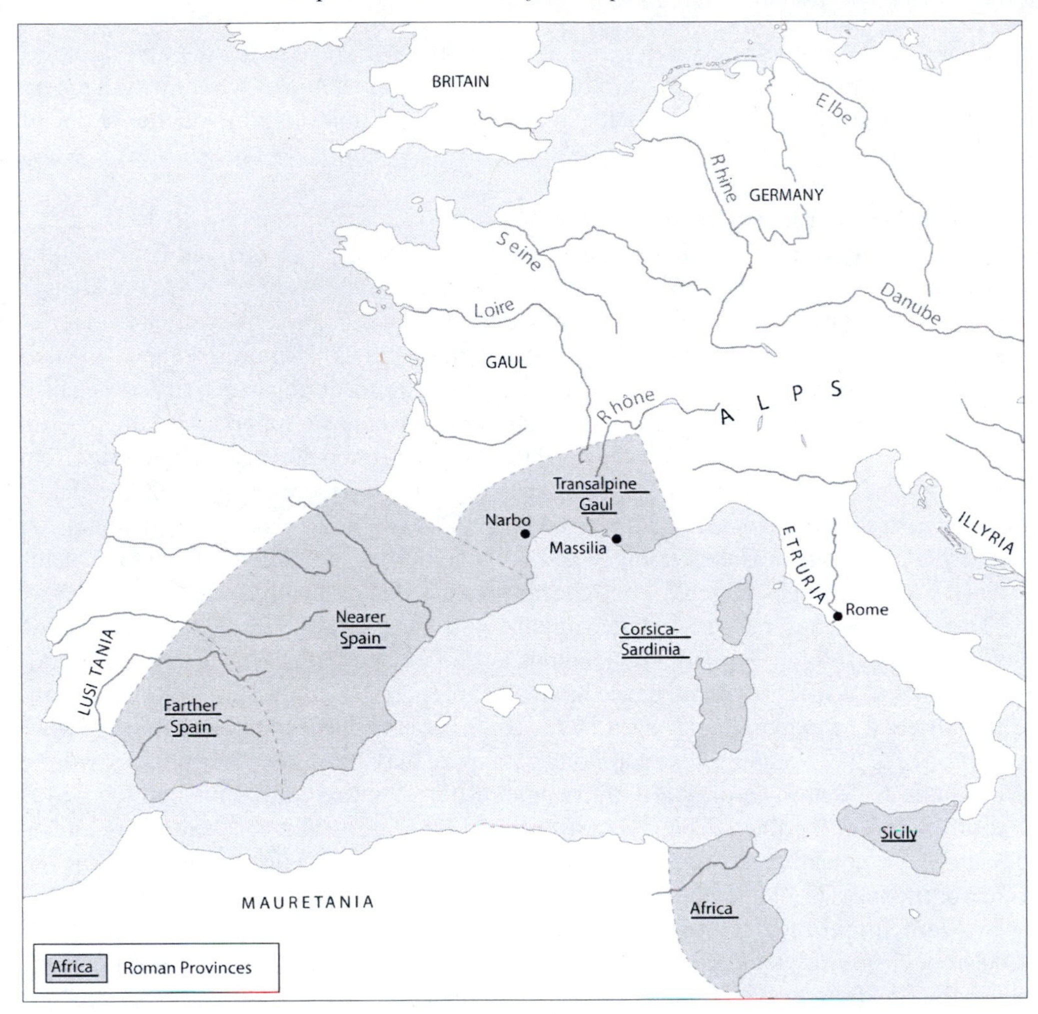


The West at the Time of Julius Caesar

ence with greater efficiency than did the English at a later date when they were confronted with similar belligerent tribal societies in Scotland, Wales, and Ireland.

## The Collapse of the Alliance

Although Caesar's command was the most prolonged and the most spectacular, the other members of the alliance also had their military commands during this period. Crassus and Pompey were consuls again in 55 B.C. and were granted the provinces of Syria and Spain, respectively, for five years. Collectively the three men had control over most of the military resources of the empire. At the end of 55 B.C. Crassus went off to Syria in an attempt to refurbish his military reputation, but two years later he was killed by the Parthians at the disastrous battle of Carrhae. This event, coupled with the death in 54 B.C. of Pompey's wife, Caesar's daughter Julia, led to the disintegration of the alliance. Rome was now left with two dominant figures, one of whom was in an extraordinarily strong position and in the middle of putting the finishing touches to one of Rome's most successful and profitable imperialistic ventures. Pompey's laurels were, by contrast, old and decayed.

Over a two-year period communication between Caesar and Pompey gradually broke down. The core of the optimate oligarchy was irreconcilable to Caesar and demanded he abandon his command when his five-year proconsulate came to an end in 49 B.C. Though Pompey was hardly less of a dynast than Caesar, he was not in as strong a position as his rival and was gradually won over to the side of Cato and the oligarchs. There was complex maneuvering in the Senate regarding the legality of Caesar's position, during which Caesar engaged in massive bribery and succeeded in winning over to his side an important tribune, Curio. When Curio proposed that both Pompey and Caesar should step down simultaneously from their commands, 370 senators voted in favor of the measure to a mere 22 opposed. The majority wanted to avoid civil war, but when a rumor spread that Caesar was already marching on Rome the consuls approached Pompey and unilaterally begged him "to defend the state" against Caesar. Pompey now passed irrevocably to the side of the *optimates*.

To avert war Caesar suggested he would be willing to give up Transalpine Gaul if he could retain Cisalpine Gaul with two legions until the beginning of his promised consulship in 48 B.C. While he wanted peace he was not prepared to come back to Rome unconditionally and be automatically tried by his enemies as had long been threatened. Other compromises were proposed, and although Pompey may have been willing to go along with them, Cato and the die-hard optimate consuls Claudius Marcellus and Cornelius Lentulus were determined to have a confrontation. The opposition was leaderless, and on January 7 the consuls persuaded the Senate to pass the "ultimate decree" to see to the defense of the state. Caesar's supporters, among them tribunes, Curio, Cassius, and Antony, were warned that their safety could not be guaranteed, and so left the city and joined Caesar in Cisalpine Gaul. Recognizing that compromise was impossible Caesar crossed the Rubicon, the small river that divided his province from Italy, saying as he did so "the die is cast" (Plutarch, *Caesar*, 32). Unlike Sulla's officers, all but one of Caesar's officers stayed with him.

## The Civil Wars

The civil war that followed the breakdown of relations between Caesar, Pompey, and the Senate lasted from 49 B.C. to 45 B.C. Pompey was defeated at Pharsalus in Greece in 48 B.C. and was murdered shortly afterward while seeking refuge in Egypt. There were two other major engagements, at Thapsus in Africa and Munda in Spain, and in 45 B.C. Caesar returned triumphantly to Rome. There were no proscriptions, and Caesar generously extended clemency to his defeated foes. At the same time, he made it clear that the traditions of the Republic were at an end. Early in 44 B.C. he had himself declared Perpetual Dictator and commented that Sulla had committed a major political blunder when he resigned the dictatorship in 79 B.C. He received what seemed to be divine honors. The Ides of March soon followed.

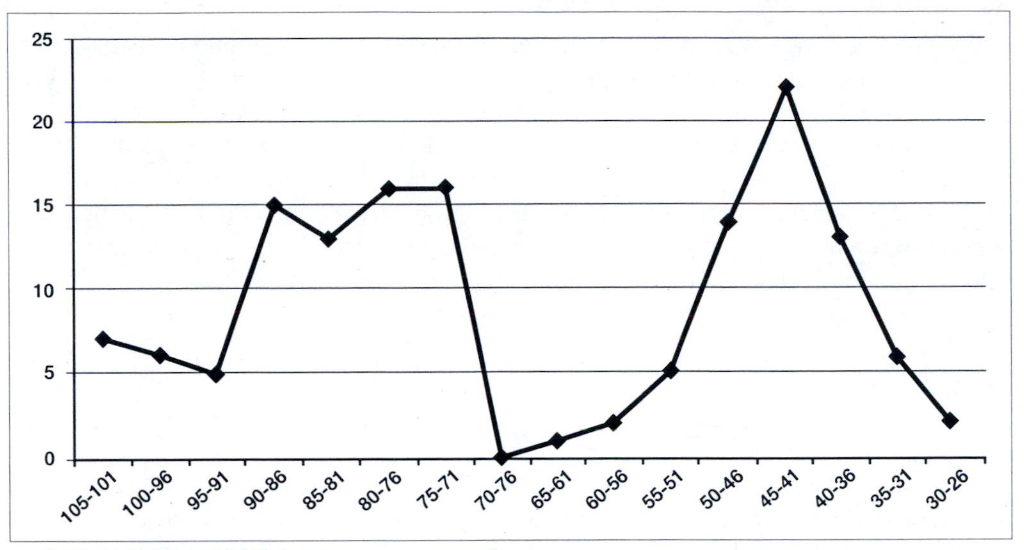


**Coin Hoards and History**

*Coin hoards, plotted in five-year periods from 105 to 26 B.C., demonstrate the impact of the civil wars of the first century on the lives of individual Romans. Coin hoards were deposits of coins hidden by owners who, for a variety of reasons, did not return to claim them. Some owners may have either perished while on military service or in the proscriptions, but others may have simply forgotten where they buried them.*

CAESAR'S REFORMS Between 47 B.C. and 44 B.C. Caesar initiated a huge number of programs, many of which were incomplete at the time of his death. One of the deep-rooted social and economic ills of the late Republic was the problem of debt, which affected all levels of society. The civil wars, however, had the effect of turning what was a problem into a crisis. People hoarded their cash, and a serious shortage of coins developed. As confidence evaporated lenders called in their loans. Borrowers began to agitate for the cancellation of debts, not just their postponement. Caesar's solution was to offer something to both creditors and debtors, but he was unable to achieve anything like the elimination of the problem. The settlement of veterans had been a challenge to Rome since the second century, and there were fears that Caesar would repeat Sulla's violent confiscations and proscriptions. Instead he settled most veterans along with many of the poor of Rome overseas on land that already belonged to the state as a result of war. His most ambitious project was the resettlement of the abandoned sites of Corinth and Carthage.

One of Caesar's immediate aims was to reduce the level of violence in Rome. This was addressed in part by reducing the number of grain recipients from 320,000 to 150,000, banning neighborhood colleges (*collegia*) and sending many freedmen to Corinth and Carthage. Elections had frequently been scenes of disorder in the late Republic. While Caesar did not ban them he did exercise control over them by nominating his own candidates. Recognizing from his own experience in Gaul the danger to the state of allowing provincial governors to have extended terms in office, he limited the terms of propraetors to one year and of proconsuls to two years.

Caesar increased the size of the Senate from 600 to 900, which led traditionalists to grumble about his appointments and claim that he admitted Gauls (supposedly, these Gauls had to ask directions to where the Senate House was and had to discard their trousers for togas). In fact most of the new members were from the equestrian class and the municipal aristocracy of Italy. He did not introduce any Greeks. To meet growing administrative needs in Rome and the provinces he increased the number of quaestors from 20 to 40 annually, and the number of praetors from 8 to 16. Caesar was criticized for making appointments to magistracies years in advance and for treating the office of consul cavalierly. According to Plutarch,

> when the consul Maximus died in office, Caesar made Caninius Rebilus consul for the one day that remained of the term. When many people, as we are told, gathered to congratulate him and escort him to the forum, Cicero said, "We'd better hurry or he will be out of office before we get there" (*Caesar* 58).

The calendar was badly in need of attention. The Roman civic calendar had only 355 days, and to bring it into harmony with the solar year an extra month had to be inserted or "intercalated" periodically. This process was heavily affected by politics because manipulation of the calendar could aid the campaigns of candidates and affect the passage of legislation. By the late Republic the calendar was ahead of the solar calendar by three months. In his capacity as *pontifex maximus* Caesar intercalated enough days to bring the two calendars into harmony, borrowed the Alexandrian solar calendar of 365 days and adjusted the civic calendar so that each year would have 365 days, with an additional day added in leap years. This "Julian" calendar survived in Europe down to Pope Gregory XIII in 1582 when the calendar was once more adjusted. The Gregorian calendar remains in use to the present.

He seems to have had plans to make Rome not just the political capital of the Mediterranean but also a center of culture and education. He granted Roman citizenship to Greek doctors, lawyers, rhetoricians, and teachers of the higher disciplines if they agreed to settle in Rome. He planned to build a library in imitation of the great library of Alexandria, which had been built by the Ptolemies, and commissioned the antiquarian Marcus Varro to make a comprehensive collection of Greek and Latin books. Roman law was to be codified. A huge building program was projected with the aim of providing Rome with an appearance suitable to its standing. He recognized the need for public space in central Rome and began buying up land for a new forum adjacent to the original forum. This project was partially completed before his death, and he dedicated the new forum and the Temple of Venus in 46 B.C. It was completed by Augustus. Similarly a new Senate House (*curia*) was started by Caesar but finished by Augustus.[3] There were plans to do something about the flooding of the Tiber, drain the Pomptine marshes, and build breakwaters along the coast to protect shipping coming into Ostia. None of these were even begun by the time of his assassination.

Caesar did not have any plans for basic constitutional reforms except to graft his divine and hereditary rule to the existing system. When it became clear that this was his intent, an all-too-visible chasm opened between him and his fellow aristocrats. Confined to Rome

[3]This building was destroyed by fire in A.D. 283 and restored by the Emperor Diocletian. It is this building that we see today in the forum.

and well aware of the poisoned atmosphere, Caesar planned to escape by going on campaign against the Parthians. His enemies, remembering the disruption caused by his absences during the civil wars, forestalled him. They did not want to be ruled for years from afar by a divine monarch. On the Ides of March in 44 B.C., Caesar was struck down by a group of senatorial assassins led by M. Junius Brutus, Cato's nephew, and C. Cassius Longinus. Almost immediately, a whole new round of civil wars broke out.

**Mark Antony**

*Gold signet ring with image thought to be of Mark Antony.*

OCTAVIAN: CAESAR'S LEGACY Caesar's most important legacy undoubtedly was his selection over other potential candidates of Gaius Octavius, his sister Julia's grandson, as his heir. In his will Caesar adopted him with the name of G. Julius Caesar Octavianus. From a contemporary's viewpoint it looked like a bad choice. The son of a *novus homo* Octavian was a mere 18 years of age and was often was sickly. Yet he had already given evidence of his character and talents when he campaigned with Caesar in Spain in 45 B.C.

Octavian reacted decisively to the death of Caesar in 44 and quickly consolidated his position as one of the principal leaders of Caesar's faction. He wooed Caesar's veterans and found himself in conflict with Mark Antony, one of Caesar's most trusted officers, but their difficulties were worked out and together with another of Caesar's generals, M. Aemilius Lepidus they established themselves as a ruling Triumvirate. Among their first acts was to purge their many enemies in a bloody proscription, including Cicero and a number of their own relatives and friends. They then divided the Roman world between them and set out to settle accounts with the murderers of Caesar, M. Junius Brutus and G.Cassius Longinus. Both were eliminated at the battle of Philippi in 42 B.C. In 40 B.C., to strengthen the alliance, Antony married Octavia, Octavian's sister. Thereafter the Triumvirs ruled in an uneasy alliance. Lepidus was dropped in 36 B.C., and the two remaining partners, Octavian and Antony inevitably began to drift apart.

Luck ran against Antony. While Octavian was able to consolidate his hold of Italy and the west, Antony failed in a campaign against the Parthians. On his return he found himself more and more dependent on the resources of Egypt as well as on its capable ruler, Cleopatra. Antony's relationship with Cleopatra and his divorce of Octavia enabled Octavian to launch a successful propaganda campaign against him. He accused Antony of immorality and treachery, but the most damaging allegation was that Antony wanted to transfer the capital of the Empire to Alexandria. In 32 B.C., Octavian obtained an oath of loyalty from all of Italy which had the symbolic value of conferring legitimacy on him as sole ruler and the practical value of providing him with manpower resources and land with which he could reward his followers. Matters came to a head in 31 B.C. Octavian formally declared war against Cleopatra, not on Antony; this was not to be another civil war but a war against a foreign enemy. That same year at Actium in Greece, Antony and Cleopatra were decisively defeated and the following year both committed suicide. The civil wars were finally over, and Octavian, or Augustus, as he is better known to us, was left alone on stage; with access to the wealth of Egypt he was in an unassailable position.

## 2. SOCIAL AND CULTURAL TRANSFORMATIONS

No aspect of Roman society or culture escaped the impact of Rome's acquisition of an empire. Although the deepest effects were felt in Rome's political life, Rome's society and culture were also profoundly impacted if not transformed. With Rome's tradition of intertwined political, social, and cultural realms it was impossible to alter one without also affecting the rest. The influx of money, the importation of luxury goods from the east, and the specialists needed to sustain Rome's increasingly affluent lifestyle—the architects, skilled artisans, parfumiers, teachers and professors, actors and actresses, painters , mosaicists, muralists and furniture makers—inevitably had an impact on its cultural life. Households were affected in other ways. Many of them of them ceased to be sites of economic production. The death of many Romans in war and the absence from home on lengthy overseas campaigns of male members of the household all took their toll on the family.

Cultural and social influences, however, worked in both directions. Roman colonies throughout Italy and increasingly in other parts of the Mediterranean were little Romes embedded in the societies of their host countries. It was not possible to ignore the social and cultural ways of these intruders. The Romans were the winners in the great game of Mediterranean history, and there was little evidence that, at least in the near future, anything would change that. Elites in particular, as is their wont, were ready to make accommodations with the conquerors. Rome had the money and the power, as well as an undefeatable army.

### Religion

RELIGIOUS DECLINE? Previous discussion showed how intimately the civic religion of Rome was entwined with its political culture.[4] Scholars have wondered whether Roman religious culture was dragged down in the same way that Rome's political culture was during the long fall of the Republic. Was the late Republic a period of religious decline accompanied by crumbling temples and neglect of the gods and the festivals and rituals that were their due? There is some evidence that this was the case, but there is an equal amount of uncertainty about the trustworthiness of the sources. Some of those, such as Cicero, who seem to be chronicling a decline in religiosity, are the same ones who were lamenting what they regarded as the disappearance of the old order. They may thus not be the most believable sources for what was really happening in religious affairs. There is also the problem of the influence of the later ideological claims of Augustus, the legitimacy of whose regime was based on its supposed restoration of the Republic and the old morality. A key element in this ideology was Augustus' claim to have rebuilt ruined temples and shrines and to have reinstated the old rituals that had fallen into disuse during the last years of the Republic. Lodged

[4] A part of Chapter 5, section 6, which is called "The State Religion."

in this claim is the implication that the Republic had gone through its travails because of its neglect of the gods, whereas Augustus' restoration manifestly—because it was successful—had the approval of the gods. This was a fine piece of propaganda and hard to argue against because Augustus, as the victor in the last of the civil wars, was able to shape the historical record better than his (dead) opponents.

ASSIMILATION OF THE NEW A more profitable line of approach may be to assume that the connection between religious and political life was as intimate as ever in the late Republic, but that as political life changed, religious practices took on new forms and were adapted to the changing needs of the political culture. As Rome expanded in the Mediterranean it assimilated some cults and rejected others. If a new cult was to be accepted by Rome it had to be examined, discussed, and endorsed publicly by the appropriate public bodies, primarily the Senate. Thus the cults of Aesculapius and Cybele (the Great Mother goddess), which came to Rome in the third century B.C., received state sanction and were welcomed by official representatives of the state. However, the cult of Cybele only became acceptable after it was considerably modified. Its self-flagellating, self-castrating priests, for example, were unacceptable to Roman sensibilities.

The cult of Dionysus (the Bacchic cult) was also difficult for Romans to accept because it violated a number of basic politico-religious principles. The first of these was that responsible members of the elite were supposed to be in charge of religious affairs. For that reason Rome had a number of priesthoods, each of which had responsibilities for particular aspects of the state cult. By contrast, the cult of Dionysus, which appeared in Italy in the early second century B.C., was conducted in privacy by non-state-appointed priests. It consisted of initiations into secret rituals, held at night. Its membership included free and slave, men and women. From the viewpoint of the government this cult represented a two-fold threat: It operated outside the approved format of religion and, probably more dangerously, seemed to offer an alternative form of society to its members. Hence it was savagely repressed. For the same reasons the shrines of Isis in Rome were destroyed in the 50s and 40s B.C. Astrology, too, was suspect because its practitioners had specialized knowledge and corresponding influence. It, too, operated outside the confines of the state religion. Astrologers were expelled from Rome in 139 B.C. and again in 33 B.C.

Yet despite repression of the cult of Dionysus in the second century B.C. and Isis in the first, both remained popular. The great mural found in the Villa of the Mysteries at Pompeii suggests how widespread was the cult. This famous frieze, which depicts various aspects of initiation, was painted in about the middle of the first century B.C. Likewise, despite the destruction of the shrines of Isis in the 50s, in 43 B.C. the Triumvirs decreed a temple in her honor. The worship of Dionysus and Isis, as well as other mystery cults, represented alternative, more personal ways of approaching the divine. They offered new sources of knowledge about the cosmos and human nature and new forms of relationships with the gods. The mystery cults were different from the state religion but not opposed to it. Eventually the state came around to this belief and granted the cults legal standing. At their start the mystery cults were patronized by immigrants and were largely confined to cities, but in time they spread widely. What we see happening in the field of religion in the late Republic is a deepening—or at least an enlarging—of religious sensibilities and at the same time a corresponding expansion of what was legally and politically acceptable.

TEMPLES Temple building, a good indication of religiosity, continued in the late Republic as the great military dynasts followed ancient precedent in honoring the gods under whose guidance they believed they had won honor and glory for themselves and Rome. Pompey erected temples to Hercules and Minerva, but his most significant building in Rome was a large theater-temple complex in the Italian tradition of such buildings, in honor of Venus Victrix (Venus the Giver of Victory).[5] Caesar went one better than Pompey with an entire forum dedicated to Venus, under the title of "Genetrix"—Venus the Ancestress of the Roman people and, more to the point, ancestress of his own gens, the Julii.[6]

POLITICAL THEATER What nowadays might be called political theater was a longstanding Roman practice. It frequently had religious overtones. In 143 B.C. when the Senate refused to authorize his triumphal procession, Appius Claudius Pulcher went ahead with it anyway. To ensure there would be no interference he had his daughter Claudia, a Vestal Virgin, ride in his triumphal chariot with him. When an outraged tribune tried to drag Appius from the chariot, Claudia held on to him and the parade continued. A Vestal Virgin's immunity trumped even the tribune's intervention.

In 57 B.C., after he had managed to get his archenemy Cicero exiled, Clodius had Cicero's house torn down to symbolize the annihilation of Cicero, his family, and his memory. In its place he erected a shrine to Liberty (*Libertas*) as a stinging criticism of Cicero's execution without trial of the Catilinarian conspirators in 63 B.C. When the political situation changed and Cicero was recalled from exile there was a problem: What about his house? As was proper the Senate referred the case to the college of pontiffs where there was a discussion. Both Clodius, defending his actions and the shrine to Liberty, and Cicero, supporting his claim to his property, gave speeches. In the end the judgment of the college favored Cicero on the grounds that the consecration of Cicero's house (i.e., its destruction) had not been authorized by the Roman people.[7] Cicero's original quarrel with Clodius had been initiated by another piece of political theater. Clodius had allegedly intruded on the Bona Dea festival, which was restricted to women. Why Clodius did this is unclear, but it may have been a political statement of some kind. Clodius in any event was put on trial and Cicero gave damaging evidence against him. Although Clodius escaped he felt that his *dignitas* had been damaged by Cicero. Hence the vendetta. Caesar, at whose house the Bona Dea festival was being celebrated, divorced his wife on the grounds that "Caesar's wife should be above suspicion."

A more serious matter was the use of religion to block the legislation proposed by Caesar and his supporters Crassus and Pompey in 59 B.C. During the tumultuous assemblies at which the legislation was passed, Caesar's colleague, the consul Bibulus, declared

---

[5]See Chapter 8, page 62 for reconstruction of Pompey's theater and temple to Venus and page 216 for Caesar's forum and temple.

[6]Aeneas, the Trojan hero, was the son of Anchises and Venus. Aeneas' son Iulus was appropriated by the Julii as their ancestor.

[7]Cicero's speech, *On His House*, survives. Unfortunately Clodius' does not.

that he would "watch the heavens" for signs of divine displeasure (*obnuntiatio*). Technically, this should have brought the assembly to a halt. When Caesar went ahead anyway, challenges to the legality of his acts were later raised based on the grounds that he ignored Bibulus' *obnuntiatio*. The matter, however, was never presented to the augural college for a decision, and the Caesarians presented a counter-argument: Because Bibulus did not obnuntiate in person at Caesar's assembly, his divination was invalid. Caesar's laws, even if dubiously legal, remained in effect.

THE DIVINE CAESAR: *DIVUS JULIUS* Perhaps the most significant expansion of Roman religious sensibilities in the late Republic was the divinization of Caesar. Before his assassination he was given the right to have a priest (a *flamen*) conduct his cult, and after his death he received altars, a temple, and sacrifices. In 42 B.C. he was declared divine: *divus Julius*. From the time of the granting of these honors they have been the subject of debate. Just what did it mean to declare someone a god? Was it like the triumphing general, who as part of the ritual, impersonated Jupiter by donning the god's garments and shoes? Was it more like Rome's founder, Romulus, who was believed, in one tradition, to have been swept up into heaven at the end of his life and to have become a god?[8] Or was the process analogous to the divinization of Hellenistic kings with appropriate borrowings from that cult practice?

Again, perhaps it is better to see Caesar's divinization as the logical, if extreme, extension of a development that had been going on for some time. Soldiers, given their exposure to danger and the unpredictability of the battlefield, are understandably superstitious. Generals have often tried to reassure their troops and sustain their morale by cultivating some supernatural quality or association with the divine. Polybius reports a tradition regarding Scipio Africanus, the victor over Hannibal, that he "made his men more confident by instilling in them the belief that his plans were divinely inspired" (10.2). He was, supposedly, so intimate with Jupiter that the guard dogs of the Capitoline temple did not bark when he visited the god's shrine. In the late Republic campaigns lasted for years, and generals spent a great deal of time in the field with their armies, far from home, surrounded by enemies. It made sense for them to follow Scipio's example and cultivate a belief in the commander's closeness to the divine. Thus Sulla claimed that Venus (Aphrodite in Greece) was his special patroness and guided him in all his actions. He advertised this in the coins he issued and took an additional cognomen, "*Felix*," blessed by the gods. Pompey similarly issued coins displaying his attachment to Venus and erected the magnificent temple complex to her in Campus Martius in Rome on his return from his eastern campaigns. Caesar was able to outdo both Sulla and Pompey with his forum and temple to Venus Genetrix because his family had from time immemorial claimed actual descent from the divine ancestress of Rome.

There was a long tradition in the Greek world of bestowing divine honors on successful generals and great benefactors. To people brought up in the religious cultures of monotheistic faiths such behavior looks like outrageous—or more likely, cynical—flattery, and sometimes it was. On the other hand, the line between the divine and the human among an-

[8]An alternate version had him torn to bits by the senators who, allegedly, took pieces of his body away with them for burial. Both version are found in Livy 1.16.

**Caesar's Forum and Temple to Venus Genetrix**

*Caesar's forum followed the tradition of Roman temple-building inherited from the Etruscans. Unlike synagogues, churches, and mosques, the Roman temple was not a place in which but before which worshipers gathered. The temple building itself was simply the house where the cult statue was kept. The true temple was the space in front of the "house." It was there that the altar was located and where the community gathered and sacrifices and prayers offered. Both temple and altar were usually placed on a high, raised platform often located at the end of a large, colonnaded enclosure as here. Only the scantiest ruins of Caesar's Forum remain, but at its prime it must have been impressive. High on its podium the temple immediately drew the worshipers' attention to it. At the same time the Temple and its enclosure subordinated the individual worshiper to the order and symmetry of the buildings and to the gods of the state who inhabited them.*

cient Mediterranean peoples was not as starkly drawn as it is in the monotheistic tradition. The divine in some form or another was always immanent, ready to burst into the lives of individuals and nations. It manifested itself most clearly in the great victories of generals. Even apart from these spectacular revelations of divine intervention it could always be assumed that some god or spirit was at hand and showed his or her presence in innumerable ways to the religiously observant. The Gracchi and Caesar were given clear signs of danger yet ignored them and so went to their deaths.

In the light of this tradition it is not surprising that Caesar received divine honors. What is surprising is that it happened not in the east where it was customary, but rather at Rome where it was not. The fact that something like divine honors seem to have been offered to him before his death and certainly afterwards shows how far Roman political culture had shifted from the collective rule of competitive peers to the rule of a single, possibly divine, or at least divinely favored individual. To that extent Roman religious sensibilities had kept in step with political reality.

DEMOCRATIZATION OF RELIGION? Democratization of the priesthoods had been a matter of contention between the patrician elite and the people since the fourth century B.C. The issue was still alive three centuries later when Sallust pointedly put in the mouth of the radical tribune Memmius the following words making clear the importance of priesthoods in the politics of Rome:

> The nobles strut in grandeur before you the people, flaunting their priesthoods and their consulships—as if these were honors and not stolen goods (*Jugurthine War* 31.10).

Membership in the priesthoods had been gradually pried open over the years. The *lex Ogulnia* of 300 B.C. abolished the monopoly of the patricians and added places for plebeians. But this did not mean that priests were chosen popularly, only that the colleges of priests were no longer restricted to patricians. As in the past the colleges themselves picked new members by cooptation. In the third century B.C. this process was modified in the case of the selection of the chief priest, the *pontifex maximus*, who was chosen henceforth by a limited form of popular election in which 17 of the 35 tribes voted, a process extended in 104 B.C. to all priests. The candidates continued to be nominated by the colleges, but each member of the college had to nominate a candidate and no more than two priests could nominate the same candidate. This suggests that there was an effort to provide real choice. Thus a fairly typical Roman compromise was achieved. On the one hand full popular control of religion was rejected while on the other these influential colleges were made more open and subject to a degree of public control.

## The Household and the Family

DECLINE OF THE HOUSEHOLD The transformation of the Italian economy due to its monetization and the development of cash-crop farming had a major impact on the character of many households. Most of the evidence concerns elite households, and it is relatively easy to see how they fared in the new economy, but we can only guess at what happened to the much larger number of subsistence-level households that were affected. For many at the lower end of the income spectrum the household ceased to be an economically independent unit that supported the family from generation to generation. Unknown numbers of uprooted, landless families were forced off their own land by powerful neighbors who were consolidating their estates and had to find a living for themselves either as tenants of the rich in the countryside or as part-time laborers in the cities. Equally unknown numbers were drawn to Rome because of the possibility of employment other than agricultural labor and because of the attractions and excitement of urban living.

To modern eyes this has a familiar appearance. An inevitable concomitant of modern economic development has been this disappearance of subsistence farming and mass emigration to cities. There is a major difference, however, between ancient and modern economies. In the developing economies of the contemporary world factories soak up most of the uprooted emigrants, whereas in the ancient world there were no such productive sectors of the economy, only the service sector. Emigrants to Rome could count on subsidized or free grain, but beyond that they had to scrape out an existence in competition with masses of freedmen and slaves. Little is know of how these families fared. They are visible at best in the historical record only as the mobs, organized or otherwise, that made life so miserable for the politicians of the late Republic. In the Empire they were to make their noisy and aggressive presence felt at shows held in the city's theaters, amphitheaters, and circuses.

RURAL AND URBAN WOMEN As in the past, wives were essential parts not just of the reproductive but also the economic aspects of the rural household. The Roman writers on agriculture, Cato, Varro, and Columella, mention the activities of the wives of the slave managers of the estates they write about and assign them high levels of responsibility. Undoubtedly the same work was performed by free wives as well. High levels of skill were necessary for much of this work as is clear from Cato's instructions:

> The farm manager's wife must be clean and see that the farmhouse is kept tidy and clean. The hearth is to be swept every night before going to bed. On the Kalends, Ides, Nones she is to put garlands over the hearth and pray to the family Lar [*the household god*] for prosperity. She must make sure that there is food cooked and ready for the manager and the slaves. She should keep plenty of hens for the sake of the eggs. She should have supplies of dried pears, berries, figs, raisins and stewed berries. Pears, grapes and apples, as well as preserved grapes and grape pulp are to be kept in floor-sunk kitchen pots [*dolia*]. Fresh Praenestian nuts are to be kept the same way. Yearly she must store in *dolia* Scantian apples and other berries and fruit that customarily are kept as preserves as well as wild fruits. She must know how to grind good flour and how to grind spelt finely (Cato, *On Agriculture*, 143).

Apparently households of this type ate rather well at least where eggs, bread, and fruits were concerned. Many examples of the *dolia* mentioned in the quote have been found *in situ*. They are often the only indication of the presence of a farmhouse.

SLAVES We have no equivalent source of information for ordinary, non-elite urban households. Much of the economic life of Rome of the late Republic lay in the hands of freedmen and foreigners. Huge numbers of slaves were employed in elite households and a large service sector existed to supply the needs of these households. Household slaves, while often better off than their rural counterparts, still found themselves in humiliating situations where they were vulnerable to the attentions of husbands, wives, household freedmen, or of other but more powerfully placed slaves in the household. A leaden curse tablet from the late Republic is inscribed by a woman named Eutychia, probably herself a freedwoman, who directs a demon to destroy "Danae the new slave maid" who has besotted her husband Soterichus. One can only imagine what happened to Danae when Soterichus lost interest in her. There was a large "hospitality" industry in Rome in the form of inns, taverns, and brothels, the latter mostly serviced by slaves. The entertainment industry was also well represented in Rome. Party-giving was a high art among the elite (and imitated by all other levels), and talented entertainers were always in demand. Among the many thousands of funerary epitaphs found in Rome is one put up to honor a child actress by the name of Eucharis. Apparently gifted as a dancer, singer, and musician, she died at 14 leaving a grieving father and a patroness, probably a freedwoman actress herself, who paid for the quite lengthy inscription.[9]

EMANCIPATED WOMEN? Scholars point to the high visibility of some elite women in the late Republic as evidence for the emancipation in general of women from patriarchal family restraints. There is no doubt battlefield deaths and the absence due to military service of husbands and other males of the household for extended periods left many women to manage their households on their own. There is also a great deal of evidence that, legally at least, women were a good deal freer of male supervision than they had been in the past. It was easier for them to inherit and use their inherited wealth without too much male interference. On the other hand it is hard to know how much of a break this represents with the past or whether it is merely a function of the diversification of households and the prominence of elite households in the historical record. We know little of how rural or non-elite households functioned. It is unlikely that in terms of patriarchal sway there was a huge shift from the past. Traditional ancient households were much more complex than their modern counterparts and had to be functionally authoritarian—wherever the authority actually lay, whether with husband or wife or both—in order to exist.

Women in Roman society were never segregated. They attended religious festivals in which they sometimes had public roles. They had their own, female-only festivals such as the *Bona Dea*. One of the most important priesthoods, the *flamen Dialis*, was actually a joint priesthood of husband and wife. The *flamen Dialis* had to be married and his wife, the *flaminica*, had several religious functions to perform jointly with her husband. If she died, the priesthood ceased until another couple was appointed. Following Etruscan tradition Roman women participated in integrated dining and drinking parties.

THE INTERCESSORY POWER OF MATRONS Elite matrons always seem to have some kind of intercessory role even in the political realm. The tradition was ancient. Romans believed that at the founding of their city the legendary Hersilia reconciled Sabines and Romans by leading the abducted Sabine women into the middle of the battle between the two sides. Another ancient model was Veturia, the mother of the traitor Coriolanus. She intervened with her son to save Rome when it was about to fall to him and his Volscian allies.

At the height of the war with Hannibal the Senate decided to smooth over class differences by forbidding rich women from riding in carriages, wearing purple clothes, and displaying too much jewelry (the *lex Oppia*). However, after the war when there was a move to abrogate the law in 195 B.C., masses of women came from the countryside to support the legislation. They blocked the streets leading into the Forum and besieged the houses of the tribunes. The abrogation succeeded. While it is true that the women would not have been involved in what amounted to a riot unless their male kin approved, the fact that they appeared en masse in the streets set (or maintained) the precedent for occasional female intervention in public affairs. The point of public intervention is noteworthy because it is a presumption that behind the scenes, as members of the family *consilium*, women always exercised considerable influence. Perhaps, therefore, it is better to see the more spectacular

[9] The inscriptions cited above can be found in A. Degrassi, *Inscriptions Latinae Liberae Rei Publicae* II, 1145, 803.

displays of independence evidenced by some elite women in the late Republic as an evolutionary development rather than a radical break with the past.

## Roman Literature Comes of Age

In the midst of the roiling changes of the late Republic Latin literature came of age. In part this was due to the emergence of a kind of un-Roman, apolitical leisurely class among the elite. Nevertheless, the traditional devotion of the Roman upper classes to a life of public service, although weakening, also had a hand in the final shaping of Latin literature.

It should not be imagined that the Roman elite was boorish or cultivated anti-intellectualism because martial values and public display ruled supreme in Rome. On the contrary, the leadership of Rome placed considerable emphasis on literary culture precisely because the possession of such a culture on the one hand distinguished its members from the rest of society, and on the other allowed them to enter the cosmopolitan world of Greek culture and society on an equal footing. The possession of a literary education was to be an enduring characteristic of the Roman ruling class down to the fall of the Empire.

With the self-assurance that came with the conquest of much of the Mediterranean the Romans of the second century B.C. began to appropriate the literary tradition of the Greeks. As we saw in chapter 8, section 2 this did not mean merely imitating Greek models of history, poetry and plays, but the creation in Latin of a parallel, if not entirely equal body of literature. No other people of the Mediterranean with which the Greeks were in contact made even attempted—let alone succeeded—in such an undertaking. The Etruscans may have begun to produce a literature in their own language, although this is disputed, but in any case the process was terminated by their early conquest and incorporation in the Roman commonwealth. The Celts remained largely outside the influence of Mediterranean literate culture and what little literature there is in any Celtic language dates from centuries after the fall of Rome. The Carthaginians produced practical handbooks such as those devoted to agriculture, but nothing that could be identified as a true body of literature. Invariably, if non-Greeks wrote about their own people they did so in Greek, not in their native vernacular. Only the Romans developed a well rounded literary corpus in their own language that included multiple genres of poetry, plays, history, biography, speeches, letters, and philosophical works. One scholar has commented that what had taken Greece four centuries to create was created by Rome in four generations. Inevitably Latin literature fell far short of Greek literary accomplishments in terms of depth and breadth, but the fact that it came into existence at all is significant. The final compliment paid to the success of Latin literature was when Greeks began to read it and even to write in Latin. The finest piece of historical writing in the fourth century A.D. was by a Syrian Greek by the name of Ammianus Marcellinus writing in Latin, and the best poetry in Latin in the fifth century A.D. was by a Greek from Alexandria in Egypt, Claudius Claudianus.

ORATORY In *polis* political life the ability to communicate had always been an essential adjunct of a political career, but in the early centuries of the Republic there was little opportunity or necessity for the practice of public oratory. However, in the late Republic the

Senate gradually ceased to be the locus of decision making and public issues increasingly began to be discussed in the courts, assemblies, *contiones* (special meetings called by magistrates to explain legislation), the campaign trail and in army camps. These new venues provided an opportunity for the development of public oratory and it was in this context that Latin prose was molded. In particular new men such as Cicero rose on the strength of their ability to communicate well with the public, and the members of the old elites quickly learned that the mastery of words could speed their advance through the *cursus honorum*.

Cicero developed his talents while addressing courts and assemblies and in due course the Senate. Fifty eight of his speeches survive. It is often claimed that it was his ear for the music of Latin and his sense of its rhythms that gave the language a form that fitted it as a vehicle of thought and expression for other writers for all time. Beyond his speeches hundreds of his letters survive. Cicero's literary ambitions ranged widely. He aimed to provide Latin readers with a body of philosophic literature that would replace the works of Greek philosophers on whom Romans had been to this point dependent, and to a large extent he was successful. His writings covered such topics as political theory, statecraft, ethics, rhetoric, epistemology and theology. More than any ancient writer Cicero's body of work brings to life the concerns, personalities, and emotional conflicts of the late Republic. For 40 years he produced an unending flow of material. No other figure of the ancient world revealed so much of himself as Cicero. There were, of course, many other great orators such as the Gracchi in the second century and Q. Hortensius and M. Antonius in the first, but only fragments of their work survives. Caesar was also a fine speaker and cultivated a very effective but much plainer variety of oratory than Cicero.

THE USES AND ABUSES OF WRITING At an early date members of the Roman elite recognized that the ability to write well had other than literary usefulness; it could also be employed as a potent political weapon. In the second century B.C., for example, Gaius Fannius, a consul and former supporter and friend of Gaius Gracchus, wrote a history of the Gracchan revolution from the viewpoint of the ruling oligarchy. It so successfully exculpated the murderers of the Gracchi that it swamped the Gracchan viewpoint and became the accepted version of the history of those turbulent times. In the next century contemporary history of this kind merged with autobiography and, on occasion, with pure propaganda, when a host of public figures wrote justifying or laudatory accounts of their careers. Rutilius Rufus, an ex-governor who had been exiled after a notoriously unjust trial, wrote a defense of his tenure in office, blackening his enemies. Marius and Sulla produced inflated, self-congratulatory autobiographies. The biased memoirs of Sulla were used in turn by the historian Cornelius Sisenna as a source for his equally biased account of the Social War (90–88 B.C.) and the civil wars that followed. Sallust, a member of Caesar's faction, picked up where Sisenna left off. Although Sallust's histories have perished except for fragments, two of his monographs, *The Jugurthine War* and the *Conspiracy of Catiline*, have survived. His venomous portrait of the times, when read together with Cicero's and the poet Catullus' images of public and private corruption, leave an indelible, if distorted, impression of the age. Caesar wrote the *Commentaries*—terse, written reports to the Senate—from Gaul. They are masterpieces of both Latin literature and political astuteness.

With Livy's *History of Rome*, Roman historical writing reached maturity. We are lucky that considerable amounts of his history survive. Because Livy came at the end of a long period of historical development he was able to draw on the work of earlier historians and biographers. He was candidly moralistic in attitude, and his history abounds with edifying examples of virtue and dismal portrayals of vice. In his introduction he invited the reader to

> examine closely the lives, the customs, the kinds of men and the means they used in politics and war to first win and then retain our empire; next to see how, with discipline gradually weakening, morals at first became as it were discordant; then how they began to disintegrate rapidly and finally collapse in ruin until we come to our own times when we can neither endure our vices nor accept the remedies needed to cure them. The study of history is a healthy and worthwhile activity. It presents to the reader a huge variety of models to be followed or avoided, and it does so with complete clarity. It works equally well for the individual and for the state. (*History of Rome*, 1.1)

Because of his narrative ability and literary talents, Livy's work overshadowed and soon replaced the histories of his predecessors.

LIBRARIES AND ANTIQUARIANISM From the second century B.C. onward, libraries were of increasing importance to Romans. Aemilius Paullus, who had a deep interest in Greek culture, brought the library of Perseus back to Rome with him as part of the loot from the Third Macedonian War. Similarly, from the sack of Athens Sulla brought the library of Aristotle to Rome. It became fashionable for the elite to have, along with fishponds and aviaries, a private library or two. Trimalchio, the freedman who features in the novel the *Satyricon*, boasted he had both Greek and Latin libraries. Julius Caesar planned a great public library and appointed the antiquarian, M. Terentius Varro to be its head.

In an age of increasing historical awareness more people became conscious of the obscurity and archaic character of many Roman customs, religious practices, place names, and the like. Varro responded to this need for information with a great outpouring of books on a huge variety of subjects. Of the 490 books he is credited with, the titles of 55 titles are known. He wrote on agriculture, architecture, astronomy, geography, history, language, law, medicine, music, and religion. He was a key figure in establishing standards of scholarship in Latin and his work was an invaluable source of information for later writers. Only two of his works, one on the Latin language and the other on agriculture, survive. Many other antiquarians and encyclopaedists struggled to make sense of Roman laws, customs and history. Cicero was stimulated to write a history of oratory, and Caesar wrote works on astronomy and grammar.

POETRY AND THE THEATER The theater declined in the first century B.C. as low-grade, popular farce and mime drove out tragedy and comedy. On the other hand personal poetry, epigrams, love elegies, and lyrics reached extraordinary heights of excellence in the poetry of Catullus, Propertius and Tibullus. Tibullus tweaked Roman martial attitudes by proclaiming that although he hated war, he was a "good general and soldier in the service of love," and Propertius claimed that "the conquest of people is worth nothing in comparison to love." Lucretius wrote on the materialistic philosophy of Epicurus from an ethical viewpoint. According to Epicurus fear of the gods and fear of death were the two most serious obstacles to human happiness. Lucretius structured his poem—written in magnificent verse—in such a way as to give emphasis and at the same time alleviate these two sources of human anxiety. All these poets wrote at a time when the horizons of the elite classes while contracting politically were broadening culturally. From a preoccupation with the competitive aspects of political life, the elites found new satisfactions in the expenditure of wealth, the enjoyment of art, literature, music and architecture. A private life of self-cultivation and luxury became an alternative to the ferocity of traditional Roman political culture.

The old culture was not entirely moribund however and in Virgil's great epic, the *Aeneid*, Rome found a reassertion of the old ideals of selfless dedication to the Republic and its needs. The *Aeneid* tells the story of the wanderings of the Trojan hero Aeneas and his search for a place to found a new Troy. Unlike Homer's heroes who were full of zest and spontaneity but lacked introspection, Aeneas was a thoroughly modern figure, complex, often confused and unsure of what he was doing. He knew destiny had something in store for him but had difficulty in discovering what it was. In an age when Rome's old moral consensus was fracturing Virgil was able to show through Aeneas how the virtues of the past could still be relevant. Aeneas ends up in Carthage and thinks about marrying Dido and settling down to a life of luxury and comfort but rejects the temptation and continues on what seems like an endless and possibly pointless journey. Yet he refuses to yield to his own weaknesses or the weaknesses of others. Midway through the poem, as a result of a journey to the underworld, he discovers what providence has in store for him. In the underworld he learns that his descendants will found Rome and will extend "its authority (*imperium*) to the ends of the earth and its spirit to the heights of Olympus" (*Aeneid* 6.782). Romans are warned to avoid civil war. Their destiny is "to rule nations… and establish peace… to be merciful to the conquered and to put down the haughty" (*Aeneid* 6.851).

## 3. SUMMARY: THE FALL OF THE ROMAN REPUBLIC

This section is a summary of potential causes of the fall of the Republic, not a conclusion. It does not attempt to provide an answer for why the Republic fell, but rather to suggest ways of thinking about this huge and important subject.

It is easy enough to bundle together what are thought to be the causes of the fall, but hard to disentangle them and make a coherent argument for any one of them, though of course this is what historians do and have been doing for centuries. Some causes are clearly more important than others. Some might be better classified not as causes but as conditions (i.e., circumstances without which the underlying causes would not have gone into effect) or occasions (i.e., opportunities for acting). Perhaps a useful exercise for the reader might be to go through this section with these distinctions in mind, sorting out conditions from occasions from causes and seeing, if in the end, a single principal "cause" can be identified—or not.

Changes in the wealth, cultural sophistication, education, and values of the elite had an important bearing on the transition from Republic to Empire. So did the transformations of finance and agriculture that accompanied Rome's rise to world power. But there were other factors. The Senate, which need to increase in size to reflect Rome's growth and the changes in the composition of the ruling class, was first doubled by Sulla and then increased again by Caesar. Its cohesion, however, declined precipitously. After the Social War the citizenship expanded enormously and Rome had difficulty assimilating the new members of its commonwealth. There were problems with the way armies were raised, funded and pensioned off; with the courts; with debt and the maintenance of order in Rome and the Italian countryside. There was a lack of discipline in virtually every segment of society.

MILITARY AND DEFENSE ISSUES For many reasons, Rome was reluctant to undertake a great deal of direct responsibility for the lands it conquered throughout the Mediterranean. Cyrene, for example, was not organized as a province until 20 years after it had been bequeathed to Rome by its ruler. Nevertheless Romans never gave up their conquests or forgot their legacies. They did not allow other power centers to rise or permit lands they had conquered to fall into the hands of others. As a result, despite its slowness to create new provinces, Rome found itself committed to the perpetual military defense of its acquisitions and the general maintenance of order in the Mediterranean.

The internal contradictions of these policies could only be resolved by the creation of a number of standing armies in key areas of the empire. These in turn, however, forced a resolution of the question of where the legionaries were to come from and who was to pay them. There would either be large numbers of draftees who could be quickly rotated in and out of the legions, or fewer, long-term volunteers. However, Rome's tradition of fulfilling its manpower needs only from the ranks of property owners initially ruled out the alternative of an all-volunteer army. In the course of the first century it became clear, however, that the traditional method of recruitment, whether because of a decline in the number of property owners or because of increasing resistance to military service, or for other reasons, was no longer viable. The draft still operated in the first century but it no longer restrained ambitious commanders. Charismatic leaders dangling the possibility of a war that could lead to much booty always attracted volunteers. Volunteer armies in turn created other problems. What was Rome to do with the demobilized veterans of such armies? The Senate was never able to find a satisfactory solution to this issue. By default military commanders and the popular assemblies took responsibility for the veterans. Thus the Senate, which had controlled the draft in the past, lost control of the state's manpower reserves. Power shifted to the legions and their commanders. These soldiers were not conscious revolutionaries and there was no rebellion, in Marxist terms, of the proletariat in the legions against the state. Rather, the decline of the draft and the weakening of the authority of the Senate and of the elite in a more general sense, gave the landless an option. They could choose to fight or not to fight, and they could select the leader for whom they would fight. In the 18 years between the outbreak of the civil war in 49 B.C. and Octavian's victory over Antony at Actium in 31 B.C. there were an astonishing 25 mutinies. For the Republic this was a fatal melding of ambitious, unrestrained commanders with troops willing to follow them even against their fellow citizens.

If the Mediterranean and European worlds of the late Republic had been more peaceful the old system might have righted itself without civil war and the eventual collapse of the collective rule of the aristocracy into one man rule. However, from the time of Marius both large and small wars gave repeated opportunities to ambitious and unscrupulous commanders to conduct campaigns practically at will. The Senate was unable to restrain them. In times of peace after the armies had been demobilized there was a possibility that the Senate might have been able to reassert its authority but in that eventuality the more successful commanders could always combine their resources against the Senate—as Pompey, Crassus, and Caesar did in 60–59 B.C.—at which point their will was irresistible. The power of commanders in the field tended to increase, not decrease. Extended commands in a province meant years of continuous patronage and direct access to provincial resources. Marius was consul five times in a row from 104 to 100 B.C., Sulla held *imperium* from 88 to 79 B.C., and Caesar had nine straight years in Gaul. With long term commands came the power to appoint officers, dispense funds, and divide booty. Political affairs in Rome could be manipulated from afar. Senators and individual voters could be bought, leased or rented as needed. The age of the dynasts of the late Republic was an age of individualists who were restrained not by the larger interests of Rome or their colleagues' disapproval but only by their vision of what, and how much they wanted.

INTERNAL AFFAIRS At the same time that external affairs presented opportunities and challenges to Rome there were internal developments within Rome itself that were equally challenging. The Social War made possible the unification of Rome and Italy but it was difficult to overcome the many obstacles that had for so long made that unification impossible. The Roman elite were very conscious of the competition that aristocrats from the Italian municipalities presented. There was always a limit on how many candidates could reasonably expect to compete for the handful of magistracies available annually. After as before the Social War there were, annually, only two top jobs in Rome. Perhaps had Rome had been more generous earlier or had approached the problem of integration with greater imagination or had the infusion of the Italians occurred at a less chaotic time, the state might have been able to cope with the influx. Unfortunately, time had run out. The Roman oligarchs were no better equipped to cope with the increase in the number of equestrians who were eligible for admission to the senatorial order than they were with the Italian elites. It needed someone like Caesar who was willing to surround himself with equestrians, or his adopted son and heir, Octavian, who was of equestrian stock himself, to recognize the potential of incorporating the equestrians in his coalition. Only Caesar, out of all the contending dynasts had the foresight and the skill to combine Italians, equestrians, new senatorial houses, the urban plebs and the common soldiers in a single coalition. On this combination of disparate groups and interests Octavian (later named Augustus) built a new state.

Complementing the newly emerging political order was a cultural revolution of significant proportions. Rome was transformed during the chaotic years between the Gracchi and Augustus from a provincial city-state with a *polis*-style government into the sophisticated capital of a world empire. The city overflowed with Greek works of art. Philosophers, rhetoricians, literary figures, doctors, architects and skilled craftsmen of every kind came from the east and found employment in the households not just of the upper aristocracy but throughout the elite. New ideals of what constituted the good life competed with the old ideals of service and subordination to the state. The transformation was not achieved with ease. Legally weak but morally powerful bonds of kinship, patronage, friendship, and duty had in the past united the various strands of Roman society. The newly emerging society was more fragmented. What was left of the old patriciate clung to its privileges and attempted to lord it over the newcomers. They found to their dismay they were in contention for public recognition with elements of the new imperial nobility that included provincials, equestrians, freedmen, equestrians, and families from the Italian aristocracy. Some in the newly emerging elite sought only to avoid political entanglements and enjoy their riches in peace and quiet. Many women of the ruling classes achieved independence as a result of the upheavals of the late Republic and the decline of the rigid patriarchal system. They acquired riches and education and moved with freedom at the highest levels of society. As the new groups evolved they developed their own individual codes of behavior, and the simpler consensus of the past faded. The intermingling of society and the state, so characteristic of the Republic and one of its great strengths, vanished and was replaced by more complex sets of social relations. The private sector of society expanded enormously in size and attractiveness. Roman society below the level of the ruling elite was depoliticized, and in due course also demilitarized.

Despite the fact that the fall of the Republic had important social and cultural underpinnings, most scholars think it was in essence a political not a social or cultural revolution. If that is the case then the question to be addressed is why the Senate and the ruling political class generally lost control? While this narrows the focus rather than answers the question of why the Republic fell, it highlights the next great act in Roman history: The reconstitution of the Republic by Augustus. But to use the term "reconstitute" is to predetermine the answer. Perhaps Augustus did not "reconstitute" the Republic so much as complete the work of demolition that had been begun by his talented, perceptive adoptive father, Julius Caesar?

# Part Three

# The Republic Restored: The Principate of Augustus

## 1. INTRODUCTION AND OVERVIEW

### Rome Reinvents Itself—Again

Just as Rome evolved its own hybrid version of the *polis* after the expulsion of the kings, so Romans created a new state—an idiosyncratic form of one-man rule—out of the chaos of the late Republic. In its early stages it lacked the obviously despotic characteristics of the traditional kingdoms of the Middle East—Assyria, Babylon, Persia, or Egypt—or even the more recent Hellenistic kingdoms of Alexander's successors. Nor was it like the tyrannies with which many Greek cities were familiar, where an individual strong man, usually with popular support, ruled by his own dictates and was protected from his enemies, inside and outside the city, by armed mercenaries loyal to him alone. In typical Roman fashion one-man rule as it evolved under Octavian (who later acquired the title of Augustus) was complex, multi-layered, legalistic, practical, and overlain with a good dose of theatricality.[1] It was so complex that most—but not all—contemporaries of Augustus were unable or too cautious to identify it as a form of monarchy. It took several generations of Romans looking back on the period of Augustus' rule for the claim to be established among the elite that it had been a form of one-man rule from the beginning.

[1]For the sake of simplicity I will use the term "Augustus" for Octavian (Gaius Julius Caesar Octavianus) even before he received the title in 27 B.C.

THE PLAYERS Rome's form of popular sovereignty was not solely the product of Augustus' statesmanship. He was, it is true, the presiding genius who guided this most recent version of Rome's self-reinvention, but by necessity all the elements of Roman society were called upon to play important roles. Anyone of them could have brought the evolving process to a halt.

There were several elements in the new regime. The first player of importance was the senatorial order, the most politically active part of the elite—which now included large numbers of the Italian aristocracy and even some members of provincial elites from places like southern Gaul and Spain, which had been Romanized generations earlier. To a surprising extent, given its 500-year-old visceral history of resistance to one-man rule, there was relatively little opposition to Augustus from the Senate. There were a few attempted coups, but for the most part senators went along with his reforms. Next came the elite in its more extensive form, the equestrian order, which also by this time included many notables from the *municipia* of Italy and the provinces. Augustus was himself of equestrian origin as were his closest advisors, Agrippa and Maecenas. The *equites* had major roles to play in Augustus' reforms, filling essential administrative and military positions that for one reason or another could not be assigned to senators. Another major player—in a sense the principal audience for the reforms of Augustus—was the people of the city of Rome itself, a boisterous self-confident, diverse mass used to voicing its opinions and having them respected. Ways had to be found to co-opt or at least contain this volatile segment of Roman society, which could take to the streets in moments. Rome had a long tradition of resistance to a state-run police force, and mobs were an ever-present danger to public order. Then, finally, there was the army, that is to say those Romans who formed an organized, armed body, conscious—at times—of its latent power. During the late Republic the army had been evolving from a citizen militia into a professional military without whose cooperation neither the Senate nor military dynasts nor emperors could rule. For Augustus, and even more so for his successors, the army was a more essential but in the end also a more dangerous constituency than the Senate, the equestrian order, or the people. It was especially important for Augustus to find a secure place for it in his evolving strategy of restoring stability to the tottering state.

## 2. HISTORIOGRAPHY

### The Good and the Bad Augustus

TACITUS In ancient times views of the deeds of Augustus broke down into two basic categories, conveniently assembled by the senatorial historian Tacitus (ca. A.D. 56–117). We have first the "good" Augustus who restored the Republic, respected law, extended the rule of Rome, and accomplished much more:

> Intelligent people spoke variously of his life with praise and blame. Some said that dutiful feeling toward a father [*the duty to avenge his adoptive father, Julius Caesar*], and the necessities

of the state in which laws had then no place, drove him to civil war, which can be neither planned nor conducted on any right principles.... the only remedy for his distracted country was the rule of a single man. Yet Augustus had reorganized the state neither as a monarchy nor as a dictatorship but under the rule of the First Man in the State [princeps, *a traditional designation for a prominent senator*]. The ocean and remote rivers were the boundaries of the Empire; the legions, provinces, fleets—all things were linked together; there was law for the citizens; there was respect shown for the allies. The capital had been beautified on a grand scale; only in a few instances had he resorted to force, simply to secure general tranquility.

Then, on the other hand, there were those who held a different and negative opinion of Augustus:

It was said, on the other hand, that filial duty and state necessity were merely assumed as a mask. His real motive was lust for power. Driven by that, he had mobilized the veterans by bribery and, when a young man with no official position, had raised an army, tampered with a consul's legions, and pretended attachment to the faction of Sextus Pompey. Then, when by a decree of the Senate he had usurped the high functions and authority of praetor... he at once wrested the consulate from a reluctant Senate and turned against the Republic the arms with which he had been entrusted to use against Antony. Citizens were proscribed and lands divided.... Even granting that the deaths of Cassius and Brutus were sacrifices to a hereditary enmity (though duty requires us to ignore private feuds for the sake of the public welfare), still Sextus Pompey had been deluded by the phantom of peace, and Lepidus by the mask of friendship. Subsequently, Antony had been lured on by the treaties of Tarentum and Brundisium and by his marriage with the sister of Augustus, and he paid by his death the penalty of a treacherous alliance. No doubt there was peace after all this, but it was a peace stained with blood.

Tacitus' own opinion was more in line with those who took a negative view of Augustus:

When after the destruction of Brutus and Cassius there was no longer any army of the Republic.... Augustus won over the soldiers with gifts, the populace with cheap grain, and all men with the attractions of peace. So he grew greater by degrees while he concentrated in himself the functions of the Senate, the magistrates, and the laws. He was wholly unopposed, for the boldest spirits had fallen in battle or in the proscription, while the remaining nobles, the readier they were to be slaves, were raised the higher by wealth and promotion, so that, aggrandized by revolution, they preferred the safety of the present to the dangers of the past. Nor did the provinces dislike that condition of affairs, for they distrusted the government of the Senate and the People because of the rivalries between the leading men and the rapacity of the officials, while the protection of the laws was unavailing, as they were continually upset by violence, intrigue, and finally by corruption.... At home all was tranquil, and there were magistrates with the same titles; there was a younger generation, sprung up since the victory of Actium [*the battle in 31 B.C. that eliminated Octavian's last rival, Antony*], and even many of the older men had been born during the civil wars. How few were left who had seen the Republic. Thus the state had been revolutionized, and there was not a vestige left of the old-style virtue. Stripped of equality, all looked up to the commands of a sovereign without the least apprehension for the present.[2]

[2]Tacitus, *Annals* 9, 10, 2, 3, 4. Based on the translation of A.J. Church and W. J. Brodribb, *The Annals of Tacitus* (London, 1906).

## Augustus' Image Problem

Writing more than a century after most of Augustus' reforms had been put in place, Tacitus had the advantage of historical perspective and the experience of serving under several emperors. That perspective, however, was vitiated by the fact that he wrote as a survivor with a guilty conscience regarding the treason trials in which he had participated under the emperor Domitian (A.D. 81–A.D. 96). On the other hand, Romans who lived at the time of Augustus had to judge by their immediate experience of the man. It would have been hard for them, at least initially, not to have thought of him as just another one of the power-hungry, glory-seeking military dynasts who had dominated the Roman political scene since Sulla. After all, Augustus was himself the adopted successor of Julius Caesar, the last and most powerful of these dynasts. As Caesar's heir he was the inheritor of Caesar's name, his fortune, his faction, and most importantly, of the duty to avenge his adoptive father's murder. That involved him, along with the other triumvirs, in a long list of judicial murders and property confiscations throughout Italy. He disgracefully betrayed Cicero, who had helped him in a period of political weakness immediately after Caesar's murder. With his fellow triumvirs he waged a bloody civil war of revenge against the conspirators. When they were disposed of, he and Antony exiled Lepidus and then fell to quarreling among themselves. Yet another round of civil wars followed. How could his contemporaries—especially those who ended up on the wrong side—forget such awful deeds? Of course they could not. To suppress this poisonous legacy would have been impossible, but Augustus had to neutralize it in some way. It was one of the major accomplishments of his reign that he was able to insert a counter-version in the media of the time—rhetoric, literature, art, architecture, and coinage—that made it impossible for his enemies and later hostile writers such as Tacitus, to restrict the story of Augustus to the bloody days of his triumvirate. If nothing else Augustus' media triumph was a masterpiece of public relations and political skill. However, it had more substance than that. It could celebrate the achievement of order and stability, and it bestowed on later ages classics of literature and the visual arts that remain impressive to the present day.

## The *Res Gestae*: Augustan Ideology and Self-Justification

Augustus wrote an autobiography, which has not come down to us. As part of his will, however, he left the *Res Gestae* ("Deeds Accomplished"), a terse account of his long stewardship of the Empire. This document was intended to be read in the Senate after his death and was inscribed in bronze on pillars set up at the entrance to his mausoleum in the Campus Martius and in front of temples in the provinces. The bronze was melted down long ago, but luckily a copy of the *Res Gestae* carved on the walls of the Temple of Rome and Augustus at Ancyra (in modern Turkey) has survived. In essence this document is a statement of the ideology of Augustus' reform program and an unapologetic defense of his reign.

LEGALITIES In the *Res Gestae* the record of the bloody triumvir Octavian disappears. For that matter, the other triumvirs are barely mentioned and none of them by name.

Nothing is said of Cleopatra. Instead Augustus devotes a great deal of attention to the legal justifications of his actions from the time he accepted the will of Julius Caesar and formally became Caesar's adopted son to the time of the writing of the document. It begins with the brief statement: "When I was 19, on my own initiative and at my own expense, I raised an army to restore the liberty of the Republic [*rem publicam in libertatem vindicavi*]. At this time it suffered under the tyranny of a faction [*that of Mark Antony*]" (*RG* Pref.). These are almost exactly the same words Sulla used nearly a century earlier to justify his march on Rome to free the state from the alleged tyranny of Marius. They immediately suggest that Augustus' aim was to justify his acts by appeal to the long established Republican tradition, going back to the expulsion of the kings, that the recovery of the liberty of the Republic was a noble, good, and above all, legitimate thing. This was not the deed of a private individual acting without the authority of the law. Thus he says his revenge of his father's murder was a publicly sanctioned act and that he never accepted any power offered him "which was contrary to the tradition of our ancestors" (*RG,* 6).

**Augustus**

*Could a man who looked as benign as this really have murdered hundreds of his fellow citizens, friends, political allies and relatives in cold blood? Augustus' sculptural program was as carefully calculated as of all his other projects.*

AUGUSTUS' *AUCTORITAS* Augustus' great *auctoritas*, he asserts, did not rely only on his purely legal powers—as a triumvir or consul or tribune—but on his overall proven military and political ability. This was the way in which the great *principes* of the Republic made themselves eminent. Their greatness depended on their *virtus* and their long and distinguished service to the state; it was not just a result of the offices they held. A golden shield was put up in his honor in the Forum Julia (Julius Caesar's new forum) inscribed with the virtues of *clementia, iustitia,* and *pietas*—precisely the qualities he claimed to have been represented by his regime. His control of the state came about as the result of the *consensus universorum*—the agreement of everyone—when all of Italy swore an oath of allegiance to him before the battle of Actium. Then in 27 B.C. he transferred full control of the state back to the Senate and people of Rome. At various times the Senate and the people conferred on him the titles of First Citizen (*princeps senatus* in 28 B.C.), *Augustus* (in 27 B.C.), and Father of the Fatherland (*pater patriae* in 2 B.C.). He is at pains in the *Res Gestae* to point out that he settled demobilized soldiers legally by compensating landowners. He emphasizes the vast sums of money he generously bestowed on people and soldiers as their *patronus* and the honors that, in return, the entire community of Romans bestowed on him. The great military successes of his regime were the successes of Rome, and his legacy was a *patria*, a country of which Romans could be proud. The message is that he was not a warlord like the dynasts who preceded him, whose conquests were for the sake of personal glory and power; the conquests of Augustus were wholly for Rome.

The *Res Gestae* is many things: It is at once a list of accomplishments, an *apologia*, a statement of ideology, a political testament, and an epitaph. Tacitus and historians who share his view of human nature tend to dismiss the difficulty and challenges of the Augustan restoration by means of clever epigrams, cynicism, and studied witticisms. The *Res Gestae*, a summary of nearly half a century of work, suggests, however, that the Augustan reform program cannot be so easily summed up or, for that matter, dismissed.

## Other Ancient Writers

Contemporaries of the Princeps other than Augustus himself also wrote of his rule. Velleius Paterculus, a somewhat younger contemporary of Augustus and an official under Tiberius, the successor of Augustus, welcomed wholeheartedly his reforms:

> There is nothing that man can desire from the gods, nothing that the gods can grant to a man, nothing that wish can conceive or good fortune bring to pass which Augustus ...did not bestow upon the Republic, the Roman people, and the world. The civil wars were ended after twenty years, foreign wars suppressed, peace restored ... Validity was restored to the laws, authority to the Senate; the power of magistrates was reduced to its former limits ...the old traditional form of the Republic was restored. Agriculture returned to the fields, respect to religion, to mankind freedom from anxiety, and to each citizen his property rights were now assured. (2.89)[3]

Livy wrote until 9 B.C., but unfortunately the books that would have covered Augustus to that date survive only in the form of very brief summaries. Their principal emphasis seems to have been on the wars of conquest conducted by Augustus. The surviving books of Livy's history suggest an independent viewpoint, but one that was in large measure in accord with Augustus' aims. Tacitus, for example, says that Livy felt free to praise Brutus and Cassius without offending the Princeps. This is the same Tacitus who asserted that there were plenty of talented historians who might have written about Augustus but were deterred by "a rising tide of flattery" (*Annals* 1.1).

POLLIO, CORDUS, APPIAN Asinius Pollio, consul in 40 B.C., a friend of Virgil and Horace and a supporter of Julius Caesar, wrote a history of the civil wars that went from 60 B.C. to the battle of Philippi in 42 B.C. For Asinius Pollio the last free year of the Republic was 60 B.C. the year Pompey, Crassus, and Caesar plotted to enforce their wishes on an unwilling Senate. He is reported to have said: "It is not easy to write of a man [*meaning Augustus*] who has all the means of punishment at his disposal" (Macrobius, *Sat.*,2.4.21). Another chronicler was the senator Cremutius Cordus whose account of the civil wars and the Augustan regime went down to 18 B.C. Like Livy he felt free to praise the republicans Cicero, Brutus, and Cassius, calling the latter "the last of the Romans." For him the Republic ended at Philippi with the death of Brutus and Cassius. Except for fragments the histories of Asinius Pollio and Cremutius Cordus have not been preserved. Their writings were probably known to Appian, an Alexandrian Greek, who wrote a general history of Rome in the

[3] *Velleius Paterculus*, tr. F. W. Shipley (London, 1924).

second century A.D. Books 17 to 21 of his *Histories* cover the civil wars and are valuable because they contain material that reflect works, such as the histories of Pollio, that are now lost. He was an admirer of Rome and a convinced monarchist.

SUETONIUS, PLUTARCH, DIO CASSIUS The biographies of Caesar and of Augustus by Suetonius are important sources for the period. Suetonius held important posts in the imperial administration in the early second century A.D. and had access to archives that allowed him to quote verbatim from letters of Augustus. He did not pass himself off as an historian. As a biographer his aim was to collect material, often gossipy, illustrating the personalities of the emperors he studied and to measure their performance accordingly. He and Plutarch, also writing in the early second century A.D., made Julius Caesar the first monarch and Augustus the second. Plutarch's *Lives of Caesar* and *Antony* are among the best of his biographies. A century later, a senatorial historian, Dio Cassius, divided Augustus' regime into three periods. The first period lasted from the time Octavian accepted the will of Caesar in 43 B.C. to the battle of Philippi in 42 B.C., where Brutus and Cassius were defeated. During this time the Republic was still in existence. In this assessment Dio Cassius agreed with Cremutius Cordus, who also believed that the Republic ended with the Battle of Philippi. In the second period, from 42 B.C. to 27 B.C. Augustus behaved like an all-powerful dynast. The last period, from 27 B.C. onwards, saw the establishment of the monarchy under which subsequent Romans lived to Cassius'own time. Contemporary poets such as Virgil and Horace are obviously not historians, but their poems do constitute a large body of material that historians regularly mine for information about attitudes towards the Principate of Augustus.

Josephus and Philo provide insights into Jewish history, religion, and life, while the various books of the New Testament provide information about early Christianity as well as life in Palestine and the eastern Mediterranean in the first and second centuries A.D. Non-historical literature in the form of the poetry of Ovid, Lucan, Statius, and Martial, in addition to their own literary value, offer insight into the cultural and social life of the Early Empire. Inscriptions, coins, papyri, and archaeology illustrate many facets of imperial life that are at best hinted at in the literary sources. Use has been made in Chapter 15 below of the extraordinary archaeological finds made at a fort on Britain's northern frontier with Scotland (pages 346–347). These discoveries give a vivid picture of the kind of life led on that distant frontier by auxiliary units of the Roman army.

## Modern Views

Broadly speaking, modern historians fall into one or other of the two categories—the good and the bad Augustus—on which Tacitus reported. Their opinions correlate—roughly—with the levels of their commitment to republicanism (i.e., constitutional government). Judgments of Augustus seem to invite authors to weigh up the amount of chaos they think a society can endure while still remaining free and obedient to law. How much freedom is too much? How much chaos can be tolerated? When does law cease to be law and become instead a façade for dictators? For some societies and their historians very little chaos is tolerable. In the 1930s, following the disorder created by the First World War, some continental European governments idealized Augustus as the man who rescued his homeland from mayhem, disciplined its people and extended its borders militarily—just as they hoped to do or had already done in their own countries. Historians sympathetic to these viewpoints produced accounts that dwelt on the problems faced by Augustus, glorified his success in overcoming them, and celebrated his autocracy.

In reaction to these trends one of the greatest historians of the twentieth century, Ronald Syme, composed *The Roman Revolution*, published in 1939. For Syme and those influenced by him, Augustus was no benevolent Princeps but only a cold, calculating, chameleon-like figure who was supported by a small coterie of talented but self-interested, ruthless upstarts. At the heart of all government, Syme believed, must be sought the small group of individuals who run it. "In all ages, whatever the form and name of the government, be it monarchy, republic, or democracy an oligarchy lurks in the façade." Hence, the principate of Augustus with all its pretensions to institutional legality was a "necessary and salutary fraud."[4] Since the 1970s there has been a reaction against Syme's elitist view of history and his consequent neglect of the roles played by others—such as the people and the army—in the reconstitution of the state. Since Syme's time much work has been done in the fields of art, architecture, and archaeology, and as a consequence studies in these fields have considerably added to our knowledge of the extent and depth of Augustus' program. Modern works tend to reflect this new knowledge and are generally more sympathetic to the tasks Augustus faced and the adroitness and appropriateness of his solutions to them.

**Time Line of Augustus**

| | |
|---|---|
| 63 B.C. | Birth of Octavius |
| 44 B.C. | Adoption of Octavius by Julius Caesar; Assassination of Caesar |
| 43–33 B.C. | The Triumvirate |
| 42 B.C. | Battle of Philippi |
| 40 B.C. | Antony marries Octavia |
| 38 B.C. | Octavian marries Livia |
| 32 B.C. | Antony divorces Octavia |
| 31 B.C. | Battle of Actium |
| 30 B.C. | Deaths of Antony and Cleopatra |
| 27 B.C. | Octavian restores the Republic and receives the name of Augustus |
| 23 B.C. | Augustus resigns the consulship and receives tribunician power. Agrippa receives proconsular *imperium* for five years. |
| 23 B.C. | Death of Marcellus |
| 21 B.C. | Agrippa marries Julia |
| 20 B.C. | The Parthians hand over Crassus' standards |
| 19 B.C. | Augustus receives *imperium consulare* |
| 18 B.C. | Agrippa receives proconsular *imperium* and tribunician power for five years. |

[4] *The Roman Revolution* Oxford, 1939, 7; 516.

| | |
|---|---|
| 17 B.C. | The *ludi saeculares.* Augustus adopts Gaius and Lucius Caesar |
| 13 B.C. | Agrippa's powers renewed. |
| 12 B.C. | Death of Agrippa; Augustus elected Pontifex Maximus |
| 11 B.C. | Tiberius marries Julia |
| 9 B.C. | Death of Drusus |
| 6 B.C. | Tiberius receives tribunician power for five years; retires to Rhodes |
| 2 B.C. | Exile of Julia; Augustus proclaimed *pater patriae* |
| A.D. 2 | Death of Lucius |
| A.D. 4 | Death of Gaius. Augustus adopts Tiberius who receives tribunician power for 10 years. |
| A.D. 6 | Military treasury and the Vigiles created |
| A.D. 6–9 | Pannonian revolt |
| A.D. 9 | Varian disaster |
| A.D. 13 | Tiberius' tribunician power renewed |
| A.D. 14 | Death of Augustus. |

# 12

# The Augustan Settlement

## 1. BREAK UP OR RESTORATION?

### Not Many Alternatives

After his victory over Antony and Cleopatra at Actium 31 B.C. Octavian was faced with the colossal task of restoring Rome to a functioning state.[1] It was not a foregone conclusion that he would succeed. Writing in 38 B.C., the poet Horace thought that "this city might die by its own right hand… and this impious generation of fated blood perish and the land belong once again to wild beasts" (*Epodes*, 7.10; 16.9). Given the disfunctionality of Rome's government for over a century it seemed more likely that far-flung provinces with no deep or long-term connections with Rome would break off and go their own way given the opportunity and the means. In any case it was clear to most Romans that a firm hand was needed to prevent internal and external actors from destroying the empire that generations of earlier Romans had created at so much cost to themselves and their neighbors. The only question was how firm that hand was to be and whose—an individual's or the Senate's or some as yet undiscovered combination of the two.

THE CAESARIAN SOLUTION Julius Caesar's solution—to the extent he had one—to the problems that plagued the late Republic was an improvised form of one-man rule. At the pinnacle of his power he issued decrees and orders and consulted his friends but never the Senate, which he scorned.

[1] Octavian's full name after accepting his adoption by Caesar was Gaius Julius Caesar Octavianus. Sometime before 38 B.C. he added the praenomen "Imperator" to his title and became "Imperator Caesar." This title emphasized military and dynastic claims respectively. All later emperors (*imperatores*) assumed it.

He mainly kept busy with administrative tasks, building projects, reforms (such as the reform of the calendar), and preparing for a campaign against the Parthians to recover the standards lost by Crassus at the battle of Carrhae. As a result Caesar increasingly found himself isolated from traditional Roman political culture. We do not know whether or not he thought he could reform the constitution in a fundamental way; with his quick intelligence he may have decided it was beyond remedy—at least by him. Perhaps he knew his own character too well. He was far too impatient to do the hard work of bridge-building—to persuade, flatter, and compromise—that is at the heart of politics. The Senate was an exclusive club full of men from ancient Roman families and new men trying to make their presence felt. Their outsize egos—many of them matched with second- or third-rate characters—needed constant stroking. Caesar was not the kind of man to provide that kind of attention. He had spent too many years on campaign, far from the irritations and political wranglings of Rome. No wonder he wanted to get out of the city and wage war in the east.

Even apart from long-standing traditions of Roman political culture it would have been difficult for Caesar to sustain himself for long without building a government in which his friends, who rightly expected to be rewarded, found positions of power and honor. Not even the most powerful of autocrats works alone. Syme was right to insist that all governments are oligarchies at their core. Caesar needed many helpers. To do that, however, meant working within the existing political order. The prestige of the Senate, despite its manifold failures, was immense. Institutionally there was no alternative to it. It was impossible to govern a Mediterranean-wide empire without officials, and these had to come from somewhere. Where else could Caesar find people with the necessary background and qualifications for governance and command except in the Senate, which acted as a kind of screening filter for the Roman government? When Caesar chose his great-nephew Octavian as his heir perhaps he saw in him the qualities he found lacking in himself. What Winston Churchill is supposed to have said of Franklin Delano Roosevelt—that he was a man with a second-rate mind but a first-rate personality—might also be said of Octavian.

## 2. INSURMOUNTABLE PROBLEMS?

### The Army

The most pressing problem facing Octavian after Actium in 31 B.C. was that of the army. The empire needed a standing army for its defense and to maintain internal order. There was general agreement on these two points, but other questions remained. How large should the army be, and—a connected question—how large an army could Rome afford? How was it to be funded, and from where were the recruits to come? How long were they to serve, and most importantly, who was to command them? Dio Cassius reports a speech between two of Augustus' closest advisors on how best to answer some of these questions. Interestingly Agrippa, the Princeps' military man, advocated maintaining the traditional system of recruiting conscripts for short periods of time, arguing that a standing army was a perpetual threat to stability. This kind of recruitment would keep the costs down and maintain the connection between civilians and soldiers. Maecenas, a wily and cultivated politician and diplomat, with perhaps short-term solutions in mind, argued for a volunteer army of professionals serving for long periods of time. His argument carried the day.[2]

The experience of the late Republic had taught the ruling class the danger of large-scale special commands. Some way of preventing generals doing what generals did from Sulla to Augustus himself—namely turning the armies of the Republic into private armies—had to be found. If not, the cycle of civil wars would be repeated until there was nothing left to fight over.

DEMOBILIZING THE LEGIONS In 31 B.C. there were 60 legions under arms. Many, perhaps most, of these soldiers had been drafted into the legions by one or other of the two sides in the recent civil war and were anxious to be demobilized. They had to be found land and settled quickly before trouble erupted in the ranks. Even a beloved commander like Julius Caesar had to face down mutinies in 49 and 47 B.C. by soldiers who wanted to return home.

The standing army was to be built around those professionals who had no interest in returning to civilian life. Between 31 B.C. and 13 B.C. Augustus reduced the 60 legions to 28 legions. He claims to have sent home or resettled 300,000 veterans in colonies (*Res Gestae,* 3). Under Sulla, resettlement had been financed by a bloody proscription; fortunately, the means for accomplishing Augustus' enormous resettlements were supplied by the treasures of Egypt, which Augustus seized after the defeat of Antony. In the *Res Gestae* Augustus underlines the difference between his method of settling veterans and those of his predecessors. After noting that in Italy he "paid 600,000,000 sesterces for land and in the provinces 260,000,000," he goes on to say, "I was the first and only one to do this of all those who up to my time settled colonies of veterans in Italy or the provinces"(*RG* 16).

TERMS OF SERVICE Length of service, pay scales, and discharge benefits were all regularized. In A.D. 6 a special military treasury (*aerarium militare*), funded by a sales tax and death duties, was set up to pay retirement bonuses to the 6,000 or so veterans who were discharged annually. Augustus draws attention to the fact that he provided the initial funding of 170,000,000 sesterces for the *aerarium militare* out of his own pocket, or as he put it, "out of my own patrimony" (*Res Gestae*, 17). Service was to be for 20 years with five years in the reserves. The discharge bonus was fixed at 12,000 sesterces for ordinary soldiers, equivalent to about 14 years of pay.

A BAD BARGAIN The new taxes were naturally highly unpopular, but the alternative—land grants and confiscations—were even more unpopular. The taxpayers grumbled but in the end accepted the Augustan solution. It was a necessary, but bad bargain. Military service and citizenship in Rome now became detached from each other. Army service and the ownership of land were the traditional and inseparable foundations of civilian power in a constitutional state. The theory of such states was that those who took on themselves the

[2]Or something like that argument. The speeches are not historical in the sense that they would have been had Dio Cassius been present at the debate and taken notes he later worked up into a facsimile of the original. But they reflect ideas that were commonplace since the emergence of the *polis* and were undoubtedly on the minds of any Romans who gave a minute's thought to the dilemmas the city had faced since the second century B.C.

risk *and* costs of war deserved to decide who and whether they were going to fight. To turn the immense responsibility for the defense of the state over to a paid professional military necessarily involved ceding much power to the army. After all, why should those who were unwilling to take on the miseries of war be able to dictate to those who were? Shaking off military responsibilities has some immediate satisfaction and pleases a number of constituencies. Historically, however, societies that have had large standing professional armies have usually paid a very high price for them beyond the actual cost of their maintenance. It was not that these facts were unknown at Rome, as the discussion between Agrippa and Maecenas (see above, pages 238–239) indicates. It may have been that, as with so much else in the Rome of this time, the principle had been abandoned long before to imperial needs. An immediate solution was necessary. Agrippa was right in principle, Maecenas in terms of expediency.

## Augustus, the Elite, and the Constitution

THE CONSTITUTIONAL PROBLEM OF THE ARMY The constitutional problem of the army was not easily solved. Somehow Augustus had to find a legally acceptable means of keeping control of the army without having to remain dictator in perpetuity (Caesar's choice), or alternatively, being consul every year. This was in addition to the political problem of how to keep tight control of commanders in the field who, if particularly successful, could become instantaneous competitors for the Princeps' own job. The alternative—having incompetent commanders—was obviously not a viable solution. Romans expected victories in the field, not defeats. When the army of Varus was wiped out in Germany in A.D. 9, Augustus had to worry not just about the danger caused by the loss but also about the political fallout—senators muttering about incompetence and bungling on the Palatine (where Augustus had his house) and reminding themselves that Varus had been the son-in-law of that scheming intimate of the Princeps, Agrippa and was now, or had been until his death, married to a grand-niece of Augustus himself. Augustus took the loss hard, "leaving his hair untrimmed for months and often beating his head on a door exclaiming, 'Quinctilius Varus, give me back my legions!'"(Suet. *Augustus*, 23).

In 36 B.C. during his struggle with Antony, Octavian had offered to give up his triumviral powers and return the government of the Republic to the Senate and people—provided Antony did the same thing. The offer was something more than a ploy to embarrass his triumviral colleague. It demonstrated that Octavian was aware that he had to consider a constitutional solution to the ongoing crisis of government. With Antony out of the picture he was in a position to actually fulfill his offer of 36 B.C. Having held the consulship continuously from 31 B.C., Augustus renounced his powers in 27 B.C. In a carefully choreographed drama he returned control of the state to the "will of the Senate and the Roman people" (*RG*, 34). Pressed by the Senate, he retained the consulship and also consular control (*imperium consulare*) through legates over the legions in the frontier provinces of Gaul, Spain, and Syria, as well as Egypt. The Senate retained control of pacified but important provinces such as Africa, Illyria, and Macedonia with a few legions. Although this solution had at least constitutional form, it was not completely satisfactory. As in previous years when Augustus held the consulship it halved the number of consular positions available to the nobility and saddled Augustus with many routine duties. From Augustus' viewpoint this was only a partial solution to some key political issues, but it did cut the ground from under those who complained that something needed to be done about their leaders' excessive powers in light of the fact that the emergency had ended.

Insofar as the army was concerned, the Princeps continued to exercise control over the bulk of the legions. Because they were located in the frontier provinces he could engage in expansionary policies that would enable him to appeal to the army while at the same time portraying himself to Romans in general as an expander and defender of the Empire. This could be turned to good political capital—except, of course in the case of a military setback. The next chapter will deal more fully with Augustus' frontier policies and issues of imperial administration.

MAIUS IMPERIUM In his ongoing search for ways to finesse the problem of retaining military command while respecting constitutional traditions, Augustus in 23 B.C. gave up the consulship after holding it for nine years in a row. He did not hold it again except on rare, mostly honorific, occasions. This provided the elite with two chief offices instead of one, while adding to the Princeps' patronal power.[3] As part of his understanding with the Senate Augustus could recommend (or block) candidates for the office. Instead of losing power by this move Augustus actually gained power. Now being able to recommend an additional candidate every year strengthened his power within the senatorial aristocracy.

The problem of control of the army could have been complicated by Augustus' abandonment of the consulship, but this issue was fixed by having the Senate grant him special proconsular power that was greater than that possessed by any proconsul (*maius imperium*). This new arrangement once more extended the Princeps' powers because now he could legitimately intervene in all provinces, including those under senatorial control, whenever he thought it necessary.

The separation of the power of the office from the actual office itself was a clever arrangement and shows the flexibility of Rome's unwritten constitution. The action had important consequences. Normally office holders were subject to the veto of their colleagues (*collegiality*), the annual time limit (*annuality*), and the geographical limits of the assigned province. Augustus was now freed from these restrictions. Needless to say the Senate was well aware of the implications of its actions, but it also knew the dangers that insufficiently controlled armies posed to Rome's stability. There was no alternative to one-man rule in this respect. The only question that remained was what form—the modality—one-man rule would take. What the Princeps was proposing must have seemed to most senators about as good a solution as they could hope for at this point in time. *Maius imperium* thus became one of the legal pillars of the new constitution.

AUGUSTUS' ILLNESS That same year (23 B.C.) Augustus became seriously ill, and on what seemed to be his deathbed gave his signet ring to Agrippa and his papers to his con-

[3]The consuls of the year, called *consules ordinarii*, had more prestige than suffect consuls (i.e., senators who were appointed consuls for a portion of the year). The *ordinarii* gave their names to the year.

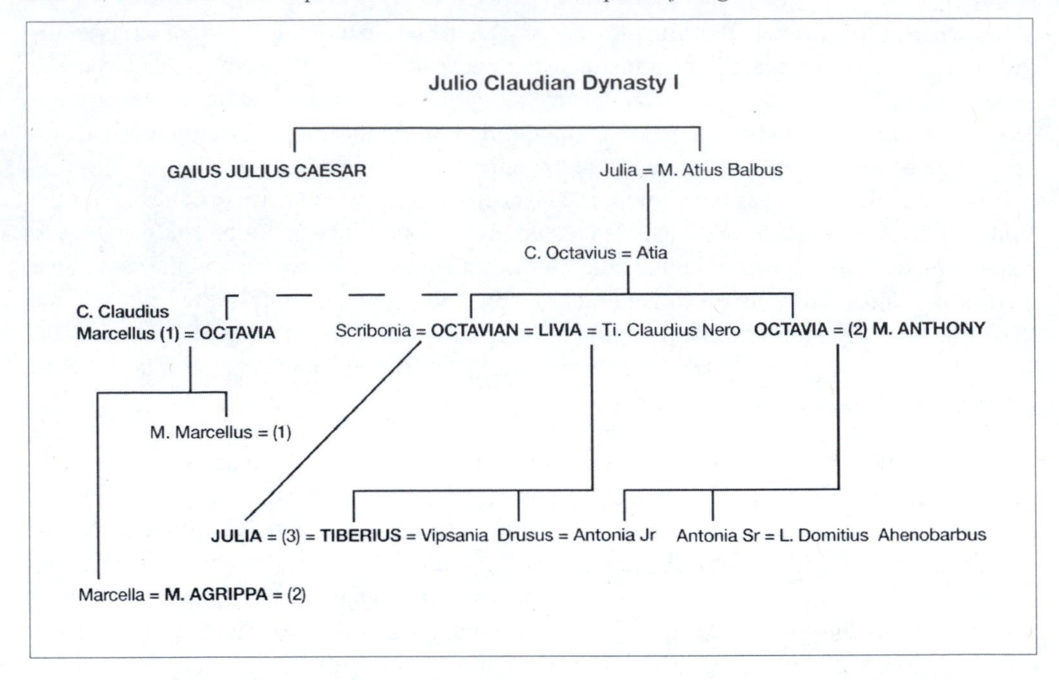


sular colleague, Calpurnius Piso, a convinced republican constitutionalist. His presumed heir, his nephew Marcellus, received nothing. It seems likely that up until this unexpected illness the resignation of the consulship and the choice of Piso as the Princeps' colleague had been a well-prepared scenario intended to convince doubters that he was serious about restoring the formalities of senatorial rule. Augustus' reaction to his illness suggests, however, that his republicanism was not entirely a farce. If he were to die at this point it seems Augustus wanted to be remembered as one who acknowledged the values and traditions of the Republic. Had he designated Marcellus as his heir he would have given more than the appearance of turning his rule into an overt, hereditary monarchy where, at the death of the king, the kingdom passed like so much real estate to the heir-apparent. The 18-year-old Marcellus was obviously unqualified to step into the shoes of his uncle, although Augustus' preference for him was shown by the fact that in 25 B.C. he had married his daughter Julia to him.[4] As it happens, the Princeps recovered, but his brush with death must have brought to the forefront, if it was not already there, the thorny issue of what was to be done when Augustus did eventually pass from the scene. As it turned out this was the great conundrum for legitimate one-man rule at Rome. These issues will be treated in greater detail in the next chapter.

TRIBUNICIAN POWER In the course of seeking suitable legal forms for his extraordinary powers, Augustus selected one constitutional form from the old patrician state and one from the plebeian. The first, as we have seen, was proconsular *imperium*, which gave him control of the army. The second was tribunician power (but not the office of tribune, for

[4]The unfortunate Julia, Augustus' only child, was married to Agrippa after Marcellus' death and then, when Agrippa died, to Tiberius, Augustus' stepson.

which, as a patrician, Augustus was ineligible), which was voted to him in 23 B.C. Together they were to be the legal foundation of the new state.

There were multiple reasons for Augustus' request for tribunician power. Tribunician power was soft power and was particularly popular with the people. It did not have the coercive edge of true magistracies such as the praetorship or the consulship. For centuries the people had turned to their tribunes for the redress of all kinds of grievances, and now they could turn to their tribune-emperor. It was also a good choice from a purely practical, constitutional viewpoint. Acting with the power of a tribune, Augustus could veto or enact legislation, intervene on behalf of individuals, hold court, or call the Senate into session, yet the office had none of the tyrannical connotations of the kingship or even, from the people's view, of the consulship. De facto, however, Augustus rarely actually exerted these powers.

PERSONAL RELATIONS WITH THE ELITE Relations between Augustus and the upper classes were considerably eased by his concern for constitutional formalities, but he exploited other, less formal approaches with great ingenuity and apparent genuineness. For example, whereas Caesar had little patience with the Senate and offended it unnecessarily, Augustus went out of his way to be deferential. He did not flaunt his power, and maintained a simple and modest standard of living. He wore homespun togas and lived in a dwelling that any of the nobles might have possessed. In the matter of titles, which were so important at Rome, his preference was for informal *princeps*, or "elder statesman." In the Republic this term had been applied to ex-consuls whose prestige and authority were such that they were able to lead the Senate and the government, though not in any formal or legal sense. Augustus' use of the title implied that he ruled in a similar traditional way, by his authority and not by virtue of any alteration in the constitution. Although no one could overlook the fact that Augustus' *auctoritas* was greater than any previous *princeps*, after 50 years of bloodshed the upper classes were willing to close their eyes to the reality of his power as long as they did not also have to face the external trappings of an autocracy.

In other respects, Augustus managed relations with the Senate with tact and dignity. Its numbers were gradually reduced from 1,000 to 600, and membership in the senatorial order was made hereditary, although Augustus retained the right to nominate new members. The census qualification was put at one million sesterces, but special emphasis was placed on integrity and capacity for public office.

The powers and jurisdiction of the Senate and of Augustus tended to overlap in a number of areas, and the lines of demarcation were left deliberately vague. Both made appointments to the provinces, but the Senate sent governors to the peaceful, senatorial provinces, whereas Augustus sent his governors to the remainder, the imperial provinces where the legions were stationed. Governors were now paid regular salaries, and their terms were extended from one year to three to five years. The temptation to exploit their positions was thus reduced, and their lengthened tenure allowed them sufficient time to acquire expertise in the exercise of their duties. By these means and by the judicious reform of the tax-collecting system, Augustus was able to establish the provinces on a sound administrative basis. The provinces and Augustus' frontier policies will be treated at greater length in the next chapter.

## The People

THE PEOPLE OF ROME Constitutional niceties were not the first priority of the inhabitants of the city of Rome. As in most cities, the main concern of Rome's population was for its safety and general well being, beginning with a dependable supply of food and water. Street crime had to be repressed, the danger of fire contained and the trash removed. Boredom was a danger in an economy where masses of people were chronically underemployed. Idling crowds, especially the well informed, self-conscious mobs of Rome, needed to be distracted, especially from politics. In the old days of the Republic the assemblies, the courts, the *contiones*—the information meetings that were held by magistrates before voting and electing assemblies met—provided, if not entertainment, at least stimulating occupation on a regular basis for the the *plebs urbana*. Politics of this kind was now over. The firm grip of the Princeps had eliminated the kind of noisy, public canvassing by candidates that had been the norm in the run up to the annual elections of magistrates. Augustus relieved the aristocracy from this demeaning—but entertaining—activity. Turning the energies of the Roman people from politics to something else must have been a topic to which the Princeps and his advisors devoted much time.

NEEDED: AN URBAN ADMINISTRATION As in most of Augustus' programs there were plenty of guide posts to be found in the precedents of the past. All he needed to do was elaborate or, more often, simply enlarge their scale. The poet Juvenal, writing at about the same time as Tacitus, summed up the approach as "bread and the circuses" (*panem et circenses*). This is a useful but far too cynical epigram. Romans were not dependents of the state and did not think of themselves that way. They were neither the groveling subjects of a king nor the playthings of an aristocracy but rather free and independent citizens. They assumed that if they had fought and won an empire they had a right to be proud of themselves for having won it—and to benefit from it. There was no debate among them about what an empire was for. What Rome badly needed—and under Augustus received—was a proper urban administration.

BREAD As tribune (123 to 122 B.C.) Gaius Gracchus had passed a measure to provide the urban plebs with subsidized grain. Support for the food supply was neither aimed at relieving poverty nor was it for humanitarian concerns. The rights of citizens rather than the needs of the poor was the underlying motivation. Those who benefited from Gracchus' subsidy were citizens. They were the target of his legislation because as citizens they had the vote.

As Rome expanded from a population of around 250,000 at the time of Gaius Gracchus to around 1,000,000 by the time of Augustus, the more general need to regulate the food supply became paramount. The city had long outgrown the productive capacity of Latium and Etruria, and grain now came from different parts of Italy, Sicily, Sardinia, Africa (meaning Tunisia), and eventually Egypt. Administrative necessity, however, did not replace the original political principle. In 58 B.C. the tribune Clodius Pulcher took the process a step farther when he made the monthly ration of grain free. Again, the target constituency was the citizenry, not the poor per se. Augustus set the number of those eligible to receive

**The Food Supply: The Warehouses of Ostia**

*Much of the grain and other goods needed by Rome came through the harbors of Ostia and Portus at the mouth of the Tiber, a little over 20 miles from the city. Ships were offloaded there and their cargoes barged up the Tiber to Rome. Ostia was largely abandoned in the fifth century A.D. due to the decline of Rome's population, silting and presence of malaria. The site was not overbuilt and is today one of the best preserved Roman cities in Italy. Shown here is a warehouse of Ostia.*

the grain at 200,000 and issued them tickets (*tesserae*), wooden tablets with the day of the month on which the recipients were to receive their grain inscribed on them.[5] He appointed an equestrian official, the *praefectus annonae,* the Prefect of the Food Supply, to watch over the supply chain and on one occasion took over control himself when there was danger of a famine. In the *Res Gestae* Augustus proudly notes that on that occasion "I so administered the grain supply (*annona*) that I freed the entire people, at my own expense, from the fear and danger they were in" (5). Because the grain supply largely depended on private entrepreneurs, the Princeps had to act as a kind of Federal Reserve ready to inject money into the system to maintain its liquidity when that became necessary.

WATER AND AQUEDUCTS There was a long gap between the building of the aqua Tepula in 125 B.C. and the next major undertaking, the aqua Julia in 33 B.C. by Agrippa, dur-

[5]The figure of 200,000 suggests that the free, citizen population of Rome was only about 25% of the population in Augustus' time. Nevertheless, it was a key constituency for the reasons previously noted, namely, its self-confident political awareness.

ing which time the population of Rome exploded. This period was also one of unprecedented disorder during which, among other things, the water supply of Rome was neglected. Infrastructure maintenance, especially where decay tends to be invisible as in the case of bridges and aqueducts, is rarely a priority with any government until a crisis is reached. The same was true of Rome. Fixing the channels of aqueducts did not gain politicians the credit that new projects did. It is significant that the first major aqueduct to be built in nearly a century, along with the repair of three of the old ones (Appia, Anio Vetus, Marcia) and an expansion of the fourth (Tepula), occurred in the period of the buildup to the confrontation with Antony.

The building of the Julia and the repairs of the others were undertaken, among many other projects, by Agrippa, Augustus' closest confidant (after Livia, his wife), when he was aedile in 33 B.C. It was thus not a private benefaction of the Princeps but a typical republican activity that aediles and censors carried out over the centuries. Part of Agrippa's mandate from the Princeps was to set up an administrative system to maintain the entire water supply of Rome under the director of a *curator aquarum*, a job that was important enough for Agrippa himself to undertake. In 19 B.C. he added a large new line, the aqua Virgo, the largest aqueduct to be built until the time of Claudius. It served the western part of the city.[6] The Virgo and the Julia together doubled Rome's water supply. Later Augustus had another aqueduct, the aqua Alsietina, built across the Tiber in what is now Trastevere to supply water for his naval games. The construction of these showy aqueducts had multiple aims. Their building supplied an obvious need for water and provided a lot of work for the underemployed. They also reinforced Augustus' claim to republican credentials. He, as Princeps, was supplying what republican magistrates supplied in the past but in a more efficient, timely manner.

**The Water Supply: The Aqueducts of Claudius**

*The emperor Claudius built the Porta Maggiore gate to carry his two new aqueducts, the* aqua Claudia *and the* aqua Anio Novus *over the Via Praenestina and the Via Labicana. The* Anio Novus *at nearly 60 miles in length was the longest of the Roman aqueducts. Some of its arches were over 100 feet tall. Fragments of the arches of both aqueducts can still be seen outside Rome.*

[6]Of all the old aqueducts the *Virgo* is the only one still in service.

BATHS Augustus, however, had additional plans in mind for the water supply of Rome. During the late Republic bathing had become an increasingly popular habit among Romans. One reason for this was functional. Masses of people who moved to Rome from other parts of Italy or overseas were crammed into unhealthy, dirty living quarters where staying clean and disposing of waste was a chronic chore. Enterprising businessmen opened baths to serve these needs among them, interestingly, the grandfather of M. Junius Brutus, Caesar's assassin, who inherited a bath house from his father.

These privately owned baths had limited usefulness, among them was their cost. Public money, however, tended to go to more traditional projects such as roads, bridges, aqueducts, temples, and walls. Breaking with this tradition, Agrippa built a large bath, which he willed to the people in 12 B.C. It is likely that one of the purposes of the aqua Virgo was to serve this project. From this time onward, the building of baths (and also public latrines), was an important undertaking by emperors. Some of the most remarkable ruins that can be seen scattered around Rome are the remains of imperial baths. The only one to survive in anything like its original condition is the *tepidarium*, the medium-hot room, of the baths of Diocletian, a few minutes walk from the main train station.

CASH The food supply for Rome, outside emergencies or times of political necessity, was not subsidized by taxes paid by the citizens of Rome or Italy, but by the people of the provinces from where the grain came. The grain supplied by these regions was the tribute paid by conquered subjects to their conquerors. That was the point of having an empire. The people, however, in addition to their expectation of food coming to them from their overseas subjects as a right, also expected periodic handouts from the rich. This was one of the ways, ironically, the people of Rome were able to assist its elite in displaying its generosity. Like the majority of *polis* peoples, Romans did not believe in charity and despised pity. Despite regarding themselves as a free people, they had no qualms about accepting cash hand-outs from the upper strata of their society on the grounds that the honor and respect they bestowed in return was an adequate quid pro quo. A senator or knight (*eques*) with a reputation for generosity could expect friendly greetings as he and his entourage made their way through the streets or when he and his family appeared in the theater or the arena. A further bonus for the generous was security. In the narrow, unsafe byways of urban Rome the reputation for being generous might buy the well-off protection as well as recognition. The rich did not generally live in segregated neighborhoods, so it paid to have friendly neighbors even though the slaves and dependents of the well-off served as bodyguards and night watchmen for their owners' homes.

The new style of popular politics in the first century B.C. elevated expectations on the part of the people of Rome to new levels. The pandering of the great dynasts and the rising expectations of the people appalled Romans of the old school, leading to assertions that not just the elite, but all of the population had become corrupt. Moral decay may indeed have been at work, but underlying the generosity of the wealthy lay the immense income from the empire. In the absence of a redistributive tax system the expectations of the people that the rich provide them with handouts, entertainment, and buildings to use and admire was not unreasonable. It would have been foolish for the wealthy to think they alone could enjoy the profits of empire.

Under Augustus the expectations of the people remained unchanged except that with the Princeps acting as supreme patron they could expect more. Their expectations were not disappointed. Augustus devotes more lines of the *Res Gestae* to his generosity than he does to constitutional matters, which is a good indication of what he thought of the importance of the expectations of the people. A convenient summary at the end of the document, made perhaps by one of the local notables at Ancyra, gives a total of 600,000,000 sesterces for his handouts.[7] Veterans settled in the colonies around the Mediterranean were not neglected. On the occasion of his triumph over Cleopatra in 29 B.C. he gave 400 sesterces to each of the plebeians at Rome but 1,000 sesterces to the 120,000 veterans in the colonies (*RG*, 15). In pointing to these huge outlays, Augustus none too subtly was drawing attention to the new order of things. Members of the nobility might also be generous in their outlays, but none could compete with the Princeps, whose resources far outdistanced theirs.

## Order in the City

POLICE AND FIRE BRIGADES In *polis*-societies the existence of a police force was thought to be incompatible with the freedom of citizens. *Polis*-citizens found the idea of one citizen arresting another repugnant. At Rome, with its strong aristocratic tradition, maintaining order by way of a police force was even more repugnant. Who would control it? To whom would it be responsible? Hence the suppression, investigation, and prosecution of crime were left to the self-help initiative of individuals, their family, kin, and neighbors. Good relations with others was a correlate of safety and public order. So it was in Rome until toward the end of the Republic. Street crime and small-scale disturbances were expected to be taken care of by local residents and passers-by. Security was one of the points of having a large body of retainers. It was only when disturbances evolved into riots and began to have political dimensions that the authorities became involved. It took nearly a century of disorder in Rome to overcome the antipathy to a police force, and when it came into existence its threat to freedom was recognized.

THE URBAN COHORTS The police became part of Augustus' plan to institutionalize the administration of the city. Known as the urban cohorts, the police came in the form of a body of armed men, organized into three cohorts, each about 500 strong under the command of the prefect of the city, the *praefectus urbi*. During the Republic this official was a stand-in for the consuls and praetors on the rare occasions they were all out of the city.

Under Augustus the prefect's position was upgraded. He was always an experienced man, a senator, often an ex-consul. His main job was to maintain order in the city, for which responsibility he possessed *imperium* giving him command of the urban cohorts. He had his own court, which grew in importance in the coming centuries. The urban cohorts had such duties as maintaining order at the theater, at the games, and at the circus. Surprisingly, most disorder came in connection with the theater where the followers of pantomimes clashed with each other, rather than at the other two venues.

[7] On coins and the value of sesterces see box, Chapter 8, page 166.

**The Administration of the City of Rome**

| *Area of Responsibility* | *Personnel* | *Rank* |
|---|---|---|
| Public Order | *Praefectus Urbi* | Consular senator |
| | *Aediles* | Senators (4) |
| | *Tresviri capitales* | *Vigintiviri*–presenate post (3) |
| Fire | *Praefectus vigilum* | Equestrian |
| | *Subpraefectus* | Equestrian |
| Food Supply (Annona) | *Praefectus Annonae* | Equestrian |
| | *Praefectus frumenti dandi* | Praetorian senator |
| | *Procurator ad Miniciam* | Equestrian |
| Water Supply | *Curator aquarum* | Consular senator |
| | *Procurator aquarum* | Equestrian |
| Public Works | *Curatores operum publicorum* | Consular senators (2) |
| | *Subcuratores operum publicorum* | Equestrian |
| | *Procurator operum publicorum* | Equestrian |
| Streets | *Aediles* | Senators |
| | *Procurator viarum* | Equestrian |
| Tiber and Sewage | *Curatores alvei Tiberis riparum et cloacarum Urbis* | Consular senators (5) |
| | *Procurator ad ripas* | Equestrian |
| Libraries | *Procurator bibliothecarum* | Equestrian |
| Festivals | *Procurator ludi magni* | Equestrian |
| | *Subprocurator ludi magni* | Equestrian |
| | *Procurator ludi matutini* | Equestrian |

THE *VIGILES* A body known as the *vigiles*, under an equestrian prefect, was created to act as a fire brigade. This was yet another departure from tradition. In the past even an organized firefighting force, let alone one as large as this under the new organization, was thought to constitute a danger to individual freedom. The *vigiles* started out as a body of 600 slaves, which were first under the command of the aediles and then the local regional magistrates, the *vicomagistri*. Over time they became a body of seven cohorts distributed throughout the city. They were now recruited among freedmen. They went on regular nightly patrols, and in addition to fire prevention they supervised building regulations. The number is uncertain, possibly 3,500 but perhaps as high as 7,000.

THE PRAETORIAN GUARD The praetorian guard (*cohors praetoria*) was originally the bodyguard of a commanding general in the field. During the triumviral period each triumvir had, for good reasons, a large bodyguard who accompanied him in and out of Rome. After Actium, Augustus maintained his bodyguard and made it a regular part of the city administration. It was made up of 19 cohorts or about 4500 men, but originally only three cohorts in civilian dress were kept in the city to avoid giving offense. Republican sensitivities to the presence of armed men in the city were still part of the political culture of Rome, especially among the elite. The remaining cohorts were stationed in towns within easy reach of Rome. They were the only troops regularly stationed in Italy. They were better paid and equipped than the regular legionaries and received larger handouts.

CURATORS Numerous officials called curators (*curatores*) were appointed by Augustus to supervise particular administrative functions of the city. Most of these were experienced exconsuls or ex-praetors. Thus in 22 B.C. he established a praetorian curator for the grain supply. In 20 B.C. there was a curator for the highways, and in 11 B.C., as we have seen, a curator of the water supply was appointed. Flood conditions were monitored by the *curator riparum Tiberis*, the curator of the banks of the Tiber river.

The construction of Agrippa's bath shows the forward-looking vision of the Princeps and the republican context in which it occurred. In the past the great aristocratic patrons took care of their clients and friends in whatever way they could, but these were mostly private benefactions. Augustus in his position of patron of the Roman people took this tradition a step farther by making what were mostly private functions into public ones under his control. The benefactions were reciprocal. The people appreciated the concern of their ruler, whether it was in the form of guaranteeing the food and water supply or maintaining order and securing property rights. It was less a subversive than a necessary process than Tacitus maliciously claimed when he said that Augustus "won over the soldiers with gifts, the populace with cheap grain and all men with the sweets of repose, and so grew greater by degrees" (*Annals*, 1.2). Functionally, emperors were better situated to deliver these social services than the hit-or-miss system of the past. At the same time, grabbing hold of these services made the people more dependent on the emperors and less on individual aristocrats.

## 3. THE BUILDING PROGRAM OF AUGUSTUS

Architecture and art are mirrors of a society. Rarely in history have both been so effectively pressed into the service of the state as by Augustus. Along with poetry they were exploited by him to convey to Romans and provincial alike the message that Rome had been restored to its traditional balance. A new age—a Golden Age—was in the process of being inaugurated. The Augustan program in art and architecture emphasized peace, prosperity, family and societal cohesion, orderly government, the restoration of religion, and traditional morality. De facto, Augustus' program created an entirely new ritual of power that in visual terms corresponded to the new political arrangements. His accomplishments in art and architecture need to be understood in this context.

### Creating an Imperial City

AN ARCHITECTURAL CHALLENGE Livy reports that in the second century B.C. Macedonian courtiers mocked the appearance of Rome because, as the historian said, "it was not yet beautiful in either its public or private areas" (40.5). The comment was probably an understatement. Rome of the Republic was an old city with unplanned, narrow winding streets, haphazardly placed monuments, temples, shrines, and statutes, much like Europe's medieval cities so much admired by tourists but impossible to actually live in. There were few open spaces to which the inhabitants of the city crammed into rickety buildings could go. Rome had spread far beyond the original Servian walls and now sprawled on both sides of the Tiber. The tendency for generals to erect temples as a result of vows made in the heat of battle added to the confused appearance of the city.

To remedy this architectural confusion was a challenge that only someone with supreme power, unlimited resources, and a vision of how the city should look could address. He would also need a great deal of time. As it so happened, Augustus was just such a person. As in all of his undertakings he had multiple aims in his reshaping of the urban fabric of Rome. Perhaps first among them was the creation of a capital worthy of an empire. It did not take the sneers of Macedonian courtiers for Romans to know that their city did not compare with any of the great new Hellenistic metropoleis such as Pergamon in Asia Minor, Antioch in Syria, or Alexandria in Egypt. Augustus went out of his way to establish in a wholly visible way that Rome was the uncontested capital of the Mediterranean. No other city could be allowed to compete with it. There was rationality behind this calculation. The impressions people take away from a country, and especially its capital, have a way of percolating down to the rest of society. What the capital looks like is taken as emblematic of the whole country. It was important that visitors, especially those from among the elites, should go away with the right impression of Rome. It would not be good if foreigners forgot the might of Rome. Just as the pyramids overawed ordinary Egyptians—not to mention visitors—the grandeur of Rome was intended to overawe all, natives and aliens alike.

A LIVABLE ROME Not only did Augustus successfully transform the constitution of Rome and lay the foundations for the Empire, he lived long enough and had the resources to transform the city of Rome into a capital worthy of its empire. That Rome became a more livable city for the masses was a secondary but important aim of the Princeps. Mainly the city was intended to project power and so it has to the present.

From a purely practical rather than an aesthetic or propagandistic viewpoint, what Augustus did was to turn the old center of Rome into a spacious, pedestrian-friendly environment made up of interconnected, colonnaded fora and green belts. He did this by focusing on a number of pre-existing urban nodes belonging to the old city. For example, a pedestrian could start at the Tiber bank near the theater of Marcellus and walk in a matter of minutes to either the great complex of buildings and parks in the Campus Martius or the collection of fora that filled the space below the Capitoline and Palatine Hills. In either case the pedestrian could walk for miles without leaving a covered colonnade for more than a few minutes. The walkability of downtown Rome only increased as later emperors such as Nerva and Trajan added more fora and more colonnades. In the oppressive heat of a Roman summer or in the cold and wet of winter the colonnades would have been a welcome relief to all who had to navigate central Rome. Strabo of Amaseia (in modern Turkey), a contemporary of Augustus and a frequent visitor of Rome, gives an idea of the effect the city could have on a visitor:

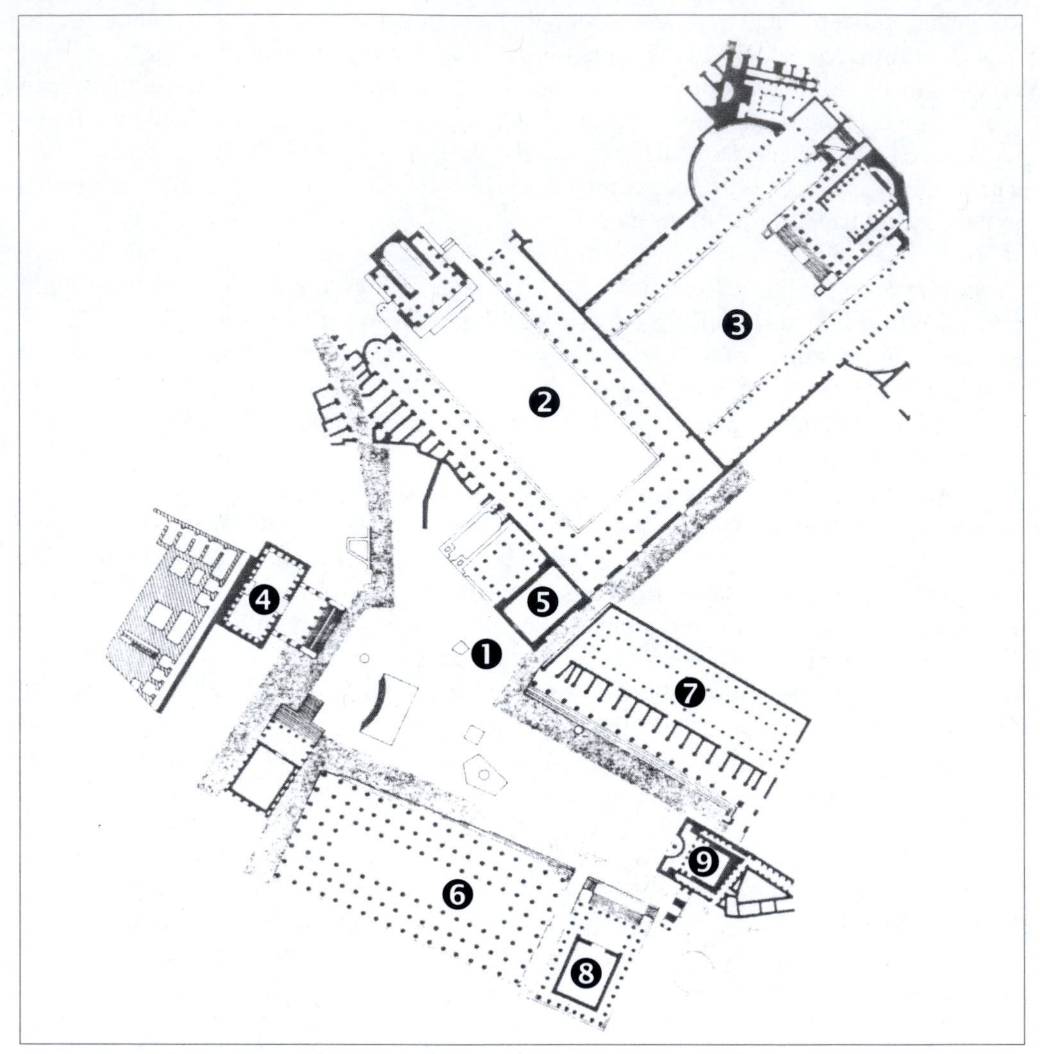


**Augustan Rome**

**1.** *Roman Forum.* **2.** *Forum of Caesar.* **3.** *Forum of Augustus.* **4.** *Temple of Concord.* **5.** *Senate House (Curia).* **6.** *Basilica Julia.* **7.** *Basilica Aemilia.* **8.** *Temple of Castor and Pollux.* **9**. *Temple of the Divine Caesar (Divus Julius).*

If, after passing through the Roman Forum you saw one forum after another ranged alongside the old one, and basilicas and temples, and the Capitolium [*the huge temple to Jupiter, Juno and Minerva on the Capitoline Hill*] and Livia's Portico, you would easily become oblivious to everything outside the city. Such is Rome (5.3).

Augustus' rather ostentatious remark that he built his forum and the temple to Mars the Avenger that dominated it using the spoils from war, and that "on ground I purchased for the most part from private individuals I built the theater which was to bear the name of my son-in-law Marcus Marcellus" (*RG*, 20) was a reminder that he was not a tyrannical ruler

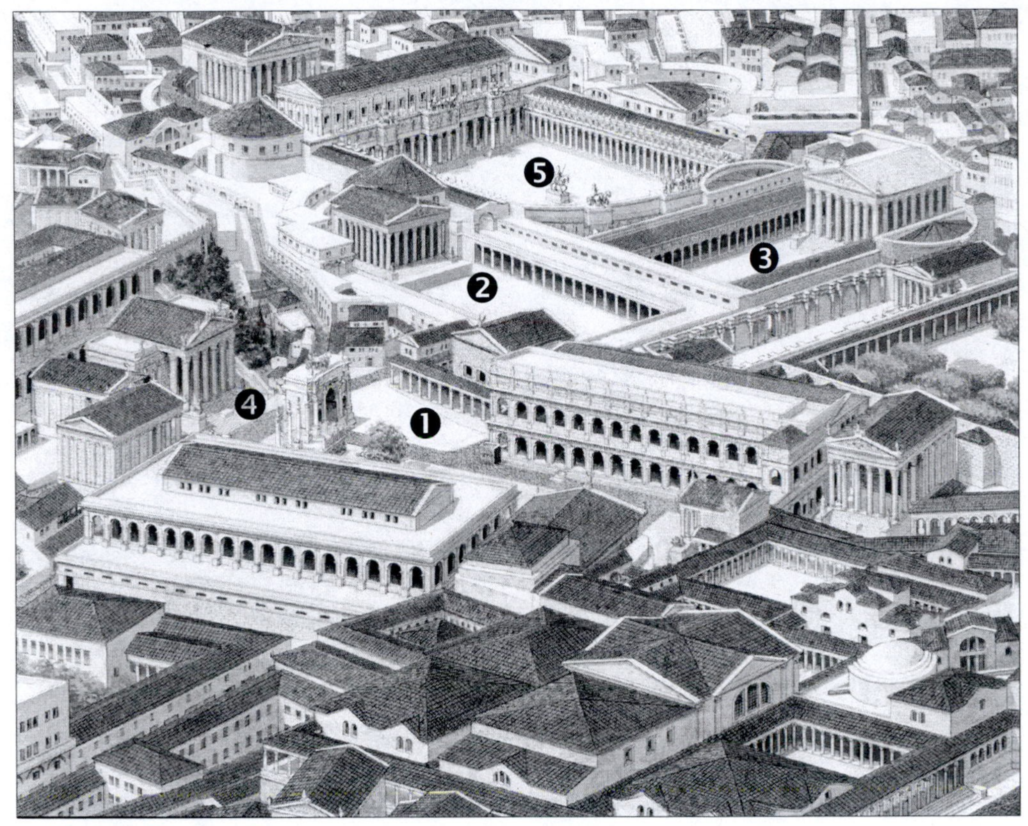


**Model of Central Rome**

**1.** *Roman Forum* **2.** *Forum of Caesar* **3.** *Forum of Augustus* **4.** *Temple of Concord* **5.** *Forum of Trajan*

who ignored property rights and expropriated private owners at will. In general we hear few complaints from those who inevitably must have suffered from his version of urban renewal.

## Architectural Messages

One of the sayings ascribed to Winston Churchill is a remark to the effect that nations first create their built environments and then these environments shape their nations' cultures. By Augustus' time Rome was a heterogeneous city made up of a minority of its original inhabitants, a much larger contingent of migrants from throughout Italy, and a good number of people from elsewhere in the Mediterranean. A high percentage of the population was either slave or freedmen. Whether or not it was included in the Princeps' long list of aims for the architectural enhancement of the city, the effect of his work was certainly to mold this mass of people into a self-conscious citizenry of Rome. Living in a city of monuments, most of them labeled and inscribed, made it inevitable that, consciously or unconsciously, literate or not, its inhabitants absorbed the history and values that inspired the city's creation.

THE TEMPLE OF CONCORD A stroll through the Roman forum was a history lesson conveyed by the place itself and the buildings that surrounded it. But it was a jumbled message made up of centuries of accumulated monuments, each with its strong historical associations. There were, for example, the complex but ambiguous messages of the prominent Temple of Concord on the side of the hill overlooking the forum on the way up to the Capitolium. It had originally been erected by Camillus in 367 B.C. to celebrate the Concord of the Orders, the *concordia ordinum*, achieved between patricians and plebeians at the time of the passage of the Licinian Sextian laws. It was later restored by L. Opimius, who as consul had authorized the wholesale slaughter of Gaius Gracchus and his followers in 121 B.C., a turning point for the worse in Roman social relations. It was here, too, that Cicero called the Senate together to pass summary judgment on the Catilinarian conspirators, yet another controversial event. Still another level of meaning was added in A.D. 10 when Augustus' designated successor Tiberius, some years after his adoption by the Princeps, transformed the temple into the "Temple of the Concord of Augustus." This suggested to anyone who looked or studied the sculptural decorations in the temple that the concord of the state and the concord of the imperial family were closely related, if not the same thing. It was a subtle message that conveyed multiple meanings. As later history of the empire was to show, the desirability of concord within the imperial family was of huge importance to the stability of the state and indeed something to be prayed and hoped for, even by those who cherished strong republican sentiments.

THE FORUM OF AUGUSTUS A visit to the forum of Augustus, inaugurated in 2 B.C. (the day the Senate and the People voted him the title of "Father of the Fatherland") gives perhaps the clearest picture of the message the Princeps wanted Romans to imbibe. His approach, as in all his monuments, was not by means of crude or obvious propaganda but by the clever manipulation of a system of symbols that were familiar to all Romans.

A visitor entered the forum from the southwestern end. It is impossible today to get an idea of what the forum looked like originally because one of Rome's busiest roads, the *Via dei Fori Imperiali*, passes through it, and on all sides lie heaps of rubble from excavations, pools of stagnant water, and sprouting weeds. The impression of the forum in antiquity, however, would have been impressive. It would have appeared, first, as an island of tranquility set amid the downtown bustle, separated from the surrounding city by its high walls. The forum itself was awe inspiring, dominated by the tall temple of Mars Ultor located on a high platform. Its thin, elongated columns, each over 55 feet tall, ended in elaborate Corinthian capitals, emphasized its height. Statues of Venus, Mars, and Fortuna stood in the pediment, flanked by Romulus and the personification of victorious Roma. In the middle of the forum stood Augustus in a bronze chariot placed on top of a plinth. This was the monument to him as "Father of the Fatherland" (*pater patriae*). It was voted, as he proudly notes in his *Res Gestae* "by the Senate, the equestrian order and the entire Roman people. They decreed that this title should be carved on the vestibule of my house and in the Curia [*the Senate House*], and the Forum Augustum beneath the chariot erected in my honor by decree of the Senate" (34). With this entry Augustus closes his *Res Gestae*.

The temple of Mars had been originally vowed by Octavian before the battle of Philippi in 42 B.C. The primary message of the forum and temple was thus that Mars had, through

**A.** *Façade of the Temple Mars Ultor in the Forum of Augustus.* **B.** *Mystery building (for identity see List of Illustrations, p. 494).*

Augustus, taken revenge on Caesar's assassins and that Augustus had fulfilled his vow of *pietas* to his adoptive father. A secondary message was that revenge had also been wreaked on the Parthians who had given up the standards taken from Crassus at the battle of Carrhae. These standards were now on display in the inner sanctum of the temple.

There were other messages, however, on display in the forum. On either side of the forum were long, colonnaded galleries. Lining the inside walls of these were statues of the *summi viri*, the great men of Roman history. Each statue had a plaque in front of it detailing the achievements of each of these heroes. Two exedrae towards the top of the forum, closest to the temple platform, were decorated with statues of Aeneas and his descendants, most prominently the Julii, the *gens* of the Princeps. In the facing excedra across the forum were statues of Romulus. Even the illiterate could "read" Augustus' program, while the literate, many of whom would have read Virgil's recently published *Aeneid*, would have received an enhanced message. The forum, like all the other fora of Rome, conveyed the majesty of the Roman state and its intimate relationship with the gods who guaranteed its greatness. It was a precinct sacred to the gods with whom peace was a precondition of the stability of the state.

Beyond that generic message, the Forum Augustum spelled out in detail the claim that Rome was entering a new age that had been prepared for it by destiny from the foundation of the city. Rome's history to the present was the work of the innumerable great figures (the *summi viri* memorialized in the colonnades), but the new age was the work of the Caesars, Julius Caesar and his adopted son Augustus, the founders of a reinvigorated and powerful Rome. Mars the Avenger was given pride of place, reminding Romans they were the descendants through Romulus of Mars, and that Mars was not a god of peace but of war.

Romulus, who had a prominent place in the forum, reminded them that as Rome had been founded in civil strife—the murder of Remus—so the new state also had its founding in fratricide. This was a hard but realistic message. Fratricide could revive if the newly established order was disturbed—or challenged. Perhaps softening this harsh image to some extent was the reminder that if Mars was the warlike ancestor of the Romans, the Princeps was the familiar, reassuring *paterfamilias* of Rome, the *pater patriae*. The image was borrowed from the traditional symbol of order and authority in society. The Roman family was whole once more, secure from the excesses of the children of the previous generation.

THE CAMPUS MARTIUS A stroll to the Campus Martius would have provided a more relaxed but complementary message to that of the imperial fora. Cutting diagonally through the Campus Marius—like a Broadway—was the Via Flaminia, the old route that led from Etruria and Cisalpine Gaul into Rome. A visitor coming from that direction would cross the Tiber at the Milvian Bridge and pass under a commemorative arch, which acted as a kind of symbolic northern gate to the city. Arches were used by Romans to indicate transitions between one area and another and in their triumphal form forced users of the highway to pass under them in silent acknowledgment of the supremacy of Rome.

On the left as the visitor headed toward the city would be Rome's first green belt, the gardens of the Acilii, Sallust, and Lucullus. Next, on the right, in the direction of the Tiber was the large mausoleum built for Augustus and his family. This monument had a marble base of 270 feet in diameter with a superimposed earthen mound planted with trees, of 150 feet. On top was a gilded statue of Augustus. In its bulk and height it dominated the flat Campus Martius. For the cognoscenti, the mausoleum referenced similar circular tombs found elsewhere in the Mediterranean, including that of Alexander the Great. It was surrounded by park-like gardens open to the public. Continuing down the Via Flaminia on the right hand side the visitor would encounter the Altar of Peace (*Ara Pacis*), a jewel-like marble masterpiece, commemorating peace and prosperity—and the Julian family. Beside the *Ara Pacis* was the *Horologium* of Augustus, a great sundial that used an expropriated Egyptian obelisk as its pointer—a reminder of the conquest of that great land by Rome.

The aqua Virgo came next, Rome's most recent major public works project. It supplied the nearby baths of Agrippa, which were open to the public. In addition to the baths, patrons could enjoy the gardens that surrounded it, or they could stroll along the paved walk bordering the canal that drained this low-lying area of the Campus Martius. The canal (known as the Euripus) was crossed at various places by little bridges raised three steps above the pathways, somewhat smaller versions of the bridges that charm visitors in present-day Venice. Alternately they could enjoy walking in the park—later stocked by Nero with exotic birds—created on the banks of the artificial lake used in connection with the baths. A block or so away the voting precinct known as the Saepta offered a mile of colonnaded walkways. Tired of that exercise, one could visit the Pantheon, the Temple to all the Gods, built by Agrippa, and later rebuilt by Hadrian. Hadrian's version survives as one of the best-preserved of all Roman monuments in the city. On the opposite, eastern side of the Via Flaminia was the portico of Vipsania, built by Agrippa's sister. This was a

**The Gardens of Augustan Rome**

*In the second century B.C. aristocrats such as Scipio Aemilianus began to create private pleasure parks of terraces, walkways, fountains, and groves of trees around their townhouses. By the first century private gardens formed a loose green belt around the city. Pompey planted a large garden around his villa in the Campus Martius* **(1)** *and Caesar laid out a huge park on the east side of the river* **(2)**. *Augustus continued this tradition adding gardens to the temple of Apollo on the Palatine, around his mausoleum, the porticus of Livia, and elsewhere in the city. Famous gardens to the north* **(3)** *were those of Lucullus and Sallust. These private* horti *were in addition to the sacred groves and kitchen gardens that already existed in the city.*

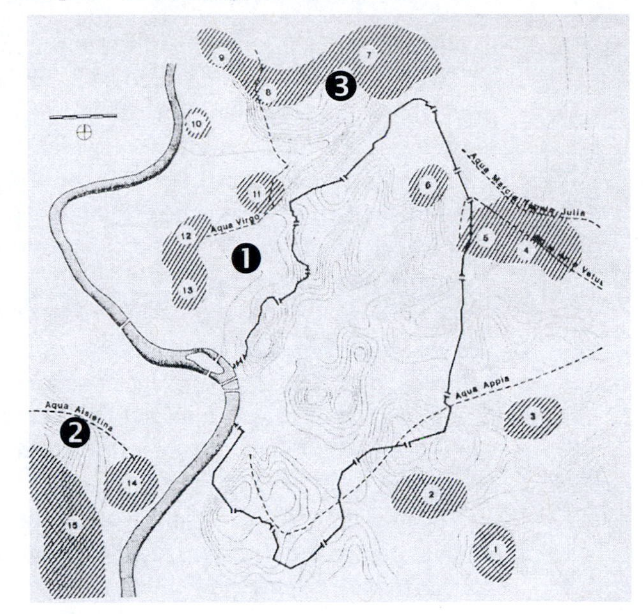


large garden-like enclosure planted with laurels and surrounded by colonnaded walks. Within its colonnades was a detailed map of the world erected by Agrippa showing the extent of Rome's empire.

A few minutes' walk from these buildings was the great theater-temple of Pompey and another theater, built by the Spanish-born Cornelius Balbus and bearing his name. Someplace nearby—its location is uncertain—stood the amphitheater of Statilius Taurus, erected by one of the Princeps' most distinguished generals. Also in this area was yet another, larger theater, that of Aemilius Scaurus. It had a capacity of 20,000 while Pompey's theater could hold 11,000. According to the encyclopaedist Pliny, 3,000 bronze statues adorned the first story of Taurus' theater.

From this area one could walk through the portico of Octavia, built by Augustus' sister, to the theater dedicated to the Princeps' nephew Marcellus. It still stands despite the battering it received during the Middle Ages when it was the headquarters of the Fabii, one of Rome's feuding noble families whose rivals, the Frangipani, occupied the Colosseum. At this point the visitor arrived at the banks of the Tiber and could turn northeast towards the Roman forum or continue along the banks of the river. If he chose the latter he could view the impressive mouth of the *Cloaca Maxima*, the great sewer that drained the forum area, which is still visible. After that he would enter the commercial area of Rome, the forum Boarium, with its docks and warehouses.

## 4. RELIGIOUS AND SOCIAL REFORMS

Augustus attempted to stem the rising tide of moral change that had developed in the late Republic by enacting a comprehensive program of social, religious, and moral reform. Because many men and women of the upper classes preferred to remain childless, Augustus enacted penalties for childless couples while creating special benefits for those with children, although later he was compelled to reduce or even remove the penalties and increase the benefits. To cope with adultery, which was widely condoned among the elite, and to extend the power of the state over the family, Augustus made adultery a public crime to which severe penalties were attached. Sumptuary laws were enacted to control luxury, and attempts were made to control the haphazard manumission of slaves and the number of the poor eligible for free grain.

The Princeps placed special emphasis on the traditional religion and morality of Rome. His very title, *Augustus*, had religious connotations and could be taken to mean that his rule had been inaugurated with all due concern for the augural requirements of Roman religion, or it might have drawn attention to his authority, the word for which was derived from the same Latin root. Eventually the title came to be seen in the broader context of the inauguration of not just the rule of the Princeps but of a new age of Rome.

The idea that prosperity and peace in the state depended on the pious fulfillment of religious duties to the gods was an ancient one in Rome, and in the Republic the magistrates had taken particular responsibility for maintaining the *pax deorum*, the peace between gods and men. Augustus made a point of stressing his concern for this traditional belief by restoring temples—82 by his own account—and becoming a member of the sacred colleges of pontiffs and augurs. He suggested that the calamities of the recent civil wars had been caused by neglect of the gods, and part of his ideology was his claim to have revived many cults and ancient practices.

## The Priesthoods

The importance of the priesthoods to the careers of Roman politicians has been discussed in Chapter 5, Section 6 (pp. 97–99). These offices constituted a kind of coordinated career track parallel to the magistracies they sought. The priesthoods had the added advantage over the magistracies that they could be held for life. Therein lay their political importance, a significance that was, of course, taken into consideration by the Princeps. By way of controlling their influence and extending his control over the state religious apparatus, Augustus had himself elected, over a period of time, to all the priestly colleges, despite the long-standing tradition that only one priesthood could be held at a time.

AUGUSTUS AS CHIEF PRIEST An important turning point in the Princeps' carefully scripted take-over of the religious levers of power came in 12 B.C., when Lepidus, the third member of the triumvirate and the current *pontifex maximus*, died. Augustus assumed the office. From this date onward he was not only the secular but also the religious head of the state. Soon after their accession to power all his successors automatically assumed the office. The perceptive senator Dio Cassius commented: "From the fact that the emperors are enrolled in all the priesthoods and moreover can grant most of the priesthoods to others, and that one of them, even if two or three emperors are ruling jointly, is *pontifex maximus*, they control all sacred and religious matters" (53.17).

Important consequences flowed from Augustus' position as head of the Roman state religion. As *pontifex maximus* he was automatically responsible for the shrine of Vesta in the forum and for the Vestal Virgins who were responsible for keeping the fire of Rome's hearth burning continually. By tradition the *pontifex maximus* was supposed to live in the official, publicly owned house attached to the precinct of Vesta, but Augustus got around this inconvenience by having his house on the Palatine designated public property and constructing within it a shrine to Vesta. A radical, though logical, consequence followed this action. Tradition had it that Aeneas had brought with him the sacred fire from Troy along with the *lares* of Troy. These, along with the cult of Vesta had been transferred from Alba Longa by Romulus when he founded Rome. Romulus, it should be recalled, was himself a son of a Vestal Virgin by Mars, and Augustus was a descendant of Aeneas. Although the original hearth of Rome remained in the shrine of Vesta in the forum, a connection between Augustus' private hearth and that of Vesta had been established. Ovid put it this way: "Apollo has part of the house [*referring to the temple of Apollo, which had been constructed out of a part of Augustus' house*] as does Vesta. The remaining part is occupied by Augustus himself" (*Fasti*, 3.699). The public hearth of Rome and the private hearth of the emperor were now closely connected if not fused into one.

## Reaching the People Administratively and Religiously

During the Republic the city of Rome had been divided into four districts (*vici*) with shrines to the *lares*, household gods or spirits of the area, located at every crossroads. Sacrifices were offered annually at these shrines by colleges made up of people from the local *vici*. Like all sacrifices, these rituals brought the people together for the celebration and also to share the meat of the sacrifices. In the late Republic the colleges had become focal points of political discontent, and efforts were made to rein them in. Caesar tried to suppress them. Augustus took a radically different approach. He co-opted the colleges by extending his personal patronage to them and by bringing them within his newly created administrative system. The method he used to achieve this was to increase the number of districts from four to 14 and by converting the *lares* of the individual shrines into the *lares* of his own family and of his *genius*, his spirit. Precedent for doing this may have come from the practice of honoring the Gracchi and Marius, popular heroes of the people, at these shrines. In this way Augustus broke down the purely local identity of the *lares* and extended a familial relationship to all the inhabitants of the city, a point to be later emphasized when the title *pater patriae*, Father of the Country, was bestowed on him in 2 B.C.

## Festivals and Games

The young Octavian when he returned to Rome in 44 B.C. to claim his inheritance from his adoptive father, Julius Caesar, showed himself fully aware of how the Roman public could be reached. When frustrated at every turn by the jealous consul Antony, Octavian gave two sets of games, the Ludi Ceriales and the Ludi Victoriae Caesaris. This put him in direct contact with the people. When they learned that to finance the games in honor of Caesar he was forced to sell his own property he earned a lot of good will. In 33 B.C., before the final confrontation with Antony, lavish games were given by Agrippa at which "tokens were rained on the heads of the people, some of which were good for money, others for clothes, others for something else"(Dio Cassiuis 49.43). In his *Res Gestae* Augustus devotes two full chapters (22 and 23) to the games and spectacles he sponsored. "About 10,000 men," he says, fought in eight gladiatorial games that he gave either in his own name or the names of his sons or grandsons. In one spectacular show 3,000 men fought in a naval gladiatorial battle staged in a specially excavated lake across the Tiber that got its water from a newly built aqueduct. "Thirty beaked ships, triremes or biremes and a large number of smaller vessels," he says, were involved. He put on sixty-three non-gladiatorial, that is theatrical or circus, games. In one of these 3,500 animals were slain.

## Expanding the Religious Calendar

In all of his games the Princeps had plenty of precedent provided by the games of dynasts of the late Republic when the celebration of festivals in honor of the gods became more and more lavish. As the years went by, however, Augustus added many new feasts to the religious calendar. These allowed him to demonstrate his showmanship to the fullest. Actium, Augustus believed, was won through the intervention of Apollo, so in addition to the temple erected to him on the Palatine, a festival to celebrate the victory was established. Another festival was initiated for January 7 to celebrate the day Augustus received his *imperium*. September 3 was a festival honoring a naval victory won during the civil war. The Augustalia were games given to thank the gods for his safe return from Syria in 19 B.C. After the dedication of the Forum Augustum in 2 B.C. a series of games, the Ludi Martiales, in honor of Mars the Avenger, were instituted and celebrated each May 12. Augustus' birthday was celebrated September 23. The date of his election as *pontifex maximus* was celebrated as a festival. These new festivals were, of course, in addition to all the old ones so that over time a larger and larger portion of the year was devoted to festivals and games. As Suetonius remarked in his biography, Augustus "surpassed all his predecessors in the number, variety, and magnificence of his games" (Suet., *Aug*., 43).

THE SECULAR GAMES The high point of Augustus' religious renewal program came with the celebration of the Secular Games in 17 B.C., a carefully orchestrated event proclaiming the inauguration of the New Period or Age (*saeculum*). Secular games dated from the time of the Republic and were supposed to have been performed every 100 years, though early records are sparse. They came under the supervision of the college of the *quindecemviri* of which Augustus and Agrippa were members. They required the consultation of the Sibylline Books, now thoughtfully lodged in Augustus' temple of Apollo beside his house. The celebration usually consisted of three nights of sacrifices and games in honor of the gods of the underworld, but Augustus added three daytime celebrations in honor of Jupiter, Juno, Apollo, and Diana. Some scholars think the Secular Games may have been connected with the festival of the Parilia, which celebrated the founding of

Rome. In that case the Secular Games would have been regarded as rituals marking the rebirth of the city and aimed at drawing the population into a renewal ceremony of Rome's founding. If that is the case, Augustus' celebration may have been aimed at suggesting the games marked not just the passing of an era, but the birth of a new one under his auspices. The poet Horace was commissioned to compose a hymn, the Secular Hymn (*Carmen Saeculare*) sung by 27 boys and 27 girls in the temple of Apollo. It stressed the central importance of Augustus and brought into prominence Augustus' patron god Apollo. The three days and nights of religious activities were followed by seven days of celebration, mostly, it seems, in the form of plays, put on in the theaters and the circus Flaminius. The next time the games were celebrated was in A.D. 47, 800 years after the founding of the city. As in so much else, Augustus established the basic framework for religious practice in Rome that was to endure for centuries.

## 5. CHIEF EXECUTIVE OFFICER: HOW AUGUSTUS RAN THE EMPIRE

### What Kind of CEO?

In building new sets of relationships with the elite and the people Augustus addressed the political and legal issues of the new regime. What remained was to figure out how he was going to administer the empire. What was the executive branch to look like? Was it to be modeled on the courts of Middle Eastern monarchs, Greek tyrants, or Hellenistic kings? As in all of his creations, the executive shaped by Augustus was a typically Roman blend of tradition and innovation.

In the Republic the Senate and its annual magistrates had been Rome's chief executive agency. That role was now, obviously, at an end. Augustus had to find a replacement and quickly. For instance, he had 28 legions and needed to find commanders, officers, and centurions for them. Where were they to be found? How was he to vet their competence? This was not an insignificant personnel matter. There were dozens of financial administrative positions to be filled at Rome and in the provinces. The numbers were not large compared to modern governments, but an executive quickly runs out of the names of people he knows personally and feels he can trust. He begins to have to rely on the recommendations of others and what he hears of the reputations of potential candidates. For instance the future emperor Vespasian owed his advancement to the fact that a powerful freedman in the imperial household, Narcissus, drew the then emperor's attention to Vespasian. Besides personnel and money to run the government, the Princeps needed information. How was that to be gathered, sifted and evaluated? Who was to do that? We have seen how Augustus established many boards of curators to look after flooding, sewage, the water and grain supply, buildings, the maintenance of roads, and the like. They had to be staffed with competent people. Contracts had to be let out for supplies for the army. By his political choices Augustus had made himself personally responsible for all the headaches that administrations usually farm out to already existing, well-staffed permanent departments of diplomacy, national security, personnel, accounts, correspondence, intelligence, and so on.

ROME'S DISLIKE OF BUREAUCRACY Rome had no tradition of bureaucracy. The preferred model of administration was the family. The aristocracy resisted the idea of creating agencies staffed by tenured professionals. There was plenty of evidence that such departments easily gained power that escaped the political oversight of whatever council of state was supposed to be supervising them. In the Republic the family or patrimonial style of administration was both the belief and the practice. A tiny handful of administrators ran the Empire. According to one calculation 100 elite Romans (army commanders, governors, etc.), ran the Empire in the first century A.D. In the Republic it had been half that number.

Augustus inherited this understandable rejection of independent, unsupervised power centers. For him the dislike of such agencies was compounded. The delegation of key decisions such as the appointment of generals and army officers to an independent department of defense would have required abdication of power to that agency. That left him with the dilemma: How was he to combine efficient, competent administration to which he had pledged himself without suffering crippling loss of power? The key to the survival of the Princeps and his successors was not to let independent departments develop but retain control of all key decision-making within his own family.

One further difficulty stood in the way of creating a working executive for the Empire. It was below the dignity (*infra dignitatem*) of senators or equestrians to serve the emperor in salaried positions. Members of these classes theoretically possessed the best qualified people to assist the emperor, but such individuals could not be treated as long-term employees to be ordered around and hired or fired at will. The emperor needed professionals, but to be a professional meant total dedication to a particular occupation to the exclusion of all else. Such positions in ancient political thought were for slaves or ex-slaves.

HOUSEHOLD MANAGEMENT The natural model at hand that could potentially address all these problems was the traditional Roman household. One of the main responsibilities of the great nobles of the Republic was the management of their huge estates, which they ran as self-sustaining, privately held corporations. The *paterfamilias* held title to all the resources of the household, whether material or personal. He ran the corporation with the assistance of his family members, first and foremost his wife. Slaves and freedmen executed the directives of the householder.

A key agency in the management of the household was the family *consilium* or council, which acted as a kind of senate to the two permanent family magistrates, the *pater* and *materfamilias*. Depending on the seriousness of the issues at hand, family councils could be made up of the parents, in-laws, married children of both sexes, and friends. They ranged from chatty gatherings to serious courts. On one occasion a wealthy *paterfamilias* by the name of Tarius called on Augustus to serve as a member of his *consilium*. The issue concerned a plot by Tarius' son aimed at killing his father. Interestingly, the emperor was expected to come to the house of the *paterfamilias*, not the other way around. If the council met at the emperor's house the council—in this case acting as a private court—would have been taken to be the council of the emperor. The emperor in fact came to Tarius' house, and the council deliberated the case. At the end of the discussion Augustus asked for a secret ballot to prevent those present from following the Princeps' verdict. The decision of the council was that the son should be sent into exile in southern France. His father leniently continued his son's allowance.[8]

Informal councils like the family council were used in other circumstances. Praetors, for example, who were responsible for the administration of the legal system during the Republic, took advice from councils of friends and relatives who had experience in legal affairs. Provincial governors took groups of relatives and friends with them to act as their advisors when they went to their provinces. When the governor held his court, the members of their council sat beside him and assisted him in making decisions.

**The Epigrammatic Trap**

*The great historian Edward Gibbon, author of* The Decline and Fall of the Roman Empire, *was an admirer of Tacitus and shared his sour view of human nature. Here is a sample of Gibbon's portrait of Augustus.*

> The tender respect of Augustus for a free constitution which he had destroyed can only be explained by an attentive consideration of the character of that subtle tyrant . . . His virtues, and even his vices were artificial; and according to the various dictates of his interest, he was at first the enemy [i.e., *when he was triumvir*], and at last the father, of the Roman world (Chapter 3).

*CONSILIUM PRINCIPIS* Augustus used these models—the model of the family council and the informal advisory councils of magistrates and governors—to provide the basic format for his privy council. It was known as the *consilium principis,* the council of the Princeps. The participating senators and equestrians were designated *amici Augusti*, friends of Augustus. The council also included key appointees from the administration such as the Praetorian Prefects. Freedmen and slaves belonging to the imperial family staffed the administrative apparatus and were entrusted with the execution of the decisions made by the emperor and his advisors. Augustus thus administered the Empire the way an old-fashioned aristocrat of the Republic administered his family and estate. Control of all essential decisions—and all essential information—remained within the family of the Princeps, and of course Augustus throughout his life depended on the advice of his intelligent, strong-minded wife, Livia, and other family members.

## 6. THE MASK OF AUGUSTUS: REFLECTIONS

The embittered senatorial historian Tacitus portrayed Augustus as a ruthless, duplicitous, mask-wearing ruler. This image provided the senator with plenty of material for clever epigrams. Undoubtedly these epigrams tell us more about Tacitus and his age than they do

[8]The full story can be found in Seneca's *On Clemency*, 1.15.

about Augustus. Epigrams, while often quotable and entertaining, are also in the end dismissive. They stop rather than encourage thought.

There is no doubt that Augustus wore a mask. Near death he quipped: "Have I played my part in the mime of life well enough?" (Suetonius, *Aug.*, 99). To be a good mime on the Roman stage took enormous talent. Audiences were sophisticated and highly critical. Because he had a huge range of parts to play a mime needed versatility and exquisite sensitivity to audience response. He had to be knowledgeable about human nature. According to the critic Lucian the mime must "not be ignorant of anything that is told by Homer and Hesiod and the best poets—and above all by tragedy" (*On Dance*, 71). Maecenas was supposed to have advised Augustus: "You will live as in a theater in which the spectators are the whole world" (Dio Cassius, 52.34).

## Mask-Wearing: A Cultural Necessity

Augustus wore many masks and knew full well he was acting parts. But then, everyone else knew this too and expected it. Mask-wearing on the part of politicians was an essential part of Roman political life just as it is of all politicians in well-developed political cultures. Augustus was a superb actor-politician who knew he had multiple roles to play. Luckily for Rome he played most of them well.

In this respect he was merely following the example of the political figures of the past who also knew they had roles to perform as warriors, judges, priests, politicians, patrons, fathers, husbands, friends, and so on. The handbook on electioneering ascribed to Quintus Cicero, the brother of Cicero, was written to guide aspiring politicians of the Republic. It describes in detail how a candidate for office should present himself to the multiple constituencies that made up the Roman voting public and without whose support he could not expect to be elected. However, it was also assumed there had to be some substance behind the mask. A Roman magistrate was expected actually to be a brave warrior, a good councilor in war and peace, a generous patron, a dependable friend, a strict father and husband. Even if by natural endowment he was none of these, his education prepared him to live up to the roles his position demanded. The Roman educational system was in some respects the reverse of ours. Children at all levels of society were assigned roles in life and were expected to perform them rather than to look inside themselves for their true talents and then find suitable roles to play in society. Character in Roman educational theory was formed by role-acting. You became what your place in society assigned you.

AUGUSTUS' ROLES Augustus' job was to combine all the roles of the traditional Republican politician-general-priest-patron-father into one without tripping himself up. Most of his successors were not as successful as he was in doing this. Tiberius hated playing roles and was cordially disliked in return. He soon withdrew from Rome to the quiet of his villa on Capri. Emperors like Caligula, Nero, and Commodus were popular because they played their roles to the hilt. Unfortunately they got so deeply involved in their roles that they were overwhelmed by them and were eventually destroyed.

The reader can judge for him- or herself whether Augustus' work was a success or not, bearing in mind that a true restoration of the Republic was not an option. Augustus, for all his maneuvering, never claimed to have restored the Republic.[9] The key question to be asked in reviewing the deeds of Augustus is this: What were the alternatives? Rome of the period of the fall of the Republic was as full of talented politicians as it ever was. It had a well-established political culture that celebrated freedom. Nothing external prevented the discovery of a political solution. There were no serious military threats, no looming financial crises. Rome's elite is usually thought by historians to have been remarkable for its knowledge, intelligence, and flexibility. The people of Rome were not a down-trodden, ignorant, apathetic peasantry subservient to their betters. They were citizens who celebrated a centuries-long tradition of asserting their liberties and rights. Yet in that nearly two-century period during which crisis followed crisis, no politician or group of politicians—neither elite nor people—were able to find just the right formula to address the crises that accompanied Rome's shift from city-state to world-state. That Rome had the energy, after a century of on-and-off civil wars, seditions, riots, assassinations, and proscriptions, to find a leader who could persuade the multiple squabbling parties of old aristocrats, new men, Italians, rural and urban peoples, and provincials to accept a new constitution was not a miracle but a tribute to Rome's deeply established political culture. Rome was lucky, of course, to find leadership of the caliber of Augustus, his wife Livia, his adopted son Tiberius, his friends Agrippa, Maecenas, and a host of others, but leaders have to have followers and supporters. Everyone, senators, knights, and people had to be willing to engage in new rule-making and then obey the rules when they were made. Augustus was the affable impresario under whose nearly half-century reign these rules were made.

Another question, which will be addressed to some extent in the following chapters, is *cui bono*?—for whose good was all this work of Augustus and his supporters done? Was it only for the Roman people? Or did the people of the Empire, Rome's subjects, benefit also? Who paid for the adornment of Rome—its transformation from a city of brick to a city of marble? Was it worth the cost? Did Rome become just a great parasite city on the Tiber, draining off the resources of the Mediterranean? Or did it give back anything in return? And, finally, what price, if any, did the Roman people pay for the bargain they made with the Princeps and his successors?

[9] Only Hollywood has its heroes call for a *res publica restituta*, a restored republic.

# Part Four

# Making Permanent the Augustan Settlement

## 1. INTRODUCTION AND OVERVIEW

### The Succession: The Argument against Institutionalization

Revolutions need to be institutionalized, or they die. Augustus' replacement of the Republic with one-man rule was a dazzling combination of ad hoc arrangements and artful adaptations of Republican institutions and legalities. The test would come after his death. Would it—could it—survive? The odds were against it. Despite the length of the Princeps' long rule the Republican traditions he utilized were deeply established in Rome. Augustus never dreamed of abolishing the Senate and creating a substitute council made up of his cronies and kin folk. The Senate, however, demonstrated again and again that it was incapable of constructive collective action. It could not lead; it had to be managed. The larger elite class, the equites or knights, had their own vested interests and huge amounts of money. The Princeps could not rule without them, any more than he could without the support of the armies, which had their interests. The question therefore was whether the successors of Augustus could hold all the strands of government together. It is a tribute to the strength of the government that had taken shape under Augustus that despite occasional failures the principate survived for approximately two centuries before a combination of external pressures and internal weaknesses combined to produce yet another remaking of itself by Rome.

## Inheriting Rome

One of the most important responsibilities of government is to arrange for the peaceful transition of power from one administration to the next. Augustus must have frequently pondered the matter of the succession from early in his career. What if he were suddenly to be swept away by disease, accident, or assassination? In such a scenario the likelihood of the succession being determined once again by civil war was high. Yet the passing of his power to another, especially a family member, was a tricky business. Such an arrangement might have pleased the *plebs urbana* and the armies, who did not care much about constitutional niceties, but it was a good deal more than the elite, and a substantial segment of the rest of the population, could stomach. The Empire was not a piece of real estate or a house, and Romans were not slaves and retainers who could be passed on by will from father to son. The passing of power this way was incompatible with Rome's political culture—or, at least until that culture was substantially modified.

THE NATURE OF THE PRINCIPATE There was another problem: The principate as it evolved under Augustus was not an office or a position.[1] There was no such thing as the institution of "The Principate." The position held by Augustus as Princeps was a collection of powers and honors gathered over a period of time accompanied and sustained by his accumulated *auctoritas*. *Auctoritas* was the sum of magistracies held, successes won in courts, on the battlefield, and so on. It was the accumulated respect of one's peers and fellow citizens built up over a lifetime. As such it could not be passed on—except as a hope—to an heir. Ideally if an heir could be identified ahead of time then it might be possible to build up the same *consensus universorum*—the agreement of all—that sustained Augustus. It could be arranged for the heir to hold the right offices, wage wars, give games, honor the nobility, put up large buildings—just as Augustus had—and so, in time find acceptance. It would be hard for society to deny preference to someone on whom it had already repeatedly conferred offices and honors. The problem with this approach was that it took a huge amount of luck and a great deal of time.

THE CRISIS OF 23 B.C. In the delicate minuet that the Princeps was performing with the elite of Rome he could not afford to be thought to be designating formally a successor, especially someone from within his own family. That would be tantamount to declaring himself king and no one, neither Augustus nor the elite of Rome, at this point in time, wanted that. As long as the dance continued both sides could pretend to be satisfied with the arrangement—and in fact it worked well for both—but the Princeps' illness of 23 B.C. forced ev-

[1]The difficulty of identifying the nature of the principate is revealed in the following description provided by the distinguished historian Fergus Millar: "One could describe the Roman system of the first century as an autocracy, as an empire, as a constitutional monarchy, as a nation-state, as a city-state, as a *res publica*, even as a sort of democracy, in which constitutional power could only be conferred by the votes of the people. Few political systems have been quite so complex a mixture of old and new, autocratic and popular, monarchic and communal," Fergus Millar, *The Roman Republic and the Augustan Revolution*, (Chapel Hill, 2002), 376.

eryone to think of what might happen when the music stopped. As we have seen, when close to death he handed his official papers to his consular colleague Piso and his signet ring to his closest advisor, Agrippa, signifying that Piso and Agrippa between them were to carry on the government. There was nothing for the potential heirs of Augustus, his nephew Marcellus and his step-son Tiberius, each 18 years old in 23 B.C.

A solution to Augustus' dilemma, however, was already in the making. By 23 B.C. one thing was clear. The holding of *maius imperium* and *tribunicia* potestas described legally the power of the current Princeps. Both powers had been detached from the actual office from which they derived so that it was not necessary for the holder of either power actually to be consul or tribune. What was to prevent Augustus from requesting from the Senate similar powers for a defined period of time—say five years—for someone else who in due course might become the Princeps' successor? Clearly such a person would have to demonstrate his worthiness to have these powers bestowed on him, and the timed bestowal would act as a kind of probationary period during which the elite and the ruling First Man could decide whether the designee was ready for the job. It can be assumed that most of the elite was as concerned as was the Princeps that the succession be smooth and would be willing to go along with such a solution. Any alternative was worse. Fear of the chaos of the late Republic was still an active memory. The sudden death of Augustus would plunge the Senate into a battle between its competing factions, each formed around a potential new Princeps. It could also be assumed that the armies of the frontiers would almost immediately become involved, perhaps choosing their own senatorial commanders (if they liked and respected them) as their candidates. It would be hard for the senators in Rome to stand up to such candidates and their armed backers. Thus the battle for the new leader would or at least could degenerate into a battle between the armies of the frontiers and their generals, and in fact this is what happened in A.D. 68 when the Julio-Claudian dynasty ended.

## 2. INSTITUTIONALIZING THE PRINCIPATE

For the reasons outlined above Augustus had resisted institutionalizing the principate. However, once a series of peaceful successions from one emperor to another took place successfully it was inevitable that the collection of powers that constituted the principate should eventually move from being personal, familial, ad hoc powers to actual legal powers. This occurred in A.D. 70 with the accession of a new dynasty, the Flavians, which had no aristocratic claims to the family prerogatives of the Julio-Claudians and so needed the powers and prerogatives of the Princeps to be spelled out in detail. Custom established in the years of Augustus and his successors, the Julio-Claudians, became law. From this time onward, when the Senate and people of Rome ratified the choice of a Princeps they were doing more than approving an individual but conferring legally valid powers on him. The political culture of Rome, still deeply Republican in Augustus' time, had changed. By A.D. 70 and the accession of Vespasian the character of the principate had taken on a clearly identifiable institutional form.

Although the role of the Princeps was now well established, the means by which he administered the Empire were still evolving. Down to the end of the Julio-Claudian dynasty the principal bureaucratic offices remained within the family of the ruling Princeps, administered by freedmen and slaves. There had already been some movement in the direction of having equestrians staff various posts, but again it was the accession of the Flavian emperors—Vespasian, Titus, and Domitian—that accelerated the process by which men of equestrian rank took over the highest positions rather than freedmen or slaves.

## 3. SOURCES

Some of the sources for this period—Suetonius, Tacitus, Plutarch, and Dio Cassius—have already been mentioned in the introduction to Chapter 12. From Tacitus, who is one of the main sources for the period, we have a biography of his father-in-law, Julius Agricola, governor of Britain for seven years; an ethnography of the Germans heavily laced with moral comments; the *Histories* which, when complete, covered the years A.D. 69 to 96; and the *Annals*, which dealt with the Julio-Claudians. Unfortunately only parts of these last two works survive. Josephus and Philo provide insights into Jewish history, religion, and life, while the various books of the New Testament provide information about early Christianity, as well as life in Palestine and the eastern Mediterranean in the first and second centuries A.D. The *Historia Augusta* or Augustan History is an incomplete series of quirky, untrustworthy biographies of second- and third-century emperors. The biographies are

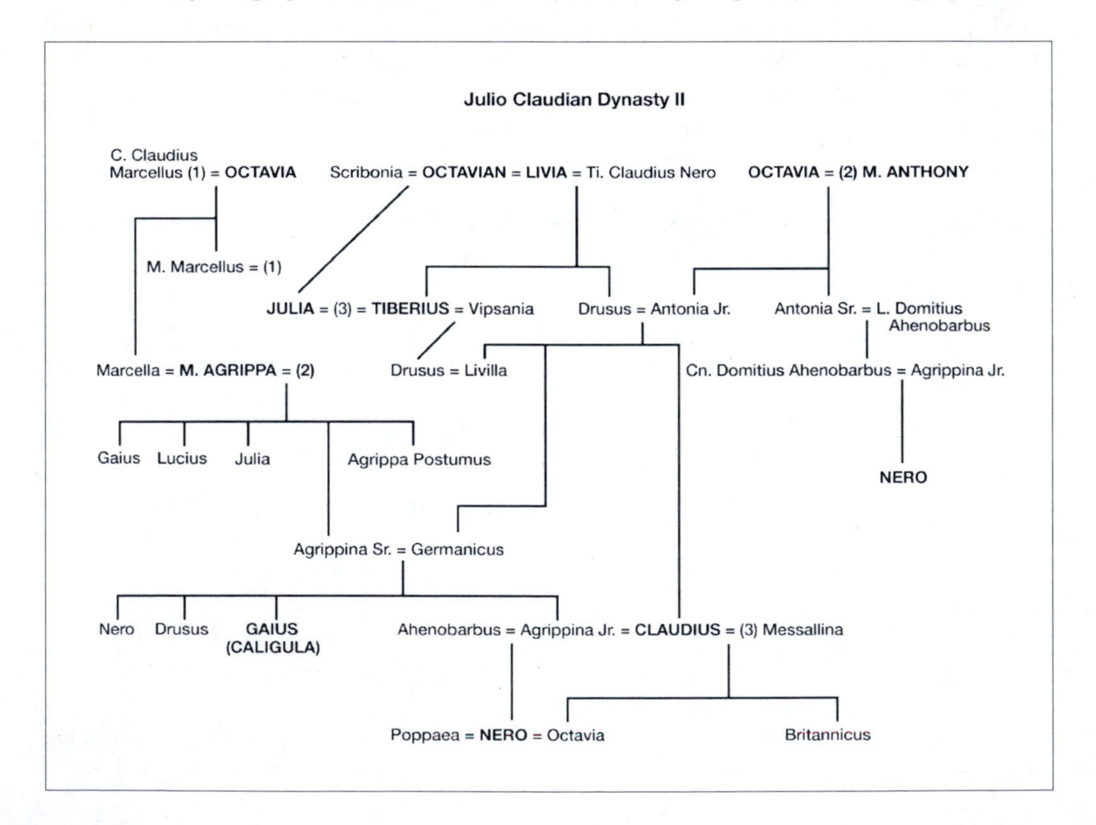

modeled on the *Lives* of Suetonius and contain, in imitation of Suetonius documents such as letters from emperors and senatorial decrees, but most are now thought to be forgeries. The history was written in the late fourth century A.D. and shows sympathy towards the Senate and is opposed to hereditary monarchy and the interference of the army in politics. Non-historical literature in the form of the poetry of Ovid, Lucan, Statius, and Martial, apart from their own literary value, offer insight into the cultural and social life of the early Empire. Inscriptions, coins, papyri, and archaeology illustrate many facets of imperial life that are at best hinted at in the literary sources.

# 13

# The Julio-Claudians: Tiberius to Nero

## 1. SUCCESSION: THE CANDIDATES

### Agrippa

The succession plan evolved by Augustus was slowly put into effect. An interval was allowed to elapse after the crisis of 23 B.C. Then in 18 B.C. Agrippa received tribunician power for five years and possibly also *maius imperium* at the same time. Hence, if Augustus dropped dead there was a proven, non-family, competent successor at hand, already legally empowered, to take up where the former Princeps left off. Legal niceties of this type may seem both hypocritical and hair-splitting. After all, Agrippa was Augustus' son-in-law. But such subterfuges are often how governments, political factions, and businesses operate. Augustus' solution to the problem of continuity—given the complexities of existing Roman political traditions—was a work of genius. After it was in place the majority of the elite, not to mention the First Man, his family, friends, and retainers, must have breathed a collective sigh of relief. Property owners must have slept more soundly. The likelihood of a new round of civil wars and more confiscations was ended—for the time being. Nevertheless the whole constitutional arrangement required a great deal of civilized pretense in public and cooperation behind the scenes to make it work. At best it was a rickety system.

### Tiberius

Agrippa was around 45 years of age when he was given tribunician power, and although healthy, thought had to be given to additional candidates in the event of his death or inca-

**Agrippa and Livia**

*Agrippa and Livia from the Ara Pacis. One of the aims of the sculpture program of the altar was to demonstrate the unity of the imperial family.*

pacitation. Both Marcellus and Tiberius had begun accelerated careers prior to 23 B.C., but late that same year Marcellus died and Agrippa himself died in 12 B.C. Once more the potential dangers of an unprepared transmission of power were revealed.

As a teenager Tiberius had shown military talent when he campaigned with Augustus in Spain. At 20, to further his experience, he was put in charge of a prosecution of conspirators at Rome. Two years later he was sent on an important diplomatic mission to the east to recover the standards from the Parthians and install the new king of Armenia. The deal had been negotiated by Augustus, but Tiberius was entrusted with the job of representing Rome in that important region of the world. He was advanced to the praetorship in 19 B.C. and then campaigned successfully in southern Germany. In 13 B.C., at age 29, he was elected consul. A year later he campaigned in Pannonia. On his return Augustus publicly demonstrated his confidence in Tiberius by marrying his daughter Julia, previously married to Agrippa, to him. Whatever the political advantages of such a union it was an unhappy marriage for both. Tiberius was forced to divorce his wife Vipsania, Agrippa's daughter, to whom he was genuinely attached. Julia was a freer spirit than the serious Tiberius could tolerate.

## Gaius and Lucius

By 6 B.C. Augustus seems to have decided that Tiberius had proved himself to the public at large. By this date Tiberius was thoroughly familiar with the Empire, having travelled over much of it. He was a solid supporter of the regime. Augustus had the Senate bestow tribunician power on him for five years, but then something went wrong with the plans. Personal relations between the two men, given their different characters, may never have

**Lucius as Child From Ara Pacis: The Sorrows of Augustus**

*Augustus adopted his grandsons Gaius and Lucius hoping one of them would be his heir. Both, however, died young. Here Lucius Caesar, grandson and possible heir of Augustus, clings to the toga of a family member.*

been warm, but now they seem to have soured badly. Tiberius unexpectedly withdrew from public life and went to live on the Greek island of Rhodes. Like most palace spats the reasons for the breakdown in the relationship between the two men and Tiberius' departure from Rome are obscure. One likely explanation is that Tiberius recognized that Augustus had begun to favor his grandsons, Gaius and Lucius, over him. Both had been adopted by the Princeps in 17 B.C., and Tiberius rightly thought it would be prudent to get himself out of the way while they began their public careers and developed their reputations as he had. The shadow in Rome of an older, successful commander and potential successor closely related to the Princeps' household would have created political problems for the whole family. Senators and others among the elite were always on the lookout for fissures to exploit within the ruling family and would have begun immediately to calculate which of the potential successors of Augustus would actually be successful. It was not an idle game. For prominent members of the elite the stakes in such calculations were high. It was vital not to end up on the wrong side of a succession dispute if there was one. Augustus, of course, hewed to his policy of avoiding giving the impression that he was planning a dynastic succession. By now, however, such a policy must have been regarded as a transparent pretense.

As it happened, Augustus' grandsons Gaius (born 20 B.C.) and Lucius (born 17 B.C) died early. Lucius died in A.D. 2 while on the way to Spain to begin his military career, while Gaius died of a wound received while campaigning in the east against the Armenians two years later. The wisdom of having multiple heirs now revealed itself. Tiberius resurfaced as the most competent and proven candidate and was adopted by Augustus as his son in A.D. 4. Tiberius in turn was forced to adopt his own nephew, Germanicus. Augustus himself adopted Agrippa Postumus, the last surviving son of Agrippa and Julia. Both adoptions were probably aimed at preventing Germanicus and Postumus from becoming centers of intrigue that might jeopardize the position of Tiberius. As a result of their adoptions both were now safely lodged inside the ruling family. Under such circumstances it would be much harder for members of the Senate to lure them into heading factions in opposition to the regime.

## Augustan Precedents

Everything that Augustus did as Princeps established a precedent, and that included his solution to the problem of the transmission of power. Fortune favored Rome. Augustus had a daughter but no sons. As we have seen, heirs chosen from other blood relatives—his nephew and grandsons—died prematurely. The Princeps was finally forced to adopt a non-family member, Tiberius, as his heir. Thus the precedent was accidentally established that future rulers should look for the theoretically most competent successor and then adopt him. This meant acknowledging that the Senate had some role in the search for the Princeps' successor. On the whole it was an effective arrangement. The adoption preserved the dynastic principle that reassured the people and the soldiers that there was family continuity and dependability. At the same time the elite, in particular senators, were assured that the ruler would not act as a dynastic monarch passing on his position to his son in violation of the Senate's claims and rights. Ideally a successor would have to have passed muster, as Tiberius did, with the elite. Tiberius had in fact proved himself an acceptable—if not particularly popular—candidate with both Augustus and the elite. It was not a huge concession on the part of the Princeps—he got the successor he wanted—but it was sufficient to allay the sensibilities of the elite. The danger would come when a ruling emperor had a son. At the same time the elite's acceptance of Tiberius revealed its willingness to submit to the regime of a by-now-less-than-fully veiled autocracy. The elite accepted the new rules and the limitations the new rules imposed on its traditional powers. It was of this that Tacitus was thinking when he referred with his habitual cynicism to senatorial servility. The members of the elite, he said, submitted to Augustus because they "preferred the safety of the present to the dangers of the past" (*Annals*, 1.2). Yet, as Tacitus himself knew well, it was not an unreasonable bargain, and it was certainly one to which he was a part as a prominent senator of a later generation.

## 2. EXPANDING THE EMPIRE UNDER AUGUSTUS

### Glorifying Rome the Traditional Way: By Conquest

Augustus' assumption of control of the frontier provinces allowed him to conduct aggressive policies of expansion and consolidation on behalf of Rome. He could thus play to the hilt the traditional republican role of defender and enlarger of Rome's possessions. This also kept the military involved at a distance from Rome so that the armed might of the legions might not appear, at least not too obviously, as the means by which the Princeps maintained his power. It also kept the troops busy. Augustus was able to portray his significant conquests not as the achievements of his generals but as his own achievements on behalf of the Roman people.

Under Augustus the fragmented conquests of the Republic were rounded out and consolidated. Historians debate whether there was or was not any genuine strategic thinking behind these acts. One opinion holds that Augustus established a hegemonial empire that used client states as buffers and kept the legions in key positions in the provinces where they could either back up the client states or put down rebellions within the Empire itself. Unfortunately we lack the kind of internal documentation that would prove that Augustus sat down with his advisors and generals, studied maps, read reports, and calculated the costs and risks that would have led to such strategic planning. The more common opinion is

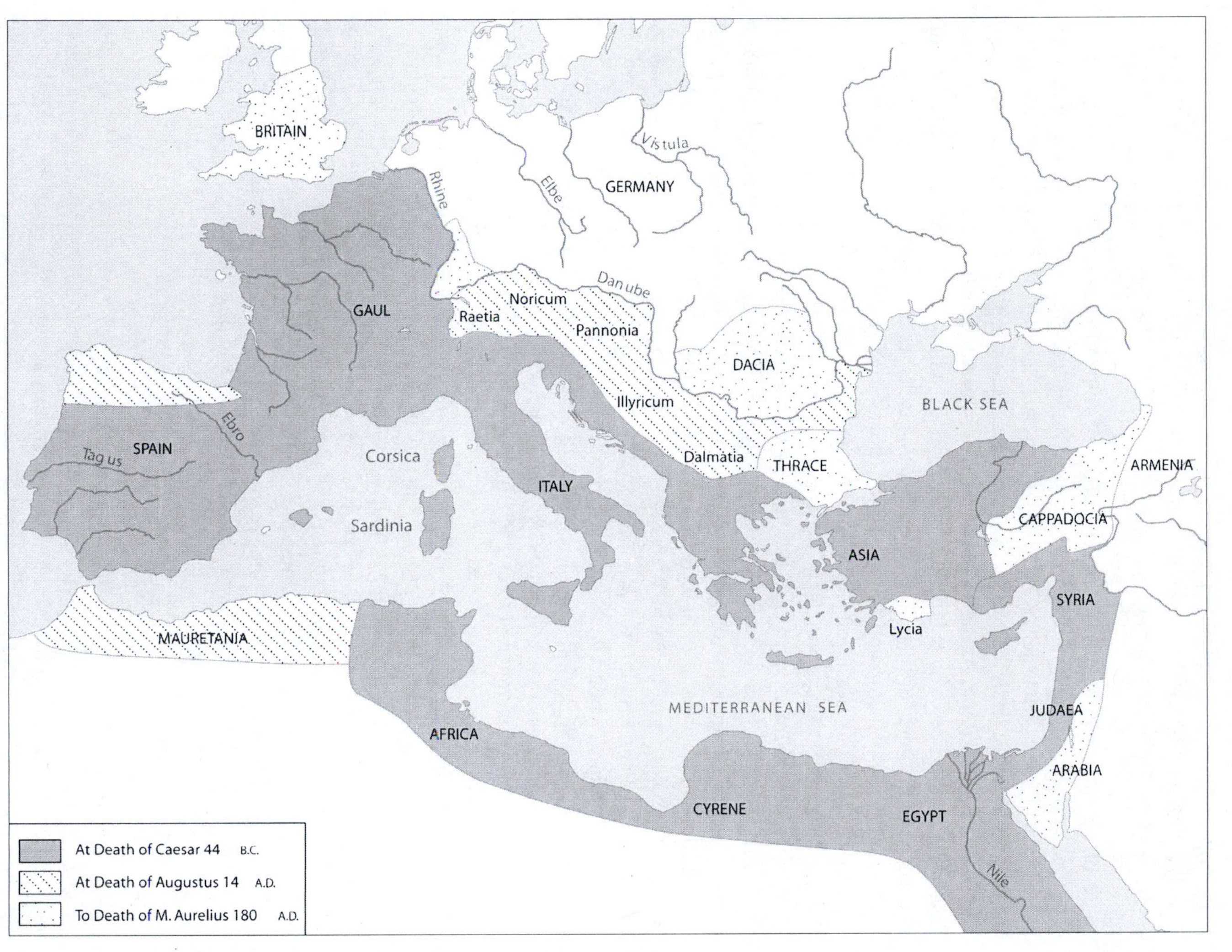


Expansion of the Roman Empire from Caesar to M. Aurelius

that Augustus dealt with the strategic needs of the empire as necessity demanded. That necessity was not always military. At times it included the political need for military success on his own part as well as on the part of his potential successors.

AUGUSTUS' NEED FOR MILITARY SUCCESS Agrippa already had an excellent military reputation established during the civil wars, but Augustus' was weak. Members of the aristocracy noted cattily that he tended to be sick at crucial moments, such as the time he was ill at the battle of Philippi. Thus the need to establish his credentials probably underlay some of the campaigns he undertook. At the same time it is hard to imagine that these campaigns were just randomly chosen or dictated exclusively by political necessity. For instance, Augustus chose to deal with the Parthian Empire diplomatically rather than by seeking revenge for the defeats suffered by Crassus and Antony. He was not averse to using displays of force and firm diplomatic communiqués as long as he got what he thought the Empire needed in that part of the world, namely, a secure border and a promise not to interfere in key Roman areas of influence such as Asia Minor, Syria, Palestine, and Egypt. The return of the lost standards was also important. All of these successful negotiations gave the Princeps the right to boast of his successes in the east, claiming as he did in the *Res Gestae* that "I forced the Parthians to restore to me the spoils and standards of three Roman armies [Crassus in 53 B.C., Antony in 40 and 36 B.C.], and to seek as suppliants the friendship of the Roman people. These standards I deposited in the inner shrine of the Temple of Mars Ultor" (29). This narrative reminded everyone of Antony's failures while it was of little importance to the Parthians that they were portrayed as being coerced into returning the lost standards. The "victory" validated the message of success Augustus was trying to sell the Roman people.

The west was a different matter entirely. In fairness to the Romans, if they had been confronted by unified, militarily powerful states such as Parthia in the east, they might have conducted themselves differently. But the west was characterized by a few developing states such as those of Burebistas in Romania and the Marcomannic state of Maroboduus in Bohemia and southern Germany, but more often the reality was hundreds of vaguely defined tribes. The Greek term *ethnos* and its Latin equivalent *natio* were used to describe such peoples. The terms implied cultural and social similarities such as languages, family relations, economic practices, clothing, and food customs. Their level of political organization was low in comparison with their Mediterranean neighbors to the south. Their stability was shaky as their communities were headed by elders and prominent individuals, some of whom had pretensions to chieftainship, which often only meant leadership in war. With such peoples it was hard to establish dependable, long-lasting diplomatic relations. Friendships could be maintained, but they were an undependable basis for a sustained relationship. The situation brought out the worst on both sides. The weaknesses of these tribal peoples were exploited by the Romans who had long experience with similar groups in Italy. Sometimes raids conducted into Roman territory or against "Friends of the Roman People" provoked retaliation. At times when internal Roman reasons for success on the battlefield became dominant, there was no equivalent to the might of Parthia to restrain Roman war-making. As Livy noted in a previous century, the news of the revolt of a tribe was a sufficient pretext for a Roman campaign.

WARS IN THE WEST The results were predictable. Long and bloody campaigns such as those Rome had conducted in the second century B.C. in Spain, and by Caesar in Gaul in the first century, were waged under Augustus in northwestern Spain, which remained unconquered from republican times; Illyricum (a large region covering a good portion of the Balkans); the Alps (Switzerland and southern Bavaria and Austria); and Germany. An inscription set up near Monaco listing the names of no less than 46 tribal peoples subdued by Augustus gives an idea of the magnitude of the task the Romans set for themselves. Motivations for the different campaigns varied. Those in Illyricum in 35 B.C. to 33 B.C. were conducted to keep pace with Antony's campaigns in the east and demonstrate Octavian's military capacity. Later the value of the Danube as a route from southern Germany to the east became apparent, and wars were conducted in that region by Tiberius from 12 B.C. to 9 B.C. and again in A.D. 6 after a major revolt there. Two new provinces, Dalmatia and Pannonia, were created, and a large command farther east known as Moesia, which reached the Black Sea. The Alpine campaigns of 16 and 15 B.C. burnished the reputations of Augustus' step-sons Tiberius and Drusus and were essential from strategic viewpoints for safe communications between Italy, the Rhine, and Illyricum.

Prima Porta Augustus

*Augustus is portrayed in military garb as the conqueror of the Parthians. Eros riding a dolphin at his feet alludes to Augustus' divine ancestor Venus. His shoes, hard to see in this image, recall those of gods and heroes, not humans. The cuirass shows cosmic representations of a new world order of peace and, naturally, Roman supremacy.*

The interior of Gaul, though conquered by Caesar, had not yet been properly organized; it was now divided into three new provinces. The proximity of a not wholly pacified Gaul to Germany created a problem for the Romans. The Rhine itself was not a military barrier and there was no significant cultural difference between the peoples who lived on either side of the river. "Germany" was a cultural construct, not an ethnic or national reality. As in Caesar's time immigrations and raids from across the Rhine created disturbances in Gaul. We hear of problems there on and off from the 30s B.C. to the teens B.C. In 17 B.C. a coalition of German tribes crossed the Rhine, looted and plundered Gallic territory, and inflicted a serious defeat on the legate M. Lollius. Augustus led the Roman response in person. He could not afford to allow the appearance of military failure on such an important frontier to undermine his political standing in Rome. He spent three years in Gaul righting the situation. This was followed up by four campaigns conducted by his step-son Drusus between 13 B.C. and 9 B.C. in an attempt to terrorize the Germans and suppress Gallic unrest. During the last campaign in 9 B.C. Drusus reached the Elbe but on his return had the misfortune to break a leg in a fall and died on the way back to the Rhine. His brother Tiberius was sent in 8 B.C. to sustain the momentum and demonstrate that the death of the Roman general had not caused Rome to rethink its plans for Germany.

AUGUSTUS' GERMAN STRATEGY What these plans were is unclear, and modern scholars argue at length about even the existence of a plan to conquer Germany to the Elbe or beyond. Some scholars think that Augustus was an expansionist and aimed at extending Roman boundaries to the ends of the earth. Through a mistake in geographical understanding, the Romans thought that Asia was not much more distant from the Rhine than the Rhine was from Spain. According to this view Augustus planned to add Germany and probably everything else east of the Rhine to the Empire. In A.D. 6 a massive pincer movement from the upper Rhine and the Danube, involving 12 legions, was organized to incorporate Germany up to the Elbe, but just as the offensive was about to get underway, Illyria to the south revolted. By A.D. 9 Tiberius had finally suppressed this revolt, but the same year the three legions in Germany under P. Quinctilius Varus were wiped out in a surprise attack. According to these scholars this brought to an end Roman plans for the conquest of Germany, and the lands to the east of the Rhine were evacuated. Others think Augustus' plans were based on a defensive posture and that he had no intention of annexing Germany, only establishing practical, defensible frontiers. Whatever theory is preferred, it cannot be forgotten that Augustus' main focus was not conquest per se (as seems to have been the case of his adoptive father), but rather creating a new and lasting system of government in Rome. Foreign affairs in general and military victories in particular were always subordinate to the political needs of the primary undertaking. Victories large or small or non-existent could be dressed up to bolster the regime. Major defeats, however, were intolerable and had to be reversed as soon as possible.

Augustus' handling of both east and west suggests a flexible, prudent approach to foreign affairs. Some advances were strategic—such as the conquest of the Alps and Illyricum—which improved Rome's central military position considerably. Others were motivated by fear of greater dangers. Repeated raids across the Rhine by booty-seeking German tribes could lead to disturbances in Gaul. The appropriate response here was intimidation, and it worked. The presence of two Roman armies of four legions each in upper and lower Germany (the southern and northern sections of the Rhine) led to lavish military spending on the legions and military infrastructure such as roads and fortresses. The influx of money stimulated economic development on both sides of the Rhine, especially in Gaul. Trade with "Free Germany," that is Germany outside Roman control, flourished. For several generations the Rhine frontier was relatively quiet, and Gaul remained undisturbed, giving the province a chance to develop stability.

Augustus' conquests and consolidations doubled the size of the Empire. They impressed the people of Rome as they were intended to. The glamour of exotic geography added to the impression of the size of the Empire. Romans were told that Britain, on the other side of the ocean no less, had been intimidated. They heard of invasions of *Arabia Felix*, "Blessed or Fortunate Arabia," and even farther off Ethiopia. Germany and Illyricum had been pacified. Distant Armenia was brought within the Roman orbit. Embassies were paraded from Parthia and India, from the peoples of the steppe lands north of the Black Sea and from the Caucasus. Agrippa's map propagated the idea that the whole inhabited world was Roman or at least dominated by Rome.

## 3. THE JULIO-CLAUDIAN EMPERORS

Augustus set a high bar for his successors, so high that none of them was able to reach it. His successors, Tiberius, Gaius (Caligula), Claudius, and Nero, the so-called Julio-Claudians, were sustained in good measure by the prestige Augustus had built up for his house and regime.

During the transitions from emperor to emperor Augustus' legal and administrative arrangements held firm as did his conquests. Nevertheless, a huge burden fell on the shoulders of all his successors. They had to have proved themselves successful in military affairs, prudent in domestic and foreign policies, adept in the choice of their advisors and generals, and popular with the people and armies. They had to run their own households without undermining their prestige by scandal. Most importantly, they had to find worthwhile successors. This was a lot to ask of any one human being.

### Tiberius, A.D. 14–37

Tiberius was more at home in the army camp than in the suffocating confines of his house on the Palatine hill where he had to live in unrelenting proximity to family members, senators, and most despised of all, the people. All of these took for granted the easy informality and accessibility of his predecessor, the amiable Augustus. Tiberius was neither amiable nor sociable. He was cynical and suspicious in manner, and affected Roman *severitas*. He spoke Greek fluently, was well read, and enjoyed conversing with Greek philosophers. He was not a good actor as was his adoptive father, and could not conceal his disdain for the fawning, scheming senators or the fickle, pleasure-seeking mobs of Rome. His mother, the redoubtable Livia, was also a problem. She now enjoyed the title of "Augusta" conferred on her by her husband's will and hoped to have a hand in shaping the policies of the new regime as she had under Augustus, but Tiberius was able to ease her into a resentful retirement. There were suspicions she had greased his way to the throne. Tacitus saw the "step-motherly malevolence" of Livia at work in the disposal of the direct heirs to the throne. Tiberius was determined to end the speculation that she might be his guiding spirit when he was in power. He vetoed an attempt by the Senate to confer on her the title *Mater Patriae*, mother of the country, and forbade her deification after her death.

TIBERIUS' ISOLATION Unlike Augustus, Tiberius had no advisors he felt he could trust. He had no Agrippa or Maecenas, and perhaps most importantly, no Livia. He had been forced to divorce Vipsania, the wife he loved and trusted and marry Julia, Augustus, daughter, who cuckolded him. When her *paterfamilias* Augustus discovered her crime he had her banished. She died in A.D. 14. Tiberius' brother, Drusus, whom he had trusted, died on campaign in Germany, as we have learned. His son Drusus showed promise in putting down a mutiny among the Balkan legions, but he died unexpectedly in A.D. 23. His adopted son and imperial heir, Germanicus, was, by contrast to the morose Princeps, highly popular but of dubious talent. He put down a rebellion in Germany by giving in, Tiberius thought, too readily to the demands of the mutineers. While touring in the east Germanicus quarreled with the governor of Syria, Calpurnius Piso, Tiberius' watchdog. When Germanicus died of a fever in A.D. 19 Piso was suspected of poisoning him and after a spectacular trial in Rome, committed suicide. Germanicus' widow Agrippina was convinced Tiberius had been the real instigator of her husband's death. Adding to this conviction was the fact that Tiberius refused to allow her to remarry. Her children, being the descendants of Augustus, constituted possible focal points of danger and a new husband, not being a member of the imperial household, would have come with his own extended network of connections, any one of which might have caused problems. Finally, there were the people. Unlike Augustus, Tiberius did not believe in spending large sums of money on games and festivals, nor did he enjoy attending them, thereby stirring up the peoples' resentment of him.

As Tiberius became more and more isolated he thought he had found a confidant in the person of the Praetorian Prefect, Aelius Sejanus, whom he made sole commander of the guard.[1] Prefects were regular members of the emperor's advisory council (*consilium principis*) and so were present during all policy deliberations and military planning. One of the prefects and a detachment of the guard accompanied the emperor when he travelled or was on campaign. Under such circumstances it is not hard to see how an emperor might find himself relying on his prefects for much of his advice.

THE PLANS OF SEJANUS After the death of his son Drusus and his adopted son Germanicus, and with the encouragement of Sejanus, Tiberius withdrew to a villa located safely on the island of Capri in the Bay of Naples. Capri was close enough to Rome for Tiberius to return to the capital if necessary and receive regular dispatches, but it also allowed him to screen his visitors. In fact he never returned to Rome. Once he sailed up the Tiber, but a distant view of the city was enough for him to order the ship turned around.

Sejanus' larger plan now began to unfold. When Tiberius' mother Livia died in A.D. 29, the emperor did not return to attend her funeral. With the influential Livia out of the way, the way was open for Sejanus to begin eliminating potential heirs to the throne. Agrippina, the widow of Germanicus, was arrested on charges of conspiracy. She and her two eldest sons died in prison. A son, Gaius, and three daughters, Agrippina ("the Younger"), Drusilla, and Julia survived. Sejanus' next target was Gemellus, Tiberius' grandson. To get control of him Sejanus suggested to Tiberius that he marry Gemellus' mother, Livilla, but the emperor refused, having decided to name Gemellus and Gaius as his heirs. At this point Antonia, Gaius' grandmother, became suspicious and sent Gaius to Capri to alert Tiberius to the danger. Convinced by Antonia of the danger to the regime, Tiberius acted swiftly, first to secure the loyalty of the Praetorian Guard and then to denounce Sejanus to the Senate. The senators, having suffered long enough under the autocratic upstart Sejanus, gladly condemned him and his family to death. Before committing suicide Sejanus' wife managed to get in one last blow at the emperor. She sent a note to Tiberius claiming that her husband

[1]There were normally two prefects, but at times emperors chose to rely on a single commander.

Livia

*Livia, wife of Augustus and mother of his successor Tiberius ably supported her husband in his plans to remake Rome. She played the role of an old-fashioned* materfamilias, *running the emperor's household with firmness, dignity, tact, and intelligence. Here she is portrayed in a simple, severe style that might be used to depict just any Roman woman, not the powerful wife of the* Princeps. *A hostile tradition caste her as a ruthless intriguer who successfully disposed of Augustus' heirs so that Tiberius, her own son by a previous marriage, could become emperor. She was the grandmother of another emperor (Claudius) and great grandmother of a third (Gaius).*

had seduced Livilla, and that Livilla and Sejanus had then conspired to poison Drusus, the emperor's son and husband of Livilla.

## Gaius (Caligula) A.D. 37–41

Gaius and Gemellus were made joint heirs in A.D. 36. When Tiberius died the next year, Gaius, with the support of the new Praetorian Prefect, Macro, was proclaimed emperor. Tiberius' will appointing Gemellus as co-heir was ignored.

The new emperor had spent much of his childhood in army camps with his parents, Germanicus and Agrippina, and had acquired the nickname Caligula ("Little Boot") from the miniature uniform and its hob nailed boots (*caliga*) he wore as a child. Gaius had been brought up to believe that Tiberius had been responsible for the death of his father. He then witnessed the campaign waged against his family by Sejanus, which saw the deaths of his mother and brothers. Despite this dreadful childhood Gaius' reign began well and his unstable character did not manifest itself immediately. His accession was welcomed by both Senate and people. He was exceptionally intelligent and a gifted orator, but he had a cruel and cynical wit and enjoyed arguing and rebutting the speeches of well-known orators. His sense of theatricality pleased the people, and he made appearances as a Thracian gladiator, a singer, a dancer, and fought with real weapons. He drove chariots in regional circuses.

His relationship with the senators was another matter. On one occasion in the dead of night he called three senators of consular rank to the palace. When they arrived half dead with fear, expecting the worst, they were led to a stage on which amid blaring flutes and heel taps Caligula suddenly appeared, dressed in cloak and ankle-length tunic. Having performed a song and dance he disappeared as suddenly as he had appeared.

After the death of his grandmother Antonia (who acted as a restraining influence on him), followed by a serious illness, Caligula's actions became increasingly erratic. The illness, as in the case of Augustus, probably raised the inevitable question of who was to succeed him, and rumors of plots began to circulate. He had Macro, the Praetorian Prefect, and Gemellus, Tiberius' grandson and his co-heir, executed. On campaign in Gaul in A.D. 39 to 40 a conspiracy was in fact discovered and its leader, the commander of the army of the Upper Rhine, Gaetulicus, was executed. His sister, Agrippina the Younger, mother of the future emperor Nero, was implicated as a co-conspirator and banished. She was recalled after the emperor's death. In constant danger of assassination, Gaius became more brutal and erratic. In A.D. 41 he was murdered, together with his wife and infant daughter by Praetorian officers.

A hostile tradition portrayed Caligula as mad, possibly as a result of illnesses. He was alleged to have committed incest with one of his sisters and to have sadistically tortured prisoners. There were rumors that he intended to make his horse a consul and that after training maneuvers for an invasion of Britain he had marched the legions to the English Channel only to order them to pick seashells. He was accused of wild extravagance just as his predecessor, Tiberius, was criticized for the opposite, his miserliness. Senators were hard to please. Caligula was, it is true, autocratic and accepted honors that came close to deification. His short rule, however, did no permanent damage to the Empire. His supposed extravagances included games, the maintenance of roads in Italy, the launching of two new aqueducts that were completed by his successor, harbor improvements to ensure the dependability of the grain supply, and a circus on the Vatican on the other side of the Tiber.

### Tiberius in His Own Words

Tiberius hated flatterers... and if anyone spoke of him too fulsomely he interrupted them and corrected their language on the spot. Once when addressed as "Lord" (*dominus*) he warned the man never to speak again in this insulting fashion ["*dominatio" was the power an owner had over his slaves*]. Another spoke of "Your Sacred Duties," and yet another said that he had "approached the Senate by the Emperor's Authority." Tiberius made them change "sacred" to "laborious" and "authority" to "advice." He was unperturbed and patient in the face of abuse, slander or of lampoons of himself or his family and would often say: "Freedom of speech and thought is the test of a free country." When the Senate asked that those who had offended in this way should be prosecuted he said, "We do not have the time to become involved in any more affairs. If you open that window there will be no time for anything else. Everyone will take the opportunity to air some private feud" (Suetonius *Tiberius*, 27, 28).

## Claudius A.D. 41–54

Among the plotters who brought down Caligula was a powerful freedman by the name of Callistus, who had earlier persuaded Caligula to spare his uncle Claudius, who was supposed to be an inoffensive non-entity. After the assassination Claudius was hustled off to the Praetorian camp where he was saluted as emperor by the guardsmen. Negotiations with the Senate began. Some senators spoke of restoring the Republic, but there was little support for the proposal either inside or outside the Senate. The Praetorians extorted a huge donative or bonus of 15,000 sesterces per man for their efforts—equal to 15 times the yearly salary of an ordinary legionary soldier and 15 times the amount of the legacies left by Augustus and Tiberius. Suetonius comments that this was the first time an emperor openly purchased the loyalty of the military. The emperor's generosity, which clearly manifested his weakness and dependence on the Guard, did not end there. Every anniversary of Claudius' coming to power he paid each Praetorian 100 sesterces. The special treatment of the Guard angered the legionary soldiers who now, undoubtedly, began to wonder why this lucrative form of king-making should be left to the Praetorians alone.

GROWING UP IN THE PALACE Claudius was generally considered unfit for Roman public life because of a congenital weakness that caused him to limp and, when agitated, to slobber. He stammered and his head shook. Livia, his grandmother, and Augustus despised him as a disgrace to the imperial household, and Caligula made him the butt of jokes. He had not even been adopted into the Julian family (the family of Julius Caesar) and was practically unknown outside the palace. To escape these miseries Claudius turned to drink and books. He studied history under Livy and became an avid antiquarian and an expert on religious matters. He wrote a history of Rome down to 44 B.C., circumspectly avoiding the delicate issue of Octavian's bloody triumvirate. He also wrote on Carthage and Etruscan history. None of his works survive.

CLAUDIUS AS EMPEROR In A.D. 47 Claudius celebrated the Secular Games, mainly with the aim of reassuring the people of the continuity and success of the regime. To gain military prestige and consolidate his support with the army, he decided to annex Britain and was briefly present at the invasion. He made a good choice of commanders, placing Aulus Plautius, with four legions, at the head of the invading army. Among Plautius' legionary commanders was the future emperor Vespasian, who owed his position to the influence of Narcissus, one of Claudius' freedmen. Initially the invasion went well, and Roman control of the south was quickly established (A.D. 43–47). The conquest of Wales and the north of Britain was a different story, and it was to be another 30 years before the rest of Britain was secure. He increased the number of provinces by adding two in Mauritania as well as Thrace and Lycia in Asia Minor.

Claudius proved to have unexpected administrative abilities and organized permanent departments of finance (*a rationibus*), correspondence (*ab epistulis*), and petitions (*a libellis*) headed by freedmen who ran them efficiently but whose great power won many enemies for their master. At Ostia he built a new port to better provide Rome with grain and merchandise from overseas. He treated the Senate with respect and consulted it regularly, but his relationship with it was prickly. Against opposition he advocated the admission of Gauls to the Senate. Claudius' insecurity as Princeps led him to take quick action against real or imagined threats and offenders were often tried in private with only a few advisors present. His participation in trials conducted by the Senate was regarded by senators as meddling in their prerogatives.

Because of his upbringing Claudius lacked the kind of network of kin and friends that sustained Augustus. This lack, combined with poor relations with the Senate, led to increased dependence on the advice of his wives and freemen. The power of freedmen in the administration tended to grow as their responsibilities grew, and proportionately the ability

Caligula and his Three Sisters
*It is perhaps understandable that given the terrible experiences Gaius had while growing up in the imperial household he should have wanted to emphasize the solidarity of his family. Thus in commemorative coin issues he honored his renowned father Germanicus and his equally redoubtable mother Agrippina the Elder. His three sisters were also honored. They appear with him as* SECURITAS *(Agrippina the Younger);* CONCORDIA *(Drusilla); and* FORTUNA *(Julia) in coins of* A.D. *37. However, this was the last time the three sisters appeared on his coinage. Drusilla died in* A.D. *38, and Agrippina and Julia were exiled on suspicion of treason. So much for family solidarity.*

of an emperor to supervise them declined. Two freedmen in particular, Narcissus and Pallas, accumulated immense riches and influence and were deeply resented by senators and other members of the elite who found access to the emperor blocked by these two men. Claudius married four times, but his last two wives, Messalina and Agrippina, were the most influential and, as it turned out, the most dangerous. Messalina was the mother of his only surviving son, Britannicus. Despising her husband she planned a coup to overthrow him, but the plot unravelled and Narcissus urged the emperor to execute her. He reluctantly agreed. Pallas then persuaded Claudius of the political necessity of another marriage and proposed Agrippina, whose father was the popular Germanicus, Claudius' brother, and whose mother was a descendant of Augustus. It was Claudius' and his son Britannicus' misfortune that Agrippina had a son, Nero, from a previous marriage, some three years older than Britannicus. He seemed to show promise, and she determined to place him on the throne. Apparently besotted by Agrippina, Claudius in A.D. 50 adopted Nero as a partner with Britannicus, and three years later agreed to a marriage between Nero and his daughter Octavia, which effectively promoted Nero over his own son. Intensely ambitious, Agrippina lined up the support of the philosopher Seneca (who became Nero's tutor), the Praetorian Prefect Burrus, and the freedman Pallas. Claudius died in 54, allegedly poisoned by Agrippina, and Nero succeeded to the throne. The Senate declared Claudius a god, and Agrippina was made his priestess.

**Problems with Palace Gossip as a Source of History**

*It is hard to tell how far outside the palace the outrageous things that happened or were supposed to have happened there circulated. The senator, Dio Cassius, writing in the third century A.D., draws attention to the problem of knowing what was actually going on among the small circle of people who ran the Empire from the time of Augustus onward. His comments are obviously true for all closed ruling systems, ancient or modern. He describes the events of 27 B.C., when Augustus proclaimed the restoration of the power of the Senate and People, and goes on to say:*

> In this way the government was changed at that time for the better ...for no doubt it was impossible for the people to be safe under a republic. Nevertheless, the events that happened at this time cannot be recorded in the same manner as those of previous times. In the past, as we know, all matters were reported to the Senate and to the People, even when they happened at quite a distance. Hence everyone learned of them and many recorded them. As a result, the truth regarding them, no matter to what extent fear or favor, friendship or enmity, colored the reports of certain writers, was always to a certain extent to be found in the works of the other writers who wrote of the same events, and in the public records. But after this time, most things began to be kept secret and concealed, and even though some things are by chance made public, they are distrusted just because they cannot be verified. It is suspected that everything is said and done with reference to the wishes of the men in power at the time and of their associates. As a result, much that never occurs circulates widely and much that happened beyond doubt remains unknown. In the case of nearly every event a version gains currency that is different from the way it actually happened. Furthermore, the very magnitude of the Empire and the multiplicity of things that happen, render accuracy in regard to them most difficult to establish (53.19).

## Nero

Nero's reign began promisingly. In his first speech, which was written by Seneca, Nero promised to rule as Augustus had ruled, without undue interference by freedmen and without trials behind closed doors. He announced that clemency would be the motto of the regime. For at least the first five years tradition claims he ruled well, leaving most of the work of government to his mother, Seneca, and Burrus. Together they effectively managed imperial affairs, court intrigue, public relations, and patronage.

**Chronology: The Julio Claudian Emperors**

| | |
|---|---|
| Augustus | 27 B.C.–A.D. 14 |
| Tiberius | A.D. 14–37 |
| Gaius (Caligula) | A.D. 37–41 |
| Claudius | A.D. 41–54 |
| Nero | A.D. 54–68 |

DECLINE Nero had plans of his own but was willing initially to accept the guidance of Seneca and Burrus because they helped restrain the domineering Agrippina. Agrippina, however, had a tendency to overplay her hand. As a way of keeping control of her son she reminded him on occasion of the danger of potential challengers to his position from descendants of Augustus, and in A.D. 55, when she seemed to show favoritism to Britannicus, Nero had him poisoned. Four years later she showed her displeasure with an affair Nero was conducting with Poppaea Sabina, wife of the senator Salvius Otho (later briefly emperor in A.D. 69). Nero "finally came to the conclusion that wherever Agrippina was she was a menace to him" (Tacitus, *Annals*, 14.3) and decided to get rid of her. He tried first to have her drowned in a contrived accident while she was travelling by ship to attend a festival at Baiae near Naples. Though she suffered a shoulder injury, she still managed to survive by swimming to land. Nero then had her stabbed to death in her home.

When Burrus died in A.D. 62 Seneca's influence came to an end also, and Nero emerged as an irresponsible, amoral dilettante whose principal, although genuine, interests were the theater, music, literature, and athletics. He was uninterested in military affairs, and never visited the armies. As the reign advanced his eccentricity increased, provoking conspiracies that further contributed to the downward spiral of his influence. A disastrous fire in A.D. 64 that lasted nine days destroyed all but four of the 14 regions of Rome. Nero introduced a new building and fire code but also took the opportunity to seize land in the burned area for parks and a huge palace he planned to build there, the Golden House, thereby alienating many landowners among the elite. He deflected rumors that he had instigated the fire by blaming the Christians, who were thought to be a Jewish sect. He had many of them burned as an appropriate punishment for their supposed crime, but the Roman masses were not taken in and sympathized with the unfortunate scapegoats. However, he never lost his popularity with the people who appreciated his patronage of the games and his generosity to them. A failed conspiracy to assassinate him in A.D. 65 led to the execution of many of the elite, including Seneca, the poets Lucan and Petronius, and the Stoics Thrasea Paetus and Barea Soranus. The senators, as was their wont, cooperated with the emperor in betraying and condemning their peers.

ADMINISTRATION AND WAR Despite the intrigues of the palace, excellent governors were appointed to the provinces. Major wars were fought in the east by some of the best generals Rome had produced in many years. In a series of campaigns against the Parthians, Cn. Domitius Corbulo brought Armenia within the Roman sphere of influence and gave Nero an opportunity to stage and preside at an elaborate coronation of its king in Pompey's theater in Rome, which was gilded for the occasion. Maladministration of Britain led to a major revolt in A.D. 60 led by the queen of the Iceni, Boudicca; the rising continued until A.D. 67. In Judaea, mishandling of provincial affairs by successive Roman procurators provoked a major revolt in A.D. 66 and required the dispatch of a full-scale expedition to put it down. While Nero was on tour in Greece performing in the festivals—and winning first prizes in 1808 of them, even in ones in which he did not compete—T. Flavius Vespasianus (Vespasian) was appointed commander of the Judaean expedition. His career, after successful service in Britain under Claudius, had suffered a setback because of his unfortunate habit of falling asleep at Nero's recitals. Perhaps more important was the fact that Narcissus, his freedman patron in the palace, had opposed the union of Claudius and Agrippina, so for both men passage into political oblivion followed inevitably upon Nero's marriage. Vespasian pressed the war in Judaea efficiently and had practically ended it when civil war broke out over Nero's successor.

**Nero and His Mother**
*The prominence of Agrippina in this depiction of mother and son is emphasized by the fact that her name and title appear beside her and Nero's heads. Nero's name and title, by contrast, appear on the less prestigious reverse side. Such a depiction had never before occurred. Except for commemorative issues the obverse always showed the ruling Princeps.*

Most of Nero's irresponsibilities had had little effect on the provinces or the armies, but in A.D. 67 he came to suspect his generals of treason and ordered Corbulo and the commanders of the Rhine legions to commit suicide. In Gaul Julius Vindex rose in revolt. At first Nero paid no attention. He called senior senators and advisors to meet with him in the palace, but after a brief discussion of the situation in Gaul "devoted the rest of the session to showing a completely new water organ and explaining the mechanical complexities of a number of other models" (Suet., *Nero* 41). The governor of Spain, Galba, joined Vindex in revolt, and other commanders followed suit. Vindex's revolt did not last long, but it was sufficient to start the movement that led to Nero's downfall. When the gravity of the situation finally sank in, Nero panicked. One of the Praetorian Prefects, Nymphidius Sabinus, told the Praetorians that Nero had fled and bribed them to declare for Galba. Emboldened, the Senate declared Nero a public enemy and recognized Galba as emperor. Nero fled to the villa of one of his freedmen and there committed suicide, supposedly lamenting "What an artist dies with me" (Suetonius, *Nero*, 49).

# 14

# From the Flavians to the Death of Commodus

## 1. THE YEAR OF THE FOUR EMPERORS: A.D. 69

### Arcana Imperii: *The Secrets of Empire*

According to Tacitus the death of Nero agitated "all the legions and their commanders because the secret of the empire had been revealed—that emperors could be made elsewhere than Rome" (*Histories* 1.4). Some of the agitation was the result of moral outrage at the excesses of Nero. The coinage of Vindex in Gaul, for example, called for the restoration of the *genius* of Rome, for freedom, military vengeance, and the primacy of the Republican institutions—the Senate and People. After the Senate accepted Galba as emperor the eight Rhine legions proclaimed their general, Vitellius, emperor. Galba got to Rome first accompanied by an early supporter Otho, the governor of Lusitania (modern Portugal). Galba, aristocratic, elderly, miserly, and a stickler for discipline, had a poor grasp of how to handle things when he got to Rome. He began by enraging the Praetorians by refusing to pay the large donative they had been promised by their prefect Sabinus. He canceled public games and so upset the populace. He then alienated Otho, who had expected to be adopted as Galba's heir but was passed up in favor of a relatively unknown aristocrat named Piso. Otho promptly turned on Galba and persuaded the Praetorian Guard by bribes and promises to switch sides and back him. Galba and Piso were murdered in the Forum and the Senate and People then accepted Otho as Princeps.

When the Rhine legions of Vitellius crossed the Alps into Cisalpine Gaul Otho marched to meet them but was defeated near Cremona in northern Italy with massive losses on both sides. Suetonius, whose father served in one of Otho's legions, reports that Otho committed suicide to try to put an end to the civil war. Meanwhile the legions in Syria under Licinius Mucianus and those in Judaea under Vespasian proclaimed Vespasian emperor and their lead was followed by the Danubian legions. Vespasian also had the support of a key ally, Julius Alexander, prefect of Egypt, whose adherence was important because Egypt provided a good portion of the grain for Rome and the legions in the east. Mucianus now began his march on Rome while Vespasian went to Egypt to receive the adherence of Alexander, leaving his son Titus to continue the siege of Jerusalem. Being closest to Italy the Danube legions under their commander, Antonius Primus, got there first and defeated the Rhine legions of Vitellius at Cremona. The ancient colony was sacked and Primus' men advanced on Rome, where after severe street fighting they captured it. During the struggle the Capitoline temple was burned. Vitellius was captured and executed, and Vespasian was recognized as emperor in late December. Soon afterwards Mucianus, the commander of the Syrian legions, arrived in Rome as the new emperor's principal representative. On January 1, A.D. 70, Vespasian entered the office of consul with his son Titus as his colleague. The dynasty of Augustus was at an end, and a new one had been installed. Titus remained in Judaea to finish the siege of Jerusalem, and in August of that year the city was captured and the temple destroyed.

## 2. THE FLAVIAN EMPERORS

### Some Consequences of the Year of the Four Emperors

THE SECRETS OF EMPIRE The civil wars of A.D. 69 and the accession of the Flavian dynasty threw into bold relief a number of unsettling aspects of the Principate. The Praetorian Guard revealed that it was a dangerous, destabilizing force but also that its power to make emperors was limited. When the frontier legions intervened the guardsmen were no match for them. The Senate showed it still had some authority when it declared Nero a public enemy. The people demonstrated they too had influence when they failed to rally to Galba. The legions, however, were revealed as the ultimate kingmakers. It was not a revelation that generated much pleasure. The precedent might have been bad enough had the armies acted as one in choosing an emperor, but they did not. The regional armies behaved like rivals and fought each other in savage battles. At the first encounter at Cremona 40,000 men are said to have lost their lives. The old colonial city of Cremona was sacked with great loss of life, and Rome itself suffered heavy damage. Farms and villages on the routes of the armies were looted by all sides. For the first time in generations the inhabitants of Italy and the city of Rome were confronted with the reality of war and what a brutal, undisciplined soldiery could do to the fabric of civilian life.

### The Succession

Vespasian had two sons, Titus and Domitian. Titus had already demonstrated his competence, and Domitian had been launched on his career. He also showed promise. If there was any doubt about the dynastic nature of the Principate before this, it was now clear that it was a hereditary monarchy. In some quarters this was welcomed. A peaceful succes-

**Rome Experiences War: The Occupation of the City by Vitellius**

*It is hard to tell which Tacitus despised more: the undisciplined legions or the degenerate mobs of Rome. Many in his class shared his views of the military of which they knew little, and of the people of Rome which they knew too much.*

The inhabitants of Rome stood by and watched the combatants as though they were an audience at a show, encouraging first one side, now the other by shouts and applause as if they were attending a mock fight in the arena. ...It was a terrible and hideous sight that presented itself throughout the city. Here raged battle and death; there baths and taverns were crowded. In one spot there were pools of blood and heaps of corpses while close by were crowds of male and female prostitutes. The vices of a luxurious peace were so closely intermingled with the horrors and cruelties of a sacked city that an observer would be ready to believe that the people was simultaneously mad with rage and lust. ...As if it were a new entertainment added to their holidays, the mob exulted in and enjoyed the scene, indifferent to which side won, and rejoicing over the suffering of the commonwealth (*Histories*, 3.83).

sion seemed assured, and the state would not have to face, at least in the near future, the kind of chaos brought about by Nero's irresponsibility. The belief that the Princeps should also be the best man, not necessarily the son of the present ruler, was still current but was now in the background. Many clung to this theory but Vespasian in his blunt way told the Senate on one occasion that his sons would succeed him: "My sons will succeed me—or nobody will" (Suet., *Vesp*., 25). Titus was promoted rapidly to prominence as the designated heir. He held 7 consulships and had tribunician power conferred on him from A.D. 71. Domitian had behaved poorly—"playing the emperor's son"—according to Tacitus (*Hist*., 4.2), in the chaos of A.D. 69, and although he held the consulship in A.D. 73 and again in A.D. 80 he had never commanded troops in the field as had his brother Titus. When Titus died unexpectedly in A.D. 81, Domitian had to build up his image as a military figure by leading campaigns against the Germans on the Rhine and against a particularly stubborn enemy, the Dacians, in what is today Romania.

**Praetorian Guardsmen in Parade Uniform**

*The Praetorians thought of themselves as emperor-makers but the real power to make emperors lay with the frontier legions as the civil war of A.D. 69 proved.*

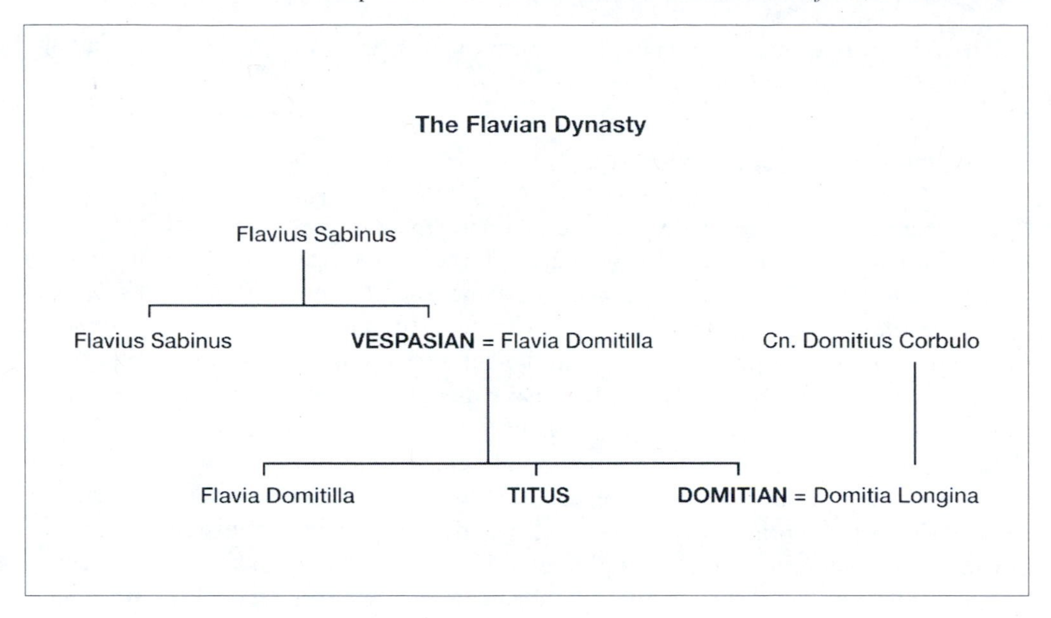


## Legitimation: Legal Aspects of the Succession

Although mostly a formality, every emperor's position rested upon investiture by the Senate. Generally either reigning emperors designated their successors or the choice was made by the winning army in a civil war. Nevertheless, action by the Senate was accepted as an essential part of the designation and legitimation of a new ruler. Prior to the Flavian period the process of conferring power on a new emperor may well have been spread over time and required a number of different decrees, but a law passed in late A.D. 69 ( the *lex de imperio Vespasiani*) made the powers of the Princeps a matter of legal statute. After that date, when the Senate and People ratified the choice of a new Princeps they not only endorsed the individual but conferred on him specific legal powers such as *imperium*, tribunician power, the right to make treaties, to call the Senate into session, and so on. Other prerogatives such as the name of *imperator* and the office of *Pontifex Maximus* may also have been included in this omnibus grant of power.

Augustus resisted this kind of institutionalization of the Principate for reasons that were valid in his time, but the assumption of imperial powers by successive emperors had become so firmly entrenched in tradition that they had acquired the force of law. The fact that Vespasian lacked the kind of *auctoritas* that his Julio-Claudian predecessors possessed as a kind of birthright may have had something to do with the passage of the law. The point is illustrated in an anecdote from Tacitus. When Nero ordered the Praetorian Prefect Burrus to send Praetorians to kill his mother Agrippina, the prefect replied that he could not vouch for their obedience. Their loyalty, he said "is to the whole house of the Caesars, not to Nero alone" (Annals, 14.7). The Flavians could make no such claims to the greatness of a family name and the *auctoritas* it enshrined. The *lex de imperio* of A.D. 69 recognized the sober reality that emperors could be made in places other than Rome and by powers other than the Senate and People of Rome. They might also come from different social strata. By the third century emperors were brazen enough to usurp titles without waiting for senatorial approval as Dio Cassius complained (63.29).

## The Administration of the Flavians

Many senators had perished under the trials of Nero and in the recent civil wars. Their number had shrunk from around 600 to about 200. The need to bring the Senate up to strength gave Vespasian and his son Titus, who with his father shared a join censorship in A.D. 73 to 74, an opportunity to create what amounted to a new party and a new aristocracy. New senators were appointed, especially men from the equestrian order and from the provinces. Northern Italy (Cisalpine Gaul) supplied many as did the province of Narbo (southern France) and Baetica (southern Spain). Tacitus came probably from Narbo in southern France. Pliny the Younger, another important senator and literary figure, came from Comum in the Po valley. Specialization in the *cursus honorum* was recognized so that men who had experience principally in civilian life and in municipal administration might be advanced to senatorial rank. Examples of this were two later emperors, Nerva and Antoninus Pius. Likewise men whose special talents lay on the military side of things such as Trajan and Hadrian, also later emperors, would not be held back. Vespasian was active also in extending grants of citizenship and the Latin right, a kind of halfway stage to citizenship, to various individuals and communities in the Empire. Spain was the most noticeable beneficiary. During this period the Latin right was extended to all of Spain. The *ius Latii*, as it was called, conferred Roman citizenship on the magistrates of local cities and conferred Latin municipal status on their communities. Since Claudius, the permanent departments in Rome, such as finance and correspondence, had been in the hands of freedmen, but these were now transferred to the care of equestrians—the first step in the creation of a civil service outside the traditional framework of the Senate.

## Campaigns of the Flavian Emperors

A considerable amount of repair needed to be done in the provinces. Despite the capture of Jerusalem in A.D. 70 the war continued for another five years. The great palace fortress of Herod at Masada fell in A.D. 73 after years of siege. The fall of Jerusalem allowed Vespasian to celebrate a 30-day triumph advertising the restoration by the Flavians of order in the Roman world. To exhibit the booty he built the Temple of Peace on land reclaimed from Nero's Golden House.

With the departure of the Rhine legions for Rome in support of Vitellius, a nationalist revolt broke out in northeastern Gaul. It was led by two Roman citizens, Gaius Julius Civilis, a Batavian (modern Netherlands) chieftain, and Julius Classicus. Both leaders were prominent in their own communities and officers in the Roman army as commanders of their own auxiliary troops stationed in that area. Classicus, for example, commanded a cavalry wing recrutied from among his own tribe, the Treveri. Together they attempted to create a Gallic empire with some assistance from German tribes from across the Rhine. They forced captured Roman soldiers to swear allegiance to an *imperium Gallicum*. The revolt was quickly

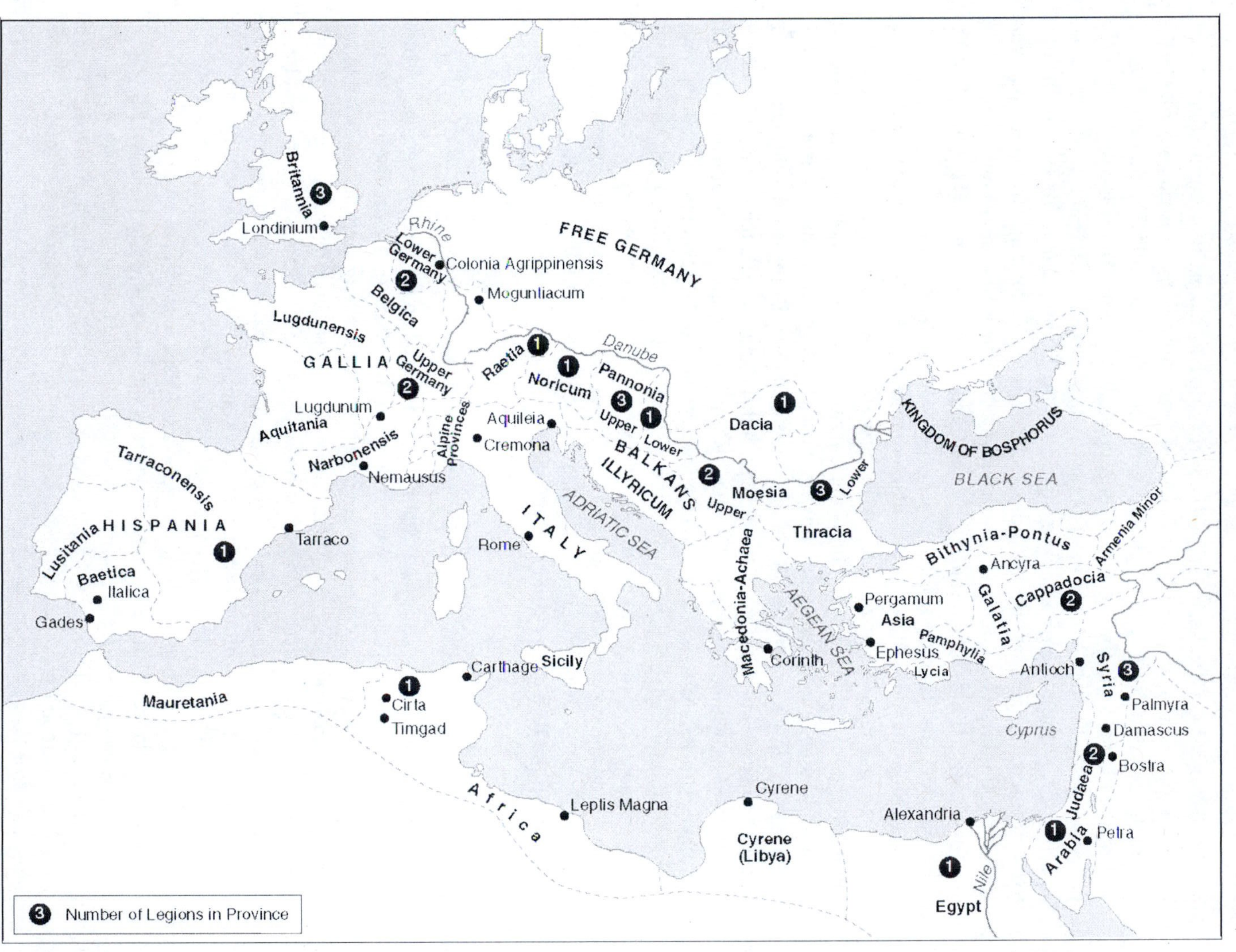


The Provinces and Legions of the Roman Empire at the Time of Marcus Aurelius

put down by Petilius Cerialis, but its outbreak revealed the danger of using auxiliary forces in the same areas from which they came. One of the reforms of the Flavian emperors was to ensure that auxiliaries served in regions other than their homelands. Another reform initiated by the Flavians was the breakup of large concentrations of troops, such as the eight legions that served in the Rhine area. The new policy spread legions and their supporting auxiliary troops more evenly along the frontiers of the Empire. An important modification to the northern frontiers was the creation of a *limes*, a road behind an earthen rampart with forts at regular intervals, connecting the headwaters of the Rhine and Danube. The cutting and fortification of this road through the forests expedited and improved communications between Rhine and Danube armies.

Under Domitian the conquest of Britain continued under the competent leadership of Julius Agricola, father-in-law of Tacitus. In the east, fear of the Parthians led to an increase in the number of legions in Syria. In all these frontier provinces a considerable amount of attention was paid to infrastructure investment in the form of roads, bridges and camps. The first emperor to campaign in person since Claudius, Domitian fought successfully against the German Chatti in the Rhine area, but the main challenge of the period came from the lower Danube, where the Dacian kingdom of Decebalus had begun to expand into Roman territory in Moesia. Domitian campaigned successfully there in A.D. 89, but pressure in Pannonia from the Iazyges, an Iranian-speaking tribal people, forced him to make peace with Decebalus and shift emphasis to the west. After the loss of a legion in A.D. 92 the invasion was contained. This period saw the beginning of the barbarian pressures on the northern frontiers, which were to continue for centuries until Rome's defenses finally crumbled in the fifth century and the western Empire came to an end.

## Relations with the Senate

The Flavian dynasty that Vespasian established was based on the rural bourgeoisie of Italy, and thus it was in marked contrast to the aristocratic and eccentric Julio-Claudians who had ruled up to the time of Nero. The new emperor's forbears belonged to an equestrian family that engaged in tax collecting. Vespasian himself had made his career in the army. He was probably appointed commander in Judaea by Nero on the assumption—wrong as it turned out—that a man of such modest background would not be likely to betray him. Because of this background the new rulers were regarded by some members of the elite as provincial intruders. The emperor found himself patronized by some of the old senators, such as Helvidius Priscus who offered advice on the assumption that Vespasian was not up to the job.

The tone of the new regime was one of modesty, simplicity, and strict adherence to the old ways. Vespasian seemed ideally placed to be a new Augustus, the restorer of peace after a period of bitter civil war. There was a fair amount of truth to that assessment. Actium had been a decisive moment in Roman history, and Rome was lucky to find an Augustus who, like the future emperor Vespasian, was of equestrian background. Some of Vespasian's coins depict him as the founder of a new Rome, another Romulus, but others stress continuity with the past, emphasizing traditional slogans such as Peace, Security, Fortune, Victory. Dynastic references were stressed to build up confidence in the new regime's stability and continuity.

| **Chronology: The Flavians** | |
|---|---|
| Vespasian | A.D. 69–79 |
| Titus | A.D. 79–81 |
| Domitian | A.D. 81–96 |

Titus succeeded to the throne when his father Vespasian died of a fever in 79, but he died suddenly before any clear judgment could be made of him. He was unmarried at his death in A.D. 81, and Domitian had already been designated his heir. Domitian's reputation is refracted through the lens of a hostile senatorial tradition found in the writings of Tacitus, Pliny the Younger and to a somewhat lesser extent in Suetonius' biography of the emperor. Domitian had little patience with the kind of respectful handling that the elite had come to expect as their due since the time of Augustus. He had an authoritarian understanding of his role as Princeps and did little to conceal it. He preferred to be addressed as "Lord and God" (*dominus et deus*) and began a letter, which was intended for general circulation, with the words "Our Lord and God orders you to do this" (Suet., *Dom*., 13). His father, too, had been authoritarian, but he was shielded from much of senatorial resentment because of his personal modest manner and the recognition that he had saved Rome from chaos as well as adroitly managing the consequences of the catastrophes of A.D. 69.

If Domitian was neglectful of the kind of care the touchy senators expected, he had no misunderstanding whatsoever of the importance of the army or the people. The people were entertained by frequent banquets and spectacles, and the recently completed Colosseum

**The Flavian Amphitheater or the Colosseum**

*The Colosseum, the largest amphitheater in the Roman world could hold up to 50,000 spectators. Audiences assembled outside the amphitheater in an area marked by bollards. Their tickets directed the spectators to one of 79 arcades, which admitted them by means of a series of elaborate staircases to the auditorium.*

amphitheater was put to good use. He knew the army had to be kept busy, successful, and well paid. He raised the pay of the legionaries by a third to 1,200 sesterces and proved himself a successful leader in campaigns on the Rhine and Danube against serious enemies. When Antonius Saturninus, a legate in Upper Germany, attempted to lead a rebellion he found little support among the troops. It was easily put down by the governor of Lower Germany, the future emperor Upius Trajanus. Thereafter, however, Domitian became increasingly suspicious, verging on paranoia, and a reign of terror descended on Rome. Domitian imagined plots everywhere, complaining "that all emperors necessarily lead miserable lives because they cannot convince people that plots against them are real until one actually succeeds" (Suet., *Dom*., 21). Real and imagined traitors were put on trial, and as always the Senate obliged with the requisite sentences of death. The purge of one of the Praetorian prefects and other administrators panicked others into a real plot. The following year Domitian was killed in the palace by conspirators, among whom may have been his wife Domitia, daughter of Nero's great general, Domitius Corbulo and the two Praetorian prefects.

For some senators looking back on the Flavian dynasty it was a time of restoration; for others it was, at least under Domitian, a period of the worst kind of tyranny. Certainly Tacitus the historian and Pliny the Younger looked back on these years as a time of humiliation and terror. Nevertheless, the consensus Augustus established remained as the foundation of the Principate. Whether this consensus could survive serious external threats to the Empire or extended civil wars was yet to be seen.

## 3. THE ADOPTED EMPERORS

### *Nerva A.D. 96–98*

Domitian's successor was the elderly senator M. Cocceius Nerva, a descendant of one of the few surviving noble families that could still trace its ancestry back to the Republic. His choice by the Senate occurred with such swiftness after Domitian's murder that collusion between Nerva, senators, and the assassins seems likely. Domitian's memory was condemned (*damnatio memoriae*). His statues were ordered destroyed and his name erased from official monuments. The Senate's choice did not sit well with the military, with whom Domitian had campaigned for many years. Restive generals and an unruly Praetorian Guard frightened the childless Nerva into adopting as his son the commander of the Rhine army, Ulpius Traianus (Trajan), by way of insurance against a coup. The move, fortunately, forestalled a repetition of the unhappy events of A.D. 69 when the Rhine legions had been among the main instigators of rebellion.

Trajan was a native of Italica in Spain, the descendant of Italian settlers in that region. He was Rome's first, but by no means last, emperor of provincial origins. Trajan's father commanded a legion under Vespasian during the Jewish War and was governor of Syria in the 70s. The future emperor served with his father in Syria and afterwards commanded a legion in Spain. He was appointed consul by Domitian in A.D. 91, and Nerva made him governor of Upper Germany in A.D. 97.

Nerva's adoption of Trajan accidentally revived the principle favored by the Senate that the current Princeps should select his successor not from his immediate family but from the best candidates for the position, who were all, naturally, senators. For the next 97 years this method of selecting the new emperor was adhered to until the reign of Marcus Aurelius, an emperor who actually had a natural son. Merit, as we shall see, rarely entered into the equation. Yet for nearly a century the dangers of assassination and civil war were avoided and the Empire entered into a period thought of by ancient and modern commentators as a Golden Age.

## Trajan A.D. 98–117

After a short reign, Nerva died and was succeeded by Trajan. Trajan was fortunate to have trusted friends, among them a fellow Spaniard, Licinius Sura, an able general and councilor. He persuaded Trajan to conciliate the Senate and pass himself off as an Augustan-style Princeps. In contrast to the despotic and arrogant Domitian who wished to be addressed as *dominus et deus*, Lord and God, Trajan let it be known he was satisfied with *optimus princeps,* Best First Man. Nevertheless, Pliny the Younger responded with a fawning panegyric to the emperor. Ever circumspect, Tacitus, who once considered continuing his history of the Flavians to include Nerva and Trajan, thought better of it and switched to chronicling the more distant and therefore safer Julio-Claudians. Despite the benevolent appearance of the new regime, the prudent Tacitus recognized that Trajan's power was every bit as absolute as Domitian's, under whom he and other senators had been forced to collaborate in the disposal of supposed enemies of the state. Trajan's relations with the Senate were good, but Pliny's letters reveal a Senate incapable of collective action. When the senators received the privilege of a secret ballot for their deliberations from the emperor some could not restrain themselves from writing witticisms and obscenities on their ballots (Pliny, *Letters*, 3.20/4.25).

THE CONQUEST OF DACIA Trajan was first and foremost a military man. He was glad to inherit Domitian's wars against the troublesome Dacians—although it took him several campaigns and the building of a huge, 60-foot-wide bridge built on 20 piers across the Danube as well as a canal to get around the problems of navigation posed by the notorious Iron Gorge, to accomplish the job. Decebalus, who had outlasted several emperors, was finally defeated in A.D. 106 and committed suicide. His capital, Sarmizegethusa, was occupied and turned into a Roman colony with the name of Ulpia Traiana. Unfortunately, only a few words of Trajan's own account of the wars survive, but one of Rome's greatest surviving monuments, Trajan's column, displays a pictorial account of the war in 155 segments. The column originally formed part of a library and basilica complex, which allowed viewers to see the carvings close up from several galleries. The basilica itself was the focal point of a magnificent forum, the largest in Rome, now a depressing ruin. Two centuries later the emperor Constantius visited Rome and was overwhelmed by the magnificence of Trajan's forum.

### The Problem of "Ruling Men Who Cannot Bear Either Absolute Slavery or Absolute Freedom"

*The following speech of the emperor Galba gives the reasons for the preference for adoption among the elite as a means of securing the best candidate for emperor. The speech is reported by Tacitus. It was given at the adoption of Piso by Galba in A.D. 69.*

If our immense empire could stand by itself and keep its balance without a ruler I would not be embarrassed to return the government to a republic. As it is we have reached a point where my old age can confer no greater benefit on the Roman people than a good successor.... Under Tiberius, Gaius, Claudius we were the legacy, as it were, of a single family so that the adoption of an emperor at this point in time will seem to be a kind of freedom. The dynasty of the Julii and the Claudii has come to an end and adoption will find the best successor. To be born and bred of emperors is a matter of accident—and is valued accordingly. But in adoption unclouded judgment is involved. ... The most practical and fastest method of deciding between good and bad policies is to imagine what you would or not approve under another emperor. Rome is not like one of those nations that are ruled despotically, where there is a distinct ruling family and everyone else is a slave. You [*Piso*] have to rule over men who cannot bear either absolute slavery or absolute freedom (*Histories*, 1.16).

As a result of the Dacian war the legions on the Rhine were reduced from seven to four, and those on the Danube rose to 12. The war made little strategic sense and left the Empire with a vulnerable salient north of the Danube, exposed to attack on three sides and over time necessitated a disproportionate legionary presence. With more sense Arabia Petraea ("Rocky Arabia") was carved out of the Negev desert as a province in A.D. 106, and the string of desert oasis cities from Palmyra in the north, through Damascus and Bostra to Petra in the south, entered into a period of great prosperity as their ruins, still impressive to the present, attest. Militarily less successful than the Dacian campaign was Trajan's attempt to occupy the buffer state of Armenia and to extend the Empire beyond the Euphrates to the Tigris. After initial successes and the capture of Ctesiphon, the Parthian capital, a major revolt in his rear in northern Mesopotamia forced him to retreat.

Contributing to the problems of Trajan's Mesopotamian campaign was a revolt of the Jews of Egypt, Cyrenaica (modern Libya), Judaea, and Cyprus that began in A.D. 115. It seems to have begun in Egypt where tensions between Greek and Jewish communities existed as far back as the time of Augustus. In Cyrenaica an insurgent was proclaimed King of the Jews, suggesting that the revolt, at least there, had a messianic quality to it. There were massacres on both sides, and it is thought that upwards of a million people perished. Prosperous Cyrenaica never recovered.

**Reconstruction of Trajan's Forum**

*Ammianus Marcellinus, a native of Antioch in Syria, lived in Rome for many years. It was his opinion that the Forum of Trajan was "the most exquisite structure under the canopy of heaven, which even the gods admired." Most of it collapsed in an earthquake in the early Middle Ages and it was used as a quarry by the people of Rome for their houses, palaces, and churches.*

## Hadrian A.D. 117–138 and Antoninus A.D. 138–161

A TRICKY SUCCESSION Retreating from Mesopotamia, Trajan arrived in Antioch, where he had a stroke. He continued his journey, hoping to reach Rome, but died en route in Cilicia (A.D. 117). No heir had been designated even though Trajan and his wife Plotina had no children. A likely successor was Hadrian, Trajan's cousin and ward, who was married to Sabina, Trajan's grandniece. Hadrian had the support of Trajan's wife Plotina, was popular with the troops, and at the time was advantageously placed as governor of Syria. He was not, however, popular with the faction among the generals favoring Trajan's expansionist policies. One of the foremost of these was Lusius Quietus, a Moor (i.e., a Berber) from Mauretania in north Africa who had served Trajan well in the Dacian and Mesopotamian wars with his Moorish cavalry (they appear on Trajan's column). Plotina, however, had the advantage of proximity to the emperor and plotted with the Praetorian Prefect Attianus to conceal the death of Trajan until the favored Hadrian could be summoned from nearby Syria. The story was given out that Trajan had adopted Hadrian on his deathbed. It naturally aroused suspicions, but Hadrian had the all-important support of the Syrian legions. A few years after his accession to power, Hadrian had Quietus removed from his command of the Moors, and with three other senators he was executed for a supposed conspiracy against the

**Trajan and His Wife Plotina**

*Although she had no children, the forceful Plotina engineered a peaceful succession by stage-managing Hadrian's adoption at Trajan's death.*

emperor. Hadrian chose not to renew the war against the Parthians and abandoned Trajan's conquests in Mesopotamia. He also seems to have thought of abandoning Dacia but was persuaded that Roman settlement there was too far advanced to be reversed.

With the execution of Quietus and the other consulars who had been part of Trajan's circle, Hadrian's relations with the Senate started out poorly. To mollify this important body Hadrian promised that henceforth senators would be judged only by their senatorial peers. He promoted talented members of the equestrian order to senatorial rank as had his predecessors so that gradually the distinction between the two orders was eroded. Suetonius the biographer and a protégé of Pliny is an example of this process.

HADRIAN'S CULTURAL INTERESTS Hadrian was a true lover of all things Greek. He enjoyed debating with sophists, and he wrote poetry, painted, and designed buildings. He ordered the reconstruction of the Pantheon, producing in the process one of the gems of Roman architecture in terms of its innovative design and the use of concrete. The span of its dome is larger than the dome of St. Peter's and its design enabled it to withstand the earthquakes that brought down much of the Colosseum and other Roman landmarks. Hadrian's innovative spirit can also be seen in his villa at Tivoli and in the Temple of Venus and Roma in the Forum, which he designed.

HADRIAN'S TRAVELS In contrast to Trajan, Hadrian had no intention of expanding the boundaries of the Empire but was content to ensure that the armies were up to the job of defending it effectively. To that end Hadrian spent the years A.D. 120–131 touring the Empire, often making unannounced visits to remote outposts, checking account books, observing and participating in military exercises. These tours were not easy, even for an emperor. Between A.D. 121 and 125 he visited Britain, Spain, Gaul, Germany, Raetia, and Noricum (parts of modern Bavaria, Switzerland, Austria) in Europe, and Mauretania (Morocco and Algeria), Africa (Tunisia), and Cyrene (Libya) in Africa. While in Britain he launched the building of the 80-mile long wall that bears his name, and in Upper Germany he had palisades erected, making this Rome's first fixed, artificial frontier. Between A.D. 125 and 131 he was in Greece, Asia Minor, and Africa, but mostly in the east where he visited Syria, Phoenicia, Palestine, Arabia, and Egypt. One of his tours unfortunately led to a catastrophe for the inhabitants of the province he was visiting. After seeing the desolate state of Jerusalem he announced plans to rebuild the city and settle a veteran colony there. A temple to Jupiter was to be erected on the site of the Second Temple. A convinced and chauvinistic Hellenist, he forbade circumcision. Neither decision may have been intended as provocations, but that is exactly what they were. Soon after the emperor left Judaea a messianic figure by the name Simeon Bar

**The Pantheon**

*If the design of the Pantheon looks familiar it is because it is one of the most copied architectural forms for buildings of all sorts. In the U.S. (among many) there is Jefferson's home at Monticello, the library at the University of Virginia and the beautiful rotunda in the National Gallery of Art. In Europe innumerable churches, opera houses, museums, libraries, university buildings, palaces, and private homes enshrine the design of the Pantheon in one form or another.*

Kochba ("Son of a Star") rallied the Jews, and a war waged with great ferocity by both sides resulted. The revolt may have begun in A.D. 131–132, and when it ended in 135 the Jewish population of Palestine was greatly reduced and Jews were forbidden to enter Jerusalem. Dio Cassius claims that nearly 600,000 rebels perished. Judaea was renamed Syria Palaestina.

Hadrian's decision to refound Jerusalem was part of a more general policy to foster urban life throughout the Empire. In the Danube valley he encouraged the reconstruction of old cities and the founding of new ones with the aim of creating a prosperous, settled hinterland for the defense line of the Danube. In Africa he encouraged oil production on reclaimed land. Elsewhere he founded new cities or embellished old ones with baths, theaters, temples, and aqueducts. The aqueducts he built for Carthage had a combined length of over 130 miles and supplied the city with nearly 10 million gallons of water per day.

ANTONINUS PIUS One of Hadrian's most important contributions to Roman history was his success in negotiating not just the smooth transition to his successor, but also to his successor's successor. His first choice of a successor, Lucius Ceionius Commodus, who took the name of Lucius Aelius Caesar, died prematurely. Shortly afterwards he adopted a respected, wealthy but unambitious senator of Gallic origin named Antoninus on condition that Antoninus, who was childless, adopt a young but impressive youth by the name of Marcus Annius Verus (later Marcus Aurelius) and Lucius Ceionius Commodus, the son of the recently deceased Aelius. On his death Hadrian was succeeded smoothly by Antoninus. The Senate, still disliking Hadrian, debated whether to deify him or not and annul his acts, but the new emperor persuaded them to think otherwise, thus earning the title "Pius," and so he is known to us as Antoninus Pius.

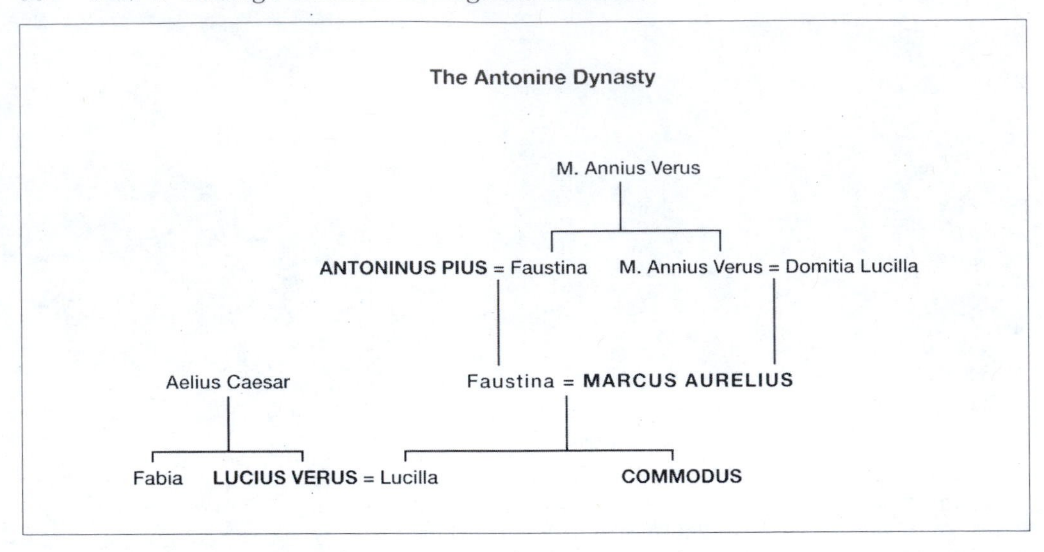


Antoninus never had to leave Rome, and nothing remarkable happened during his 23 years of rule. He was content to live the life of a Roman aristocrat, attending the Senate, dining with friends, and working on his correspondence. The rhetorician Aelius Aristides says with exaggeration: "The emperor can stay quietly where he is and rule the whole world by letters which arrive at their destination almost as soon as they are written" (*To Rome*, 33).[2] Antoninus was no doubt able to lead this civilized existence because he was the beneficiary of Trajan's aggressive military policies and Hadrian's care for the army. There were no major wars during his reign. The emperor had excellent relations with the Senate. "His manner was never harsh or merciless or blustering.... All business was nicely calculated and divided into its times as by a leisured man. Every item was handled in a calm, orderly, vigorous and consistent manner" (Marcus Aurelius, *Meditations*, 1.16). There were no significant family problems in the imperial household, and when he died after a long, dull, and peaceful reign, he was succeeded by Marcus Aurelius as Hadrian had planned. Marcus' reign, however, was anything but peaceful or dull.

## Marcus Aurelius A.D. 161–180 and Commodus A.D. 180–192

Marcus Aurelius' father died at an early age, and the young man was raised by his grandfather, a native of southern Spain and a relative of Hadrian. He received an excellent education in Greek and Latin. Many of the letters between Marcus and one of his tutors, Fronto, survive. Marcus was serious minded and from his youth showed an inclination towards philosophy, particularly Stoicism and Epicureanism. His *Meditations,* a kind of philosophic diary written in Greek while campaigning on the frontiers, reflect a mix of these philosophies together with a dose of Platonism.

[2]Important messages could be relayed at a rate of 160 miles a day, but the normal transmission of news was slow. The median time it took to get the news of an emperor's death from Rome to Egypt was 52 days, R. Duncan Jones, *Structure and Scale in the Roman Economy* (Cambridge, 1990, 8–9).

**Marcus Aurelius**

*When a new emperor acceded to the throne, images of him were sent from Rome or some provincial capital to other cities of the Empire. This repoussé gold bust of Marcus Aurelius was found in 1939 in the city of Aventicum (mod. Avenches) in what is today Switzerland. Only two other gold busts of emperors survive. It was through works of art such as this that Greco-Roman art was introduced to Europe north of the Alps.*

From childhood Marcus was a favorite of Hadrian and at age 15 was betrothed to the daughter of Lucius Aelius Caesar, Hadrian's first choice for his successor. This betrothal ended when Aelius died, and on Hadrian's death Marcus was betrothed to Antoninus' daughter, Faustina. He was only 17 when adopted by Antoninus Pius in A.D. 138. At 19 he was made consul for the first time, and he was 25 when he received tribunician power and proconsular *imperium* (A.D. 146). On Antoninus' death he insisted that his adoptive brother, Lucius Ceionius Commodus, renamed Lucius Aurelius Verus, serve with him as co-Augustus or co-regent, a first in Roman imperial history. Marcus as *Pontifex Maximus*, and the possessor of greater *auctoritas*, was the senior partner.

CAMPAIGNS AGAINST THE GERMANS Almost immediately the joint emperors were faced with a series of crises in Britain, Germany, along the Danube, and most seriously in the east when in A.D. 162 the Parthians seized Armenia. Marcus sent his co-Augustus Verus to lead the counter-attack in the east, accompanied by an experienced staff. Verus stayed in Antioch while his generals waged war, recovering first Armenia and then defeating the Parthians in Mesopotamia. Parthia's principal Mesopotamian cities, Seleuceia and Ctesiphon, were seized, and the palace of the Parthian kings at Ctesiphon, was razed to the ground (Dio Cassius, 71.2). The victorious armies returned, however, infected with a highly communicable disease that eventually spread throughout the Empire causing great loss of life and economic damage. Despite their good health practices, the disease seems to have done considerable damage to the legions. The virulence of the disease may have been generated in part as a consequence of the spectacular growth of cities during the Principate. Ironically, prosperity contributed to undermining Rome's Golden Age.

The eastern campaign had barely ended when assaults along the Danube frontier, weakened by the sending of three legions to the east, began. Two new legions were raised and Marcus auctioned off imperial property to pay for the campaign. Both emperors campaigned in A.D. 168, but the following year Verus died and Marcus spent the next 11 years alone in almost continual warfare on the Danube. In the worst crisis since the invasion of the Cimbri and Teutons at the end of the second century B.C. the Germanic Marcomanni and Quadi crossed the Alps and besieged Aquileia in northern Italy in A.D. 170. They were soon driven out, but more invaders found their way as far south as Athens in Greece, while Spain was ravaged by

Moors who crossed over from north Africa. From A.D. 170 to 174 Marcus campaigned against the Marcomanni and Quadi carrying the war successfully into the invaders' own territory north of the Danube. Captives from the wars were settled in Roman territory in the Danube valley and possibly also in Italy to supplement populations thinned by the plague. In A.D. 175 Marcus warred against the Sarmatian Iazyges in the Hungarian plain but was forced to give up the campaign when the governor of Syria, Avidius Cassius, apparently hearing and believing a rumor that Marcus was dead, revolted. After a few months the revolt collapsed, but Marcus felt the need to tour the east in person. Perhaps to end the uncertainty about the succession he named his son Commodus as Augustus in A.D. 177. In the following years Marcus and Commodus continued to campaign successfully on the Danube.

PROBLEMS WITH THE SUCCESSION Marcus and Faustina had spectacularly bad luck in the survival rate of their male offspring. Of the possibly 15 children they had Commodus was the sole surviving son. He was only 16 when appointed Augustus and 19 when he inherited power on his father's death in Vienna in A.D. 180. Unfortunately for Rome Commodus was no Octavian who also began his career at 19. Instead of evolving Commodus sank. For all his other accomplishments Marcus failed in one of the most important tasks of an emperor, the appointment and education of a suitable heir apparent. Commodus quickly made peace with his German adversaries, abandoned his father's conquests, and returned to Rome where he celebrated a triumph. Given the poverty of our sources it is hard to know whether or not this was in accordance with Marcus' plans. Perhaps the frontiers had been sufficiently stabilized by Marcus' and his armies' heroic efforts in the previous decades so that it was now possible to retrench and give the Empire a chance to recover.

COMMODUS The first emperor to have been brought up in the palace since Nero, Commodus almost immediately demonstrated what a poor environment that place was for raising children. Tall and athletic, he rejected his father's steely intellectuality and dedication to the laborious work of running an empire. Rather than be an emperor, Commodus wanted to be the impresario of the games at Rome. He also wanted to be an active participant—a star in fact—in them. A century earlier Nero had appalled the elite and charmed the mob with his artistic performances and chariot racing, but Commodus outdid his predecessor. For 12 years he entertained audiences with exhibitions of skillful shooting of wild beasts and performances as a gladiator in the arena. Among the thousands of animals he killed were elephants and ostriches. There was more than a little method in the emperor's madness. Audiences could identify with his impersonation of Hercules, the slayer of monsters, human and otherwise, that threatened human civilization. The emperor, as his viewers recognized, was first and foremost the sustainer of the thin veneer of order and civility that overlay Roman society. Despite what the elite thought, the emperor was the people's *deus et dominus*—God and Lord. They wanted him to be their semi-divine hero Hercules.

Commodus provided more indications of the progression of his insanity when he began to give himself new names and then went on to reform the calendar in accordance with these names. It was not sufficient for him to change the names of a few months as had been the case when Quintilis and Sextilis were renamed July and August in honor of Julius Caesar and Augustus respectively. August became Commodus, September Hercules, October Invictus, and so on. A wholly new beginning had to be given to Rome. With senatorial approval Rome itself was to be renamed *Colonia Commodiana*, and Romans were to become Commodians. Many senators and other members of the elite died in a number of futile, poorly organized conspiracies. As Commodus sank deeper into his lunatic role-playing, however, his actions began to impinge on the safety of the immediate members of the imperial household, who were best positioned to generate an effective end to his misrule. The plot that finally succeeded was supported by the Praetorian Prefects, the emperor's favorite mistress Marcia, and various trusted palace attendants. When poison failed to kill the athletic emperor, his personal trainer was brought in to finish the job by strangling him. As with the murder of Domitian, the Senate intervened to make one of its own members emperor, incensing the Praetorian Guards who, after disposing of the Senate's choice, had someone more to their liking installed as emperor. In a repetition of A.D. 69 the frontier armies objected to the Praetorians' choice, and within months a legionary general was seated on Rome's imperial throne.

**Commodus**

# Part Five

## The Roman Empire: What Held it Together?

### 1. INTRODUCTION

The natural tendency of the area we call the Roman Empire was toward anarchy. It had neither geographical nor cultural unity. It was a gigantic mosaic of languages, cultures, and people then as it is now. Some of the peoples of the Empire had traditions of literacy and urbanization going back 3000 years before Rome appeared on the scene. In other regions people clung to their ancient, Iron Age, oral cultures and resisted urbanization as an intolerable infringement on their freedoms. There was never a time before Rome when Britain and Egypt, Tunisia and Austria, and France and Syria were unified under a single political system. After the collapse of Rome these regions were never subsequently united.

If we include the Mediterranean Sea, the geographic extent of the Roman Empire at its height was only slightly less than that of the continental United States. Roman administrators and troops were thinly spread over these regions, and the task of visiting and supervising them was close to overwhelming. Throughout its history, time and distance were the secret enemies of the Roman peace. Despite the high quality of its 53,000 miles of road, the transportation network and the general economy of the Empire remained that of an underdeveloped country. In the Late Empire a 1200 pound wagonload of wheat doubled its price over a journey of 300 miles. The great historian Edward Gibbon was right when he said that the story of the fall of the Empire was "simple and obvious" and that therefore "instead of

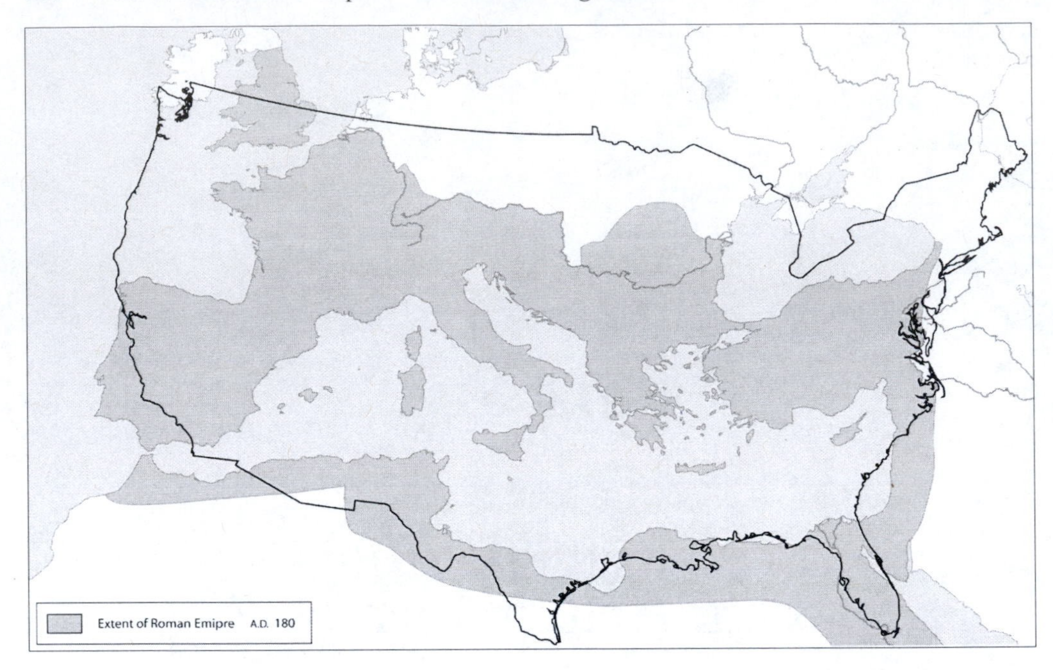


inquiring why the Roman Empire was destroyed, we should rather be surprised that it had subsisted so long."[1]

## The Cement of Empire

The cement that held the Empire together for as long as it did was social, cultural, political, and military in character. Of these four elements, the military component was the most fundamental. On it rested the security of the Empire. Ultimately the fate of Rome depended on the ability of the army to intimidate or, at times, inspire, the inhabitants of the Empire and those outside it who might threaten it. The army in turn depended on the willingness of the people of the Empire to foot the bill for its expenses. It was a simple enough equation, amounting to a tacit understanding between the elites of the Empire and the imperial government that costs would not exceed benefits, or at least not for long periods of time. When they did, as began to happen in the third century A.D., the foundations of the Empire were shaken. This was particularly true in the west which was, compared to the east, less developed and more geographically exposed to barbarian invasions. Consequently, it had difficulty sustaining the increasing costs of defense. In the east the equation between costs and benefits was better maintained, and the Roman Empire survived there in some form for nearly 1000 years after it disappeared in the west.

Although the army was ultimately the bedrock of imperial rule, Rome did not govern by force alone. Far from it. Without the ability to build some kind of consensus among the heterogeneous and competing elites of the Empire, there was no way that the army could have ensured Roman overlordship for very long. Rome had neither a systematic ideology of em-

[1] *The Decline and Fall of the Roman Empire* (London, 1901), 4.161.

### The Case for the Roman Empire: Order or Chaos?

*Gibbon characterized the Empire as a "dreary prison." Realistically, however, what were the choices? As the following reading points out the alternative to Roman rule in the west at least was constant inter-tribal fighting and invasions from Germany and Britain. Tacitus puts the case for Roman imperial rule in the form of a blunt speech given by the Roman commander Cerialis to a number of Gallic tribes. They had recently revolted against Rome and were reconquered.*

*Cerialis called an assembly of the Treveri and Lingones and spoke as follows:*

> I am not one for words; instead I have always maintained the power of Rome by force of arms. But since words mean a great deal to you people, and you judge things to be good or evil not as they really are but as agitators say they are, I have a few things to say....
>
> Gaul always had its petty kingdoms and wars until you submitted to our power. Although often provoked, we have used the right of conquest to burden you only with the cost of keeping the peace. For peace among nations cannot be maintained without armies; armies cost money, and money can be raised only by taxation.
>
> We hold everything else in common. You often command our legions; you rule these and other provinces; you are not segregated or excluded by us. You benefit from good emperors though you live far away, while we who live close by, suffer from evil ones. Accept the extravagance and avarice of your masters just as you put up with bad harvests and floods and other natural disasters. There will be vices as long as there are men. But they are not eternal, and they are counterbalanced by better times....
>
> If the Romans are driven out—Heaven forbid!—what else can there be except wars among all these nations? Eight hundred years of the divine fortune of Rome and its discipline have produced this federal Empire and it cannot be pulled apart without the destruction of those attempting to do just this.
>
> You are in a most dangerous situation. You have gold and wealth— the main causes of war. Therefore, love and care for peace, and also love and care for that city in which victors and vanquished alike share on an equal basis. Learn the lessons of fortune for good or evil: Do not choose obstinacy and ruin in preference to submission and safety (Tacitus, *Histories*, 4.73–74).

pire nor any strong belief in the power of bureaucracies to govern. In the task of ruling the Romans used what they knew best, their own relatively open social system with its hierarchical organization of society based on wealth and public service. Personal patronage allowed connections to be established across class and cultural lines. Careers in the army and civil service encouraged the able and the ambitious of the Empire to rise to high office. At the local level Rome's key to success was its ability to involve the elites of the Empire in the basic day-to-day tasks of maintaining order and collecting taxes. Based on Rome's uniform socio-political system, members of the elite, whether they originated in Syria, Africa, or the Balkans were able to find membership in the club of clubs, the Roman Senate, and rise to the highest offices the Empire offered. Indeed, some of the most successful imperial dynasties, such as that of the Severans from Leptis Magna, an old Phoenician city in Libya, were not even from Italy, let alone from the old Roman heartland of Latium. The great dynasts of the late third century A.D. who saved Rome from ruin were from the Balkans.

Not all of the elements that held the Empire together were Roman inspired or engineered. Rome was fortunate in the absence of a strong sense of national identity among most of the peoples of the Empire. The one exception, the Jews of Judaea who rebelled against Roman rule in the first and second centuries A.D., were savagely put down. The Greeks possessed a common culture and language but lacked political unity or even the desire for a Greek national state. Most other peoples had a sense only of local or regional identity. Even in supposedly unified Italy many of its peoples remained outside the mainstream of imperial life, isolated by geography, poor communications, and preferences for ancient local cultures. From its predecessors Rome inherited a Mediterranean that possessed a well-developed, ancient urban culture. In Greek high culture, and its own Latin adaptations of it, Rome found an important force for uniting the disparate cultures and ethnicities of an otherwise culturally chaotic world.

# 15

# What Held the Empire Together: Institutional Factors

## 1. THE IMPERIAL OFFICE

The emperor who presided over the sprawling mass of the Roman Empire was no autocrat whose well-oiled machinery of government enabled him to rule despotically over docile subjects. Despite the claims of Hollywood, Roman emperors did not have the surveillance resources or the powers of a modern totalitarian regime at their disposal. The emperors claimed that power came to them from the Senate and the People of Rome. As late as the sixth century A.D. Pope Gregory the Great, nostalgically echoing this ideological belief, could say that the difference between barbarian kings and Roman emperors was that the latter were the lords of free men. Until the third century the people of Rome were called into session to ratify decisions of the Senate.

### The Power of the Emperor

It is true that the emperor was extremely powerful. He was the ultimate court of appeal. His decrees had the force of law. He was richest man in the Empire and its principal patron. He was the head of the Roman religion. From him flowed concessions, privileges, judgments, gifts, and appointments. Indeed, the maintenance of the emperor's role demanded a constant outflow of gifts. A senator who had uttered a treasonable remark begged the forgiveness of Augustus, but on receiving it he went on to ask for a substantial sum of money commenting, "Otherwise no one will believe I have been forgiven." Gifts like this helped sustain the Emperor and established an image of him as a generous person. For several days Caligula threw coins to the people from the roof of the Basilica Julia in the Forum. At games given by Nero, tokens were given "for different kinds of food, free grain handouts, clothes, gold, silver, gems, pearls, paintings, slaves, cattle and trained animals; and finally for ships, blocks of apartments and land" (Suetonius, *Nero*, 11). The emperor in turn expected gifts, especially from the rich in their wills and from the cities of the Empire in the form of gold crowns on his accession to power or after major victories.

The emperor was the commander-in-chief of the armies of the Empire. To him all the other generals swore allegiance and could be removed at his whim. Sometimes this was the fate of Rome's most successful commanders, such as Corbulo, who was ordered to commit suicide by the insecure Emperor Nero. On the other hand, with good reason, emperors always feared the power in the hands of their commanders and governors in far-off provinces. They constantly wondered what plots were being hatched against them, knowing how easily the soldiers of the legions could be swayed by charismatic personalities, not to say by promises of pay increases and bonuses. The emperor Domitian, who in fact fell to a plot, used to complain that no one took a ruler's worries about plots seriously until after one succeeded. Commodus, having survived one plot, fell to the machinations of another, which involved among others his mistress and his personal athletic trainer.

## Imperial Responsibilities

If the emperor's power was significant, his responsibilities were overwhelming. Any administration, ancient or modern, stands or falls by the qualities of its appointees, and it was the emperor's main job to find the right governors, legionary commanders, financial managers of imperial possessions, and key positions in the city administration of Rome itself.

The first and foremost responsibility of the emperor was the defense of the Empire against outside aggression and internal disorder. For this the army had to be maintained in constant readiness over thousands of miles of frontier. New recruits, armaments, and supplies had to be shipped to the farthest corners of the world in a regular, dependable fashion. Suitable officers from generals to centurions had to be selected, trained, and appointed—no easy task in an army of 350,000 to 400,000 men spread over 45 provinces. The military responsibilities alone would have taken all the time of an emperor, as in fact they did in times of invasion or civil war. Military responsibilities, however, were only part of the emperor's responsibilities. He had to maintain peace within the Empire as well as without, peace within his own family, peace with the Senate and with elites throughout the Empire, and peace with the ordinary people, especially of Rome and the cities of the Greek East.

In the Republic it was evident that the Senate was in control of foreign affairs even though governors had considerable freedom in their provinces. In the Empire the emperor, through his coins, statues, inscriptions, and the imperial cult, made it clear that he was in charge with the result that the people of the Empire, when dissatisfied with the treatment they received from local governors, city councils, and the like, felt they could turn to the emperor directly and personally for help. They did this by sending or sometimes delivering in person petitions, *libelli*, which the emperor in fact received, read, and replied to in a note at the bottom of the petition. Cities and villages sent delegations, but sometimes individuals sought the emperor out, such as did the fisherman from a small town in Africa who traveled to meet Augustus in 29 B.C. to seek relief from tribute. Sometimes, swamped by the mountains of correspondence, emperors delegated others to reply. Governors either at a loss for what to do in a particular case or covering themselves in case they made a mistake, sent letters asking emperors for advice. In irritation the emperor Trajan replied to a request from his governor Pliny in Bithynia for an architect: "You can have no lack of architects; every province has experienced and talented people. Don't assume it is easier to send to Rome for one" (*Letters*, 10.40).

## The Importance of the Imperial Image

Roman emperors inherited from Augustus a difficult set of relationships. The imperial office had a Janus-like quality well summed up by the philosopher Epictetus:

> No one fears the emperor himself—but they do fear death, exile, confiscation of their property, imprisonment or loss of rights. Nor does anyone love the emperor unless he is of unusual merit. But we do love wealth, a tribunate, a praetorship, or a consulate (*Diss*., 4.1.60 )

Emperors had to be affable and approachable while maintaining their dignity. In his own twisted way the emperor Caligula got one side of this Janus-like quality of the emperor right when he said: Let them hate me as long as they fear me. Maintaining the other side of their image, their benevolence, was more complicated.

Appearance—"face"—was always a central element of Roman political culture. Aristocrats of the Republic were exceedingly conscious of their status, not as we might think, because they were vain, as undoubtedly they were, but because their power—their social and political capital—depended on the image they conveyed. All the terms used in Latin to convey this sense of status—*dignitas*, *honos, gloria, auctoritas*, etc.—continued into the Empire and were inherited by the emperor in a disproportionately large way. As the Chief Aristocrat of Rome he had always to be conscious of his dignity. The emperor had to be friendly but not overly familiar with senators, equestrians, and other members of the elite. He had an image to maintain. But for an emperor the image was a lot larger and more complex than it was for even the most exalted of Roman aristocrats of the Republic.

TITLES AND THE MEDIA One of the best ways an emperor could burnish his image was by defeating foreign enemies, the more exotic and farther off the better. Even in the Republic generals advertised their success in putting down Rome's distant enemies by adding titles such as Africanus, Asiaticus, Creticus, and Macedonicus to their names. The emperors followed suit with Arabicus, Armenicus, Britannicus, Dacicus, Germanicus, Parthicus, and Sarmaticus. Augustus' *Res Gestae* contains a total of 55 geographical names, many appearing in Latin for the first time. Who knew—or cared—where Media or Scythia was as long as they were not nearby? Enemies with outlandish names such as Bastarnae and Sugambri (*RG*, 31–32) must surely live on the fringes of the inhabited world, clearly nowhere near Rome—and that was good. Emperors proclaimed their military victories and titles on triumphal arches throughout the Empire, on coins, medallions, statues, buildings, even on milestones. They were the Pacifiers of the World and the Expanders of the Empire.

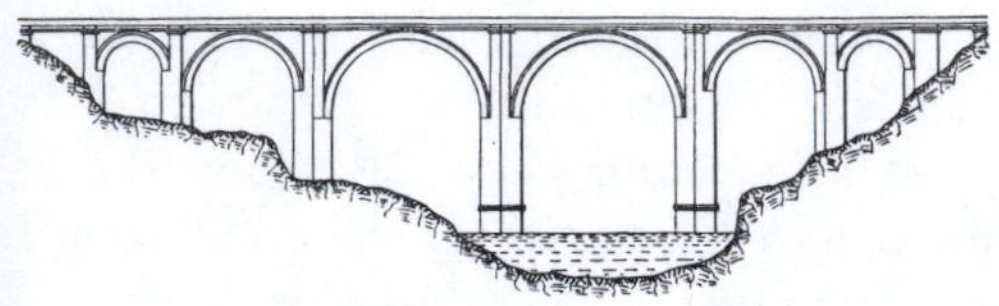

**Trajan's Bridge over the Tagus at Alcántara (Spain)**

*Great building projects such as bridges and aqueducts also conveyed messages of Roman power. The still-functioning bridge at Alcántara over the Tagus River was built by orders of the Emperor Trajan in* A.D. *104–106. The inscription on it reads: "A bridge that is to last through the ages" and so it has.*

Trajan was: *Optimus, Maximus, Sacratissimus* (Best, Greatest, Holiest). Antoninus Pius went one better: to Trajan's list he added "Of all Ages." One milestone has the following inscription to the third century emperor Caracalla, sounding like a parody of Rome: "To the Emperor Caesar Marcus Aurelius Severus Antoninus, Pious, Blessed, Augustus, Victor over Arabia, Victor over Adiabene, Greatest Victor over Parthia, Greatest Victor over Britain" (*CIL*, 13.9129).

Even in a world without newspapers, radio, or TV, let alone the Internet, the imperial message was successfully conveyed to the fringes of the Empire and beyond. Roman coins show up all over free Europe and as far away as India and Vietnam. These carefully contrived media-messages from the emperors were all the more effective at the time because there were few or no competing counter-messages of an equivalent quality, quantity, or ubiquity being propagated from any other source. In authoritarian states control of the media is all important to the regime's survival. Except in a few instances to be discussed in later chapters, the emperor's control of the Roman media went unchallenged. Even today the battered triumphal arches of the Roman world, the huge amphitheaters and theaters, the broken aqueducts, the inscriptions and vast quantities of coins, some of great beauty, convey what the emperors wanted to convey, namely, that Rome was unchallengeable.

THE NEED FOR VICTORY The army Tiberius inherited from Augustus was an army of professionals, bound not to their generals, but rather to their emperor by an oath of allegiance. There was, however, a lot more to the relationship between emperor and army than an oath. On the part of the emperor there had to be demonstrated competence or at least a manifest interest in the troops. Neither competence nor interest, unfortunately, could be inherited, though to be the son of a previous emperor was a good starting point. Troops were loyal to families.

**Pont du Gard**

*Some of the best examples of Roman hydraulic engineering are to be found in the provinces. The Pont du Gard in France is one such example. It was part of a 30-mile-long aqueduct to provide water to the city of Nemausus (mod. Nîmes) in southern France. Built entirely without mortar and having arches built to allow for the winds that howl down the valley of the Gard, the aqueduct is still in excellent condition. The water conduit at the top is six feet high and four feet wide. Guided tours allow tourists to walk through its 300 yard length.*

Tiberius had no need to establish his military credentials with the army when he stepped into Augustus' shoes. Later emperors, however, often did. Gaius had weak military experience and Claudius none at all. Nevertheless they understood full well that the image of military invincibility had to be maintained. The emperor had to be seen as having either advanced the boundaries of the Empire or having taken revenge for an injury (*iniuria*) inflicted by some unworthy neighbor or unruly subject who needed to be disciplined. For Augustus, recovering the lost standards from the Parthians was not strictly a military necessity but it was politically expedient. It was also inexpensive. Claudius' invasion of Britain was militarily unnecessary and ruinously expensive. Dio Cassius provides an anecdote regarding the Celtic British chief Caratacus who, after his capture, was brought to Rome and supposedly exclaimed when he saw the city, "Why do you, who have so much, covet our little tents?" (60.33). Yet, from a public-relations viewpoint the conquest of Britain was a spectacular success. Rome's legions had crossed mysterious Ocean and conquered a people who were, so far as anyone knew, at the ends of the earth. "There are no peoples beyond us," said the Britain chieftain Calgacus in Tacitus' reconstruction of his speech to his followers, "there is nothing past us but the waves and the rocks" (*Agricola* 30). Trajan's expansion of the Empire, the reduction of Dacia to a province, was not strictly a military necessity either, but it was essential to take revenge for the reverses inflicted by the Dacian king Decebalus on Roman arms under Domitian. Rome's reputation was at stake. Unlike the addition of Britain, the reduction of Dacia to a province surprisingly turned out to be a big financial success and thus another proof of the virtue and goodness of the emperor. Lest his success be forgotten, Trajan built his gigantic forum out of the loot of his victory.

THE POINT OF BOOTY There were other benefits to campaigns to expand the empire or put down rebellions. The procession of prisoners and booty from a distant frontier had multiple target audiences and aims. It spelled out the message that Rome would ruthlessly repress rebellion no matter what the cost. The passage of wretched prisoners, triumphant Roman armies, and piles of loot being transported to Rome through various provinces had the effect of reminding everyone en route who was in charge. The message to the gawking crowds who lined up to see the passage of Jewish slaves on their way to Rome in A.D. 70 was that Roman arms had triumphed somewhere—it did not really matter where. Finally, the arrival of the triumphal army with its booty and prisoners was a reminder to all of Rome—Senate and people alike—of the power of the army and its commander, the emperor. The Romans were very conscious of rituals and their power. A showy triumphal procession once or twice a generation would go a long way toward sustaining enthusiasm for and fear of Rome in the minds of provincials and Romans alike.

Recognizing that people have short memories, booty was deposited in key public places. Thus the standards recovered from the Parthians were put in the Temple of Mars Ultor and the booty from the victory in Judaea was lodged, ironically, in Vespasian's Temple of Peace. The candelabra from the sack of the temple in Jerusalem, carved on the triumphal arch of Titus, are still viewed by visitors as they enter the Roman Forum from the east. Not a temple in Rome was without some reminder of the power of Roman arms. Statuary drove home similar messages.

World-wide the iconography of conquest is remarkably consistent over the centuries. A favorite scene of conquest in pharaonic Egypt was that of the Egyptian king standing majestically with drawn bow in a chariot that rolls over the bodies of the dead. Assyrian victory friezes are particularly graphic in their portrayal of the destruction of towns, the impaling of leaders, and the parading of prisoners. To the chagrin of Washington commuters, heroic Civil War generals on prancing chargers clog the traffic on some of the city's busiest thoroughfares.

## 2. THE IMPERIAL ADMINISTRATION: CREATING A NEW POLITICAL CULTURE

Both Senate and equestrian elite had to find new ways of interacting with the reality of one-man rule initiated by Augustus. *Civilitas,* tact, was always the key. In many respects adjustment to the new political culture was hardest on the first generation of Romans after the civil wars. There were no existing norms or customs governing the relationship between senators, equestrians, and the new kind of Princeps Augustus clearly was. In the Republic there had always been senatorial *principes* or leaders to whom deference was due.

**Triumphant Emperors: Hadrian and Marcus Aurelius**

*The cultured Hadrian appears in many surviving statues as a grim-visaged general in full military dress with one massive foot placed on the head of a rather small barbarian. The equestrian statue of Marcus Aurelius originally showed his horse trampling a barbarian.*

**The Spoils of Jerusalem on the Arch of the Emperor Titus**

*The capture of Jerusalem in A.D. 70 by Titus, son of the emperor Vespasian, was a turning point in Jewish history. The temple was destroyed, the walls torn down and the priestly class all but disappeared. In this scene from Titus' arch the spoils of the temple are carried in triumphal procession.*

But among all senators, even if there were differences in *dignitas* and *auctoritas*, there was a shared basis of mutual, if competitive, honor and respect. This was not the case in the new world of the Principate, where there may still have been prominent leaders, but they were no longer leaders in the old sense. Now there was only one leader, one single Princeps, one politician. Politics had been drained from the relationship between senators and Princeps. That left a problem: What was the status of the senators? How were they to act when all their traditional instincts told them to act politically? What were the new rules? Finding out how to behave in each other's presence was hard for both emperor and senators. Proper forms of interaction had to be discovered or invented as the regime progressed. This happened in due course, but a great deal of pain was involved. It was hard to undo the old ways. Augustus' *civilitas* was credible, but Tiberius' was not. He was uncomfortable with the elite and it with him. He feared and hated the flattery of the Senate, regarding it as servile and insincere. In his early years he tried to accommodate the sensibilities of the Senate in his appointments. Competence had to be taken into account but it was mediated through honor and status:

> In giving out offices Tiberius considered the nobility of the candidate's ancestors, his military renown, and the brilliance of his civil accomplishments to establish that there was no one better qualified.... The emperor entrusted imperial property to such as were most distinguished—sometimes to men he had never met, strictly on the grounds of their reputation (Tacitus, *Annals*, 4.6).

Tiberius, however, complained of the ill will he generated whenever he made an appointment, because to make one appointment he had to pass over others (Tacitus, *Ann.*, 2.36). Game-playing of this kind soon exhausted his patience. Emperors sometimes found it easier to give a position to someone from an undistinguished background than to a touchy aristocrat who was concerned that his appointment might not measure up to his expectations, let alone his lineage. Vespasian was made governor of Judaea by Nero because "he was energetic but not to be feared because of the lowliness of his lineage and name" (Suetonius, *Vesp.*, 4.5). Despite the difficulties inherent in the peculiar relationship of emperors and senators, Roman political tradition did have a way in which the emperor could grant favors without stirring resentment: the conferral of friendly kindnesses, *beneficia*.

## Imperial Patronage

In the Republic friends were forever doing favors (*beneficia*) for each other without the least bit of servility being involved. That was how friendships were built and maintained. In the Empire the same reciprocities were expected of emperors, who had an enormous range of benefits at their disposal. They could, for instance, allow favored households to tap into the public aqueducts or use the public transportation system. On request they granted citizenship, exemptions from the obligation of marriage and the raising of children, or from military service. They could bestow freedom on slaves or grant promotions to equestrian, senatorial, or military ranks. Pliny the Younger wrote on behalf of a centurion to Trajan:

> Sir, a centurion by the name of Publius Accius Aquila has requested that I send you a petition requesting your intervention in the case of his daughter's status as a citizen. It was difficult to refuse, especially as I know how readily you give a sympathetic hearing to your soldiers' requests.

Trajan responds:

> I have read the petition which you forwarded for Publius Accius Aquila, centurion in the sixth cavalry cohort. I have granted his request. I have granted his daughter Roman citizenship and am sending you a copy of the order to pass on to him. (Pliny, *Letters*, 10.106–107)

Pliny's many recommendations of individuals to the emperor were not based on an impartial evaluation of his candidates' abilities or competence, but rather on qualities of character. He touted, for instance, their *probitas* (i.e., their uprightness); their *industria* (they were not slackers); their *humanitas* (they were civilized, decent people); their *innocentia* (integrity); and their *modestia* (circumspection). Irrespective of the office the same virtues were repeated in the letters of commendation. This was not a meritocratic system in the modern sense of the term. Essentially what men like Pliny were saying in their testimonials was: "This person is a friend of mine and hence a worthy character. I am going surety for him. I would not recommend him if I did not have full confidence in him. Trust my judgment." Unlike other empires, which established schools to train professional administrators or held standardized examinations, Rome trusted its ancient patronage system, which it knew well. Character, in Roman eyes, counted more than technical competence or cleverness.

CIRCLES OF PATRONAGE Although the emperors usurped the kind of patronal resources the famous families of Rome used to dispense in the Republic, their trusted inner circles were allowed to build up clientships of their own. In addition to ensuring the loyalty of their closest adherents, the emperors bound to themselves, through them, their clients throughout the Empire. In this way numerous provincial elites were brought within the web of imperial patronage. Everyone benefited. Senators acted as brokers of imperial favors and they themselves benefited. As Pliny put it when requesting a promotion for his client Rosianus Geminus: "Sir, I ask you that you please me by increasing the *dignitas* of my former quaestor. I mean to say, you will increase my *dignitas* by showing your favor to him" (*Letters*, 10.26). By this system generation after generation of provincials were co-opted and brought into the imperial system.

Learning how to behave with the Princeps was one thing; learning to work with him and his administration was another. The way towards a working relationship between the elite and the emperor was smoothed by an ancient Roman institution, the *cursus honorum*.

## The *Cursus Honorum* in the Principate

In the Principate the senatorial *cursus honorum* had lost the political significance that had made it central to the public life of the Republic. Nevertheless, the *cursus* still led, as it did in the past, to magistracies, governorships of provinces, the command of legions, and major administrative offices in the city of Rome and elsewhere. These were the honors the ambitious among the elite craved, but the emperor did not give them to just anyone. They were not purely personal gifts or benefactions. Only senators who had passed through the *cursus* were eligible for imperial appointments. Even if the emperor was the master string-puller, there was still an orderly process in the selection of officials. With all his power the emperor was often at the mercy of those, like Pliny and Fronto and hundreds of others, who made recommendations of candidates to him.

There was a second *cursus*, however, over which the emperor exercised a much closer supervision. This was the *cursus* of the equestrian order, the second tier in the Roman elite. The equestrian career track was an imperial innovation that produced something that came as close to a meritocratic administration as Roman political customs would allow. The use of the term "bureaucracy" or even "administration" should not, however, conjure up images of masses of government employees toiling invisibly in a scatter of alphabet agencies. As in the Republic, the administration in the Empire, such as it was, hewed to its libertarian principles. At the managerial level there were a scant 163 equestrian procurators by the end of the second century A.D. when the bureaucracy reached its final form.[1] Rome, a city of about 1,000,000, had a similarly spare managerial cohort of less than 40.[2] Not counted in these figures are the freedmen and slaves who worked under the equestrian and senatorial appointees.

## The Senatorial *Cursus*

In the Empire the *cursus honorum* looked a lot like the *cursus* of the late Republic in structure. There were the same offices in the same order. The difference was that the emperor exercised, depending on the importance of the office, greater or lesser control over the candidates and the electoral process. There was also a stronger hereditary character to the senatorial order than there had been in the Republic.

Young men of about 20 who were interested in a senatorial career and had the requisite census qualification of 1,000,000 sesterces and the right to wear the *laticlavus* (i.e., the wide stripe on the toga that indicated membership in the senatorial order) could compete. The right to the *laticlavus* came by being born into a senatorial family or by grant of the emperor. This grant came as a result of either individual application of a candidate to him or, more often, by recommendation from some well-placed friend or relative.

These young men began their careers by first holding one of 20 junior positions in what was known as the *vigintivirate*. With the emperor's approval they next moved on to the military tribunate. There were six military tribunes per legion, one of which was reserved for a *laticlavius*. The job was administrative and did not involve the command of individual units. The other six were reserved for equestrians whose rank was indicated by the narrow stripe (*angusticlavus*) they wore on their togas. After their military service, which might take a number of years, the *laticlavius* was eligible for one of 20 quaestorships. These were elective offices with year-long administrative, usually finan-

[1]Comparisons with modern bureaucracy are clumsy and misleading, but it might be worth mentioning that the state of California has 360,000 state employees alone, not counting municipal and federal employees. There are more police in the city of New York than there were bureaucrats in the entire administrative system of the Roman Empire with its population of 50 million or more.

[2]See figure 17, page 249 in Chapter 12 for the details.

cial, responsibilities. Some quaestorships were more important than others. For instance, two of the 20 elected quaestors were assigned to the treasury in Rome (*aerarium Saturni*), four to the consuls and two to the emperor himself. The rest were scattered around Italy and the provinces.

The next step in the senatorial *cursus* was the aedileship (six slots), or tribune of the plebs (ten slots). As can be seen, the number of available positions narrowed somewhat after the quaestorship and there seems to have been some genuine competition for these and for the next position, the praetorship (18 slots). The praetorship was of real importance because it opened up a large number of significant Empire-wide appointments such as the command of legions and the fleets. By this time the candidates were about 30 years of age. The next position, the consulship, was the pinnacle of the senatorial career. The number of ordinary consuls was two as in the past, but under the Principate it was customary for these two to resign halfway through their term of office and for others, suffect consuls as they were called, to be appointed in their places. The number of suffects varied, but was usually in the range of eight to ten. There were 19 under Commodus. One final comment on the *cursus* under the Principate: The emperor as censor could "adlect" anyone he chose to a senatorial rank (e.g., the rank of quaestor or praetor—without the individual having to hold the office itself or its preceding steps).

THE SIGNIFICANCE OF THE SENATORIAL *CURSUS* The *cursus* acted as a kind of human resources department for imperial officials. It gave emperors and other members of the elite an opportunity to examine over extended periods of time the behavior of potential candidates for a wide variety of offices. It was noted, for example, that while Pliny was doing his military tribunate in the east he had a head for figures. This led to his career as prefect of the military treasury, prefect of the public treasury in Rome, and later to a special commission tasked with reining in the extravagant expenditures of some of the cities in Bithynia (in modern Turkey).

The *cursus*, on the other hand was a big help to the young men who planned a senatorial career. The serious responsibilities that went with a number of the *cursus* postings helped young men mature quickly. When they joined the Senate the first thing they learned was how to interact with their peers and watch how their peers dealt with the emperor. Failure at that level made progress in the *cursus* next to impossible short of an intervention by the Princeps or some very well-placed individual. These young careerists travelled widely and became privy to a great deal of information about the peoples of the Empire, the conditions of the legions and the provinces, systems of taxation, and so forth. They made contact with provincial elites that often had a major impact on their later careers. They would learn how to deal with competent as well as incompetent governors and generals.

THE EMPEROR AND HIS HELPERS There were 600 members in the Senate from the time of Augustus on and each year the emperor, theoretically at least, had to look over as many resumes as were needed to find candidates for the 64-odd magistracies that had to be filled, not counting the many candidates who sought the *laticlavus* to begin their careers. If he only looked at a short list of, say, three resumes per position, this would have amounted to nearly 200 resumes. The vetting of the *cursus* could not be allowed to become a full-time job, yet it was one of the most important responsibilities emperors had and one that they constantly fretted over.

Many of those to be elected to the junior magistracies must have been selected on the basis of senatorial recommendations or the recommendations of the emperor's own family and freedmen, especially the latter, because they had control of the personnel files of the candidates. The emperor would know few of these men personally. As the field narrowed for the senior positions of praetorship and consulship, the scrutiny and debate in the imperial household must have become a lot more intense. Here is where family members, and especially the emperors' wives, must have had a lot of say. Life among the elite was highly social. Emperors invited senators and equestrians and their wives to dinner and were themselves invited in return. Mistakes in choosing candidates at the high levels of the administration could have lasting effects. One appointment we know Augustus regretted was that of Varus who was married to his grandniece. Varus, it will be recalled, was the negligent general who managed to lose three entire legions in Germany as well as his own life. This was a black eye for the regime and its carefully fostered image of competence.

SENATORIAL POSTS For what kinds of positions did a senatorial career prepare a candidate? Obviously the first and most important was the imperial office itself. Until the third century A.D. all emperors were men of senatorial rank who had either gone through the usual step-by-step process of the ordinary senatorial *cursus* or an accelerated version of it in the case of imperial heirs. Next in importance came the governorships of provinces of which there were around 40 in this period (setting aside provinces under equestrian administration). The larger imperial provinces (i.e., those directly under the emperor that had the majority of the legions) were ruled by senators of consular rank with the title *legatus Augusti propraetore* (i.e., as delegates of the emperor with praetorian rank). They combined supreme civil and military responsibilities under their commands. Smaller imperial provinces were governed by an ex-praetor who also commanded whatever armed forces were in his province. Senatorial provinces under the control of the Senate were governed by proconsuls chosen by lot for one-year terms. After Gaius' rule none of the Senate's provinces possessed any legions, although they might have detachments of troops. Governors of imperial provinces had an appointment that usually lasted about three years.

In addition to these posts there were the commands of individual legions in those provinces, such as Germany, the Danube area, and Syria, which had multiple legions. In the city of Rome there were major positions available to senators such as the prefectures of the city and the food supply (see figure on page 249). In total, around 60 military and civilian positions requiring senatorial rank had to be filled with the direct or indirect approval of the emperor, a few annually, the majority over somewhat longer periods.

## The Equestrian *Cursus*

The equestrian order was the second of Rome's two topmost classes. It had a minimum census qualification of 400,000 sesterces, and despite its second-rank position was still a very exclusive group by any measure. Senators and equestrians shared the same cultural interests and were often interrelated by marriage. In its broadest, empire-wide form the equestrian order was much more numerous and heterogeneous than its senatorial counterpart. At Gades in Spain, for instance, 500 men qualified for equestrian status. In the Principate the majority of equestrians may be equated with the large land owners of Italy and the most urbanized provinces around the Mediterranean. Most were satisfied to play the role of local aristocrats and powerbrokers rather than becoming involved in what might be called in the U.S. a federal career, that is, in the case of Rome, a role in the imperial administrative and/or military service since the two were closely intermingled.

THE EQUESTRIAN MILITARY *CURSUS* Claudius, trying to bring some order to the equestrian pattern of officeholding, decreed that the sequence should be: *praefectus cohortis* (commander of a unit of auxiliary, non-Roman citizen infantry), *tribunus militum* (military tribune, see above), *praefectus equitum* or *alae* (commander of a unity of auxiliary cavalry). Most equestrians would have been in their late 20s or early 30s on appointment to these positions. These three military commands, sometimes abbreviated to *tres militiae,* prepared an equestrian for the next important post, a civilian procuratorship, or a military command requiring equestrian rank.

Annually there were about 360 posts available for the *tres militiae*. Not all of the 360 equestrians, however, came from the land-owning class. A percentage was senior centurions who had reached the top grade, *primuspilus* (First Javelin), in the ranks of the legionary centurions. Of the equestrian military commands the most important was the prefect (or, at times, prefects) of the Praetorian Guard, the prefect of the *vigiles* at Rome, the prefect of Egypt and the prefects or commanders of the fleets based at Ravenna and Misenum. Pliny the Elder, a naturalist and scientist by avocation, was the prefect of the fleet at Misenum at the time of the eruption of Mount Vesuvius that buried Pompeii and Herculaneum in A.D. 79. Determined to observe the event close up he had himself rowed over from Misenum but was overwhelmed by the gases and died. His nephew, Pliny the Younger, behaving prudently as was his wont, stayed at Misenum with his mother and watched the catastrophe from a safe distance. His graphic account of the event survives (Pliny, *Letters*, 6.16).

PROCURATORS After their *tres militiae* the better connected, more talented or ambitious equestrians went on to serve in procuratorial positions. These were appointments ranging from the governorships of minor province such as Judaea, Corsica, and Mauretania to adjunct positions in the treasury or food supply departments (see figure on page 249).

Next in importance came those procurators who were responsible for the collection of taxes, the payment of troops and the supervision of the emperor's properties in both imperial and senatorial provinces. These procurators could hold court in fiscal matters and in emergencies substitute for provincial governors. Their reports provided the emperor with a separate, not always unbiased, source of information about their governors, the condition of the legions, the provinces and so on. Naturally there was the potential for overlapping jurisdiction and room for plenty of tension between procurators and governors. In Britain the tough-minded and experienced governor Suetonius Paulinus put down the revolt of Boudicca with what the procurator, Julius Classicanus, thought was excessive force.

### Titus Flavius Germanus: A Procuratorial Career

*This inscription reveals as much about Roman society as it does about procuratorial careers. Germanus was probably the descendant of freedmen. Obviously a talented and industrious individual, he held many responsible positions at Rome, some under the emperor Commodus whose name was erased after his assassination. One of these positions was procurator for the distribution of money to poor families in southern Italy. The aim of this program was to encourage the poor to raise rather than to expose or sell their children. Possibly after his successful career at Rome he settled at Praeneste, an important town about twenty miles south of Rome, where he held many municipal positions.*

[This inscription is set up to honor] Titus Flavius Germanus, son of Titus, curator of the outstandingly successful German triumph of [*Emperor Commodus*],* honored [*by Emperor Commodus*]* with the most illustrious priesthood, the Pontifex Minor; procurator of the 5% inheritance tax; procurator of inherited estates; procurator of the great games; procurator of the morning games; procurator of the city districts with the additional responsibility for paving streets in two parts of the city; procurator of the 5% inheritance tax from Umbria, Etruria, Picenum [*gap*]... and Campania; procurator for child assistance in Lucania, Bruttium, Calabria, and Apulia; curator for the repair of public works and sacred buildings. Aedile; duovir; priest of the deified Augustus; duovir quinquennalis [*one of two censors at Praeneste*]; patron of the colony. This memorial was erected by his freedman Cerdo to his incomparable patron, together with his sons Flavius Maximus, Germanus and Rufinus, who have been honored with equestrian rank. H. Dessau, *Inscriptiones Latinae Selectae* (Berlin, 1893), 1420.

*There is a gap in the inscription at this point where the name of the hated Commodus had been chiseled out. Commodus suffered the ultimate indignity of the condemnation of his memory (*damnatio memoriae*).

Classicanus wrote to Nero complaining of Paulinus' behavior, and the governor was withdrawn. In A.D. 69 he threw his support to Vitellius.

A RATIONALIZED ADMINISTRATION? It would be a mistake to think that the evolution of the equestrian *cursus* was part of an inevitable "rationalization" of the Roman administrative system. As has been remarked on more than one occasion, the Julio-Claudian emperors administered the Empire through their own *familia*, that is the staff of freedmen and slaves of their own private households. This was done for a number of reasons, one of which was that the political culture of the time would not permit gentlemen of the landed class—senatorial or equestrian—to serve even an emperor in what was deemed to be a servile position. One of the consequences of this cultural obstacle was that men of both classes found themselves complaining impotently that men of lesser status than they—mere freedmen or worse, slaves—often wielded real power while they only played at exercising power. It took until the Flavians for freedmen and slaves to begin to take second place to equestrian gentlemen who now managed to swallow their *dignitas* sufficiently to act as full time administrators in the palace. Tacitus complained of the servility of senators, but the equestrians were guilty of making their own accommodations with the new, evolving political culture.

It was another half century or more, before the equestrian administrative system was fully articulated under Hadrian. By mid-second century A.D. there was a regular hierarchy of positions based on pay grades ranging from *sexagenarii* (60,000 sesterces per year) through, *centenarii* (100,000 per year), *ducenarii* (200,000 per year) to—rarely— *trecenarii* (300,000 per year). By the first century A.D. there were about 60 equestrian procurators, and by the end of the next century the number had increased to an estimated 163. By then the political culture of Rome had been so changed that there was no shame, indeed there was honor, at least for an equestrian, in holding an appointment with a generous salary in the service of the all-powerful chief administrator, the emperor. With powerful positions, however, went proportionately great dangers. The closer equestrians (or senators for that matter) came to the center of power the greater the risks they and their families faced. Sejanus and his family under Tiberius were not the last powerful equestrians to run afoul of their chiefs.

THE IMPERIAL *PATRIMONIUM* Yet another of the responsibilities of the emperor that could—like reading the resumes of candidates and the reports of governors, legionary commanders, and procurators—eat up all his time, was the management of his *patrimonium* or *res privata*, his own personal estate. This job was delegated to equestrian procurators who in turn generated more information than any emperor, even the diligent ones like Antoninus Pius, could digest.

The imperial *patrimonium* was a vital asset for an emperor, enabling him to maintain his position as Chief Aristocrat and Patron. It provided him with an income that allowed him to reward, bribe or bail out friends or enemies at will. It allowed Augustus, for example, to intervene 12 times during the food panics of 23 B.C. supplying food for the population "bought at my own expense" (*RG*, 15). The imperial *patrimonium* was huge and continued to grow throughout the Principate, and by the end of the second century A.D. a substantial percentage of the real estate of the Empire was incorporated in the imperial *res privata*. It consisted of hundreds of properties scattered all over Italy and the provinces, encompassing mines, forests, and quarries as well as agricultural land. The entire Thracian Chersonese (Gallipoli) constituted a single imperial property. Some properties that ended up in the imperial patrimony had been willed to emperors by rich members of the elite in the hope that the remainder of their estates would pass intact to their heirs and not be sequestered by hard-up emperors. Other properties ended up there as a result of confiscations of the estates of those accused of traitorous behavior.

OVERWHELMED BY PAPERWORK Is it any wonder that, in the face of the paperwork alone—not to mention campaigning in squalid, uncivilized frontier provinces—some emperors might have thrown up their hands and decided to devote themselves to less onerous imperial responsibilities such as supervising the games at Rome? It is not difficult to see how an emperor with the disposition of Antoninus Pius would be content to read reports or, more likely, digestible summaries of reports, prepared for him by trusted aides. Conversely, it is understandable that Nero or Commodus could decide he was better equipped to entertain the masses, which was also an imperial responsibility, than kill barbarians or put down rebellions. The wonder is that during the reigns of Nero and Commodus the administration ground on anyway and some excellent appointments were made under both rulers.

## 3. THE PROVINCES AND PROVINCIAL ADMINISTRATION

The basic goals of the Roman imperial system were simple, and its administrative apparatus rudimentary. Its aim was to maintain law and order in the provinces and collect taxes. Rome had no interest in interfering to any significant degree in the social and economic lives of its subjects. The system of taxation was un-standardized and varied considerably from province to province. It was also undersupervised. By any measure the Roman Empire was undergoverned. Proportionately the Chinese Empire employed perhaps 20 times the number of functionaries that the Romans used.

### Governors: The New System

Under the Republic governors had the illusion—and sometimes the reality—of independence when they went off to govern their assigned provinces. They had responsibility not to some one individual, a commander in chief who was their legitimate superior, but to their senatorial peers as a collective body. A governorship in the Republic was part of a political career, a step up the ladder, or a consequence of having held an office. In the Principate this all changed. Political advancement with Rome as the main theater and one's peers and the people of Roman as the audience was no longer the aim. The governor was now an administrator working on behalf of someone else, not a politician trying to make a name for himself by currying favor with the provincials or alternately, looting the province to continue financing his career. "Administrator" is probably too strong a term. Perhaps "associate" or "colleague" would more accurately reflect how governors and other highly positioned senators and equestrians thought of themselves, and emperors certainly played along with the game by honoring their appointees with flowery titles.

The connections between governor and emperor were not based wholly on legalities. A governorship was an honor received at the hands of the Princeps. It indicated to all his peers that he had been reviewed, his loyalty and competence examined and judged sufficient. Presumably he was chosen over others who were judged less loyal or competent as that term was understood. In Roman political culture the acceptance of honors or favors put the person receiving them under obligation to the one conferring them. Governors were thus honor-bound to support their rulers and their rulers' policies no matter what were their private beliefs or ambitions. "All that is left to us," moans one of the figures in Tacitus' history "is the glory of obedience" (*Annals* 6.8). Whether as governor of a province or as a legate commanding a legion the senator had to answer to the Princeps who appointed him. Even when in the field or in his province he might be under the surveillance of an agent of the emperor. We have already seen the case of Suetonius Paulinus, the governor in Britain who efficiently put down the revolt of Boudicca but whose equestrian procurator urged Nero to recall him. Success was no guarantee of a favorable reception in Rome. It might even have the opposite effect with insecure or jealous emperors. Success undid such talented generals and governors as Domitius Corbulo under Nero and Lusius Quietus under Hadrian.

RESPONSIBILITIES In the frontier provinces governors had the combined task of ruling the civilian population and commanding whatever armed forces happened to be there. In Syria or the Rhine these might consist of several legions whereas in Austria there might only be a few auxiliary units. Because he was chief administrator, judge, and general, the governor needed as much political ability as military.

The governor's main responsibility in the peaceful provinces was the maintenance of order. He had to accomplish this task with a minute staff, no existing bureaucracy and no military support to speak of. He had perhaps three or four paid assistants and the rest had to be made up of friends. Fronto, the friend and tutor of Marcus Aurelius, was appointed governor of Asia in the mid–second century A.D. and set about collecting his staff by asking some friends from Cirta, his hometown in Africa, to come along with him, as well as some rhetoricians from Alexandria and a military specialist from Morocco.

Governors were not directly responsible for the finances of a province. The maintenance of aqueducts, roads, city walls, temples, sewers and so on was left to the cities and their city councils. City magistrates were also responsible for collecting the two main taxes demanded by Rome, the poll tax and the land tax. When collected these taxes were passed on to Roman fiscal agents, the quaestors and procurators for transmission to Rome.

The political position of the governor was all important. The peace of the province depended largely on his ability to maintain good relations with the ruling oligarchies of the cities. His efforts to do this could be complicated by collusion between local elites and other Roman officials already in the province, such as imperial procurators who reported directly to the emperor. It could be assumed that some local aristocrats had personal contacts with members of the Senate at Rome. There were always complicating factors such as whether the defendants in cases that came before a governor for trial were Roman or whether they belonged to the upper or lower classes (*honestiores* or *humiliores*) because different penalties applied to the two categories. What was a governor to do when he discovered corruption in his province? How was he to handle exploitation by the local elites of their fellow citizens? Should he take the risk of being told by well-connected local oligarchs that he was no friend of Caesar's if he defended the poor or unpopular individuals against their better placed oppressors? Even the most conscientious of governors must have been frequently perplexed when confronted with issues like these.

## Appeal: Provocatio

In the Republic appeal, by Roman citizens living in the provinces or provincials was to the Roman people. In the Empire the appeal was *ad Caesarem*, to the emperor. *Provocatio* was the cornerstone of the political liberties of the Roman people in Rome during the Republic. Within the city and up to the first milestone a citizen could appeal to the people, *ad populum*, for redress of grievances by approaching a tribune of the people whose house was to be open day and night for such appeals. The tribune could provide *auxilium*, help to the person seeking assistance. In the Empire the problem was: What about Roman citizens who lived outside Rome? What about non-citizens? Could they appeal? As time went by the number of Romans in the provinces grew considerably, making the issue of *provocatio* an urgent one.

In the case of Roman citizens, the thinking seems to have been that as citizens they could appeal to the emperor because his tribunician power was valid throughout the Empire. The first known case occurred in the reign of Claudius when the apostle Paul, who was born a Roman, made his appeal from a local court in Judaea.[3] Paul was accused of inciting a riot in Jerusalem and was brought before the local governor, Antonius Felix, who kept him in prison for two years until relieved by his successor, Porcius Festus. Paul, fearing a lynching during a hearing of his case before Festus, appealed to Caesar and was in due course shipped off to Rome for trial. *Acts* ends with Paul under house arrest in Rome. There are no details of his trial. Tradition has it that he died in the persecution of Nero in A.D. 67.

The case of Paul involved a Roman citizen, but as early as 6 B.C. there is evidence that even non-citizens could get a hearing in Rome. In that year Augustus agreed to hear a case from the Greek city of Cnidos in Asia Minor. Euboulos, a citizen of that city, and his wife Tryphera (neither one was a Roman citizen) had a falling out with some family members and were literally besieged in their home. In the course of the siege a slave was told to dump the contents of a chamber pot on the besiegers. The slave lost control of the pot—whether deliberately or not was in dispute—and it fell, killing one of the relatives. Euboulos and his wife were accused of murder by the Cnidian authorities and fled to Rome fearing they would not get a fair hearing in the city. Augustus ordered an investigation and after hearing the report declared in favor of Tryphera (Euboulos had died in the meantime) and wrote a letter to the Cnidians to that effect. The letter, carved on a marble pillar, survives. Scholars debate whether or not this was technically an appeal; the main point is that de facto it was treated as an appeal to the Princeps who handed down a judgment, which merited a permanent posting in a public place.

## Roman-Style Bureaucracy

The foregoing survey might easily lead to a misunderstanding of the nature of Roman rule. The modern terms "administration," "bureaucracy," and even "government" have connotations that do not quite fit the nature of Roman-style rule and suggest a level of formality the Romans would have found alien. The term procurator, for instance, came from the realm of household or estate management, not public law. Before the term entered into wide usage in the Empire it referred to someone who took care of (*cura*) something for someone else. A procurator was an agent, a deputy, a manager of an estate, a steward. The emperor, the great *paterfamilias* of the Roman family, took care of that family by delegat-

[3]The well-known case is presented in detail in *Acts of the Apostles* in the *New Testament*.

ing others to act on his behalf. They in turn were responsible directly to him for their good or bad administration.

It must surely seem strange that the master of the world, Augustus, with everything else he had to do, had time to adjudicate personally a case of manslaughter by chamber pot that occurred in a distant, unimportant city. Yet the case was not wholly atypical. Perhaps the only thing all of these cases had in common was that they involved members of the elite, some of whom were Roman citizens and some of whom were not. They got their cases before the emperor, not because of the merit of the cases, but because of their connections, a process that fits a personal and familiar style of government rather than one dominated by impersonal juridical and bureaucratic norms and procedures characteristic of modern states. There were no prosecuting attorneys because none existed; there was no established hierarchy of courts, which passed the cases formally, by well-trodden legal procedures, from one to the other as happens in modern legal systems. The cases were not settled by careful references to precedent or even the facts of the cases but by considerations of equity and the necessity of maintaining social norms. Augustus, for instance, comments disapprovingly on the level of hostility of the Cnidians to the defendants. The Cnidians needed to be reminded of the danger of summary justice as well as the fact that there was a court of appeal beyond the city magistrates. According to the *lex Iulia de vi publica* of 18 B.C. a governor or other official who punished a man in defiance of *provocatio* was subject to capital punishment. In his comment, Augustus was sending a message, not just to the Cnidians but to other cities as well that governors should make their judgments with great care, at least where it concerned the kind of people who had the wherewithal to make an appeal to the emperor. Litigious Greeks needed to be taught that their petty squabbles, while they needed to be dealt with, could not be allowed to disturb the tranquility of provincial life. Augustus' main responsibility was the peace of the Empire and neither he nor his successors would allow the cities of the Empire, which were the Empire's main means of keeping order, fall into social chaos as had so easily happened in the past. The people of the Empire, or at least the elite of the Empire, were to be treated as part of a large community of people who shared the same culture, the same interests, and presumably the same respect for law and order. Therefore, in cases of disputes between peers strict legal formalities were not the only matters at issue. The norms of honor and decency needed to be maintained. Litigants were not to pursue their claims to the bitter end. The emperor was in a position to make such decisions and of course his decisions had the force of law and entered the rapidly increasing case book of precedents.

## 4. THE ARMY

### The Real Costs of a Professional Army

The army of the Principate looked and acted much like the army of the Republic. It had the same tactical organization and followed the same military doctrines as its predecessor. It was still an army of heavy infantry trained to seize and hold ground in high-intensity, close-quarters combat. Most of the officers were still upper-class civilian amateurs who served a few years in mostly administrative capacities and then returned to their homes in Rome, Italy, or the provinces. The legions were brigaded with approximately equal numbers of auxiliary troops who provided specialized arms such as cavalry, archers, slingers, and light infantry. The legions were composed of Roman citizens and are thought to have numbered about 150,000 men. There were an additional 30,000 in the fleet and 9000 in the Praetorian Guard stationed in Rome. There were about 220,000 auxiliaries for a total army of about 400,000 men.

HOW PROFESSIONAL WAS THE ARMY? Appearances, however, were deceiving. The army of the Empire below the rank of military tribune was a professional army made up of long-term enlisted men. The legionaries were no longer civilians who were cycled in and out of the army as need dictated. As professional soldiers they had a distinct sub-culture of their own that set them apart from the rest of the Roman community. They lived far from Rome in a self-contained universe of camps and fortresses with their own routines, ceremonies, dress, music, habits, reward systems, and values.[5] The loyalty of the legionaries was first to their *contubernales*, their tent-sharers, then to their particular century and cohort. Next in order of importance came the legion itself with its sometimes centuries-long history, its sacred standards, and individual traditions. The legionary commander could expect the loyalty of the legionaries as could the emperor and his family. Very low down in that list came the abstraction of "Empire." Once the soldiers of the legions ceased to be civilians in the old sense, the political-cultural shift that had been underway since the later Republic was complete.

The rest of the Roman community took little interest in these men except when, as happened in A.D. 69, rough soldiers from the Rhineland and Danube regions and later detachments from Syria suddenly appeared in Italy, destroying the ancient colony of Cremona and capturing Rome (for the full story, see Chapter 14, pages 290–291). By that date Italy was largely demilitarized. Recruiting, except for officers and praetorians, took place in Spain, southern Gaul, and Noricum. Later recruitment shifted even farther afield to the frontier regions where the armies were based. Gradually the whole Mediterranean littoral was demilitarized. A cultural distance, an anti-military mentality, developed between the safe inner core of the Empire and its far-away protective shell. This, however, was not a wholesale revolution, and Romans had not given up on the idea of citizen soldiers. The officer corps was not professionalized. There was no West Point for the formation of officers who would devote their whole lives to the army and in the process rise to command it. Nor had Rome reached the point where it was paying non-citizens—barbarians—to fight on its behalf, at least not yet. Nevertheless, the move to an all-volunteer force below the rank of officer altered the political-social contract that had previously lain at the foundation of the Roman constitution.

*POLIS* IDEOLOGY In the traditional *polis, citizens subsidized the cost of defense with their time, their enthusiasm, and their own resources such as food, arms, and armor. In polis*

[5]There were some regional differences. In Egypt, for example, detachments were spread among the population. Syrian legions tended to be near or at cities.

ideology the idea of paying someone else to defend one's homeland, apart from hiring some very specialized units such as archers or slingers, was repugnant, dangerous, and costly.

It was repugnant because it represented a rejection of the most fundamental aspect of *polis* life, namely, the intimate connection between military service and political power. The burden of soldiering was the price of citizenship and the political rights that went it. Citizenship and soldiering were convertible; they were the opposite sides of the same coin. It was dangerous because even in the case of paid citizen-soldiers it was uncertain whom they would accept as commanders and whom they would obey. It was logical to expect they would prefer tried commanders from their own ranks—people they knew well and trusted—rather than some perhaps unknown senator sent out from Rome for a few years and then another after him. There was always the question of whether the troops would fight if they were not paid or not paid enough. No one had forgotten the innumerable mutinies, most of them caused by the bad conditions and lack of pay, in the late Republic. There was a sharp reminder of this when the Pannonian legions revolted in A.D. 14 on the death of Augustus, despite the fact that Tiberius, whom the troops knew, had been eased into Augustus' position as his successor. The late second century A.D. emperor Septimius Severus summed up the problem of unruly troops when he was supposed to have advised his sons who were to be his successors, to "pay the soldiers and forget about everything else" (Dio Cassius 76.15).

**What Inspired the Legions in the Civil War of A.D. 69**

*Like the supporters of two football teams calling each other names, the armies of Otho and Vitellius clashed outside Cremona in northern Italy. They were not inspired by their leaders, who seem almost incidental to the fight. Otho's army was composed of Praetorian Guardsmen and other units. The Rhineland legions made up the Vitellian army. The Praetorians were recruited in Italy, while by A.D. 69 only a percentage of the Rhine legions would have been of Italian origin.*

Both armies were stimulated by the call of honor and glory, but they had different sources of motivation. One side stressed the power of the legions and the army of Germany, the other the prestige of Rome's garrison and the praetorian cohorts. The Vitellians reviled their opponents as flabby and indolent soldiers, demoralized circus fans and theatergoers, while the Othonians spoke scornfully of their enemy as a lot of foreigners and barbarians (Tacitus, *Histories*, 2.21).

Obviously the costs of maintaining an all-volunteer army would be high. Where was the money to come from, and who would pay? A related question was whether citizens safe within the cocoon of the peaceful Empire would be willing to pay for soldiers in far-away provinces. An Alexandrian in Egypt might legitimately wonder whether it made sense to spend his tax money on a frontier in Scotland, that is, assuming that the money even reached its destination and was not siphoned off someplace along the way. Why Scotland anyway? The more informed might wonder: why bother defending Britain? Was Dacia really necessary?

THE IMPERIAL DILEMMA All of these factors were fully understood by the Roman leadership—obviously a lot better than we understand them—but the leadership also knew that Rome had long since ceased to be a *polis*, even though many of the forms of the *polis* remained. In choosing to replace a citizen-militia with an all-volunteer force, the Roman state in the person of Augustus proposed a new constitutional bargain to the people of Rome and indirectly to the Empire. The principal terms of the bargain were as follows: Except in emergencies Roman citizens would not be drafted, but in exchange for passing the burden of military service to other citizens, they had to agree to pay enough in taxes to sustain the army. The burden of taxation was to be divided among the special military treasury (*aerarium militare*), the general treasury (*aerarium Saturni*), and the emperor's own private revenues (his *fiscus*, literally his basket or money bag). The *aerarium militare* paid the retirement bonuses (*praemia*) to the legionary veterans and was funded by a tax on Roman citizens consisting of a five percent inheritance tax on estates and a one percent tax on goods sold at auction. The yearly pay of the soldiers was paid from the general treasury, which drew on a wide range of taxes from the Empire, but principally in the form of a land tax (*tributum soli*), a personal or poll tax on individuals (*tributum capitis*), and the emperor's *fiscus*. The distinction between the emperor's private revenues and *aerarium Saturni* was never clear, and eventually the two sources of income became one single imperial treasury.

THE SIZE AND COST OF THE ARMY This bargain generated a number of difficult questions for Augustus and his advisors. Their solution was critical to the survival of the Principate. The first had to do with the size of the army Rome needed to maintain internal and external order. This was really two questions: What was the optimal size of the army—what were the actual defense needs of the Empire—and secondly, could the Empire afford such an army? Then, assuming the Empire had the resources to fund the optimal army, could its inhabitants be persuaded to pay its costs? As can be readily seen the questions were as much political as financial or economic. Augustus and his successors had to make a guess at not so much what the Empire could afford, but at what it could be willing to pay on a regular basis, emergency situations aside, over a long period of time. Once that was established then it would then be possible to make a reconciliation with the other side of the equation, namely, the defense needs of the Empire. Although bookkeeping was primitive and a budget infeasible, the emperors and their advisors had a pretty good idea of the amount that came in through taxes and went out on military expenditures. Beyond that they must also have had a sense of how much tax could be extracted from the Empire without creating a backlash on the part of rich and poor alike. The problem is illuminated by the experience of Domitian. When he decided to increase the pay of the army he found that the only way he could do so was by reducing the numbers of soldiers in the legions, for which he earned the rebuke of Dio Cassius, who complained that Domitian had "harmed the state greatly, having made its guardians too few and too expensive at that" (67.3). Suetonius adds that even then the emperor could get his hands on the necessary cash only by confiscations from the rich, ruthless exactions in the provinces, and vigorous enforcement of the special tax on Jews (Suet., *Domitian*, 12.). Domitian's heavy-handed tax collections led to at least one serious revolt, that of the Nasamones, a Numidian tribe in Africa.

AN EMPIRE NOT A NATION There seems to have been an understanding, at least at the elite level, that there was a connection between taxation and defense needs. One of Tacitus'

**Conditions of Service and the Revolt of A.D. 14**

*On the death of Augustus the legions in Pannonia mutinied. Tacitus provides a highly rhetorical account of a speech given by a rabble-rousing soldier by the name of Percennius who was part of the leadership of the mutiny. Tacitus had a typical upper-class disdain for the troops and gave the worst possible explanation for the soldiers' unhappiness. They were mere opportunists, he claimed, seizing the moment to squeeze what they could out of the situation of uncertainty created by Augustus' death. Their commander had allowed them to live in comfort and idleness with the result that discipline had dissolved. Percennius addresses the soldiers listing their complaints. Despite Tacitus' disdain there is no reason to disbelieve Percennius' catalog of grievances:*

"Old men, with bodies mutilated by wounds are still enduring 30 or 40 years of service. Even after your official discharge your service is still not over because you have to stay in the reserves, still under canvas. And if you survive alive after all these hazards you are then dragged off to some remote part of the world where under the name of "land" you are settled in some swamp or on a barren mountainside. Truly, soldiering is inherently a harsh and unrewarding profession. Body and soul are reckoned at two and a half sesterces a day [*less than a denarius, the normal daily pay for a laborer*], and with that you have to buy your own clothes, weapons and tents and bribe centurions if you want exemptions from chores. We all know that lashes and wounds are always our lot as are harsh winters and laborious summers, cruel war and unprofitable peace. There will never be relief until our service is based on fixed rules, pay of four sesterces [*a denarius*] a day, 16 years of service with no recall, and our gratuity (*praemium*) to be paid in cash before leaving camp." (Tacitus, *Annals*, 1.17)

speakers makes the point explicitly with the blunt comment: "Peace among nations cannot be maintained without armies; armies cost money, and money can only be raised through taxation" (*Histories*, 4.73). Indisputable in principle, such assertions do not change the hard truth that the extraction of taxes is at best a difficult art for all governments, past as well as present.

Though it is hard to make generalizations for the whole Empire, pay seems always to have been just barely adequate until the third century A.D. In theory the Empire should have been rich enough to support a properly funded military, but apparently Augustus and his advisors thought a relatively small army was all that the Empire could be expected to sustain over a long period of time. After Actium, Augustus decided to retain only 28 legions under arms, and that number dropped to 25 after Varus' catastrophe. By the end of the first century the number had risen to 30 and stayed at that number until the end of the second century when it went up to 33. There must have been some rational calculation underlying these numbers since by most standards of measurement the Empire was at its highest level of economic prosperity during these years. The most likely factor restraining expansion is cost. Yet there is general agreement that, at least by modern standards, taxes in the Empire were not high.

An explanation that accounts for the low tax-generating capacity of the Empire is that as a whole it was not sufficiently cohesive socially or politically to bear the burden of the actual costs of imperial defense. The Empire was not a compact nation-state of the kind that made its appearance in the nineteenth century and whose wealth, coherence, and willingness to make self-sacrifices make it possible to draft and arm citizen-soldiers on a massive scale and then sustain huge losses in men and materiel on the battlefield. Nationalistic fervor at least temporarily subsidizes the cost of war in terms of casualties. In addition, modern nations are able to do something that ancient powers could not do: lessen the present pain of war by fobbing off its financial costs on future generations. The Roman Empire had neither the national cohesiveness of a modern nation state nor the financial means of funding wars by means of bonds and inflationary policies. Perhaps it might not have made much difference. Modern nations, despite their wealth, populousness, and cohesion, seem not to be willing to sustain heavy casualties indefinitely, as the examples of France and Britain in the run up to World War II indicate. They did not want to repeat the slaughter of the First World War.

The Roman leadership understood that imperial defense was a long-term proposition. After all, according to imperial propaganda, Rome was eternal. Defense could not be treated as though it were a crusade involving national survival as was the case during some of the wars fought during the Republic. Defense of the Empire could not be made to depend on unpredictable or momentary enthusiasm. There could be no substitute for prudent calculation of the tax needs of the army, which in turn was a function of political calculation. Given the longevity of the Principate it should be acknowledged that Augustus and his advisors made excellent estimates regarding imperial defense, reconciling military requirements and the Empire's need for an equitable tax system. In the end the argument might be made that the Roman Empire survived as long as it did not because the legions were so formidable—although they were—or because the Empire was rich, but because Rome's elite was so good at politics. This, however, is a different topic and will be taken up in the next chapter.

BEYOND TAXES There were other connected reasons that made imperial defense a challenge for emperors. All tax systems suffer from flaws. High rates of taxation encourage taxpayers to hide their income. The powerful are more adept at lowering their tax burden than the less powerful. Corruption is hard to avoid. The tax system itself may be inefficient. Tax money, like electricity during transmission, simply disappears. In the Empire all these factors were at work, but there were others peculiar to Rome. Many taxes were never collected at all or were forgiven by emperors when it was either politically necessary to make concessions or when it was clear the taxes could never be collected. Emperors had a political need to be thought of as benevolent, kindly, and generous. Hadrian calculated that a cancellation of debt would boost his political standing and canceled 900,000,000 sesterces (HS) worth of old debts owed the main treasury. He could then boast of his liberality in his coinage, one issue of which shows a lictor burning tax records. Finally, there was a moral reason underlying the dilemma of increasing troop pay to proper levels. A good portion of the elite, not necessarily the best informed or the wisest, believed that, as a matter of principle, large donatives to soldiers as was customary at the accession of new emperors and at

**Army Pay Rates**

The total cost of the army (legionaries, auxiliaries, navy) in the first century A.D. may have amounted to over 400 millions sesterces, by far the largest part of the Empire's disposable income. Any increase in pay could put strains on the Empire's resources as was the case from the time of Septimius Severus (A.D. 193–211) onward. Nevertheless, that cost, measured by weight in silver or tons of wheat was *less* than the amount of the budget of the college of a large modern university. The per capita cost of the army was low but so was the surplus out of which it had to be maintained. All amounts are in sesterces.

| *Emperor* | *Legionary Infantry* | *Legionary Cavalry* | *Auxiliary Infantry* | *Auxiliary Cavalry* |
|---|---|---|---|---|
| Augustus | 900 | 1050 | 750 | 900 |
| Domitian | 1200 | 1400 | 1000 | 1200 |
| Septimius Severus | 2400 | 2800 | 2000 | 2400 |
| Caracalla | 3600 | 4200 | 3000 | 3600 |
| Maximinus | 7200 | 8400 | 6000 | 7200 |

other times, was an evil in itself. It amounted to buying the army's loyalty, rewarded avarice and destroyed discipline, or so it was claimed. In this version of Roman imperial history bad emperors were invariably those who purchased their troops' loyalty with money.

It is not that these members of the upper classes were in the grip of a miserly aristocratic ethos; quite the contrary. They were not averse to giving away large sums of money as part of their social role as leaders, especially in their native cities. The problem was that the armies were far away, and the life of the camp was alien to most of the elite of the Empire. What they knew of it—or thought they knew of it—inspired fear and loathing. Even if senators and equestrians had familiarity with the military, the elite of the Empire as a whole was much larger and broader than the senatorial and equestrian classes, and it saw only the worst side of soldiers and armies as they passed through their provinces, if they saw them at all. Unfortunately for Rome it was on the shaky loyalty and reluctant willingness of this group to pay and collect taxes that the Empire's safety depended. In good times—when the frontiers were not under severe pressure—the elite went along with the bargain devised by Augustus. It was a different matter when the good times ended in the third century, but Augustus deserves the credit for establishing a formula that worked for at least two centuries. He could hardly be blamed for the catastrophes of the third century, many of which were not of Rome's making.

RATIONALITY Rationality did not always enter into the calculus of imperial defense. The military strategy of the emperors, beginning with Augustus, had multiple aims, not all of them the result of a rational cost–benefit analysis. In this regard Rome was no more exceptional than any other state in history. The Romans were well aware that some provinces were

**A Modern Scholar Unravels the Roman Tax System**

"[T]he wealth amply present in the empire found expression through conspicuous consumption to a quite remarkable degree—which was privileged, which was the way of life among the ruling classes and emperors themselves, and which could not be touched. To this was added the freedom, almost the obligation, to spend and give as a grand patron. So government never saw a tenth or a fifth of the taxes demanded because it must magnani- mously cancel all arrears. It never saw another tenth or fifth which was lost to various kinds of perquisites allowed the emperor's servants.... The need for money at the center, in which we might expect to find the determinant of pressure felt in the provinces, thus followed rules of its own. Those rules were set by many considerations having to do with façade rather than function; or perhaps it would be better to say that free spending, arbitrary benevolence, indulgence of petitioners even if corrupt, were all part of a façade that also had a function: namely, to answer to popular expectations of Greatness embodied."

Ramsay MacMullen, "Tax Pressure in the Roman Empire," *Latomus* 46.4 (1987), 745.

a waste of money. Sufficient taxes could not be extracted from them to pay the costs of their defense. This was a given for the historian Appian writing in the second century A.D., who says in the preface to his wide-ranging history: "On some subject peoples the Romans expend more on them than they receive, thinking it dishonorable to give them up even though they are so costly" (Appian, *Pref.*, 7). Claudius' weak political position needed to be bolstered by military success; hence the attempt to make Britain a province. Yet, having acquired Britain the Romans did not cut their losses when they saw that it was no threat and had no economic value. They clung tenaciously to it and spent more money on it. Three to four legions were regularly based there. In this instance, at least, economic issues did not win out over the value of honor and image. The Empire and the emperor had their reasons. At times they may be opaque to us, but they deserve to be respected. Perhaps *honos* and *fides* were worth the cost of a few legions.

## Military Matters

THE NATURE OF FRONTIERS The Roman Empire had over 6,000 miles of frontier to defend, from Hadrian's Wall in Britain to the deserts of North African and Arabia. Some of the frontiers were rivers, such as the Rhine and the Danube, along which the army had constructed an elaborate chain of military roads and fortress towns and in carefully selected places watch posts, palisades, ditches, and walls. In Syria another network of fortresses existed to defend the eastern half of the Empire against Parthia, the only major organized state with which Rome had to contend. In Africa constant vigilance was needed to keep the desert tribes from pillaging the settled areas. Nevertheless we should not think of the Roman frontiers as we do of frontiers between modern nation-states, which are intended to demarcate one state from another. Even in its relations with Parthia the Roman frontier was extremely fluid, consisting largely of jointly shared territories occupied by Arab tribesmen, some of whom claimed allegiance to Rome and others to Parthia and who often changed allegiances.

Most of the frontiers, whether in Europe, Africa, or the Middle East, were simply zones of supervised contact between the peoples of Roman provinces and peoples who lived beyond them. Many of the trans-frontier peoples did not recognize settled boundaries and with good reason. For millennia Celts in Britain, Germans and Dacians in central Europe, Berbers in north Africa, and Arabs throughout the East had moved freely in response to seasonal pastoral needs, population pressures, or natural catastrophes such as famine or flooding. From the viewpoint of these peoples the provinces of the Empire were artificial obstacles having no intrinsic legitimacy. Needless to say the Roman authorities and the bulk of the provincials took a different view.

As a practical matter the frontiers were set up mainly to channel the movements of trans-frontier peoples in ways that would create the least disturbance for the settled provinces of the Empire. Walls, ditches, palisades, roads, and bridges were used as means of directing moving populations to where they could be supervised and counted, since one of the key elements in the Roman defense of Empire was the possession of accurate information. Frontiers were thus supervised corridors or regions of economic and social exchange, not fortified, exclusionary zones. Nor did Romans think that the frontiers restricted their ability to move beyond them. They expected to use the frontier areas as jumping-off points for periodic campaigns of intimidation or conquest. Hadrian's Wall in Britain, for instance, was a lightly held chain of fortresses, walls, and ditches, while the main legionary forces were encamped at York miles to the south. Roman power extended for perhaps a hundred miles to the north of the Wall.

Under the Flavians and their successors, the Roman frontier gradually lost its fluid outlines and came to possess clearly identifiable boundaries. The old client-states, which had been used as buffers, were absorbed, and the new defensive aim was to provide security against small-scale infiltration as well as much larger incursions. The advantage of this policy was that it allowed even the border provinces to develop cities and agriculture along Mediterranean lines, and places such as the Danube valley, once remote and undeveloped, now began to flourish.

STRATEGY: THE CHALLENGE OF GEOGRAPHY Unlike the Republic's position in Italy, Rome of the Empire lacked the kind of internal lines of communication on land that would have helped it defend its frontiers. Transportation was good in the Mediterranean, and troops could be moved from place to another if the campaigns were near the coast, but the problem was with the northern frontiers. The overall form of the Empire was oblong, a difficult shape to defend. If Rome was lucky it would not have to face major incursions at opposite ends of the Empire at the same time. It was easy enough for the Rhine legions to back up the Danubian or Moesian legions and vice versa, but much more difficult for these forces, except those in Moesia, to reinforce the Syrian legions. Rome, however, could not always depend on the fickle goddess Fortuna. Under Marcus Aurelius, as we have seen, this policy was put to the test. Although he and his generals stemmed the tide of invasion in both east and west, the experience demonstrated that the frontiers could only be maintained by transferring units from one frontier to another. There was no strategic reserve.

## The Strategic Reserve

Under the Julio-Claudians the legions tended to be grouped in combined legionary armies with regional responsibilities. There were eight legions split between upper and lower Germany, and four legions in Syria. However, after A.D. 69 when the danger of legions being concentrated in one place revealed itself, the legionary groups were divided up and spread out over larger areas. The double legionary bases in Germany, such as those at Vetera (Xanten), Colonia Agrippinensis (Cologne), and Mogontiacum (Mainz) were replaced with single-legion bases. Regiments of auxiliaries were spaced out between the major legionary bases.

The logic behind the disposition of Rome's military forces seems obvious enough. Gaul, recently pacified, needed to be insulated from the disturbing potential of so-called "Free Germany." Similarly the restive Balkans needed to be insulated from tribes across the Danube. Syria needed a strong Roman presence to hold Parthia at bay—hence the concentration of forces in these areas. Egypt was too valuable to be left without a legionary presence. Spain, too, needed a legionary presence, having only been recently pacified. The problem behind this logic was that a serious invasion in any one frontier region, as opposed to minor infiltrations, could not be stopped by the local forces. Other regions would have to send support, but that in turn weakened the frontiers in their areas. It was not always easy to determine whether an infiltration was large or small and where it was headed. If it was large it would take time to concentrate the forces to cope with it.

ON THE MARCH Other scenarios besides large invasions had to be considered. At times the emperors judged that major aggressive campaigns of intimidation or conquest were necessary. In that case calculations had to be made regarding the number of troops and supplies needed. Orders then had to be transmitted to begin the slow process of assembling the striking force. Legions or units of legions as well as auxiliaries had to be taken from one area and marched to the point where the attack was planned. Under Tiberius, for example, *legio IX Hispana* was transferred from Pannonia to Africa to help the legion based there, *III Augusta*, put down a rebellion. When Corbulo campaigned against Armenia in A.D. 62 he had among his forces a legion borrowed from Germany. In a campaign planned in the east under Nero, *legio XIV Gemina*, which had been victorious over Boudicca, was ordered transferred from Britain. It was in transit in the fateful year A.D. 68, returned to Britain for two years, and was then on the Rhine frontier from A.D. 70 onward.

DISTANCE The distances soldiers had to march are staggering. From Antioch in Syria to the Rhine is somewhat over 3000 miles. For short periods of time a lightly burdened Roman army could make up to 20 miles a day, but a more realistic figure for extended marches was 10 to 15 miles per day. Thus the 3000-mile march from Germany to Antioch could take the better part of a year. In addition to soldiers there was a baggage train to consider. The tent of each *contubernium* of eight men was carried by a mule, which gives a total of about

650 mules per legion. Centurions and officers required their own pack animals. Vegetius, our main source for these matters, adds that each century had its own light-bolt shooter, probably mounted on a cart drawn by mules, and each cohort a larger stone-throwing engine carried in a four-wheeled wagon. This amounts to 59 carts and 10 wagons drawn by a total of about 160 draught animals per legion. These hundreds of animals had to be fed, watered, and periodically replaced. The standard ration issued for individual soldiers was three pounds of bread, one pound of meat, two pints of wine, and about a cup of oil per day. The calculation of the amount of water, flour, fuel, fodder, wine, and oil required every 15 to 20 miles was not so much the challenge as collecting and transporting it to the right place every day. Forage by a legion on the march was an alternative to an organized supply system, but it would have slowed the army to a crawl, not to mention alienating every community within a few miles of the line of march. Understandably only on the rarest of occasions were such long distance transfers actually made. These calculations leave out other, more personal considerations that had a major impact on legionary transfers. As the years went by the legions tended to be concentrated for long periods of time in particular areas where the soldiers, although prohibited from marrying, nevertheless established families. Soldiers were understandably reluctant to leave their families and march away, possibly never to return. One solution to this problem was for only a part of a legion, a vexellation, to be transferred, but this too had its obvious disadvantages.

PROBLEMS OF THE RESERVE All of these factors suggest that Rome needed a strategic reserve if it was not to strip the frontiers someplace and so generate problems for itself in the area weakened by the departure of legions or parts of legions. It seems likely that the idea of a strategic reserve of some kind must have crossed the minds of Rome's accomplished generals from the time of Augustus onward. Some scholars think that the issue was not that Rome's military lacked vision but that the Empire's existence had not been challenged to the point where a compelling case could be made for such a fundamental change. It could reasonably be hoped that the existing system would be sufficient to meet all known threats. After all, the world did not end when Commodus made a deal with the Germans and returned to Rome to perform less onerous tasks than campaigning in the wilderness of central Europe. Other scholars wonder whether the presence of a large strategic reserve stationed, for example, in northern Italy might not have been seen as a permanent threat to the political stability of Rome. The behavior of the Praetorian Guard since its founding was sufficient proof of the danger of any military presence in or near the capital. Perhaps supreme self-confidence in its own fighting abilities was the explanation. Armies are by their very nature conservative organizations. The Romans had always muddled through; why change a proven formula for success? There was no enemy—yet—who had caused them serious problems.

## The Officer Corps

The legions were unlike modern fighting units in a number of ways. As we have seen in the section on the army in the Republic, the centurions came somewhere between commissioned officers and enlisted men. Commanding 80 men, they would fit between lieutenants commanding platoons (40 men) and captains commanding companies (175 men) in the U.S. Army. Like non-commissioned officers in modern armies, centurions were promoted from the ranks. They did not form or belong to a separate, culturally distinct body from the enlisted men as officers do in modern armies.

SENATORIAL OFFICERS The officers of the legion were not professionals but rather members of the Roman elite who, as part of a career pattern, were expected to spend time in the army. Depending on one's status or choice of career, a young man could begin either in the army or with civilian posts and then move on to other military and civilian positions. Legionary commands usually lasted three years and governorships about the same length of time. Such brief stints with the army, often in different parts of the Empire, guaranteed that not many senators developed long-lasting relationships with the legions or any truly deep levels of professionalism. As in the Republic, the principal requirements of a general were courage, initiative, and leadership abilities. He had to be able to inspire his men with an aggressive spirit and encourage them in battle where he was an active, directing participant.

EQUESTRIAN OFFICERS Below the legates were the military tribunes, one of senatorial rank (*laticlavius*), and five of equestrian (*angusticlavius*). The military tribunes had administrative duties and did not command individual units. In the command hierarchy of the legion the prefect of the camp came between the senatorial military tribune and the equestrian tribunes. He was a thorough-going professional with long experience, having passed through the ranks of the centurionate and reached the status of First Centurion (*primus pilus*).

Most equestrians were working their way through their three tours of duty (*tres militiae*), having served previously as prefect of an auxiliary cohort (*praefectus cohortis*) and then after their military tribuneship would go on to command of a wing of allied cavalry (*praefectus alae* or *equitum*), but some were promoted centurions. Like the legionary commanders, the appointments of the military tribunes were temporary and a majority of the equestrians after their *tres militiae* returned to their home cities to continue their lives as local notables—*domi nobiles*. In any case they were not professionals who lived their entire careers attached to a particular legion. For that matter centurions did not spend all of their lives attached to a single legion, but passed from legion to legion as need or opportunity suggested.

SOCIAL FLEXIBILITY OF THE MILITARY The intermingling by Romans of civilian and military spheres of activity may seem strange to modern eyes accustomed to regard the two as naturally separate. Populations deriving from a *polis* culture, however, saw nothing strange in the combination, in fact just the opposite: They believed that the separation of military and civilian responsibilities inevitably led to the subordination of the latter to the former.

The influx of educated civilians from the towns of Italy and the provinces provided much of the talent necessary for the cohesion of the Roman army. The movement of officers throughout the different provinces of the Empire and the promotion of ordinary soldiers provided a form of unity to the scattered legions and auxiliary units. The civilian nature of the equestrian officers opened the army to whole classes of educated people whose careers might otherwise have terminated with a minor magistracy in their home towns. Men of talent and ambition were able to transfer the expertise they acquired in their civilian careers to the army and find a whole new world of imperial service opened to them. The connection between the military and civilian administrations helped to keep the army an integral part of elite Roman life and guaranteed that it would not become overly professionalized. This relationship also had its weaknesses, but at least in peaceful times it proved an rough solution to the problem of how to integrate the diverse regions of the Empire. Although integration of this type was not its aim the Roman army became the prime agent of social unity and mobility in the Mediterranean world. During the later centuries of the Empire the connection between civilian and military cultures frayed to the point where there was little or no connection between the two, especially after transfrontier warriors came to constitute the majority of soldiers in the Roman army.

## The Fighting Qualities of the Army

REPUTATION At a tactical level the effectiveness of the army was the result of a number of factors. During the Republic the army had developed a reputation for invincibility. Of equal importance was the widespread knowledge that the army was backed by a state known for its tenacity in the face of disastrous setbacks, its deep reserves of manpower, and its willingness to expend them. It was not a state that shied away from the use of violence. These were invaluable assets that gave the Romans a pre-emptive edge over most of their would-be enemies who always had to wonder whether they could successfully combat an army that had defeated such mighty and diverse enemies as the Carthaginians, Macedonians, Germans, and others. This was essentially the argument Herod Agrippa used in his futile attempt to prevent his fellow Jews from revolting against Rome in A.D. 66:

> You are not richer than the Gauls, stronger than the Germans, nor cleverer than the Greeks … When almost all nations under the sun have prostrated themselves before the arms of Rome will you alone make war against them? … What allies do you hope for in the coming war? You must expect them from the uninhabited wilds, for the inhabited world is all Roman (Josephus, *Jewish War*, 2.358–388).

Genuine fighting capabilities sustained the image of invincibility of Roman arms. Its heterogeneous composition and flexibility have already been noted. It could borrow from others what it lacked in terms of specialized arms such as cavalry, archers, slingers, and skirmishers. As a result, it was never dependent on a single manpower pool, which when exhausted, would have brought the state to its knees. A Roman army could thus consist of a legion or a number of legions with whatever number of auxiliary units and borrowed legionary cohorts were deemed necessary for the campaign. Without changing the basic commitment to heavy infantry, the Roman army was able to find flexibility by employing the special skills of the auxiliary units, which were commanded by Roman officers but fought according to their own style.

A MOBILE ENGINEERING ARMY As discussed in the chapter on the Republic the Roman army was pre-eminently a shock force designed to seize and hold ground. The army

**Rising Through the Ranks**

*Marcus Vettius Valens rose through the ranks, beginning as a private in the Praetorian Guard at Rome and ending up as procurator, or personal agent and representative of Emperor Nero in Lusitania (Portugal). He may have gotten his first appointment as the result of the recommendation of a patron, but thereafter his own abilities and the opportunity to "network" at Rome advanced his career smoothly.*

This inscription is set up to honor Marcus Vettius Valens, son of Marcus of the Aniensis tribe, patron of the colony of Ariminum [*in Italy*]. He began his career as a private in the 8th Praetorian Cohort [*at Rome*] and was clerk of the Praetorian Prefect. He was recalled for the campaign in Britain [*under Claudius*] and was decorated for bravery. He was then promoted centurion of the 6th Cohort of the *Vigiles*; next, centurion of the 16th Urban Cohort; next, centurion of the 2nd Praetorian Cohort; enrolled as a member of the Emperor's special escort; centurion, *legio XIII Gemina* in Pannonia [*modern Hungary-Slovenia*]; First Centurion [*with equestrian rank*], *legio VI Victrix* in Spain; decorated for successfully waging war against the Asturians; Tribune, 5th Cohort of *Vigiles*; Tribune, 12th Urban Cohort; Tribune, 3rd Praetorian Cohort; First Centurion for the Second Time, *legio XIV* in Pannonia; Procurator Nero Caesar Augustus at the ducenarius level in the Province of Lusitania [*Portugal*].

H. Dessau, *Inscriptiones Latinae Selectae* (Berlin, 1892), 2648.

could function equally well on rough terrain as on level ground. But it was also an engineering army. On the march it built camps on a daily basis. When territory was secured permanent bases were established, roads and bridges built, swamps drained, and supplies amassed. The legions were largely self-sufficient. They had their own workshops that produced weapons, armor, carts, wagons, and catapults. They had the largest concentrations of masons, carpenters, armorers, architects, bridge builders, and engineers in the Empire. Over time a sustaining infrastructure came into existence in frontier provinces that allowed legions in the most remote regions to draw upon supplies from local resources as well as from more distant supply centers.

As a result of its engineering and logistics capacities Rome could project power efficiently with a relatively small army and at relatively low cost. Caesar built a bridge across the Rhine in 10 days, crossed it with his army, and campaigned for 18 days on the right bank. Then he withdrew and tore the bridge down. His point was to show the German tribes that the Romans had the technical ability to cross the Rhine or any other river at will. A century and a half later, Trajan built a magnificent bridge across the Danube to facilitate his invasion of Dacia and overawe the Dacians. It was 60 feet wide, balanced on 150-foot-high stone piers, each set 170 feet apart. Caesar invaded Britain in part to show that Roman arms could cross even Ocean; no land, in other words, was outside the reach of Rome.

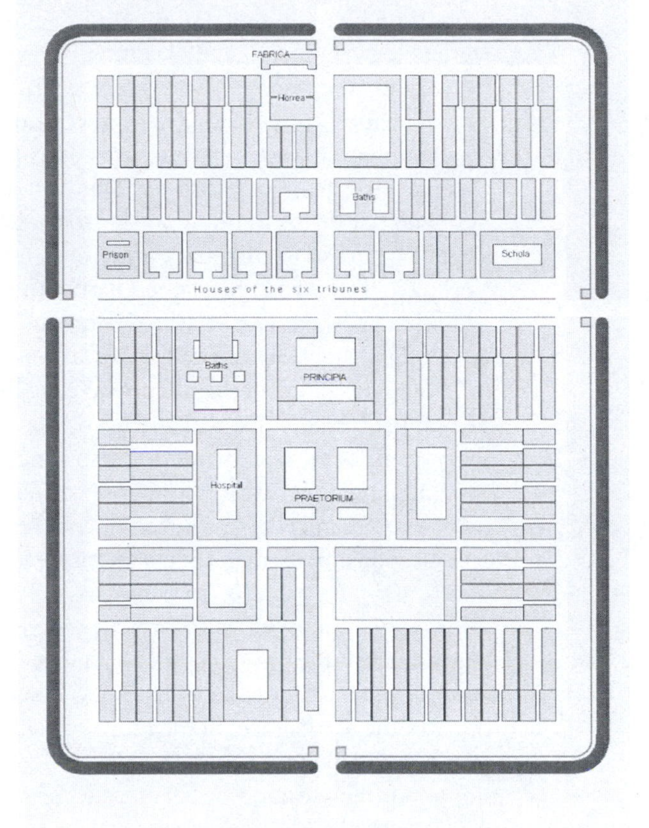


**Plan Roman Army Camp at Neuss**

*This well-equipped camp at Novaesium (modern Neuss) in Germany was first established by Drusus, adopted son of Augustus, and rebuilt in stone as a single-legionary fortress under Claudius for legio VI Victrix. The praetorium was the commander's house and the principia was where the senior officers were billeted. The horrea were the granaries and the fabrica the workshop. The schola was a conference room. For more information go to http://www.livius.org and click on "Rome" and then "Germania Inferior."*

Roman permanent camps were themselves marvels of engineering. They were supplied with water by aqueducts that fed their baths and helped maintain levels of hygiene not seen until modern times. Hospitals were designed to provide quiet for the patients and reduce infection. Some of the main buildings in the camps were heated with hot air flues in their floors and walls.

*Legio III Italica* built and sustained an entire city in the midst of the wilderness of the Atlas Mountains in Algeria where it still stands as a monument to Roman stubbornness and strategic vision. At an unfinished legionary camp deep in hostile territory in Scotland, hundreds of miles from the nearest base, 10 tons of iron nails intended for the construction of permanent barracks, baths, hospital buildings, and so forth, were found. In the east, *legio XII Fulminata* left stone inscriptions on the shores of the Caspian Sea some 1000 miles from its home base at Melitene in what is today Eastern Turkey.

COMMUNICATIONS An underestimated technology that sustained the strength of the Roman army was its mastery of communications. All great armies in history have been dependent on good paperwork, and generally speaking the more efficient the military bureaucracy, the more effective the army. The Roman army had a huge advantage relative to its enemies in that it possessed a developed military bureaucracy in which documentation was integral to its functioning. The ability of the army to keep track of unit strengths and the acquisition and distribution of supplies made possible what the Confederate general, Nathan Bedford Forrest, said was essential to winning battles, "Get there fustest with the mostest." Literacy, down to the level of low-grade officers and even enlisted men, was built into the system and enabled the army to function at an extraordinarily high level of efficiency, disproportionate to its actual numbers. As a result, relatively few legionaries and auxiliaries were able to police gigantic swathes of territory.

Recently the discovery of extensive written documentation for the activities of the garrison of the fort of Vindolanda in northern England has provided insight into how a relatively small number of troops were able to control large, hostile territories. The fort at Vindolanda was part of a chain of fortresses that kept an eye on the fluid border between Britain and Scotland before the building of Hadrian's Wall (A.D. 120–126). These fortresses acted as a kind of trip wire for the main army unit, *legio IX Hispana,* based 80 miles to the south at York. The forts were garrisoned by contingents of non-Roman auxiliaries. In the case of Vindolanda the auxiliaries were Batavians and Tungrians from the lower Rhine area (modern Holland and Belgium). They were commanded by their own officers, and in the case of the Batavians much of the documentation deals with their commander, a man by the name of Flavius Cerialis. He was the descendant of recently enfranchised Batavians. Interestingly, some of the documentation also concerns his wife and her plans for a birthday party.

Vindolanda was well built and had facilities that included permanent barracks for the men, a command center, a hospital, bath houses, workshops, and storage facilities for food and weapons. In many respects the fort was self-sufficient and even produced a surplus of goods that were peddled to outsiders. It had its own arms specialists who may have produced a good number of the arms needed by the garrison. The fact that one of the documents records the presence of 100 pounds of sinews in storage suggests that the fort built or at least maintained its own catapults. Some 343 soldiers were assigned to work in one or other of the workshops. Some retail activity took place in the fort, because members of the garrison had money to spend and there were merchants at hand to supply them with the luxury goods they wanted. An elaborate communications network allowed the importation of goods from the Mediterranean, such as fine quality wine to supplement the fort's own locally produced beer. Olives and olive oil are also mentioned. Interestingly, pepper, which came from India or southeast Asia, is listed among the condiments and spices.

Vindolanda was the center of a node of roads and tracks connecting it to smaller forts and outposts. The garrison was not significant, but its disposition gave the impression that it was much larger. One document tells us that the strength of the unit stationed there was 752 men, but that of these more than half were actually assigned in small detachments at seven different places. A further 46 men were on loan to the governor as part of his bodyguard; 25 were sick; six wounded. Only 265 were left to man the fort itself. It is presumed that the other forts in the region were similarly garrisoned, so that 20 or so forts, each with a complement of about 800 men, were able to police a territory stretching through rough terrain, from one side of England to the other and as much as 100 miles north of the line of defense.

What enabled this system to work was its developed, sophisticated communications system that allowed the commanding officers to have a clear idea of where all the individual units were and what their current strength was. This capacity, wedded to the ability of the Romans to construct and maintain buildings and roads the like of which the natives had never seen and to employ cost-effective weapons such as catapults, helped deter the indigenous population from challenging Roman overlordship. That auxiliaries from recently subdued Gaul could possess such high standards of living and technical abilities gives a hint of

**The Romans Have Subjugated the Whole World By No Other Means Than Through Training**

*In his description of the Roman army the historian Josephus notes that the legionary was equipped with breast-plate, helmet, sword, and dagger. In addition he carried a javelin, an oblong shield, a saw, a basket, a shovel, an ax, a leather strap, a scythe, a chain, and three days food supply. "As a result," Josephus goes on to say, "the legionary soldier differs little from a loaded pack mule." (Josephus,* A History of the Jewish War, *3.107–108). The fourth century military writer Vegetius, describes how recruits were trained*:

> The Romans have subjugated the whole world by no other means than through training in the use of weapons, strict discipline in camp and experience in warfare.
>
> From the start of their training new recruits must be taught the military pace. Keeping their ranks while moving must be carefully checked whether on the march and or in battle. This cannot be done except by constant practice, for an army which is broken up and lacks orderly ranks is always in danger from the enemy. Therefore twenty Roman miles [i.e., about 18 or 19 U.S. miles] at the military pace should be completed in five hours during summer time. At the quicker full pace twenty four Roman miles should be completed in the same time
>
> The recruit must be trained to jump ditches … he must learn how to swim for there are not always bridges over rivers, and in retreat or in pursuit an army is frequently forced to swim. In sudden rainfalls or snowfalls, streams become torrents and dangers arise from not knowing how to swim as well as from the enemy… vaulting onto horses should be practiced strictly and constantly, not only by recruits but also by trained soldiers… young soldiers must be frequently required to carry loads up to sixty pounds and to march at the military pace… every recruit must know how to construct a camp. Nothing else is more advantageous and necessary in war. If a camp is built correctly, the soldiers spend their days and nights securely inside the rampart, even if the enemy besieges them. It is like carrying a walled city around with you wherever you go (Vegetius, *Epitoma rei militaris*, 1).

the even-higher standards of the legions to the rear, not to mention the army's capacity to integrate fully non-Romans into its units.

## The Genius of the Roman Military (and Empire)

The Roman army fought well above its weight for the reasons outlined above. It managed, heroically at times, to overcome huge obstacles of time and distance. Good planning, efficient logistics, and the existence of a well designed network of all-weather roads gave it a

**Keeping Records**

The administration of the legion, whether in terms of special services, military services or pay is recorded daily in the acts with an even greater precision than is the case with military and civil taxes which are kept in official files. Even in peacetime soldiers from all the centuries do night watches and sentry duty and so that no one is overburdened or escapes his duty, the names of all who have done their stints are written in lists. Likewise the name of anyone who receives a furlough is written down along with the length of time it is good for (Vegetius, *Epitoma rei militaris*, 2.19).

degree of mobility not matched until modern times. Its internal organization, force structure, and military doctrine allowed a small army to defend for centuries gigantic swathes of territory against internal and external threats.

The social, political, and cultural infrastructure sustaining this army was also a work of genius. Without the success of the Empire's social engineering the army would quickly have fallen apart. Most empires built on a single homeland eventually run out of enthusiasm, manpower, and talent. Rome's genius was to base the Empire not on a geographically defined territory or single dominant ethnic group but rather on a network of diverse elites and their willing collaborators, bound together by a common citizenship and sense of community. When Italy ceased to be a recruiting ground as it did by the end of the first century, recruits were found elsewhere. For centuries elites from most parts of the Empire (there were some significant regions that failed—Gaul for example—in this regard) threw up talented and ambitious leaders. More than once they saved the Empire from destruction and even guided Rome to several new self-inventions whose magnitude were to parallel those that occurred in Rome's earlier history.

# 16

# What Held the Empire Together: Social and Cultural Factors

## 1. *MUNICIPIA*, COLONIES, AND DIASPORA

The previous chapter emphasized the minimal presence of Romans in the Empire outside areas where the legions were located. Yet someone had to govern—to settle disputes, chase down criminals, maintain order, and pass necessary legislation—in the thousands of cities and non-urbanized communities that constituted the Roman Empire. Theoretically Rome could have sent out masses of its own citizens to act as rulers over the peoples of the Empire, but under Rome's prevailing minimalist political culture this style of overlordship was impossible.

The answer to how Rome ruled its vast possessions from the time of Augustus on lies not in some new development but in the redeployment of old ruling techniques. When it came to governing themselves or others, Romans were most comfortable with face-to-face, personal contacts. From the early days of the Republic Rome was reluctant to annex too much territory and so multiply its responsibilities. At the same time it was unwilling to let go of its conquests. Its solution to this self-imposed dilemma was to rule conquered territory indirectly through local elites who carried the burdens of maintaining order, collecting taxes, and supplying auxiliary troops for the army. These elites received their reward in terms of ties of friendship, grants of citizenship, marriage alliances, and most important, support when their ruling position was challenged from within their own cities. Eventually their communities received municipal status, which brought them even closer to the Roman commonwealth. This was the gentler, soft-power side of Roman imperialism. However, lest the elites of Italy forget that there was also a hard edge to Roman imperialism there were colonies located at strategic sites around Italy connected to the metropolis by all-weather roads. In places there were large communities of individual Roman settlers. Ideologically Rome cultivated a reputation for unfailing fidelity to its friends and allies and its opposite, a reputation for never letting go of conquered territory and inflicting heavy punishment for disloyal allies.

All of these aspects of Republican political culture carried over into the Empire and were adapted to the needs of the Principate. From its experience in ruling and eventually assimilating all of Italy Rome possessed a range of political, legal, and social instruments that gave it flexibility in dealing with the huge variety of communities it encountered throughout the Mediterranean. Armed might may have been the ultimate bedrock of Roman dominance, but force alone is far too crude an instrument for long-term rule in any imperial undertaking. History and its own inventiveness had provided Rome with an instinctive understanding of what it took to deal effectively with different forms of political organization from chiefdoms to sophisticated urban governments.

## Romans in the Empire: Where Were They?

In some respects Roman presence in the Early Empire (Principate) looked a lot like its presence in Italy before the Social War (91–89 B.C.). Just as most Romans in the Republic before the Social War could have been found in the Roman heartland of Latium and Campania, and in a scatter of colonies throughout Italy, in the first centuries of the Empire most Romans (outside army bases) were to be found in Italy, in colonies around the Mediterranean, and in a highly mobile diaspora wherever opportunity for economic, social, or political advancement presented itself. Eventually that situation changed, and in the third century A.D.—just as in Italy after the Social War—all the inhabitants of the Empire became, technically speaking, citizens. In this period, however, thinking in terms of Romans in Italy during the Republic may help understand how the Empire cohered.

MUNICIPIA The development of the *municipium* has already been discussed at length in the chapters on the early Republic, where it was argued that it was an essential institution of Rome state-craft in dealing with non-Roman peoples. It remained a potent administrative technique in the Empire, especially in the West where urban life was not well developed.

Under Caesar many communities in Spain were rewarded for their loyalty by the grant of municipal status, which gave the rulers of these communities Roman citizenship and the rest of the community Latin standing (*ius Latii*), a kind of probationary or partial form of Roman citizenship. Augustus regularized the process with a law, the *lex Iulia municipalis*, which also provided a model charter for imitation elsewhere. In the course of time Latin standing was extended to communities widely throughout the West as a favor or reward from the emperor. While the *municipium* aimed at introducing Roman law and political customs in areas where they did not exist, the *municipium* had the attraction for local peoples, and especially their elites, of providing them with a workable way of making contacts with the power-brokers in the imperial aristocracy and through them with the emperor himself. Many *municipia* eventually were elevated to the status of colony.

COLONIES In the Republic the Romans established heavily fortified colonies at strategic locations throughout Italy. Their main aim was to defend Roman territory, hold down conquered areas, provide land for land-hungry Romans, and help friends and allies throughout the peninsula. These colonies were simultaneously the fetters of Italy and the defensive-offensive bastions of Rome. In a somewhat similar way from the time of Caesar to the second century A.D. Roman emperors planted colonies of Roman veterans around the Mediterranean. In the West, for example, Caesar and Augustus between them established 12 colonies in Mauretania (Algeria-Morocco), 15 in Africa (Tunisia), and 18 in Spain. They resettled the sites of Corinth and Carthage, uninhabited since their destruction by Rome in 146 B.C. Both were strategically located and had good harbors.

The aim of colonization in the Empire was somewhat different from what it had been under the Republic. Strategic defense of Rome was not a primary concern. That was now the army's responsibility. Colonies, however, did have a secondary role in Rome's defense program. The veterans could be depended on to serve as a back-up for the legions in times of trouble, maintain Roman presence in key areas, and over time, provide recruits for the army. The initial aim was economic, namely, securing good agricultural land for veterans. For obvious reasons it was easier to find land in the conquered provinces than in Italy where it could only be obtained by unpopular confiscations or by costly purchases. There were some instances, however, where land overseas was purchased.

The colonies, even if not originally intended as such, quickly also became advertisements of Roman cultural presence. Unlike colonies in Italy, they were authorized to issue their own coinage, a potent means of propagandizing on behalf of Rome. Colonial elites tended to reproduce in as monumental a scale as they could afford, the urban amenities of Rome. They built aqueducts, markets, temples, baths, amphitheaters, and theaters. Where feasible they laid the colony out on a grid pattern. Colonists were culturally far more conservative than the citizens of the capital and were often more Roman than was Rome itself. This was a favorite theme of Tacitus. A colonial himself he regarded Rome as culturally decadent, while provincials like himself—Pliny the Younger was another example—maintained the virtues of the Romans of old.

Reception of the colonists varied from region to region. The communities in which colonies were embedded had no difficulty in sizing up their new guests. Greek cities saw them as useful conduits to the center, to Rome itself, and a way of acquiring privileges and benefits for themselves. In some recently conquered provinces such as Britain, Roman colonies were hated and with good reason. Their arrival undercut the power of native chieftains and led to the confiscation of much of the tribes' best land. During the revolt of Boudicca in A.D. 61, one of the main targets of the rebels was the colony at Camolodunum (Colchester), which was razed and its inhabitants killed. In Africa, Syria, and Pannonia Roman colonies were often welcomed as forces for stability and order, as well as centers of prosperity and urban life. This was especially true in double colonies (i.e., colonies founded alongside a previously existing native city or community as in Apulum in Dacia or Thamugadi [modern Timgad] in Numidia).

THAMUGADI: AN OUTPOST IN THE WILDERNESS Thamugadi was built on the Sahara side of the Atlas mountains in what was then a rich agricultural environment. It was

**The Colony of Thamugadi (Timgad)**

*Thamugadi (modern Timgad) shows the typical grid pattern the Romans followed in laying out their army camps and colonial foundations. This aerial view of Timgad demonstrates well how triumphal arches functioned in a Roman city. Set at a crucial node in the city's transportation network Timgad's arch forced all travelers to pass by or under it, reminding everyone, residents and visitors alike, who was in charge.*

founded in A.D. 100 by Trajan as the home of veterans retiring from *legio III Augusta*, which was based about 15 miles away at Lambaesis. With a population of between 10,000 and 15,000 people. Thamugadi was not a large city, but it had all the amenities of cities found in the faraway heartland of the urbanized Mediterranean. Its construction in a region that had never seen a city before, let alone one as magnificent as Thamugadi, was a stunning achievement. Its construction had the purpose of overawing the local tribes in addition to providing a decent home for the veterans.

Thamugadi's elite grew wealthy on trade and agriculture and, like elites elsewhere, made large benefactions to the city. The city was laid out on a strict grid pattern. Its streets were paved with local blue limestone or sandstone. It had a forum lined with porticoes and shops, and facing each other on opposite sides were a basilica for business transactions and trials and a senate house (*curia*) where the local council met. The city had numerous fine temples and shrines of the gods. Built into a hill was a theater that could accommodate about 4000 spectators. The city had a library, several markets, and an industrial quarter with workshops for the production of glass, bronze, and pottery. No less than 14 baths,

**Cuicul (Djemila)**

*Cuicul (modern Djemila) was founded as a colony by the emperor Nerva (A.D. 96–98). Protected by the presence of legio III Augusta at Lambaesis it flourished as did the other cities of central Numidia. It boasted two fora, baths, temples, and arches. In the later Empire two Christian basilicas were built there. Many of its larger homes were adorned with extensive floor mosaics.*

ranging from small to huge, served the population. Most of the larger private homes were built with peristyles around interior courtyards and had their own piped water. The city, the legionary base, and the fertile agricultural territory that sustained both constituted an oasis of stability in the lawless wilderness of the Atlas mountains, preventing or at least hindering the local tribesmen from their perennial raids on the rich agricultural coastal areas to the north. Many centuries later, long after *legio III Augusta* had disappeared, the tribesmen had their revenge. Thamugadi was sacked, and the life of the region reverted to its pre-urban ways. Eventually the sands of the deserts invaded it and covered it to a depth of several feet.

AFRICANS AND MOORS IN THE IMPERIAL SERVICE Protected by Lambaesis, sometime around A.D. 100 four colonies founded by Augustus—Cirta, Rusicade, Milev, and Chullu in central Numidia—combined together to form one large, prosperous colonial federation of roughly 800 square miles in extent, reaching from Cirta, 200 miles inland, to the coast. Even if Romanization was not an aim of colonial establishments in the Empire such a federation must have had an important cultural impact on the province. The political, social, and cultural vigor of this region of Africa is demonstrated by the number of members of the local elites who went on to serve in various capacities in the equestrian and senatorial aristocracy of the Empire. The sudden—or what appears to be sudden—appearance of a native of Cirta, Cornelius Fronto, as the tutor of Marcus Aurelius, heir apparent to the throne, occurred because of a series of antecedent connections between the Cirta area and Rome. Fronto in turn promoted the careers of his townsmen, several of whom became consuls. By the second century A.D. the imperial aristocracy had more Africans per capita than citizens from any other part of the Empire. Belonging to the Empire had its rewards.

Not all of those who made it so high were of colonial origin. Lusius Quietus, whom we have already met, was a member of the elite of Mauretania (modern Morocco). He served first under Domitian as the commander of an auxiliary light cavalry unit, but he made a name for himself under Trajan during the war against the Parthians in Mesopotamia. Trajan, who valued his talents, advanced him rapidly, enrolling him in the Senate with the rank of praetor, then promoting him to suffect consul and governor of Judaea. His prominence apparently led to his fall under Hadrian, Trajan's successor. The greatest African success story within the imperial aristocracy was the rise of the Severan dynasty (of which there will be more in the next chapter). The Septimii Severi belonged to the elite of the old Phoenician city of Leptis Magna in Libya and during the first century A.D. established contact with elite circles in Rome. By mid–second century two members of that family were serving in the Senate and one of them secured senatorial rank for a promising relative, Lucius Septimius Severus. Severus went on to a distinguished career, becoming governor of Pannonia and then emperor.

Because Roman colonies were, justly or unjustly, viewed as authentic representations of Rome in the provinces, it became the ambition of all cities to acquire the title of *colonia*. After Hadrian the actual planting of Roman colonies became rare, but the number of cities that acquired the status of colony continued to rise. One second-century author explained why:

> They [*i.e., non-Roman cities*] are eager to become colonies because that status… carries with it very great prestige, owing to the grandeur and majesty of the Roman People. Colonies convey the impression of being miniatures and reproductions of Rome itself (Gellius, *Attic Nights*, 16.13)

But there was more to it than honor. Prestige had practical benefits. When it came to entrance into the senatorial order, men from colonies had a better chance of appointment than others in provincial cities not so well placed. If the colony acquired the *ius Italicum*, a not-very-common right, by which the colony was regarded as Italian, it escaped the two usual taxes imposed on provincials, the *tributum soli* and *tributum capitis*. It is understandable that this right was not given out often, but it was a useful reward to encourage local aristocracies to remain firm in their friendship to Rome. By the late second century the possession of the title "colony" did not imply much by way of Roman culture. The granting by Marcus Aurelius of the title of colony to Edessa and Singara and by Septimius Severus to Nisibis—all in strategic Mesopotamia—had more political objectives in mind than the supposed Romanness of these ancient cities, which remained what they had always been, ancient Semitic-speaking communities.

THE DIASPORA Colonies and army bases were not the only places where Romans could be found in the Empire. From the second century B.C. onward there had been a slow trickle of Romans and Italians from Italy into the provinces. They followed on the heels of the legions contracting for services such as the provision of food, clothing, transportation, the purchase of slaves, and the sale of goods needed or sought by the soldiers. Others were members of the tax companies of the publicans (*societates publicanorum*) that were hated everywhere. They were so numerous that in 88 B.C., after the invasion of the Roman province of Asia by Mithridates, it was claimed that over 80,000 Romans and Italians were killed in a series of massacres. Overseas the distinction between Italians and Romans was quickly lost, and the inhabitants of provinces where they were present simply regarded them all as Romans.

During the first century B.C. there were particularly large influxes of Romans and Italians into Africa, Spain, southern Gaul, and to some extent Asia Minor, where good agricultural land and urban amenities were available. These immigrants were not there to spread Roman culture but to exploit economically whatever advantages their Roman citizenship put in their way. They were to be found in the smallest of cities where they advertized their presence under the all-purpose designation of "businessmen" (*negotiatores*). As one example, in Thinissut in Africa the "Romans who do business" there made a dedication "to the god Augustus under the curatorship of L. Fabricius" (*ILS,* 9495). Although only a small town, Thinissut was located near the coast in the agriculturally rich Cape Bon peninsula, and presumably a sufficient number of enterprising Romans found it worth their while to establish themselves there. In another case, in an out-of-the-way town in Numidia the Romans identified themselves as the "*conventus* (association) of Roman citizens who lived in Masculula" (*ILS*, 6774). This designation had legal connotations, and it is hard to guess what the Romans were doing there because Masculula was not located near any major road or town. Perhaps they were involved in some way in the development of agriculture in the area. We know that as a result of secure conditions made possible by the presence of Roman military forces, local tribes began to settle down to profitable sedentary agriculture. The cultivation of the vine and particularly the olive spread in the region. Exports went to Italy and other parts of the Mediterranean. It may have been that the *conventus Romanorum* of Masculula represented the most significant agency capable of promoting city life in an area where there was little or no tradition of urbanization. In the East, which had been urbanized for millennia, the Roman diaspora tended to end up in long-established Greek, Syrian, or Phoenician cities. To cite just one example, in Mantinea in the Peloponnese (southern Greece), "the Romans who do business" honored Euphrosynus—son of Titus and his wife Epigone—for building a market for the sale and distribution of agricultural products in the city (*Sylloge*, 3.783).

THE POWER OF THE ROMAN DIASPORA The Roman diaspora of the Early Empire was unlike those of other periods such the Jewish, Chinese, or Armenian diasporas. Unlike these others, Roman immigrants were not mere guests in an alien community. Their situation was the reverse; they had power relative to their hosts. They were Roman citizens, who spoke Latin and understood the culture of the ruling power. They may have had contacts with local military camps or fortresses to which they provided supplies; with the governor or imperial procurators in the area; and in the case of the very well connected, with members of the equestrian or senatorial elite in Italy itself. They made natural partners for the local native elites with whom they did business and socialized. The more important the provincial city the more important the *conventus Romanorum* who lived there. If civic traditions were weak the immigrant Romans might well become dominant, though what that meant in terms of Roman culture after a century or so of assimilation is hard to tell.

When the emperor thought of the Empire he must have thought of it in terms of a mosaic of Roman cities abroad, of colonies, *municipia*, and provincial cities in which groups of Romans constituted a very useful source of local knowledge and contacts if not actual political power. Through these usefully placed Romans he could funnel his *beneficia*, which were considerable. Citizenship was an important reward for deserving provincials, but the emperor had even richer benefits to offer. He could, for example, make appointments to equestrian or senatorial positions or confer a military tribuneship or the prefectship of an allied contingent. He could grant the status of a magistrate such as a quaestorship or praetorship, which in turn could lead to important positions elsewhere in the Empire.

THE USEFULNESS OF IMPERIAL SERVICE The opportunity for imperial service worked to the advantage of Romans as well as provincial elites. For the latter, imperial service was an escape from provincial narrowness and rural boredom. In the imperial aristocracy ambitious and able provincials could find a way to mix with the mightiest figures in the Roman Empire. For Rome, with a long tradition of opportunistically drawing on outside talent, enthusiastic provincials were a counterweight to old and dying senatorial families from previous generations.

One example will have to suffice: Julius Severus, an important member of the elite of Ancyra in Galatia (modern Turkey) was by ancestry a descendant of the Tectosagi Celts who invaded Asia Minor in the third century B.C. and who had gradually assimilated Greek culture and settled down to an urban life. It may be recalled that the Temple to Rome and Augustus in Ancyra contains the most complete version of Augustus' famous *Res Gestae*. In the winter of A.D. 113–114 when Trajan was moving troops from the west in preparation for the war against Parthia, Severus made them welcome at his own expense. He thus performed a doubly useful civic function. On the one hand he pleased the Roman high command, which was always conscious of the impact on local communities of the passage of armies through the provinces, but he also buffered his own people from the costs of supplying the legions on their march. As a reward his fellow citizens put up an inscription and a statue in his honor—a commonplace reward for a commonplace action by a local aristocrat. However, Severus' generosity also attracted the attentions of the emperor Trajan and his cousin Hadrian, who promoted him to the Senate with the status of tribune. Severus made the most of the geographical position of Ancyra, which was located at a key node in the highway network linking Europe and the east, but clearly he was also a man of talent and ambition. We know of some hundreds like him through inscriptions and an occasional mention in our literary sources, but there must be thousands of whom no record survives. These were the provincials who kept the Empire going generation after generation, long after the Italian contingent in the imperial elite declined in numbers and importance.

UPWARD MOBILITY: THE AUXILIARIES Most of the examples cited so far have been of success at high levels of provincial society. There were also, however, opportunities for

**An Auxiliary Soldier Makes Good**

To the departed spirits of Gaius Julius Dexter, veteran and soldier of a cavalry wing, clerk (curator) of his squadron, overseer of the arms, and standard bearer of the squadron. He served 26 years and having completed his time was honorably discharged. He was a member of the Board of Two of his colony of Thelepte (in Africa). He lived 85 years and was cremated here. The wife of Julius Dexter, Tutia Tertia lived 70 years and was cremated here (*ILS*, 2518).

non-elite provincials to escape the restrictions of provincial life, rise socially, and acquire some economic self-sufficiency. Auxiliary units were integral parts of the Roman army and a key element of its success. Troops in these units were long-term enlistees, professionals in their particular kind of warfare whether light cavalry, slingers, archers, or light-infantry skirmishers. There were some exceptions, but they were usually commanded by Roman equestrian officers with the title of prefect of a cohort or of a cavalry wing. The service of auxiliary units could take them from one end of the Empire to the other. We have already met the Mauritanian Lusius Quietus who took his unit of cavalry with him from Africa first to Dacia (modern Romania/Hungary) and then to Mesopotamia (modern Iraq). Auxiliaries were paid almost as well as legionaries and on discharge received the Roman citizenship after their 25 years of service. During their terms of service they could pick up Latin, become numerate and literate, and make contacts with upper- and middle-class Roman officers who might prove useful later. Provincial Syrians, Africans, Gauls, Germans, or Britons might start out uneducated and penniless in the auxiliaries and later emerge with a rough education, citizenship, some money, and new status. Many settled in the regions to which they had been assigned, but some returned home to awe the youth of their native towns and excite the jealousy of their peers. Discharged at the rate of 6000 a year, the auxiliaries constituted an important addition to the Romanized population of the Empire and a continuing source of recruits for the army, because sons regularly followed their fathers into the old units.

## The Roman Senate and the Provinces

The Senate needed replenishment from the provinces. By the time of the Flavians all the old patrician families of the Republic had died out and only 15 plebeian noble families were still extant. The Emperor Claudius, a strong proponent of bringing provincials into the imperial aristocracy, claimed that in pushing this policy he was merely following the precedent of Augustus and Tiberius who "wished that there be in this House (the Senate) the flower of the colonies and municipalities everywhere, namely, all good and rich men" (*FIRA*[2], 43). Senatorial families disappeared at a rate of 75 percent per generation. Why there was such a high rate of turnover is unclear, but it may have had something to do with inheritance customs that limited family size. In any case, the tendency for the Roman aristocracy not to reproduce itself led to a large number of openings in the Senate in every generation. These openings were filled by members of the elite, first from the towns of Italy and the longer-settled provinces of the west, southern Gaul and southern Spain, Numidia (Algeria), and Africa (Tunisia), and then, gradually, from the eastern Mediterranean.

By the time of Commodus about 60 percent of the senators were of eastern Mediterranean origin. The majority of those who entered the equestrian or senatorial orders came from regions previously colonized by Roman citizens. For example, of the 69 members of eastern provenance who became senators between Augustus and Commodus, 55 came from colonies or places where there were Roman settlements. The distinction is worth noting but it may not be very helpful. The difference between the elite of Greek cities, who had acquired Roman citizenship, and the elite from cities founded or colonized in previous centuries by Romans naturally faded over time.

From the first century A.D. Greeks from the east served in important equestrian posts. Claudius Balbillus of Rhodes received the citizenship under Claudius and was prefect of Egypt under Nero. Tiberius Julius Alexander was an Alexandrian Jew who was made procurator of Judaea by Claudius, served with Corbulo when on campaign in Armenia in A.D. 66, and was finally made prefect of Egypt. In A.D. 69 his support was crucial to Vespasian's successful bid for the imperial throne. Other areas of the Empire also provided Rome with talent. Another Julius Severus, this man a native of the colony of Aequum in Dalmatia (modern Croatia) was, according to Dio Cassius, one of Hadrian's most capable generals. He commanded *legio XIV Gemina* in Pannonia, and then in sequence was governor of Upper Dacia, Lower Moesia, and Britain. From Britain he was summoned to Judaea to suppress the Jewish revolt of Bar Kochba, which he did with great efficiency and brutality. He stayed in Judaea which was renamed Syria Palaestina after the revolt before becoming governor of Syria.

## Cultural Unity of the Imperial Elite

The Roman Empire, although de facto multicultural, was not institutionally or legally so. It was not like Canada or Belgium or Switzerland, countries which recognize and prize the quasi-independent standing of different ethnic and linguistic groups. While the Romans had no difficulty in acknowledging the existence of innumerable cultures throughout the lands they ruled, they accorded these cultures no special formal or informal standing. They took for granted that if elites across the Mediterranean wanted a say in Roman affairs they would have to subscribe to Greco-Roman culture and be proficient in Greek and Latin. When foreign kings came to visit Augustus in Rome they put aside their royal robes and donned togas, and when Augustus visited the provinces "the kings attended his morning audience as clients" (Suetonius, *Aug.* 60). There was no pretense regarding the equality of cultures. Greco-Roman political, literary, artistic, architectural and philosophical culture was regarded without a moment's hesitation as superior to all others.

THE SPREAD OF GRECO-ROMAN CULTURE One of the most remarkable features of the imperial period was the way Greco-Roman culture was assimilated by the diverse peoples of the Empire. The Roman satirist and poet Juvenal complained that too many intellectuals and literary figures in Rome came from the east. He was right. Roman and Italian natives found themselves in a highly competitive cultural environment. Many of the greatest masters of Greek and Latin time were provincials, many from the east. Lucian, the brilliant satirist who wrote in Greek, was Syrian; the historians Arrian and Dio Cassius were from Bithynia in Asia Minor (modern Turkey), as was rhetorician and moralist Dio Chrysostom; Apuleius—novelist, philosopher and orator—and Tertullian—lawyer, ethicist, and Christian apologist—were African.

The upper-classes who shared the common heritage of Greek and Latin could travel comfortably in the knowledge of being able to find people like themselves everywhere. Between them and the masses of the people, however, a great educational divide yawned. There was an important difference between the practical literacy of a soldier, merchant, or ordinary town councilor and the literate, the bookish education of the cultured upper-classes. The acquisition of a classical education was long, expensive, tedious, and for many incredibly boring. Only the elite could afford the time and the cost, but the possession of such an education was an important social marker that instantly identified an individual as upper class. That kind of social identification was worth a lot.

In the formal system of Greco-Roman education only two languages, Greek and Latin were studied. Other languages and their literature—no matter how ancient and venerable—were regarded as barbaric and thus ignored. The Jewish scriptures, although remarkable, did not reflect the civic values of the *polis*, nor did they possess the kind of secular poetry, philosophy, history, and theatrical works that characterized the literatures of Romans and Greeks. Adding to the specialized character of Greco-Roman literary education was the fact that the languages of current use were not studied but rather the Greek and Latin of the classical authors. In Latin these authors were Virgil, Terence, Sallust, and Cicero, and in Greek Homer, Thucydides, the Attic tragedians, and Demosthenes. These masters were accepted as canonical authorities and students were expected to model their styles after them. Imagination and originality were actively discouraged. Form and style were considered more important than content. After all, who could surpass Cicero or Demosthenes in rhetoric, Sallust or Thucydides in history, Homer or Virgil in poetry? Technical proficiency was prized above all. The classical texts were dissected line by line, and the rules of grammar and syntax learned by memory. Generations of students went through untold suffering to master the nuances of a classical style. Saint Augustine, the great bishop of Carthage and a great literary figure in his own right, used to recall with horror his early days in school. Death, he used to say, was preferable to what was suffered by children in their childhood studies—which only goes to show that the problem of the best way to educate children was as intractable 1500 years ago as it is today.

THE PRACTICALITY OF EDUCATION Appearances to the contrary, there was a practical side to the educational system. Stripped of its ideological superstructure its ultimate goal was to provide mastery of the spoken, not the written word. The conduct of an active civic life and the art of public speaking were intimately connected. Because the educated regarded a career of public service as their normal lifetime occupation, some level of oratorical ability was indispensable. Private matters also required the ability to speak well. Business and legal affairs that today might be handled in writing or by telephone conversations or by emails were then conducted in person and often in public. Audiences were impatient with inarticulate speakers because they were used to hearing the smooth delivery and logical arguments of trained orators. There was a reasonable expectation that the average middle or upper-class person could expect to have to speak at one time or another in public before magistrates, fellow city councilors, jurors, the people at large or, during their military career, groups of soldiers. The most effective speaker was one formally trained in rhetoric. St. Paul had the reputation of being well able to defend himself, so that when he was put on trial before the local Roman governor in Judaea the authorities in Jerusalem, feeling they were not up to the task of prosecuting him themselves, hired a rhetorician by the name of Tertullus to argue their case (*Acts* 24.1).

During the so-called "Second Sophistic" (approximately A.D. 60–230) speech making, or to be more precise, declamation, became an art form in its own right. Resident teachers of rhetoric and touring eminences in the field had the capacity to draw large crowds to hear their carefully crafted presentations, filling lecture halls and even theaters. Pliny the Younger tried out his *Panegyric* to Trajan on his friends in a recital that lasted three days, and suffered equally at their hands. Aelius Aristides, one of the major figures on the declamation circuit, could be heard on such subjects as the history of classical Athens and the greatness of Rome. He composed hymns to the gods, polemical essays defending rhetoric against Plato's attacks on art, and a lament for the city of Smyrna after a devastating earthquake. Over 40 of his speeches survive, the longest running to 240 modern pages. Sophistic declaimers were far from useless. They were valuable assets who could be sent by their cities to congratulate and entertain new emperors on their elevation to the purple, to seek privileges or, on occasion, pardon for failures on the part of their communities. They were influential in settling disputes in their own cities and the squabbles between neighboring cities over boundaries, debts and the like.

ENDOWED CHAIRS The cities of the Empire were keenly interested in higher education, and any city that thought anything of itself provided publicly funded chairs of grammar and rhetoric. As patrons of the arts the emperors endowed salaried chairs at Rome and Athens. Antoninus Pius was said by the somewhat untrustworthy *Augustan History,* to have founded such chairs throughout the Empire. There was, naturally, great competition for these positions. Besides salaries and the honor of holding an endowed chair there were additional benefits. Vespasian gave rhetoricians the privilege of immunity from holding expensive city offices. Despite encouragement given at high levels to culture no thought was given to the idea that formal education could or should be used as a tool for socialization in the modern sense. Literary and rhetorical education was narrowly conceived as the prerogative of a small elite that had the time and the money for it. Extending this kind of education broadly would have seemed absurd as well as impractical. The main institutions of education were, as in the past, the household and the community itself. They were fundamental and irreplaceable.

BOOKS Furtherance of one's education was made possible by the existence of libraries, bookshops and a lively book trade. Textbooks of all kinds were readily available. Summaries of architecture, history, geography, philosophy, medicine, and many branches of science, could be picked up from any decent bookseller. There were handbooks on practical subjects such as anatomy, the construction and maintenance of aqueducts, the practice and theory of medicine, building and engineering, town planning, and all aspects of warfare and weaponry. Some survive to the present including Celsus' epitome of medicine, Vitruvius' survey of architecture, and Euclid's handbook on geometry which was used up to the twentieth century. If a person needed a quick update on Roman history, but was short on time there was no need to read all of Livy's 142 books on the history of Rome because quite digestible booklets one tenth the size of the original were available. Polybius who wrote 167 books on Greek and Roman history was even heavier going than Livy as ancient critics attest and a good deal of what he wrote has not survived. The result, unfortunately, is that much of the story of the Roman Republic cannot be told. Even the education of the supposedly well-educated people tended to consist of odd bits of information—mythological, antiquarian, and historical—and their knowledge of mathematics, the sciences, and philosophy was minimal, even by ancient standards. Some Romans—maybe many more than the elite would have liked to have admitted—thought that a formal, traditional education was actually a waste of time. The writer Petronius (first century A.D.) in his satirical novel the *Satyricon* has his protagonist boast:

> I didn't waste my time learning geometry or literary criticism or any other rubbish like that. I learned how to read public notices, how to deal in percentages, weights, measures and currency (*Satyricon* 58.7).

ELITE TASTE Beyond literary and rhetorical training the elite shared broad common cultural interests and especially a common quest for luxury. Among the upper-classes diet, speech, dress, manners and conduct became standardized. Their possession became more important than ethnicity or descent. Mediterranean elites came to share similar tastes in domestic architecture and art. They learned to drink wine rather than beer, used olive oil liberally even in areas where it was not produced locally, employed entertainers and patronized musicians and athletes. Their tastes encouraged the spread of the vine as far north as it could be cultivated and of the olive all over the Mediterranean. The desire of the upper-classes for classical art—any classical art—led to the industrialized production of statues and pottery which were shipped in great quantities all over the Empire and which are today to be found as prized possession of museums worldwide. Mosaic floors graced public buildings and private homes. Wall paintings, which for obvious reasons have had a lower survival rate than statues or mosaics, were also highly popular and tended to share common artistic themes.

## 2. RELIGIONS OF THE EMPIRE: UNITY IN DIVERSITY

### Diversity and Coherence

DIVERSITY Religion was a force for both diversity and coherence throughout the Empire. Every city, town, village, and rural community had its own sets of deities and cults and a corresponding calendar of holy days and festivals. It was the community's special mix of gods, goddesses, spirits, and heroes that defined its identity and distinguished it from its neighbors who, naturally, had their particular forms of religiosity and their special characters. The religious calendar of each community structured the year and gave meaning to daily life. The main festivals were not optional events; they were as necessary to the ordering of things as sowing grain and bringing in the harvest. Neglect of the festivals or their improper or inadequate performance would bring disaster. Not incidentally they also provided opportunities for socializing, banqueting, and doing business. It is understandable that when the Romans established new colonies or municipalities they also provided in the city's charter rules regarding appropriate rituals, how they were to be performed, and who was to perform them. Being Romans they specified how much was to be spent on the festivals. The gap between the religions of individual peoples was to some extent bridged by syncretism and fusion. In north Africa, Saturn was associated with Jupiter; in Gaul, Mercury was identified with the native Celtic deity Lug and Jupiter with Taranis. At Bath in Britain, Minerva was identified with the local spring goddess, Sulis. Yahweh, the god of Israel was sometimes identified with Zeus. Syncretism, however, could only go so far in transcending the differences between the religions of the diverse peoples of the Empire. It enabled visitors to attend each others' festivals, but it did not make them members of the community that was actually putting on the celebration. Diversity was one of the main attractions of the festivals of the different cities.

It would be a mistake to think of these rituals as mere "formalities," in which only the ignorant and superstitious believed, empty of "real" meaning. In the psychology of ancient peoples rituals shaped character and taught people how to behave properly in their relationship to the gods. It was the life-long, annual repetition of the same rituals that made for the effectiveness of the educational curriculum of the community. Not to know how to pray, dance, and sing in honor of the gods was to be uneducated, misanthropic, and lacking in the kind of moral formation that made a good citizen. Without this kind of moral formation personal and civic life would descend into barbarism.

ATTRACTIONS OF THE CIVIC RELIGIONS Most of the civic religions, as the religions of the individual cities and communities are called, were low in doctrinal and ethical content but high in local appeal and personal satisfaction. When there was money available the ritual of the civic religions could be very impressive indeed and served to bring all members of the community together in the worship of the individual gods who looked after that particular community. It is understandable that the emperors seized on great festivals as a very public and popular way of asserting their authority, flaunting Roman power, and drawing the different strands of society together in a common, unifying activity (see Section 3: The Games). It also explains why they put so much money into them.

Everywhere the ancient festivals and sacrifices required the financial support of the cities and the upper classes for their suitable enactment. The celebrations included sacrifices, banquets, dancing, music, games, plays, and processions, and their grandeur depended on the wealth of the cities and the generosity of the elites. Thousands of people sat or stood in theaters, amphitheaters, town squares, or temple steps to witness religious spectacles of one kind or another. The shrine of the healing god Asclepius at Epidaurus in Greece had a theater that could accommodate 15,000, and in other parts of the Empire theaters were specially built adjacent to temples to accommodate worshipers at festival times. At times there were theatrical re-enactments of religious or mythological events. Many of the mystery cults, such as those of Eleusis, also staged large-scale, dramatic affairs attracting thousands. Religious festivals were widely publicized outside individual cities in the hope of attracting worshipers (or just tourists, because both would pay). The more magnificent the celebration, the larger the crowds. Pilgrims and tourists alike carried the word of these religious celebrations far and wide.

THE WEAKNESSES OF CIVIC RELIGION The strength but also the weakness of the cults and civil religions of the Empire lay in their close ties to the communities in which they were embedded. When their fortunes rose, so did those of the cults: the temples were maintained or embellished, the festivals were splendidly celebrated. The reverse was also true. When cities and communities declined, so did their ability to maintain the cults, which unsustained by public support, faded. Gods not worshiped ceased to be gods or degenerated to the level of local superstitions. There is little evidence that in the Early Empire the traditional cults failed to satisfy the religious needs of the people. At least in the cities, if the local cults did not appeal or were not conducted according to one's tastes, there were other choices. The unity and relative peacefulness of the Empire promoted the spread of religions and made exotic alternatives available everywhere. The weakness of the civic religions was their localism. They worked well to preserve coherence in their individual communities but were not as effective promoting social unity regionally let alone in an empire-wide capacity. There were panhellenic sanctuaries and games, which appealed to a wide group of votaries, but the one cult that transcended locality and provided a unifying religious activity for the whole Empire was the worship of the emperor.

## Emperor Worship as a Force for Unity

The emperor was the high priest and head of the Roman state religion, and as such was responsible for maintaining right relations—the peace of the gods (*pax deorum*)—between the gods and humankind. While alive he was a semi-divine intermediary between human beings and the gods, and when dead he was a god himself. From the time of Augustus onward the emperor took a prominent role in offering sacrifices, and in public depictions of the ritual only the emperor or his immediate family is shown presiding. Scenes of imperial sacrifice of this type were common on imperial coinage, aiming to drive home the message that the emperor was the divinely appointed, if not quite divine, intermediary, the patronal-broker, between the gods and the people of the Empire.

In the east, rulers had long been worshiped as being more clearly sources of divine power than the sometimes remote deities of traditional belief. It made good sense politically to honor a man-god ruler, for this conveniently combined cult and homage in a single act. In the Republican period the Greeks had identified the goddess *Roma* as the source of Rome's power and worshiped her, sometimes along with an individual Roman general. Thus the cult of *Roma* and the general T. Quinctius Flamininus, who "liberated" Greece from Macedonian domination in 197 B.C., was established at Chalcis, where it survived for more than 300 years. When Rome swept away the Hellenistic kings the cities and leagues of the Greek-speaking east turned naturally to the new king—the Roman emperor—who had replaced them. During the Principate the cult of Rome and Augustus, replete with temples, altars, and priests, spread throughout the eastern provinces and eventually, following prodding by the emperors, to the west as well. In Italy and Rome homage was paid to the *genius*, or "spirit," of the emperors following the tradition of the cult of the *genius* of the *paterfamilias* (the head of the Roman household) within his own family. Logically, other members of the imperial family were incorporated in the cult of the reigning emperor. Thus, all the peoples of the Empire could be viewed as being members of a single family, with the emperor as their kindly but firm *paterfamilias*. It made sense to pray for his prosperity and to seek his favor.

THE ROLE OF THE ELITE Diversity characterized the way the cult of the emperor was carried out; there was no single, mandated form of worship. The cult of the emperor and of Rome involved the erection of temples and shrines in their honor, together with sacrifices and banquets on the birthdays and accessions of emperors. Religious activities of this kind were traditionally the special province of the upper classes whose job it was to represent the community in its relations with the gods. They alone had the resources to supplement city funds for the erection of monuments or sponsoring the multiple festivals of the religious calendar. The gods, it was understood, appreciated lavish sacrifices, banquets, processions, plays, and all the other activities that were part of religious culture, and of course so did the people. To these activities were added specifically Roman religious cultural features such as gladiatorial combats and wild animal hunts. In taking on priesthoods, members of the elite knew that they were going to take a heavy hit in their wallets. Such priesthoods, however, were recognized by them as an essential part of city-life and that without them the cultural life of the cities would shrivel and decline.

The elite of the Greek world was happy to add the imperial cult to the other religious activities of their cities and to spend lavishly on its celebration. The sacrifices, processions, games, and plays allowed the sponsors an opportunity to parade in new ways their generosity to the people. In return they expected to be honored by their fellow citizens and noticed by the emperor and the imperial aristocracy for their expressions of loyalty to Rome. They vied among themselves to be appointed priests of the imperial cult. The highest honor was an appointment to the High Priesthood of a province to which a title such as Asiarch (for Asia) was attached. There was no hypocrisy in this blending of religious and purely secular functions. In the world of the *polis* as we have seen in the chapters on the Republic religion, politics, social, and cultural life were inextricably mixed with each other in ways that only seem odd to societies where religion and the secular world are seen as two separate, mostly incompatible, spheres of activity. In this context Jesus' claim that one "should render to Caesar what is Caesar's and what is God's to God" (*Matthew* 22.15; *Mark* 12.13; *Luke* 20.20) was revolutionary. It is the modern Western world, not the ancient world, that is unusual in this regard.

## Augustales and the Imperial Cult

Although there were many slaves in Roman society liberal traditions of manumission produced a large class of freedmen. They were often very wealthy because much of the trade, shop keeping, and manufacturing of the Empire lay in their hands. In addition to being wealthy they were also ambitious to advance within Roman society. This created a problem for the Roman elite. Although freedmen became citizens upon manumission, law and ancient custom prevented them from fully entering civic society. They could not hold magistracies or enter the *cursus honorum* which was at the center of the system of honors and rewards among the upper classes. Their sons might, but they could not. The dilemma for the elite was how to integrate this important group of men. It would not be safe to leave them outside and besides the wealth of freedmen made them natural candidates to share the huge burdens of the liturgies—the festivals, the aqueducts, the baths and theaters and so on the elite was supposed to underwrite, endow or build—but which also drained their fortunes.

By a clever and typically Roman sleight of hand the elite found a way to achieve this desirable goal while preserving existing legalities and customs. They created a kind of parallel aristocracy and a parallel *cursus honorum*, the order and college of *Augustales*. *Augustales* had their own magistracies, council and rules of precedence. Its members were allowed to wear the purple bordered togas that distinguished the elite from the masses of society whether freeborn or servile. Its more outstanding members were granted the insignia of the public offices of the city though they were not allowed to occupy the office itself. At a stroke the elite solved the problem of leaving an important well-off group outside the usual boundaries of society while at the same time tapping a resource to help it with its burden of running city affairs.

The college of *Augustales* was a social and religion corporation, found mainly in the western Empire. Its main responsibility was the maintenance of the imperial cult. Members were chosen by the local city council. Usually *Augustales* served for a year in office but they remained members of the order of *Augustales* for the rest of their lives. Their numbers varied from city to city and it is hard to make quantitative judgments from surviving inscriptions. At Herculaneum, one of the cities buried after the eruption of Vesuvius, a fragmentary list gives the names of 450 individuals divided into different units (*curiae*) who constituted the order of *Augustales* in that town. Like city magistrates in cities empire-wide *Augustales* paid a large fee upon entry into their society and were expected to contribute lavishly to the expenses of city activities. Their rewards were the same as for freeborn magistrates: public honor and recognition, applause at the festivals and games, and the erection of statues and honorary inscriptions. Their names can be found in association with all the usual benefactions. They sponsored banquets, games, and festivals; they built baths and arenas; and in smaller ways, they supplied the wood and oil necessary for the functioning of the baths. Their vulgarity was a popular literary theme, but despite the sneers of the elite they enjoyed the same publicity as their freeborn peers and suffered the same reduction of their fortunes at the hands of the masses who knew how to extract something in return for the only thing they had to offer or withhold: their applause and recognition.

## The Weakness of the System

In the end the worship of the emperor did not contribute strongly to imperial coherence. It was welcomed, as was to be expected, by the Roman diaspora and in Roman colonies since it

**The Advantages and Practicality of Urban Living**

*The basilica* **(A)** *and the stoa* **(B)** *were two kinds of buildings that typified the urban landscape of the Roman Empire. The basilica was a large rectangular indoor hall intended for meetings, court sessions, and all kinds of business affairs. Basilicas were often located near or on the forum. If its floor plan looks like that of a Christian church it is because from the fourth century onward Christians found the basilican form most suited their worship needs. The stoa was a roofed colonnade lined with stores of all kinds. It provided cover in both hot and rainy weather and was used by city people for shopping, strolling, and meeting each other. Basilicas were more common in the west, stoas in the east. The stoa illustrated here is a modern reconstruction on the site of an ancient stoa that stood in the agora (the Greek equivalent of the Roman forum) of Athens.*

helped boost Rome's prominence locally. The cult had a strong, practical appeal to native elites. The ordinary people of the Empire might have noticed its existence in minor ways or were at least grateful for an opportunity to receive an additional slab of sacrificial meat when the reigning emperor's birthday was celebrated or a new emperor installed. The temples of the emperors and their related festivals were additions, not substitutions, for the communities' traditional religions. The primary identity of the cities and communities of the Empire remained the local gods, goddesses, heroes, spirits, and festivals associated with them.

Despite this reservation, the imperial cult still had an important role in maintaining the social structure of the Empire. Sacrifices and ritual were not just about "religion," they were also about political power and social standing. The inclusion of the worship of the goddess *Roma* and the divine emperor in the pantheon gave Rome a cultural presence in local social and political hierarchies and sanctioned the legitimacy of Roman rule. The point becomes a little clearer when the behavior of the Jews and Christians is considered. When they refused to offer sacrifices to the emperor (or sacrifices on behalf of the emperor) they were believed to be fundamentally undermining the whole complex structure of Roman rule. From the pagan viewpoint they were not merely being irreligious but were doing something more fundamental: they were threatening the very basis of society and its relationship to the gods on which the Empire was built. This explains the anger Gaius expressed to a Jewish delegation that came to him from Alexandria hoping to be relieved from orders to sacrifice to the emperor. When they claimed they sacrificed regularly *on* his behalf he responded: "What's the merit of that? Why do you not sacrifice *to* me?" (Philo, *Embassy*, 353).

**The Roman Theater at Bostra**

*Bostra (or Bosra), 75 miles south of Damascus in Syria, was made the capital of the province of Arabia by Trajan and was the base of legio III Cyrenaica. It was equipped with the usual amenities of baths, plazas, temples, fountains, and the fine, well-preserved theater shown here.*

## 3. URBANISM AND IMPERIAL COHERENCE

Rome ruled through a network of urban centers. In the East there were hundreds of them. Asia Minor (Turkey) alone had 300. Each city had its own carefully defined and often disputed territory, and was ruled from within by an oligarchic elite according to its own laws, which might date to its foundation. Elsewhere non-Greek cities existed alongside later Greek foundations, as in Palestine, Lebanon, and Syria, or there were Greek cities with large numbers of non-Greeks in their populations. This complexity was guaranteed to test the flexibility of Roman governors and administrators, who in their careers might at one stage be in contentious Alexandria, which was always ready to erupt into riots between Greeks and Jews, in peaceful Sicily, where nothing ever happened, or in tribal Britain or Africa. Each region had its own particular set of problems—military, cultural, and social. It was a fine training ground for tolerance or, perhaps more usually, benign neglect. There was never a time when an emperor was without large groups of delegates from cities and communities all over the Empire waiting for an opportunity to hand their petitions to him and get his response, preferably in person. In the west cities were slow to develop beyond the coastal regions. During the Empire period the Romans encouraged and where necessary coerced communities to give up their old rural haunts and inaccessible fortresses and settle in cities in the valleys and plains.

**What the Rich Owed Society: The Career of Pliny**

*While the rich had clearly defined privileges in society, they also had some well-defined obligations. These included, first and foremost, personal service to the local municipality and then to the imperial government. They were expected to stand for election to local offices; serve in the local senate or council; perform the duties of patron (which included handing out cash); and perform military service. For some, service in the imperial administrative system and the Roman Senate was a tradition. The inscription provided here works back and forth chronologically, starting with Pliny's highest offices, then going back to earlier ones, and ending with his benefactions to Como, his hometown in northern Italy.*

Gaius Plinius Caecilius Secundus, son of Lucius, of the Oufentina tribe, consul [A.D. 100]; augur; legate with propraetorian power of the province of Pontus and Bithynia [parts of modern Turkey], having been sent there by decree of the Senate with consular power, and by the Emperor Caesar Nerva Trajan Augustus Germanicus Dacicus, Father of the Fatherland. [He was] Curator of the Course and Banks of the Tiber and of the Sewers of the City of Rome; Prefect of the Treasury of Saturn; Prefect of the Military Treasury; Praetor; Tribune of the Plebs; Imperial Quaestor; President of a Squadron of Roman knights; Tribune of the Soldiers of legio III Gallica; member of the Commission of Ten for Decisions on Civil Status.

By his will he ordered the construction of baths for the municipality [of Como] costing ... [the amount is lost through a gap in the inscription], with a further 300,000 sesterces for their decoration ... [another gap] and 200,000 sesterces for their upkeep; likewise he bequeathed 1,866,666 sesterces to his city for the support of his 100 freedmen. The interest on this amount he directed to be afterwards devoted to the feeding of the plebs of Como ... [another gap]; likewise, during his lifetime, he gave 500,000 sesterces for the support of the boys and girls of the urban plebs; he also gave a library and 100,000 sesterces for its upkeep (H. Dessau, *Inscriptiones Latinae Selectae* (Berlin, 1895), 2927).

## The Attraction of Cities

Urban living may not have offered a higher standard of living to ordinary people and may, in fact have been unhealthier than the countryside. For some, however, cities were a refuge from deep rural poverty or violence. For others they were places of opportunity and excitement.

It is hard to make generalizations about the cities of the Roman Empire since they varied enormously in size, age, and in the range of amenities they offered. In general, unlike modern cities ancient cities were designed for pedestrian use. Vehicles were often limited to night use of streets and in some cities, as at Pompeii, there was a system of one way traffic which aimed at avoiding congestion. Older cities were often a maze of narrow, twisting alleys, but the new cities founded by Rome were laid out in an open grid pattern and had a fairly standardized appearance. Main streets led logically to the city center where concentrations of buildings such as theaters, basilicas, porticoes, baths, markets and temples were to be found. The main roads were lined with colonnades, shops, and blocks of houses and apartments and usually passed under arches which helped define the layout of the city. Although major cities had aqueducts that supplied water to the baths and the fountains of the city center and to a few other locations, only the wealthy had running water. Baths usually had public latrines which were flushed with water from the baths themselves, but human waste was mostly deposited in cesspits or collected by night soil merchants. At Rome and perhaps elsewhere large pots were located at street corners for convenient urination. Their contents were collected by fullers, the city's laundrymen, who used them for cleaning and shrinking cloth.

**The Amphitheater at Verona**

*Amphitheaters were common throughout the west and Africa but less so in the east where other buildings could be adapted for gladiatorial games and shows. The amphitheater at Verona in Northern Italy accommodates 22,000 spectators and is still in use for theatrical performances.*

Most provincial cities of the Empire ranged in the thousands rather than the tens of thousands of inhabitants so there was a greater sense of community there than in Rome or in the other metropolitan cities of the Empire. People met each other in the markets and shops of the forum areas where most public business was transacted. Here the local city-councils met, trials were conducted, elections held, and public announcements made. People met each other again in the theaters, amphitheaters, gymnasia, and baths. Religious festivals which were the central features of daily life brought the whole city together to banquet after sacrifices, and to attend theatrical performances, athletic contests and in rich communities, gladiatorial fights. The well-to-do classes were not segregated elites who had little contact with the rest of the community. The ideals of urban life demanded an interchange between the classes. Town councilors and magistrates as well as Roman imperial officials could be easily identified and approached. Benches in the market place, in front of taverns and near fountains encouraged idling townsmen and women to sit and chat. Gossip and rumor which functioned as the media of ancient town-life carried tales all over the city. Since underemployment was chronic there was always a large consuming audience for this type of entertainment. Ancient cities were built on a human scale and their architecture was intended to be enjoyed by their inhabitants who, because they walked, had the time to appreciate the design and workmanship of buildings. Imperceptibly the built environment shaped the culture and the character of the city's inhabitants. Rightly the sixth century A.D. historian and palace official Procopius called the Romans "the most city-proud people known" (*Gothic Wars*, 8.22.7).

## The Games: Institutionalized Terror

The amphitheater was a Roman invention and most examples of it are to be found in the west, not the east. One scholar lists 186 with an additional 86 probable. There were 20 in Tunisia alone, most of them small. Those at Carthage and Thysdrus (El Djem), however, were each able to accommodate about 30,000 people each. The great Flavian Amphitheater at Rome, the Colosseum, could hold 65,000. Greek cities had to make do, for the most part, with their theaters.

The amphitheaters were primarily places where gladiatorial fights and wild beast hunts were given and sometimes places of public executions. Most, because of their size, were situated outside of towns. In the city of Rome itself huge resources were lavished on the games. During the reign of Augustus, the Roman calendar had 77 days of public games (*ludi*) and within two centuries the number had risen to 176. Some months were practically given over to the games. April, for instance, had the *Ludi Megalenses* (honoring the Great Mother), which lasted from April 4 to10; the *Ludi Cereales* (for the goddess of cereal grains), which went from April 12 to 19; and the *Ludi Florales* (for a fertility goddess), which went into May, from April 28 to May 3. Another good month was September, with the *Ludi Romani* from the fifth to the nineteenth. The festivals were not entirely devoted to gladiatorial and wild animal hunts. A majority of the time was given to sacrifices, banquets, processions, plays and other forms of recreation. Additional popular entertainment was provided by the chariot races in the Circus Maximus, which held up to 250,000 people. Theaters could also accommodate large numbers of people. Pompey's theater, Rome's first stone theater, could entertain 11,000 spectators per show and the theater of Marcellus (still standing) could seat 13,000 people.

Rome, however, was not typical of the cities of the Empire. The vast majority of these cities lacked the wealth and sometimes the will to put on gladiatorial fights or wild beast hunts. The Cynic philosopher Demonax, a disciple of Epictetus, argued the Athenians out of staging gladiatorial fights claiming that they would have to first give up their Altar of Pity before they could introduce such contests. Later, Athenians gained a taste for blood and were condemned by the orator Dio Chrysostom for their "crazy infatuation" with the games (31.121). After Domitian official permission was required for gladiatorial fights outside Rome.

How a society invests its resources says a great deal about the priorities of that society, and there is no doubt that the *ludi* were a fundamental institution of Roman life. No buildings were larger than the amphitheater or more eye-catching, and it has often been noted that amphitheaters dominated many cities the way Gothic cathedrals dominate so many European towns today. On no other non-military activity did the emperor and the elites of the Empire lavish so much of their resources than on the apparently useless extravagance of the games. In addition to the slaughter of human beings, extraordinary numbers of exotic animals—tigers, crocodiles, hippopotami, ostriches, not to mention bears and bulls—per-

**Union Station, Washington**

*Oddly it is easier to get a feel for the style of Roman imperial baths in the U.S. than it is in Rome, where most of the baths are just giant, crumbling heaps of brick and concrete. Union Station in Washington D.C. gives a very close approximation in terms of looks and feel, both inside and out, of what an imperial bath building might have looked like in its heyday.*

ished in arenas all over the Mediterranean. Yet the popular events won huge amounts of prestige for the emperors and elites who put them on. No one, of course, could compete with the emperor who had the resources of the Empire at his disposal. Augustus nonchalantly notes in his *Res Gestae*:

> On three occasions I gave gladiatorial shows on my own behalf and fifteen times for my sons and grandsons. About 10,000 men fought in these games . . . . On twenty-six occasions I put on wild beast hunts for the people in the circus, forum or amphitheater in which about 3,500 animals were killed (Augustus, *Res Gestae* 22).

In a throwaway comment Dio Cassius says that in the celebration of his victories Trajan gave shows that lasted 123 days during which 11,000 wild and tame animals were killed, and 10,000 gladiators fought (68.15.1).

## Baths

An integral part of all urban life in the Empire was public bathing. It was not a Roman invention since the practice had long been a part of Greek gymnasium ritual. Romans, however, had their own traditions, believing that a good sweat in front of the kitchen stove or oven could cure flu and colds. In many farmhouses in Campania and Latium a room was specifically designated for that purpose. With increasing urbanization these rural traditions developed into formal institutions, and bathing facilities became an essential mark of any city or town worthy of the name. Even villages may have had public baths. Pliny the Younger remarks that near his villa at Laurentium there was a village that had no less than three baths that he would be willing to use if his own were not available, implying there were others he would not think of using (*Letters*, 2.17). Households, urban or rural, that could afford a bathhouse had one, and to the present day archaeologists use the presence of heating flues (or hypocausts) built into foundations and walls to identify baths from other types of buildings.

There were two types of baths. *Balneae* were small bathing establishments privately owned and often incorporated into buildings shared with other businesses. They sometimes catered to the particular tastes of their customers. Pompeii had a number of baths, one of which advertized the availability of both fresh and sea water. *Thermae* were owned by the state or the city. These latter were large public baths built in open areas, supervised by a corps of professional *balneatores* who cleaned the baths, provided towels and linens for the bathers, kept the furnaces fueled, and the metal fixtures and marble polished. One of the great attractions of the baths or at least the better ones was that because floors and walls were heated large numbers of people could find a place in cold weather that was always warm. The baths of Caracalla, one of the great imperial baths at Rome, achieved a form of air conditioning by inducing convection currents in the air that flowed through the building. Rome had 11 *thermae* and 967 *balneae* according to one Late Empire source. No such precise figure is available for the rest of the Empire, though references to nearly 400 have been found in the sources.

The baths were as much—and maybe more—social and recreational institutions as they were a means of maintaining personal hygiene. Because of this emperors took a special interest in the building and subsidizing of baths for the public at large, seeing in them an opportunity to win the good will of the masses. Baths like those of Trajan and Caracalla were monumental complexes set in enclosures containing lecture halls, libraries, eating facilities, running tracks, and gardens. Everyone, free or unfree, male or female, had access to the baths. Even emperors used the baths on occasion. The generosity of the emperors was imitated by provincial elites. To this day the ruins of the public baths are, along with the remains of amphitheatres and theaters, the most imposing buildings to survive from the imperial age and not just in Rome but all across the Empire.

## What Kind of a State Was the Roman Empire?

One way to summarize these two chapters on the subject of what made the Empire cohere without repeating too much of what has already been said is to try to define what kind of a state the Roman Empire was. It is, however, easier to say what it was not rather than what it was.

Rome in the imperial period had a government and an identifiable territory, but it was not a nation or a people let alone a nation-state. It did not aim to be one. Its inhabitants were not, and could not be, a people the way the inhabitants of France or Japan, for example, are French or Japanese. Italy was important and had special privileges, but the Empire did not have a heartland the way France and Japan have clearly identifiable heartlands. It is commonplace to say Rome was a multicultural, multilingual empire and such it was, but only up to a point. It was not multicultural in the way some modern states are with their constitutionally recognized ethnic and linguistic divisions. Greco-Latin culture was supreme and exclusionary. Rome tolerated and did not interfere with local cultures, but an individual could go no place in the imperial system, no matter what his standing and education in his native culture, without a good knowledge of Latin and Greek and immersion in Greco-Latin culture.

It is difficult to find modern analogues for the Empire. Rome of the imperial period was more an idea or a complex of ideas than anything else. Socially and politically it was a network of participating elites. Being Roman, *Romanitas*, was an elastic concept transcending ethnicity, culture, language, and even territory. It was infinitely expandable. By the second and third centuries A.D. the truest "Romans" were not the people of Italy, let alone Rome itself, but groups of individuals from Africa, Spain, Greece, Syria, and elsewhere who chose to identify with Rome. Technically from A.D. 212 on all the inhabitants of the Empire were Roman citizens, but some were, in reality, a good deal more Roman than others. Elites could and did opt out of the network at the same time other elites were joining the network.

Outlined in the chapters above were the principal means by which Rome perpetuated itself. There were many Romes. There was the world of the emperor, the imperial court, and the elites, the latter easily identifiable by their bearing, dress, manners, speech, and culture. There was the Rome reflected in its look-alike provincial cities with their theaters, libraries, baths, public buildings, aqueducts, and paved roads. The power and cruelty of Rome was advertized in amphitheaters while its civility was reflected in its basilicas, baths, theaters, and fora, in its law courts and libraries. There was the Rome of imperial statues, triumphal arches, inscriptions, milestones, roads, and a coinage that circulated from Syria to Britain. There was the Rome of the army and its supporting ethnic units, the auxilia. The army was not, however, the bedrock of the Empire or the source of its cohesion. The Empire depended on the army, but to an even greater extent the army depended on the Empire; it required a river of silver to survive. This dependence of the army on the Empire was not just economic, but also social and cultural in character.

To say the Empire was a complex entity is not to exaggerate. Paradoxically, as a state it was simultaneously both strong and weak. In some respects it was a very fragile entity indeed. All-powerful Emperors often could not get their commands obeyed outside their own palaces—or at times even within their palaces. Patronage worked only as long as there were reciprocal benefits to dispense. Much depended on the willingness of the masses and elites of the Empire to buy into the idea of *Romanitas*. There was always a cost-benefit analysis at work. For some it made sense to identify with the ruling power, but it was not automatically a case of the wealthy and powerful identifying with Rome and the poor seeking "freedom" from oppressors. The poor who appealed directly to the emperors for justice did so because justice at the local level had failed them. For the unemployed or underemployed of the countryside service in the military was an alternative to poverty, drudgery, or simple boredom. To the ambitious the imperial administration and army represented an opportunity to escape from the suffocatingly narrow confines of their native cities where local elites were securely in control.

Gibbon was right to say the explanation of the fall of the Empire was simple but that it was difficult to account for its coherence. In the end Tacitus' mordant comment (cited in full, Chapter 15, page 311) was an accurate portrayal of the realities of life in the scattered and often anarchic provinces of the Roman Empire:

> If the Romans are driven out ... what else can there be except wars among all these nations? Eight hundred years of the Divine Fortune of Rome and its discipline have produced this federal empire and it cannot be pulled apart without the destruction of those attempting to do so.... Therefore, love and care for peace, and also love and care for that city in which victors and vanquished alike share on an equal basis. Learn the lesson of fortune for good or evil: Do not choose obstinacy and ruin in preference to submission and safety (*Histories*, 4.74).

For the speaker, the general Cerialis, the choice, put simply, was order or chaos. Apparently a large number of the inhabitants of the Empire thought so too. However, the depth of their commitment to the Empire was to be tested in the crisis of the third century, discussion of which follows next.

# Part Six

# Rome on the Defense: The Third Century A.D.

## 1. INTRODUCTION

The Severan dynasty (A.D. 193 to A.D. 238) was either the tail end of the Principate and Rome's Golden Age, or the prelude to the military and political disasters of the third century when the Empire almost disintegrated as a result of external assaults and internal chaos. Whichever way we choose to view it, the dynasty represents a period of transition, from the equilibrium of the Empire under the Principate, to the anarchy that came after it. By the end of the Severi it was clear that the balance among the multiple constituencies of the Empire, so brilliantly achieved by Augustus and maintained by his successors for the next two centuries, was now lost.

### Loss of Balance: The Imperial Succession

The proof that the Empire's instinct for equilibrium was gone is most easily seen in the failure of the imperial succession. Between the death of Alexander Severus in A.D. 235 and the rise of Diocletian in 284 when the Empire found a new beginning, there were 27 emperors, not counting numerous pretenders to the throne. Of these, 17 were murdered, all but one by their own troops; two committed suicide; three were killed fighting; and one died a prisoner

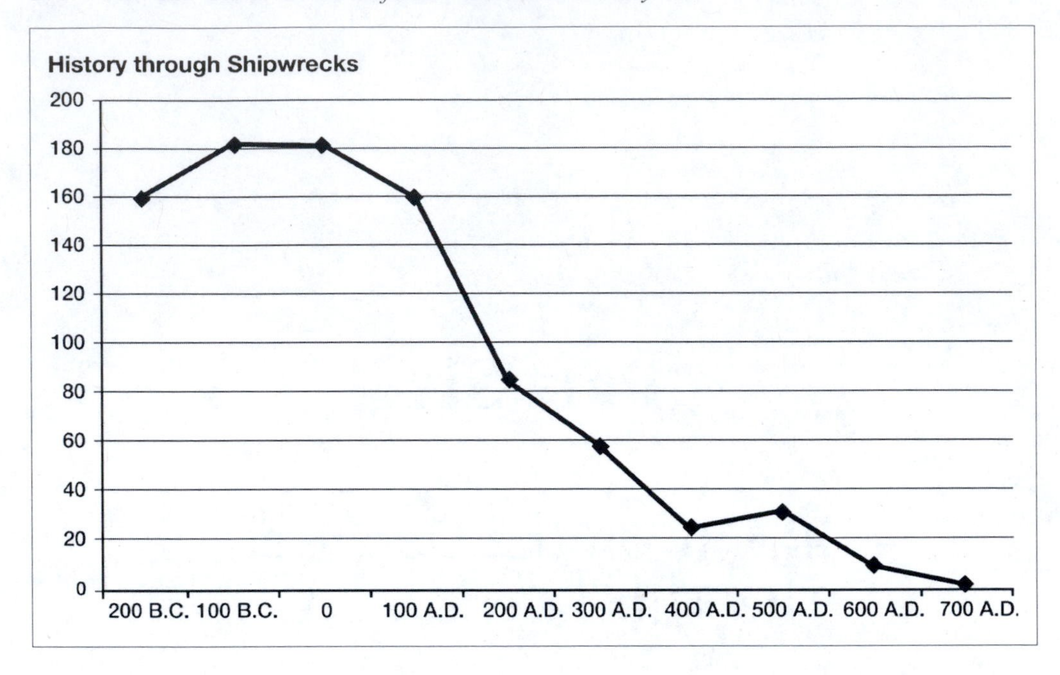


**History through Shipwrecks**

*The graph tells its own story of the decline of the Roman Empire. The tipping point seems to have been around A.D. 150. The decline stabilized around A.D. 450 before declining to practically zero around A.D. 750.*

in the hands of his enemies. Only four died natural deaths. On one notorious occasion six claimants to the throne were killed within a five-month period (A.D. 238).

Simultaneously with the collapse of the imperial office there were multiple invasions of both the Western and Eastern Empire. This was potentially a strategic worst-case scenario for Rome. In the East the crumbling Parthian Empire was replaced by a vigorous new Persian Empire that laid claims to the lands of the old Achaemenid Empire that had been destroyed by Alexander the Great. This included land such as Asia Minor, Syria, Palestine, Egypt, and Cyrenaica that had long been part of the Roman Empire. The Persians began systematic assaults that were to last for centuries, in fact until the fall of Persia to invading Muslim armies in the seventh century. In the west German invaders broke through the imperial defenses numerous times. In A.D. 269 a German federation of tribesmen, the Alemanni, advanced close to the city of Rome itself. The Balkans were the main scene of Germanic attacks, but the invaders were also able to make their way into the eastern Empire by way of the Black Sea. In A.D. 253, 256, and 267 they were looting and burning Rome's richest province, Asia Minor. Athens and Sparta were sacked in A.D. 268.

By A.D. 270 it looked as though the Empire had begun to revert to its pre-conquest, fragmentary condition. What was left of Rome's presence in the east was being maintained by an independent kingdom that had sprung up in the city of Palmyra in the midst of the Syrian desert. In the West another independent kingdom had begun to take shape. Only the central section was to some extent still under the control of Rome. Yet, by the end of the century under the vigorous leadership of the Illyrian (Balkan) Emperors, both east and west had been recovered. Shortly afterwards a world-historical step was taken by Constantine's extension of tolerance to Christianity and his subsequent promotion of that religion.

The questions to be addressed in this section have to do with the nature of the anarchy of the third century and the new Rome that appeared at the end of the century. Why did the Roman government lose its sense of balance? What went wrong? Was the disorder that was so clearly evident in the imperial succession the cause of the anarchy of the third century or the result of it or some combination of both? Were the numerous defeats suffered by Roman armies in both east and west due to the political disorder of the Empire or to a failure of the military to keep up with changing conditions? What about cultural and religious factors? In the midst of the crisis emperors Decius and Valerian were sufficiently concerned with the state of religious culture to insist that the gods be honored by universal sacrifices throughout the Empire (A.D. 249–251 and A.D. 257–260). In the case of Valerian's attempt at religious revival the hierarchy of the Christian church was a principal target. What brought about this change of attitude on the part of the authorities who, up until the mid–third century, were content to let local authorities handle religious deviance?

## 2. HISTORIOGRAPHY

This extraordinary tale of disaster and recovery is, unfortunately, hard to tell. Our sources for the period are among the worst for any period of Roman history except perhaps for its earliest. There are no surviving contemporary chronological narratives for the main events of the century, and the story of these years has to be pieced together from the untrustworthy *Historia Augusta* previously discussed; from Byzantine sources that had access to contemporary Greek accounts, now lost, and a few brief histories written in Latin in the late fourth century. Dio Cassius ended his history with the death of Alexander Severus in A.D. 235. Another Greek historian, Herodian, overlaps Dio Cassius, but also ends early in the century with the accession of Gordian III in A.D. 238.

The lost contemporary account is that of an Athenian historian by the name of Dexippus, quoted in the *Historia Augusta*, who wrote on the period from A.D. 238 to 270. Historians have concluded that he neither had access to good information nor was critical in what he had to say about the information he had. The Byzantine texts are the work of Zosimus, writing from an anti-Christian viewpoint in the sixth century, who used as sources Eunapius of Sardis (fourth century) and Olympiodorus of Thebes (fifth century). Eunapius' work began where Dexippus left off around A.D. 270 and continued to A.D. 404. John Zonaras wrote in the 12th century but had access to works that have since, like so much of the rest of the sources for the period, perished. John Malalas' *Chronicle of Antioch* is useful for information about Syria. Finally there is the trilingual inscription of the Persian king Sapor, carved at Naqsh-i-Rustam, which is useful for the period 244 to 260, and another inscription of a Persian King Narses from northern Iraq for events after Sapor's death. Eutropius (fourth century) published a very brief survey of Roman history written in Latin, up to A.D. 364, and Aurelius Victor wrote a book titled "On the Caesars," also in Latin, that gave brief biographies of the emperors from Augustus to Constantius II (A.D. 360). His career spanned the last half of the fourth century.

The early fourth century is relatively well documented but the sources are complicated by the appearance of writers who took strong views on Constantine's adherence to Christianity. Lactantius' On the *Deaths of the Persecutors* emphasizes the bad ends to which those who persecuted Christians came, especially the emperors of his own time. Eusebius (d. A.D. 339), bishop of Caesarea in Palestine, wrote a history of the Church from earliest times as well as a panegyric to Constantine. The church historians Socrates Scholasticus (fourth/fifth century) and Sozomen (fifth century) extended Eusebius' narrative down to A.D. 439.

One of the great gaps in our source of information for the third and early fourth centuries is the reduction in the number of inscriptions. For whatever reason, the so-called "epigraphic habit"—the practice of putting up masses of inscriptions by individuals and governments—tails off in the third century. Archaeology shows that while some areas such as Africa and Britain flourished, other regions did not do so well. Legal codes are useful for information about social habits but are difficult to interpret. If one finds a law prohibiting an activity, for example, was the activity a widespread phenomenon? Or, conversely, was the law a response of an emperor or some other authority to an atypical situation?. The tone of the laws tends toward harshness, but again it is hard to know what conclusions we should draw. Was it, for example, a period of great change to which officialdom responded harshly? The evidence says more of the ineffectiveness of the authorities and the inappropriateness of their responses than of the changes themselves. The coinage of the Empire remains a major source of information. It continues to proclaim that Rome was eternal and unconquerable and celebrates, ironically, "perpetual security" and "perpetual hope."

# 17

# Rome on the Defense

## 1. THE SEVERAN EMPERORS

### Pertinax and the Praetorians: A Repeat of A.D. 69

Commodus' replacement, the elderly senator Pertinax, was a highly competent general who had served as the governor of two of the Danube provinces, Upper and Lower Moesia, as well as governor of Dacia and Syria before being appointed emperor to replace Commodus. His career is a good example of how new men were able to make their way in the imperial aristocracy. Although a distinguished senator and at the time of his elevation the holder of the Prefecture of the City—the highest post that a senator could have—Pertinax was the son of a freedman from northern Italy and had served in the equestrian service before becoming a member of the Senate. His reputation as a rigid disciplinarian and his service in the frontier legions made the Praetorians wary of him, fearing he would force military discipline on them, and he had difficulty raising the money needed to pay the bonus that had been promised on his accession. The palace staff, which had grown influential under the indolent and erratic Commodus, was also afraid of the old-fashioned emperor who held their lifestyle in contempt. "He failed to understand," said Dio Cassius, "that it is impossible to reform everything at once" (73.10). After a rule of a mere 87 days the Praetorians murdered him, encouraged by their commander. The Guard then proceeded to what amounted to an auction of the Empire to whoever would pay them the largest bribe. This was not wholly unprecedented, as a somewhat similar situation occurred on the death of Caligula in 41 when Herod Agrippa acted as broker among Claudius, the guard, and the Senate. The highest bidder was senator M. Didius Julianus, who paid each guardsman 25,000 sesterces.

CIVIL WAR On hearing of the death of Pertinax, the frontier legions took matters into their own hands, and a four-year civil war ensued. The troops in Syria proclaimed C. Pescennius Niger emperor; those in Britain, D. Clodius Albinus; and the Danube legions, their commander, L. Septimius Severus. Ignoring for the moment his rivals in the east and west Severus calculated he could reach Rome before they did, as had the Rhine legions in the last civil war in A.D. 69. Abandoning the frontier he marched his legions into Italy, declaring himself to be an avenger of Pertinax and adopting the murdered emperor's name. When news of the march reached Rome the Senate condemned Julianus to death and the Praetorians entered into negotiations with Severus, hoping to be rewarded for not repeating the actions of their predecessors in A.D. 69. Instead Severus disbanded the existing Praetorian Guard and replaced it with veterans from his own ranks. He had the former emperor deified and held a magnificent funeral in his honor. He now had to deal with his other legionary rivals. Proclaiming Albinus his heir in the West, in order to secure his rear, he set off for the East, where he defeated Niger in A.D. 194. Antioch, which supported Niger, was sacked and lost its position as the capital of Syria. Byzantium, which had also resisted him, was razed. On the other hand, Tyre, which supported him, was made a colony. Turning west, he then took on Albinus and after a struggle defeated him. The city of Lugdunum (Lyon) then suffered the fate of Antioch and Byzantium, and—because a number of senators had supported Albinus—Severus turned on the Senate, executing many of its members and confiscating their estates. At the same time he announced his adoption as the son of Marcus Aurelius and declared his sons Caracalla and Geta his heirs.

## Septimius Severus and His Family

SEPTIMIUS SEVERUS During the reign of the Antonine emperors—Antoninus Pius, Marcus Aurelius, and Commodus—many north Africans were promoted to high positions in the army and the imperial administration. Among these were members of the Severan family from the ancient Phoenician city of Leptis Magna in Libya. Their most prominent member was Lucius Septimius Severus who rose to prominence under Marcus Aurelius and Commodus. There was an old slander that he spoke Latin with an accent which may reflect the fact that he was the first genuine provincial to ascend the throne. Septimius' wife, Julia Domna, was also a provincial from a prominent Syrian family whose family held the hereditary priesthood at Emesa. It is noteworthy that all three of the contenders for the throne in A.D. 193 were the first members of their immediate families to have been consuls.

Under the Severi the primacy of the army among the constituencies of the Empire came to the forefront. Septimius, the founder of the dynasty, possessed worthwhile military credentials, but his success in winning the loyalty—not just of his own Danube legions but all the legions—was due to the fact that he increased the pay of all the soldiers everywhere by a significant amount. How much the increase was is unclear, but it was at least 50 percent and may have been as much as 100 percent. He also removed the prohibition against soldiers marrying. Septimius was conscious of the need to cultivate the people of Rome. On the tenth anniversary of his accession he divided two hundred million sesterces among the populace, the largest donative that had ever been made by an emperor. With the Senate he had poor relations, understandable considering the fact that he had executed 29 of the supporters of the pretender Albinus and criticized the Senate as a body for its hypocrisy and loose living, as Dio Cassius, who was present, reports (Dio Cassius, 75.8).

| The Severan Emperors | |
|---|---|
| Septimius Severus | A.D. 193–211 |
| Caracalla | A.D. 211–217 |
| Elagabalus | A.D. 218–222 |
| Severus Alexander | A.D. 222–235 |

The pay increase, along with the promised donatives, created a strain on the income of the Empire and heightened the need for silver and gold for the coinage required to pay the army, the equestrian bureaucracy, and the expenses of maintaining Rome's gigantic food and entertainment bill. The percentage of silver in the coinage declined from 90 percent under Trajan to 45 percent under the last of the Severans. The debasement of the coinage was not a consequence of inflation but rather an indication that the state was having difficulty finding the necessary specie to meet the large increase in coins necessary to meet the army's payroll.

In A.D. 197 Septimius turned his attention to the East where he sacked the Parthian capital of Ctesiphon and made Mesopotamia a province garrisoned by three legions. Dio Cassius criticized the campaign, claiming that the addition of the new province was a mistake: "Mesopotamia has been the source of constant wars and enormous expense for us. It yields little and costs a great deal. It provides for people who are closer to the Medes and Persians. In one way or another we end up always fighting their wars" (75.3). Dio Cassius was probably right, though not for the reasons he gives. The new province, located on the east side of the Euphrates, created a dangerously exposed salient that was difficult for Rome to defend. Six years later Severus set out for Britain with the intention of finally incorporating Scotland in the Empire or at least intimidating the natives. The task proved more difficult than he anticipated, and in A.D. 210 he arranged a peace and withdrew the legions behind Hadrian's Wall. He died the following year.

CARACALLA When he was dying Septimius was supposed to have urged his sons "not to quarrel with each other, to enrich the soldiers and ignore everything else" (Dio Cassius, 76.15). His advice was only partially heeded. Caracalla soon murdered his brother Geta and to conciliate the troops increased their pay. He then went on to campaign successfully in Germany against the Alamanni and afterward in the east against the Parthians. His wars and pay increases caused financial problems and to address them he extended the Roman franchise in A.D. 212 to all free inhabitants of the Empire. He then proceeded to double the inheritance tax to which only citizens were liable. This act, known as the Antonine Constitution, was a blatant ploy to raise income, but it also had symbolic value. Since the time of Alexander the Great philosophers dreamed of creating a single world community of citizens. Caracalla's initiative seemed to fulfill this dream. From now on Rome was to be the common home of all the scattered inhabitants of the Empire and its survival was to be linked with the emperor's own fortunes. It is indicative of the evolving nature of the Empire that the man who extended Roman citizenship so widely was a descendant on his father's side of Rome's old enemies, Phoenician settlers in Africa, and on his mother's of Syrian aristocrats.

ELAGABALUS On campaign against the Parthians in A.D. 217 Caracalla was murdered by the Praetorian Prefect Macrinus. Like the Severi, Macrinus was a north African, though unlike them he was by descent a Berber. Shocking the senatorial class, he became the first equestrian rather than a senator to ascend the throne. Senators could see the danger of the precedent. It meant that the Senate, which had been losing power for a long time, was now in an even weaker position. However, Macrinus was no match for the wiles of Julia Maesa, the sister-in-law of Septimius Severus, who announced to the troops that her grandson, Varius Avitus, priest of the sun god Elagabal at Emesa, was the son of Caracalla. He was renamed M. Aurelius Antoninus. The legionaries, loyal to the Severan dynasty, killed Macrinus and declared M. Aurelius Antoninus, or as he is better known, Elagabalus, emperor in his place.

Elagabalus turned out to be more than even his own family had bargained for, and the people of Rome who thought they had seen just about everything were in for a surprise. The god Elagabal was identified, as was the Great Mother, with a black meteorite, which was brought with great acclaim from Emesa to Rome. On his arrival there the new emperor declared that Jupiter had been replaced and that Elagabal was now the chief god of the Roman pantheon. Pallas Athena was declared his consort and the Palladium, the ancient statue of Athena that was supposed to have been brought by Aeneas from Troy, was moved to the new temple of the sun god on the Palatine. The emperor then divorced his wife and married a Vestal Virgin. The Romans were not sufficiently multicultural to accept this treatment of their gods and, after being persuaded to adopt his cousin, Severus Alexander, as his heir, Elagabalus was disposed of by the Praetorian Guard—at his own grandmother's suggestion. What seemed to the Romans bizarre behavior on the part of Elagabalus was not exceptional in the context of the henotheism that was common among Semitic religions. In henotheistic belief a single god is recognized as predominant and rules over all other divinities whose existence is not denied but whose inferiority to the one (Greek, *hen*) god is affirmed.

SEVERUS ALEXANDER When he ascended the throne Severus Alexander was only 14. Throughout his reign he was firmly under the thumb of his mother, Julia Mamaea and palace offcials. The Praetorian Prefect, the distinguished legal scholar Ulpian, and a number of senators in the emperor's council were good influences on the young man, but they did not constitute a sufficiently wide basis of power. Ulpian, despite his eminence as a scholar, was politically inept. Because of his youth Alexander had had no military experience, and having his mother in the camp with him did not endear him to the soldiers. On the eastern front he obtained what amounted to a draw with the Persians and on campaign in Germany in A.D. 235 against the Alamanni he made the mistake of attempting to negotiate with the enemy. The troops, who had come back from the eastern front to find their homes ransacked by the Alamanni, were enraged that revenge was not going to be taken. They mutinied, and as they killed him referred to him as his "mother's cowardly brat" (Herodian, 6.9). His mother, Julia Mammaea, perished with him.

## The Problem of Underage Emperors and the Power of the Palace

The problem of succession, which had plagued Rome since the time of Augustus, was brought to the fore with the rise of teenage emperors. Augustus had been lucky in his successor Tiberius, who was well groomed to succeed him, but thereafter the succession was hit or miss. Nero died without a successor, and a civil war followed. Domitian was also without an heir, and his murder almost led to a repeat of the civil war of A.D. 69. The adoptive policy of Trajan, Hadrian, and Antoninus was more happenstance than policy. None of them had heirs. Marcus Aurelius had a son and, despite the fact that Commodus was already showing character weaknesses that made for comparisons with the unhinged Caligula of the first century, designated him his successor. Commodus succeeded his father at age 18. The problem became more acute under the Severi. After the murder of Caracalla, the 14-year-old Elagabalus was proclaimed emperor and on his assassination in A.D. 222 Severus Alexander, who was 14, succeeded to the throne. A few years after Severus' dispatch another 13 year old, Gordian III, was on the throne, and after a brief reign (A.D. 238–244) he too was murdered.

The case of Commodus was not as severe as those of the young Severi or Gordian III. Commodus despite his obvious failings belonged to a revered family and was a known quantity to the main constituencies of the Empire: the elites, the people of Rome, and the armies. These attributes were sufficient to keep him in power. His removal was not the result of the dissatisfaction of the armies or the people but of disgruntled members of the Senate and of palace insiders. Even by comparison to Commodus, Elagabalus, Severus Alexander, and Gordian III were under severe disadvantages. They were strictly creatures of the palace. Beyond family ties they had no appeal to the army, the elite, or even the people of Rome. That meant that power was wielded by those around them, particularly by the women of the palace and high officials who were likely to be lawyers rather than military men. It was a weak base from which to rule, and in some respects it anticipated the future concentration of power in the palace and the bureaucratic apparatus attached to it, primarily the power of the growing equestrian administration.

## The Severan Legacy

Under the Severans the Empire entered a new phase. Septimius Severus extended the frontier in Syria, Arabia, and north Africa. The army became more professional and even democratic to the extent that the old, well-established connection between the upper classes and the officer corps was weakened as large numbers of able provincials and men of the lower classes entered its ranks. Three newly recruited legions were given equestrian commanders, as were all the provinces in the east. One of these legions, *II Parthica*, was based at Alba, just a few miles from Rome. Together with the newly staffed Praetorian Guard, Septimius had under his direct control an army of some 30,000 men. This large body of soldiers guaranteed his personal safety in Italy or in any other part of the Empire for that matter and constituted the core of what might be considered a strategic reserve.

PROVINCIALIZATION AND LAW The administration was democratized in a somewhat similar way to the army. It grew as the equestrian class was given emphasis over that of the senatorial and through the addition of provincials. By one estimate, 60 percent of the imperial procurators or financial administrators were from either Africa or the Greek speaking east. Italy, and the city of Rome with it, continued to lose ground. Under a suc-

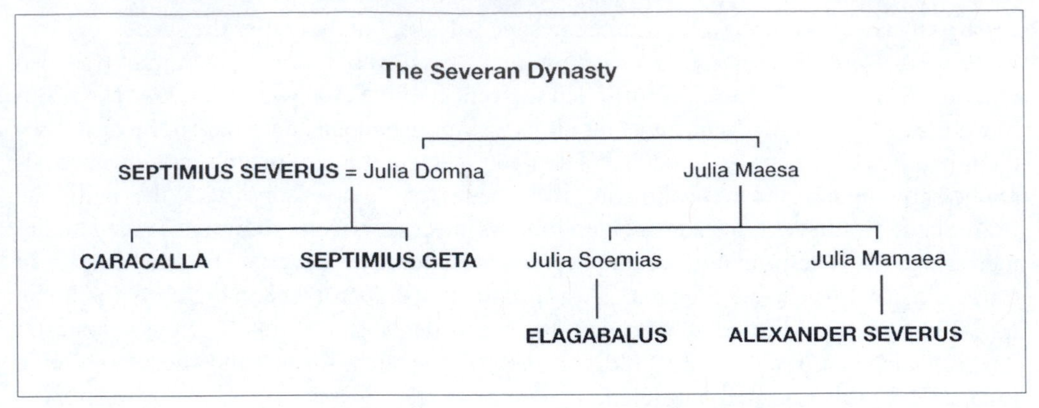


cession of brilliant lawyers who held the position of Praetorian Prefect, Roman law began to be systematically organized. These pioneering endeavors were ultimately to provide the foundation on which the emperors of the later third century were able to restore much of Rome's power and give it one more opportunity to reinvent itself. The three great lawyers of the Severan period—Papinian, Ulpian, and Paulus—account for more than half of the entries in the compilation of Roman law in Justinian's *Digest*, published in the sixth century. Their work, as it passed through the hands of Justinian and the revivers of Roman law in the twelfth century A.D., lies at the foundation of continental European law to the present.

## 2. THE THIRD-CENTURY CRISIS

From the end of the Severan dynasty the Roman Empire found itself in almost perpetual political chaos and in a state of increasing economic dislocation. Simultaneously, the eastern and western halves of the Empire came under attack. At times invaders managed to penetrate far into the interior of the Empire. Yet certain key provinces such as Egypt and Africa remained untouched. For more than half a century the pressures continued until finally a series of great emperors from the Balkans succeeded in bringing Rome back from the brink of destruction and restoring peace in what amounted to a refounding of the Empire.

### Imperial Security: A Fine Balance

THE ESSENTIAL EQUATION The equilibrium of the Roman Empire depended on a balance between frontier pressures and the success of the legions in resisting them, and between the costs of war and the resources of the state. An essential ingredient in this equation was the success of the imperial succession, and that clearly failed in the third century. The consequence of Rome's inability to pass on power peacefully from one regime to the next was chaos in key areas of the Empire as Roman armies, each supporting its own candidate for the throne, fought each other and abandoned the frontiers.

THE NEW ENEMIES At the same time that Roman armies were engaged in civil wars with each other, the probing of northern frontier by groups of barbarians changed in character. In previous centuries the invading groups were relatively small raiding parties, but in the second century A.D. larger confederations, such as the Germanic Quadi and Marcomanni and the Iranian Iazyges came into existence. Even before the time of chaos in the third century some of these confederations managed to advance significant distances into the Empire. One of them, for example, was able put Aquileia in northern Italy under siege before being driven back beyond the frontiers. In the third century similar confederations were able to cause far greater troubles for the Empire. In A.D. 233 the Alamanni attacked across the upper Danube. Bands of Goths, Sarmatians, and Iazyges concentrated in the lower Danube and Black Sea areas. The Rhine and lower Danube frontiers were attacked by the Franks and Vandals. A century earlier the senatorial historian Tacitus, writing in admiration of the warlike character of Celts and Germans, had opined:

> We have had no weapon stronger in our wars with the strongest [*Celtic*] nations than their inability to cooperate among themselves. Rarely do more than two or three states combine to repel a common danger; fighting one by one they are conquered wholesale (*Agricola*, 12, ... I pray that the Germans—if they do not love us—may long persist in hating one another. Fortune grants us no greater gift than the disunity of our enemies (*Germania*, 33).

The barbarians remained divided, but they were able to combine in larger groups than in the past. Nevertheless their attacks were not planned by some coordinating council of Germanic chieftains. The confederations were not long-standing ethnic groups but warrior bands that came together under the leadership of charismatic chiefs, and could disappear as quickly as they had appeared. They could also change sides at a moment's notice. Whole peoples seen to disappear from the historical record as the result of some minor setback. War bands were more suited for hit-and-run raids than for open warfare and were as often engaged in intertribal warfare as they were in raiding the Empire. Unfortunately, we have no directly relevant information from the varied groups of invaders themselves as to what was going on among them. Archaeology is of some help, but it is inadequate to give a general picture of what was happening in the *barbaricum*, as the Romans called the areas beyond the frontiers. After centuries of contact with the developed south the ancient, anarchic, pre-state traditions of northern Europe began to give way. The invasions of the third century are in fact evidence that the peoples of northern Europe were slowly accommodating themselves to the organized, territorial state. Some federations such as the Alamanni—the "All Men"—lived in such close proximity to the Empire that a kind of symbiotic relationship between the federation and the Empire developed. The Romans provided subsidies and goods for the Alamanni, and the tribesmen in turn provided warriors for the army. For long periods they were as much collaborators and allies of Rome as enemies. This kind of relationship was also true of other Germanic groups, and during the next several centuries we find instances of Romans and Franks fighting against other Franks, and Romans and Alamanni combining against federations that threatened both of them. As in the past Romans were adept at employing foreigners in their auxiliary units, and the warring German tribes provided an endless supply of well-qualified recruits. The process

**A Fortress of the Sasanids**

*The great Sasanid fortress of Narin Kala overlooks the Caspian Sea at Derbent (Daghestan, Russia). It was built in the sixth century* A.D. *by order of the Persian Shahanshah, "King of Kings," Khosrow I. The eight-acre fortress anchors an elaborate array of fortifications intended to block the passage into Iran of nomad tribesmen, among them the Huns, along the narrow passageway between the Caucasus and the Caspian Sea. The fortress worked so effectively it was occupied down to the nineteenth century.*

worked in the other direction also. Warriors who served Rome returned home with valuable knowledge of Roman resources and military practices.

THE SASANIDS: THE NEW PERSIAN EMPIRE Unfortunately for Rome the northern frontiers were not the only source of difficulty for the Empire. After a series of losses to Rome, the old Parthian dynasty fell in A.D. 226 and was replaced by the Sasanids, a vigorous new regime from Persis in southern Iran. The Sasanids reorganized the old Parthian state on an efficient basis and under them Zoroastrianism (or Mazdaism) became something close to a state religion with a priestly hierarchy and strongly developed ideas of orthodoxy and heresy. The regime promoted the idea of a culturally and politically united Iran. In A.D. 231 the Sasanids invaded the eastern provinces of the Empire in an attempt to recover regions that had once belonged to Persia back in the time of Darius and Xerxes.

ECONOMIC ISSUES Beginning with Caracalla's increase in the pay of the army inflation took hold of the economy and the Roman currency collapsed. The silver content of the coinage was lowered from 45 percent at the time of Alexander Severus to one percent by the time of Claudius II (A.D. 268–270). The price of grain rose from two denarii per measure in A.D. 200 to 330 in A.D. 301. The government was hit hard by these increases because its taxes came as fixed money payments. Because it had to feed and supply the legions, it eventually had to fall back on requisitions in kind.

Developments that had been underway in the second century were rapidly advanced by crisis of the third century. The role of the army in choosing emperors was now paramount; correspondingly the role of the Senate was marginalized. Emperors no longer made any pretense of being the first citizen, or Princeps. They were military men and autocrats, and their courts began to assume a proportionately larger role than they had in the past. More and more key personnel were drawn from the ranks of the equestrians until, under Gallienus (A.D. 253–268), senators were excluded from all military commands and most civilian positions. The number of Italians in the Senate continued to decline, their places being taken by provincials, especially from Africa and the east. As the state increasingly intervened in local affairs the burdens of municipal administration which were born by the city senates of the Empire increased out of all proportion to the rewards of membership. At the same time it was the relentless effectiveness and continuity of the imperial administrative services during the anarchy of civil wars and invasions that held the Empire together.

RELIGION The most important social and cultural changes of these years occurred in the field of religion and in particular in the development of monotheism. Rabbinic Judaism evolved in Palestine and the diaspora throughout the Roman Empire in the years following the fall of Jerusalem in A.D. 70. About a generation earlier Christianity made its appearance in the same areas and rapidly spread throughout the urban areas of the Empire. By the third century it was beginning to find widespread acceptance among the middle classes of the Empire and to build up a respectable intellectual presentation of its tenets. At the same time the organization of the church grew considerably. Individual churches communicated freely with one another and met in provincial councils to discuss their common needs and attempt to settle doctrinal and disciplinary disputes. Iranian dualistic influences had been significant in the evolution of both late Hellenistic Judaism and early Christianity, and Iranian monotheism was a major factor in the growth of the Sasanid empire.

## 3. POLITICAL ANARCHY

The successor of the Severans was C. Julius Verus Maximinus, a soldier's soldier. He was probably a descendant of Roman settlers in the Danube region but was dubbed a barbarian herdsman and a Thracian by hostile senators. This was a typical upper-class slander of the army and there is no doubt he rose through a number of equestrian postings before being elevated to the throne.

### The Problem with the Army

The trouble with all such pretenders to the throne was that they represented only the army group or legion to which they belonged and had great difficulty in winning the support of other army groups. One sure method of currying favor with the army as a whole was to increase its pay as Severus and Caracalla had done, but this kind of approach could not be carried on indefinitely. There was a limit to the resources of the Empire. After Maximinus raised the pay of the troops his financial demands provoked a rebellion in Africa, which was supported by the Senate at Rome. Two Africans, Gordian I and his son Gordian II were proclaimed emperors, and when they were slain in battle by troops of *legio III Augusta* which remained loyal to Maximinus, two senators in Rome, M. Clodius Pupienus and D. Caelius Balbinus, were proclaimed joint emperors. They adopted Gordian's grandson as their heir. In attempting to recover Italy, Maximinus was murdered by his own troops after an unsuccessful siege of Aquileia. Next, Pupienus and Balbinus were murdered by the Praetorian Guard, who then elevated Gordian III to the throne. On campaign in the east, the youthful Gordian died, though how is unclear since there are four different versions of his death. His Praetorian Prefect Philip was accused of murdering him, but he may have been innocent. Other versions are that he died after being wounded in battle with the Persians or was slain in a mutiny. Philip claimed Gordon died of natural causes, and he took over in A.D. 244. It says much about the integrative power of Rome that Philip, an Arab from Shahba south of Damascus was the emperor to whom fell the special honor of celebrating with great pomp in A.D. 247 the millennium of the founding of Rome.

Philip was succeeded by one of his generals, Decius, in 249. The new emperor tried to reinvigorate the cult practices of the old religion and thereby pacify the angry gods. An inscription put up to honor him designated him as the *restitutor sacrorum*, a restorer of the old forms of worship. He ordered sacrifices to be offered to the gods throughout the Empire and thus launched the first empire-wide persecution of the Christians. Those who sacrificed were issued a certificate that they had done so, and apparently many Christians simply bought a certificate while continuing with their own worship in private. The bishop of Carthage, Cyprian, lamented that many of his flock succumbed to the temptation. The main victims of the persecution were the most visible representatives of the church, the clergy. To the persecuted Christians it seemed like divine restitution when the Goths crossed the Danube, invaded Moesia and Thrace, and slew Decius in battle in the lower Danube area.

## A Divided Empire

The successors of Decius were Trebonianus Gallus and his son Volusianus, and they in turn were followed by the Moor Aemilianus. The next emperor was Valerian, the commander of the Rhine legions. At the suggestion of theSenate he appointed his son Gallienus as a second Augustus, or co-emperor, in A.D. 253. For the first time responsibility for the Empire was divided between two emperors, and while Gallienus remained in Gaul, Valerian went to the east to repel the Persians. In A.D. 257 Valerian launched another empire-wide persecution of the Christians, which was called off by Gallienus in 260 when his father was defeated and captured by the Persians. In the same year a usurper by the name of Postumus succeeded in gaining control of most of the western half of the Empire, including Britain, Gaul, the Rhineland, and Spain. In the east Palmyra, under its ruler Odenathus followed by his widow, Zenobia, proclaimed its independence and was recognized as a client-kingdom by Gallienus.

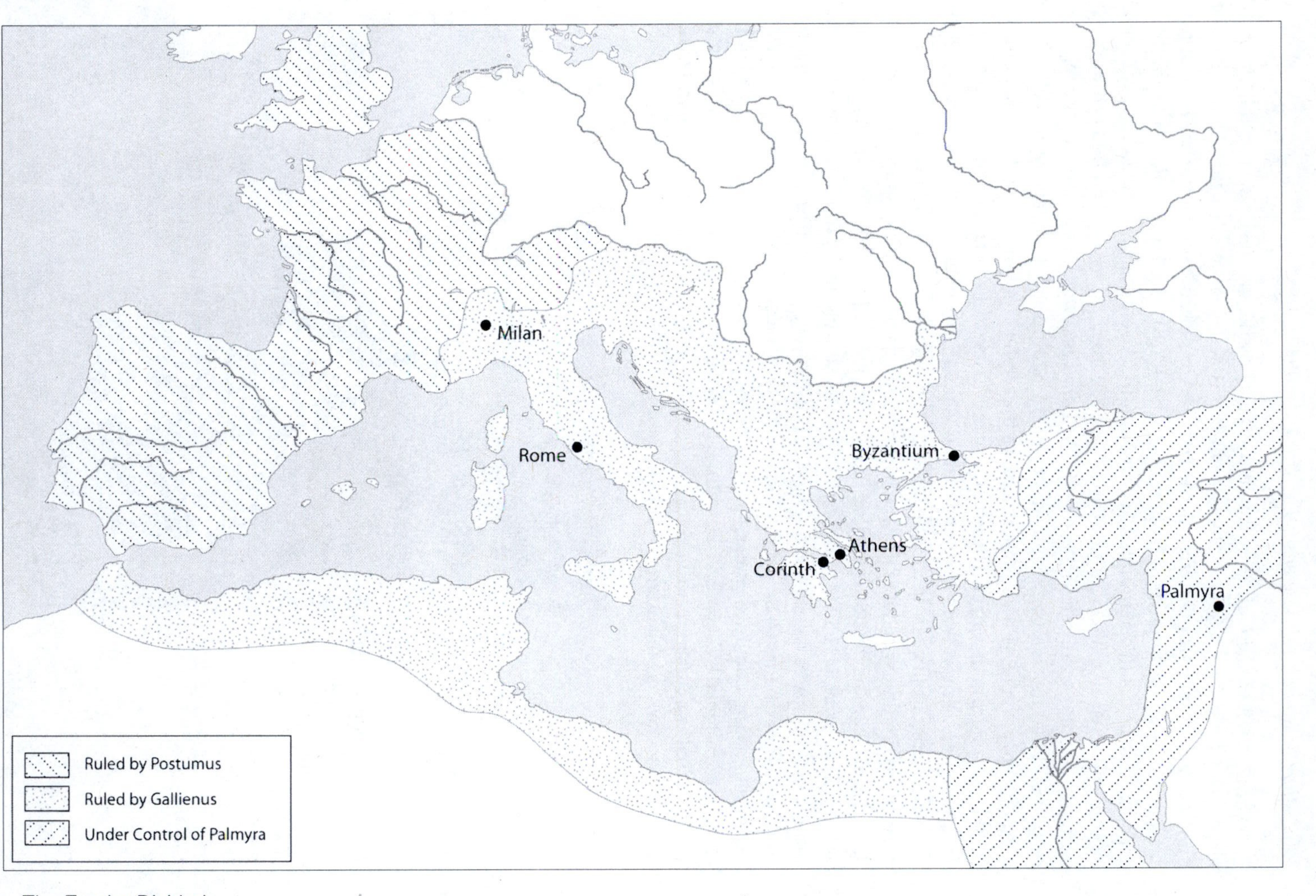


The Empire Divided

GALLIENUS Under Gallienus Rome was beset by the greatest disasters it had yet suffered. In A.D. 262–263 Gothic fleets from the Black Sea ravaged the Aegean, sacked Ephesus and burned its great Temple of Diana. Around 267, the Heruli, a German tribe, captured and sacked the cities of Byzantium, Athens, Corinth, Argos, and Sparta. Gallienus coped as best he could and initiated a series of military reforms that placed emphasis on the mobility of cavalry units (*vexillationes*), which were combined into a body of troops attached to him personally (his *comitatus*). The *comitatus* was independent of the legionary system and had its own command structure. He established his headquarters at Milan in northern Italy where he had quick access to the Danube provinces while protecting Italy from invasion from the north. The cavalry seems to have been made up of a hodgepodge of Syrian archers, Moors from Mauretania, and Dalmatians recruited locally. Under Severus the officer corps had been opened up to an extent to promotions from the lower ranks, and the process continued under Gallienus who expanded the career prospects of ordinary soldiers. More than his predecessors Gallienus appointed equestrians to commands that had previously been reserved for senators. Most of these were men who had spent their entire careers in the army and were thoroughgoing professionals. The times could no longer sustain the luxury of a transient corps of upper-class officers for whom military service was just part of a larger political career. One source, Aurelius Victor, goes so far as to claim that Gallienus excluded by decree senators from high commands. In point of fact the inclination of individuals to pursue almost exclusively military or civilian careers had begun to manifest itself as early as the reign of Hadrian, and the tendency may simply have reached its

**The Aurelian Walls of Rome**

*The walls of Rome, of which extensive sections survive, were begun by the emperor Aurelian in A.D. 271–272 and finished ten years later. The wall is of concrete faced with brick front and back, 16 feet thick and 22 feet high with towers every 330 yards. In the fourth century the height of the walls was doubled.*

logical conclusion with Gallienus. A side effect of this development was that equestrians who wished to advance to high commands and governorships of provinces could by-pass the Senate and go straight from a strictly military career to a provincial governorship without having to take time off to hold senatorial administrative posts in Rome. Conversely, senators were able to devote themselves exclusively to civilian career tracks without the requirement of having to serve as legionary commanders.

AURELIAN AND THE ADVENT OF THE ILLYRIANS Gallienus won a major victory over the Goths in 268 at Naissus in the Balkans but was assassinated the same year by the Illyrian generals Claudius and Aurelian. With the defeat of the Goths and the advent of the Illyrian emperors, Rome's fortunes began to rise again slowly. Claudius II was succeeded by Aurelian in A.D. 270, and the process of reuniting the Empire began. The Palmyrenes were defeated in 273, and in 274 Postumus' successor in the west, Tetricus, surrendered. Aurelian was able to claim the title of *Restitutor Orbis*, the Restorer of the World. Under Aurelian Dacia (modern Romania) and the Agri Decumates, the region between the headwaters of the Rhine and the Danube, were abandoned as undefendable. Great walls were built around the city of Rome.

Aurelian also attempted to reform the currency. He proclaimed the sun god as the universal god of the Empire and promoted the cult of *Sol Invictus*, "The Unconquerable Sun." His coins featured the legend "Born Lord and God." In A.D. 275 Aurelian was assassinated and was succeeded briefly by the aged senator Tacitus (not the historian, although he claimed descent from him). Tacitus' died of natural causes—strange in those bloody times—and another Illyrian, Probus, succeeded to the throne. In 282, discontented with his rigid discipline, the troops rebelled and killed him and the Praetorian Prefect Carus became emperor. Two years later troops proclaimed the one-time Illyrian shepherd Diocles emperor, and as Diocletian he began the work of the refounding of the Roman Empire.

## 4. THE EMPIRE AND THE EMPEROR: "HOLDING A WOLF BY THE EARS"

The emperor Tiberius used to complain that an emperor was like the man in the proverb who was holding a wolf by the ears: he could neither let go nor hold on (Suetonius, *Tiberius*, 25.1). The years A.D. 69 and 193 had shown what happened when the rulers in Rome lost their grip on the ears of the wolf—in this case the armies. After the civil wars of 69 Tacitus talked candidly about the "secrets of empire"—the *arcana imperii*—that were revealed by the events of that year. Yet, nothing, so to speak, was done to address the problem. It was not that emperors and elites were too slow-witted to understand what was at stake but rather there was little they could do about it.

The imperial succession was always the chink in the armor of imperial Rome. The problem was in part cultural. Roman armies had a long tradition of independent action going back to the last century of the Republic, when they frequently ordered about the generals who were supposed to be their commanders. Under the Empire the symbolic capital of im-

| Chronology: Third Century Emperors | | | |
|---|---|---|---|
| Maxminus the Thracian | 235–238 | Aemilianus the Moor | 253 |
| Gordian I | 238 | Valerian | 253–260 |
| Gordian II | 238 | Gallienus (son of Valerian) | 253–268 |
| Balbinus | 238 | Claudius II (first of the Illyrian emperors) | 268–270 |
| Pupienus | 238 | Quintillus (brother of Claudius) | 270 |
| Gordian III | 238–244 | Aurelian | 270–275 |
| Philip the Arab | 244–249 | Tacitus | 275–276 |
| Decius | 249–251 | Probus | 276–282 |
| Trebonianus Gallus | 251–253 | Carus | 282–283 |
| Volusianus (son of Trebonianus) | 251–253 | Carinus and Numerian (sons of Carus) | 283–284 |

perial dynasties such as that of the Julio-Claudians, the Antonines, and the Severans counted for a great deal in maintaining the loyalty of the armies, but after the death of the last of the Severans in A.D. 238 no dynasty was able to command the loyalty of all of the armies, and there was not enough money to purchase their loyalties. Had the third century presented Rome with fewer strategic and tactical military challenges the imperial succession might not have been so chaotic, and any one of the many competent emperors thrown up by the regional armies might have been able to establish sufficient authority to command the obedience of the whole army. He might then have been able to pass his legacy of authority to his successor, whether an adopted or natural son. Gallienus and Aurelian showed great talent and energy and had strong leadership abilities, but neither had a sufficiently strong grip on the imperial office to be able to restore the stability of the imperial succession. At the end of the third century Diocletian thought he had found a solution when he divided the responsibilities of the Empire between two co-emperors (Augusti) and their two designated successors (Caesars). However, that approach failed too, and civil war and occasionally dynastic succession continued to be the politically crude and unsatisfactory way in which emperors came to power.

There were other issues of a quite different nature that were erupting just below the surface of the Empire and that until the third century had received scant attention from the authorities. This was a cultural change of major proportions in the form of the acceptance of a version of monotheism by an important minority of the Empire's population. The main, but not the only, protagonist of this religious development was Christianity, which by the third century, had developed an alternative narrative to the Roman state's ideological claims as well as an effective alternative to the state's civic religions. In the second century B.C. the Senate of the Republic had come down hard on the followers of the god Dionysus (the Bacchic Conspiracy) because they seemed to be proposing an alternative way of life, if only on a minor scale, to that approved by the state. Yet in the form of Christianity, with its well-developed organizational structure, its attractive forms of small-scale social interactions, its satisfying doctrine, and what was beginning to be a respectable intellectual outreach to Greco-Roman philosophy, the Roman state faced a far more formidable challenge than it did from cells of the Bacchic cult. Monotheism in its Christian format was the first movement that had the potential to replace the civic ideology of the *polis* that had been the foundation of Roman society and culture since the founding of the city. Whether this potential would ever be realized was hardly something that either emperors or even bishops can have given much thought to during the chaos of the third century, but in the next century it came to the fore when Constantine made his surprising choice at the battle of the Mulvian Bridge. The following chapter traces the development of monotheism in some of its forms in the Empire.

# 18

# The Challenge of Monotheism

## 1. THE CULTURAL SETTING

The previous chapter dealt primarily with the political, administrative, and military developments of the third century. It would be a mistake, however, to regard these events as central to the history of the period. Beneath the surface a major cultural revolution was developing that was to emerge, challenge, and eventually replace most of the cultures of the Mediterranean and Middle East. It was itself of ancient origin and very much part of Middle Eastern, but not Greco-Roman culture. Its homeland was Egypt, Iran, Judaea, Syria, Mesopotamia, and Asia Minor.

### The Middle East, Greece, and Rome

In the fourth century B.C. the Middle East was conquered militarily by Alexander the Great and for centuries much of it, including such lands as Syria, Palestine, Mesopotamia, and Egypt was under the control of his successors. By the first century B.C. what remained of Alexander's conquests fell into the hands of the Romans, and so it remained until the Arab invasions of the seventh century A.D. Greco-Roman presence was strongly represented in the form of hundreds of cities founded or colonized by Greeks or Romans from the time of Alexander onward. Some of the archaeologically best-preserved remains of Greek cities are to be found, not in Greece proper, but in the area of Syria-Palestine and even in the heartland of the old northern kingdom of Israel. An impressive Greek city by the name of Antiochia Hippos, for example, was built on a 1000-foot hilltop overlooking the Sea of Galilee. Hippos, also known as Sussita, belonged to a group of other Greek cities in the area known as the Decapolis, the Ten Cities, and represented a major presence of Greek culture and influence in the area. Traditionally Egypt was much less urbanized than the great

Mesopotamian kingdoms, and Hellenization took a different form there than in other parts of the Middle East.

A CULTURAL POWERHOUSE Although overwhelmed militarily, and politically subject to non-native rulers for centuries, indigenous Middle Eastern culture remained powerful. Different regions reacted differently to Greco-Roman cultural presence, and cultural interaction varied considerably. Syria and Mesopotamia, by the period of the Roman Empire had become a particularly rich mix of cultures with strong influences from Iran to the north and the Buddhist lands to the east. The Jews of Judaea resisted the Hellenizing efforts of the Seleucids of Syria in the pre-Roman period and rebelled on numerous occasions against Roman overlordship after the Romans took over from the Seleucids. The Jews of the dispersion (or diaspora), as opposed to the Jews of Judaea, had a somewhat different set of problems from their kinsmen in Judaea. The Jewish diaspora was strongly represented in Mesopotamia, Syria, and Egypt and to a lesser extent throughout the Greek and Roman cities of the Mediterranean. Some of these communities were ancient, having existed since the time of the exile from the northern kingdom of Israel in the eighth century B.C. and from Judaea after the destruction of Jerusalem in the sixth century B.C. Jews of these lands had to contend in a more immediate way with the culture of both the Greeks and their other non-Jewish neighbors throughout the Middle East than did their kinsmen in Judaea. Obviously, the Law could not be as easily or exactly observed in a non-Jewish environment as in the homeland, and its demands had to be adjusted accordingly. There were three precepts of the Law—circumcision, the observance of the Sabbath, and the avoidance of pork—that became the most obvious cultural characteristics of Jews outside Palestine. These were perhaps the most visible distinguishing marks of the Jews of the diaspora but Jewish monotheism and Judaism's clear moral standards also distinguished Jews from their neighbors and made socializing difficult and participation in the civic religions of the *polis* impossible. In other areas of life the divide was not so stark. Jews appropriated the traditional Greek moral language of the virtues and applied it to their own ethical teaching. There was even some borrowing in theological matters. Jews found Stoic arguments against polytheism and idolatry useful and adapted them, along with Stoic demonstrations of the existence of God, to the defense of their own beliefs.

ALEXANDRIA A major center of Jewish culture in the Greek-speaking world was located in Alexandria in Egypt. There Jewish intellectuals sought to refute pagan criticisms of Judaism and to present it as an ancient and reasonable faith. A great deal of apologetic literature was composed, most of it with the object of keeping the Jews of the diaspora loyal to their faith amid the temptations—moral, religious, and intellectual—of the Greek world. For the benefit of Jews who knew little Hebrew the Hebrew Scriptures were translated into Greek in a version known as the Septuagint. Later translations into Latin were made from the Septuagint. A leader in the movement to reconcile Judaic and Hellenistic cultures was the great philosopher-mystic Philo (late first century B.C.) who, along with the historian Josephus was the most significant writer in the field of Jewish-Greek literature. Philo developed a method, later borrowed by Christians that tried to demonstrate that the Jewish Sacred Scriptures contained in revealed and perfected form the philosophy and ethics of what was best in Greek thought.

## Rabbinic Judaism

Throughout the first centuries B.C. and A.D. many competing—though interacting—forms of Judaism existed in Judaea and among Jews outside Palestine. In Judaea there were two dominant schools or parties, the Sadducees, who came from well-to-do families and played a leading role in the Temple, and their principal opponents, the reform-minded Pharisees who aimed to provide an alternative to the Temple's rituals as a basis for Jewish identity. The schools differed doctrinally over the immortality of the soul, punishment after death, the resurrection of the body and other issues. Sadducees took a literal approach to interpreting the Scriptures and the Law. They insisted that only the written Scriptures were acceptable sources of revelation, whereas Pharisees claimed that the Torah (the Law) came in two forms, the one written and the other oral, each necessary and complementary to the other, each divinely inspired. In addition to these two main parties which were further divided into sub-sects, there were numerous other groups of ascetics, revolutionaries, mystics, and believers in apocalyptic restoration. Among these the most important were the separatist Essenes and the Qumran, or Dead Sea community. Yet other variants of Judaism were to be found among the many communities of the Diaspora.

When the Second Temple in Jerusalem was destroyed by the Romans in A.D. 70 and further devastation followed the Bar Kochba Rebellion of A.D. 132 to 135 Judaism experienced a spiritual upheaval comparable to the one that followed the destruction of the original Temple of Solomon (the First Temple) by the Babylonians in 586 B.C. Rabbinic Judaism emerged out of this searing experience. After A.D. 70 the power and influence of the Sadducees who were closely connected to the Temple faded. The Qumran and Essene sects were destroyed or scattered. Apocalyptic movements were discredited after the Bar-Kochba rebellion. In the absence of the Temple, the synagogue became the central focus of Jewish religious life. The rabbi replaced the priest as the wise man and interpreter of the law and the scriptures. Prayer became a surrogate for animal sacrifice. Of the surviving traditions of Judaism, Pharisaism proved to be the most adaptable in responding to the needs of post-revolt Judaism, and it was from Pharisaim in particular, though not exclusively, that Rabbinic (or as it is sometimes called, Normative) Judaism developed. To the question of who was a Jew the Pharisaic tradition responded that a Jew was the person who faithfully followed the Law, meaning by that both the written Torah that went back to Moses and the unwritten or oral law that went back to the same time and had the same authority. The proper interpreters of the law, both written and oral, were the rabbis who, after the revolt of Bar Kochba, were the sole voice of Judaism.

MISHNAH AND TALMUD After the revolts of the second century A.D. the vigor of Hellenistic Judaism declined and the Jewish community entered into a period of defensive consolidation. There was a gradual disengagement with Hellenism and a revival of Hebrew and Aramaic. The Greek translation of the Bible, the Septuagint, was abandoned in favor of the original Hebrew versions of the Scriptures. The oral tradition of the Pharisees was written down and edited. It received definitive form around A.D. 200 in the work known as the *Mishnah*, the basic document of Rabbinic Judaism. It contains statements of the Law and the original commentaries of the rabbis. The bulk of the *Mishnah* derives from the first two centuries A.D. although it contains some material going back to earlier centuries. Loosely organized groups of scholars in Palestine and Babylonia commented on the *Mishnah* between A.D. 200 and approximately A.D. 500. Their work led to the creation of two other fundamental documents of Rabbinic Judaism, the Palestinian and Babylonian Talmuds. In rejecting claims that Christianity represented the true Israel the rabbis argued that the oral law found in the *Mishnah* was the possession of Jews alone. By the end of the second century A.D. a new Jewish political identity emerged, built around Hebrew, the national language; the Hebrew Bible which provided a history and a comprehensive system of law; social institutions such as the synagogue and Sabbath worship; and the existence of the rabbis as a body of authoritative interpreters of the Bible and the law. A leader, the *nasi* or prince, represented the community to the political authorities both inside and outside the Empire and was categorized by the Romans as an ethnic representative or ethnarch. In Roman law the Jews were both an ethnic group (*natio*) and a religious community (*religio*), but one that deviated from the norms of religion familiar to the peoples of the Greco-Roman world. Jews lived as a community apart with their own laws and religious traditions and did not participate in the civic religions of the Empire as other peoples did.

## Forms of Monotheism

JEWISH ETHNIC MONOTHEISM Since the sixth century B.C. Jews were in possession of what was potentially a cultural time-bomb, though it would be several centuries before its influence would be felt by the larger Mediterranean and Middle Eastern world under the influence of its offshoot, Christianity. Monotheism developed over a period of centuries in Israel, making its first fully evolved appearance in the sixth century writings of the unknown author or authors of the book known as Second and Third Isaiah (chapters 40–66 of Isaiah). By the second century B.C. strict monotheism was accepted by Jews as a religious doctrine, a social and cultural marker, and a philosophical proposition. Jews everywhere derived their identity from their adherence to the belief in the existence of a creator god, at once infinitely removed from matter and human affairs and at the same time intimately bound up with both. Yahweh was both distant and near at hand. He was beyond space and time, yet he was also the Lord of History who intervened at specific times and places in human history on behalf of the people he chose for himself. These interventions were most noticeable in the calling of Abraham and his descendants out of Mesopotamia and then the command to Moses to lead the Israelites out of Egypt. Yahweh guided the Israelites to Canaan, the Promised Land, and then brought them back to it in a new Exodus after they had been expelled by the Babylonians in 587 B.C.

The contradictory nature of Yahweh who was at one and the same time immaterial and immovable, whose essence was "to be," and yet who was attainable by prayer, sacrifice, moral behavior, and adherence to a code of natural as well as revealed law, was never resolved and remained a conundrum for Judaism as for the other major religions claiming descent from Abraham, namely Christianity and Islam. For Jews the problem was compounded by the belief that the revelation of God's uniqueness was limited to them alone. The argument could be made that it was thus not true monotheism, but only a form of henotheism—the worship of one god without denying the existence of others—or ethnic monotheism, the worship of one's own god while ignoring or fending off the gods of other peoples.

HENOTHEISM The fourth century A.D. emperor Julian drew attention to the ethnic character of Jewish monotheism when he pointed out that Yahweh, a god who disinherited the majority of the human race, could hardly be regarded as universal. The only way to true monotheism, he argued, was by reaching to the god who stood above all ethnic gods and was "the common father and king of all peoples" (Contra Galilaeos, fr. 21.115d), namely Jupiter or Zeus. This was a clever debater's point, but it could not conceal the intrinsic weakness of polytheism which could only be resolved by adherence to true monotheism, a point made by his predecessor the emperor Constantine. In a frequently repeated speech Constantine commented that polytheism encourages multiple rulers in heaven as on earth. If everything in heaven and earth is not subject to a single ruler then there will be "sharings and divisions of the elements ...envy and avarice, gods dominating according to their power, marring the harmonious concord of the whole" (*Oratio Constantini*, 3.2). Julian was a former Christian who wanted to restore polytheism, but he was up against impossible odds because polytheism was by definition local and additive rather than universal and exclusionary.

Julian like many defenders of polytheism wanted to have it both ways. He wanted to retain the multiple gods of humanity while claiming that they were merely aspects or manifestations of the One True God and thus subservient to him. However, Julian's kind of henotheism was rejected by Romans at the time the emperor Elegabalus tried to make his solar deity the supreme god of the Roman pantheon, not because they thought the idea of henotheism was wrong but because they were satisfied with their tried and true Jupiter and did not wish to see him replaced by an exotic outsider god of whom they knew nothing. This was a practical problem henotheizing emperors could not overcome. They may have had monotheistic inclinations and aspirations, but henotheism has only the appearance of monotheism. It was not a threat or substitute for polytheism as real monotheism would have been. It was, rather, a kind of religious and political effort to tidy up and bring order to the chaotic pantheon of competing deities and make their worship easier for the authorities to manage.

THE SEARCH FOR A NEW IDEOLOGY The setbacks of the third century accelerated the search for a religion more universal than polytheism. As the emperors lost control of the frontiers and disorder plagued the armies the basis for their power was progressively weakened. If the emperor could not defend his own possessions and his own people why should he be worshiped? What kind of a god was he? Some more potent alternative to the imperial cult had to be found. The emperor Aurelian proposed the worship of *Sol Invictus*, the "Unconquerable Sun God," and a new college of pontiffs, independent of the old pontifical college, was created to serve his needs. A great new temple to him was erected at Rome. The official title of the emperor became Deus et Dominus, God and Lord, and everything having to do with the emperor was to be considered sacred—his household, his palace, his decrees and pronouncements.

PHILOSOPHICAL MONOTHEISM Besides henotheism there other possibilities of finding a universally satisfying religion that would avoid the disadvantages of polytheism, or at least that is what some philosophers thought. Philosophical monotheism, the knowledge of the existence of a supreme but unreachable deity acquired by the observance of the cosmos and the use of reason alone, was common in one form or another among the educated classes of the Empire, especially as a form of Platonism. Plato's dissatisfaction with what he regarded as the imperfections and instability of governments and laws led him to reject the reality of the material world and seek permanence in the realm of the divine, which alone was real and unchanging. According to his definition, things apprehended by the senses are mutable and finite and therefore unknowable by the mind; only the essences of things are unchanging and therefore the proper objects of knowledge. Even essences shared only partially in the highest three categories of Being: the One, the Good, and the Beautiful. The most elevated and humanly satisfying task that anyone could engage in according to Platonic belief was the pursuit of these categories and beyond them their highest embodiment, the Unknown and Undefinable God. This essentially private, highly intellectual concern with the divine was light years removed from the very material religiosity of the old *polis,* which was largely a matter of humanly satisfying ritual. Philosophical monotheism of this elevated form had little currency outside a small, although influential, class of intellectuals. It was as hard to wed this form of monotheism of the philosophers to the polytheism of ordinary people as it was for the emperors to persuade their subjects to see the value of imperial henotheism. The gap between theory and practice was too immense to be bridged no matter how great the political or intellectual needs of the Empire.

In diluted forms Platonic, Aristotelian, Epicurean, Stoic, and Cynic beliefs were widespread among the elites of the Empire. According to Seneca, philosophy:

> aims to achieve happiness and guides us thither and opens the way for us. It demonstrates to us what things are evil and what things only appear to be evil. It strips our mind of foolish illusions ...and reveals to us what the gods are and what kind they are.... It unlocks not a village shrine but the vast temple of all the gods, the universe itself (Letter, 90.27–29).

Philosophy of this kind was a vague kind of monotheism along Platonic lines, or a pantheism that saw the divine immanent or embedded in the material universe. The divinity in the form of a shaper or modeler of matter—the term for god was "demiurge"—brought order out of the original chaos, infused matter with its own natural laws and sustained its marvelous order and harmony. Happiness consists in discovering these laws of nature and especially the laws of human behavior and in living in accordance with them.

MAZDAISM OR ZOROASTRIANISM The founder of Mazdaism was the Persian prophet Zoroaster (the Greek form of the Iranian Zarathustra) who is thought, most probably, to have lived around 1200 B.C. Early generations of scholars, however, placed him in the first half of the sixth century B.C. In addition to being a priest of the Iranian religion he was a prophet, teacher, and reformer. Some parts of the Persian sacred scriptures, the Avesta are thought to go back to him. These are a series of hymns in the form of meditations on the rituals for which he was responsible as a priest. Because Zoroaster left nothing in writing most of what he taught comes to us secondhand, filtered through the oral traditions of his followers. Scholars disagree regarding the date when the first collection of his teachings was made. The text as it has come down to us suggests several episodes of collection, destruction and re-assemblage. One stage in this process seems to have occurred during the Achaemenid period (559 B.C.–331 B.C.) though the present text of the Avesta dates from the Parthian and Sassanid periods (ca. 250 B.C.–A.D. 651). About a quarter of the original Avesta survives. The rest was destroyed in the period following the Arab invasion of Iran in the seventh century.

DUALISM According to Zoroastrianism all of humanity is involved in a great cosmic struggle between two great principles, Ahura Mazda and Ahriman represented respectively by truth and falsity, light and darkness, loyalty and treachery, stability and chaos. All humans at some point in their lives have to make a choice between one side or the other-between the Ahura Mazda and Ahriman, between the Truth and the Lie. After death each person will be judged individually and when history comes to its close in the final triumph of Ahura Mazda, there will be a general judgment of all of humanity.

Zoroastrianism was not fully monotheistic. Besides Ahura Mazda there were other gods such as Mithra, the sun god; Anahita, the goddess of water and fertility; Mah, the Moon; Atar, fire, and many others. Fire, earth, and water were sacred elements. The burial of bodies defiled the earth and corpses were to be exposed on towers specially built for that purpose. Afterwards, the remains were to be deposited in mausoleums built above the ground or in tombs cut from the rock. Persian religion was administered by a priestly caste, the Magi, whose responsibilities included the maintenance of the Sacred Fire, the interpretation of dreams, the education of the royal family, and the celebration of sacrifices.

Zoroastrianism influenced many of the religions of the Middle East and through them religions world-wide. Echoes of its emphasis on the opposition between truth and falsehood, light and darkness, its apocalyptic imagery of war between good and evil, its stark moral clarity, its emphasis on personal responsibility, its ideas of immortality, resurrection, heaven and hell, are to be found in many religions including Judaism, Christianity, and Islam. As Mithraism, Iranian dualism spread west into the Roman Empire where it was a particularly popular cult of the army. With the rise of the Sasanian dynasty in second century A.D. Iran, Mazdaism was given the status of a state religion and its priests, the Magi, acquired special privileges and great power. In return, Mazdaism provided the state with a strong religious identity and at times a proclivity to persecute rival cults.

THE PROPHET MANI The reach of Iranian religion was extended in the second century A.D.when the prophet Mani successfully combined tenets of Zoroastrianism, Christianity, and Buddhism to form a new, universal religion, Manichaeism. Mesopotamia by the second century A.D. was a great mixing bowl as well as, at times, a battleground of competing philosophies, religions, cults, and sects. Christianity, Judaism, Zoroastrianism, and innumerable forms of polytheism were all represented there in the form of strong, indigenous communities. A native of Babylon in central Mesopotamia, Mani (A.D. 216–276) grew up in a community that adhered to a form of early Gnostic Jewish Christianity, which in common with other gnostic sects, believed that redemption was achieved by initiation into secret knowledge (*gnosis* in Greek) regarding the universe. After a series of visions that led Mani to believe he was a manifestation of the Holy Spirit or Paraclete ("The Comforter") promised by Jesus, he was expelled from his gnostic community. As he continued to receive revelations he travelled to India or at least Pakistan, where he preached and then returned to Persia where, on the basis of his reputation for wisdom and wonder-working, he enjoyed good relations with the Iranian aristocracy and the Persian king Sapor. He sent missionaries west where his teaching attracted the attention of Queen Zenobia of Palmyra. A century later Saint Augustine became an adherent of Manichaeism before his conversion to Christianity. An essential part of Mani's program to extend the knowledge of his revelation throughout the world was writing, and his many books were collected, expanded on, and circulated by his followers. After the death of King Sapor Mani fell out of favor with the Zoroastrian priests who regarded his syncretistic religion as a challenge to their power in the Sasanid Empire. He was executed, and his followers represented his death as a crucifixion.

MANICHAEISM Mani's message was a complex synthesis of Iranian dualism, Gnosticism, Christianity, and Buddhism. As in Mazdaism there was an eternal, cosmic struggle between Light and Darkness. All creation, all matter is evil. The world with all its miseries and horrors exists only to prevent the particles of Light that had been imprisoned in matter from returning to Paradise. Mani's mission was to reveal the truth of this reality to humans so that they could set free the Light trapped in their own bodies and allow It to be reunited with the forces of goodness. Only when the majority of the particles of Light had been liberated would there be a definitive battle between good and evil ending with the final separation of Light from Darkness. Mani's followers were to continue his mission of liberating the Light from its imprisoning evil matter by initiating people into the mystical knowledge (*gnosis*) of the struggle and how it was to be waged. In Mani's words:

> My Hope [i.e., my teaching] will go towards the West, and she will go also towards the East. And they shall hear the voice of her message in all languages, and shall proclaim her in all cities… . My Church shall spread in all cities, and its Gospel shall reach every country.[1]

The Manichaean church consisted of the Elect who were destined for salvation, and the Hearers who could hope for rebirth as a member of the elect by the observance of moral rules. The members of the Elect, who were guided by an all-male hierarchy, were to devote their lives entirely to the struggle with Darkness and were denied all worldly occupations and possessions. They were to be guided by five commandments: obedience to truth; the observance of non-violence; sexual abstinence; abstinence from meat; and finally abstinence from food and drink that were considered impure. Mani's religion spread with extraordinary rapidity from its Mesopotamian heartland westward into the Roman Empire and east into central Asia and as far as China where it had a presence until the fourteenth century. Diverse, mostly fragmentary texts in Greek, Parthian, Persian, Syriac, Coptic, and Chinese testify to the importance of the written word for Mani and his followers and its geographically widespread character.

[1] Kephalaia 154, tr. Stevenson.

# 2. REVOLUTIONARY MONOTHEISM

## Why Middle Eastern Monotheism Was Revolutionary

IT IS EXPEDIENT THAT THERE BE GODS The heart and soul of pagan culture was religion. The festivals of paganism with their sacrifices, communal feasting, dancing, and singing structured the life of all communities everywhere. The innumerable gods, goddesses, spirits, and heroes of paganism were accessible at all times and in all places on individual and at group levels. Homes were full of representations of the gods and were themselves sacred. Cities were sacred places and their shrines and temples were even more sacred. The countryside had its own forms of the sacred. There were holy rivers, wells, forests, trees, mountains, and hills. From childhood a map of the sacred was impressed on minds of the inhabitants of the Roman Empire and everyone knew how to navigate it. This involved a developed sensitivity to what was needed to be done to please the gods from childbirth to death, in work and war and politics. No sphere of human activity was exempt from religious influence. If people need to know what gods should be approached or what rituals should be used, there were experts who could provide the necessary information.

Needless to say the more educated classes tended to have a higher percentage of scoffers and skeptics among them than the rest of society and ridiculed what they regarded as the "superstitious" behavior of the unrefined, backward masses. The emperor Vespasian joked as he was on his deathbed "I think I'm becoming a god." But the educated elite was slow to proclaim its disbelief publicly, and the more thoughtful of its members worried that the widespread scepticism in which they indulged could be ruinous to society if it spread widely outside their class. The disbelieving masses would no longer conform to the laws or their strictly defined places in the social hierarchy. Ordinary people would be without moral anchors since they lacked the kind of pseudo-religious philosophies that provided alternate moral codes for the enlightened. Hence even the most extreme skeptics found it expedient to maintain the festivals and participate in them, share in public sacrifices, and offer libations to the gods. Cicero justified the role of religion:

> Piety (*pietas*), like the rest of the virtues, cannot survive as just outward show and pretence. Without piety holiness and religion will likewise vanish. And when they are gone life will be just a welter of disorder and confusion. I do not doubt that the disappearance of piety towards the gods will lead to the disappearance of trust (*fides*) and social cohesion among men as well as justice, the most excellent of all the virtues. (*On the Nature of the Gods*, 1.4)

The poet Ovid summed up this attitude in his aphorism: *expedit esse deos*—it is expedient that there be gods.

THE CHALLENGE OF TRUE MONOTHEISM Unlike henotheism or philosophical monotheism the monotheistic faiths challenged head on the civic religions and polytheism of the Empire. If there was a single Supreme Divinity who had infallibly revealed himself not only through creation but also through revelation, then no other gods could be tolerated. The so-called gods of paganism were not truly divine but rather dangerous distractions from the One True Divinity. Because they were non-existent these gods had no need of worship, temples, festivals, prayers or sacrifices. Polytheism did not deserve respect because it was intrinsically a perversion of true religion.

If any one of the monotheistic faiths—Judaism, Christianity, Mazdaism or Islam—achieved dominance the result would, inevitably, be the same, namely, the elimination of polytheism and the civic religions. Their practices would be replaced by those of whichever monotheistic religion was victorious, together with its sacred scriptures, rituals, forms of prayer, moral codes and social customs. Not all the monotheistic faiths, however, were equally well equipped to challenge the existing religious and civic order. Mazdaism was too closely related to Iranian imperialism and ethnicity to become a truly universal monotheistic religion. Judaism too was closely identified with a particular ethnic group and a specific territory and temple. Its two offshoots, Christianity and Islam, however, were truly cosmopolitan. In their basic theologies both were universal and proselytizing. Their adherents believed they had a command from God that obligated them to spread their versions of monotheism to all peoples everywhere. In means and approach Christianity and Islam differed considerably, but not in their belief that monotheism was incompatible with polytheism. What that meant in practice varied over time and from place to place and from religious community to community.

CULTURAL AND INTELLECTUAL IMPLICATIONS Besides their purely religious practices the monotheistic faiths brought with them other challenges to the existing order. They clashed directly with the fundamental polytheistic belief that the gods and the cosmos were inseparable. Monotheism posited just the opposite: God was outside and completely independent of the material universe which he created out of nothingness (*ex nihilo*) not out of existing matter, a point noted as significant by the important pagan doctor Galen. Rivers, forests, trees, or oceans were not the dwelling places of gods or spirits. The sun, the moon, the planets and the stars were not gods. Fortune or Chance which dominated the thought of even pagan non-believers was not some inexplicable impersonal force that ruled the universe including even the gods. "Providence" for the monotheists was an all-knowing, all-caring deity who, although standing apart from the universe sustained it, and directed history, however mysteriously, to its final end. Matter was not eternal, self-perpetuating. Time was not endless or circular or repetitive. It had a beginning when God created the universe and would have an end when the universe came to an end.

These assertions contradicted classical belief systems and offered an alternative explanation. Monotheism demystified, demythologized—and simplified—the universe. The material world did not exist for its own sake but for human use. Made in the image of God himself humans stood at the peak of the material hierarchy. The world was to be subject to humans not the other way around. Humanity's end or purpose, however, was not encompassed within the created world. True human fulfillment was possible only in the next life. Monotheists were in, but not of this world.

It has taken centuries, even millennia, for the radical implications of these beliefs—especially their inherent egalitarianism—to be worked out or even recognized. Many, perhaps most of the implications were apparent in early years neither to the monotheists themselves nor to their bewildered opponents. With the advantage of hindsight some of these evolutionary developments can now be seen with some clarity and will be discussed in greater length in chapter 20.

## 3. EARLY CHRISTIANITY

### Christian Origins: The Sources

The destruction of Jerusalem in A.D. 70 constitutes a kind of a wall which prevents a clear understanding of how rabbinic Judaism and Christianity evolved out of late Second Temple Judaism. The earliest post destruction document of rabbinic Judaism, the *Mishnah*, dates to about A.D. 200, and with the exception of Paul's letters and possibly the gospel of Mark, most Christian literature postdates the fall of the city. The Sadducees, the priestly aristocratic party that controlled the Temple left no literature of their own. Most of what we know about the Pharisees, apart from New Testament references, comes from after A.D. 70. Fortunately new light has been thrown on this murky world by the discovery in 1947 and in following years of a large collection of documents known as the Dead Sea Scrolls

### The Dead Sea Scrolls

In 1947, just north of the Dead Sea, a Bedouin shepherd stumbled on a cave containing a cache of ancient scrolls dating from before the time of the destruction of the Temple at Jerusalem in A.D. 70. Ultimately 11 caves in the same area were found to contain some 900 scrolls written on leather, papyrus and in one case, copper. A few scrolls were well preserved and largely intact, such as the scrolls of Isaiah, but most were fragmentary. One cave (Cave 4) alone contained the remnants of more than 500 manuscripts in 15,000 fragments. The state of this cave's contents suggest the magnitude of the task facing scholars who have the job of reassembling the fragments in their original form—as though they were working on 500 jig-saw puzzles at the same time—preserving, publishing and interpreting them. The tale of the discovery of the scrolls, the battles between the finders and the purchasers and the scholarly debates and intrigues that followed, is a story straight out of a Hollywood script. Most of the texts contain excerpts from biblical books but there are also biblical commentaries and a number of sectarian writings including the rules for belonging to a strict sectarian community of uncertain identity. The scrolls date from approximately 250 B.C. to A.D. 70 and perhaps later. The majority of them were deposited in the caves during or shortly after the revolt of A.D. 66–70.

Needless to say the impact of the finds on the religious world was huge. Broadly speaking we know that the Judaism of the first century B.C. to the first century A.D. was not monolithic; it was, rather, highly diverse. It was also in a state of upheaval. A core group of authoritative books—the Torah (the Pentateuch or first five books of the Hebrew bible), the Prophets and Psalms—were accepted as Scripture. Beyond these there was no fixed canon that could be said to have constituted a "bible," let alone an agreed upon text for the books of that bible. Interpretation of what was thought to be Scripture was wide open and

Saducees, Pharisees, Essenes, Samaritans, the followers of John the Baptist and Jesus, various revolutionary movements such as the Zealots and the Sicarii, all had widely differing views on the correct ways of interpreting Judaism and what was proper worship.

Collectively the Dead Sea Scrolls provide the clearest insight into this world of these competing interests. There are two principal theories regarding the origins of the scrolls. One is that they are a random collection of texts from different Jewish communities that were collected and deposited in the caves when it became clear that Jerusalem was going to be destroyed by the Romans. The other is that they were the library of a single sect, possibly Essene, which lived in the nearby site of Qumran. A middle view holds that the scrolls reflect a restricted range of interests and are best explained as a partisan collection of a sect of Judaism not otherwise historically attested. Early interpretation saw the Dead Sea Scrolls as the intellectual and religious precursors of Christianity. It is true that are points of contact between the New Testament and the scrolls but more recent scholars see Dead Sea texts as more generally reflecting the multiplicity of sects and viewpoints that characterized late Second Temple Judaism. At most the similarities show the deep roots of Christianity in that world.

## The Christian Scriptures: The Formation of the Canon

The earliest scriptures for Christians were the Septuagint. As mentioned previously, the Septuagint was a kind of proto-canon of the Hebrew scriptures translated into Greek by the Jews of Alexandria in the second and first centuries B.C. For the first century and a half when Christians referred to "the scriptures" they meant this Greek Alexandrian Bible.

It took several centuries for Christians to agree on the list or canon of what constituted their own holy books. From the beginning, however, certain writings came to have special value in the eyes of the adherents of the new religion.

PAUL'S WRITINGS Chronologically the earliest Christian writings were the letters of St. Paul (see below for Paul's role in the establishment of the church). His letters, which constitute the earliest source of information about Christianity and Jesus, were written on an ad hoc basis to various churches he founded in Asia Minor, Greece, and Rome. The first letter, the letter to the church in Thessalonika (I *Thessalonians*), was written not much more than a decade or so after the death of Jesus, sometime in the early 50s A.D. Not all his letters have survived. Two written to the Corinthians, for instance, and one to the Laodicaeans, have been lost. By the end of the first century A.D. his surviving letters were in circulation throughout the scattered Christian communities of the Mediterranean and Middle East, and were read publicly –as they were intended—at gatherings of Christians. They were also studied, disputed, and commented upon. The author of the letter known as 2 *Peter* thought that "some things in them were hard to understand" and that this led to confusion among "the ignorant and the unstable" (3.16), an apt if condescending description of the all-too-vigorous religious life of the Early Churches.

Apart from revealing Paul's own views on the Gospel, his letters constitute an invaluable source of information on the organization of the Early Church, the kinds of doctrines that were being taught by various missionaries other than Paul, and the interpretations that were being developed of who Jesus of Nazareth was and what was the meaning of his message. They also provide a vital source of information regarding the under-represented, non-elite classes of the Empire and a useful corrective to the classical sources, which uniformly ignore the lowly kinds of people found in the New Testament. Paul wrote in a vigorous, ordinary Greek rather than the stilted, rhetorical Greek of the elite, and in the past his style was regarded with disdain because it did not conform to elite norms. In recent years, however, scholars have come to appreciate the special kind of rhetorical artistry that characterizes his writings.

NON-PAULINE WRITINGS Other letters ascribed to Paul, John, James, and other apostles soon made their appearance and were accepted into the list or canon of the New Testament. One great letter, one of the most profound theological reflections of the Early Church, the *Letter to the Hebrews*, came from an unknown hand and was variously ascribed to Paul or Barnabas, one of Paul's companions in his early journeys, or others, and was of such weight that although there were doubts about its authorship it was revered at an early date and so made its way into the canon of the New Testament. Meanwhile, by way of oral transmission, stories about Jesus and collections of his sayings and parables began to accumulate in the various developing centers of Christianity around the Mediterranean, principally in Palestine, Syria, Egypt, and Asia Minor. Some of these collections were written down at an early date, possibly at the same time Paul was writing his letters, that is between A.D. 50 and 65. Drawing on these sources four individuals known to us as Matthew, Mark, Luke, and John composed interpretative biographies in the mode or style of the Scriptural Sacred History. These biographies, known as gospels, "stories of the Good News," were destined for specific communities of readers. Like Paul's letters these four accounts quickly won widespread approval and were used beyond the original communities for which they were intended. The first gospel, Mark's, addresses an issue that was of great concern to his readers, namely the lack of recognition of Jesus as the messiah by the majority of Jews not just during Jesus' own time but afterwards. Matthew's gospel seems to have been composed within a Jewish-Christian setting while Luke's was aimed at Gentile Christians. The Jesus portrayed by Luke is the messiah of the gentiles, detached from earthly politics and traditional Jewish revolutionary messianism. God's kingdom for Luke is a kingdom of peace and righteousness; it is the church. *The Book of Acts*, the history of the expansion of the Early Church, is also ascribed to Luke. John's gospel is very different from the other three. Its author worked at two levels, the purely historical and the "true" context which is beyond the merely temporal, historical events being described. For example, the dialogue of Jesus with the woman at the well from whom he asks for a drink of water begins with a reference to ordinary well-water which Jesus asks her for, but then moves on to a different kind of water, "living water that wells up forever" (*John* 4.17). "Living water" has strong scriptural resonance and would remind its readers of the water that Moses brought miraculously from the rock during the Exodus, of Jeremiah's lament that "they have forsaken me, the fount of living water" (*Jeremiah* 2.13), the *Song of Song*'s "well of living water," and many others references.

The four gospels quickly entered into the canon of the New Testament and were frequently cited by other writers of the first and early second centuries such as Clement and

Ignatius. A dozen or so gospels (ascribed to Peter, Mary, Thomas, and other figures around Jesus), various Acts (Acts of Andrew, John, Paul, etc.), and Apocalypses (of Paul, Peter, Thomas, and others) did not make the cut and thereby constitute a body of writings known as the Apocryphal New Testament.

THE MANUSCRIPT TRADITION The canonical New Testament has a remarkably strong and abundant manuscript tradition. In antiquity all writings had to be laboriously copied out by hand, and when worn out the scrolls on which they were written were discarded. There was no equivalent to the modern printing press, which produces thousands of identical copies of the same work. The result was that unless books were continuously used and recopied they tended to disappear. Understandably, most of the manuscripts of the great classical writers are from a late date. The earliest manuscripts for Aristotle's great work, the *Politics*, for example, date from the fifteenth century A.D., or over 1700 years after the death of its author. The manuscript tradition for his *Ethics* is somewhat better; its earliest manuscript dates to the tenth century A.D. By contrast, fragments of the New Testament are found as early as 30 to 40 years after their composition and full manuscripts are available from the fourth century. Codex Sinaiticus, for example, which was found at St. Catherine's monastery on Mt. Sinai, dates from around A.D. 350 and contains the whole New Testament. There are about 75 papyrus fragments that contain portions of the New Testament, some of which date to a century and a half before Codex Sinaiticus. One papyrus fragment dating to around A.D. 135 has four verses from the gospel of *John*, chapter 18 (Rylands Papyrus, 457).

## 4. THE FOUNDERS

### Jesus of Nazareth

Jesus was born about 4 B.C. and died in about A.D. 30. His early life was spent in an insignificant village in Galilee, an area of primarily Jewish population but also the home of large numbers of non-Jews. From the top of the hill on which Nazareth was perched Jesus could see, just a few miles away, the important city of Sepphoris, of which impressive remains survive. Phoenician Tyre was only 40 miles away and Sidon about 25 miles up the coast. The evangelist Mark says Jesus visited the regions around both of these cities as he did the area of the Greek cities of the Decapolis (*Mark* 7.31). Among its cities that are mentioned in the New Testament were Gadara and Gerasa, and anytime Jesus visited the Sea of Galilee he could see Hippos perched on its hilltop to the east. Jesus was thus not someone who grew up in an isolated, provincial setting, a simple rustic who knew nothing of the world. Through Galilee and the Decapolis passed all the land trade and travel between Egypt and Syria and Mesopotamia, and throughout history it was an area of military and commercial importance. It was also rich agriculturally. What little we know of Jesus' education shows he was literate and thoroughly familiar with the Scriptures. He had travelled to Jerusalem for the festivals. We can imagine that he knew some Greek as well as his native Aramaic and Hebrew.

Jesus' ministry began around A.D. 26, and he quickly gathered a group of followers or disciples whom he trained. The main sphere of his activity was Galilee, but he also made

**Approximate Dates of Composition of Books of the New Testament**

| *50's A.D.* | *60s A.D.* | *70's–80's A.D.* | *90's A.D.* | *100–125 A.D.* |
|---|---|---|---|---|
| 1 Thessalonians<br>2 Thessalonians<br>Galatians<br>1–2 Corinthians<br>Romans | Philippians<br>Philemon<br>Colossians<br>Gospel of Mark | Ephesians (?)<br>Gospels of Matthew, Luke<br>Acts<br>Hebrews (A.D. 65–100) | Gospel of John<br>Apocalypse<br>James<br>Non-Canonical: 1 Clement<br>Didache | 1–2 Timothy, Titus, 1 Peter, 1–2–3 John, Jude<br>2 Peter (?)<br>Non-Canonical: Letters of Ignatius |

several visits with his followers to Judaea. His miracles and teaching drew the attention of the authorities who feared an insurrection. Jesus' clearing of the Temple of the sellers of sacrificial victims heightened this fear and, after being arrested and given a summary trial, he was handed over to the Romans for execution. Two days later his tomb was found empty and his disciples reported seeing apparitions of him. Soon afterwards they began to proclaim Jesus as Messiah and Savior, first in Judaea and Galilee but not long afterwards throughout the metropolitan centers of the Empire and the Middle East, addressing first the Jews of the Diaspora and then the gentiles. So it was that in Syrian Antioch the followers of Jesus were first called Christians.

THE MESSAGE OF JESUS Christianity had its origins as one of many reforming movements in Second Temple Judaism, and its founder's message and mission have a lot in common with the world of late Jewish eschatology. Like many of his contemporaries, Jesus believed that the world was enthralled to demonic influences and that liberation would come through the intervention of God, who would overwhelm the forces of evil and set up his own kingdom over which sin and death would have no power. In the past, God had acted in a preliminary way to deliver his people from bondage in such historical events as the call of Abraham, the Exodus from Egypt, and the end of the Babylonian captivity. Now, however, he was preparing to act in a final, decisive manner.

Jesus' gospel did not involve the introduction or invention of a new ethical or moral system. Jesus did not regard himself as a teacher, a rabbi, a wise man, a military revolutionary or a counter-culture figure. His ethical message was not particularly original; much of it could be found in traditional Jewish teaching or even in pagan ethical theory. His mission was, rather, to proclaim the coming of a new period in Sacred History, the inauguration of the Kingdom of Heaven among men. This Kingdom was not to come into being by human means, such as the violent overthrow of governments, or by the exact observation of laws or ethical rules, but by the active intervention of God in human affairs in the person of Jesus. God had entered into human history in the past and was now about to do so again, but this time with finality. Jesus was no king in the ordinary sense of that word but the Suffering Servant figure of the prophet Isaiah whose agonies would atone for the sins of Israel. He was the scapegoat whose sacrificial death would usher in the Day of the Lord. During the Last Supper discourse Jesus again drew on the symbolism of Israel's past. His death would initiate a New Passover. Just as the Exodus was a mighty act by which God freed the Israelites from slavery in Egypt and made them his people, so Jesus' death was to be his "passover," or passage in triumph to the next world. It would be a New Exodus leading to a New Covenant and the formation of newly redeemed People of Israel. As a result of this New Passover, the reign of God was to be finally initiated. Humankind would be freed not merely from oppressive human rule as were the ancient Israelites in their liberation from Egypt but from what truly oppressed and enslaved the human race: sin, death, and the power of the demonic world.

The earliest Christians believed that the Kingdom was ushered in not just by Jesus' sacrificial death but also by his resurrection from the dead and his ascension to heaven. New members were initiated into the Christian community by the ritual of baptism, which identified them with the key events of Jesus' life, his death and resurrection. As St. Paul put it: "All of us who have been baptized into Christ Jesus were baptized into his death. We were buried with him by baptism into death, so that as Christ was raised from the dead... we too might walk in newness of life. For if we have been united with him in the likeness of his death, we shall be united with him in the likeness of his resurrection also" (*Romans* 6.3). The religious life of the early Christians revolved around scripture readings, singing of hymns, common meals, prayer, preaching, and ecstatic prophecy. Stories regarding the sayings and deeds of Jesus were told and retold. The common meal shared by early Christians took on the overtones of Jesus' Last Supper with his apostles and became the setting for discussions, readings, and interpretations of Jesus' life and actions.

## Paul of Tarsus

Among the major issues settled in the early years of the Christian community was the question of whether Jesus' message was to be limited to Jews or could be extended to gentiles as well. Was the ethnic, historical monotheism of Israel to be transcended and become the possession of all peoples, not just the Jews? Were all the peoples of the world to become the people of Yahweh? One of the principal figures in this momentous debate was a Hellenized Jew, Paul of Tarsus. The decision of the first generation of the Early Church in favor of a wider audience had vital implications for its future as well as for world history.

Born in the town of Tarsus, near the modern border between Syria and Turkey, Paul was a perhaps slightly younger contemporary of Jesus of Nazareth. He was raised as a Jew of the Greek Diaspora but with close contacts with the Palestinian homeland. His family was well off, an inference from the fact that Paul could claim to be a Roman citizen by birth, in addition to being a citizen of Tarsus, an unusual status in that part of the world in the first century A.D. According to his own testimony he belonged to the tribe of Benjamin and was a Pharisee of the strictest observance. After a conversion experience he initiated a series of missionary journeys that took him to parts of Anatolia, Asia Minor, Macedonia, Greece, and eventually Rome.

PAUL'S TRAVELS The pattern of his missionary journeys was as follows: He usually traveled with a few companions such as Barnabas, Mark, Timothy, or Titus and first made contact with the local Jewish community in the towns and cities he visited. Where synagogues had not yet been established, he usually met his fellow Jews in private homes and presented or, as he preferred to say, "announced" the good news of the activities of Jesus of

Nazareth—his life, death, and resurrection—which had inaugurated the Kingdom of God. Its fulfillment was to come at the end of times whose nearness or distance could not be foretold since it would come "like a thief in the night," although Paul himself thought it was close. Paul's proclamation of the good news—the Gospel—was not merely preaching. It was an authoritative announcement, an historical act of Salvation History accompanied by great signs and miracles such as the revival of the dead, the casting out of demons, and the healing of the sick. These signs and the consequences of his preaching for his converts guaranteed the authenticity of his mission, which was not something he took on by himself but was imposed on him by Jesus himself.

Paul's proclamation of the Gospel often created controversy and sometimes civic disturbances when communities fractured over the new beliefs. Some, sometimes many, Jews of the local community were converted to the new belief and were baptized "into Jesus Christ" and became members of the new sect. Sometimes gentile admirers of the Jewish community were converted and sometimes it was only gentiles who adhered to the new movement. Despite the small size of these communities, their impact was large. Converts were not restricted to the poor, the disenfranchised, and women, but included a wide segment of the urban population of the cities where Christianity was proclaimed. The new movement claimed the full inheritance of Judaism, its rituals, many of its social practices, its Sacred Scriptures, its tradition of preaching, scripture reading, and commentary. In essence Christianity in the diaspora at first saw itself as a reforming movement within the Jewish community, the "true Israel," not a new religion.

HOUSE CHURCHES Members of the newly founded Christian communities met in each other houses primarily for religious but also for social purposes. Wealthier converts provided patronage for the new movement in the form of donating portions of their homes for religious use, sponsoring the community meals that formed a central aspect of the new community's social and religious activity, and contributing to the support of the poor, widows, and orphans. These house churches might have from 30 to 50 members. We know of six at Corinth during Paul's time.

Over the years of Paul's ministry the network of house churches, micro-communities of Christians founded by Paul, were in contact with their founder, his representatives, other missionaries, and each other by personal visits and by letter. Paul made three visits to Corinth and wrote a number of letters to the Corinthian church of which two survive, as well as sending his emissaries Titus and Timothy to visit the new community. The Corinthians in turn communicated with Paul by letter and by delegates such as the servants of the household of Chloe, a wealthy Christian.

PAUL'S GOSPEL By its very nature Christianity presented complex and novel ideas and generated among its adherents novel and complex problems. For instance, the community at Thessalonika was distressed when some of their members died before the Second Coming of Christ and wanted Paul to say whether the dead would be resurrected or only the living. For many early Christians the degree to which Christianity was Jewish was an enormous puzzle. Should new converts be circumcised and follow all the dietary regulations required by the Law? What kind of interaction with non-Christians was acceptable?

How was the Christian community to interact with its non-Christians neighbors? What was the nature of the resurrection? What kind of bodies would the resurrected have? What was "redemption"?

It was to these kinds of issues that Paul addressed himself in his letters. He was not the author of an overarching theology of Christianity but rather the responder to specific theological and disciplinary questions, some of which did involve the assertions of fundamental principles that later became essential aspects of Christian belief. Paul's main role as the Apostle to the Gentiles, as he called himself, was to articulate the message of Jesus in terms of practical, down-to-earth responses to daily life issues of the new believers. The overall context of his proclamation was a version of late Jewish apocalyptism. The human race since the fall of Adam was condemned to suffer pain, disease, and death. Due to Adam's sin the original harmonious relationship between God and humankind had been destroyed. This was not to say that fallen human was incapable of doing good; quite the contrary. Paul asserted that humans possessed natural reasoning capacity that enabled them to formulate a genuinely good natural morality in conformity with human nature. But this capacity was limited and generally defective. Humans by their own unaided efforts were unable to rebuild the relationship with God that had been destroyed by Adam's failure. It took a new Adam, Christ, to restore this relationship by his self-sacrifice on the cross. This was salvation or redemption. His subsequent resurrection was proof of the restoration of good relations, since it demonstrated that death no longer had mastery over humankind. While all humans were still liable to the effects of Adam's sin, namely suffering and death, all humans were offered the opportunity to participate in the new Adam's victory over sin and death, beginning on earth and reaching completion at the end of time with the second coming and the resurrection of the body.

## Other Missionaries

Paul was not the only proclaimer of the acts of Christ as savior of humanity. In his own letters he refers to others—the eloquent Apollos for example—who had been educated in Alexandria. There was Cephas or Peter and his own helpers of various periods, Barnabas, Mark, Timothy, Titus, and Silvanus. There were women such as Phoebe, a wealthy patron who carried a letter from Paul to the Christian community at Rome, and the also well-educated couple Aquila and Prisca (or the diminutive Priscilla) to whom one scholar has ascribed the authorship of the important *Letter to the Hebrews.* The other apostles and disciples of Jesus were active also, some in Palestine but also outside Palestine. Eventually the communities of Christians throughout the Mediterranean and Middle East including such major cities as Alexandria in Egypt, Antioch in Syria, and Rome in Italy were all to claim that they were originally founded by one or another of Jesus' apostles or their duly authorized delegates.

PROBLEMS TO BE SOLVED With such a complex theology as Christianity possessed there were bound to be differing interpretations. Questions of what to do with those communities or individuals who deviated from the proto-orthodoxy that emerged in the first generation of Christians were problems that plagued Christianity from the beginning. For example, when persecutions began a critical question was what was to be done with Christians who fell away but later repented and wanted to return to the Church. What of those who committed serious sins such as adultery, or fell back into the worship of idols—what was to be done with them? Could they be received back into the community? The strong currents of Greek philosophy, which by definition questioned everything from the nature of the universe to all forms of human behavior, forced Christians into an analytic mode regarding their own religion. Who or what was Christ? Was he really human? Was he divine? If so, in what sense was he divine? Was he merely a "Son of God" in the sense of being an especially favored creature of God or was he really the Son of God in a more concrete fashion? Was Mary the mother of the human Jesus or was she also "Mother of God"? Galen, a prominent intellectual and a physician, was the first Greek critic to draw attention to the philosophic problem raised by the first chapter of Genesis, namely, creation out of nothing.

Abstruse as they may seem, these theological questions were fundamental to shaping the culture that was to evolve in the Roman Empire in the centuries to come. These were serious intellectual as well as religious issues. Some were extraordinarily daring and raised new questions about human nature and what constituted a human "person." They challenged the compatibility of faith and reason. The mere fact of existence of these conundrums—they were not present in either Judaism or Islam—stimulated philosophic thought among Christians leading to "heresies" or different, not necessarily unorthodox, schools of thought. In the end, most of them, in addition to their intellectual interest, also raised questions of authority. Who was in a position to decide them and give an authoritative response? Were the responses to be generated within the individual community by discerning individuals or by specific prophetic revelation? Were answers to be provided by the study of authoritative texts such as the letters of Paul or the letters of other apostles or the Gospels? Given the inherent theological and moral complexity of Christianity it is understandable that disputes raged within and between Christian communities about what constituted orthodoxy (correct belief) and orthopraxy (correct behavior). These battles became so fierce that at times the secular authorities were drawn into the disputes to act as mediators and, after Constantine, as enforcers. It took many centuries for the present forms of developed orthodox Christianity to emerge.

## 5. ROMANS AND CHRISTIANS

### The Difficulty of Identifying Christians

Christians of the Early Empire were at first difficult to distinguish from Jews, and the Romans were not sure what to make of them. They were much less numerous than Jews but were widely dispersed throughout the cities of the Empire. Around A.D. 100 it is thought that there were about 5,000,000 Jews and perhaps 50,000 Christians. Christians, like Jews, met in each other's houses for social and religious purposes. Again, like Jews, they entertained a way of life that was independent of the social life of their fellow citizens. The non-Christian

Natalis in Minucius Felix's dialogue the *Octavius* is made to complain about Christians, "You do not attend our festivals or take part in our processions. You are absent from our public banquets and shrink in horror from our sacred games" (12). The same charges were leveled against Jews. The difference, however, was that Christians represented a deviant sect or heresy within or outside Judaism. Jews were a known quantity and had legal standing as a people (*natio*), an ethnic community with a homeland, a temple, ancient traditions, and rituals. Christians had no homeland, no temple, no standing—at least in the eyes of the authorities—as an ancient people. The anonymous author of the *Epistle to Diognetus* (probably mid–second century A.D.) puts the Christians' view of themselves as follows:

> Christians are distinguished from other men neither by nationality, language, nor custom. They do not live separately in cities of their own, nor do they have their own special language . ... Rather, while inhabiting Greek as well as non-Greek cities, according as the lot of each of them has determined, and following the customs of the inhabitants in respect to clothing, food, and the rest of their ordinary conduct, they display to us their wonderful and admittedly striking way of life. They dwell in their own lands—but simply as sojourners. As citizens they share in all things with others, and yet endure all things as if foreigners. Every foreign land is to them as their homeland, and every homeland as a land of strangers. They marry, as do all others; they beget children; but they do not commit infanticide. They share a common table, but not a common bed. They are in the flesh, but they do not live after the flesh. They pass their days on earth, but their citizenship is in the heavens. (Footnote 5: Epistle to Diognetus 5–6. Based on the translation of Alexander Roberts and James Donaldson, The Ante-Nicene Fathers (Edinburg, 1867), 26–27.)

This belief system and its corresponding way of life left Christians in a difficult position. Although they claimed their traditions were inherited from Judaism and therefore ancient, they were not able to convince the authorities of their claims once the authorities were able to make a distinction between the two religions. Tacitus, for example, did not believe that Christianity had ancestral legitimacy. The superstition, as he calls it, originated with "Christus who was executed in the principate of Tiberius by the governor Pontius Pilate" (*Annals*, 15.44). Pliny, when governor of Bithynia (northwest Turkey) seems to have shared his friend Tacitus' view of the illegitimacy of Christianity.

PLINY AND THE CHRISTIANS OF BITHYNIA Pliny had been appointed governor of Bithynia by Trajan in A.D. 109 and had been conscientiously working his way around the province inspecting the cities and holding court. At some point in his circuit accusations against Christians were brought to him for adjudication. As he explained subsequently to Trajan he had proceeded as follows. "I ask them if they are Christians and if they admit that they are, I repeat the question a second and a third time, warning them of the punishment that will follow if they persist" (*Letters*, 10.96). Those who continued to maintain that they were Christians he sent off for execution. Citizens who were Roman citizens he designated to be shipped to Rome for trial. As soon as his judgment against the Christians became known anonymous lists were brought to him and informers provided other names. Working from these lists Pliny continued his diligent course of justice. Afterwards he seems to have had some qualms about his procedure and wrote to the emperor to ask whether he should make distinctions between male and female, young and old, and whether those who recanted should be spared. He also reported he had not found, after examination under torture, the kinds of crimes he had expected to have been committed by this secretive sect. He does not specify what crimes he had in mind, but rumors were common that Christians practiced promiscuous sexual intercourse at their love feasts; that they murdered infants and made meals of their bodies, which they declared to be the body of Christ, and generally behaved in wanton and immoral ways. On the contrary those who repented and those he tortured told the same story:

> The accused claim that the totality of their guilt was that on a certain fixed day they were accustomed to meet before daylight and to sing by turns a hymn to Christ as to a god, and to bind themselves by oath—not for some criminal purpose—but that they would not commit robbery, theft, or adultery; that they would not betray a trust nor deny a deposit when it was called for. When this was over, their custom was to disperse and to come together again to partake of food of an ordinary and harmless kind (*Letters*, 10.96).

Trajan, in his reply to Pliny said that if Christians were brought to him appropriately they should be punished, but that he should not act on anonymous reports nor should Christians be hunted down. "Such actions," Trajan said, "created the worst kind of precedents and are completely out of keeping with the humane spirit of our times" (*Letters*, 10.97). What Trajan seems to have in mind was the danger of social or even political disturbances in Bithynia that might be generated by private animosities and accounts-settling made easy by the complacent Pliny's willingness to act on anonymous charges.

*COLLEGIA*: COLLEGES Whatever we might say about Pliny's casual execution of Christians simply because they admitted to being Christians, a genuine concern for public order lay behind his actions. To people such as Pliny non-participation in civic life was proof of irrationality or worse, atheism. The same charge was leveled against Jews and for the same reasons. There was, however, another reason that the Roman authorities were suspicious of Christians.

From the first century A.D. burial societies (*collegia*) were permitted by the government and rapidly spread all over the Empire. The purpose of these societies was to bury the dead and honor their memory with inscriptions and with celebrations at banquets at which all the members gathered. Each society had its own charter and by-laws, elected its own officers, and had its own patron deity in whose honor it gathered. Members paid an entrance fee and gathered periodically to eat a banquet or celebrate a festival of the god. The societies could own property, and the wealthier ones owned shrines, meeting houses, and gardens where they held their events. It was considered one of the civic duties of the curial classes and of the *Augustales* to give gifts to or endow these burial societies. Such benefactors were then honored by being elected patrons of the society—the usual Roman social trade-off. There was a practical side to this custom. The Roman cult of the dead was deeply ingrained, and its perpetuation was of the utmost importance. If a family should die out, the burial society would indefinitely continue to honor the memory of its deceased, especially if they were benefactors.

There were potential dangers, however, in these harmless-looking associations. In the late Republic one of the reasons for the disorder that developed in Rome was the politicization of the associations or *collegia* of artisans, tradesmen, and shopkeepers. Originally these associations had been legitimate groups that met for professional, social, and religious reasons. They came together to celebrate religious rites in honor of the god or goddess of the association, to honor patrons who provided money for the colleges' feasts, for members' funerals, birthdays, and the like. Greek cities also had a long history of such groups, and when they became involved in local politics they were often the cause of rioting. The emperors were particularly sensitive to this danger to public order. Trajan, for instance, forbade the establishment of a firefighter's *collegium* in a Greek city in Asia Minor, not because such a service was not necessary but because of the danger of politicization.

## Churches and Colleges

From the Roman perspective Christians appeared to be organized as colleges. They had their elected rulers, bishops, presbyters, deacons, and others ministers, their own self-generated charters, rules, and social norms. Socially and religiously they behaved like *collegia*. They looked after the burial of their dead, took care of the sick, widows, and orphans. They were also, however, a lot better organized than the similar ad hoc associations found in the cities of the Empire. In individual cities Christian associations were in contact with each other, exchanged membership, and helped each other. Even more alarmingly, they were in contact by letter and embassies with similar associations in other cities of the Empire. As early as the 90s A.D. the church in Rome sent the quarrelsome Corinthian church "faithful and well-balanced men who have lived without blame among us from youth to old age to serve as witnesses between us and you. We have done this so that you should know that our concern for you was and is to establish peace among you quickly" (*First Clement*, 63). Early in the next century the Bishop of Antioch, Ignatius, wrote to the church in Ephesus:

> I am not issuing orders to you as if I were someone… but, since love does not allow me to be silent about you, I decided to encourage you to act together in harmony with the mind of God. … It is fitting that you act in harmony with the mind of your bishop (*episkopos*)… for your presbytery is attuned to the bishop as to a lyre. Thus Jesus Christ is sung in your harmony and symphony of love (*Letters* 3,4).

The same Ignatius encouraged the church at Smyrna to send a delegation to the church at Antioch with a letter congratulating its members on the resolution of a conflict within it. The letter was to enable them to "rejoice with them in the tranquility that has come to them from God, because they have already reached a harbor as a result of your prayers" (*Letters*, 11). Ignatius was martyred around A.D. 110. Another martyr in whom there was great interest was Polycarp, bishop of Smyrna, who according to tradition was a follower of the evangelist John. Polycarp was martyred in old age in the 150s A.D. The account of Polycarp's death was composed by someone called Marcion and sent on behalf of the church at Smyrna to another church in Asia minor at Philomelium in Phrygia. At the end of the account Marcion encourages the Philomelians to "send our letter to the brethren who are farther afield that they may glorify the Lord" (*Martyrdom of Polycarp*, 20). In short, the Early Churches around the Mediterranean were doing what Paul and the other proclaimers of the

Gospel were doing nearly a century earlier, namely, sending letters and delegations from one house church to another and consulting on mutual problems.

WHAT DID THE AUTHORITIES KNOW? It is hard to know exactly how much the Roman authorities knew of the internal organization of the Early Church. Pliny had heard about Christians and apparently had heard the rumors that circulated about them, but not much more. As the Church became more and more visible throughout the second and third centuries it is safe to assume that the authorities became much better informed. Most of the persecutions of Christians in the first two centuries of the church's existence were more like local pogroms than officially organized attempts at repressing the institution. When empire-wide persecutions began in the middle of the third century the authorities were sufficiently well informed to make the organizational structure of the church—its bishops, priests, deacons, and so on—their targets, along with prominent laymen and women, and the Scriptures.

## 6. THE QUEST FOR LEGITIMACY

### A New Ideology?

The set-backs Rome suffered in the third century called into question not just the military and political competence of the imperial government but key assumptions about its authority. Since Augustus the claim of the emperors to a monopoly of power was acknowledged as justifiable for at least as long as they were able to protect the inhabitants of the Empire from aggressive outsiders and internal disorder. That was why, in the early Empire, such a heavy emphasis was placed on themes of victory and governmental omnipotence. It was advertised widely that rebellions would be ruthlessly crushed and invasions punished with attacks on the homelands of the invaders. Preemptive strikes were regularly undertaken to maintain the image of the Empire as all-conquering, ever victorious.

The civil wars and invasions of the third century made that image difficult to maintain and emperors were forced to cast around for a new means to shore up their authority and legitimacy. Military and political reform was first in order of importance, but by themselves they were insufficient. It was obvious to more than just the rulers that the old formula, the bargain between ruler and ruled worked out by Augustus, was fraying. The imperial cult had its uses but it was a weak basis for imperial unity. At its best it was an addition to the polytheistic rituals of the Empire, not a substitute for them. Imperial propaganda could only go so far in shoring up the emperors' claim to rule. Hence the importance of finding a new way, preferably a new ideology, to bolster the authority of the struggling rulers and justify their legitimacy in the eyes of elite and ordinary people in general. It was unclear, however, what form that ideology—if one could be found—and its corresponding political structure would take. We have seen how this search began under the Severans and continued through the third century, but it was left for the great fourth century emperors Diocletian and Constantine and Constantine's son Constantius II to find a formula that worked and allowed Rome to reinvent itself successfully.

# Part Seven

# Late Antiquity: Rome Reinvents Itself

## 1. THE TRANSFORMATION OF THE EMPIRE

The story of Late Antiquity (ca. A.D. 300–700) is the tale of yet another remaking of itself by Rome. This time, however, its reinvention was far more thoroughgoing and complete than it was at the time of Augustus' makeover of the Republic in the first century B.C. or of any of Rome's previous makeovers in the early and middle Republic.

### Multiple Transformations

SOCIAL AND CULTURAL TRANSFORMATIONS In the fourth century A.D. not only was there yet another revision of the political, administrative, and military system, but this time Roman society and culture was also deeply altered. The reforms of Diocletian and Constantine, especially of the latter, were more transformations than reforms. Augustus had reorganized the government but left Roman society and culture untouched. That was not the case with Rome after Constantine. The transformation of that time went to the heart of traditional society. The old civic values of the *polis* that had dominated the Mediterranean for a millennium were challenged, and when not replaced found themselves co-existing with a new system of values based on Judeo-Christian principles of monotheism. Ambition might still direct men to serve their city or the Empire, but it could equally impel them to become bishops or retire from society altogether into yet another form of society, the self-regulating, autonomous monastery. Women found new roles for themselves independent of families, husbands, or children. These were changes that would not have been dreamed of—let alone tolerated—by the Romans of the age of Augustus. The Church as a state-within-a-state, women retiring into convents, men wandering off into the wilderness to live as anchorites or monks, ignoring their multiple family, civic, and military responsibilities, would have been quickly suppressed by the outraged authorities.

MILITARY AND ADMINISTRATIVE TRANSFORMATIONS Beginning in the third century and brought to completion by Diocletian and Constantine, the army was enlarged and re-armed to cope with the Persian threat in the east and the Germans in the north and west. In turn an administrative system was developed to generate the necessary taxes, collect the materiel, and round up the recruits needed for the expanded military. The command and administrative structure of the Empire was revised and divided between east and west. The imperial office itself was surrounded with pageant and ceremony. Intentionally it became more remote and authoritarian.

At the most basic level, the central administration was never able to persuade reluctant municipal elites and even more reluctant peasants in the peaceful parts of the Empire that defending the remote Rhine or Danube frontier or northern England was in their self-interest. The Empire held together only when the external pressures were not too great and the demands on its inhabitants not too heavy. But at some point the demands began to be seen as outweighing the benefits, and then the decay began in earnest.

GEOGRAPHICAL TRANSFORMATION By the fourth century (A.D. 300–400) the axis of the Roman world had shifted away from the Mediterranean. Italy had become a backwater, and Rome itself was rarely visited by the emperors. They now needed bases closer to the danger spots on the frontiers. Trier on the Moselle (in present-day Germany) was an important western capital. Milan in northern Italy, Sirmium on the Danube, Byzantium (soon to be renamed Constantinople), Caesarea in Turkey, and Antioch in Syria were all major administrative centers or regional capitals. These were the regions where the armies were located and where the emperors were active. They were also the regions that absorbed most of the surplus of the Empire. By a commonly accepted calculation the military needs of the Empire absorbed 75 percent of the imperial budget.[1]

While the new geography was a visible manifestation of the conditions Rome now faced, it was an even more graphic demonstration of how power—political as well as military—had migrated from the Mediterranean interior of the Empire to its militarized frontiers. The "Augustan Bargain" of the first century B.C and first century A.D. allowed Roman citizens to pass the burden of military service to a professional army. A consequence of this, although not immediately evident at the time, was that the central regions of the Mediterranean were progressively disarmed and demilitarized. By the third century the Empire's soft inner core had neither the will, the inclination, nor the means to defend itself. When the

[1] Compared with 1 to 3 percent for modern states. Although probably correct the figure is not very helpful since imperial defense was the principal—really the only—item in the budget. There were no such categories as Medicare, Social Security, Education, Highways, and debt servicing in the Roman budget, the items that with defense constitute the bulk of current U.S. budgets.

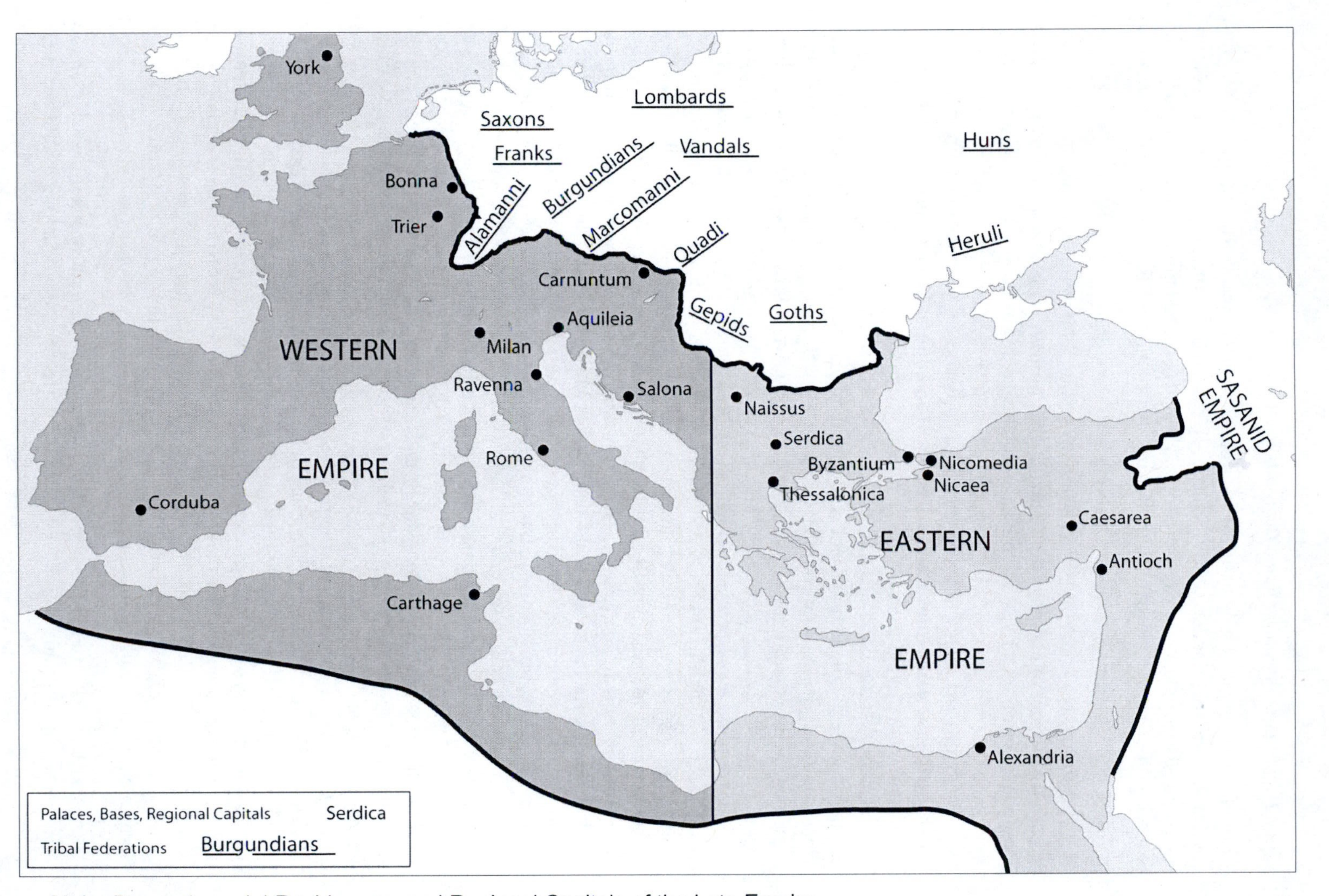


Major Bases, Imperial Residences, and Regional Capitals of the Late Empire

Visigoth Alaric invaded Italy in 401 he was opposed by Germano-Roman forces under the command of the able Vandal general, Stilicho. To defend Italy Stilicho withdrew troops from Raetia, the Rhine, and as far away as Britain. He also enrolled numbers of recently defeated barbarians, but he did not dare draft Italians and publicized the fact (Claudian, *Bellum Gothicum*, 463).

DESTABILIZING INFLUENCES The flow of resources into the northern frontier provinces had a number of perverse, destabilizing effects on the non-Roman, mostly Germanic peoples of the frontiers. Even without the problems caused by the instability of the imperial succession the existence, side-by-side, of two unequally developed societies would have created tensions as a steady flow of goods and people moved between them. From the interior of the Empire came finished luxury goods of all kinds and money in the form of bribes and subsidies that were used by the chieftains to hold their fractious societies together. Going in the other direction was a stream of slaves and warriors and, in times of overpopulation or famine, whole families and groups of families seeking new land or simply sustenance. However, it was Rome's incessant civil wars from the third century onward that caused the main instabilities on the frontiers. These wars, which paid well and offered opportunities for advancement, drew ethnic warrior groups into the Empire. Warrior bands of all kinds formed a quasi-permanent relationship with the Roman army as civil conflicts encouraged the contending armies to enlist as many recruits from across the frontiers as they could afford. Thus Constantine recruited Alamanni and Franks in his battle with Maxentius and then turned to the Goths for his clash with Licinius. Later in the fourth century Theodosius recruited Alans, Arabs, Goths, Huns, and Iberians (warlike peoples from the Black Sea area), for his civil war against Magnus Maximus. Sometimes the interaction of warrior-bands and Romans worked in the other direction. In the late fourth century one band of Goths under its chief, Fritigern, found itself losing to another under its chief, Athanaric. Fritigern turned for help to the emperor Valens. Valens obliged and Fritigern won.

We may well wonder why Rome's recruitment of non-Romans in the Late Empire was any different from similar recruitment patterns in the past. From the earliest days of the Republic Roman legions fought alongside brigades of auxiliaries drawn from allied peoples. So what was new in the later Empire? In the past the Roman homeland was the source of legionary power, and the legions were always in a dominant position relative to the allied contingents that fought alongside them. There was no doubt as to who was in control. By the Late Empire no recruits could be found in Italy or for that matter anywhere in the Mediterranean littoral. All recruitment took place in the militarized peripheries of the Empire. By A.D. 450 the bulk of the Roman army in the West was made up of barbarian federates. As larger and larger numbers of partially Romanized and wholly un-Romanized trans-frontier people served in the Roman army and for longer periods of time the question of who was actually in charge came to the fore. It was inevitable that a tipping point would come when German chieftains realized this and took over the rulership themselves.

EAST AND WEST In the East the Roman Empire had a much stronger base than in the West. More populous and more deeply urbanized, richer, and with a long tradition of submission to autocracy, the East was more receptive to the reforms of Diocletian and

Constantine. After the loss of its western provinces to the Germans, the Roman Empire now consisted of parts of the Balkans, Greece, Anatolia, Syria-Palestine, Egypt, and Libya. Its center of gravity was the city of Constantinople, which was able to fend off the invaders and at the same time provide a stable administration for the remaining provinces. But this eastern Roman Empire (or, more commonly, Byzantine Empire) was a much-altered Empire from its predecessor Roman state. Its language and culture were Greek, not Latin, and its geographic orientation was towards the south and east (i.e., toward Egypt and Mesopotamia). The core of the imperial state remained the emperor, his court, the army, and the civil service. To these, however, were now joined in close alliance the authority and organizational resources of the Church. Yet, although the Church contributed to the stability and legitimacy of the Byzantine state it added in some ways to its potential for fragmentation. The challenge of interpreting the complex doctrines of Christianity led in time to whole provinces drifting away culturally from the imperial Church. By the time of the Arab invasions in the seventh century A.D. Egypt and Syria were so alienated from Constantinople that they offered little resistance.

THE ARAB INVASIONS The seventh-century Arab invasions of the Mediterranean paralleled the Germanic invasions of the west some two centuries earlier. However, while the Germans attacked opportunistically, Arab armies were unified by a vision of the world provided them by one of the world's most important historical personalities, the prophet Muhammad. Before his death in A.D. 632 his armies had conquered Arabia and unified its formerly anarchic tribes. After A.D. 632 Muslim armies engaged in one of the most rapid and permanent conquests in history. The Eastern Romans or Byzantines were routed in A.D. 636 and Syria fell the following year. Egypt was absorbed in A.D. 642, and by 711 all of north Africa and Spain had been overcome. The east was conquered with equal rapidity. The Persian Sasanid empire fell in 637 and by the end of the century Arab armies reached the frontier of China in central Asia. Only the Byzantines held out and in the process prevented Europe from falling under Muslim sway. Constantinople was besieged in A.D. 677 and again in 717, but in both cases the attacks were beaten back. The end of the Eastern Roman Empire did not come for another seven hundred years and then only when the walls of Constantinople were battered down by the artillery of the Ottoman Turks in A.D. 1453.

## 2. HISTORIOGRAPHY

The historiography of the transformation of the Roman Empire covered in this chapter is plagued by a number of problems. The period was one of warfare in many different areas, yet while we are relatively well informed about these wars from the Roman viewpoint, what we know from the German, Sarmatian, Hunnic, or Iranian viewpoint is essentially nothing. The northern peoples were illiterate and kept no records. For a brief period the Sasanids maintained an inscriptional record of the deeds of their kings, but that soon lapsed. Later Arab sources are untrustworthy. The absence of a secular non-Roman perspective creates a problem for all subsequent historians and has tended to lead them, consciously or otherwise, to take the Roman point of view of the period as normative. When we say "Roman" it should be understood that that term refers mostly to elite Roman viewpoints. There is further discussion of this problem below.

## The Roman Sources

The early fourth century is relatively well documented, but the sources are complicated by the appearance of writers who took strong views on Constantine's adherence to Christianity. Lactantius' *On the Deaths of the Persecutors* celebrates the triumph of Constantine and emphasizes the bad ends to which those who persecuted Christians came, especially the emperors of his own time. Eusebius (d. A.D. 339), bishop of Caesarea in Palestine, wrote a history of the Church from earliest times to his own day as well as a panegyric to Constantine. The Church historians Socrates Scholasticus (fourth/fifth century) and Sozomen (fifth century) extended Eusebius' narrative down to A.D. 439. Ammianus Marcellinus was a Greek-speaking native of Syria who served under the emperors Constantius II and Julian. After serving in the army he retired to Rome where he wrote his history of Rome in 31 books down to the battle of Hadrianople in 378. He is the last of the great chroniclers writing in Latin. Eutropius (mid–fourth century) served under Julian and Valens and dedicated his 10-book compendium of Roman history (the *Breviarium*) to the latter. It has useful information on the third and fourth centuries. Many of the works of the last pagan emperor, Julian, survive and provide a vivid self-portrait of the man. Orosius (late fourth and early fifth centuries) wrote after the sack of Rome by Alaric in A.D. 410 to refute claims that neglect of the gods led to the fall of the city. The work is in seven books and goes down to A.D. 417. Like Eutropius, the early sections are of little use, but he provides useful information for contemporary affairs. Zosimus (early sixth century) wrote of Roman imperial history from a pagan viewpoint, blaming the problems of the fourth century on the adoption of Christianity. His history breaks off just before the fall of Rome in A.D. 410. The correspondence of Symmachus, a member of the old senatorial aristocracy of Rome, survives as do his reports (*relationes*) to the emperor Valentinian II. The latter provide useful information on the administration of the city of Rome where he was prefect in A.D. 383 to 384. A bishop by the name of Theodoret (fifth century) wrote a history of the Church from the time of Constantine to A.D. 428, borrowing heavily from Socrates Scholasticus but including useful documents. The panegyrics and letters of another bishop, Sidonius Apollinaris (fifth century), shed light on Roman relations with the German invaders during the fall of the western Empire. The poems of Claudian also provide information on the Roman west during the last days of the Empire there.

## Religious Sources

Between A.D. 200 and 700 authoritative Jewish oral commentaries on the Scriptures (the "Second Torah"), in the form of the Mishnah and the Talmud, were written down, edited, and disseminated among Jewish communities throughout the Mediterranean and Middle East. Normative, or rabbinic, Judaism as it is known today, stems directly from this period.

During this same period the canon of the New Testament was finalized and the whole Bible, both its Hebrew and Greek portions, were translated into Latin and transmitted to all of western and central Europe. This translation—the Vulgate—remained the standard text of the Bible in western Christendom for the next millennium. Translations in others languages, such as Armenian, Coptic (Egyptian influenced by Greek), Ethiopic, Gothic, and Syriac (closely connected with Arabic), were made, and translations into Slavic and other languages soon followed. There was a gigantic outpouring of philosophy, theology, sermons, hymns, liturgical compositions, histories, poems, and religious tracts in Coptic, Greek, Latin, and Syriac by the "Fathers" of the Christian Church. This period, known as the "Patristic Age," established the basic doctrines of Christianity that remain to the present the foundation of belief in both eastern and western branches of the Church (i.e., in the east the Orthodox Church and in the west Catholic and Protestant Churches). Finally, between approximately A.D. 610 and 632 the Quran, the holy book of Islam, was transmitted by Muhammad to his followers. According to Muslim tradition a final written version of the *Quran* was produced in A.D. 650 at the time of the third caliph, Uthman. By about A.D. 700 congregations of one or other (and sometimes all three) of the Abrahamic religions could be found from Ireland to Bengal, from Sudan to central Asia.

## Modern Views: An Age of Iron and Rust

Writing in the third century and looking back to the age of the great emperors Trajan, Antoninus Pius, and Marcus Aurelius, the senator Dio Cassius wrote sadly: "Our history now descends from a Kingdom of Gold to One of Iron and Rust" (Dio Cassius, 71.36). The poet Claudian who died about A.D. 400 returns to the theme of rust in his description of Roma, the personification of the city, as a feeble, unkempt old woman "whose weak shoulders can barely support her unpolished shield, while her badly fitting helmet shows her gray hairs and her spear is a mass of rust" (*de bello Gildonico*, 1.21-25). About the same time as Claudian the historian Ammianus Marcellinus picks up on the theme of old age though he took a somewhat more optimistic view: Despite the set backs of the third and fourth centuries Rome, although "now declining into old age," still commanded the respect of nations.

The gloomy opinions of Dio Cassius and Claudian, and Ammianus' designation of his own time period as Rome's old age, took hold of the imagination and prejudices of the writers of the Enlightenment period and through them entered the western cultural mainstream. From Diocletian and especially from Constantine onward culture in all its forms is portrayed as having been in rapid decline. Superstition and dogmatism replaced the inquiring minds of tolerant, philosophical Greeks; art became crude; literature was lost or slipped into barbarism; the state became totalitarian. For the next thousand years or more the West was dominated by a culture of credulity, oppression, and backwardness.

Since the 1960s, however, a less elitist and less ideologically driven view of the period has generated an alternate narrative of the reforms of Diocletian and Constantine. It is now recognized that the period from 200 onward coincided with a much more socially open and diverse military and administrative system than the one that had preceded it. It was this openness to talent from below that so irritated aristocrats like Dio Cassius and other commentators on the period. The history of the later eastern Roman Empire is no longer seen as a stagnant pool of water left behind by the receding high tide of a vibrant classical culture. Previously ignored nations and peoples within and on the periphery of the Empire from Ireland to Nubia are seen as having played autonomous roles in imperial history and are acknowledged as having made original and different, rather than inferior, contributions to western culture.

Taking these perspectives into consideration recent scholars have come to regard Late Antiquity as an independent period of immense creativity at a number of levels. The Roman state successfully reinvented itself and in its eastern incarnation lasted a thousand years, benefiting western and central Europe by fending off repeated Islamic assaults. The eastern Roman Empire preserved priceless manuscripts of classical authors and developed its own forms of art and architecture. In the west, while the period can be seen exclusively from the viewpoint of the collapse of the Roman government in the face of "barbarian" invasions, on a larger canvas it can also be seen as the period when Mediterranean culture was passed on to, and accepted by, the invaders. After centuries of resistance to the state, the peoples of central and northern Europe embraced forms of the state originally pioneered in the Mediterranean, along with the rule of written law, philosophical thought, literature, and religion. They abandoned their oral culture in favor of literacy. Paradoxically, it was the Christian Church in both East and West that now became the most vital mediator between the newcomers and the classical, *polis*, past. The first book to be translated into German was a quintessentially Middle Eastern cultural product, the Bible. Latin remained the language of learning, Roman law was the law of the Church, and its theology, couched in Greek philosophical language, was unintelligible without a background in Greek philosophy. By embracing Christianity the peoples of northern Europe made a choice to embrace the culture of the Mediterranean and the Middle East.

# 19

# Recovery and Transformation

## 1. DIOCLETIAN

### The Tetrarchy

With the accession of Diocletian to the throne the Empire found peace again. The emperor campaigned successfully in the east and in the Danube area while his general Maximian drove invaders out of the west. Maximian was rewarded with being made "Augustus," or senior co-emperor in A.D. 286. The imperial college of emperors was expanded to four in A.D. 293 when both Diocletian and Maximian adopted as "Caesars," or junior emperors and successors, the generals Gaius Galerius and Flavius Constantius, respectively. This arrangement is known as the tetrarchy or the rule of the four. Its aim, at least on paper, was to put an end to the tradition of succession by assassination and civil war, which had been the dominant means of selecting emperors in the previous century. The two Augusti adopted the titles Iovius and Herculius respectively to emphasize their quasi-divine authority. Diocletian was Jupiter (Iovius) advising and directing his Hercules, Maximian, whose job was to execute heroically his assigned tasks. To cement the tetrarchic relationship, Constantius put away his common-law wife Helena (the mother of the future emperor Constantine) and married Theodora, Maximian's step-daughter, while Galerius married Diocletian's daughter Valeria.

KINGS ONCE AGAIN The pretense that emperors were appointed by the Senate and people of Rome was discarded. From now on the emperors' sovereignty was bestowed on them by the gods. Their public appearances were carefully choreographed. When commoners entered the divine presence of the emperor they had to prostrate themselves while members of the elite knelt. In the Principate the emperor wished to convey to the elite the

**A New Artistic Direction**

*Art reflected the social and political transformation of the Late Empire. According to one school of thought the plebeian artistic tradition that had always existed alongside the more upper-class Hellenizing tradition, came to the fore in the fourth century. The classical, humanistic style that had been characteristic of imperial portraiture gives way to the typological. The depictions of Constantine* ***(A)*** *and the Tetrarchs* ***(B)*** *show a significant change in this direction. Frontality and simplicity of modeling dominate. The function of the eyes is accentuated, interest in anatomical correctness disappears as does concern for the portrayal of personal likenesses. The individual is suppressed in favor of the type.*

appearance that he was a great aristocrat of republican vintage. When he sat in judgment his *consilium*, or council of fellow aristocrats, sat with him. Under the new system the emperor's council now stood and the name of the council was changed to "consistory" (*consistorium*) to reflect that alteration. There was no longer even the suggestion that the emperor was simply the most prominent among equals.

Finally, after eight and a half centuries, the royal crown reappeared. Crown, scepter, orb, purple cloak, triumphal regalia, and jeweled shoes became the standard symbols of the emperor's office. As in many courts eunuchs became key figures in the palaces of the emperors. The cycle had come fully around. Roman history began with the rule of kings, passed through the free Republic and the popular monarchy of the Principate, and ended with an undisguised autocracy. The allegiance of the people no longer had a secular, political basis. Power came to the emperor from on high. Some of Constantine's coins (ca. A.D. 330) illustrated this by showing a hand from the heavens handing him a crown. During the Republic magistrates had held priesthoods and understood they were responsible for maintaining good relations with the gods, the *pax deorum* or the Peace of the Gods. In the Empire the Princeps as *pontifex maximus* was responsible for this duty, and when Constantine became a Christian, he maintained this tradition and regarded the *pax deorum*, now simplified as the *pax Dei* (the Peace of God) as perhaps his prime responsibility. He also continued to hold the office of *pontifex maximus* as did his successors down to the time of Gratian (ca. A.D. 375). By extension the care of the Church and its good order became his responsibility also even if this involved suppressing incorrect belief or indiscipline. From the emperor's viewpoint he was not merely entitled but obligated to intervene in Church affairs. What the Church thought of this right or duty was another matter.

The multiplication of emperors permitted a more effective defense of the Empire, and Roman armies were able to beat back their enemies on all the frontiers. From A.D. 298 there was a general lull in wars and rebellions. Maximian and Constantius spent most of their time in the west, while Diocletian and Galerius campaigned in the east. Each of the tetrarchs had his own *comitatus* or mobile field army, court, and staff. An idea of how much territory could be covered by the emperor and his *comitatus* can be gleaned from the activities of the Augustus Licinius, successor of Galerius, in A.D. 313. In early February he left the legionary base of Carnuntum on the Danube (roughly midway between Vienna and Budapest) for Milan, where he married Constantine's sister Constantia. In April he was back in the Balkans, where he defeated a challenger, Maximinus Daia at Adrianople in Epirus (modern Albania). He fought Maximinus again in the fall near Tarsus in Cilicia (modern eastern Turkey), and from there he continued to Antioch where he prepared to campaign against the Persians—more than 1600 miles in a single year.

**The Tetrarchy**

| *West* | | *East* | |
|---|---|---|---|
| Maximian | A.D. 286–305 | Diocletian | A.D. 284–305 |
| Constantius Chlorus | | Galerius | |
| Caesar | 293–305 | Caesar | 293–305 |
| Augustus | 305–306 | Augustus | 305–311 |
| Severus | | Licinius | |
| Caesar | 305 | Augustus | 308–324 |
| Augustus | 306–307 | Maximinus Dia | |
| Maxentius | | Caesar | 305–308 |
| Augustus | 308–312 | Augustus | 308–313 |
| Constantine | | | |
| Caesar | 306–308 | | |
| Augustus | 308–337 | | |

## The Reforms of Diocletian

THE ARMY It hardly needed to be demonstrated that the army needed strengthening. Under Diocletian its numbers, which had been slowly rising, rose to almost double what they had been at the beginning of the third century, reaching perhaps 600,000 to 650,000 men. The complement of the individual legions was reduced to about 1000, but the number of legions was increased. The emperor also undertook a major building campaign on all the frontiers to shore up the peripheral defenses of the Empire. He does not seem to have pursued Gallienus' development of a permanent strategic mobile reserve. Like a new Augustus he set about a thorough reorganization of the Empire in every area—military, administrative, fiscal, and economic. Fortune favored him as it did the original Augustus. His 20-year-long reign was sufficient to implement the majority of his reforms. He also chose well in his successors, although his complex scheme of succession was unable to prevent a civil war after his retirement.

THE BUDGET During the crisis of the third century requisitions in kind had become the principal source of income for the state. Diocletian successfully reorganized the collection of goods into a regular system of levies (*indictiones*) as part of the creation of a true budget for the Empire. He abolished the old taxes and replaced them with a uniform system applicable throughout the Empire. There were two measures, the *iugum* and the *caput*. The *iugum* referred to the productive capacity of the land and the *caput* the productive capacity of an individual. Thus, for example, in Syria five acres of vineyard, 20 acres of arable land, or 50 acres of lesser quality land were evaluated as one *iugum*. The *caput* stood for the laborers who worked the land and also for cattle. Once a census had been taken it was possible for the central government to have a good idea of what its income might be in any given year and theoretically at least impose an equitable tax on everyone. A side effect of this new system was an effort by the government to tie laborers to the land in order to make the census, which was conducted regularly, manageable. In principle Diocletian's reforms would logically lead to a highly regimented society, but in practice the ability of the citizens to avoid the consequences of the new laws was almost boundless. Corruption, which was always a problem, found even more deft ways for avoiding the regulations while at the same time engendering a spirit of cynicism and distrust. Diocletian also tried to fight inflation by strengthening the currency and issuing an edict fixing the prices of goods on the theory that prices rose because of greed. As with all price fixing edicts in history it failed.

THE QUEST FOR CULTURAL UNITY Following the logic of imposing fiscal and economic uniformity on the Empire, Diocletian also tried to establish cultural unity by outlawing what he and his advisors took to be non-Roman practices. Among the major obstacles to such unity two religions of eastern origin, Christianity and Manichaeism, were identified. Both were banned. In the case of Christians churches, where they existed, were destroyed, the Scriptures burned, the hierarchy targeted. When these measures proved ineffective the next step was to force all the inhabitants of the Empire to offer sacrifice. The edicts were enforced with more or less rigor depending on the region. They were most vigorously pursued in the east and in Africa, where most Christians were to be found, and less so in the west, where there were fewer of them. The persecutions lasted 10 years but failed to achieve their aim of suppressing the two religions.

THE NEW ADMINISTRATIVE APPARATUS The administration of the Empire was now expanded and professionalized to provide the necessary taxes, manpower, and supplies for the reconstituted state. Until the third century the government of the Empire depended on an informal system of aristocratic government supervised by the emperor, who had more immediate control over the equestrian civil service. In this system upper-class provincials (curials or decurions) were responsible for the administration of their cities and the collection of imperial taxes. The development of a true bureaucracy made up of career officials whose loyalty was to the state and sovereign and which was largely independent of the cities and the magistrates was slow to develop. Even after Diocletian's reforms, when the administration had developed considerably, the local curial classes were still responsible for the collection of imperial taxes, although their supervision was increased greatly.

The new system looked a lot like an expanded version of the old. When Diocletian became emperor there were approximately 50 provinces, but many of these were inefficient administrative units. The province of Asia, for example, had a single governor responsible for supervising 250 cities. Diocletian's solution was to divide provinces into smaller units, each headed by a governor (*praeses*) with a staff of about 100, so that ultimately the number of provinces came to a hundred grouped in 13 dioceses under vicars (*vicarii*). The sudden multiplication of imperial administrators created a need for uniform administrative policies and in the 290s imperial rescripts were gathered and issued in the form of two law codes, the Gregorian and Hermogenian, named after their compilers.

With the exception of Asia and Africa, which were governed by senatorial proconsuls, all the governors were equestrian. Diocletian's reorganization took place only at high levels in the administration, and there was much less proliferation at the lower echelons. It has been calculated that there were about 30,000 civil servants by the end of the fourth century, still a minute number considering that the Empire had a population of perhaps 50 million.

## 2. CONSTANTINE

### Constantine's Rise to Power

When Diocletian and Maximian retired in A.D. 305, civil war broke out again. Diocletian's co-Augustus, Constantius, died the following year, and his son Constantine was proclaimed Caesar in his place. Maxentius, the son of Maximian entered the contest but was defeated by Constantine at the battle of the Mulvian Bridge in A.D. 312. Constantine dreamed that he would win if he painted on his soldiers' shields the emblem of the superimposed Greek letters *chi* and *rho* which for Christians was the monogram for Christ. For his pagan legionaries the sign would not have been unfamiliar because the letters were an abbreviation for a common term, *chrestus*, meaning "auspicious."

Constantine ascribed his victory over Maxentius to the Christian god and was convinced that he needed to retain his support. At Milan in A.D. 313 he and his co-Augustus, Licinius

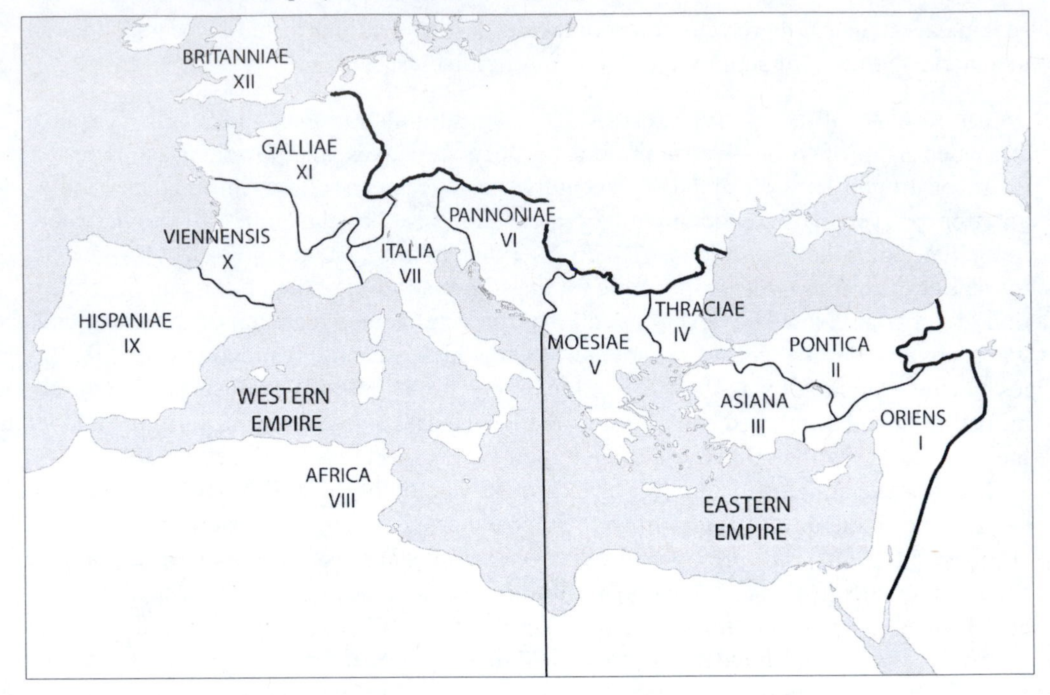


Dioceses of the Late Empire

extended toleration to Christianity, returned properties confiscated in the recent persecution to the churches, and granted Christian clergy exemption from obligatory curial service, a privilege enjoyed by pagan priests.

THE DONATISTS Upon assuming the throne Constantine discovered that the Church was riven by theological and disciplinary disputes and in particular that the African church was split between the rigorist Donatists and the more forgiving orthodox. The problem at issue was whether sacraments such as baptism could be validly administered by clergy who had fallen away from their faith during the persecutions. The orthodox position was that they were legitimately administered and that furthermore clergy who repented could be readmitted to union with the Church. The Donatists rejected these concessions as unpardonable laxity. They honored martyrs as uncompromising heroes, denounced landowners for their riches, criticized bishops for waffling during the recent persecutions, and insisted that the sacraments depended for their efficacy on the holiness of those who administered them.

The Donatist controversy drew attention to an organizational and disciplinary problem that was to plague the Christian Church throughout its subsequent history. When Christians were few in number and their congregations could be numbered in the dozens rather the hundreds or thousands it was relatively easy to insist on the highest standards of behavior. Those unable to meet the standards took themselves out of the congregation or could be shamed out. It is a management truism that standards and membership change when an organization grows. Rules that may have worked well in small-group settings may not work when the scale of the organization changes. By the fourth century, after 40 years of peace since the time of Gallienus, interrupted only by Diocletian's persecution, the number of Christians at every level of society had grown. There were perhaps six million of them by this date, still a small number relative to the population of the Empire as a whole, but they were located mostly in cities of the east and Africa where they had disproportionately more influence. As the membership grew the clergy were faced with a difficult problem. How strictly were they to enforce discipline—and who decided what was appropriate disciplinary action? What sins should be forgiven, and after being forgiven should sinners be readmitted to full communion and under what circumstances? Should they be made to do penance? Should confessions be public or private? From an organizational viewpoint the answers to these questions would determine whether the organization—in this case the Church—would grow and become more forgiving—or lax—depending on one's viewpoint, or more restrictive and stay small? Thus at issue in the Donatist controversy was not just a minor point that could be easily settled, but one that went to the heart of what Christianity was about. Was it to grow and become a mass, universal religion as the orthodox argued or was it to remain a small minority cult of the very rigorous and the very devout? St. Augustine said the Donatists thought of themselves as Noah's Ark, which contained only clean creatures and was walled off from the flood waters. As an orthodox leader he understandably preferred the gospel image of the kingdom of heaven as a net that caught both

**Image of Chi Rho**

good and bad fish. The fact that the dispute went on for generations, long after Constantine tried and failed to settle it, suggests that both sides realized there was a great deal at stake.

LESSONS OF THE DONATIST CONTROVERSY Constantine learned a lot from his involvement in the controversy. He discovered the difference between those who were uncompromisingly intransigent and impossible to work with, and those who were willing to recognize that politics and compromise were essential to all institutions, even religious institutions. The orthodox were the kind of leaders with whom Constantine could work. They understood that public order and social peace had to be taken into consideration in settling disputes. Constantine's initial efforts to diffuse the problem by assigning adjudication to the bishop of Rome (A.D. 313) and then calling a council of bishops at Arles (A.D. 314) in Gaul all failed. So did coercion. In the end Constantine counseled patience (A.D. 321) and left it to God to decide:

> Indeed it is by this that the judgment of God appears manifestly greater and more righteous in that he bears them [*i.e., the Donatists*] with equanimity and condemns them by his patience, enduring all things that come from them. God indeed promises to be the avenger of all. Thus, when vengeance is left to God, a harsher penalty is exacted (Optatus, *Appendix*, 10).

IMPERIAL PROBLEMS Although Licinius was Constantine's brother-in-law, the two Augusti were jealous of each other and quarreled over territorial issues. Relations between the rulers deteriorated but a peace between the two was patched together in A.D. 316. By its terms Constantine was given control of the western half of the Empire while Licinius took responsibility for the east. Their sons were declared Caesars with the right of succession. Some years later, when Licinius turned on the Christians in his court and in his army Constantine declared war on him and overcame him (A.D. 324). After 40 years the Empire was now in the hands of a single ruler who believed in dynastic succession and had no time for Diocletian's collegial system of rule by tetrarchs.

Although he planned to have his sons succeed him, Constantine's family was plagued with difficulties. His favorite son and heir, Crispus, was the offspring of a relationship with a concubine, whereas his present wife Fausta, daughter of Maximian, promoted the fortunes and careers of her own sons by Constantine. In 326 she accused Crispus of assaulting her, and the emperor, without proper investigation, had his son executed. Later Constantine's mother Helena persuaded him that Fausta had lied and the emperor had Fausta executed, though her sons remained in line to succeed Constantine. Remorse and grief filled the emperor's later years which he attempted to expiate by lavish gifts to the Church. He waited until close to the moment of death to be baptized so that he could enter heaven with a soul washed clean of sin.

After the defeat of Licinius, Constantine turned his attention to a great theological battle that was raging in the east between Athanasius, the bishop of Alexandria, and one of his priests, Arius regarding the relationship between Christ and God the Father. The disagreement was troubling because it had split the churches of the eastern half of the Empire. Employing the experience gained during the Donatist controversy Constantine began by trying personal persuasion, and when that failed he called a council of the whole Church to

**Coins of Constantine and Fausta**

meet in 325 at Nicaea. His aim was not to settle theological issues but to restore order to the Church and prevent the conflict from affecting imperial unity. At Nicaea he personally directed the council until a moderate formula was created.

The fact that so much time seems to have been absorbed by Constantine in religious affairs deserves special attention along with discussion of the endlessly debated question of the emperor's conversion to Christianity. The focus of this discussion, however, will not be the sincerity of Constantine's conversion or his knowledge of Christianity but rather the political and administrative issues involved in his choice of Christianity as the religion of the Empire and the consequences that flowed from that choice.

CHURCH ORGANIZATION By the time of Constantine mainstream Christianity was already organizationally well developed. Whether this tendency was inherent in the religion from its beginning is debated. The traditions, however, are unanimous that Jesus chose twelve men (the apostles) as a kind of council out of a much larger group of followers (the disciples), and among the twelve he selected what might be termed an executive committee of three, Peter, and the brothers James and John. These three men were involved in key events, such as the transfiguration and the agony in the garden, from which the remainder of the twelve were excluded. Peter had some kind of leadership role. There is also agreement that Jesus entrusted to his followers a command to proclaim the Good News widely. He was not a rabbi who expounded the law or a counter-culture figure who through aphorisms proclaimed freedom from convention, or a prophet in the tradition of the prophets of old whose aim was to arouse his hearers from their religious torpor. Rather, he authoritatively ordered his follows to announce that the Kingdom of God had arrived. If these two principles—personnel and mission—are combined, it should not be surprising that some kind of organizational structure can be detected early in the Church's history. The pastoral letters attributed to Paul in the New Testament and the writings of Clement, Ignatius, and Polycarp all make clear that by the end of the first century and the beginning of the second bishops, elders, and other ministers were taking responsibility for managing a variety of Church affairs.

Foremost among these was the collection of money for the poor, an activity Paul himself engaged in on behalf of the church at Jerusalem. When his enemies accused him of mismanaging the collected funds he insisted that independent delegates be chosen from the churches that made the contributions and that these delegates accompany him on his journey to Jerusalem and supervise the deposition of the funds. At an early stage, again visible in Paul's writings, lists of the needy were kept by the churches and prioritized by category. Widows, orphans, and poor consecrated virgins came first, then the aged and the sick. Cash, clothes, and goods in kind were handed out directly by a bishop or his deacons or manager (the oikonomos). Thus from the start the Church was involved in the management of affairs and the settling of disputes that naturally occurred as they do in all organizations. Throughout its early years the collection of alms was one of a bishop's main responsibilities, and the success of a bishop was in good measure judged by how well he could extract large contributions from the rich. In this activity public speaking was an essential tool so that eloquence along with management ability and holiness were among the main qualifications sought in bishops.

THE ROLE OF BISHOPS Bishops also had to be good at resolving disputes, disciplinary as well as theological. The first battle in the early Jerusalem Christian community was between its Greek and Hebrew constituents who squabbled over the unequal way their respective widows were being treated. This occurred within months of the death of Jesus. The problem was resolved by the creation of the order of deacons who were made responsible specifically for the kinds of tasks the dispute had brought to light. Another early issue that had to be resolved involved a husband and wife who joined the community but instead of turning over all their possessions to the apostles kept some back and were duly punished (*Acts* 5 and 6). Disputes of one kind or another were constant. One of the main problems in the Donatist controversy involved a wealthy woman by the name of Lucilla who presided over a salon at Carthage frequented by social climbers including members of the clergy. The bishop Caecilian made the mistake of rebuking her publicly for the superstitious habit of kissing the bones of some alleged martyrs before receiving communion. She never forgave him. When the Donatist controversy heated up she encouraged her friends among the clergy to hold a synod at Carthage at which Caecilian was deposed on grounds that the bishops who had consecrated him bishop had not stood firm during the recent persecutions. He was duly removed and replaced with one of Lucilla's friends.

DEBATING ORTHODOXY There were other practical considerations that contributed to the development of organizational structures within the emerging churches of the Empire. It was taken for granted that Jesus' message was the same for all people, and that therefore the community of Christians should be one. Christian communities, however, were scattered all over the Empire as well as outside the Empire. At the same time, as we have seen, complexity was built into the very nature of the new religion. Paul often spoke of the deep mysteries of Christianity of which converts needed to be aware. Jesus' message needed interpretation and explication, but how this was to be done was a matter of dispute. Should interpretations depend on the inspiration of prophets who spoke in individual communities?

What role did the authority of the original apostles and their lineal successors have in providing definitive answers to difficult questions? Within years of the death of Jesus the important question of whether gentiles could be admitted to the community of Christians and on admission whether they would be required to obey the precepts of the Mosaic Law, arose. Paul proposed one solution, but there were others who opposed him. A definitive answer was finally provided by a meeting of the leaders of the church at Jerusalem who decided in favor of the admission of the gentiles and their freedom from observance of most elements of the Law. These early precedents established a modus operandi of the early Church communities. They were not to free lance or attempt to settle issues of doctrine and discipline on their own. There were higher authorities involved, but these authorities in turn needed to pay attention to the long-established traditions of the individual churches, especially those of the major congregations in the cities of Antioch, Carthage, Jerusalem, Alexandria, Rome, and Constantinople. In time the citation of the gospels or the letters of Paul or other apostles came to have great weight and eventually led to the formation of the canon of the New Testament. Letters on controversial issues were exchanged among the churches, and groups of delegates travelled from one church to another. Periodic regional meetings were held.

## Heresies and the Growth of the Church

MARCION AND HIS HERESY By the second century there was a well-established mainstream form of Christianity that adhered, with some local variations, to an essential core of doctrine, moral behavior, and discipline. However, disputes over what constituted this proper belief (orthodoxy) and proper behavior (orthopraxy) were an integral part of the evolution of this essential core. Among the major issues debated and settled in the early second century A.D., for example, was the relationship between Judaism and Christianity and between the Hebrew Scriptures (*Old Testament*) and the Christian Scriptures (*New Testament*); another matter was Gnosticism and its version of salvation.

These issues were raised by Marcion (ca. A.D. 110–160), son of the bishop of the city of Sinope on the Black Sea, who argued that there was a fundamental difference between the God of the Jews and the God of the Christians. The creator of the world, Marcion claimed, was not Yahweh, the God of the Hebrew Bible, but the "Demiurge" (Greek for maker or artificer), an inferior being created by God. It was this agent of God that was responsible, on his own, for creating humans and then denying them the knowledge of good and evil, driving them out of Eden, and keeping them in slavery by means of the precepts of the Law of Moses. Finally, the true but invisible God sent his Son to liberate humankind from enslavement to the Demiurge and the Law. Unlike Jesus of Nazareth, however, this Savior-Son was not truly human. He merely seemed to die on the cross. According to Marcion all the apostles except Saint Paul mistook this Savior for a prophet of the Demiurge. Marcion rejected the whole New Testament except for 10 of Paul's letters and a very shortened version of the *Gospel of Luke*, which suited his beliefs.

Marcion's critique provoked a vigorous response from the orthodox community, which formally affirmed the continuity of the Old and New Testaments and the identity of the God of both. This affirmation was in reality no more than an endorsement of the ongoing, long-time practice of reading lessons from both the Hebrew Scriptures and New Testament at Eucharistic services and of the assumption that the Hebrew Scriptures were an integral part of the Christian Scriptures. From the orthodox perspective Judaism and Christianity shared a common ancestry, Scriptures, forms of worship, and morality. Judaism should and could not be rejected. Jews and Gentiles were both called by God to be members of the Kingdom and would, in the end of times, share that Kingdom. In his letter to the Romans Paul asked rhetorically: "I ask, then, has God rejected his People [*meaning the Jews*]? By no means… through their trespass salvation has come to the Gentiles…. Now if their trespass means riches for the world, and if their failure means riches for the Gentiles, how much more will their full inclusion mean?" (*Romans* 11.1 and 11–12).

DOCETISM AND GNOSTICISM Along with the rejection of Marcion's interpretation of Judaism was the orthodox rejection of Marcion's docetist or gnostic interpretation of Christ. Docetism was an adaption of the widespread belief that goes under the name of Gnosticism, a popular mystical blending of elements of Greek philosophy and Middle Eastern religious dualism (for discussion of dualism see Chapter 18, Section 1, page 400). In one form or another it continues to the present day.

According to Gnosticism good and evil derived from two fundamentally opposed principles, spirit and matter. The material world was evil, and the soul was a spark of the divine lodged in a material body that dragged it down. God was not and could not have been the creator of the material world, which was rather the work of an errant "emanation" from God. Escape from enslavement to the body and the material world was achieved by a form of superior, spiritual knowledge or wisdom (*gnosis* in Greek) revealed by God only to a small inner circle of the initiated.

Gnosticism had many forms, but in its docetic Christian form it challenged the idea that Christ was the Son of God—in the orthodox sense that he was a real human being who possessed a true body and who really died. Such beliefs were rejected by gnostics because, as a matter of principle, they denied the goodness of matter and found repugnant the idea that the Divinity could assume matter in the form of a human body. Hence for docetists Christ only "appeared" (the term docetism derives from the Greek for "appear" or "seem") to be human and hence could not have died on the cross as the orthodox asserted. For the same reasons resurrection of the body was dismissed as repugnant to Gnostic principles. Equally abhorrent to ancient (and modern gnostics) was the existence of a visible church that claimed to possess authority over the message of Christ and over his followers.

The decisions taken within the orthodox community regarding gnosticism were a critical part of the evolution of Christianity as a culture. By endorsing the goodness of matter as created by God Christians affirmed that nothing material was to be rejected out-of-hand as unclean or unworthy simply because it was matter. Spirit and body were not opposed but complementary principles. The eating of certain foods was thus not prohibited as at variance with Christianity. Art could be used in the service of the Church as could philosophy in the service of theology. Forms of government were indifferent but could be infused from within by Christian principles. Labor was not unworthy of free human beings as many pagans thought; it was painful as a result of human nature's fallen state, but it was honorable and had intrinsic moral value.

ARIANISM The principal heresy that Constantine found wracking the Church in the fourth century was also a dispute about the nature of Christ and the reality of his humanity. It was, however, a good deal more subtle than docetism and involved genuine problems of understanding the nature God, of fallen humanity, and correspondingly, the nature of salvation.

For Arius, a leading priest of the Church of Alexandria, the problem derived from the nature of God himself. Since there was but one God He could not communicate His being since to do so would imply that He was divisible. Thus Christ, Son of God, could not be God in the strict sense of the term. For Arius the Word of God or the Son of God had to have been created. He was an instrument of the divine will, an intermediary between God and the world, and only the "Son of God" in an adoptive sense. Followers of Arius accused the orthodox of Tritheism—the belief in three gods. (Jews, Greek philosophers, and in due time Muslims had similar reactions to the doctrine of the Trinity). The orthodox responded by pointing out that if Christ was not God in the proper sense of the term then humanity could not be saved. Only a God-Made-Man could successfully bridge the chasm between God and fallen humanity.

The issue threatened to split the Church more fundamentally than any dispute to date, and Constantine intervened to force a decision, calling an ecumenical ("world-wide") Council at Nicaea in 325. At Nicaea, under the prodding of Constantine, the orthodox put forward the formula "*homoousios*"—of the same substance—to describe the nature of the Son in relation to the Father. This interpretation was adopted by the Council, and opposing views were condemned. While the western bishops found this term acceptable there was suspicion among eastern bishops that the term implied that Father and Son were not truly distinct *hypostases* or persons. Another formula that circulated but did not find favor was "*homoiousios*"—of like (but not the same) substance.

These and similar terms were debated for centuries in an attempt to define the relationships within the Trinity. The issues are not easily dismissed as theological hair-splitting since from a philosophic point of view they involved a redefinition and enlargement of the terms used for "person" in Greek philosophy. Adding to the theological difficulties of defining the nature of the Trinity was the problem of finding suitable words in Latin for Greek philosophic terms.

In general the Arian formulation of the doctrine of the Trinity was easier to comprehend than the orthodox and had a large following, but it gradually lost out over time to the older and more deeply established orthodox creed. Arianism had a revival when the missionary Ulfilas converted the Goths to a form of Arian Christianity, but that movement ended when the Franks under their king Clovis converted to orthodox Christianity and defeated the Goths. The orthodox formula hammered out at Nicaea remains lodged in the Nicene Creed to the present.

## Constantine's Choices

From the time of the Severi emperors had been looking for a more effective way than the imperial cult to unify ideologically the people of the Empire. The need grew stronger during the third century as the political authority and prestige of the imperial office ebbed as a result of endless civil wars and invasions. Polytheism, however attractive and satisfying it was at the local level was hopelessly chaotic and quite beyond rational organization. Decius, Valerian,

Diocletian, and Galerius tried, with mixed results, to prop up their religious authority by ordering sacrifices to the gods throughout the Empire. Their orders were often ignored or generated even more corruption as masses of people tried to find ways to avoid them. Where enforced they often created dissension. Africa, one of the most important provinces in the Empire, was divided for a century as a result of the Diocletianic persecution. Constantine could see the need for a unifying ideology as well as, if not better than, his predecessors. He could also see that coercion was, more often than not, counter-productive.

POSITIVE OR NEGATIVE? The question for him, setting aside issues of his sincerity and religiosity, was whether encouraging Christianity would be a positive or negative gain for him and his successors and for the Empire. On the negative side was the fact that most of the elite, the army, and the administration were not Christian, and at least some of them were hostile to the upstart religion. The majority of the population of the Empire was rural and thoroughly pagan but largely indifferent to what religious policies the emperors pursued. Then there was the consideration that there was not really one organizationally unified Church, but a mosaic of churches, some of them riven by strife. Encouraging Christianity could be risky.

On the positive side was the opportunity to neutralize Christianity as a disruptive force. Romans had a long and successful tradition of co-opting their enemies and there was much in Christianity that could meet the immediate needs of the Empire. Christianity's claim to be religiously universal coincided with the emperor's claim to universal authority; empire and Church could support one another to their mutual benefit. The claim of divine appointment of the emperors from the time of Aurelian on would be strengthened. There was, however, more to neutralizing the threat; there was the opportunity of winning the support of the most energized and motivated people in the Empire. The Christian Church was a large, autonomous organization, the only genuine supra-local organization currently outside the reach of the imperial administration. Its adherence could bring many benefits to the Empire. If, as seems likely, Constantine conducted a cost-benefit analysis he might well have concluded that the risk was worth it. The army did not care which god or gods the emperor worshiped as long as he kept winning battles and Constantine had long ago demonstrated he was good at that. The elite was different but there were already Christians among the elite and had been for a considerable length of time. Christians, in fact, were everywhere. They had long ago invaded the schools and universities. Sharing a similar educational background they debated with pagans on an equal footing. The unorganized people of the countryside, the *pagani*, did not count. It was a case of a strongly organized minority being in a position to have a disproportionate influence. Constantine must also have given some thought to what might happen after he passed from the scene unless he was succeeded by one of his own designated heirs. But here too Constantine could hope for a successful continuation of his policy, and if that failed the Empire would not be any worse off since, ideologically, there seemed to be no other solution at hand.

As his rule progressed Constantine showered privileges on the Church, welcomed bishops in his court, and personally rejected paganism without persecuting pagans. He exempted the clergy from the burdens of decurial service to their cities and encouraged disputing parties in civil law suits to take their cases before bishops if at least one of the parties so requested. The policy guaranteed, so St. Augustine said, that there would always be someone angry with the bishop and who would be ready to accuse him of taking bribes. Constantine's policy had the double benefit for the Empire of tying the bishops to its fate and at the same time relieving the Empire of some of its judicial responsibilities. The bargain Constantine enacted between Church and Empire had analogies to the bargain worked out by Augustus with the citizens of his day. Each side paid a price and gained something. Whether it was a good or bad bargain for the two parties involved—the Church and the secular authorities of the Empire—is a debate that continues to the present.

## Administration and Defense

Under Constantine the separation of civilian and military powers continued. A large mobile field army was built up under the control of cavalry and infantry commanders. Its soldiers who had the title of *comitatenses* received higher pay and more privileges than did the frontier troops, the *limitanei*. Praetorian Prefects now had exclusively civilian responsibilities. The Praetorians were replaced by a new group, the *scholae*, and a corps of couriers and spies (*agentes in rebus*) was created. Constantine revived the fortune of the senatorial order by opening up many civilian offices to senators and by giving out the rank of senator freely. He revived the title of patrician, which had died out in the third century, as a personal honor given in recognition of service to the Empire.

CONSTANTINOPLE There was considerable logic to establishing a major military and administrative presence near both the Euphrates and Danube frontiers. The step was taken by Constantine in A.D. 324. He first considered Sirmium and Serdica in the Balkans, and possibly Thessalonika in Greece, but finally chose the ancient Greek city of Byzantium on the Bosporus. It had an ideal location at the strategic and easily defended crossroads between Europe and Asia. The city could be supplied by land as well as by sea, and it straddled the vital west-east road that led from the western provinces down the Danube to the Bosporus, then over the Anatolian plateau by way of Nicomedia, Ancyra, and Caesarea to Antioch. Economically it could enrich itself from the trade that flowed through and around it. Its shortage of drinking water was remedied by the emperor Valens who added an elaborate series of aqueducts and reservoirs. The walls originally built by Constantine were torn down in A.D. 413 and rebuilt farther away, doubling the size of the city. Constantinople was also close to the great cultural and intellectual centers of Greece, Asia Minor, and the east. In 425 professorial chairs in Greek and Latin rhetoric, grammar, philosophy, and law were established there.

The founding of Constantinople (the City of Constantine) as Byzantium was renamed had profound historical consequences. It was founded not as a pagan but as a Christian capital. It therefore lacked the statues of the gods and had no temples or shrines or any other reminders of the old civic religion. Bloody animal sacrifices were not performed there. Its senators, unlike those of old Rome, were not the inheritors and sustainers of a thousand years of ancient Roman religious practice. After a major Church council was held there in A.D. 381 the bishop of Constantinople acquired great prestige and claimed that "he should have primacy of honor second only after the bishop of Rome" because Constantinople was

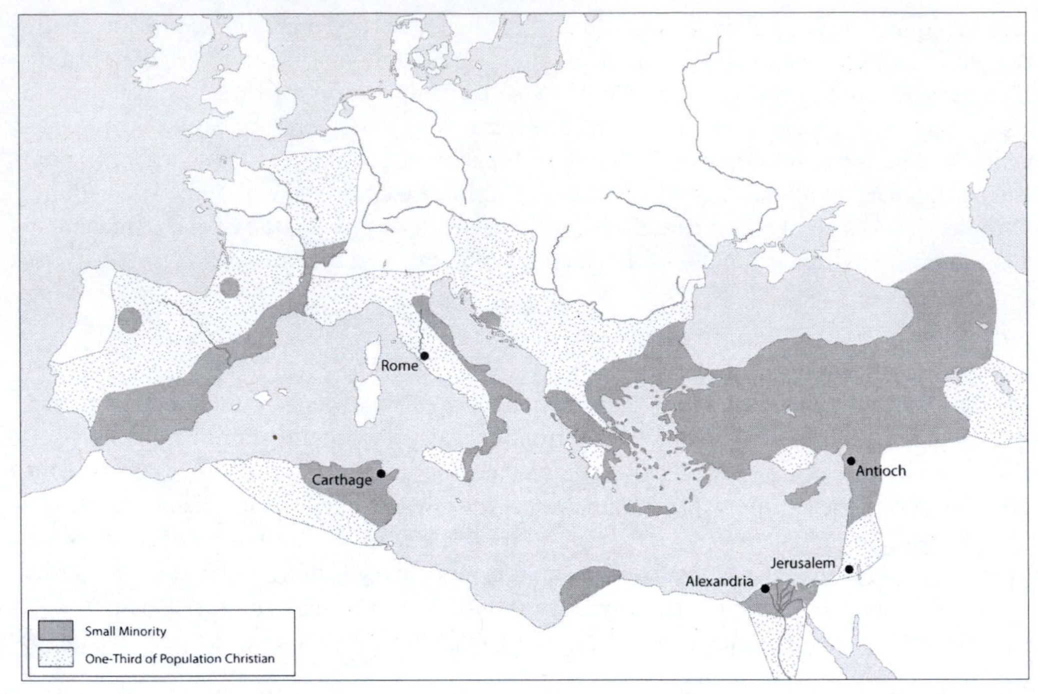


The Spread of Christianity

the New Rome. Whether it was Constantine's intention or not, the new city provided a focus for a kingdom quite unlike the one that was developing in the western half of the Roman Empire under Germanic influence. The language and culture of the region were Greek. It had large economic resources, and even its class structure offered more hope for permanence because land was divided more equitably among the different strata of society. The eastern senatorial aristocracy was not dominated, as it was in the west, by an old core of great landowning nobles. There was a different appreciation, too, of the role of the emperor that helped promote a more stable, unified political system. Culturally, the east was far more deeply urbanized and Hellenized than the west. Even areas that had previously not been noted for their contributions to Greek culture, such as Cappadocia, rural Syria, and Egypt, now began to produce figures of intellectual significance. In the great convulsions of the fifth century, the east was able to fend for itself, whereas the more vulnerable and weaker western half of the Empire collapsed before the onslaught.

# 20

# Final Transformations East and West

## 1. AFTER CONSTANTINE

### The Struggle for the Succession

When Constantine died in A.D. 337 he left the Empire to his three sons and two nephews, an arrangement which inevitably generated a struggle for power among the heirs. In a similar situation three centuries earlier Augustus had better luck in having an older, adopted son, the well-seasoned Tiberius to succeed him. Constantine's sons were all young: Constantine II was 21 and ruled on behalf of his father in the west (Spain, Gaul, Britain); Constantius II was 17 and ruled in the east. Constans at a mere 14 was responsible for Italy. In 353 after a series of civil wars, bloody purges, and assassinations Constantius II emerged as sole ruler. Two years later increasing imperial needs led him to appoint Julian, Constantine's only surviving nephew, as Caesar in Gaul. There Julian was successful in a campaign against the Alamanni, and when Constantius demanded that Julian lend him his Gallic legions for a war he planned to conduct in the east against the Persians, the soldiers rebelled and proclaimed Julian Augustus. Before civil war could break out Constantius died and Julian became sole emperor (A.D. 361–363).

CONSTANTIUS' POLICIES Constantius continued to pursue the policies of his father Constantine. Aiming to strengthen Constantinople's claims to prominence as well as to consolidate his own power Constantius established a second Senate there of 300 members in A.D. 340. It grew rapidly, reaching almost 2,000 by the end of the century. He continued the policy of favoring the senatorial over the equestrian order and more offices were elevated from equestrian to senatorial rank. With the decline of the equestrians, the expansion of the army and the administration, the decurion class, the moderately well-off class on which the administration of the Empire depended, came under extreme pressure. Instead of struggling to be promoted to the equestrian order decurions now aimed for senatorial rank. The wealthy, whenever they could, bought the title. The reasons for seeking the higher rank were the same as before—exemptions and privileges, especially the exemption from the obligation of extremely burdensome curial services. Senatorial rank also gave its holders added security against the demands and arbitrary acts of the growing numbers of imperial governors and government agents. The administration recognized that exemption from curial responsibilities was a major problem, and by 436 the privilege was restricted to those with the highest senatorial rankings.

DECLINE OF THE DECURIONS As the senatorial order expanded and as the rank of senator was bestowed more frequently, the equestrian order gradually died out or was merged with the senatorial order. By the beginning of the fifth century the equestrians had vanished and in their place was a much larger—and cheapened—senatorial class. The number of decurions, the backbone of the Empire, gradually declined as some were able to move up into the exempt classes while their poorer or less unlucky colleagues were forced into the lower classes and numbered among the *humiliores*. Over time this process of simplification of society reduced the classes of the Empire to two. The first comprised the large, expanded senatorial order, the clergy, and the functionaries of the state, all privileged and, in varying degrees, well-off. The second was made up of the masses of the Empire, all unprivileged and extremely poor.

JULIAN Julian had for years been a secret pagan and enjoyed dabbling in magic. Although raised a Christian he was impressed by the wonder-worker Maximus of Ephesus who awed him with séances and miracles. Upon accession to the throne he publicly proclaimed his loyalty to the ideals of Hellenic civilization and the ancient religion, which he restored as the official cult. In the process he defined religious dissent as treason to society and the Empire. He sought to reverse the inroads of Christianity by attempting to put paganism on a similar organizational footing and by demanding high moral standards of its ministers. He hoped to drive a wedge between Christians and the educated classes of the Empire by banning Christian teachers of Greek and Latin. As did his predecessors he became involved in the continuing struggles between the Arians and the orthodox in the eastern half of the Empire. He restored the troublesome patriarch of Alexandria, the famous Athanasius, and then deposed him again. As religious turmoil increased, Julian turned his attention to the frontiers. While on campaign against the Persians in 363, he was mortally wounded in battle, and his successor, Jovian (A.D. 363–364), was forced to make a humiliating peace and surrender all territories won by Rome since the time of Diocletian. With Julian's death the dynasty of Constantine the Great came to an end.

## 2. THE LAST EMPERORS IN THE WEST

Jovian reigned only briefly and on his death a Pannonian general by the name Valentinian succeeded to the throne and immediately appointed his brother Valens Augustus of the

**Emperors of the Late Roman Empire**

| *West* | | *East* | |
|---|---|---|---|
| Constantine II | 337–340 | Constantius II | 337–361 |
| Constantius II (sole emperor) 351–361 | | | |
| Julian (sole emperor) 361–363 | | | |
| Valentian I | 364–375 | Valens | 364–378 |
| Gratian | 375–383 | Theodosius I | 379–395 |
| Valentian II | 383–392 | | |
| Theodosius I (sole emperor) 394–395 | | | |
| Honorius | 395–423 | Arcadius | 395–408 |
| Valentian III | 425–455 | Theodosius II | 408–450 |
| | | Marcian | 450–457 |
| Majorian | 457–461 | Leo I | 457–474 |
| Anthemius | 467–472 | Zeno | 474–491 |
| Romulus Augustulus | 475–476 | Anastasius | 491–518 |
| | | Justin | 518–527 |
| | | Justinian | 527–565 |
| | | (Other emperors to A.D. 1453) | |

East. As yet another upstart Balkan emperor, Valentinian was despised by the educated classes of the Empire, but in the eyes of the army he was an emperor in the competent, soldierly tradition of Diocletian and Constantine. He was a stern disciplinarian and a conscientious administrator. He attempted to protect the poor against the injustices of the rich and was impartial in the on-going theological disputes within the Church. He drove the Alamanni out of Gaul and went on to ravage their homeland across the Rhine. In Britain and Africa order was restored by his general Theodosius.

## The Valentinian-Theodosian Dynasty

THE DISASTER OF ADRIANOPLE In the middle of the fourth century the Huns, a nomadic people of the Eurasian steppe, appeared in Ukraine where they overwhelmed the Alans and the Goths whom they drove before them into the Empire. In A.D. 375 two groups of Goths petitioned for refuge and Valens allowed both to cross the Danube and settle in vacant land. Soon, however, the excessive demands of imperial officials drove them to revolt, and in 378, at the disastrous battle of Adrianople, they overwhelmed the emperor and his army. Later these two groups of Goths coalesced with others to form the Visigoths under the leadership of Alaric.

To some extent the situation was stabilized when Gratian, Valentinian's successor in the west, appointed the able Spanish general Theodosius to succeed Valens and make a settlement with the Germans. Theodosius was able by diplomacy and military force to bring peace to the Balkans and rebuild the eastern Roman army, incorporating in the process large numbers of the invaders in the army and giving particular emphasis to cavalry.

Gratian and Theodosius were both active in the battles between Christians and pagans and between the orthodox and the Arians. Persuaded by Ambrose, the powerful bishop of Milan, Gratian dropped the ancient title of *pontifex maximus* and removed the Altar of Victory from the Senate at Rome. For his part Theodosius, an adherer of the Nicene Creed, legislated against the Arians and in 381 convened the Second Ecumenical Council of Constantinople, which reaffirmed traditional orthodox beliefs. Ten years later he closed pagan temples and forbade all pagan rites. His religious policies reflect a step in the growing alliance between Church and State.

THE SACK OF ROME When his co-ruler Gratian was assassinated in A.D. 383, Theodosius defeated the usurper in battle. He kept Gratian's half-brother, Valentinian II, as his colleague in the west but when Valentinian was in turn murdered, Theodosius had to fight another costly civil war from which he emerged in 394 as the last sole ruler of the united Roman Empire. His reign as sole emperor, ironically, lasted only five months. After his death in 395 he was succeeded by his young and, as it turned out, ineffectual sons, Honorius and Arcadius. Honorius took responsibility for the west and Arcadius for the east, but both quickly fell under the control of advisors and generals who conducted savage campaigns for power among themselves just when the Empire most needed strong central control. The Goths under the charistmatic Alaric took advantage of the weakness of the Empire to raid Greece, and stopped only after they were encouraged to move westward by Arcadius' principal advisor, the wily eunuch Eutropius. For a time the commander of the western armies, the Vandal general Stilicho was able to control the Visigoths, but after his assassination in 408 no one was able to stop their maraudings. In A.D. 410 they sacked Rome itself and its fall sent reverberations throughout the Empire. The Visigoths eventually left Italy and settled in southwestern Gaul as the presumed subjects of the Romans but in fact as an independent people. The Roman army in the west gradually disintegrated. Britain was told by Honorius to "look to its own defense" (*Zosimus* 6.10) in 410. The army's units in Spain and Africa disappeared in the 450s and its last contingents in France were gone by 486. The biographer Eugippius describes how the surviving regiments in Austria received their last installments of pay in the 480s and were let go:

> While the Roman Empire still stood, soldiers were maintained with public pay in many of the towns for the defense of the frontier, but when that custom lapsed the military units were abolished together with the frontier (*Vita S. Severini*, 20).

## 3. THE RISE OF THE GERMAN KINGDOMS

After driving the Goths and Alans out of Ukraine the Huns moved westwards, establishing themselves in the great plains of Hungary. From there they raided northwards, displacing more Germans and driving them westwards towards Gaul. In the winter of A.D. 406 large numbers of Germans crossed the frozen Rhine and forced their way into central Gaul. Among the invaders were the Vandals who passed through Gaul into Spain and from there crossed over into Africa (Tunisia) where they established an independent kingdom at Carthage. From there they raided Italy, sacking Rome in 455.

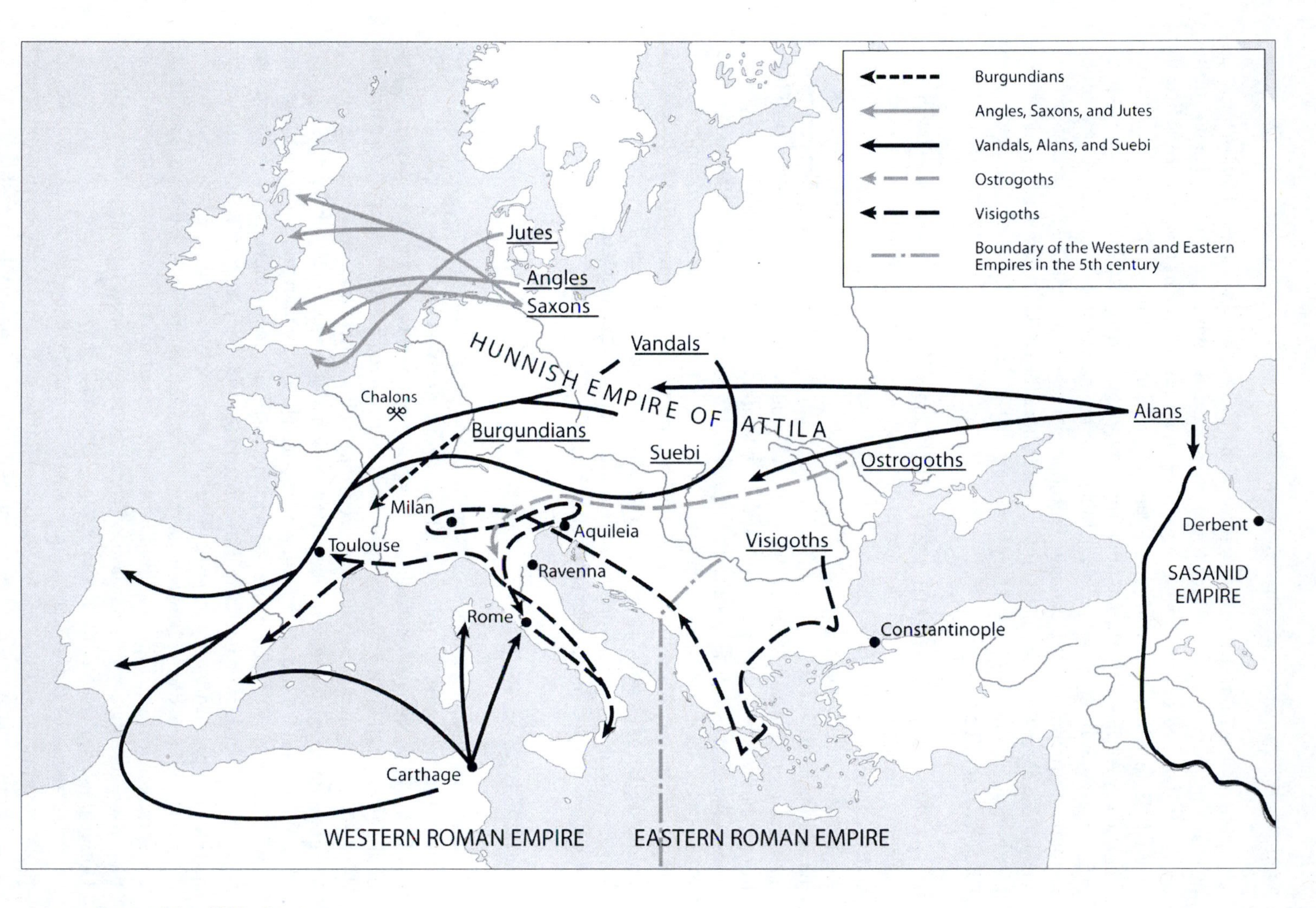


Invasions of the Fifth Century A.D.

By the middle of the fifth century most of the west was in the hands of Germanic peoples, and the hazy outlines of Medieval Europe were beginning to emerge. Roman influence in Britain had been declining long before Honorius warned its inhabitants the Empire could do little to help them and by mid-century the island was in the process of being overwhelmed by Angles, Saxons, and Jutes from northern Germany. In Gaul the Franks, a powerful federation of Germans, was established in the northern and central areas. To their south the Burgundians settled along the Rhône in a region that still bears their name. The Visigoths were in Provence and Aquitania. Still, both Romans and Germans could appreciate a common danger, and in 451 they united against the Huns of Attila and defeated them at Chalons east of Paris.

THE END OF THE EMPIRE IN THE WEST For the next 20 years a series of shadow emperors controlled by German chiefs ruled in the west. In 476 the mercenary captain Odoacer ended the farce of Roman rule and deposed the current puppet emperor Romulus Augustulus, and returned the imperial insignia to Constantinople. In this uneventful way the administration of the Empire in the west came to an end. No one at the time seemed to have been much disturbed by the event or even paid much attention to it. In A.D. 490 the troublesome Ostrogoths (the "East" Goths) under the leadership of their chief Theodoric were authorized to depose Odoacer and invaded Italy. Odocacer was defeated and killed in 493 and Theodoric ruled Italy ostensibly as the representative of the eastern emperor as had Odoacer. In reality the arrival of Theodoric and the Ostrogoths meant that Italy was now simply the latest Germanic kingdom to be carved out of Roman territory. The process of transforming the western Empire from a unified state into an unstable group of quarreling, petty Germanic kingdoms was now complete.

## Romans and Germans

Scholars argue among themselves over the character of the Germanic occupation of the western Empire. Were the Germans who settled in the west migrating peoples or warrior bands or some combination of the two? A strong argument can be made at least in the case of the Visigoths that they were a warrior band that evolved into something like a nation under the leadership of Alaric and his successors Wallia, Theoderic, and Euric. Initially the Visigoths emerged as a result of the amalgamation of three previously independent groups of Goths around the strong leadership of Alaric. They were then joined by other Germans as well as peoples of the Empire. As was the case with many other German groups, the Visigoths had been in contact with Rome for a long time. They had served in its armies, and had been impressed by the majesty of its imperial façade. Gradually these experiences eroded the cultural barrier between the two sides. Alaric's brother Athaulf declared he had come to recognize that the "undisciplined barbarism of the Goths made it impossible for them to create a state without the laws of Rome." He now wished, he said, to use the glory of Gothic power to "restore the Roman name" (Orosius, 7.48).

The breakup of the western Empire was thus accomplished with less violence than might be expected. In much of the west life continued as it always had and in some respects it may actually have improved as a result of the disappearance of the grinding but largely ineffective tax system of the Empire. In parts of Italy and Gaul German soldiers were stationed in cities, not the countryside. Whether these soldiers were maintained out of income generated from state resources or from land allotments is disputed. If the former case is true, then taxes that would otherwise have gone to the imperial treasury were directly assigned to individual soldiers so that the only real loser was the tax collecting apparatus which was now largely bypassed. Individual cities were administered locally by elected defenders (*defensores*). Legal practice was the same as in the past. Instead of working for the imperial civil service Roman judges and advisors now served in the courts of German kings. The Theodosian Code promulgated between 429 and 438 on the authority of Theodosius II (died A.D. 450) was the principal reference work of the law throughout the Empire and was intended to supplement the Gregorian and Hermogenian codes of the previous century by adding a collection and codification of all the laws that had been passed since time of Constantine. Much of the Theodosian code was later incorporated in Justinian's *Corpus of Civil Law*.

ACCOMMODATING THE INVADERS At least in these regions the image of hordes of savage barbarians descending from beyond the Rhine and Danube on the civilized Empire dressed in fur, destroying with fire and sword and eventually settling down to a miserable

**A Typical Italian Mountain Town**

*Before the development of cities in Italy around 700 B.C. most of the peninsula's inhabitants lived in easily defended settlements on hilltops. Once urbanization took hold and the countryside became safe, these were gradually abandoned. The reverse process took place at the end of the Empire. As conditions in the countryside deteriorated and cities declined, the rural inhabitants returned once more to defensible hill top settlements. The many hilltop towns that can be seen throughout Italy today are testimony to the unsettled conditions that followed the fall of the Empire in the West.*

existence in ruined cities and country villas is false. The number of Germans was not large, and they were far from their homelands. It is estimated that their warrior bands never consisted of more than 5,000 to 15,000 warriors. There may not have been more than 3,000 Burgundians. After centuries of contact they were used to Roman ways, and it made sense for them to work out a modus vivendi with the local Roman populations and their ruling elites. Germans and Romans alike—especially the large Roman landholders—had a common interest in maintaining existing institutions and some level of order. Over time a new Roman-Germanic coalition of rulers, administrators, soldiers and landlords emerged. The Visigoths and Burgundians each produced law codes in which they either incorporated or juxtaposed Germanic and Roman enactments. The Visigothic *Lex Romana Visigothorum* (the Roman Law of the Visigoths) contained about a quarter of the Theodosian Code. There is some archaeological evidence that supports the theory that the integration of Romans and Germans was relatively peaceful. In some places excavated graves show a full mingling of Roman and German military artifacts such as belts, buckles, and weapons. Other evidence suggests that Germanic warlords worked their villas and estates just as Roman landlords did.

In Britain and in some parts of Spain and Africa, however, the transition to Germanic rule was not peaceful. In Britain urban life had been crumbling long before the central administration abandoned the province in 407. The Church was not strong there, and the native British (i.e., Celtic) population seems to have been in decline before the arrival around A.D. 450 of large numbers of migrating German speaking Angles, Saxons, and Jutes. Unlike many other parts of the western empire there was a decisive break in Britain with the Roman past. The Latin language, Roman law, and institutions did not survive, as they did in Gaul and Spain and elsewhere after the dissolution of the imperial administration and the disappearance of the legions.

## The Germans and the Church

In the west the main problem the Empire faced in the fourth and fifth centuries A.D. was not the threat of Christianity to Greco-Roman high culture but the very real possibility that both pagan and Christian cultures would alike be destroyed in the anarchy created by the barbarian invasions. Even before the invasions of the late Empire the veneer of high culture and centralized state control in the west was thin and easily fractured.

Throughout Roman imperial history a number of different frontiers ran through the Empire in the west. There was the frontier of the military zone, which coincided roughly with the Rhine and Danube rivers. There was the language frontier that ran between the Celtic- or German-speaking country people and the Latin-speaking urban dwellers. There was the frontier between the literate elites and illiterate masses of the people. There was the frontier between the great landowners and the bulk of the peasants who worked their vast estates. Overall there was an uneasy balance between those who accepted the Mediterranean and Middle Eastern version of city and state championed by Rome and those inside and outside the Empire, who actively resisted it.

From the time of Caesar Celtic resistance to Rome was strong in northern France, Britain, western and southern Germany, and the Balkans. Despite the centuries-long incorporation of these regions in the Empire, city life was weakly established there and the Roman state received only lukewarm support from the native populations. In the case of Britain, as we have seen, the Roman presence there was easily erased. Resistance was even stronger in the lands beyond the Rhine and Danube. Rome's great effort to bring the peoples of temperate Europe within the fold of Middle Eastern type institutions failed – or at least seemed to have failed.

THE CHURCH AS A BRIDGE Paradoxically the Christian Church succeeded where the Roman state failed. Roman pagan civil institutions had proved themselves unable to control barbarian violence and disorder. The rough invaders appalled educated pagans. Pagans could think of no way to bridge the gap between their own rarified, bookish culture and the illiterate, pre-political Germans other than by the unlikely assimilation of the Germans. From the pagan viewpoint the task of raising boorish German warriors to being able to appreciate the subtleties of Virgil or the thousand year old Greek of Homer was an impossible task. It was not even worth the effort. The Church, on the other hand was well equipped to build a bridge between classical and Germanic cultures through its message, leadership, and institutions. When the news of the fall of Rome to the Visigoths in A.D. 410 reached Augustine, the bishop of Hippo, he observed that "the City of God has as much room for the Goths as for the Romans." The mission of the Church was universal; Christianity was for all people, regardless of language, culture, or ethnicity.

As the state in the west declined it was gradually replaced by the institutions of the Church, which existed alongside the primitive political forms of the German kingdoms. Ordinary people needed leadership and order and the Church through its institutions was able to provide both. Some of the most able men of the time were to be found as bishops and abbots. These were individuals who combined knowledge of pagan philosophy and worldly political (and sometimes military) abilities with a secure faith. Sidonius Apollinaris was a member of the Roman elite, a leading literary, ecclesiastical, and political figure in Gaul in the fourth and fifth centuries. By marriage he was a relative of one of the last Roman emperors, Avitus, and he was prefect of Rome in 468. On his return to Gaul he was consecrated bishop of Clermont. When the city came under siege by the Goths he helped organize its defense until it was surrendered by the emperor. His poems and letters followed classical literary models but added Christian themes. His works champion traditional aristocratic values in the face of the changing conditions of Gaul and the presence of Germanic courts. Other bishops, such as St. Lupus who interceded on behalf of his congregants with Attila and St. Germanus with the king of the Alans, were also able to help mediate with the invaders.

THE MONASTIC SYSTEM: ORIGINS AND GROWTH The monastery was another institution the Church possessed that enabled it to help society survive the breakdown of state government in the west. The monasteries—for both men and women—that developed throughout the west during the barbarian invasions were bulwarks of stability and civility against the chaos of the times.

The monastic movement originated in the eastern Empire in places like Egypt and Syria where thousands of men and women retreated to remote places in the desert and the hills, cutting themselves off from secular life and devoting themselves to religious practices and ascetical exercises. They claimed to recognize no political authorities, refused to serve in the army or pay taxes. They did not marry. Their whole lives were devoted to self-mastery and the life of the spirit in a superhuman effort to transcend the limits of earthly existence and live to the full Christ's precepts. Many people thought of them as heroes, supermen of the spiritual world, models of a strict Christian life, while for others they were dangerous, anti-social fanatics. Their holiness was held up as a model to shame worldly Christians and their asceticism attracted admirers whose gifts fostered the growth of institutions which in turn opened the monks to accusations of corruption. As their reputation for holiness grew, however, so did their capacity to disrupt civil life when they chose to involve themselves in political and ecclesiastical affairs. Late in the fourth century bands of fanatical monks roamed the cities of Syria and Egypt destroying temples and statues and attacking the homes of pagan notables. Sometimes they rallied on behalf of one or other side of the various theological wars that raged in the late Empire and caused disruptions in cities from Alexandria to Antioch. The ability of the Church to tame the excesses of the monks and confine them in well regulated religious communities was one of the great achievements of the institutional Church of late antiquity. Once the monks were disciplined and brought under control they became enthusiastic and exemplary missionaries to the barbarians and eventually the guardians of much of the classical heritage of the past.

SAINT ANTHONY The first step in curbing ascetical enthusiasm was taken at the start of the fourth century by St. Anthony (A.D. 250–340) in Egypt. He devised a loose association of hermits who would leave their caves and huts periodically for community worship. By mid century another, more structured form of monasticism began to emerge. In Anatolia St. Basil of Caesarea (329–379), and in Egypt St. Pachomius (d. 348) established institutionally strong organizations of men and (in separate institutions) of women. Community life was stressed over the individual though hermits were allowed in some instances to live outside the monastic complex. In the Pachomian tradition personal property was given up and life was subordinated to a regular routine of spiritual practices, study, and work. The community was ruled by an abbot who was expected to maintain discipline and check tendencies to extreme asceticism.

SAINT BENEDICT By the sixth century the monastic movement had spread to the west where monasteries were often the only centers of literacy, Christian life, and teaching. Such figures as Martin of Tours, John Cassian, and Benedict of Nursia provided the basic organizational format for western monastic life. The rule of St. Benedict stressed a cooperative and social form of monasticism in which the monastery became a self-sustaining state in miniature. It had its own hierarchical organization together with a structured economic and cultural life. Study was an integral part of the Benedictine monastic discipline. As a consequence it was the monasteries of the west that kept alive and transmitted the classical tradition to future generations after the fall of the Empire. The rule of St. Benedict became the standard and universal type for all of western monasticism and in the ninth century all monasteries in France were obliged by royal decree to accept it.

Germanic Kingdoms and Eastern Roman Empire, Ca. A.D. 500

## What Conversion Involved

Conversion to Christianity was only in part a religious experience. The Christianity that was accepted by Germans and other northern peoples was a thoroughly Hellenized and Romanized version of the religion. What the newcomers to the Romanized parts of the Empire accepted when they became Christians was a version of Christianity that had been mediated by centuries of Greek thought and expression, and by Roman organization and legal practice. The evangelization of the Germans was not achieved by individual preaching and conversion so much as by the interaction between German tribes and the hierarchical organization of the Church. German chieftains dealt with Roman bishops as though they were dealing with the great magistrates and representatives of the old regime. When a chieftain and his council made a decision in favor of Christianity his followers accepted his decision. Thus, becoming Christian in large measure also meant becoming Roman.

ACCULTURATION OF THE GERMANS The Christianity of the fourth century was a highly developed culture possessing its own centuries-old traditions, its rituals in Latin and Greek, its Sacred Scriptures and the writings of its scholars and saints. Literacy played a central role in the religion. The Church had a strong internal organization founded on Roman legal principles and Roman respect for orderly procedures. Its doctrines were enshrined in Greek philosophical language that had been polished by several centuries of intense argument and dispute. Even in terms of dress the Church maintained the old traditions of the Mediterranean. At the time their congregants were switching to trousers the clergy resolutely continued the use of the old Greco-Roman tunic. What we think of today as ecclesiastical vestments were simply the standard clothing of the Mediterranean elite of the classical period. Architecturally Christian churches were modeled on the plans of secular basilicas. Implicitly, conversion to Christianity by the northern trans-frontier peoples involved the acceptance of forms of Greek thought and Roman traditions of law and order, art and architecture. When the Germans became Christians they, in effect, gave up their traditional resistance to literacy and complex social and political organizations and accepted the cultural ways of the Mediterranean world. With that decision the old familiar world of oral culture and the ways of thought based on it died away, surviving only in outlier regions such as the Celtic fringes of Ireland, Scotland, Wales, and the more distant parts of Scandinavia. Ironically, the collapse of the Roman administration in the west made possible the incorporation of the barbarians in the cultural world they had resisted for so long.

SOME CONSEQUENCES Modern Western traditions of popular participation in politics and social and cultural life in general owe more to the Christian belief that all of the faithful are equal members of the society of the people of God than directly to the Greek *polis* civic tradition. Oddly, our hallowed Anglo-Saxon heritage of common law was influenced more by ecclesiastical canon law than by classical Roman law. Literacy was essential to the liturgy of the Church and the functioning of the hierarchy. For the masses of the people of continental Europe who had never been exposed directly to a culture based on writing, this was a new experience. It opened up new worlds to them. Hearing the Scriptures read made them aware of the existence of ancient and distant civilizations whose long and complex history was now part of their own heritage. The history of Israel became the history of the barbarians. To what these people of the north knew of Romans and Greeks at first hand was added knowledge of Egyptians, Assyrians, Babylonians, Philistines, and other peoples—all mediated through the Bible. This information came to them not as discrete bits of academic information that they might have learned in schools but as part of a history that was personally theirs. Although it was to take centuries the masses of Europe would eventually be able to read the Scriptures in their own languages. A step in this direction occurred as early as the middle of the fourth century when a Gothic bishop by the name of Ulfilas ("Little Wolf") translated the Bible into Gothic. It was the first book to appear in a Germanic language. Some its finely written pages still survive and can be seen in the library of Uppsala in Sweden. In this unlikely and roundabout fashion one of the foundations of modern Europe was laid.

CLOVIS AND THE FRANKS In the early years of the invasions one of the main barriers between Germans and Romans was, oddly, religion. Those Germans who had converted to an Arian form of Christianity during their wanderings found themselves regarded not just as outsiders but as heretics by the native Roman population when they attempted to settle down. The barrier fell over time as the German leadership saw the wisdom of accepting the orthodox faith of the provincials among whom they lived. The conversion of the Franks from paganism to Catholic Christianity at the time of the baptism of their king, Clovis, around A.D. 500 was an important step in the process of reconciling Roman and Germanic populations. Clovis' Catholic wife, a Burgundian princess by the name of Clotilda may have been influential in his decision, but the Frankish king also appreciated the support the institutional Church could contribute to the maintenance of order and the building of the state in his realms. He recognized that it was important for him to reconcile the Roman majority of the population to his rule. In addition, by his conversion Clovis received the support of the Pope in Rome and became his ally. He was successful in unifying the Frankish tribes and in driving the Visigoths out of Gaul into Spain. With the advantage of hindsight the conversion of Clovis and his success a leader of the Franks can be seen one of the foundational steps in the shaping of western Europe.

## 4. THE RISE OF THE EASTERN ROMAN OR BYZANTINE EMPIRE

Geographically, demographically, politically and economically the eastern half of the Roman Empire was better equipped to defend itself against invasion than was the west. The east too was fortunate to have a string of strong, long-lived emperors who built up the bureaucracy, maintained the army, and retained support of the Church during the turbulent fifth and sixth centuries. In comparison to the west the east had fewer violent disruptions of the imperial succession. Theodosius II (A.D. 408–450) was able to keep the Huns and Persians at bay, and Zeno (A.D. 474–491) rid himself of the Ostrogoths by assigning Italy to them. Anastasius (A.D. 491–518), during his long reign, succeeded in fending off invasions from both east and west and in keeping peace among the competing factions within the Church and the administration..

## Justinian and the Disasters in the West

The long-lived Anastasius was succeeded by Justin (A.D. 518–527) and then Justinian (A.D. 527–565). The power of the eastern Empire grew under these leaders, and efforts were made to reunify the Empire. The Vandals were overcome in Africa and Roman armies were once again seen in Spain and southern France. Justinian made a major blunder, however, when he attempted to overthrow the Ostrogothic kingdom in Italy. Protracted and often pointless campaigns finally destroyed the economy of Italy and at the same time exhausted the resources of the eastern Empire. The conquest of the Vandal kingdom in Africa did nothing more than damage that province's flourishing urban life. According to the contemporary historian Procopius the African war resulted in five million dead, and the Italian war 15 million. These hugely inflated figures, which reflect a long-standing historiographic tradition, should be weighed against modern estimates of the actual population of north Africa (minus Egypt) at three million, and for Italy perhaps eight to ten million. Whatever the actual figures the damage, particularly to Italy, was permanent. It never recovered. When the Lombards, a new wave of Germanic invaders, arrived in Italy in A.D. 586 there was no one to fend them off. It is often said that the political disunity of Italy for the next 14 centuries can be laid at the feet of the Lombards, but it is more likely that in the absence of any truly significant political power in Italy during this period, the peninsula simply reverted to the fragmented conditions that existed there before the Romans unified the country. It has been pointed out, for example, that the Papal States of the Middle Ages corresponded approximately to the territories conquered by Rome in the fourth century B.C. The rest of Italy remained in the hands of a succession of local and foreign rulers.

CULTURAL AFFAIRS Justinian was more successful in area of the arts and administration. Roman civil law was reduced to order in the great *Corpus of Civil Law* consisting of: 1. the *Codex Justinianus*, a comprehensive collection in 12 books of the legal pronouncements of the emperors from Hadrian to Justinian and intended to replace the Theodosian Code; 2. the *Digest*, a collection in 50 books of excerpts from the writings of Roman legal experts from the first four centuries; 3. the *Institutes* in four books, was a textbook for the training of law students. The way the Code was compiled has given modern scholars huge difficulty in identifying the different authorities cited in it and trying to determine which entry belongs to which period. A fourth part of the corpus of civil law appeared in 534 containing, mainly in Greek, Justinian's further edicts or "novels" as they are called. The Code provided the legal framework for the administration of law for the remainder of the eastern Roman Empire's existence, and although it went far toward making the emperor absolute, its very existence provided checks on his power to act arbitrarily. Byzantine emperors (as historians call the rulers of the eastern Empire) were authoritarian but not despots because their actions were judged legal only when they conformed to the Code. In the west the administration of law fell on hard times during the years following the end of the Empire there, though the Institutes, which were short and simple enough to be understood, never fell out of use. In the eleventh century there was a revival of Roman law. For centuries thereafter some of the best minds in Europe devoted themselves to a study of the Digest, and Roman law was progressively used in the development of the state. Its absolutist spirit appealed to western kings and their lawyers. In the form of the Code Napoleon Roman law was extended to almost all of Europe and through European colonies to large portions of the globe.

After a great fire destroyed much of the city of Constantinople, Justinian undertook a major building program. The construction of the Church of Holy Wisdom, Hagia Sophia, was one of the principal products of that program. It was a stunning architectural achievement and still stands as a monument to the vitality of this last fragment of the Roman Empire. Another architectural masterpiece is the Church of San Vitale in Ravenna (Italy), which is adorned with extraordinary mosaics, including one depicting Justinian himself and his wife Theodora.

RELIGION AND CULTURAL IDENTITY Constantine tried to settle some doctrinal problems, but more than a century later key theological issues were hardening into more than theoretical formulas. In some instances local interpretations of Christianity became central to the cultural, and sometimes political, identity of whole regions of the Empire. The eastern Syrians of Mesopotamia and Iran adopted Nestorianism which held that there were two distinct individuals and two personalities—the divine and the human—in Christ. For Nestorians Mary could not have been the "Mother of God;" she was the mother only of Christ. In opposition to Nestorianism the doctrine of Monophysitism asserted that Christ had but one personality and a single, divine nature. The divine, Monophysites said, swallowed up the human as "the ocean absorbs a drop of water." Like the docetists, Monophysites believed that Christ's body had only the appearance of a human body. This doctrine took hold in Egypt, western Syria, and Armenia, and the churches there began to organize their identity around it. Constantinople and the western Churches held the traditional doctrine that Christ's two natures were united "without confusion, change, division or separation … the property of each being preserved in one person (*hypostasis*)," as the Council of Chalcedon in 451 proclaimed. This latter formulation became the orthodox position of the imperial Church and of later Christianity. In the west Africa was split since the time of Constantine between the orthodox and the rigorist Donatist schismatics.

When the state intervened to try to establish a uniform version of Christianity large bodies of believers were alienated and the state's authority was undermined in entire provinces. When Justinian tried to reconcile the Latin Church by making what were perceived to be doctrinal concessions, the Monophysite communities of Egypt and Syria were alienated. Although his successors struggled to find formulas that would satisfy all sides of these issues they ended up dissatisfying everyone. Eventually the problem of orthodoxy was solved for the Empire when the eastern provinces of Syria, Palestine and Egypt fell to the conquering armies of Islam in the seventh century. It was a steep price to pay. Monophysites and Nestorians became dhimmis, members of subordinate, disadvantaged minority communities. In dwindling numbers they remain in this condition to the present.

### The Slavs and Eastern Europe

One of the consequences of the migration westwards of the Germanic warrior bands who lived east of the Elbe was the emergence of a Slavic ethnic identity in that region. The eastern Romans first took note of them around A.D. 500. Wherever they appear in the sources they do so as warriors and opportunistic plunderers much as the early German invaders had appeared to the Romans of previous centuries. Eventually the Slavs came to the fore in a large swathe of eastern Europe from the Elbe to the Danube. From the Danube they migrated south into the Balkans and Greece. In 626 they combined with the Persians and another steppe people known as the Avars to put Constantinople under siege. The siege failed, and centuries later the eastern Romans celebrated August 7 as the day of their liberation from that threat. The Slavic occupation of eastern Europe from the Baltic to the Black Sea is sometimes regarded as a silent revolution because in large measure it failed to produce the kind of colorful leaders that the earlier German migration into western Europe had produced and who left such an indelible mark on myth and history. Nevertheless, the Slavs persisted, and their conversion to Christianity, like the conversion of the Germans, was a critical event in the development of Europe.

## 5. ISLAM AND THE TRANSFORMATION OF THE MEDITERRANEAN

In some respects the Arab conquests of the eastern Mediterranean, north Africa, and the Middle East in the seventh and eighth centuries look like parallels to the Germanic invasions of the west that happened two centuries earlier. Like the Germans the Arabs were provided with multiple opportunities by their opponents. In the case of the Germans it was Rome's proclivity to engage in civil wars, while for the Arabs it was a series of bloody wars between Romans and Persians that severely weakened their opponents' powers. In both cases the invasions brought to an end the predominance of classical Greco-Roman culture and led to the creation of two new mixed cultures, one based on Christianity, and the other on Islam. However, there were also marked differences between the two invasions. There was no unifying, organizing principle behind the Germanic assaults. German invasions and those of non-German groups such as the Sarmatians and others were a mix of uncoordinated, opportunistic warrior bands in search of plunder and land to settle or of peoples seeking refuge from enemies. Arabs armies were also made up of warlike tribal peoples, but they were united by their devotion to Islam and the imperative to spread Muslim beliefs by means of war.

### The Arabs

THE ARABS AND THE BIBLE Arabs are mentioned in the Bible and in Assyrian annals as early as the ninth century B.C. In Genesis, the first book of the Hebrew Bible, there is a story of how Sarah, when she was not able to conceive a child, suggested that Abraham father a son from her Egyptian slave girl, Hagar. When Sarah and Abraham thought that Ishmael, the child that was born to Hagar, was their promised heir, God told them that although Ishmael would be the ancestor of a great nation he was not to be Abraham's heir. That was to be Isaac, born sometime later. In *Genesis* Ishmael goes on to marry an Egyptian wife and one of his daughters marries Esau, a son of Isaac and a brother of Jacob. Esau became the progenitor of the Edomites of the Negev, but Ishmael fades from the picture. His sons lived, according to Genesis, somewhere to the east of Canaan. Ishmael, however, reappears in the second century B.C. *Book of Jubilees*, a re-telling of Genesis that did not find its way into the canon of the Bible. In *Jubilees* Abraham sends Ishmael to settle the region between Canaan and Babylonia. His descendants, Jubilees tell us, were called "Arabs and Ishmaelites" (20.11–13). Apparently by the second century B.C. the association of Arab and Ishmaelite was well established. In the first century A.D. Josephus, the Jewish historian, refers to the identification of the two, and for the Christians of the Middle East Arabs were either Ishmaelites or Saracens. The latter name was thought by them to be derived from Sarah.

ROMANS AND ARABS For centuries Romans and Byzantines regarded the nomadic Arabs or Saracens as a nuisance. The military officer and historian, Ammianus Marcellinus said of them that they waged war by theft and banditry rather than by pitched battles and were like "rapacious kites who were well suited for guerilla raiding" (14.4). They were a frontier problem, a known quantity, not a serious threat to the rich, settled provinces of Syria, Palestine, and Egypt. For millennia there was interaction between settled agricultural and nomadic or semi-nomadic pastoral populations. Middle Eastern records including the Hebrew Bible record the exchanges between the two populations as sometimes friendly and sometimes hostile. In the interminable conflict between Romans and Parthians (and later between Romans and Persians) the Arab tribes—when they were not fighting each other—sided sometimes with the Romans and sometimes against them. There was a steady infiltration from the pastoral periphery to the settled agricultural regions of the eastern Empire, and the stability of the Empire seems to have encouraged growth in population. Christianity was adopted by many Arab tribes including the major Ghassanid kingdom, which straddled the frontier between Rome and Arabia. According to the Muslim historian al-Tabari there was a Christian Church in Sanaa in Yemen built by stone masons and mosaicists from Constantinople. Monophysitism predominated among these Christian Arab communities. There was an even larger Jewish presence in Arabia, many Jews having fled there after the revolts of the first and second centuries A.D. By the time of Muhammad the Jewish tribes were thoroughly Arabized, speaking Arabic and bearing Arabic names.

ARABIA The geographical term "Arabia" dates from the time when the Romans began to organize their frontiers in the east and made use of earlier Greek distinctions between Fertile Arabia and Desert Arabia—Arabia Felix and Arabia Deserta. In earlier centuries the southern portion of the Arabian peninsula, ancient Saba (biblical Sheba, modern Yemen), the land Solomon of Israel traded with, had been highly developed. It possessed a sophisticated irrigation civilization similar to that of Mesopotamia and it was the site of one of antiquity's greatest hydraulic achievements, the earthen Marib dam. Located at the mouth of the Red Sea Saba was excellently located for trading with India and lands further east. Myrrh and frankincense—aromatic resins that came from trees that grew only in that region—were another source of wealth. As early as the first century A.D. or shortly thereafter observation of the monsoon led to direct transoceanic contact between Arabia, Ethiopia, and India. This in turn eventually undermined Saba's prosperity.

The western parts of the Arabian peninsula had always been a place of warring tribes, although interaction with the settled agricultural lands to the west had led some of them to create states such as Petra in the Negev and Palmyra in Syria. Both states, in due course, came under Roman control. Syria-Palestine formed one province, and Petra became Arabia. The cities of the region were Hellenized and Greek-speaking, but the country people retained the use of Aramaic, a language as close to Hebrew as, for example, Italian is to Spanish. In the third century Aramaic—the native language of Jesus and the apostles—became a literary language in which Christians, Jews, Gnostics, and pagans wrote copiously. As Hebrew declined in use among Jews, oral translations in Aramaic or Syriac (a dialect of Aramaic) were made during the reading of the Scriptures and these were eventually written down. The translations are known as Targums (targumim, Hebrew "translations"). They form a useful source of information on the early Hebrew versions of the Bible. In due course there were full translations of the Hebrew Bible and the New Testament into Syriac. Many secular Greek works were also translated into that language. Poetry in Syriac was used as a means of spreading knowledge of Christianity and reached its height in the poems of St. Ephraem, who lived in northern Syria in the fourth century A.D.

## Muhammad

The trade routes that made Saba, Petra and Palmyra rich also enriched the oasis settlements of Medina and Mecca. Muhammad was born in Mecca around A.D. 570. His parents died when he was young and Muhammad was cared for by his uncle Abu Talib who at one point took him on a trading expedition to Syria. He later became the agent of a rich widow, Khadija, whom he later married. As a townsman Muhammad was aware of the destructive tendencies of the warring Arabic tribes and felt the best way to overcome their anarchy was by way of religious and moral reform. For this he turned for help not to the native pagan gods of Arabia, but to the God of Jews and Christians. However, despite the presence of Jewish and Christian influences on Islam it would be a mistake to see Islam as a mere synthetic blending of the older religions. Both the Quran and the religion of Islam bear the clear imprint of Muhammad who viewed Judaism and Christianity as predecessor religions whose authority was superseded or abrogated by God's last and final revelation to him.

According to later Muslim tradition (there is no contemporary documentation) when he was around 40 Muhammad received his prophetic call and for the remainder of his life received revelations from God through the angel Gabriel. After his call Muhammad continued to live in Mecca and began to make converts. He drew the ire of his fellow citizens when, as a monotheistic prophet he felt obligated to condemn the pagan gods of the city. As the relationship between Muhammad and his followers and the pagan majority of Mecca deteriorated Muhammad began to send his followers to the more favorable environment of Medina. He joined them there in 622 in an event known as the *hijira* or "emigration." The year was later adopted as the first year of the Muslim era. Muhammad spent the rest of his life in Medina, continuing to receive revelations and to organize his followers. An early portion of the Quran says that the Jews of Medina were part of the community (*umma*) of Muhammad's followers, but relations soon soured and the Jews were either expelled or killed and enslaved. From Medina Muhammad waged successful war against Mecca and hostile tribes in the surrounding area. By the time of his death in 632 (year 11 of the Muslim era) most of Arabia had submitted to him. He was survived by nine wives and four daughters. Of these daughters Fatima was the most important because of her marriage to Muhammad's cousin Ali. The prophet had no surviving sons.

THE QURAN Muhammad did not think himself as the focal point of Islam as Jesus was for Christianity, but rather as someone who spoke in the prophetic tradition as the mouthpiece of Allah (Arabic for God). He was a messenger of God, not a savior. In that respect Islam is closer to Judaism than to Christianity.

In Islamic belief the Quran, the sacred book of Islam is the compilation of the revelations made to Muhammad. Its words are not those of the Prophet but of Allah himself. When the Quran was complete Muhammad repeated it back twice in its entirety to Gabriel to ensure its completeness and authenticity. Around A.D. 650, some twenty years after Muhammad's death, the Caliph ("Successor") Uthman had a definitive edition of the Quran made and ordered all non-conforming versions to be destroyed. Scholars think that, in actuality, before Uthman's time a number of scattered collections and individual sayings of the Prophet existed so that Uthman's job was essentially one of compilation. The work may not have been complete until the eighth century. The earliest securely dated complete Qurans are from the ninth century.

THE BIBLE AND THE QURAN Unlike the Bible, the Quran is not an historical narrative beginning with the creation of the world, but rather an assembly of revelations relevant to different historical occasions in Muhammad's life. For Christians the historical Jesus—who was born in Bethlehem, grew up in Galilee and, as the earliest creeds put it, "suffered under Pontius Pilate, was crucified, died and was buried and on the third day rose again from the dead"—is the revelation of God. For Muslims the Quran is the revelation. Unlike the Bible, which was mediated through the personalities, languages, and cultures of the prophets, poets, writers, liturgists, and legalists who contributed to it, the Quran was the direct word of God. In Muslim belief it is not subject to historical interpretation the way the Bible is. In fact no translation of the Quran can be considered authentic. It must be read in Arabic. One medieval Spanish Muslim scholar put it this way: "Non-Arabic is not Arabic; therefore the Quran [*in translation*] is not the Quran." One of the great debates currently underway within Islam is the degree to which the text of the Quran can be subjected to the kind of minute technical linguistic and historical analysis to which the Bible has been subject since the Renaissance. Or, to put it another way, can the Quran be treated, in secular fashion, simply as a source of history and be shown to be, as has the Bible, the handiwork of many individuals writing at different times and places and often from differing viewpoints?

## The Expansion of Islam

From the beginning the main engine of Islamic expansion was the waging of jihad or holy war. As a result of Muhammad's successful suppression of internal warfare among the Arabian tribes he and his successors were able to direct the warlike energies of the now united Arabian tribes outward. Just war for Muslims was not only a matter of raiding for booty and glory—important as they were—but also an act of consecration and self-sacrifice. To die in the "Path of God" was to achieve the highest of Islamic ideals and to be rewarded with eternal life. Apart from high levels of enthusiasm Arab armies had some practical advantages. Unlike the professional armies of the Byzantine and Persian Empires they travelled lightly and were able to move with speeds that could not be matched by their opponents.

The conquests by Muslim armies in the seventh and eighth centuries were among the largest, most rapid, and most permanent in history. In 636 Damascus surrendered to a Muslim force which soon conquered the rest of Syria. Jerusalem fell in 638 and the following year a tiny Arab army of no more than 4,000 men captured Egypt. Reinforced Muslim forces continued west across north Africa to Spain, where they easily destroyed the Germanic Visigothic kingdom in A.D. 711. The advance of Muslim armies in the west was only finally stopped in central France by the Germanic Franks at the battle of Tours in 732. In the following century Rome was sacked by Arab raiders. Saint Benedict's great abbey at

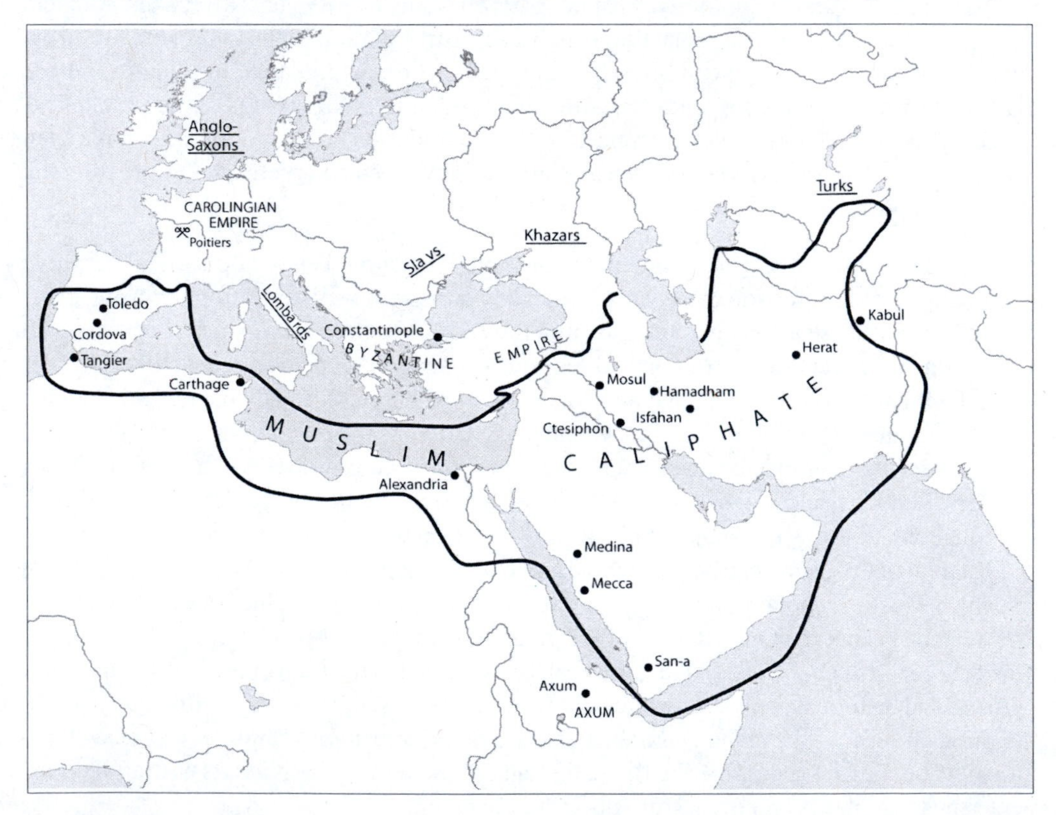


Islamic Conquests

Monte Cassino was looted and destroyed, Sicily was occupied, and raids for slaves and booty were conducted on Italian cities for centuries afterward.

In the east Muslim armies had equal success. Mesopotamia fell in 641 and the Persian kingdom of Iran in 644. The conquerors continued on into what is today Pakistan. By 715, some 80 years after the death of Muhammad, the Islamic world stretched from the Atlantic to the Chinese frontier. In size and population the land conquered by the Muslims was roughly equivalent to that of the Roman Empire at its height. The only place where Arab armies and navies were unsuccessful was in Asia Minor, where the east Roman Empire held out against them. For the next 800 years the eastern Romans were the principal—and sometimes the only—obstacle to Islamic penetration of Europe.

WHY THE EASE OF THE ARAB CONQUESTS? Enthusiasm alone does not explain the ease of Arab conquests. In all wars timing is important, and in the launching of their attacks the timing of the Muslims could not have been better. Persians and Byzantines had been at war with each other on and off for centuries, but the war that broke out after the assassination of Emperor Maurice in A.D. 601 was by far the most destructive to date. Persian armies swept through the provinces of the Eastern Empire doing enormous physical damage and destroying Constantinople's control of its richest provinces, Mesopotamia, Syria, Palestine, and Egypt. In its homeland of Anatolia cities were abandoned and their populations forced to flee to the mountains. The Romans eventually recovered and the counterattack launched by Heraclius (A.D. 610–641) was equally ferocious. The Sasanid Empire was shaken and never fully recovered. However, after Heraclius' death the Byzantine Empire itself was paralyzed by a disputed succession. It was at this low moment for both empires that the Muslim armies began their raids. Had the attacks on the Byzantines and Persians begun a generation or two earlier the results might have been quite different.

There were other factors that assisted the rapid conquests of the Muslim armies. The indigenous populations of both Byzantine and Persian Empires were alienated from their governments as a result of fiscal and religious oppression. The Persian government persecuted its dissenting religious minorities and the Monophysite and Nestorian Christians of Syria, Palestine, and Egypt had no love for their Byzantine masters. The heartland of Christianity fell to the Arab invaders without a struggle, but Muslim armies had a somewhat harder task against the Persians.

DHIMMITUDE The inhabitants of the conquered regions did not immediately convert to Islam, but rather remained as a separate category of subordinate tax payers, dhimmis. Muslims regarded dhimmitude as a concession by victors to the vanquished; there was no question of human rights involved. Jews and Christians—"The People of the Book"— were allowed to continue to practice their religion (a privilege not granted to pagans, who were forced to convert or face death). No culture of resistance seems to have developed among the Christians of the lands conquered by the Muslims. They complained but did not revolt.

ASSIMILATION When the Arabs converted to Islam they did not abandon their language or culture. On the contrary Muhammad gave the Arab language a pre-eminent place in the new religion. As a result he was only partially successful in separating Arab culture from the core message of Islam, which was universal and trans-ethnic. When Muslim armies conquered non-Arabic lands such as Egypt and Africa, they did not attempt to accommodate Islam to their inhabitants. The reverse was the case: The conquered peoples had to assimilate to the culture of the new faith. Only the Persian language held out against the conquerors although it was heavily affected by Arabic. Those Greeks, Jews, and others who did not convert to Islam were nevertheless thoroughly assimilated into Arabic culture, gave up their languages, and learned to speak Arabic. While the emphasis on Arabic cultural hegemony might have helped unite the quarrelsome tribes of Arabia briefly, their unity did not last long. After Muhammad's death many tribes refused to pay the required alms-tithe and seceded from the umma. It took the military efforts to restore control over the tribes, and even then they were reconciled only when there was an agreement to allow the huge quantities of booty taken during the wars of expansion to be distributed by the tribal chiefs in the garrison towns of the empire.

## 6. SOME REFLECTIONS ON THE FALL OF THE ROMAN EMPIRE

The fall of the Roman Empire, as Demandt's summary (see the box on the next page) suggests, has been a popular subject with historians for a long time and has produced a proportionately large number of theories. What follows is not another theory of the fall but a number of suggestions to help guide thinking on the subject.

Any theory—or combination of theories—that claims to explain the fall of the Roman Empire needs first to acknowledge that the entire Empire did not fall. Only one half—the western half—collapsed. Thus, the question of what caused the Roman Empire to fall should be phrased more like this: Why did the west fall and not the east? How did the Eastern Empire, or at least some of it, manage to survive for a further 1000 years after the collapse of Roman rule in the west? Were not both portions of the Empire subject to the same internal and external forces?

### East and West

WESTERN DISADVANTAGES: GEOGRAPHY Europe may be thought of as a peninsula of Eurasia and as the spout of a funnel through which, periodically, the peoples of the steppe poured into Europe. From the Ural Mountains in Russia to the Atlantic coast of France the Great Plain of Europe stretches unbroken by any serious natural obstacles. No imposing range of mountains intervenes to slow movement on the steppe-gradient from east to west. By geographic destiny the western half of the Roman Empire was fated to bear the brunt of any barbarian attack, while the Caucasus and the Black Sea, strengthened by the fortifications of Constantinople, protected the eastern Empire.

In the west the emperor had to guard the long frontiers of the Rhine and upper Danube. Britain was a continual distraction and a waste of resources. In the east only the lower Danube was of concern to the emperors and even if these defenses were breached the powerful

**Why Did the Roman Empire Fall?**

*Long before Wikipedia or more generally "The Internet" became available as a convenient source of information (and misinformation), German scholarship offered readers reliable information in the form of the reference handbook (*Handbuch*). The following is a very abbreviated list of 210 factors that have been alleged at one time or another to have caused the Fall of the Roman Empire.*

A -C Absolutism, agrarian slavery, anarchy, anti-Germanism, apathy, aristocracy, asceticism....Backwardness in science, bankruptcy, barbarization, bastardization, blood-poisoning, bread and the circuses, bureaucracy....Capitalism, caste, celibacy, centralization, childlessness, Christianity, civil war, climate deterioration, communism, complacency, conservatism, corruption, cosmopolitanism, crisis of legitimacy, cultural neurosis, cultural leveling....

D-F Decentralization, decline of cities, deforestation, degeneration, demoralization, depletion of resources, depopulation, deprivation of rights, despotism, differences in wealth, division of Empire ... Earthquakes, egalitarianism, egoism, emancipation of slaves, epidemics, equal rights, eradication of the best, escapism, ethnic dissolution, exploitation.... Fear of life, female emancipation. ...

G-I Gladiatorial combat, gluttony, gout ... Hellenization, hedonism, heresy, homosexuality, hothouse culture.... Idleness, immoderate greatness, imperialism, impoverishment, individualism, indoctrination, inertia, inflation, intellectualism, irrationality....

J-L Laziness, lead poisoning, lethargy, leveling (cultural), loss of discipline, loss of nerve, luxury....

M-P Malaria, marriages of convenience, mercenary system, mercury poisoning, militarism, moral cowardice... Nomad attacks... Orientalization, outflow of gold, over refinement, over expansion, ... Pacifism, paralysis of will, particularism, parasitism, pauperism, plagues, pleasure-seeking, proletarization, prostitution, psychosis, public baths....

R-V Racial degeneration, racial discrimination, racial suicide, rationalism, refusal of military service, rhetoric, resignation, religious conflict, rise of the masses, romantization of freedom, ruin of the middle class.... Semitism, sensuality, servility, sexuality, shamelessness, slavery, sloth, socialism, Slavic attacks, soil erosion, soil exhaustion, stagnation, statism, superstition....Taxation, terrorism, totalitarianism, treason, two front wars....Underdevelopment, usurpation of all power by the state.... Vaingloriousness, vulgarization (Alexander Demandt, *Der Fall Roms: die Auflösung de römischen Reiches im Urteil der Nachwelt*. München, 1984, 695).

bastion of Constantinople made it impossible for invaders from the west to reach the inner core of the eastern Empire's rich provinces. The western Empire had no such second line of defense. Once the frontiers were breached the invaders could march straight into Italy, Gaul, or Spain, ravaging at will. No wonder the western elite abandoned the cities that were targets for barbarian looting, and withdrew to their fortified villas in the countryside.

Successive emperors made valiant efforts to defend the west. It is estimated that in the late fourth century as a result of the German tribes being pushed into the Empire by the Huns the western Empire lost two-thirds of its effective troops. Valiant efforts did not stop or, at times, even slow down the flow of migrants and raiders and the disorder that attended their unwelcome arrival in the Empire. However, the differences between east and west should not be overstated. While claiming that the west had a greater burden of defense to bear than the east, this is not to play down the threat of Persia to the eastern Empire. From the third century Persia was indeed a major concern for the east, but it was not until the sixth and seventh centuries that the conflicts became truly serious and then the eastern Empire was tested severely. Nevertheless, unlike the west, which failed its test, the east survived its Persian trial and for nearly 1000 years thereafter the Muslim onslaught.

GENERAL EUROPEAN BACKWARDNESS Historically the city and state were permanently established in the Middle East and some parts of the Mediterranean nearly 4000 years before they were permanently established in western and central Europe. This is an astonishingly wide chronological gap that is not easily explained. It is not as though continental Europeans were out of touch with the well-developed regions of the Middle East; they did not live on an isolated island in the middle of the Atlantic. Although they were neighbors of people who developed complex societies and became literate by around 3000 B.C. continental Europeans remained content with their small-scale, poor, low-tech, oral cultures for millennia.

In contrast to the west, the millennia-long growth of complex societies in the east encouraged economic development, population growth, specialization, and the stratification of society. Over the centuries great wealth was accumulated, and vast amounts of agricultural land were opened to cultivation. Such complex societies were more productive, more populous and more stable than the simpler societies of temperate Europe. Because they had developed deeper roots, set-backs—whether military, demographic or economic—could be more easily righted. Roman efforts to bring large segments of Europe within the cultural orbit of the developed Mediterranean world were to an extent successful, but urbanization remained shallow. Cities were unable to sustain themselves in the face of the centuries of barbarian attacks and Roman counterattacks that turned some of the frontier provinces into battlegrounds and economic wastelands. Had the west sufficient time to evolve as did the lands of the Mediterranean and Middle East it might have been better equipped to cope with its dangerously exposed geographic location and the instability of Eurasia.

The geographic disadvantages of the west were multiplied when in the third century—for what at the time seemed to be necessary administrative and military reasons—the Empire was split in two. Unfortunately, the long-term result of this division was that the west was thrown back on its own all too limited resources while the east was relieved of the subsidy it had, in effect, paid for the defense of the west.

EASTERN ADVANTAGES For reasons other than geographic the Romans of the eastern half of the Empire were better able to defend themselves against marauding bands of invaders than their counterparts in the west. Eastern emperors could draw on more plentiful supplies of troops from within their own territories and were not as dependent on large contingents of German mercenaries as were the western emperors. The east had greater financial resources to meet the needs of imperial defense than did the more recently urbanized west. Taxes were more abundant and easier to collect. It is estimated that Egypt provided three times the revenue of Africa, the richest western province. Britain, northern Gaul, and the Danube provinces were miserably poor and under populated. Much of their territory was covered by forest and marsh.

The east too was lucky in having a string of strong, long-lived emperors during the turbulent fifth and sixth centuries. Between the accession of Diocletian in A.D. 284 and Maurice in A.D. 602 there were just five attempted rebellions in the east, all of which were put down easily and with few casualties compared to 11 in the west, all of which were serious and involved huge losses and the expenditure of scarce resources.

## Network Failure

The Roman Empire was essentially a network of cooperating local elites. This network structure of the Empire was one of its strengths but also one of its potential weaknesses. If, for whatever reason, the elites of the Empire decided to withhold their support the Empire was bound to collapse.

THE FAILURE OF THE ROMAN "BRAND" For centuries the Roman "brand" was attractive to many of the peoples of the Empire. It provided an outlet for the politically and socially ambitious. Membership in the senatorial order represented a giant step upwards in status and power above what could be attained at the local or provincial level. With privilege, however, went responsibility. The Empire relied on its network of local elites to maintain order and collect the revenues needed to run the Empire. There was a delicate balance between the rewards and responsibilities. During the third century as demand grew for more taxes and more recruits for the army the rewards declined and the responsibilities increased. In some regions of the Empire a line was eventually crossed and the cooperation of the elites declined. In many cities the decurions, the lower strata of the elite, moved either upwards into the higher echelons of the aristocracy or were forced downwards into the lower classes.

This was especially true in the west where the elites began to tear down their townhouses and retire to their great villas in countryside. They have, accordingly, been blamed for their failure to behave more patriotically, to pay their fair share of the taxes and to shoulder the burdens of local administration. This is a severe judgment and neglects the fact that the government of the Empire in the west had failed in its most important responsibility: The protection of society from violence, internal as well as external. After repeated demonstrations that the Empire was unable to provide security local elites and people alike began to look elsewhere for help. It was natural for them to seek the protection of the powerful, who were close at hand, rather than the help of a useless government and a distant emperor.

DEPOLITICIZATION AND DEMILITARIZATION It is perhaps true that had Rome appealed as effectively to its people as modern nation-states do to theirs—especially in time of war—the Empire might have survived. But Rome was not a nation-state. It was, rather, a geographical and governmental oddity, a mosaic of cultures, languages and peoples without a natural heartland, held together by a web of assenting elites and their often reluctant subjects, without a shared history—real or imaginary—that might have inspired them to higher levels of sacrifice. Indeed, instead of cultivating a sense of independence at the local level Rome felt it had to do the opposite: depoliticize and demilitarize much of its population. It believed it had no other choice. How else could it rule? It was sufficient that the demilitarized portions of the Empire pay their taxes which would go to funding a professional army. The army would then do the work of protecting the disarmed provinces. This worked as long as the professional army was up to the task of defense, but once it failed there was no back-up plan and collapse had to follow. No self-inspired local militias rose up spontaneously to defend their lands from the relatively small bands of marauding invaders as they might have in the past. The peoples of the Empire, especially in its core Mediterranean regions, had been too thoroughly pacified. For too long Rome had been the center of all politics and all decision making.

## The Role of Christianity in the Fall

The revolutionary potential of monotheism to alter the cultural world of Rome was briefly alluded to in a previous chapter (Chapter 18, Section 2). Some more of its implications were left to be drawn out here.

Arnaldo Momigliano, one of the most prominent historians of antiquity remarked in a survey of the causes of the decline of the Empire that it serves no purpose merely to echo Gibbon who attributed the fall of the Empire to "barbarism and Christianity." Momigliano continued: "What Gibbon saw as a merely destructive power must be understood on its own terms of Civitas dei (the City of God)—a new commonwealth of men for men. Christianity produced a new style of life, created new loyalties, gave people new ambitions and new satisfactions."[1]

The coming into existence of a "new commonwealth," to borrow Momigliano's term, alongside the existing state and society of Rome was at the heart of the social and cultural transformation of the Roman Empire that Christianity wrought. In this respect the decision of Constantine to embrace Christianity was a revolution with far more significant consequences than the reforms of Augustus who rescued Rome from the chaos of the late Republic. Augustus reestablished the state; he did not refashion society. Constantine did both.

NEW OPPORTUNITIES The ability of the Church to drain off some of the best talent in the Empire has been previously discussed. Such figures as Sts. Ambrose, Athanasius, Augustine, Basil of Caesarea, Gregory of Nazianzene, Hilary of Poitiers, and Jerome, were men of great ability and born rulers and would have made excellent administrators or possibly even generals had they so chosen. These men, however, were not exceptional. At much

[1]Arnaldo Momgliano, *The Conflict Between Pganism and Christianity in the Fourth Century* (Oxford: Clarendon Press) 1963, p. 6.

**A Bishop's Autobiography**

*The following document, an inscription set up during the reign of Constantine, gives a clear idea of how it was possible to transfer from the secular civil service of the state to the spiritual service of the Church without a huge psychological upheaval. Eugenius, the subject of this inscription, engaged in much the same activities while acting as a town-councilor as he did later on as a bishop. Were he a pagan he would have been building or repairing temples or aqueducts; here he is engaging in building and adorning a church. His values in this respect look little different from those of Pliny the Younger (see page 368) who also recorded for posterity his good deeds on behalf of his city. The selection of what Eugenius chooses to highlight—his service to his native city, his membership of the governor's staff, his marriage, his building activities—were just the kind of actions pagans listed in their inscriptions. There are, however, some significant differences: Eugenius records his selection as bishop and his steadfastness and suffering for his faith as also worthy of recording. He brackets the Church and his family in his concluding comment. "To the glory of the Church and my family" might previously have been "To the glory of my city and my family."*

I, M. Julius Eugenius, son of Cyrillus Celer of Kouessos, town councilor (or *decurion*) having served on the governor's staff in Pisidia (*in Asia Minor*), and having married Flavia Iulia Flaviane, daughter of Gaius Nestorianus, a senator, and having served honorably in the meantime, when an order went out from the Emperor Maximinus that Christians should sacrifice and not be allowed to resign the service (*i.e. step down as town councilor*) I endured very many torments and succeeded in leaving the service under the governor Diogenes while keeping the Christian faith. After staying in Laodicea (*in Phrygia, also in Asia Minor*) for a short time I was by the will of the all-powerful God installed as bishop. For twenty-five years I administered my bishopric with much honor, built the whole church from the foundations, and provided also all the surrounding ornamentation, consisting of porticoes and tetraporticoes and paintings and mosaics and a fountain and gateway, and fitted it all with dressed stone, and in a word with everything Being about to depart from human life, I have made for myself a plinth and a tomb, on which I have had the foregoing inscribed to the glory of the Church and my family (*Monumenta Asiae Minoris Antiqua* 1.170, tr. Fergus Millar, slightly altered).

humbler levels of Roman society there were men of similar character who regarded a career in the Church as a worthy alternative to service to their local communities. An inscription from the small city of Laodicaea in Phrygia in Asia Minor demonstrates the point and will have to stand for this widespread phenomenon of the late Empire (see box, previous page).

A TRUE COUNTER CULTURE Apart from its ability to attract men of character and talent who might otherwise have ended up in the Roman army, the imperial administration or the local curial service, and in this way undermine the Empire, Christianity possessed an ideology that was at odds in some important ways with the prevailing culture. Throughout the Roman Empire a person's identity was first and foremost derived from his or her place of origin. An individual was primarily a citizen of a particular city or community and only secondarily—if that—a citizen of the Empire. The religion of one's city was an essential constituent of one's identity. Daily life revolved around the city's calendar of religious events. Magistrates had both religious and civic functions; no one dreamed of separating the two. Festivals were by definition religious and constituted a central part of the social and cultural life of the community. They were entertainment but not "just" entertainment. Now came a religion which challenged all of these practices and presented a very different view of how religion should function, who should administer it, and what was its relationship to the community.

Christianity was by definition a non-local religion. While it could establish itself locally it was in practice a religion without a specific homeland, city or place. Its teaching transcended language, ethnicity, and culture. As a religion it could influence an existing society, but neither Jesus nor his apostles taught that Christianity was to be the basis for *a* Christian state or society. The New Testament offers no plan for a purely Christian state. The anonymous second century A.D. author of the *Letter to Diognetus* puts it this way:

> Christians are distinguished from other men neither by nationality, nor language, nor custom. They do not live separately in cities of their own, or have their own special language, or lead a life that is peculiar in any way.... While inhabiting Greek as well as non-Greek cities, according as the lot of each of them has determined, and following the customs of the natives in respect of clothing, food, and the rest of their ordinary conduct, they display their wonderful and admittedly striking way of life. As citizens they share in all things with others, and yet endure all things as foreigners. Every foreign land is to them their homeland, and every homeland as a land of strangers.... They pass their days on earth but their citizenship is in the heavens (5–6).

The author of the *Letter* does not bring out the fact that this kind of Christian cosmopolitanism was at variance with the localism of the cities of the Roman Empire and inevitably created tension between Christians and their fellow citizens. Although similar to the more cosmopolitan form of citizenship espoused by the Roman state, Christianity's version of the City of God transcended even Roman citizenship, so that Christians were in tension not only with their immediate neighbors but also with the overarching government of Rome.

WHAT IS OWED GOD AND CAESAR Christianity challenged the state in more direct ways. The distinction Christ made between what was owed to God and what was owed to Caesar limited the power of both the Church and the state. It was a revolutionary assertion.

The Church might not claim to run the state but it certainly claimed to limit its power. It insisted that the state not try to run the Church or to claim divine prerogatives for itself. It claimed, in short, the right to an autonomous space of its own within the state. In the west after the fall of the Empire the Church became an independent partner—at times a senior partner—of the state. It was an institution in its own right, independent of, and claiming spiritual superiority to, the state. It had its own churches, hospitals, orphanages, poor houses, monasteries, convents and lands. They were the property of the Church, not the state. Its numerous personnel—clergy, monks and nuns—were responsible first to the ecclesiastical authorities and only secondarily, and at times not at all, to the state. The Church, in contradiction of the principles of Roman statecraft had managed to carve out for itself an independent realm within the state over which it exercised or claimed to exercise independent jurisdiction. Under Constantine when the state worked out an arrangement with Christianity it did so in the hope of eventually absorbing the Church and extinguishing its independent standing. On numerous occasions it succeeded. In time, however, it was the autonomous realm created by the Church in opposition to the all-powerful state that allowed civil society, one of the main characteristics of Western culture today, to flourish.

THE NEW VALUE SYSTEM With the coming of Christianity new values replaced old. In the *polis* cultural world-view human flourishing could occur only in the here-and-now of active political and military involvement. It was in the public realm of the forum and the camp alone, so it was thought, that the traditional virtues of bravery, good practical judgment, justice and moderation—the cardinal virtues—could develop and be practiced to the full. True human growth was possible only in a *polis* and was not attainable by non-citizens, most women, slaves and generally people who lived in remote places out of touch with the city-state world of the Mediterranean.

This ideology had deep roots in Greco-Roman society. By the Empire the participation of poorer citizens in the civic life of the cities had dwindled to very little, but the ideology lived on. In the *polis*-world down to the fall of the Empire civic services to one's city were the activities that were honored, not the activities of the market place, the trades or the professions. These occupations were necessary, but they were not considered honorable or virtue-producing; they were not the kinds of things citizens should do. If possible these activities were to be farmed out to foreigners, freedmen and slaves. What counted was recognition by one's fellow citizens and that came from service in the public, not the private realm.

SUBVERSIVE VALUES In opposition to this ideology of civic virtues Christianity proposed a different and potentially subversive way of life. Manual labor in the Christian calculus was not regarded as degrading but rather the unfortunate consequence of sin. Work in itself was not ennobling, but performed in the right spirit and with the right intention it could be virtuous. This claim undermined *polis* values because it suggested that physical labor—what the poor and slaves did—could be taken as equivalent, in terms of value, to the public services performed by free citizens. The Benedictine monastic rule which was summed up in the words *ora et labora*—pray and work—must have seemed foolish to individuals imbued with the values of the traditional city-state. Poverty, Christians asserted, should not to be thought of as intrinsically degrading, or riches a proof of intrinsic worth.

Misuse of wealth was criticized by moralists of the *polis*-world, but the New Testament went a good deal further in reminding Christians that wealth could be a positive obstacle to what really counted, namely, true spiritual development. Good deeds were to be performed, preferably anonymously—"do not let your left hand know what your right hand is doing" (*Matthew* 6.3). Virtuous actions were not to be proclaimed in the marketplace in the style of *polis*-benefactors whose statues and inscriptions were visible everywhere and form such a large part of museum collections to the present. Treasures were to be accumulated in heaven not in this world. Small deeds like the tiny donation of the poor widow to the temple fund was worth more than the large amounts given by the rich who "gave out of their abundance whereas she gave out of her necessity" (*Mark* 12.44)

RADICAL ASSUMPTIONS At the root of the new value system was the radical implication that any one, male or female, slave or free could be as virtuous—indeed was likely to be more virtuous—than the rich and famous men and women of the city who only appeared to be virtuous. Such an ideology was mystifying to *polis*-dwellers. It inverted the traditional value system which assumed that education, wealth and status were essential to the acquisition of virtue and for which economic resources were necessary. If a person could be considered "virtuous" without these, how could society function? If women, slaves and the poor could be "virtuous" according to the new way of thinking, what was to happen to the traditional virtues of the *polis*? Who would bother to practice them? Although most of the truly radical and indeed revolutionary implications of the new ideology remained to be worked out in practice, many among the elite and in philosophical circles saw clearly the dangers to *polis*-society inherent in the new religion.

It is true that the Christian canon of virtues included the old *polis* virtues of courage, prudence, moderation, justice, fidelity, chastity and so on, but it added new ones. No citizen of an ancient *polis* would have thought that acts of humility, obedience, meekness, self-abnegation, or charity towards the poor were virtuous. Slaves and the poor were humble but why should a citizen pretend to be "humble"? A citizen was not a slave and it was important that he not act slavishly. His civic duties were self-evidently valuable and necessary for the success of the community; their excellence should be trumpeted, not hidden. Indeed the whole idea of Christian altruism was of doubtful practical and theoretical worth. In the *polis* value system one did good in order to receive benefits. The worth of doing something just for the love of God or one's neighbor without the expectation of gain was difficult to understand; it was even more difficult to believe that people—or at least people in any numbers—could ever be persuaded to act that way. The asceticism of monks and anchorites struck *polis*-dwellers as inhuman. Celibacy, which was honored by Christians, was suspect since it struck at the heart of the family. It was bad enough if a son announced his intention not to marry but the idea of a daughter refusing to do so was seen as particularly destructive. Choices of this kind undercut the assumption that the family and society had prior authority over its children, and that children had reciprocal obligations to their society. Rejecting a life of civic duty and virtue for a monastic existence seemed the height of self-centeredness and egoism. Christians retorted that voluntary celibacy was an honorable giving of oneself to God and a proclamation of the coming of the Kingdom when there would be "neither giving nor taking in marriage." Such answers, however, made little sense to the average *polis*-dweller.

## Golden Ageism

Appealing to a Golden Age to refute one's opponents has been a favorite technique used by debaters, historians, poets, rhetoricians, and philosophers since the Greek poet Hesiod gave the idea of a Golden Age currency around 700 B.C. Cleverly, the second and third century A.D. historian Dio Cassius took Hesiod's idea a step farther. For Dio Cassius the decline from the Golden Age of Antoninus Pius and Marcus Aurelius was not a slippage from gold to silver or to iron but a giant leap from gold to rust. Two centuries later the same technique enabled the poet Claudian to bemoan the rusty condition of the Rome of his own day. Nearly a millennium and a half after Claudian the famous Edward Gibbon had recourse to Golden Ageism to make "Decline and Fall" a commonplace in the English language and denigrate everything that happened after Rome's fall. Like Dio Cassius, Gibbon found his Golden Age in the second century:

> If a man were called to fix the period in the history of the world during which the condition of the human race was most happy and prosperous, he would, without hesitation, name that which elapsed from the death of Domitian to the accession of Commodus. (*Decline and Fall*, 1.2)

The viewpoint taken in this chapter is that the term "transformation" is a more accurate and less judgmental description of what actually happened in the late Empire. Yes, there was "Decline and Fall" in the sense intended by Gibbon, but there was also a lot more. The trouble with using terms such as "Decline and Fall" is that they have the effect of terminating further discussion and analysis. Once a period has been declared in "decline," then inevitably what went before must have been some kind of Golden Age, and what came after it something poorer. Why waste time on a period that was manifestly inferior to the age that preceded it? Instead of focusing on Gibbon's "Decline" a more useful approach to understanding the meaning and complexity of the end of the classical world is to look at how the two principal inheritors of Greece and Rome, Christianity and Islam, each dealt with their respective classical legacies.

CHRISTIANITY, ISLAM, AND THEIR HERITAGES Popular prejudice likes to contrast the "Dark Age" of Europe after the fall of the western Empire, with the cultural florescence of Islam in Spain, Africa, and the Middle East, forgetting (or more likely not knowing) that what provided the basis for this flourishing was classical Greco-Roman civilization. When the Arab armies invaded the old provinces of the Roman Empire they did not bring with them long and well developed artistic, architectural, literary, scientific, or philosophical cultural traditions. On the contrary they had none. Instead they found such traditions well established—in places for as much as a thousand years—among the peoples they conquered. It was not Arabs who first translated Greek texts into Arabic, but Aramaic and Syriac-speaking Christians in Syria and Mesopotamia. When the first mosques were erected they were built in imitation of already existing models of secular and religious buildings by Greek and Roman architects and builders. The inhabitants of the conquered lands—Jews, Christians, and pagans alike—were the mediators of Greco-Roman culture to their Arab conquerors. In the west, by contrast and to their detriment the German invaders found a much more weakly developed classical tradition, a poorer economic base and very little in the way of city life.

The origins of Christianity were in many ways the opposite of Islam's beginnings. Christianity began in a minor province of the Roman Empire at a time when Rome's power was at its peak. Its martyred founder Jesus of Nazareth was unlike the warrior-prophet Muhammad whose armies conquered first Arabia, and then under his successors the Middle East and much of the old Roman Empire. Christians were not initially of any significance socially and politically and suffered centuries of on-again off-again persecution before they finally found themselves in a position of power. By that time the traditions of church-state relations were well established. Church and state were distinct organized hierarchical institutions, and each possessed quite different bases of legitimacy and authority. The Church claimed to derive its authority from the mission of Christ expressed in the doctrine of apostolic succession according to which legitimate rule within the Church was established. In relationship to the state the words of Christ "Render under Caesar what is Caesar's and to God what is God's" (*Matthew* 22.21) were taken as the classic source of the difference between secular and religious authority and between distinct secular and religious realms. The west, therefore, inherited a dual political legacy, with the Church claiming to run its own affairs independent of the state, and the state claiming its own traditions of imperium, the power to rule rooted in the assent of the ruled. In the eastern Roman Empire civic and religious authorities were more closely cemented together than in the west. In the west the emperor was rarely in Rome and his power was more clearly dependent on the army than the Church, while in the east the emperor, who was a permanent resident of Constantinople, derived a considerable portion of his legitimacy from the Church in the person of the Bishop or Patriarch of Constantinople.

## Cultural Accommodations

CHRISTIAN-PAGAN ACCOMODATIONS Based on their fundamental beliefs Islam and Christianity made very different cultural accommodations with their Greco-Roman heritages. The weak political position of Christians forced them to enter into dialogue with their pagan co-citizens in areas such as art, literature, philosophy, and politics. From their Jewish inheritance they possessed a long and well developed tradition of intellectual exchange with paganism. Educated pagan converts felt the need to translate the message of Christianity into a language and a form compatible with their own cultural traditions. No taboo prevented them from doing so. When challenged by Greek philosophers Christians were comfortable in responding in philosophical language borrowed from Greek philosophy. Thus the doctrines of Christianity were shaped by centuries of Christian thinkers applying Greek philosophic and linguistic conventions to its tenets. It was felt that fundamentally religion and reason could not be in conflict since both had the same divine origin. Faith might involve mysteries that were beyond human comprehension, but the mysteries themselves were not irrational; humans were just too weak-minded to be able to understand or express their full meaning. There was no linguistic barrier between pagans and Christians. Christians spoke the languages of the Empire, its scriptures were composed and written in Greek, the language of the dominant culture and then quickly translated into Latin, the language of the ruling power. Without objection they were subsequently translated into many other languages. The Gospels adapted traditional Greco-Roman biographical forms to provide accounts of the life of Jesus. Paul and others wrote letters as did their non-Christian counterparts. Apologists debated with their non-Christian interlocutors using the same language, images and types of arguments. In the fourth century a poet by the name of Juvencus made a daring paraphrase of the Gospels in four books of hexameter verse in imitation of Virgil's great poem about Rome, the *Aeneid*. Christian poets composed their poems following long-standing Greco-Roman conventions but introduced new content. Roman political and organizational principles were absorbed by the nascent Church and became part of its administrative structure. Politically Christianity was malleable; it could adjust itself to just about any form of legitimate secular government. It is no wonder that Muhammad regarded Christianity as corrupt. From the Christian viewpoint, however, the belief that in Christ God took on human flesh, affirmed at a very fundamental level the essential goodness of the material world and the achievements of human beings. This was a basic position, but it was not always easy for Christians to decide what aspects of the material world and which of the achievements of human beings could and should be endorsed. An early example of this was the problem caused by the easy availability of meat sacrificed to idols. Christianity placed no restrictions on the kinds of food or drink that could be consumed, even food that was part of the rituals of idolatory. Christians, Paul insisted, were free of the law and those whose consciences were robust enough to allow them to eat sacrificial meat could do so—provided they did not scandalize or shock Christians who had weaker consciences. This was a form of freedom that could easily slide into libertinism as the many condemnations of it found in Christian scriptures and later writings testify.

## Islam and Its Pagan Classical Heritage

As a conquering religion Islam had no need to make the kinds of cultural and political accommodations Christians made. The victorious Arabs constituted an elite that ruled over their Greco-Roman subjects whether they were pagans, Jews, or Christians. There was no need for them to interact with them except as conquered peoples. The conquerors claimed to choose what was useful and compatible with Islam while discarding everything else. The language of Muhammad, the Quran and the ruling elite was Arabic, not Greek or Latin. It was therefore the duty of the conquered to learn Arabic. What could be of use in Latin or Greek had to be translated into the language of the rulers. There was no attempt to acculturate Islam to Greek and Roman sensibilities. Muslims had their own cultural traditions; they did not need to work within the cultures of Greeks and Romans.

For the same reasons Muslims took a very different view of the state than did Christians. For Muslims there was a seamless relationship between the state and Islam; the two were one. God's law was the state's law. God's army was the state's army. Islam's enemies were God's enemies. In the Islamic community, the *umma*, there were no independent secular spheres. Religious and secular authorities were one in all respects. Christianity by contrast was extraordinarily malleable and compatible with whatever legitimate political establishment—monarchy, oligarchy or democracy—existed. It was not tied to a particular language or culture but could incarnate itself, with certain obvious limitations, in any it encountered. Christianity could influence a political culture from within, but it did not have a developed idea of the state it needed to impose as a religious imperative.

MUTUAL THREATS The cultural legacy of the Greco-Roman world was for both Christians and Muslim both a valuable cultural treasure trove and a threat. From the enormous body of classical literature of all kinds that existed Muslims were selective in their choices and by and large restricted their borrowing of Greek works to science and philosophy, many of which they found had already been translated into Syriac, a language close to Arabic, by Christians. These works were the foundation on which they built their own important and original contributions to the development of science and philosophy during the ninth and tenth centuries. Greek literary works were largely ignored as were Greek and Roman artistic traditions when they involved the representation of the human body. Classical architecture, however, formed the basis of Islamic developments in that field.

Of all the legacies of the Greco-Roman world the rationalist tradition was the most threatening to both Christianity and Islam. As Gibbon put it: "The various modes of worship, which prevailed in the Roman world, were all considered by the people as equally true; by the philosopher, as equally false; and by the magistrate as equally useful" (Decline 1.2). Rationalism and its concomitant skepticism were potent solvents of all religious belief. If pursued with full intellectual rigor they could create as they have in the modern world a source of authority independent of religion. Among Christians and Muslims views varied as to the degree that faith and reason could be reconciled. "What does Jerusalem have to do with Athens?" was the well-known bon mot of the Christian apologist Tertullian. On the whole, however, mainstream Christianity with its incarnational (God-made-man) principal coming to the fore tended to assume that faith and reason were compatible. From early times it accepted as legitimate the use of philosophy to explore and express its doctrinal beliefs. Paul established an early position in this regard when he asserted that human reason alone, unaided by divine revelation, was able to discover the existence of God. "For what can be known about God is plain to them [*meaning pagans*], because God has shown it to them. Ever since the creation of the world his invisible nature, namely, his eternal power and deity, has been clearly perceived in the things that have been made" (*Romans*, 2.19–20). Faith could not be opposed to reason since humans were created by God as thinking beings just "a little less than the angels," as the psalmist put it. As Christians made their way in the Empire and their numbers increased, pagan intellectuals began to take note of them and challenged their beliefs. Christians were then forced either to retreat into their own private realm or to respond in similar, rationalist terms. From early in the second century a tradition of apologetics or defense of revelation by appeal to reason developed. In the fourth century Synesius, the bishop of Cyrene, could claim that not only were faith and reason not opposed but that philosophy itself was "a 'schoolmaster' or teacher [*a pedagogue was the term he used*] whose function was to bring the Greeks to Christ, just as the Law brought the Hebrews to him. Thus philosophy is a preparation, paving the way towards perfection in Christ" (Clement, *Stromata*, 1.5.28).

Muslims were not forced to run the intellectual gauntlet of the Greco-Roman philosophic tradition and its powerful defenders as were Christians. Islam addressed Greco-Roman culture from a position of political strength and military superiority. In its early centuries it embraced many aspects of Hellenic philosophy and science but in time a reaction grew among Muslims against both. Muslim thinkers began to suspect that reason was being given an improper priority over revelation. Al-Ghazali (A.D. 1058–1111), a central figure in Islamic thought, criticized philosophy in a number of influential works. His *Incoherence of the Philosophers* emphasized the inadequacy of reason and the centrality and necessity of revelation and mystical knowledge for a full human life. His skepticism was widely shared. For traditionalists, the foundation of Islam lay exclusively in the Quran, the sunna of the Prophet, and those beliefs testified to by the first generation or two of his followers. The vast majority of Muslim intellectuals were educated in schools of Islamic law (madrasas) rather than more broadly in schools where philosophy and theology had primacy over jurisprudence. From the eleventh century the predominant tendency among Muslims has been to give preference to revelation over reason. In the west the Renaissance, the Reformation, the Scientific Revolution, and the Enlightenment were movements that grew directly out of the triple legacy of Greece, Rome, and Christianity. They remained unnoticed, however, until recent times in the Islamic world.

Today both Christian and Islamic cultures confront the radical consequences of their early cultural accommodations and subsequent historical growth. Christian culture in the west has gone far in the direction of absorbing secular culture, a point made strongly by many Muslims who regard the Christian west as having slipped back into the condition of *jahaliyya*—the condition of the pre-Islamic pagan world of barbarism, moral chaos and ignorance. In their view, the Christians of the west have long since ceased to be "Peoples of the Book." The only power capable of facing the corroding and often corrupting challenge of modernity in the view of these Muslims is a reformed Islam which makes no compromises with rationalism. Whether modernity will, in the end, have the same impact on the Islamic world that it has had on the Christian west remains to be seen.

# Glossary

**Acropolis:** The citadel of a Greek city-state (*polis*). The equivalent in Roman city was called the arx.

**Aedile:** One of four magistrates elected annually at Rome. They were responsible for the general oversight of law and order in the city, the grain supply, public buildings, markets, weights and measures, and public games (*ludi*).

**Aeneas:** In the Homeric saga the hero Aeneas escaped from Troy as it was being destroyed by the Greeks taking with him the Palladium, the small wooden statue of an armed Athena which guaranteed the safety of Troy. First kept at Lavinium it was then located in the inner most part of the Temple of Vesta at Rome. Only the chief vestal could enter. It was the pledge of Rome's safety.

**Aerarium:** The Roman treasury located in the Temple of Saturn in the Forum. It was under the supervision of *quaestors* (see below). State documents such as senatorial decrees and treaties were kept there.

**ager publicus:** The publicly owned land bank of Rome made up of territory conquered by Rome. It was leased to *possessores* out by the censors. According to the Licinian-Sextian law of 367 B.C. there was a limit of 500 jugera (350 acres) per *possesor* but there is plenty of evidence that this limitation was often ignored.

**Amphitheater:** An oval building made originally of wood but later of stone for Roman gladiatorial and animal fights.

**Aristocracy:** Literally (Gk.), the "rule of the best." The term originated in the fifth century B.C. and implied rule by an elite of lineage, culture and wealth as opposed to rule by merely the wealthy (= oligarchy—see below). In this text the more comprehensive term "elite" is more often used than aristocracy.

**Asia:** The name of a small river valley in ancient Anatolia near Ephesus. The term was eventually applied to all of Anatolia and then to the lands further east.

**Anatolia:** Asia Minor, mod. Turkey.

**Asia Minor:** Corresponds to most of modern Turkey.

**Auctoritas:** The influence and prestige built up by success on the battlefield and in civil affairs by senior statesmen at Rome.

**Augustales:** Priests responsible for the imperial cult during the Roman Empire. They were usually freedmen.

**Auspices:** Divining the will of the gods from signs was referred to as "taking the *auspices*." Literally the term meant "watching the birds." The priests who were designated to look for signs were called augurs. All public acts—elections, the census, military operations, the inauguration of temples etc.—required *auspicatio*: The auspices were not thought to reveal the future but only that the gods had approved (or disapproved) of the particular action about which their opinion was sought. If approval was denied the auspices could be repeated. See also **Divination.**

**Auxilia:** Roman allies (*socii*) who fought alongside the legions. Individual units were commanded by a prefect (*praefectus*) from the city where the unit originated. The auxiliaries were often cavalry or specialized troops. Infantry units of *auxilia* were made up of cohorts of 500 men. Groups of 10 cohorts formed an "allied wing" (*ala sociorum*) commanded by Roman equestrian officers, also called prefects. The term "wing" refers to the location of the allies on the battlefield, namely, on the wings of the legions. In the Empire the term "*ala*" came to refer exclusively to cavalry.

**Barbarian (Gk. barbaros/oi (pl.):** The term used by Greeks for non-Greek speakers. As Greeks grew in self confidence during the 5th. century the term tended to acquire an overtone of inferiority. It did not necessarily have a derogatory significance.

**Beneficium:** A favor done for a friend or a legal privilege enjoyed by a particular individual or community.

**Caesar:** The *cognomen* or third name of Julius Caesar. It later became an imperial title.

**Censor:** Every five years two men were elected censor by the Centuriate Assembly for an 18 month term. They conducted the census, leased state contracts, and reviewed the Senate expelling those they regarded as unfit. The censorship was the high point of a Roman senatorial career.

**Census:** The list of Roman citizens drawn up every five years by two censors.

**Centuriate Assembly:** Roman assembly of all citizens. They voted in 193 weighted units called centuries. It had elective, administrative and judicial capacities.

**Centurion:** Commander of a company (*centuria*) of legionaries. The unit may originally have had a 100 men in it but later the number was 80 or fewer.

**Client:** A Roman citizen who had ties, moral rather than legal, to a patron, an individual of higher status.

**Cohors:** One of ten tactical units in the Roman army after the reforms of Marius.

**Coinage:** The Roman silver denarius was valued at 16 bronze *asses* or four sesterces. A denarius was roughly equivalent to the daily wage of a freeborn worker. See figure page 166 for more details.

**Collegium:** A group of people organized for political, religious, social, or professional reasons. The major priesthoods were organized into *collegia*. Minor priesthoods formed sodalities (*sodalitates*). Every magistracy was to be made up of at least two officials. The resulting "collegiality" was an important aspect of Roman political practice. An individual magistrate could veto (*intercessio*) the action of his colleague. The purpose of collegiality was to restrict the power of individual officials and force them to achieve consensus.

**Commercium:** Literally (Lat.), business. It was the term used for the reciprocal right between Romans and Latins for the conduct of business in each others' cities. Commercium allowed contracts to be enforced in each other's courts.

**Comitium:** The place of public assembly in the Forum in front of the *Curia* or Senate house. Also the term for a properly called assembly.

**Consul (pl. consules):** One of two chief annual magistrates elected at Rome with *imperium* (see below).

**Conubium:** Marriage. Also the right to enter into a recognized Roman marriage and for the right of Latins and Romans to intermarry.

**Cursus honorum:** Roman career path or ladder or race course of honors. The term referred to the succession of magistracies which were supposed to be held in a certain order ending with the highest of honors, the censorship.

**Decurion (pl. decurions):** Also known as curials or *curiales*. Members of the senates of the cities of the Roman Empire. Decurions had responsibility for maintaining order in their jurisdictions and collecting taxes. They had the potential to access the higher levels of the Roman imperial administration.

**Democracy:** In Greek political practice a democracy was a strongly egalitarian form of constitution (*politeia*) in which power was calculated arithmetically, not geometrically (i.e., one vote per eligible citizen). In a "pure" democracy the rich, the powerful, and the educated did not, at least overtly, have proportionately more power than their fellow citizens. All male citizens had equal voting rights and equal access to office. Democracies were characterized by the use of the lot rather than elections in the selection of officials.

**Demos:** Could mean either a specific territory and/or the people who lived in it.

**Denarius:** see **Coinage.**

**Dictator:** Temporary, single, emergency magistrate at Rome. The customary principle of collegiality was set aside, but the term of office was for only 6 months.

**Dignitas:** Public recognition won by public service to the state, principally military service but also service in the civilian realm of the courts, the legislative assemblies and the Senate. It was a key factor in the motivation of the Roman elite.

**Divination:** The technique of discovering the will of the gods by interpreting the flight of birds, the direction of lightning flashes or the condition of the entrails of sacrificed animals.

**Dominate:** The term given by historians to the more overtly authoritarian period in Roman history dating approximately from the time of Diocletian. Some scholars see the Dominate beginning as early as the end of the second century A.D.

**Dominus:** Latin for "Lord," or "Master."

**Druids:** Druids constituted a class of learned men among Celtic peoples. They were responsible generally for maintaining the religious, legal, cultural and historical traditions of their communities.

**Elite:** Those members of a society, ancient or modern, who have greater access to wealth, power, and education than the majority of society.

**Eponymous ancestor:** The mythical or legendary individual after whom a people is named. Thus, the Israelites were so named because of the assumption that they were the descendants of Abraham's grandson Israel. The Romans were the descendants of Romulus etc.

**Eques; Equestrian order:** Cavalryman; member of the second rank of the Roman elite. The members of the senate were chosen from among the equestrians.

**Eschatology:** Explanations purporting to explain how the world will end. Eschatological beliefs were held be peoples throughout the Middle East.

**Ethnos (pl. ethnê):** A Greek term used for people who, while they had a common identity and territory, had not organized themselves as a city-state or *polis*. From the sixth century onwards Greek *ethnê* often formed federations such as the Achaeans and Boeotians. By the fourth century such federations had evolved into well-organized federal leagues and played a major role in Greek affairs. Because of their size they had a major advantage over the smaller city-states of Greece. The Latin equivalent is *natio*.

**Ex S(senatus) C(onsulto):** "By resolution of the Senate."

**Farmstead:** A farming unit made up of land, buildings, equipment, and animals.

**Fasces:** The bundle of rods about five feet long containing an axe carried by the official attendants (*lictores*) of Roman magistrates. They were the symbols of the authority of the magistrates The absence of the axe in the bundle of rods symbolized the individual citizens right of appeal (*provocatio*). Consuls had 12 lictors and fasces, praetors six. Dictators may have had 24. Augustus had the right to 12 fasces in perpetuity and possibly 24 outside Rome.

**Fetiales:** A college of 20 priests who advised the Roman Senate on questions of war and peace. Two of them were sent to states which made treaties with Rome calling curses on the Roman people if they broke the treaty. In case of war the *fetiales* called on Jupiter to witness the wrongs done to the Romans. When war was declared a fetial priest went to the frontier of the enemy state and hurled a spear across the boundary as a declaration of war.

**Fides:** Trustworthiness, good faith. An important item of Roman social and psychological self-esteem. There was a temple of Fides located in a prominent position on the Capitol overlooking the Forum.

**Flamen:** Roman priest.

**Forum:** Equivalent to the Greek *agora*. The area of a Roman city designated for public business (political assemblies, courts) and commerce. Sometimes there was more than one forum in a city.

**Freedman:** Manumitted slave. If the proper legal forms were followed the freedman received the citizenship with some restrictions. He or she took the manumittor's name and had some residual obligations to the manumittor.

**Gens:** The group of people supposedly (and sometimes really) descended from a common ancestor. For example, the *gens Julia* to which Julius Caesar belonged claimed descent from Iulus, the grandson of the Trojan hero Aeneas who was supposed to have settled in Latium some 1200 years before Caesar. See also **Nomen**.

**Gloria:** Literally (Lat.) "glory." Glory was won by service to the state, principally through success on the battlefield.

**Hegemony:** The term which was derived from **Hêgemôn,** literally "leader" in Greek. It was given to an individual or to a state which headed an organization of independent or quasi independent states. E.g. Sparta was the *hêgemôn* of the Peloponnesian states.

**Hellas:** Name given in the classical period to Greece. Originally the term referred to just a small area of north central Greece in the vicinity of Thermopylae.

**Honestiores:** Literally (Lat.), "the more honorable people." High status members of the elite in the Roman Empire. They had special legal privileges which *humiliores* (see below) did not possess.

**Hoplite:** In Greek-style warfare, heavily armed and armored members of the infantry phalanx. Hoplites supplied their own arms and armor. They came from the core, landowning, citizen farming classes of the *polis* or city-state and were the key to its survival. Over time the weight of armor was reduced and hoplites became more mobile and the phalanx—or, in the case of Rome—the legion, more flexible. The hoplite was the dominant figure on the battlefield from the seventh century unit to the fall of the Roman Empire.

**Humiliores:** Low status people in the Roman Empire. They lacked the privileges of the *honestiores* (see above).

**Imperium:** Supreme delegated authority in civic and military realms vested in certain magistrates such as consuls and praetors.

**Imperator:** The bearer of *imperium*. More generally, a successful military commander. From the Flavian period the term *imperator* became a title of the emperor.

**Indo-European:** A linguistic term for a family of languages including European, Iranian and northern Indian languages. The term has no racial or ethnic connotations.

**Intercessio:** The right of a Roman magistrate to veto the activity of a colleague or of a lower magistrate.

**Iugerum (pl. iugera):** A measure of land. One *iugerum* = 0.25 ha. or 0.625 acre.

**Lar (pl. lares):** The protective spirits of homes, crossroads of a city and of the city itself. In homes they were placed in a shrine and prayed to daily. They are usually in the form of small statuettes holding drinking horns and libation bowls.

**Legatus (pl. legati):** Someone delegated to act on behalf of the Roman senate or on behalf of an individual such as a governor. Commanders of legions were often legates. From the time of Augustus a provincial governor appointed by him was a legate.

**League:** see **ethnos.**

**Legion:** The basic heavy infantry divisional formation of the Roman army. It was composed of about 5000 men. It was made up of men eligible for military service.

**Lex (pl. leges):** A statute passed by one of the assemblies at Rome or in the Empire period by an emperor.

**Lictor:** Attendants of Roman magistrates. They carried the *fasces* (see above).

**Limes:** The boundary or limit of Roman Empire. The term was used specifically of the system of walls and roads connecting the Rhine and Danube frontiers.

**Liturgy:** A type of indirect taxation used throughout the Greco-Roman world. Under this system the well-off were expected to perform acts of public service such as funding festivals, aiding individual citizens in need, and providing help to the community in emergencies. Pay-off came in the form of public honors such as statues and inscriptions.

**Ludi:** Public games offered at Rome by private individuals or by officials.

**Magi:** A Zoroastrian (Zarathustrian) priestly class among the Medes.

**Manes:** Spirits of the dead.

**Maniple:** One of 30 units, each made up of two centuries, out of which a legion was divided. They contained up to 160 men. They lost importance after the introduction of the cohort (see above).

**Mesopotamia:** Greek term meaning the "Land between the Rivers" (Tigris and Euphrates). Modern Iraq and parts of Iran.

**Military Tribune:** One of six middle-ranking officers in a legion. Their tasks were administrative and disciplinary not tactical. They were of equestrian rank. In the Empire period one of the 6 was of senatorial rank

**Municipium (pl. municipia):** In the period of the Roman Republic the *municipium* was a self-ruling city in Italy to which Rome extended full or partial franchise. During the Empire the bestowal of the status of municipium was used as a method of extending the citizenship and rewarding the loyalty of cities in the provinces.

**Negev:** The desert area of southern Palestine stretching from Beersheba to Aqaba.

**Nomen:** Latin. The second or *gens* (clan) name of a Roman male. In the late Republic Roman most elite males had three names: the *praenomen, nomen,* and *cognomen* as in "Tiberius Sempronius Gracchus." The *praenomen* was the personal name used at home. In formal situations a man could be addressed by *praenomen* and *nomen*, and sometimes by his *cognomen* as well. Women had only one name, their father's *nomen*, as in "Sempronia," "Julia," or "Marcia."

**Nobilis (pl. nobiles)** The term means literally "known" men and referred in general to the ruling aristocracy of Rome. By the first century it had a more technical significance, "descended from a consul," and referred to those families which had an ancestor who was a consul.

**Novus homo (pl. novi homines)** In the Roman Republic the first member of a family to become a Roman senator. In a special sense it referred to the first man in a senatorial family who reach the consulship.

**Oligarchy:** Greek for "the rule of the few." An oligarchical constitution (*politeia*) restricted participation in governance to the wealthy. Even in oligarchic constitutions, however, the rest of the citizens still had political rights which they might exercise in the assembly, the courts and the elections. Unlike democracies oligarchies were characterized by the use of elections for magistrates rather than the lot.

**Optimates (pl.):** "The best people"—as contrasted with the *populares* (see below). Supporters of the traditional aristocratic or oligarchic political system at Rome. Neither they nor the *populares* constituted a political party.

**Ovatio:** An ovation was a lesser form of triumph. Ovations were granted in cases when the requisite body count of 5000 for a triumph was not met or if the enemy was thought to be too humble or unsuitable (e.g. slaves or pirates).

**Pantheon:** A Greek term meaning "all the gods." Also Hadrian's great temple in Rome.

**Patria potestas:** "Fatherly power." The legal power of male Roman head of a family—father or grandfather—over his family and his descendants through males, including adults.

**Paterfamilias:** The ascendant male who had *patria potestas*.

**Patrician:** Probably connected with "*patres,*" "fathers." The *patres* were the heads of the leading families in early Rome at the time of the founding of the Republic. The term "*Patres*" was a collective term for all the patrician members of the senate.

**Patronus (pl. patroni):** see **Client.**

**Penates:** Spirits of the inner part of a Roman house who protected the store room and to whom the head of the household made offerings of food and drink.

**Phalanx:** The tactical formation of hoplite infantry. It consisted of hoplites in ranks of 8 deep armed with thrusting spears and shields. In the fourth century Philip II of Macedon modified this arrangement by organizing phalangites in files of 16 men deep armed with long pikes up to 18 feet long (called the *sarissa*). This new phalanx fought in coordination with light infantry and heavy cavalry.

**Plebs:** A generic term for the "people." A plebeian was a non-patrician citizen of Rome.

**Polis (pl. poleis):** Greek for "city-state" or, as some scholars prefer, "citizen-state." The *polis* consisted of a defined group of citizens, a demarcated territory, and generally some kind of urban center. The average *polis* was a small (no more than 700 to 1000 households), self-governing, self-perpetuating corporation. A *polis* may also have had many resident, non-citizen legal aliens (*metics*) and slaves. There were an estimated 1500 *poleis* in the Hellenic world.

**Pomerium:** Sacred boundary of a Roman or Latin city ritually established and marked out by stones. Armed men, except on special occasions such as triumphs, were not allowed inside the pomerium. Thus Rome's centuriate assembly which was the civil equivalent of the army met in the Campus Martius (the Field of Mars) just outside the pomerium.

**Pontifex (pl. pontifices):** Literally "bridge builders." Priests of one of the major Roman priestly colleges.

**Populares:** Roman politicians, plebeian or patrician, who acted in a popular manner, i.e. they dealt directly with the people and supposedly on their behalf. Their optimate opponents disdained this method of political activity as untraditional and demagogic.

**Praetor (pl. praetores):** Important, annually elected Roman magistrates who held military and civilian *imperium*. Their main responsibility was the supervision of the Roman judicial system and the governance of provinces. An important post in the *cursus honorum* (see above). The number increased from the original one position to eight by 80 B.C. There were 12 in the Empire.

**Praetorian Guard:** A commander's body guard and later the emperor's body guard.

**Princeps (pl. principes):** Leading member(s) of the elite in the Roman Republic. Even when not holding a magistracy the *principes* had considerable weight because of their *auctoritas*. The influence of a *princeps* was contrasted with the *dominatio* of a master over a slave. Augustus chose the term *princeps* as a title because of its traditional, non-threatening implications.

**Princeps Senatus:** In the Republic the title of a senator placed at the head of the list of senators by the censor. It was an informal, but highly prestigious title.

**Proconsul:** At the end of his year in office a consul might have his command continued or prorogued with the title of proconsul for a set time period or an assignment elsewhere.

**Procurator:** A financial administrator. In the Empire period a procurator could be the administrator of the Emperor's personal property.

**Provincia:** "Province." The generic realm of responsibility of a Roman magistrate. It could be territorial or jurisdictional. E.g. the province of a praetor was the Roman judiciary but he could also be the governor of an overseas province.

**Publicanus (pl. publicani):** Publicans were private contractors at Rome. Publicans bid for state contracts either individually or in groups called *societates*. State contracts covered such things as arms and food supplies for the army, building contracts for roads and aqueducts and the collection of the taxes of entire provinces.

**Quaestor:** Annually elected Roman magistracy and first step in the *cursus honorum*. Quaestors generally had financial responsibilities either at Rome or abroad.

**Quirites:** An ancient, probably Sabine god. Speakers addressed citizens as "Quirites."

**Rostra:** The speakers' platform in the Forum was decorated with the beaks (*rostra*) of captured ships.

**Sacrosanctity:** "Inviolability." Sacrosanctity was a taboo that protected Roman tribunes of the people and aediles against violence. A person who injured a tribune or aedile was declared "sacred" or dedicated to the gods and could thus be killed out of hand without trial.

**Semitic:** Linguistic designation for a group of languages including Babylonian, Assyrian, Hebrew, Aramaic, Syriac and Arabic. It has no racial or ethnic connotations.

**Senate:** At Rome the advisory council of the kings and later of the Republic. It was the principle source of administrators, governors and commanders in the Empire.

**Senatus consultum (SC):** Decree or resolution of the Roman Senate.

**Socius (pl. socii):** Ally of Rome. Also a companion or business partner.

**Stipendium:** The living expenses of a soldier paid by the state. By the late Republic it was synonymous with pay.

**Temperate Europe:** That part of Europe lying between the north shore of the Mediterranean and the sub-Arctic regions.

**Toga:** Undyed woolen robe worn only by Roman citizens. The togas of senators and equestrians were marked with purple bands of varying widths, wide for senators, narrow for equestrians.

**Tribune:** Roman military tribunes were elected annually from the equestrian order in the Republic. They served in the legions. Tribunes of the People, *tribuni plebis*, were the annually elected civilian officers of the plebs. They had the power of *intercessio* that enabled them to veto the activities of virtually all magistrates and assemblies. Apart from negative powers they had the right to provide help (*auxilium*) for citizens, call assemblies and present legislation or conduct trials.

**Triumph:** A procession of a victorious general through Rome along the Via Sacra to the temple of Jupiter Optimus on the Caplitoline hill where the spoils of the war were displayed. Prerequisites were: victory in a properly declared war; 5000 enemy dead; the war had to be fought in the general's province and under his auspices.

Permission to conduct a triumph depended on a decision by the Senate followed by a vote of the people.

**Triumvir:** Elected commission of three at Rome with varying types of responsibility, such as the founding a colony or the assignment of land.

**Villa:** Usually an elaborate rural dwelling made up of residential and farm buildings, workshops, and often a bath house and temple. They varied greatly in size and complexity.

# Useful Web Sites

## General gateway sites

http://www.perseus.tufts.org
http://www.stoa.org/diotima/
http://www.fordham.edu/halsall/
http://www.livius.org
http://www.attalus.org/
http://www.sas.upenn.edu/
http://classics.mit.edu
http://www.sas.upenn.edu/~ekondrat/rome.html
http://www.museum.upenn.edu/new/worlds_intertwined/etruscan/religion.shtml
http://www.britishmuseum.org/explore/galleries/
http://www.bbc.co.uk/history/ancient/romans/
http://www.roman-emperors.org/
http://www.roman-empire.net/
http://www.csun.edu/~hcfll004/nicolaus.html
http://www.pbs.org/wgbh/pages/frontline/shows/religion/
http://www.tertullian.org/fathers/
http://www.bbc.co.uk/religion/religions/christianity/index.shtml

## City of Rome

http://www.cvrlab.org/projects/real_time/roman_forum/roman_forum.html
http://www.maquettes-historiques.net/page24.html
http://penelope.uchicago.edu/~grout/encyclopaedia_romana/imperialfora/imperialfora.html
http://ancienthistory.about.com/od/cityofrome/p/ForumRomanum.htm
http://www.romanhomes.com/why_rome/panoramic_views.htm
http://www.vroma.org/~forum/forum.html
http://home.surewest.net/fifi/index50.html

http://www.isolatiberina.it/Im/im_Roma%20PreArcaica.jpg
http://www2.siba.fi/~kkoskim/imbas/roma/startpage.php?lang=en&action=1

## Art, Architecture, Coins

http://www.beazley.ox.ac.uk/index.htm
http://www.whitman.edu/theatre/theatretour/home.htm
http://corinth.sas.upenn.edu/romemapping/preview/circusmaximus.html
http://id-archserve.ucsb.edu/arthistory/152k/index.html
http://romancoins.info

# Suggested Readings


Alcock, Susan. Graecia Capta: *The Landscapes of Roman Greece*. Cambridge and New York: Cambridge University Press, 1993.

Alfoeldy, Geza. *The Social History of Rome*. Baltimore, MD: Johns Hopkins University Press, 1988.

Alston, Richard. *Soldier and Society in Roman Egypt: A Social History*. London and New York: Routledge, 1995.

Aubet, Maria Eugenia. *The Phoenicians and the West*, Second Edition. Cambridge: Cambridge University Press, 2001.

Badian, Ernst. *Publicans and Sinners: Private Enterprise in the Service of the Roman Republic*. Ithaca, NY: Cornell University Press, 1972.

Badian, Ernst. *Roman Imperialism in the Late Republic*, Second Edition. Oxford, UK: Blackwell, 1968.

Ball, Warwick. *Rome in the East*. London: Routledge, 2000.

Balsdon, J. P. V. D. *Life and Leisure in Ancient Rome*. London: Phoenix Press, 2002.

Barnes, T.D. *Athanasius and Constantius*. Cambridge: Harvard University Press, 1993.

Barnes, T.D. *Early Christianity and the Roman Empire*. London: Variorum, 1984.

Barnes, T.D. Constantine and Eusebius. Cambridge: Harvard University Press, 1981.

Beard, Mary, and Michael Crawford. *Rome in the Late Republic, Second Edition*. Ithaca, NY: Cornell University Press, 1999.

Beard, Mary, John North, and Simon Price. *Religions of Rome*, 2 vols. Cambridge, MA: Cambridge University Press, 1998.

Berkey, Jonathan P. *The Formation of Islam: Religion and Society in the Near East, 600–1800*. New York: Cambridge University Press, 2003.

Boatwright, Mary T. *Hadrian and the Cities of the Roman Empire*. Princeton: Princeton University Press, 2000.

Bowersock, Glen W. *Augustus and the Greek World*. Westport, CT: Greenwood Press, 1981.

Bowersock, Glen W. *Hellenism in Late Antiquity*. New York: Cambridge, 1990

Bowersock, Glen W. *Julian the Apostate*. Cambridge: Harvard Univesity Press, 1978.

Bowersock, Glen W. *Martyrdom and Rome*. New York: Cambridge University Press, 1995

Bradley, Keith. *Slavery and Society at Rome*. New York: Cambridge University Press, 1994.

Brown, Peter. *Augustine of Hippo: A Biography*. Berkeley: University of California Press, 1967. Revised Edition, 2000.

Brown, Peter. *The Body and Society: Men, Women and Sexual Renunciation in Early Christianity*. New York: Columbia Univesity Press, 1988. Revised Edition, 2008.

Brown, Peter. *The World of Late Antiquity, Second Edition*. London: Thames and Hudson, 1989.

Brown, Peter. *The Rise of Western Christendom, Second Edition*. London: Blackwell, 2003.

Brunt, P. A. *Italian Manpower 225 B.C.–A.D 14*. Oxford: Oxford University Press, 1971

Brunt, P. A. *Social Conflicts in the Roman Republic*. London: Hogarth Press, 1986.

Campbell, Brian. *The Roman Army, 31 B.C.–A.D. 337*. A Sourcebook. London and New York: Routledge, 1994.

Campbell, Brian. *War and Society in Imperial Rome, 31 B.C.–A.D. 284*. London and New York: Routledge, 2002.

Chadwick, Henry *The Church in Ancient Society*. Oxford: Oxford University Press, 2001.

Chadwick, Henry. *The Early Church*. London: Penguin, 1967

Chamoux, F. *Hellenistic Civilization*. Oxford: Oxford University Press, 2002.

Champion, Timothy, et al. *Prehistoric Europe*. London: Academic Press, 1984.

Clark, Gillian. *Christianity and Roman Society*. Cambridge: Cambridge University Press, 2004

Clark, Gillian. *Women in Late Antiquity: Pagan and Christian Lifestyles*. Oxford, UK: Clarendon, 1993.

Cooper, Kate. *The Virgin and the Bride: Idealized Womanhood in Late Antiquity*. Cambridge: Harvard University Press, 1996.

Cornell, T. J. *The Beginnings of Rome*. London: Routledge, 1995.

Crook, John A. *Law and Life of Rome: 90 B.C.–A.D. 212*. Ithaca, NY: Cornell University Press, 1967.

Dixon, Suzanne. *The Roman Family*. Baltimore, MD: Johns Hopkins University Press, 1992.

Drake, Hal. *Constantine and the Bishops: The Politics of Intolerance*. Baltimore: Johns Hopkins University Press, 2000.

Dyson, Stephen L. *The Creation of the Roman Frontier*. Princeton: Princeton University Press, 1985.

Dyson, Stephen L. *The Roman Countryside*. London: Duckworth, 2003.

Earl, Donald C. *The Moral and Political Tradition of Rome*. Ithaca, NY: Cornell University Press, 1967.

Eckstein, Arthur M. *Moral Vision in the Histories of Polybius*. Berkeley and Los Angeles, 1995

Eckstein, Arthur M. *Mediterranean Anarchy, Interstate War, and the Rise of Rome*. Berkeley: University of California Press, 2006.

Eckstein, Arthur M. *Senate and General: Individual Decision Making and Roman Foreign Relations, 264–194 B.C. Berkeley: University of California Press, 1987.*

Evans, John K. *War, Women, and Children in Ancient Rome*. London: Routledge, 1991.

Fagan, Garrett G. *Bathing in the Roman World*. Ann Arbor: University of Michigan Press, 1999.

Favro, Diane, *The Urban Image of Augustan Rome*. New York: Cambridge University Press, 1996.

Feldman, Louis H. *Jew and Gentile in the Ancient World: Attitudes and Interactions from Alexander to Justinian*. Princeton: Princeton University Press, 1993.

Flower, Harriet I. *Ancestor Masks and Aristocratic Power in Roman Culture*. Oxford: Clarendon Press, 1996.

Fowden, Garth. *Empire to Commonwealth: Consequences of Monotheism in Late Antiquity*. Princeton: Princeton University Press, 1993.

Gamble, Harry Y. *Books and Readers in the Early Church: A History of Early Christian Texts*. New Haven and London: Yale University Press, 1995.

Gardner, Jane. *Being a Roman Citizen*. London and New York: Routledge, 1993.

Gardner, Jane. *Women in Roman Law and Society*. Bloomington: Indiana University Press, 1986.

Garnsey, Peter. *Famine and Food Supply in the Greco-Roman World*. New York: Cambridge University Press, 1988

Garnsey, Peter. *Cities, Peasants, and Food in Classical Antiquity*. New York: Cam-bridge University Press, 1998

Garnsey, Peter. *Food and Society in Classical Antiquity*. New York: Cambridge
University Press, 1999

Garnsey, Peter. *Thinking about Property from Antiquity to the Age of Revolution*. New York: Cambridge University Press, 2007.

Garnsey, Peter. *Ideas of Slavery from Aristotle to Augustine*. Cambridge: Cambridge University Press, 1996.

Garnsey, Peter. *Food and Society in Classical Antiquity*. Cambridge, MA: Cambridge University Press, 1999.

Garnsey, Peter, and Richard Saller. *The Roman Empire: Economy, Society, and Culture.* Berkeley: University of California Press, 1987.

Garnsey, Peter, Keith Hopkins, and C.R. Whittaker, *Trade in the Ancient Economy.* London: Chatto and Windus 1983

Garnsey, Peter, and C. R. Whittaker (eds.). *Imperialism in the Ancient World.* Cambridge, UK: Cambridge University Press, 1978.

Goffart, Walter. *Barbarians and Romans: Techniques of Accommodation*. Princeton: Princeton University Press, 1980.

Goldsworthy, Adrian Keith. *The Roman Army at War: 100 B.C.–A.D. 200*. Oxford: Clarendon Press, 1996.

Greene, Kevin. *The Archaeology of the Roman Economy.* Berkeley: University of California Press, 1986.

Gruen, Erich S. *Culture and National Identity in Republican Rome*. Ithaca, NY: Cornell University Press, 1992.

Gruen, Erich S. *The Last Generation of the Roman Republic*. Berkeley: University of California Press, 1974.

Harl, Kenneth W. *Coinage in the Roman Economy: 300 B.C. to A.D. 700*. Baltimore: Johns Hopkins University Press, 1996.

Harris, W. V. *War and Imperialism in Republican Rome*. New York: Oxford University Press, XXXX

Heather, P. J. *The Fall of the Roman Empire: A New History of Rome and the Barbarians*. Oxford and New York: Oxford University Press, 2006

Heather, P. J. *Goths and Romans 332–489 A.D. Oxford: Clarendon Press, 1991*

Heurgon, Jacques. *The Rise of Rome*. Berkeley: University of California Press, 1973.

Hopkins, Keith. *Conquerors and Slaves*. New York: Cambridge University Press, 1978

Hopkins, Keith. *Death and Renewa*l. New York: Cambridge University Press, 1983.

Isaac, Benjamin. *The Limits of Empire: The Roman Army in the East, Revised Edition.* Oxford, UK: Clarendon Press, 1992.

Johnson, David, *Roman Law in Context*. Cambridge, MA: Cambridge University Press, 1999.

Keppie, Lawrence. *The Making of the Roman Army*. Norman: University of Oklahoma Press, 1998.

Kraemer, Ross Shepard. *Her Share of the Blessing: Women's Religion Among Pagans, Jews, and Christians in the Greco-Roman World*. Oxford, UK: Oxford University Press, 1992.

Lancel, Serge, *Carthage: A History*. Oxford: Blackwell, 1995.

Laurence, Ray, and Joanne Berry, eds. *Cultural Diversity in the Roman Empire*. London: Routledge, 2001.

Lazenby, J. F. *Hannibal's War*. Norman: Oklahoma University Press, 1986.

Lintott, Andrew. *Violence in Republican Rome, Second Edition*. Oxford: Oxford University Press, 1999.

MacDonald, William L. *The Architecture of the Roman Empire*, 2 vols. New Haven: Yale University, 1982 and 1986.

MacDonald, William L. *The Pantheon: Design, Meaning and Progeny*. Cambridge: Harvard Universtiy Press, (1976), 2002.

MacMullen, Ramsay. *Corruption and Decline of Rome*. New Haven: Yale University Press, 1988.

MacMullen, Ramsay. *Enemies of the Roman Order: Treason, Unrest, and Alienation in the Empire*. Cambridge: Harvard University Press, 1966.

MacMullen, Ramsay. *Paganism in the Roman Empire*. New Haven: Yale University Press, 1981.

Marrou, H. I. *A History of Education in Antiquity*. New York: New American Library, 1964.

Mattern, Susan P. *Rome and the Enemy: Imperial Strategy in the Principate*. Berkeley and Los Angeles: University of California Press, 1999.

Meeks, Wayne. A. *The Moral World of the First Christians*. Philadelphia: Westminster Press, 1986.

Millar, Fergus. *The Roman Middle East: 31 B.C.–A.D. 337*. Cambridge: Harvard University Press, 1993.

Mitchell, Thomas N. Cicero: *The Ascending Years*. New Haven and London: Yale University Press, 1979.

Mitchell, Thomas N. Cicero: *The Senior Statesman*. New Haven and London: Yale University Press, 1991.

Momigliano, A. *Alien Wisdom*. Cambridge: Harvard University Press, 1975.

Mouritsen, Henrik. *Plebs and Politics in the Late Roman Republic*. Cambridge: Cambridge University Press, 2001.

Neusner, Jacob. *Talmudic Judaism in Sasanian Babylonia*. Leiden: E. J. Brill, 1976.

Nippel, Wilfried. *Public Order in Ancient Rome*. Cambridge, UK: Cambridge University Press, 1995.

Peters, F. E. *The Monotheists: Jews, Christians, and Muslims in Conflict and Competition*. 2 vols. Princeton: Princeton University Press, 2003.

Poliakoff, Michael. *Combat Sports in the Ancient World*. New Haven: Yale University Press, 1987.

Pomeroy, Sarah B. *Goddesses, Whores, Wives and Slaves: Women in Classical Antiquity*. New York: Schocken, 1995.

Potter, D. S., and D. J. Mattingly. *Life, Death, and Entertainment in the Roman Empire*. Ann Arbor: University of Michigan Press, 1999.

Potter, Tim. *Roman Italy*. Berkeley: University of California Press, 1990.

Price, Simon. *Rituals and Power: The Roman Imperial Cult in Asia Minor*. Cambridge, UK: Cambridge University Press, 1984.

Rawson, Elizabeth. *Intellectual Life in the Late Roman Republic*. Baltimore: Johns Hopkins University Press, 1985.

Rich, John, and Graham Shipley, eds. *War and Society in the Roman World*. London and New York: Routledge, 1993.

Richardson, Emeline. *The Etruscans: Their Art and Civilization*. Chicago: University of Chicago Press, 1964.

Rosenstein, Nathan. *Imperatores Victi: Military Defeat and Aristocratic Competition in the Middle and Late Republic*. Berkeley and Los Angeles: University of California Press, 1990.

Saller, Richard P. *Patriarchy, Property, and Death in the Roman Family*. Cambridge: Cambridge University Press, 1994.

Saller, Richard P. *Personal Patronage Under the Early Empire*. New York: Cambridge University Press, 1982.

Salmon, E.T. *Roman Colonization under the Republic*. Ithaca, NY: Cornell University Press, 1970.

Salmon, E.T. *Samnium and Samnites*. Cambridge: Cambridge University Press, 1967.

Sanders, E. P. *The Historical Figure of Jesus*. London: Penguin, 1995.

Sanders, E. P. *Jewish and Christian Self-Definition*. Philadelphia: Fortress Press, 1980.

Scheidel, Walter, Ian Morris, and Richard P. Saller. *The Cambridge Economic History of the Greco Roman World*. New York: Cambridge University Press, 2007.

Schuerer, Emil. *History of the Jewish People in the Time of Jesus Christ, Revised Editdion*. Edinburgh, UK: Clark, 1973.

Sherwin-White, A. N. *Racial Prejudice in Imperial Rome*. New York: Cambridge University Press, 1967.

Sherwin-White, A. N. *The Roman Citizenship, Second Edition*. Oxford: Clarendon Press 1973.

Sherwin-White, A. N. *Roman Society and Roman Law in the New Testament*. Oxford: Clarendon Press, 1963.

Smallwood, E. Mary. *The Jews under Roman Rule from Pompey to Diocletian: A Study in Political Relations*. Leiden: Brill, 1976.

Syme, Ronald. *The Roman Revolution*. Oxford: Oxford University Press, 1939.

Talbert, Richard J. A. *The Senate of Imperial Rome*. Princeton: Princeton University Press, 1984.

Taylor, Lily Ross. *Party Politics in the Age of Caesar*. Berkeley: University of California Press, 1949.

Thompson, E.A. *Romans and Barbarians: The Decline of the Western Empire, Revised Edition*. Madison: University of Wisconsin Press, 1980.

Treggiari, Susan. *Roman Freedmen During the Republic*. Oxford: Clarendon Press, 1969.

Treggiari, Susan. *Roman Marriage*. New York: Oxford University Press, 1991.

Treggiari, Susan. *Terentia, Tullia and Publilia: the Women in Cicero's Family*. London and New York: Routledge, 2007.

Veyne, Paul. *The Roman Empire*. Cambridge: Harvard University Press, 1997.

Veyne, Paul. *Bread and the Circuses*. London: Penguin, 1992.

Wells, Colin. *The Roman Empire, Second Edition*. Cambridge: Harvard University Press, 1992.

White, K. D. *Roman Farming*. Ithaca, NY: Cornell University Press, 1970.

Wiedemann, Thomas. *Emperors and Gladiators*. London: Routledge, 1992.

Wiedemann, Thomas. *Greek and Roman Slavery*. Baltimore and London: Johns Hopkins University Press, 1981.

Wilken, Robert Louis. *The Christians as the Romans Saw Them. Second Edition*. New Haven: Yale University Press, 2003 (1984).

Wolfram, H. History of the Goths. *Berkeley and Los Angeles*: University of California Press, 1988.

Wolfram, H. *The Roman Empire and its Germanic Peoples*. Berkeley and Los Angeles: University of California Press, 1997.

Woolf, Greg, *Becoming Roman: The Origins of Provincial Civilization in Gaul*. Cambridge: Cambridge University Press, 1998.

Yavetz, Zwi. *Julius Caesar and his Public Image*. London: Thames and Hudson, 1983.

# Photo and Figure Credits

**11:** Shipwrecks and History. After A. J. Parker, *Ancient Shipwrecks of the Mediterranean and the Roman Provinces* BAR 580, Oxford: Tempus Reparatum 1983, fig. 3, p. 549. **19:** Image of SPQR from arch of Titus in the Roman Forum. Photo: Eliza Nagle. **21:** Roman Coins (Italia, Roma; Aeneas and Caesar), Courtesy of the American Numismatic Society. **29:** Villanovan situla, 8th–7th Century B.C. Courtesy of the Getty Museum. **37:** Capitoline Wolf, Musei Capitolini. Photo: Vanni/Art Resource, NY. **39:** Roman Coins (Brutus, Libertas), Courtesy of the American Numismatic Society. **45:** Plan of Early Roman Forum. **46:** Temple of Castor and Pollux Photo: author. **50:** Walls of Norba. Photo: Roger Wilson. **56:** The Seven Hills and the Servian Walls of Rome. **59:** Plan of Capitol and coin of Fides, Courtesy of the American Numismatic Society. **63:** Plan of Cosa from T. W. Potter, *Roman Italy* Berkeley and Los Angeles: University of California Press, 1987, 71. Courtesy of Sandra Potter. **76:** Plan of Houses on Palatine. After A. Carandini, *Boll. Arch.* 2 (1990), 159f. **77:** Roman noble, Palazzo dei Conservatori, Rome, late lst. century B.C. Photo: Scala/Art Resource, NY. **84:** Roman Assemblies in the Republic. **87:** The Five Census Classes. **93:** The Manipular Legion. **100:** Roman Coin (Janus), Courtesy of the American Numismatic Society. **101:** Temple of Vesta, Uffizi Gallery, Florence. Photo: Deutsches Archäologisches Institut Rome, neg. 77.1759. **113:** Carthaginian warship and coins. Courtesy of the *Sunday Times* of London. **133:** Coin of Flamininus, British Museum/Art Resource, NY. **136:** Victory Monument of Aemilius Paullus at Delphi. H. Kähler, *Rom und seine Welt, Erläuterungen*, Munich: Bayerischer Schulbuch Verlag, 1960. By permission. **148:** Economic Transformation of Italy. **A.** The so-called Porta Augusta, Perugia, Photo: T. W. Potter; B. Via Praenestina bridge, photo of J. B. Ward-Perkins, Courtesy of the British School in Rome; **C.** Villa dei Papiri, after D. Comparetti and G. De Pietra, *La villa ercolanese dei Pisoni* (Turin, 1883, pl. 24). **162:** Theater Building Was Not Welcome at Rome. Reconstruction of Pompey's Theater and Temple of Venus in the Campus Martius, from C. Meier, *Caesar,* Berlin: Severin and Siedler, 1982, fig. 41. **166:** Roman Coinage. **172:** Coin of Nerva, Courtesy American Numismatic Society. **174:** The Gracchan Coalition. **186:** Cohort Legion. **190:** Coins of Social War, Courtesy of the American Numismatic Society. **201:** Inner and Outer Peristyles at the J. Paul Getty Museum at the Getty Villa in Malibu. Photo credits: Julius Shulman and Jergen Nogai (inner and outer peristyles); Richard Ross (outer peristyles). **209:** Coin Hoards and History. After Michael Crawford, *Papers of the British School at Rome* 37 (1969), p. 79 **211:** Image of Antony, Courtesy of the Oriental Institute of the University of Chicago. **216:** Caesar's Forum and Temple, Courtesy of Fototeca Unione, Rome. **231:** Augustus, Musei Capitolini, Rome. Photo: Bildarchiv Preussischer Kulturbesitz/ Art Resource NY. **242:** Julio Claudian Dynasty 1.

**245:** Ostia Warehouse and Mosaic. Photos: author. **246:** The Aqueducts of Claudius. Photo: Tim Potter. **249:** The Administration of the City of Rome. 253: From: Peter Connolly and Hazel Dodge, *The Ancient City: Life in Classical Athens and Rome.* New York: Oxford University Press, 1998, 231. **255:** A. Relief of façade of Temple of Mars Ultor. Photo: Deutsches Archäologisches Institut, Rome, Neg. 01837. B. Supreme Court façade, Washington DC. Photo: Wikpedia Commons. **257:** The Gardens of Augustan Rome. From Diane Favro, *The Urban Image of Augustan Rome* (Cambridge and New York, 1996), fig. 81, p. 177. Drawing by Richard H. Abramson. Courtesy of Cambridge University Press. **270:** Julio Claudian Dynasty II. **274:** Agrippa and Livia from Ara Pacis. Photo: author. **275:** Lucius as child from Ara Pacis. Photo: author. **279:** Prima Porta Augustus. Vatican Museums. Photo: Art Resources. **283:** Bust of Livia. Louvre Museum, Paris. Photo: Réunion des Musées Nationaux/Art Resource, New York. **286:** Coin of Gaius and his three sisters. Courtesy of the American Numismatic Society. **289:** Coin of Nero and Agrippina. Courtesy of the American Numismatic Society. **292:** Praetorian Guardsmen. Courtesy of the Louvre Museum, Paris. **293:** Family Tree of Flavians. **297:** The Colosseum. Photo: Alinari/Art Resource, New York. **301:** Model of Trajan's Forum, Courtesy of the Getty Museum and the University of California at Los Angeles. **302:** Cameo of Trajan and his wife Plotina. British Museum. Photo: © British Museum/Art Resource, New York. **303:** Pantheon. Photo: Author. **304:** The Antonine Dynasty. **305:** Marcus Aurelius. Courtesy of the Roman Museum, Avenches. **307:** Commodus. Musei Capitolini. Photo: Erich Lessing/Art Resource, New York. **316:** Trajan's Bridge at Alcántara, Spain Photo: William L. MacDonald. Drawing of Bridge: *Encyclopaedia Brittanica,* 12th ed. **317:** Pont du Gard aqueduct, France. Photo: William L. MacDonald. **319:** Equestrian Statue of Hadrian: Photo: author. Hadrian in Military Garb. Photo: Carolyn Vout. **319:** Triumphal Arch of Titus. Photo: Eliza Nagle. **337:** Army Pay Scales in the Empire. After M. A. Speidel, *Journal of Roman Studies* 1992. **345:** Ground plan of the Roman army camp at Neuss. Courtesy of Jona Lendering. **352:** Aerial View of Timgad. Photo: Fototeca Unione, Rome. **353:** Djemila. Photo: William L. MacDonald **366:** Stoa of Attalus, Athens. Photo: Author. Basilica. Photo: Author **367:** Theater at Bostra. Photo: DeA Picture Library/Art Resource, New York **369:** Verona Amphitheater. Photo: Tim Potter. **371:** Union Station. Photos: Author. **376:** History Through Shipwrecks. After A. J. Parker, *Ancient Shipwrecks of the Mediterranean and the Roman Provinces* BAR 580, Oxford: Tempus Reparatum 1983, fig. 5, p. 549. **384:** Family Tree of Severi. **386:** Sasanid fortress at Derbent. Photo: Eric Powell. **390:** Aurelian Walls of Rome. Photo: author. **408:** The Books of the New Testament: Approximate Dates of Composition **426:** A. Constantine, Palazzo dei Conservatori. The Tetrarchs, Venice. Photos: author. **431:** The Chi Rho. Sixth century altar. Courtesy of the Louvre Museum, Paris. Photo: Author. **433:** Coins. Constantine: British Museum. Photo: © British Museum/Art Resource, NY; Fausta: Courtesy of Münzkabinett, Staatlich Museen zu Berlin. Photo: Bildarchiv Preussischer Kulturbesitz/Art Resource, New York. **447:** The town of Calcata in southern Etruria. Photo: Tim Potter.

# Index

## G

## H



## I

**M**

## Q



## R



## S

## T

### U



### V



### W

**Y**



**Z**